FOURTH EDITION

The Private Side of American History

Readings in Everyday Life

VOLUME **II** SINCE 1865

FOURTH EDITION

The Private Side of American History

Readings in Everyday Life

VOLUME II SINCE 1865

Edited by

THOMAS R. FRAZIER

*The Bernard M. Baruch College
of The City University of New York*

HBJ **Harcourt Brace Jovanovich, Publishers**
San Diego New York Chicago Austin
London Sydney Tokyo Toronto

Picture Credits

Cover: Robert Burroughs.   **6** The New York Public Library, Astor, Lenox and Tilden Foundations.   **30** Cook Collection, Valentine Museum, Richmond, Virginia. **52** Library of Congress.   **76** The Bettmann Archive.   **106** The Bettmann Archive. **136** The Bettmann Archive.   **158** Courtesy of Howard Shorr © Los Angeles Times. **182** From the collections of Henry Ford Museum and Greenfield Village, Neg. No. 0-4901.   **220** United States Weather Bureau.   **248** Library of Congress. **278** The Bettmann Archive.   **302** Wide World Photos.   **342** Wide World Photos. **372** McCullin/Magnum.   **406** Dennis Brack/Black Star.   **432** The Bettmann Archive.

ISBN: 0-15-571961-0
Library of Congress Catalog Card Number: 86-80747

Printed in the United States of America

Preface

Although there has been some change in the past decade, most studies of history concentrate on public figures and public affairs—that is, the events and people that historians consider most important and influential. What tends to be left out in these traditional presentations is the ordinary, day-to-day life of most of the members of a given society—that is, the "private side" of history. This phrase should not suggest events hidden from public view, but rather the personal incidents and the attitudes of ordinary people—especially their responses to the policies of the dominant power in their society.

This Fourth Edition of *The Private Side of American History* continues and expands on the themes of the first three editions. The essays collected here and in Volume I of this edition represent a sampling of the varied attitudes, life styles, living arrangements, and cultural conflicts that have affected the American people. The selections deal both with the mainstream culture and with cultural groups considered deviant by the mainstream. Portrayed here are people—rich and poor, black and white, male and female, old and young, powerful and weak—as they go about their daily task of trying to provide themselves with a satisfactory way of life. New topics covered in the Fourth Edition include abortion, the westward movement, the rise of the movies, Chicano-Anglo conflict, the automobile industry, the desegregation of professional sports, the Vietnam War, evangelical religion, and contemporary attitudes toward marriage.

This portrayal is necessarily incomplete, for only an encyclopedic work could encompass the complexities of everyday life throughout

American history. But the essays presented here should give the reader a taste of the manifold cultures found within American society today and in the past.

The sixteen selections in this volume, arranged in roughly chronological order from 1865 to the present, are grouped into four sections, each of which concludes with an annotated bibliography. The headnote accompanying each selection places the subject matter in its historical context. A brief introduction to the volume describes the major areas that should be considered in a historical survey of everyday life.

For scholarly assistance I would like to express my appreciation to: Elliott Barkan, California State University, San Bernardino; William R. Biles, Oklahoma State University; Richard D. Brown, University of Connecticut; Robert W. Cherny, San Francisco State University; Edward M. Cook, Jr., University of Chicago; Robert M. Crunden, University of Texas, Austin; John W. Jeffries, University of Maryland Baltimore County; Peter Levine, Michigan State University; David Nasaw. College of Staten Island (CUNY); David Rosner, Baruch College (CUNY); Ellen Skinner, Pace University; and Reed Ueda, Tufts University.

Thomas R. Frazier

Contents

1865–1900
The Gilded Age

1900–1930
The Early Twentieth Century

1930–1960
Depression, War, and After

1960 to the Present
Contemporary America

Topical Table of
Contents

Work:
Conditions and Attitudes

Education
and Recreation

Sex, the Home,
and the Family

Religion, Thought, and Values

Health, Disease, and Death

Violence
and War

Social
Control

FOURTH EDITION

The Private Side of American History

Readings in Everyday Life

VOLUME **II** SINCE 1865

Introduction

In recent years the traditional presentation of American history in schools and colleges has come under criticism. The growth of various liberation movements in the 1960s has led to a rewriting of many history texts to include material on blacks, American Indians, white ethnic groups, and women, among others. New Left historiography has brought about a reconsideration of economic and class interests both domestically and in foreign policy. A third area in which the historical record has been remiss is the one represented by the essays reprinted in this volume— the realm of the everyday life of the American people, the private side of American history. The traditional emphasis on public events has resulted in an historical record that fails to provide sufficient insight into the role of ordinary people in the development of our culture and society. Their feelings, the ways in which they responded or reacted to public events, the hopes, desires, and needs that have been the basis of their response are now recognized by many American historians as a legitimate and important area of historical concern.

In attempting to understand and write about the everyday life of ordinary people, it has been necessary for historians to draw on the theoretical and methodological approaches of the social sciences. Several of the selections in this volume, in fact, have been written by professional sociologists and anthropologists. Historians are only just beginning to apply to recent American history the new historiographical approach so well represented in the Fourth Edition of Volume I of *The Private Side of American History*, which treats America's early growth.

This second volume is concerned not so much with a growing America as with the attempts to build a national culture based on "traditional American values" in the face of serious challenges by different groups who have little desire to participate in such a value system at the expense of their own culture and perceived past. The consensus on the national culture so sought has proved to be extremely fragile and ultimately incapable of being sustained. When history is viewed from the perspective of the "movers and shakers" of the nation, as it has been in the traditional textbooks, the consensus appears to have been established. When the everyday life of the American people is examined, however, the fragility of the consensus is clear. While the people may appear quietly to acquiesce in the dominant culture of the society, they go right on living their lives, often outside its stated values.

In this volume we will examine the attempts to establish a cultural consensus and will look at those who try to pattern their lives after its perceived values. We will look more often, however, at those who live by a different set of norms, those whose continued existence challenges the dominant culture and who, ultimately, refuse to abide by the rules of what has been called "the American way of life." The groups dealt with in this volume fall, for the most part, into the category of those left out of or briefly mentioned in, the traditional texts: women, poor people, ethnic minorities, the young, and the old, among others. But the focus here is not on the causes of their oppression or the conflicts in which they engage in their attempts to come to grips with the dominant power in our society. We concentrate, rather, on the effects of their oppression and the adaptations and adjustments they have made in their attempts to live as fully as possible under often difficult circumstances. Throughout the nation's history, the majority of the people in the United States have lived outside the dominant culture; so we are, in fact, exploring here the private lives of most Americans.

What we are concerned with, then, are the things that most Americans do most of the time—the day-to-day activities and experiences that concern and shape the individual and, thus, are factors in shaping American society.

The quality of individual life is determined largely by such basic factors as work, education, family relationships, and stage in the life cycle. By examining what work people do, how they feel about what they do, what effect it has on them, and whether or not it does what they expect it to—to provide them with a living—we can see the effect employment, or lack of it, has on society as a whole. We need also to understand the impact that the various sources of education in our society—schools, mass media, advertising, family and peer group interaction, and religious institutions, among others—have on the total development of the individual. Because, traditionally, the family has been one of the major forces shaping an individual's life, we must look at the family structure in the United States and see how changes in the structure affect the lives of all its members. We should also note the impact of changes in the society on the various members of the family in their relationships with each other.

Religion is another important part of American life. The religious institutions have been a major force in the establishing of societal norms, and religious ideas have often been influential in forming counter-norms and in providing emotional support for those outside the mainstream of American culture. Therefore, an understanding of the roles religion has played in the cultural development of America is necessary to our study.

Also important are those areas of concern that are even less directly governed by the individual. Included are such factors as the effect of drought; violence, war and its aftermath; governmental policy; and social control. We can examine how the people of the United States have dealt with these crucial and, in some cases, ultimate questions. We will observe the impact of ecological disaster on critical segments of the population. We will explore both personal and institutional violence. We will look at the contradictory influence governmental decisions have on the lives of the young and on war veterans. We will also examine the means society uses to shape the individual's behavior to the desired norm. Here we will consider how the dominant society attempts to assimilate or govern the groups it considers deviant; the actions "deviant" groups take to maintain their distinctiveness—and the price they pay for their efforts; and, of particular importance, the way certain institutions such as schools and churches operate directly or indirectly as agents of social control. The areas of concern considered here by no means exhaust the possible categories for the study of everyday life, but they are at least suggestive of the kinds of experiences that must be covered in exploring the private side of American history.

In this volume, each section contains at least one selection that delineates the norms or activities of one segment of the dominant culture. The other selections describe behavior or attitudes that deviate from, or are in the process of altering, the traditional norms. The volume begins by describing the growing practice of abortion as a means of family planning for the middle-class. The growth of an immigrant population with a high birth rate prompted national policy makers to view the abortion issue as threatening to their cultural hegemony. Other topics in this section deal with the attempt of freed slaves to form a community independent of the dominant white culture. Also covered is the conquest of the open spaces and the Indian population of the West and the justification of the questionable policies that resulted from that process. Finally, this section follows the attempt of the traditional elite to escape a changing society by withdrawing into restricted enclaves where they need associate only with others of their own class.

The first selection in part two describes the changing patterns of leisure among the working class of Worcester, Massachuetts, and the second deals with the activities of newsboys as the newspaper industry changed its distribution system. Attacks on Mexican–Americans, both native and foreign-born, in East Los Angeles during the First World War are explored in the next selection, and the section concludes with an analysis of the automobile industry by focusing on the impact of Henry Ford and his ideologies.

The first essay in the third section shows how poor conservation methods combined with adverse weather conditions led to the Dust Bowl of the 1930s. Next, the state of public schooling during the Depression is examined. The impact of the Second World War on the employment patterns of female workers is evaluated in this third selection. One aspect of the racial situation in America is described in this last selection by telling the story of the desegregation of major league baseball.

The last section opens with a study of the counterculture of the sixties that had such an impact on young Americans. Following this is a study of the military during the Vietnam War. Both the lives of ordinary soldiers and the policies of the officer corps are examined. The following subject looks at the growing influence, culturally and politically, of evangelical religion. This volume concludes with an exploration of contemporary attitudes toward love and marriage, attitudes which have an important impact on the values of family life.

This volume provides but a sampling of the enormous variety of life-styles and life experiences of the groups and individuals who make up what we call the American nation. The editor has attempted to acquaint the student with the possibility of better understanding the history of the United States through a study of the many different ways in which people have shaped their lives hoping that they might live with as much of their essential humanity intact as possible. For many this has been an extremely difficult task because of the structural disorders in American society. Only if these disorders are seen for what they are, however, and seriously challenged, will the private lives of the American people improve in significant ways.

The Gilded Age

1865–1900

FIFTH AVENUE FOUR YEARS AFTER MAD. RESTELL'S DEATH.

Puck's *very comment on the suicide of Madame
Restell was this fanciful projection of what Fifth
Avenue might look like in the future; April 17, 1878.*

The Social Character of Abortion

JAMES C. MOHR

No laws governing abortion existed in the United States at the beginning of the nineteenth century. If a woman wanted an abortion and could get one, she had it. The English common law tradition, which was later adopted by the United States, however, sought to restrict the deliberate causing of a miscarriage after "quickening"—that is, the spontaneous movement of the fetus inside the woman carrying it. The state of medical knowledge at the time could not diagnosis a pregnancy; only when the fetus itself signaled its presence was a woman sure of her condition.

Some women, at all times and in most places, have made use of a variety of practices when they decided not to allow a pregnancy to come to term. Herbal and mineral compounds that caused miscarriage (abortifacients) were widely available. Folk wisdom also recommended several forms of violent physical activity to achieve the same result. In the early nineteenth century, medical manuals referred to the problem of "obstructed menses," a thinly veiled reference to early pregnancy. The most popular manuals in the Untied States, cited in Mohr, recommended "bloodletting, bathing, iron and quinine concoctions, and if those failed, a teaspoonful of the tincture of black hellebore [a violent purgative] . . . twice a day in a cup of warm water. . . . Later in pregnancy a . . . woman would try . . . violent exercise, raising great weights; reaching too high; jumping, or stepping from an eminence; strokes [strong blows] on the belly; [and] falls' " (pp 6f). Needless to say, these solutions were often ineffective, but they did have a detrimental effect on the health of the pregnant woman.

As the middle of the nineteenth century approached, three developments led to drastic changes in attitudes and policies relating to abortion. The first was an increasingly scientific medical profession. As it became possible to determine the certainty of pregnancy prior to "quickening," doctors began to favor a ban on abortion at any time, and a clear distinction was made between abortion (a deliberate act to terminate the pregnancy) and miscarriage (a spontaneous explusion of the fetus).

Following this scientific breakthrough laws began to appear which made abortion at any stage of the pregnancy illegal. But the rudimentary scientific knowledge of the time made the process difficult to prove in a court of law, allowing only occasional cases to be successfully brought to trial, therefore leaving the practice widespread.

The third development was demographic. In the early part of the century most of the women who sought abortions were young and unmarried. These women were trying to protect their reputations and prevent embarrassment to their families. Increasingly, on the other hand, by the middle of the century those seeking the services of abortionists were middle- and upper-class married women using abortion as a means of limiting the size of their families. Madame Restell, the most well-known abortionist in New York City, catered predominantly to the carriage trade. The following selection, by James Mohr of the University of Maryland (Baltimore County), describes the demographic shift that occurred and the effect this changing pattern had on abortion policy.

By the end of the nineteenth century, primarily through the efforts of the newly regularized medical profession, abortion at any stage of pregnancy was made illegal throughout the United States. It is ironic that just as medical science had developed techniques for safely terminating pregnancies (at least in the early stages), the doctors then led in the struggle to make such operations impossible to procure legally.

Abortion policy remained the same in the United States until 1973 when the Supreme Court in its *Roe* v. *Wade* decision made it possible for a pregnant woman, if she so desired, to receive a medically safe abortion in the early stages of her pregnancy. Abortion in the later stages was hedged about with qualifications, however, and this has led to the adoption of legal variations from state to state. The abortion question has not, then, been laid to rest. Anti-abortion forces are seeking to overturn the Court's decision, while pro-choice advocates continue to favor the position of a womans' absolute right to abortion if she so chooses.

Before 1840 abortion was perceived in the United States primarily as a recourse of the desperate, especially of the young woman in trouble who feared the wrath of an overexacting society. After 1840, however, evidence began to accumulate that the social character of the practice had changed. A high proportion of the women whose abor-

THE SOCIAL CHARACTER OF ABORTION   from *Abortion in America: The Origins and Evolution of National Policy* by James C. Mohr. Copyright © 1978 by Oxford University Press, Inc. Reprinted by permission.

tions contributed to the soaring incidence of that practice in the United States between 1840 and 1880 appeared to be married, native-born, Protestant women, frequently of middle- or upper-class status. The data came from disparate sources, some biased and some not, but in the end proved compelling.

Even before the availability of reliable evidence confirmed that the nation's birthrates were starting to plummet, observers noticed that abortions more and more frequently involved married women rather than single women in trouble. Professor Hugh L. Hodge of the University of Pennsylvania, one of the first physicians in the United States to speak out about abortion in anything approaching a public forum, lectured his introductory obstetrics students in 1839 that abortion was fast becoming a prominent feature of American life. Hodge still considered women trying "to destroy the fruits of illicit pleasure" to be the ones most often seeking abortions, but he alerted his students to the fact that "married women, also, from the fear of labor, from indisposition to have the care, the expense, or the trouble of children, or some other motive" were more and more frequently requesting "that the embryo be destroyed by their medical attendant." Hodge attributed a good deal of this activity to the quickening doctrine, which allowed "women whose moral character is, in other respects, without reproach; mothers who are devoted, with an ardent and self-denying affection, to the children who already constitute[d] their family [to be] perfectly indifferent respecting the foetus in the utero."

In 1844 the *Boston Medical and Surgical Journal* noted an increase in the number of openly practicing abortionists and expressed dismay that their services were "even sometimes sought after by married women." Although abortions performed for the victims of seduction or of youthful exuberance had always been forgiven by the public, the *Journal* believed married women had no "shadow of excuse . . . for their heartless depravity." The editor went on to decry the fact that Christian America would tolerate a practice he considered "still more deplorable" than the infanticide then believed to be common in heathen China. In the hoopla of sensationalism that surrounded the initial public awareness of Madame Restell's activities, Americans learned that married women of good social standing comprised a substantial proportion of her clients. A mother of two children told Dr. Gunning Bedford that she had used Restell's products and services to miscarry five different times, and "she knew a great number of females who were in the habit of applying to Madame Restell." Edward H. Dixon, who published both a medical monograph and a popular manual on sex and disease in 1847, had likewise heard that "married persons [were] adopting such means." Even among women who did not seek the services of a professional abortionist, according to Dixon, many "either . . . avoid the necessary precautions to prevent miscarriage, or . . . seek to produce it." William Alcott, a popular speaker on the lecture circuit of the 1840s and 1850s, also bemoaned the use of abortion by married women trying to hold down the size of their families.

By 1854 the *Boston Medical and Surgical Journal* declared that the situation was getting worse not better. Abortion was

> not exclusively performed upon unmarried women, who fly to the abortionist in the hope of being able to conceal from the world their shame and degradation, but even married women, who have no apology for concealment, and who only desire to rid themselves of the prospective cares of maternity, also submit themselves, far more frequently than is suspected, to hazardous manipulations, alike injurious to their bodies and subversive of all the finer sentiments of the mind. In some instances husbands have been known to aid and abet their wives in this wicked expedient, on the plea that they have children enough already, or their circumstances forbid an increase of family expenses and responsibilities.

Professor Jesse Boring of the Atlanta Medical College pointed out in an 1857 paper on criminal abortion that the practice was no longer simply the recourse of "the unfortunate only, who have been deceived and ensnared by the seducer." Now it involved "the virtuous and the intelligent wife and mother" as well. The physicians of Buffalo, New York, concurred in 1858. In the past they could look upon abortion almost with compassion, or at least with benevolent neglect, for it had saved "unfortunates" whose "happy, innocent life" would be "changed to a wild and almost unavoidable career of crime and remorse." But that was no longer the case. Abortion since midcentury had been "brought to the very heart of every family." Harvard's Professor Walter Channing reinforced that idea in 1859, and so did both the American Medical Association and the Michigan State Medical Society in the same year.

By the end of the Civil War the medical community believed that the great majority of women having abortions in the United States were married. Horatio Storer, the nation's leading anti-abortion spokesman at that time, aimed an entire volume of anti-abortion propaganda at married women in 1865 in an effort to dissuade them from continuing the practice. A year later he followed that book with another aimed not at single women but at husbands. Abortion "is practiced to a great extent by the married," concurred a Vermont physician in 1866; in 1867 physicians were "not more usually by the single than by the married" asked for abortions in Ohio; it was no longer simply an escape from illicit intercourse, but a systematic practice among the married, asserted a Detroit physician in 1867; "by all odds the most numerous are married," agreed a Detroit colleague in 1874; I. T. Dana, professor of theory and practice of medicine in the Medical School of Maine, declared that abortion prevailed there "chiefly amongst married and otherwise respectable women"; though "many of the cases of criminal abortion are young women or girls who have 'got into a scrape,' " wrote a spokesman for the Bristol Northern District Medical Society of Massachusetts in 1870, "by far the *larger* number of these cases are married women."

Dr. George E. Smith of Hillsdale, Michigan, reported a *"widespread* determination on the part of many who are married to avoid the labor of caring for and rearing children." As a result, in his words, abortion had become "so frequent . . . that it [was by 1873] rare to find a married woman who passes through the childbearing period, who has not had one or more." According to the respondents of the Philadelphia survey, married women were "numerically the chief offenders." A botanic from Grand Rapids "had, on an average [through the early 1880s], two applications a week to produce abortion, and mostly from those in married life." In 1889 a student of American abortion patterns, who had obtained the New York City stillbirth records from 1870 through 1887, reported to the New York Medico-Legal Society and later to an international congress on medico-legal problems that "probably seventy-five or ninety per cent of the abortions of our civilization are committed by the married women of the nation." This last writer, incidentally, was virtually alone among medical spokesmen in favoring the repeal rather than the further strengthening of the country's anti-abortion laws.

Most observers, then, agreed that most of the women who drove America's abortion rates so steeply upward after 1840 were married. Most observers also agreed that virtually all of the women who sought abortions in the United States during the middle decades of the nineteenth century shared at least one other characteristic: they appeared to be almost exclusively Protestants. Storer put it as bluntly as anyone: abortions were "infinitely more frequent among Protestant women than among Catholic." Respondents to the Philadelphia survey unanimously concurred and the Michigan State Board of Health laid heavy stress on the same point. Indeed, no writer put forward any qualifying suggestions and all of the available data seem to confirm Storer's conclusion. Ironically, this conclusion, never controverted and continuously substantiated between 1840 and 1880, would subsequently allow anti-abortion crusaders to appeal to legislators with a virulent, undisguised, and apparently effective anti-Catholicism.

Whether all of these married Protestants were also native born is somewhat more difficult to judge. Most physicians argued that they were and so did most compilers of state statistics. Moreover, modern demographers have demonstrated that a precipitous drop in the native birthrate, as distinguished from the birthrate for immigrant women, accounted for the overall decline in the fertility of the nation as a whole after 1840. The assertion that Catholics did not practice abortion as a form of family limitation in the way that Protestands did was nowhere challenged by contemporary evidence of any sort. But the belief of several nineteenth-century observers that immigrants as a whole, not just Catholic immigrants, also refrained from abortion is open to at least one possible qualification.

The qualification involves the Germans. Judging by advertisements in the German-language press in New York after the Civil War, abortion was apparently on a commercialized and relatively open basis in the German community by then. *Frauenarzts,* or female specialists, quite candidly announced their willingness to provide for German women the services then touted so openly in the English-language press. Many practitioners offered abortifacient preparations for sale and several made less than subtle allusions to their willingness to operate. A Dr. Harrison, for example, invited German women to his office with the promise that "all menstrual obstructions, from whatever cause they might originate, will be removed in a few hours without risk or pain." One visit was normally enough, but women requiring extended care could receive in-house board. Harrison had a number of German-language competitors, who were equally straightforward in their ads. The pres-

TO THE LADIES—MRS. BIRD, MIDWIFE, 254 Stanton, private entrance second door in Sheriff, respectfully acquaints the ladies of this city and vicinity, that from long experience and successful practice in the treatment of the various complaints to which females are so peculiarly liable, she feels warranted in asserting that the most desperate cases will speedily yield to her treatment. Hundreds of ladies can testify to her capability, having been restored from the most severe indisposition to perfect health by her mode of practice. Mrs. B. has had the great advantage of an attendance at several celebrated hospitals in Germany, and has received the most flattering testimonials from eminent medical practitioners, thus affording a guarantee for the skillful performance of the duties which she has undertaken.—General satisfaction has uniformly attended her in her responsible duties, and she cannot omit this opportunity of returning her sincere acknowledgements for the unlimited confidence reposed in her acquirements. Soothing Syrup, for children teething, ointment for sore breasts, salve, and other esteemed remedies for female complaints, to be obtained as above. Female Periodical Pills guaranteed in every case where the monthly periods have become irregular. Price $1 per box.

An advertisement for one of the earliest of the German-trained midwives who offered abortion services to women in the United States; New York Sun, Feb. 26, 1846.

ence of a German-speaking abortionist in Boston as early as 1845 may have been more than merely a unique curiosity, especially inasmuch as German-language abortion broadsides continued to appear there into the 1870s. A significant proportion of the abortionists arrested under the auspices of the New York Society for the Supression of Vice during the 1870s were German, most of them German Jews. George Ellington, in an 1869 exposé *The Women of New York,* claimed that most of the "female abortionists" there were "of foreign birth or extraction," and had risen to their present occupations "from being first-class nurses— in Germany, especially," where they had gained a rudimentary knowledge of medicine in nursing schools.

It seems likely, then, that abortion was being practiced at least to some extent among German immigrants. This does not mean that the overwhelming proportion of the women seeking and obtaining abortions in the United States between 1840 and 1880 were not native born; they almost certainly were on the basis of contemporary evidence. This is only to suggest that native-born observers, such as regular physicians, may have been unaware of what was going on within the German-speaking community and as a result they may have overlooked a partial exception to their generalization. Or it may be that physicians chose to overlook the exception, for, like anti-Catholicism, they would find nativism a valuable asset in their subsequent efforts to persuade American legislators to enact anti-abortion laws.

Opinion was divided regarding the social status of the women who accounted for the great upsurge of abortion during the middle period of the nineteenth century. While most observers agreed "all classes of society, rich and poor" were involved to some extent, many thought that the middle and upper classes practiced abortion more extensively than the lower classes. The Michigan State Medical Society in 1859 declared that abortion "pervade[d] all ranks" in that state. The Medical Society of Buffalo pointed out that same year "now we have ladies, yes, *educated and refined ladies*" involved as well. On the other hand, court cases revealed at least a sprinkling of lower-class women, servant girls, and the like. Storer's volumes of the 1860s suggested that abortion cut across class lines in the United States. From Syracuse, New York, in 1871, from Burlington, Iowa, the same year, from a special report of the Illinois State Medical Society in 1872, from the Woodford County Medical Society of Illinois in 1874, from Detroit in 1874, from Kansas City in 1884, from Philadelphia in 1889, and from many other medical observers around the country throughout the period came supporting testimony that women of all social classes practiced abortion.

Overwhelming indications that American women of all economic classes practiced abortion, however, were not necessarily inconsistent with the possibility that larger proportions of some classes were involved than of others. This may explain why several contemporaries expressed sentiments similar to those of the Ohio physician who wrote in 1867 that the "atrocious crime . . . [was] . . . most commonly found among the more intelligent and refined of our citizens." The Philadelphia survey suggested "that the crime, so far from being confined to the lower and middle strata of society—regarding them socially and educationally—finds its patrons, in large proportion, in the higher grades of society." In 1869 *The Revolution,* a feminist journal published in New York, reprinted portions of a popular lecture that claimed "Restellism" was "fashionable in the American *dress circle."* A special committee of the New York Medico-Legal Society agreed in 1872 that abortion was most prevalent "in our own day and city among the well-to-do—the so-called respectable classes." A contributor to *The Southern Practitioner* in 1887 considered it "a lamentable but well-known fact that this great sin [was] most frequently consummated in the higher strata of our society." A defender of legalized abortion in the United States hailed "the educated, refined, cultured women of this country" as the ones responsible for the nation's high abortion rates.

Physicians may have associated abortion with "the better classes," as a Michigan doctor rightly perceived in 1875, because those were the classes with which they most frequently came into contact. The same might be said of feminists. Put differently, the sort of people who contributed to medical journals or wrote for feminist magazines may have had little real knowledge of medical mores among the poor. Nonetheless, the cost of an abortion leads one to believe that abortion, though it was definitely practiced to some extent by American women of all classes, may have been proportionately most common among the middle and upper classes between 1840 and 1880.

Although the going price for an abortion varied tremendously according to place, time, practitioner, and patient, abortions appear to have been generally quite expensive. Regular physicians testified repeatedly throughout the period that the abortion business was enormously lucrative. Those doctors pledged not to perform abortions bitterly resented men like the Boston botanic indicted for manslaughter in an abortion case in 1851, who posted $8000 bond and returned to his offices, at a time when the average university professor in the United States earned under $2000 per year. The temptations to rationalize an occasional abortion on some pretext or other for a wealthy patient were almost irresistible. One doctor claimed to refuse $1000 to perform an abortion, and another turned down $500. But there is a great deal of evidence, both direct and indirect, that many regulars succumbed to generous blandishments. Only the affluent, generally speaking, could offer temptations that were worth the risk to a regular of being found out by his colleagues. The two groups of regulars most vulnerable to proffered bonuses for abortions were young men struggling to break into the viciously competitive laissez faire medical market of the 1840s and 1850s and older practitioners losing their skills and their reputations during the 1860s and 1870s, when modern medicine took long strides forward and physicians unfamiliar with the new breakthroughs began to fall behind.

When women turned from regulars to the commercial abortionists, the prices were still not cheap. Itinerants and irregulars generally tried to charge whatever they judged the traffic would bear, which could vary anywhere from $5 to $500. During the 1840s, for example, Madame Restell charged $5 for an initial visit and diagnosis, then negotiated the price of the operation "according to the wealth and liberality of the parties." In a case for which she was indicted in 1846 she asked a young woman about "her beau's circumstances" before quoting a figure, and then tried to get $100 when she found out the man was a reasonably successful manufacturer's repesentative. The man thought that was too costly, and only after extensive haggling among go-betweens was a $75 fee agreed upon. By the late 1860s Restell's fees had gone up, and her clientele was regarded both by the popular press and by popular writers as distinctly upper class and very wealthy.

An irregular practitioner was able to charge an Orange County, Vermont, farmer a $100 fee in 1858 to abort the farmer's servant girl. A fee of $25 to $50 seems to have been more usual in that period, however, and a woman in New York City was able to obtain an abortion during the Civil War for a bargain-basement price of $8.

But such sums still represented a great deal of money to most farmers and all laborers in the middle of the nineteenth century. As William Alcott somewhat wryly put it in 1866, some practitioners would perform abortions "for a very small sum; or, if not, *for a large one!*" Moreover, commercial abortionists frequently worked in unofficial partnership with cooperative boardinghouse owners. The abortionist would perform the operation in his office, which usually involved dilation of the cervix and the introduction of some irritant into the womb. The patient would then retire for up to five days in the cooperating boardinghouse, where the actual expulsion took place. The boardinghouse owner would dispose of the products of the abortion and swear to any false certificates that seemed prudent. These boardinghouse owners, needless to say, also demanded handsome sums.

The standard price of an abortion had apparently leveled somewhat by the early 1870s, provided exclusive specialists like Restell, who openly catered to the rich, were avoided. "The luxury of an abortion," noted Ely Van de Warker in 1871, in a telling phrase, "is now within the reach of the serving-girl. An old man in this city [Syracuse, N.Y.] performs this service for *ten* dollars, and takes his pay *in instalments.*" Ten dollars was also the fee charged by Mrs. Fenno of Sommerville, Massachusetts, in the late 1870s, though she tacked on an extra $5 if a return visit became necessary. That reverse incentive was unusual; most abortionists guaranteed results for an initial flat fee. They usually began with drugs, and followed up with an operation if the drugs did not work. But the initial fee covered the whole treatment.

Despite the apparent gradual leveling of prices, however, the abortion business remained a profitable commercial venture well into the 1870s. Anthony Comstock, the single-minded leader of a massive anti-obscenity campaign launched in the United States during the 1870s, kept meticulous and extensive records of all the people he helped arrest while operating as a special agent of the Post Office Department. Between 1872 and 1880 Comstock and his associates aided in the indictment of 55 persons whom Comstock identified as abortionists. The vast majority were very wealthy and posted large bonds with ease. The books of a Bleecker Street (New York City) abortionist arrested in 1873, for example, indicated an average profit of $2000 per month. Francis Andrews, an Albany abortionist who jumped $5000 bond in 1873, was "worth about $400,000," had donated $27,000 to the Albany YMCA, and had helped organize the "Quaker City Expedition to the Holy Land." Ezra Reynolds of Rochester, New York, was said to be worth $40,000 when he escaped to Canada. Sarah Sawyer, "the Restell of Boston," wore a dress valued between $1000 and $1500 to her arraignment in 1873. Madame Restell's wealth, of course, variously estimated at up to $1,000,000, was legendary. These bits of evidence, scattered and imprecise as they are, nonetheless confirm the impression that a genuinely flourishing market for abortion services existed in the United States from the 1840s through the 1870s. While some practitioners charged fees that women of modest means could afford and arranged terms of credit, big money was clearly involved in the practice, so it is likely that middle- and upper-class women could and did avail themselves of abortion services more systematically and more often than poorer women.

The geographical distribution of abortions in nineteenth-century America cannot be ascertained with much precision. The spread of abortion as a large-scale social phenomenon after 1840 appears to have been from the eastern seaboard states toward the midwestern and southeastern states, but historical demographers would expect a pattern like that even without seeing any of the evidence on abortion per se. The population itself moved along similar lines, and so, according to the demographers, did the practice of family limitation, which has in turn been generally correlated with industrialization, urbanization, and the disappearance of virgin land in any given district. To confuse matters, however, there is a great deal of scattered evidence—as many of the references in this and the preceding chapter attest—that abortion began to be used as a means of family limitation rather widely throughout all parts of the United States after 1840, even in the nation's frontier territories, although many standard demographic generalizations might not lead investigators to predict its appearance in such areas. This does not mean that the practice had a uniform social and demographic impact throughout the nation, but it does indicate that abortion as a means of family limitation after 1840 was not a regional phenomenon but a national one. By the 1860s outcries against abortion came from almost every state in the Union, and virtually every medical journal in the country viewed abortion as a serious problem in its particular area.

Similar ambiguities arise when the available evidence on abortion in nineteenth-century America is examined with an eye toward deciding whether the practice was fundamentally urban or rural. In the 1840s the discovery that married women were turning to abortion on a significant scale was often associated with the growth of urban areas, and many Americans no doubt saw in Restellism one more confirmation of their suspicions that cities were sinful centers where people went to live unnatural lives. Yet many of the women who were aborted in American cities before midcentury were not themselves urban women, as the early exposés of Restellism were at pains to point out. Several of the key court cases decided before midcentury involved women who had come from the surrounding countryside or from small towns to seek an abortion in an urban center. It is difficult to know what to make of such evidence. On the one hand, the availability of abortion services may have been associated with urbanization to some extent, at least through midcentury, which is an implication that many demographers and most economists would probably find believable. On the other hand, the influences associated with urbanization apparently reached very far and very quickly out into the rural districts. Moreover, the fact that a trip to the city offered anonymity to those women who did not wish to reveal their private lives to the informal lay healer, apothecary, or physician in their village may help explain why a few observers thought cities tended to function as abortion centers.

If abortion on a socially significant scale was initially perceived as an urban phenomenon, however, it did not retain that character for long. By the 1860s the vast majority of writers on abortion, even those who estimated the total incidence of abortion rather conservatively, reinforced the belief that the practice was common to "every village, hamlet, and neighborhood in the United States" and that it seemed to thrive as well on the prairies as in large urban centers. This may have resulted from the diffusion of family limitation practices generally, from the proliferation of irregular physicians in the countryside, from some combination of those factors, or from factors that demographers do not yet fully understand, but the number of observers after midcentury who believed that the practice of abortion was widespread throughout all districts of the United States—rural and urban, agricultural and industrial—was legion. Moreover, this almost universally held impression among contemporary observers is substantiated by the accumulating evidence of modern scholarship that fertility ratios fell just as rapidly in rural America as they did in urban America during most of the nineteenth century.

Contemporary assertions that abortion was being practiced after 1840 in the United States by married, Protestant, and for the most part native-born women, frequently of high social standing, and from all parts of the country, may be checked, at least roughly, by specific data. Medical journals frequently published individual case histories that might be of professional interest to their readers. Sometimes a new technique was tried, and other doctors might like to know how it worked out; sometimes a unique aspect of some given case puzzled the physician involved so that he wanted the opinion of others who might have faced similar situations; sometimes the journal was trying to fill space. Between 1839 and 1880, fifty-four of these case histories involved abortions. Generally the women had either botched abortions upon themselves or been the victims of a mistake by another practitioner before calling on a regular for help. Such a sample is hardly ideal and is exceedingly small. Some of the information relevant to a social profile of the women involved is missing because physicians and journals both emphasized the medical aspects of the cases rather than the personal aspects. Still, the sample is better than no sample at all, and the data support what contemporary observers claimed to be true.

Well over half of the 54 women were married; 33 were so identified, with the marital status of 6 unknown; only 15 were definitely single. Of the married women at least 60 percent already had at least one child. The evidence for most of the remaining 40 percent was either ambiguous or missing, but several were specifically identified as newly married women who openly avowed that they did not want to start a family right away. Only one woman was identified as Roman Catholic, and in the case an abortion was strongly suspected but not confirmed. Only one of the 54 was non-white. None of the 54 was specifically identified as foreign-born, though that was not the sort of information that such case histories would ordinarily contain. Data on the social status of the women were sketchy and impressionistic, but more women were described as "belonging to a respectable family," or "physician's wife," or "wife of a wealthy banker," or the like than were described as "servant girl," or "cook," or the like. The women came from all sections of the country and from rural as well as urban areas.

To summarize at this point, then, a great deal of persuasive evidence indicates that abortion entered the mainstream of American life during the middle decades of the nineteenth century. While the unmarried and the socially desperate continued to have recourse to it as they had earlier in the century, abortion also became highly visible, much more frequently practiced, and quite common as a means of family limitation among white, Protestant, native-born wives of middle- and upper-class standing. These dramatic changes, in turn, evoked sharp comment from two ideologically opposed groups in American society, each of which either directly or indirectly blamed the other for the shift in abortion patterns. On one side of the debate were the anti-feminists, led by regular physicians, and on the other side were the nation's feminists. Both groups agreed that abortion had become a large-scale and socially significant phenomenon in American life, but they disagreed over the reasons why.

Before examining the two chief explanations put forward by contemporaries for the striking shifts in the incidence and the character of abortion in the United States after 1840, two observations may be worth making. First, it is never easy to understand why people do what they do even in the most straightforward of situations; it is nearly impossible to know with certainty the different reasons, rational and irrational, why people in the past might have taken such a psychologically loaded action as the termination of a suspected pregnancy. Second, most participants on both sides of the contemporary debate over why so many American women began to practice abortion after 1840 actually devoted most of their attention to the question of why American women wanted to limit their fertility. This confirmed that abortion was important between 1840 and 1880 primarily as a means of family limitation, but such discussions offer only marginal help in understanding why so many American women turned to abortion itself as a means toward that end.

Cultural anthropologists argue that abortion has been practiced widely and frequently in pre-industrial societies at least in part because "it is a woman's method [of limiting fertility] and can be practiced without the man's knowledge." This implies a sort of women's conspiracy to limit population, which would be difficult to demonstrate in the context of nineteenth-century America. Nonetheless, there is some evidence, though it must be considered carefully, to suggest that an American variant of this proposition may have been at least one of the reasons why abortion became such a common form of family limitation in the United States during the period. A number of physicians, as will become evident, certainly believed that one of the keys to the upsurge of abortion was the fact that it was a uniquely female practice, which men could neither control nor prevent.

In a somewhat similar vein, several scholars have recently argued that the reduction in family size that took place in nineteenth-century America reflected an increased autonomy for women within the traditional framework of the family. Professor Daniel Scott Smith labels the phenomenon "domestic feminism." While his hypothesis appears rather more speculative than conclusively demonstrated, the notion of domestic feminism meshes nicely with the great upsurge of abortion in the midnineteenth century America for the very reasons that the cultural anthropologists indicate. Smith rests his case primarily upon the probable use of various methods of contraception by midcentury, but notes parenthetically that the childbirth cycles of Victorian-American women were "broken not infrequently by spontaneous abortions." The data here suggest the strong probability that many of those abortions were not, in fact, spontaneous at all, but desired, encouraged, and induced. Dr. Montrose Pallen pointed out in 1868.

> Even in cases where mothers have suffered from repeated abortions, where foetus after foetus have perished through their neglect or carelessness, and where even their own health is involved in the issue, even in such cases, every obstetrician can bear testimony to the great difficulty of inducing our wayward patients to forego certain gratifications, to practice certain self-denials, and to adopt efficient means for the salvation of the child. This is not all, we can bear testimony that in some instances the woman who has been well educated, who occupies high stations in society, whose influence over others is great, and whose character has not been impugned, will deliberately resort to any and every measure which may effectually destroy her unborn offspring. Ashamed or afraid to apply to the charlatan, who sustains his existence by the price of blood, dreading, it may be, publicity, she recklessly and boldly adopts measures, however severe and dangerous, for the accomplishment of her unnatural, her guilty purpose. She will make extra muscular efforts by long fatiguing walks, by dancing, running, jumping, kept up as long as possible; she will swallow the most nauseous, irritating and poisonous drugs, and, in some instances, will actually arm herself with the surgeon's instruments, and operate upon her own body, that she may be delivered of any embryo, for which she has not desire, and whose birth and appearance she dreads.

Other writers confirmed this opinion that American women frequently refused to take precautions that might prevent a threatened miscarriage. While such abortions would go into the record as naturally occurring, they were not exactly spontaneous and were probably avoidable.

In arguments not unlike those of the anthropologists and of Professor Smith, many nineteenth-century physicians blamed the sudden willingness of married women in America to practice abortion upon what twentieth-century writers would label a rising consciousness. Put differently, a number of male commentators believed that feminist ideology outside the home had its counterpart in the upsurge of abortion among women in the home, and that the former was partly responsible for the latter. Some put the possibility explicitly. The doctor quoted above was one of them. He considered "the whole country" to be "in an abnormal state" and believed that "the tendency to force women into men's places" was creating insidious "new ideas of women's duties." Such ideas, which included the notion "that her ministrations in the formation of character as a mother should be abandoned for the sterner rights of voting and law making," were acting and reacting, according to Pallen, "upon public sentiment, until public conscience becomes blunted, and duties necessary to woman's organization [i.e. childbearing] are shirked, neglected or criminally prevented."

Earlier in the century observers had alleged that the tract literature and lecturers of the women's rights movement advocated family planning and disseminated abortifacient information. In 1859 Harvard professor Walter Channing reported the opinion that "women for whom this office of foeticide, unborn-child-killing, is committed, are *strong-minded*," and no later writer ever accused them of being weak-minded. The following year Augustus K. Gardner published a discussion of what he considered to be the "Physical Decline of American Women" in a popular literary magazine, the *Knickerbocker*. He was convinced that one of the chief causes for the decline was the widespread practice of abortion in the United States, which he believed to be gradually debilitating the nation's women, and he therefore placed himself in open opposition to the feminists of the day, whom he considered to be dangerously leading American women toward their own physical destruction. Many of Gardner's early ideas were reiterated and elaborated in *Conjugal Sins,* his 1870 best-selling treatise against family planning. A. F. Barnes was at pains to point out that an 1869 abortion case he wrote up for the *Medical Archives* of St. Louis involved a 30-year-old married mother of three children who "strongly believed in 'woman's rights.' " While many other men alluded to the possible link between feminism and abortion, a California doctor in 1877 gave the connection probably the most extended and least subtle treatment it received. This man, Henry Gibbons, Sr., blamed the spread of abortion on the unsettling effects of social theories like those of Frances Wright and Robert Dale Owen. Indeed, before he finished his lecture, which was printed in both of the major medical journals of the West Coast, he was denouncing reform generally as having a pernicious effect upon domestic relations in the United States.

In further support of commentators like these there was some evidence that women shared abortifacient information with one another and assisted their friends in attempted self-abortions. This was true even in isolated areas. To cite but a single example, it was axiomatic to a judge on the Colorado frontier in 1870 that a girl's "mother or any other old lady" would be both willing and able to offer her information on restoring menstrual flow after a missed period. Dr. William H. Hardison of Richland, Arkansas, believed that self-abortions were quite common in his area and that they were made possible by women sharing abortifacient information with one another. H.S. Humphrey of Janeville, Wisconsin, thought the same was true in his area. As G.

Dallas Lind put it in *The Mother's Guide and Daughter's Friend:* "Many women, being refused by honest physicians to relieve them of what they consider a burden, learn from other women what to take or what to do to produce abortion upon themselves." Female undergrounds, if that phrase does not stretch the notion too far, even eliminated literacy as a necessary prerequisite for practicing abortion. Some of the principals in an 1855 abortion trial in a rural section of souther Indiana notarized their depositions with their marks, not their signatures.

Occasionally feminists confirmed the fears and accusations of the defensive anti-feminists who blamed the upsurge of abortion in America on the spread of feminist ideas. A woman from the mill county of Androscoggin, Maine, where a regular physician had reported at least four hundred abortions being performed each year, wrote to a feminist journal that it was not a lack of moral instruction but the movement for women's rights that produced the total. A previous letter writer had asserted that American women continued to abort so frequently after the Civil War because virtually all of them still believed in the quickening doctrine their mothers had taught them. If they could be educated to see that abortion at any time during gestation was murder, this earlier correspondent believed, they would stop it. But the Androscoggin writer, who signed herself "Conspirator," claimed that philosophical distinctions over the origins of life had little to do with abortion among her friends in Maine and would not deter "one out of ten, if it did one out of a hundred . . . from the commission of this deed." The aborters' "cry is 'Liberty or Death,' " and the only thing that would solve the abortion problem in America would be "liberty to women, freedom entire."

The most common variant of the view that abortion was a manifestation of the women's rights movement hinged upon the word "fashion." Over and over men claimed that women who aborted did so because they cared more about scratching for a better perch in society than they did about raising children. The dared not waste time on the latter lest they fall behind in the former. Women, in short, were accused of being aggressively self-indulgent. Some women, for example, had "the effrontery to say boldly, that they have neither the time nor inclination to nurse babies"; others exhibited "self-indulgence in most disgusting forms"; and many of the women practicing abortion were described as more interested in "selfish and personal ends" or "fast living" than in the maternity for which God had supposedly created them. Occasionally a medical writer would temper the general indictment by alluding to the deep-seated fears of pregnancy and birth among American women or by suggesting that a woman tied to a drunken or ill-providing husband who used no discretion in the exercise of his "marital rights" had enormous temptations to have herself aborted. But most medical writers continued to blame "so-called extravagance and dissipation" for a large proportion of the nation's abortions. Over and over physicians warned that the growing self-indulgence among American women represented a blow "at the very foundations of society." The practice of abortion was destroying American women physically and mentally, and, worst of all, undermining the basic relationships between them and men insofar as a willingness to abort signified a wife's rejection of her traditional role as housekeeper and child raiser. For this reason, some doctors urged that feticide be made a legal ground for divorce. A substantial number of writers between 1840 and 1880, in other words, were willing to portray women who had abortions as domestic subversives.

Another connection between abortion and the drive for women's rights was allegedly by an anonymous advocate of legalized abortion who addressed the Medico-Legal Society of New York in 1888. The writer argued that the nation's anti-abortion laws were a farce, and claimed that this was "due, doubtless, to the fact (unpleasant and unpalatable as it may sound, to state it) that [anti-abortion] was against the common and almost universal sentiment of womankind; she who was the greatest sufferer and victim of the social conditions, under which its practice became necessary and inevitable; she who dreaded more the consequences as affecting her social condition than she feared legal penalties, never in her heart respected the law nor held it binding on her conscience." He went on to advocate, in a series of rhetorical questions, "the rights" of a woman to determine "whether she will take upon herself the pangs and responsibilities and duties of maternity," citing feminist views of marriage as he went. Near the end of his discussion he challenged the antifeminist Medico-Legal Society to demonstrate "the manliness to speak one strong word for woman and womankind" on the issue of a wife's right to control her own reproductive capacities and to admit that a "hollow, shallow, mocking lie" underlay "the very base of the laws regarding abortion."

Notwithstanding the possibility that recourse to abortion sometimes reflected the rising consciousness of the women who had them, and notwithstanding the fact that some males, especially regular physicians, were distinctly uneasy about the practice because of what its ultimate effects upon the social position of women might be, the relationship between abortion and feminism in the nineteenth century nevertheless remained indirect and ironical. This becomes evident when the arguments of the feminists themselves are analyzed. One of the most forceful early statements of what subsequently became the feminist position on abortion was made in the 1850s in a volume entitled *The Unwelcome Child*. The author, Henry C. Wright, asserted that women alone had the right to say when they would become pregnant and blamed the tremendous outburst of abortion in America on selfishly sensual husbands. Wright's volume was more interesting than other similar tracts, however, because he published a large number of letters from women detailing the circumstances under which they had sought abortions.

One of Wright's letters was from a woman who had her first abortion in 1841, because her one-year-old first born was sick and her husband was earning almost nothing. She "consulted a lady friend, and by her persuasion and assistance, killed" the fetus she was carrying. When she found herself pregnant again shortly thereafter she "consulted a physician. . . . He was ready with his logic, his medicines and instruments, and told me how to destroy it. After experimenting on myself three months, I was successful. I killed my child about five months after conception." She steeled herself to go full term with her next pregnancy and to "endure" an addition to her impoverished and unhappy household. When pregnant again she "employed a doctor, to kill my child, and in the destruction of it . . . ended my power to be a mother." The woman's point throughout, however, was that abortion "was most repulsive" to her and her recourse to it "rendered [her] an object of loathing to [her]self." Abortion was not a purposeful female conspiracy, but an undesirable necessity forced by thoughtless men. As this woman put it: "I was the veriest slave alive."

All of the other letters from women that Wright published, even though one writer estimated that "six out of nine" of the women she knew well enough to ask had practiced abortion to some extent, reinforced the basic point made in the letter just cited: they hated to have to do it. Another woman, for example, who had aborted several times, looked back upon the first time and pondered the question, "How did I feel?"

> I consulted a woman, a friend in whom I trusted. I found that she had perpetrated that outrage on herself and on others. She told me it was not murder to kill a child any time before its birth. Of this she labored to convince me, and called in the aid of her "family physician," to give force to her arguments. He argued that it was right and just for wives thus to protect themselves against the results of their husband's sensualism,—told me that God and human laws would approve of killing children before they were born, rather than curse them with an undesired existence. My only trouble was, with God's view of the case, I could not get rid of the feeling that it was an outrage on my body and soul, and on my unconscious babe. He argued that my child, at five months (which was the time), had no life, and where there was no life, no life could be taken. Though I determined to do the deed, or get the "family physician" to do it, my womanly instincts, my reason, my conscience, my self-respect, my entire nature, revolted against my decision. My Womanhood rose up in withering condemnation.

Letter after letter elaborated variations on the same theme.

The attitudes expressed by Wright's correspondents in the 1840s and 1850s became the basis of the official position of American feminists toward abortion after the Civil War. As Elizabeth Cady Stanton phrased it, the practice was one more result of "the degradation of woman" in the nineteenth century, not of woman's rising consciousness or expanding opportunities outside the home. Stanton felt that the denial of children to "those [husbands] who have made the 'strong minded' women of this generation the target for gibes and jeers" was somehow tragically just. Yet Stanton and the vast majority of feminist spokeswomen were unwilling to condone abortion or encourage its practice. Virtually all feminists, even those around Victoria Woodhull, viewed the prevalence of abortion in the United States as understandable, under the circumstances, but looked forward to its elimination rather that its wholesale adoption by all women. The remedy to the problem of abortion in the United States, in their view, was not legalized abortion open to all but *the education and enfranchisement of women* which would make abortion unnecessary in a future world of egalitarian respect and sexual discretion. In short, most feminists, though they agreed completely with other observers that abortion was endemic in America by midcentury, did not blame the increase on the rising ambitions of women but asserted with Matilda E. J. Gage "that this crime of 'child murder,' 'abortion,' 'infanticide,' lies at the door of the male sex." The *Woman's Advocate* of Dayton, Ohio, put it even more forcefully in 1869: "Till men learn to check their sensualism, and leave their wives free to choose their periods of maternity, let us hear no more invectives against women for the destruction of prospective unwelcome children, whose dispositions, made miserable by unhappy antenatal conditions, would only make their lives a curse to themselves and others."

Even the so-called "free love" wing of the feminist movement refused to advocate abortion. Victoria Woodhull's spiritualist convention of 1873, for example, heard several women recount their own recourse to abortion, but treated the practice as an example of the hideous extremes to which modern marriage was driving American women, not as a right that women should be at liberty to exercise under normal circumstances. As Professor Linda Gordon has pointed out in a skillful analysis of the attitude of nineteenth-century feminists toward the notion of voluntary motherhood, even contraceptive devices were unacceptable to most feminists. Abortion was simply out of the question, at least as a publicly advocated policy. Professor Gordon found only one prominent feminist in the century who was willing to hedge on this position, and then not until 1893, when abortion was no longer a really viable alternative. Moreover, as Professor Gordon stated, "if she was [advocating legalized abortion], she was alone among all nineteenth-century sexual reformers in saying so." For most feminists the answer to unwanted pregnancies was abstinence.

Given their basic assumptions, many feminists ultimately found themselves in the anomalous position of endorsing the anti-feminist physicians' calls for anti-abortion legislation. Editorials and letters in the *Revolution* in 1869, while continuing to blame thoughtless, tyrannical husbands for the huge number of abortions in America, condemned the practice as a threat to and exploitation of women, and noted with approval the efforts of the New York state legislature that year to proscribe it more vigorously. In December 1869 Dr. Clemence S. Lozier, a leading female physician in New York City, a founder of the New York Medical School for Women, and a long-time president of the New York Suffrage Association, called the police and preferred charges against a couple who approached her for an abortion. Both the feminist press and the popular press approved.

Some of the most virulently anti-feminist physicians acknowledged the refusal of feminists to advocate abortion by explicitly conceding that the feminist analysis was not altogether wrong. They admitted that men not only condoned their wives' abortions, but frequently forced them either directly or indirectly to avoid having children. In 1866 the *Boston Medical and Surgical Journal* published a reply to Horatio Storer's *Why Not?*, which had attacked aborting wives in most unflattering terms. The reply, written by the anonymous "wife of a Christian physician," argued that "the *greatest* cause of abortion is one hidden from the world, *viz.:* unhappiness and want of consideration towards wives in the marriage relation, the more refined education of girls, and their subsequent revolting from the degradation of being a mere thing—an appendage." Far from counterattacking, Storer himself accepted the basic point and decided to make the abortifacient pressure exerted by husbands upon their wives the subject of an entire volume of public pleading, which he hoped would convince men to reduce that pressure. Many observers noted that husbands frequently became annoyed when their wives indicated that they might be pregnant and made it clear to their wives that they expected something to be done about it. John W. Trader, a Missouri physician, stated this often-repeated opinion in 1874 as straightforwardly as any feminist might:

> We do not affirm, neither would we have you think for a moment that the *onus* of this guilt lies at the feet of woman. Far from it. In a majority of cases, they are more sinned against than sinning. When the reformation begins in earnest, it must begin with us men who have been the aggressors, who in every age have first suggested the crime, and who in every age have compelled the execution of it.

Trader went on to register his disgust with the many men who "sneak" into doctors' offices to arrange for abortions upon their wives, or upon women they had seduced. George Cooper, who authored *Healthy Children* in 1875, was only one of many others to suggest that husbands like that were the real murderers; wives were only acting their properly obedient roles when they sought abortions under such circumstances.

Despite the blame and recrimination evoked by the great upsurge of abortion in the United States in the nineteenth century, some of which was directed at women and some at men, it appears likely that most decisions to use abortion probably involved couples conferring together, not just men imposing their wills or women acting unilaterally, and that abortion was the result of diffuse pressures, not merely the rising consciousness of women or the tyrannical aggressions of men. American men and women wanted to express their sexuality and mutual affections, on the one hand, and to limit their fertility, on the other. Abortion was neither desirable nor undesirable in itself, but rather one of the few available means of reconciling and realizing those two higher priorities. And it seems likely that the man and woman agreed to both of those higher priorities in most instances, thus somewhat mooting in advance the question of which one was more responsible for the decisions that made abortion a common phenomenon in mid-nineteenth-century America.

Court records provide one source of evidence for the mutuality of most abortion decisions. Almost every nineteenth-century abortion case that was written up, whether in the popular press, in medical journals, or in the official proceedings of state supreme courts, involved the agreement of both the man and the woman. There is no record of any man's ever having sued any woman for aborting his child. The woman in each case felt strongly enough about avoiding having a child that she consented to run whatever medical risks she thought were involved in the process. The man almost invariably encouraged her and cooperated with her and paid whatever expenses were incurred. Whether their respective motives were the same or different, social, financial, ideological, selfish, subconscious, or unknown, the decisions appear to have been mutually agreed upon.

Perhaps the best evidence for the likely mutuality of most abortion decisions is contained in the diary that Lester Frank Ward, who later became one of America's most famous sociologists, kept as a newlywed in the 1860s. Though Ward was unique in writing down the intimate decisions that he and his wife had to make, the couple seemed otherwise typical young Americans, almost as Tocqueville might have described them, anxious for further education and ambitious to get ahead quickly. Both Ward and his wife understood that a child would overburden their limited resources and reduce the probability of ever realizing either their individual goals of self-improvement or their mutual goals as a couple. They avoided pregnancy in pre-marital intercourse, then continued to avoid it after their marriage in August 1862. Not until early in 1864 did Lizzie Ward become pregnant. In March, without consulting her husband, she obtained "an effective remedy" from a local woman, which made her very sick for two days but helped her to terminate her pregnancy. She probably took this action after missing three or four periods; it was still early enough in gestation that her husband did not realize she was pregnant but late enough that lactation had begun. Ward noted in his diary that "the proof" she had been pregnant was "the milk" that appeared after the abortion.

Anti-feminists might have portrayed Lizzie Ward's action as diabolical, a betrayal of duty. Feminists might have viewed it as the only recourse open to a female who wanted both to further her own education and to remain on good terms with an ambitious spouse who would certainly have sacrificed his wife's goals to child-rearing, while he pursued his own. But the decision was really the result of a preexisting consensus between the two of them. Though Ward had not been party to the process in a legal or direct sense, which may go some distance toward confirming the role of abortion as a more uniquely female method of family limitation than contraception, he was clearly delighted that his wife was "out of danger" and would not be having a child. After this brush with family responsibility, the Wards tried a number of new methods of contraception, which they presumably hoped would be more effective than whatever they had been using to avoid pregnancy before Lizzie had to resort to abortion. These included both "pills" and "instruments." Not until the summer of 1865, after Ward had obtained a decent job in Washington, did the couple have a baby.

Abortion had been for the Wards what it apparently also was for many other American couples: an acceptable means toward a mutually desirable end, one of the only ways they had to allow themselves both to express their sexuality and affection toward each other with some degree of frequency and to postpone family responsibilities until they thought they were better prepared to raise children. The line of acceptability for most Americans trying to reconcile these twin priorities ran just about where Lizzie Ward had drawn it. Infanticide, the destruction of a baby after its birth, was clearly unacceptable, and so was abortion after quickening, though that was a much grayer area than infanticide. But abortion before quickening, like contraception itself, was an appropriate and legally permissible method of avoiding unwanted children. And it had one great advantage, as the Wards learned, over contraception: it worked. As more and more women began to practice abortion, however, and as the practice changed from being invisible to being visible, from being quantitatively insignificant to being a systematic practice that terminated a substantial number of pregnancies after 1840, and from being almost entirely a recourse of the desperate and socially marginal to being a commonly employed procedure among the middle and upper classes of American society, state legislators decided to reassess their policies toward the practice. Between 1840 and 1860 lawmakers in several states began to respond to the increase of abortion in American life. The laws they passed during that period are the subject of the following chapter.

Cotton remained the primary cash crop in the South
after the Civil War

The Freedpeople
Form a Community:
Promised Land, S.C.

ELIZABETH RAUH BETHEL

Even though the Thirteenth Amendment to the Constitution guaranteed the freedom of the former slaves, the future for the freedpeople was anything but clear. During slavery times their lives were stunted by oppressive laws and customs. Having been barred by law from free access to traditional institutions such as legal marriage, they entered upon freedom with almost insurmountable handicaps. Most had little or no education, had to seek normalization of family relationships, had been trained only to perform unskilled agricultural labor, and had to face continued onslaughts of discrimination and prejudice from their former overlords. In their favor was their eager enthusiasm to enjoy the benefits of their newly free condition, strong ties of kinship, the consolation and hope provided by an active religious life, and the willingness to work hard and long to free themselves from dependence on their former masters. For a few years during Reconstruction they also had the aid and support of such federal agencies as the Freedman's Bureau, which tried to assist them in adapting to the new situation in which they found themselves.

The leaders of the defeated Confederacy assumed that, even though legal slavery was gone, the traditional racial pattern of southern life would continue. Afro-Americans would constitute a dependent caste, existing to serve the needs of the dominant white society. In order to ensure that this condition would continue, southern states began in 1865 to pass black codes, systems of law which would replace the customs of slavery with a legally determined caste system. While Radical Reconstruction was able to eliminate many of the more oppressively discriminatory racial laws, it could not change the intent of the southern whites to maintain the racial barriers.

The former slaves reacted in various ways to the new situation. Many tried to exercise their new freedom by moving away from their former owners' homes, but still found themselves engaged in unskilled farm labor. Some who had developed artisan's skills during slavery were able to establish themselves as independent craftsmen. A few, whether through luck, enterprise, or skill, were able to achieve the elusive goal of almost all freedpeople—land ownership. The freedpeople and their friends realized that without economic independence, legal freedom would mean little. The way to economic independence in the South seemed to be through land ownership; the envisioned "forty acres and a mule" expressed their desire.

In the early days of Reconstruction, some plantations in the South were turned over to the freedpeople to farm. The lack of clear land titles and the hostility of the governments both North and South to land reform, however, led to a restoration of most of those plantations to their former owners or their sale at public auction. If land was to be owned by freedpeople, it would have to be bought by them. This fact alone prevented land ownership for the masses of Afro-Americans. In some cases, however, land ownership for freedpeople was made possible by the policies of Reconstruction state governments. Such a case is described in this selection reprinted from a book by Elizabeth Rauh Bethel, a sociologist at Lander College.

Professor Bethel's book describes not only the results of land ownership by freedpeople, but also a particular variety of community information. Some blacks in the South decided that the only way to survive in a hostile white environment was to have as little contact with that environment as possible, and so organized all-black towns and farm communities. Several of these towns have survived up to the present time, although they can not be said to have prospered. Still, for black people of the rural South, survival itself can be seen as a kind of prosperity. And those black communities such as Promised Land, South Carolina, Mound Bayou, Mississippi, and Boley, Oklahoma, that have survived reflect the determination of their inhabitants to live as fully as possible in a world which has denied them full partnership. The strands of kinship, religion, mutual aid, and hard work mesh in the effort to form and maintain a community life which has, for a century or more, expressed the determination of the freedpeople and their descendants to live free and independent.

For Sale: The homestead, grist mill, and 2742 acres of farmland
from the estate of Samuel Marshall, six miles from Abbeville. Contact estate
executors, S. S. Marshall and J. W. W. Marshall.
Abbeville, South Carolina Press
12 November 1869

DR. MARSHALL'S FARM

P romised Land was from the outset an artifact of Reconstruction politics. Its origins, as well, lie in the hopes, the dreams, and the struggles of four million Negroes, for the meaning of freedom was early defined in terms of land for most emancipated Negroes. In South Carolina, perhaps more intensely than any of the other southern states, the thirst for land was acute. It was a possibility sparked first by General William T. Sherman's military actions along the Sea Islands, then dashed as quickly as it was born in the distant arena of Washington politics. Still, the desire for land remained a goal not readily abandoned by the state's freedpeople, and they implemented a plan to achieve that goal at the first opportunity. Their chance came at the 1868 South Carolina Constitutional Convention.

South Carolina was among the southern states which refused to ratify the Fourteenth Amendment to the Constitution, the amendment which established the citizenship of the freedmen. Like her recalcitrant neighbors, the state was then placed under military government, as outlined by the Military Reconstruction Act of 1867. Among the mandates of that federal legislation was a requirement that each of the states in question draft a new state constitution which incorporated the principles of the Fourteenth Amendment. Only after such new constitutions were completed and implemented were the separate states of the defeated Confederacy eligible for readmission to the Union.

The representatives to these constitutional conventions were selected by a revolutionary electorate, one which included all adult male Negroes. Registration for the elections was handled by the Army with some informal assistance by "that God-forsaken institution, the Freedman's Bureau." Only South Carolina among the ten states of the former Confederacy elected a Negro majority to its convention. The instrument those representatives drafted called for four major social and political reforms in state government: a statewide system of free common schools; universal manhood suffrage; a jury law which included the Negro electorate in county pools of qualified jurors; and a land redistribution system designed to benefit the state's landless population, primarily the freedmen.

THE FREEDPEOPLE FORM A COMMUNITY: PROMISED LAND, S.C.   From *Promisedland: A Century of Life in a Negro Community*, by Elizabeth Rauh Bethel (Philadelphia: Temple University Press, 1981), pp. 17–40. Copyright © 1981 by Temple University.

White response to the new constitution and the social reforms which it outlined was predictably vitriolic. It was condemned by one white newspaper as "the work of sixty-odd Negroes, many of them ignorant and depraved." The authors were publicly ridiculed as representing "the maddest, most unscrupulous, and infamous revolution in history." Despite this and similar vilification, the constitution was ratified in the 1868 referendum, an election boycotted by many white voters and dominated by South Carolina's 81,000 newly enfranchised Negroes, who cast their votes overwhelmingly with the Republicans and for the new constitution.

That same election selected representatives to the state legislature charged with implementing the constitutional reforms. That body, like the constitutional convention, was constituted with a Negro majority; and it moved immediately to establish a common school system and land redistribution program. The freedmen were already registered, and the new jury pools remained the prerogative of the individual counties. The 1868 election also was notable for the numerous attacks and "outrages" which occurred against the more politically active freedmen. Among those Negroes assaulted, beaten, shot, and lynched during the pre-election campaign months were four men who subsequently bought small farms from the Land Commission and settled at Promised Land. Like other freedmen in South Carolina, their open involvement in the state's Republican political machinery led to personal violence.

Wilson Nash was the first of the future Promised Land residents to encounter white brutality and retaliation for his political activities. Nash was nominated by the Republicans as their candidate for Abbeville County's seat in the state legislature at the August 1868 county convention. In October of that year, less than two weeks before the general election, Nash was attacked and shot in the leg by two unidentified white assailants. The "outrage" took place in the barn on his rented farm, not far from Dr. Marshall's farm on Curltail Creek. Wilson Nash was thirty-three years old in 1868, married, and the father of three small children. He had moved from "up around Cokesbury" within Abbeville County, shortly after emancipation to the rented land further west. Within months after the Nash family was settled on their farm, Wilson Nash joined the many Negroes who affiliated with the Republicans, an alliance probably instigated and encouraged by Republican promises of land to the freedmen. The extent of Nash's involvement with local politics was apparent in his nomination for public office; and this same nomination brought him to the forefront of county Negro leadership and to the attention of local whites.

After the attack Nash sent his wife and young children to a neighbor's home, where he probably believed they would be safe. He then mounted his mule and fled his farm, leaving behind thirty bushels of recently harvested corn. Whether Nash also left behind a cotton crop is unknown. It was the unprotected corn crop that worried him as much as his concern for his own safety. He rode his mule into Abbeville and there sought refuge at the local Freedman's Bureau office where he reported the attack to the local bureau agent and requested military protection for his family and his corn crop. Captain W. F. DeKnight was sympathetic to Nash's plight but was powerless to assist or protect him. DeKnight had no authority in civil matters such as this, and the men who held that power generally ignored such assaults on Negroes. The Nash incident was typical and followed a familiar pattern. The assailants remained unidentified, unapprehended, and unpunished. The attack achieved the desired end, however, for Nash withdrew his name from the slate of legislative candidates. For him there were other considerations which took priority over politics.

Violence against the freedmen of Abbeville County, as elsewhere in the state, continued that fall and escalated as the 1868 election day neared. The victims had in common an involvement with the Republicans, and there was little distinction made between direct and indirect partisan activity. Politically visible Negroes were open targets. Shortly after the Nash shooting young Willis Smith was assaulted, yet another victim of Reconstruction violence. Smith was still a teenager and too young to vote in the election, but his age afforded him no immunity. He was a known member of the Union League, the most radical and secret of the political organizations which attracted freedmen. While attending a dance one evening, Smith and four other League members were dragged outside the dance hall and brutally beaten by four white men whose identities were hidden by hoods. This attack, too, was an act of political vengeance. It was, as well, one of the earliest Ku Klux Klan appearances in Abbeville. Like other crimes committed against politically active Negroes, this one remained unsolved.

On election day freedmen Washington Green and Allen Goode were precinct managers at the White Hall polling place, near the southern edge of the Marshall land. Their position was a political appointment of some prestige, their reward for affiliation with and loyalty to the Republican cause. The appointment brought them, like Wilson Nash and Willis Smith, to the attention of local whites. On election day the voting proceeded without incident until midday, when two white men attempted to block Negroes from entering the polling site. A scuffle ensued as Green and Goode, acting in their capacity as voting officials, tried to bring the matter to a halt and were shot by the white men. One freedman was killed, two others injured, in the incident which also went unsolved. In none of the attacks were the assailants ever apprehended. Within twenty-four months all four men—Wilson Nash, Willis Smith, Washington Green, and Allen Goode—bought farms at Promised Land.

Despite the violence which surrounded the 1868 elections, the Republicans carried the whole of the state. White Democrats refused to support an election they deemed illegal, and they intimidated the newly enfranchised Negro electorate at every opportunity. The freedmen, nevertheless, flocked to the polls in an unprecedented exercise of their new franchise and sent a body of legislative representatives to the state capital of Columbia who were wholly committed to the mandates and reforms of the new constitution. Among the first legislative acts was one which formalized the land redistribution program through the creation of the South Carolina Land Commission.

The Land Commission program, as designed by the legislature, was financed through the public sale of state bonds. The capital generated from the bond sales was used to purchase privately owned plantation tracts which were then subdivided and resold to freedmen through long-term (ten years), low-interest (7 percent per annum) loans. The bulk of the commission's transactions occurred along the coastal areas of the state where land was readily available. The labor and financial problems of the rice planters of the low-country were generally more acute than those of the up-country cotton planters. As a result, they were more eager to dispose of a portion of the landholdings at a reasonable price, and their motives for their dealings with the Land Commission were primarily pecuniary.

Piedmont planters were not so motivated. Many were able to salvage their production by negotiating sharecropping and tenant arrangements. Most operated on a smaller scale than the low-country planters and were less dependent on gang labor arrangements. As a consequence, few were as financially pressed as their low-country counterparts, and land was less available for purchase by the Land Commission in the Piedmont region. With only 9 percent of the commission purchases lying in the up-country, the Marshall lands were the exception rather than the rule.

The Marshall sons first advertised the land for sale in 1865. These lands, like others at the eastern edge of the Cotton Belt, were exhausted from generations of cultivation and attendant soil erosion; and for such worn out land the price was greatly inflated. Additionally, two successive years of crop failures, low cotton prices, and a general lack of capital discouraged serious planters from purchasing the lands. The sons then advertised the tract for rent, but the land stood idle. The family wanted to dispose of the land in a single transaction rather than subdivide it, and Dr. Marshall's farm was no competition for the less expensive and more fertile land to the west that was opened for settlement after the war. In 1869 the two sons once again advertised the land for sale, but conditions in Abbeville County were not improved for farmers, and no private buyer came forth.

Having exhausted the possibilities for negotiating a private sale, the family considered alternative prospects for the disposition of a farm that was of little use to them. James L. Orr, a moderate Democrat, former governor (1865 to 1868), and family son-in-law, served as negotiator when the tract was offered to the Land Commission at the grossly inflated price of ten dollars an acre. Equivalent land in Abbeville County was selling for as little as two dollars an acre, and the commission rejected the offer. Political promises took precedence over financial considerations when the commission's regional agent wrote the Land Commission's Advisory Board that "if the land is not bought the (Republican) party is lost in this district." Upon receipt of his advice the commission immediately met the Marshall family's ten dollar an acre price. By January 1870 the land was subdivided into fifty small farms, averaging slightly less than fifty acres each, which were publicly offered for sale to Negro as well as white buyers.

The Marshall Tract was located in the central sector of old Abbeville County and was easily accessible to most of the freedmen who were to make the lands their home. Situated in the western portion of the state, the tract was approximately sixty miles northwest of Augusta, Georgia, one hundred and fifty miles northeast of Atlanta, and the same distance northwest of Charleston. It would attract few freedmen from the urban areas. Two roads intersected within the lands. One, running north to south, linked those who soon settled there with the county seat of Abbeville to the north and the Phoenix community, a tiny settlement composed primarily of white small-scale farmers approximately eighteen miles to the south. Called New Cut Road, Five Notch Road, and later White Hall Road, the dirt wagon route was used primarily for travel to Abbeville. The east-west road, which would much later be converted to a state highway, was the more heavily traveled of the two and linked the cluster of farms to the village of Greenwood, six miles to the east, and the small settlement of Verdery, three miles to the west. Beyond Verdery, which served for a time as a stagecoach stop on the long trip between Greenville and Augusta, lay the Savannah River. The road was used regularly by a variety of peddlers and salesmen who included the Negro farmers on their routes as soon as families began to move onto the farms. Despite the decidedly rural setting, the families who bought land there were not isolated. A regular stream of travelers brought them news of events from well beyond their limitied geography and helped them maintain touch with a broader scope of activities and ideas than their environment might have predicted.

The Marshall Tract had only one natural boundary to delineate the perimeter of Negro-owned farms, Curltail Creek on the north. Other less distinctive markers were devised as the farms were settled, to distinguish the areas from surrounding white-owned lands. Extending south from White Hall Road, "below the cemetery, south of the railroad about a mile" a small lane intersected the larger road. This was Rabbit Track Road, and it marked the southern edge of Negro-owned lands. To the east the boundary was marked by another dirt lane called Lorenzo Road, little more than a trail which led to the Seaboard Railroad flag stop. Between the crossroads and Verdery to the west, "the edge of the old Darraugh place" established the western perimeter. In all, the tract encompassed slightly more than four square miles of earth.

The farms on the Marshall Tract were no bargain for the Negroes who bought them. The land was only partially cleared and ready for cultivation, and that which was free of pine trees and underbrush was badly eroded. There was little to recommend the land to cotton farming. Crop failures in 1868 and 1869 severely limited the local economy, which further reduced the possibilities for small farmers working on badly depleted soil. There was little credit available to Abbeville farmers, white or black; and farming lacked not only an unqualified promise of financial gain but even the possibility of breaking even at harvest. Still, it was not the fertility of the soil or the possibility of economic profit that attracted the freedmen to those farms. The single opportunity for landownership, a status which for most Negroes in 1870 symbolized the essence of their freedom, was the prime attraction for the freedmen who bought farms from the subdivided Marshall Tract.

Most of the Negroes who settled the farms knew the area and local conditions well. Many were native to Abbeville County. In addition to Wilson Nash, the Moragne family and their in-laws, the Turners, the Pinckneys, the Letmans, and the Williamses were also natives of Abbeville, from "down over by Bordeaux" in the southwestern rim of the county which borders Georgia. Others came to their new farms from "Dark Corner, over by McCormick," and another nearby Negro settlement, Pettigrew Station—both in Abbeville County. The Redd family lived in Newberry, South Carolina before they bought their farm; and James and Hannah Fields came to Promised Land from the state capital, Columbia, eighty miles to the east.

Many of the settlers from Abbeville County shared their names with prominent white families—Moragne, Burt, Marshall, Pressley, Frazier, and Pinckney. Their claims to heritage were diverse. One recalled "my grandaddy was a white man from England," and others remembered slavery times to their children in terms of white fathers who "didn't allow nobody to mess with the colored boys of his." Others dismissed the past and told their grandchildren that "some things is best forgot." A few were so fair skinned that "they could have passed for white if they wanted to," while others who bought farms from the Land Commission "was so black there wasn't no doubt about who their daddy was."

After emancipation many of these former bondsmen stayed in their old neighborhoods, farming in much the same way as they had during slavery times. Some "worked for the marsters at daytime and for they-selves at night" in an early Piedmont version of sharecropping. Old Samuel Marshall was one former slave owner who retained many of his bondsmen as laborers by assuring them that they would receive some land of their own—promising them that "if you clean two acres you get two acres; if you clean ten acres you get ten acres" of farmland. It was this promise which kept some freedmen on the Marshall land until it was sold to the Land Commission. They cut and cleared part of the tract of the native pines and readied it for planting in anticipation of ownership. But the promise proved empty, and Marshall's death and the subsequent sale of his lands to the state deprived many of those who labored day and night on the land of the free farms they hoped would be theirs. "After they had cleaned it up they still had to pay for it." Other freedmen in the county "moved off after slavery ended but couldn't get no place" of their own to farm. Unable to ne-gotiate labor or lease arrangements, they faced a time of homelessness with few resources and limited options until the farms became avail-able to them. A few entered into labor contracts supervised by the Freedman's Bureau or settled on rented farms in the county for a time.

The details of the various postemancipation economic arrange-ments made by the freedmen who settled on the small tracts at Dr. Marshall's farm, whatever the form they assumed, were dominated by three conscious choices all had in common. The first was their decision to stay in Abbeville County following emancipation. For most of the people who eventually settled in Promised Land, Abbeville was their home as well as the site of their enslavement. There they were sur-rounded by friends, family and a familiar environment. The second choice this group of freedmen shared was occupational. They had been Piedmont farmers throughout their enslavement, and they chose to re-main farmers in their freedom.

Local Negroes made a third conscious decision that for many had long-range importance in their lives and those of their descendents. Through the influence of the Union League, the Freedman's Bureau, the African Methodist Church, and each other, many of the Negroes in Abbeville aligned politically with the Republicans between 1865 and 1870. In Abbeville as elsewhere in the state, this alliance was estab-lished enthusiastically. The Republicans promised land as well as suf-frage to those who supported them. If their political activities became public knowledge, the freedmen "were safe nowhere"; and men like Wilson Nash, Willis Smith, Washington Green, and Allen Goode who were highly visible Negro politicians took great risks in this exercise of freedom. Those risks were not without justification. It was probably not a coincidence that loyalty to the Republican cause was followed by a chance to own land.

LAND FOR SALE TO THE COLORED PEOPLE

*I have 700 acres of land to sell in lots of from 50 to 100 acres or more
situated six miles from Abbeville.* Terms: *A liberal cash payment;
balance to be made in three annual payments from date of purchase.*
J. Hollinshead, Agent
(Advertisement placed by the Land Commission
in Abbeville *Press*, 2 July 1873)

The Land Commission first advertised the farms on the Marshall Tract
in January and February 1870. Eleven freedmen and their families established conditional ownership of their farms before spring planting
that year. They were among a vanguard of some 14,000 Negro families
who acquired small farms in South Carolina through the Land Commission program between 1868 and 1879. With a ten-dollar down payment they acquired the right to settle on and till the thin soil. They
were also obliged to place at least half of their land under cultivation
within three years and to pay all taxes due annually in order to retain
their ownership rights.

Among the earliest settlers to the newly created farms was Allen
Goode, the precinct manager at White Hall, who bought land in January 1870, almost immediately after it was put on the market. Two
brothers-in-law, J. H. Turner and Primus Letman, also bought farms in
the early spring that year. Turner was married to LeAnna Moragne and
Letman to LeAnna's sister Francis. Elias Harris, a widower with six
young children to raise, also came to his lands that spring, as did George
Hearst, his son Robert, and their families. Another father-son partnership, Carson and Will Donnelly, settled on adjacent tracts. Willis Smith's
father Daniel also bought a farm in 1870.

Allen Goode was the wealthiest of these early settlers. He owned
a horse, two oxen, four milk cows, and six hogs. For the other families,
both material resources and farm production were modest. Few of the
homesteaders produced more than a single bale of cotton on their new
farms that first year; but all, like Wilson Nash two years earlier, had
respectable corn harvests, a crop essential to "both us and the animals." Most households also had sizable pea, bean, and sweet potato
crops and produced their own butter. All but the cotton crops were
destined for household consumption, as these earliest settlers established a pattern of subsistence farming that would prevail as a community economic strategy in the coming decades.

This decision by the Promised Land farmers to intensify food production and minimize cotton cultivation, whether intentional or the result of other conditions, was an important initial step toward their
attainment of economic self-sufficiency. Small scale cotton farmers in
the Black Belt were rarely free agents. Most were quickly trapped in a

web of chronic indebtedness and marketing restrictions. Diversification of cash crops was inhibited during the 1870's and 1880's not only by custom and these economic entanglements but also by an absence of local markets, adequate roads, and methods of transportation to move crops other than cotton to larger markets. The Promised Land farmers, generally unwilling to incur debts with the local lien men if they could avoid it, turned to a modified form of subsistence farming as their only realistic land-use option. Through this strategy many of them avoided the "economic nightmare" which fixed the status of other small-scale cotton growers at a level of permanent peonage well into the twentieth century.

The following year, 1871, twenty-five more families scratched up their ten-dollar down payment; and upon presenting it to Hollinshead obtained conditional titles to farms on the Marshall Tract. The Williams family, Amanda and her four adult sons—William, Henry, James, and Moses—purchased farms together that year, probably withdrawing their money from their accounts at the Freedman's Savings and Trust Company Augusta Branch for their separate down payments. Three of the Moragne brothers—Eli, Calvin, and Moses—joined the Turners and the Letmans, their sisters and brothers-in-law, making five households in that corner of the tract soon designated "Moragne Town." John Valentine, whose family was involved in A.M.E. organizational work in Abbeville County, also obtained a conditional title to a farm, although he did not settle there permanently. Henry Redd, like the Williamses, withdrew his savings from the Freedman's Bank and moved to his farm from Newberry, a small town about thirty miles to the east. Moses Wideman, Wells Gray, Frank Hutchison, Samuel Bulow, and Samuel Burt also settled on their farms before spring planting.

As the cluster of Negro-owned farms grew more densely populated, it gradually assumed a unique identity; and this identity, in turn, gave rise to a name, Promised Land. Some remember their grandparents telling them that "the Governor in Columbia [South Carolina] named this place when he sold it to the Negroes." Others contend that the governor had no part in the naming. They argue that these earliest settlers derived the name Promised Land from the conditions of their purchase. "They only promised to pay for it, but they never did!" Indeed, there is some truth in that statement. For although the initial buyers agreed to pay between nine and ten dollars per acre for their land in the original promissory notes, few fulfilled the conditions on those contracts. Final purchase prices were greatly reduced from ten dollars to $3.25 per acre, a price more in line with prevailing land prices in the Piedmont.

By the end of 1873 forty-four of the fifty farms on the Marshall Tract had been sold. The remaining land, less than seven hundred acres, was the poorest in the tract, badly eroded and at the perimeter of the community. Some of those farms remained unsold until the early 1880's, but even so the land did not go unused. Families too poor to consider buying the farms lived on the state-owned property throughout the 1870's. They were squatters, living there illegally and rent-free, perhaps working a small cotton patch, always a garden. Their conditions contrasted sharply with that of the landowners who, like other Negroes who purchased farmland during the 1870's, were considered the most prosperous of the rural freedmen. The freeholders in the community were among the pioneers in a movement to acquire land, a movement that stretched across geographical and temporal limits. Even in the absence of state or federal assistance in other regions, and despite the difficulties Negroes faced in negotiating land purchases directly from white landowners during Reconstruction, by 1875 Negroes across the South owned five million acres of farmland. The promises of emancipation were fulfilled for a few, among them the families at Promised Land.

Settlement of the community coincided with the establishment of a public school, another of the revolutionary social reforms mandated by the 1868 constitution. It was the first of several public facilities to serve community residents and was built on land still described officially as "Dr. Marshall's farm." J. H. Turner, Larkin Reynolds, Iverson Reynolds, and Hutson Lomax, all Negroes, were the first school trustees. The families established on their new farms sent more than ninety children to the one-room school. Everyone who could be spared from the fields was in the classroom for the short 1870 school term. Although few of the children in the landless families attended school regularly, the landowning families early established a tradition of school attendance for their children consonant with their new status. With limited resources the school began the task of educating local children.

The violence and terror experienced by some of the men of Promised Land during 1868 recurred three years later when Eli and Wade Moragne were attacked and viciously beaten with a wagon whip by a band of Klansmen. Wade was twenty-three that year, Eli two years older. Both were married and had small children. It was rumored that the Moragne brothers were among the most prominent and influential of the Negro Republicans in Abbeville County. Their political activity, compounded by an unusual degree of self-assurance, pride, and dignity, infuriated local whites. Like Wilson Nash, Willis Smith, Washington Green, and Allen Goode, the Moragne brothers were victims of insidious political reprisals. Involvement in Reconstruction politics for Negroes was a dangerous enterprise and one which addressed the past as well as the future. It was an activity suited to young men and those who faced the future bravely. It was not for the timid.

The Republican influence on the freedmen at Promised Land was unmistakable, and there was no evidence that the "outrages" and terrorizations against them slowed their participation in local partisan ac-

tivities. In addition to the risks, there were benefits to be accrued from
their alliance with the Republicans. They enjoyed appointments as precinct managers and school trustees. As candidates for various public
offices, they experienced a degree of prestige and public recognition
which offset the element of danger they faced. These men, born slaves,
rose to positions of prominence as landowners, as political figures, and
as makers of a community. Few probably had dared to dream of such
possibilities a decade earlier.

During the violent years of Reconstruction there was at least one
official attempt to end anarchy in Abbeville County. The representative
to the state legislature, J. Hollinshead—the former regional agent for
the Land Commission—stated publicly what many Negroes already knew
privately, that "numerous outrages occur in the county and the laws
cannot be enforced by civil authorities." From the floor of the General
Assembly of South Carolina Hollinshead called for martial law in Abbeville, a request which did not pass unnoticed locally. The Editor of the
Press commented on Hollinshead's request for martial law by declaring
that such outrages against the freedmen "exist only in the imagination
of the legislator." His response was probably typical of the cavalier
attitude of southern whites toward the problems of their former bondsmen. Indeed, there were no further reports of violence and attacks
against freedmen carried by the *Press*, which failed to note the murder
of County Commissioner Henry Nash in February 1871. Like other victims of white terrorists, Nash was a Negro.

While settlement of Dr. Marshall's Farm by the freedmen proceeded, three community residents were arrested for the theft of "some
oxen from Dr. H. Drennan who lives near the 'Promiseland.' " Authorities found the heads, tails, and feet of the slaughtered animals
near the homes of Ezekiel and Moses Williams and Colbert Jordan. The
circumstantial evidence against them seemed convincing; and the three
were arrested and then released without bond pending trial. Colonel
Cothran, a former Confederate officer and respected barrister in Abbeville, represented the trio at their trial. Although freedmen in Abbeville
courts were generally convicted of whatever crime they were charged
with, the Williamses and Jordan were acquitted. Justice for Negroes
was always a tenuous affair; but it was especially so before black, as
well as white, qualified electors were included in the jury pool. The
trial of the Williams brothers and Jordan signaled a termporary truce
in the racial war, a truce which at least applied to those Negroes settling the farms at Promised Land.

In 1872, the third year of settlement, Promised Land gained nine
more households as families moved to land that they "bought for a
dollar an acre." There they "plow old oxen, build log cabin houses" as
they settled the land they bought "from the Governor in Columbia."
Colbert Jordan and Ezekiel Williams, cleared of the oxen stealing charges,
both purchased farms that year. Family and kinship ties drew some of

the new migrants to the community. Joshuway Wilson, married to Moses Wideman's sister Delphia, bought a farm near his brother-in-law. Two more Moragne brothers, William and Wade, settled near the other family members in "Moragne Town." Whitfield Hutchison, a jack-leg preacher, bought the farm adjacent to his brother Frank. "Old Whit Hutchison could sing about let's go down to the water and be baptized. He didn't have no education, and he didn't know exactly how to put his words, but when he got to singing he could make your hair rise up. He was a number one preacher." Hutchison was not the only preacher among those first settlers. Isaac Y. Moragne, who moved to Promised Land the following year, and several men in the Turner family all combined preaching and farming.

Not all of the settlers came to their new farms as members of such extensive kinship networks as the Moragnes, who counted nine brothers, four sisters, and an assortment of spouses and children among the first Promised Land residents. Even those who joined the community in relative isolation, however, were seldom long in establishing kinship alliances with their neighbors. One such couple was James and Hannah Fields who lived in Columbia before emancipation. While still a slave, James Fields owned property in the state capitol, which was held in trust for him by his master. After emancipation Fields worked for a time as a porter on the Columbia and Greenville Railroad and heard about the up-country land for sale to Negroes as he carried carpet bags and listened to political gossip on the train. Fields went to Abbeville County to inspect the land before he purchased a farm there. While he was visiting, he "run up on Mr. Nathan Redd," old Henry Redd's son. The Fieldses' granddaughter Emily and Nathan were about the same age, and Fields proposed a match to young Redd. "You marry my granddaughter, and I'll will all this land to you and her." The marriage was arranged before the farm was purchased, and eventually the land was transferred to the young couple.

By the conclusion of 1872 forty-eight families were settled on farms in Promised Land. Most of the land was under cultivation, as required by law; but the farmers were also busy with other activities. In addition to the houses and barns which had to be raised as each new family arrived with their few possessions, the men continued their political activities. Iverson Reynolds, J. H. Turner, John and Elias Tolbert, Judson Reynolds, Oscar Pressley, and Washington Green, all community residents, were delegates to the county Republican convention in August 1872. Three of the group were landowners. Their political activities were still not received with much enthusiasm by local whites, but reaction to Negro involvement in politics was lessening in hostility. The *Press* mildly observed that the fall cotton crop was being gathered with good speed and "the farmers have generally been making good use of their time." Cotton picking and politics were both seasonal, and the newspaper chided local Negroes for their priorities. "The blacks have been indulging a little too much in politics but are getting right again." Iverson Reynolds and Washington Green, always among the community's Republican leadership during the 1870's, served as local election managers again for the 1872 fall elections. The men from Promised Land voted without incident that year.

Civic participation among the Promised Land residents extended beyond partisan politics when the county implemented the new jury law in 1872. There had been no Negro jurors for the trial of the Williams brothers and Colbert Jordan the previous year. Although the inclusion of Negroes in the jury pools was a reform mandated in 1868, four years passed before Abbeville authorities drew up new jury lists from the revised voter registration rolls. The jury law was as repugnant to the whties as Negro suffrage, termed a "wretched attempt at legislation, which surpasses anything which has yet been achieved by the Salons in Columbia." When the new lists were finally completed in 1872 the *Press*, ever the reflection of local white public opinion, predicted that "many of [the freedmen] probably have moved away; and the chances are that not many of them will be forthcoming" in the call to jury duty. Neither the initial condemnation of the law nor the optimistic undertones of the *Press* prediction stopped Pope Moragne and Iverson Reynolds from responding to their notices from the Abbeville Courthouse. Both landowners rode their mules up Five Notch Road from Promised Land to Abbeville and served on the county's first integrated jury in the fall of 1872. Moragne and Reynolds were soon followed by others from the community—Allen Goode, Robert Wideman, William Moragne, James Richie, and Luther (Shack) Moragne. By 1874, less than five years after settlement of Dr. Marshall's farm by the new Negro landowners began, the residents of Promised Land remained actively involved in Abbeville County politics. They were undaunted by the *Press* warning that "just so soon as the colored people lose the confidence and support of the North their doom is fixed. The fate of the red man will be theirs." They were voters, jurors, taxpayers, and trustees of the school their children attended. Their collective identity as an exclusive Negro community was well established.

ONLY COLORED DOWN IN THIS OLD PROMISED LAND

Abbeville County, South Carolina
Mr. John Lomax passed through the Promised Land yesterday, and he thinks the crops there almost a failure. The corn will not average two bushels to the acre, and the cotton about 300 pounds [less than one bale] to the acre. A large quantity of sorghum cane was planted. It was almost worthless. The land appeared as if it had been very well cultivated.
Abbeville *Press*
30 September 1874

The forty-eight men and women who established conditional owner-ship of the farms at Promised Land between 1870 and 1872 were re-quired by law to place at least half of their land under cultivation within three years of their purchase. There was, however, no requirement about the crops to be planted. The men who established that cultivation stan-dard probably assumed that cotton would be the major cash crop, as it was throughout the Piedmont. At Promised Land cotton was indeed planted on every one of the farms, but not in overwhelming amounts. The relatively small cotton fields were overshadowed by fields of corn, peas, and sorghum cane; and the sense of permanence among the set-tlers was clearly evident when "they planted peach trees and pear trees and had grape vines all over" the land, which only a few years before was either uncleared of native pine forests or part of the up-country plantation system. Cotton, the antebellum crop of the slaves, became the cash crop of freedom. It would never dominate the lives of the farmers at Promised Land.

The 1870's were economically critical years for the new landown-ers. They had mortgage payments to meet and taxes to pay, but they also had families to feed. In 1870, when the price of cotton reached twenty-two cents a pound, all this was possible. In the following years, however, cotton prices declined dramatically. This, combined with generally low cotton yields, resulted in economic hardship for many of the farmers. Poverty was their constant neighbor, and their struggle for survival drew them into a cycle of indebtedness to white "lien men."

In those depression years there was little credit in the Piedmont. "The poor people wasn't able to buy their fertilize. That's what makes your cotton." Storekeepers and merchants reserved their resources for the local white planters, and the Negro farmers were forced to find credit from other sources. They turned to their white landowning neighbors and in some cases their former masters, the Devlin family in Verdery; the Tuck family, nearby farmers; and the Hendersons, Ver-dery merchants. To them the Promised Land farmers paid usurious interest rates for the fertilizer they needed "to make a bale of cotton" and the other supplies and foodstuffs they required to survive the growing season.

It was during this decade that the community farmers learned to maintain a skillful balance between a small cotton cash crop and their subsistence fields. Careful in the management of debt, most landown-ers probably used their cotton crop to meet their mortgage payment to the Land Commission and their tax bill to the county. There was never any surplus on the small farms, and a crop failure had immediate and personal consequences. At best a family would go hungry. At worst they would lose their farm.

Times were hard; and, despite generally shrewd land and debt management, twenty of the original settlers lost title to their land during the early 1870's. All migrated from Promised Land before the 1875 growing season. An advertisement in the *Press* attracted some new purchasers to the vacated farms, but most buyers learned of the land through friends and relatives. New families once again moved on to the land. Wilson Nash bought the farm originally purchased by John Valentine; both men were church leaders and probably discussed the transaction in some detail before the agreement was finalized.

Allen Goode, Wells Gray, and James Fields added to their holdings, buying additional farms from discouraged families who were leaving. Moses Wideman's younger brothers, William and Richmond, together bought an eighty-five-acre farm and then divided it, creating two more homesteads in the community. J. H. Turner, who secured a teaching position in an Edgefield County public school, sold his farm to his brother-in-law Isaac Y. Moragne. Each of the landowners had a brother, a cousin, or a friend who was eager to assume the financial burden of landownership; and none of the twenty vacated farms remained unoccupied for long. Promised Land quickly regained its population. The new arrivals strengthened and expanded the kinship bonds, which already crisscrossed and united individual households in the community.

Marriage provided the most common alliance between kinship groups. The Wilson and Wideman families and the Fields and Redds were both so related. The use of land as dowry, first employed by James Fields to arrange his granddaughter's marriage to Nathan Redd, provided a convenient and viable bargaining tool. When Iverson Reynolds bought his thirty-acre farm he also purchased a second, twenty-acre tract in his daughter's name, looking forward to the time of her marriage. "When Oscar Pressley married Iverson Reynold's daughter, Janie, Iverson Reynolds give him that land or sold it to him. But he got that farm from old Iverson Reynolds when he got married." The Moragnes, Turners, Pickneys, and Letmans were also united through land-based dowry arrangements. "The Moragne women is the ones that had the land. All them, the Turners, the Pickneys, and the Letmans—all them got into the Moragnes when the women married these men."

Marriage did not always accompany kinship bonds, for at Promised Land, like every place else, "some folks have childrens when they not married. Things get all mixed up sometimes." Still, the community was a small and intimate place, woven together as early as the 1880's by a complex and interlocking series of kin ties, which were supplemented by many other kinds of personal relationships. The separation of public and private spheres blurred; and, married or not, "when the gals get a baby" everyone was aware of the heritage and family ties of new babies. "Andrew Moragne supposed to been his daddy, but his momma was a Bradley so he took the name Bradley." Even so, promiscuity and illegitimacy were not casually accepted facts of life. Both were sinful and disgraceful not just to the couple but to their families as well. For women a pregnancy without marriage was particularly painful. "Some might be mean to you then," and many refused to even speak publicly to an unmarried woman who became pregnant. "All that stop when the baby is born. Don't want to punish an innocent baby." Legitimate or not, babies were welcomed into families and the community, and the sins of the parents were set aside. Ultimately, the bonds of kinship proved more powerful than collective morality, and these bonds left few residents of the community excluded from an encompassing network of cousins, aunts, uncles, and half-brothers and sisters.

As the landowning population of Promised Land stabilized, local resources emerged to meet day-to-day needs. A molasses mill, where the farmers had their sorghum cane ground into molasses by Joshuway Wilson's oldest son Fortune, opened in the community. Two corn and wheat grist mills opened on Curltail Creek. One, the old Marshall Mill, was operated by Harrison Cole, a Negro who subsequently purchased a vacant farm in the community. The other, the former Donalds Mill, was owned and operated by James Evans, an Irish immigrant whose thirst for land equaled that of his Negro neighbors. North Carter, the youngest son of landowner Marion Carter, opened a small general store at the east-west crossroads, where he sold candy, kerosene, salt, and other staples to his neighbors, extending credit when necessary, knowing that they would pay when they could. Long before the final land purchase was completed, the freedmen at Promised Land had established a framework for economic and social self-sufficiency.

The farms, through hard work, decent weather, and an eight-month growing season, soon yielded food for the households. A pattern of subsistence agriculture provided each Promised Land family a degree of independence and self-reliance unknown to most other Negro families in the area. Cows produced milk and butter for the tables, and chickens eggs and fresh poultry. Draft animals and cash money were both scarce commodities, but "in them days nobody ever went hungry." Hogs provided the major source of meat in the community's subsistence economy. "My mother and them used to kill hogs and put them down in salt in wood boxes and cover them so flies couldn't get to them for about five or six weeks. Take it out and wash it, put on red pepper and such, hang it up to dry, and that meat be *good*." The absence of an abundant cotton crop was not a sign of lack of industry. Prosperity, as well as productivity, was measured against hunger; and, in the never-ending farm cycle, fields were planted according to the number of people in each household, the number of mouths to be fed.

Community and household autonomy were firmly grounded in the economic independence of the land. Both were strengthened with the establishment of a church in Promised Land. In 1875, fully a decade before the final farms were settled, James Fields sold one acre of his land to the Trustees of Mt. Zion A.M.E. Church. It was a sign of the times. At Promised Land, as elsewhere in the South, freedmen withdrew from white churches as quickly as possible. Membership in the Baptist and Methodist denominations increased tenfold between 1860–1870 as the new Negro churches in the South took form. Mt. Zion was relatively late in emerging as a part of that movement for independence from white domination, but the residents of Promised Land were preoccupied for a time with more basic concerns. The fields had to be established as productive before community residents turned their energies to other aspects of community development.

The Field's land, located squarely in the geographical center of Promised Land, was within a two-mile walk of all the houses in the community. On this thinly wooded tract the men carved out a brush arbor, a remnant of slavery days; and Isaac Y. Moragne led everybody in the young settlement in prayers and songs. From the beginning of their emancipation schools and churches were central components of Negro social life; and at Promised Land religion, like education, was established as a permanent part of community life while the land was still being cleared.

NEWCOMERS AND COMMUNITY GROWTH

Most families survived those first settlement years, the droughts and crop failures, Ku Klux Klan attacks, and the violent years of Reconstruction. They met their mortgage payments and their taxes, and the years after 1875 were relatively prosperous ones. Promised Land was well established before the Compromise of 1877, the withdrawal of federal troops from the state, and the election of Wade Hampton as governor. The political squabbles among the white Democrats during the years after Hampton's redemption of South Carolina touched the folks at Promised Land only indirectly. The community was, for the most part, preoccupied with internal events.

By 1800 the community had expanded from forty-nine to eighty-nine households, an average growth of four new families each year for the previous decade. Fifty of those families were landless, attracted to Promised Land for a combination of reasons. Probably at least some of them hoped to acquire land there. Promised Land was the only place in the area where Negroes had even minimal hope of buying land after 1877. Local farmers and planters, never eager to sell land to Negroes, now grew even more recalcitrant as Democratic white rule was reestablished. Sharecropping dominated farming arrangements between whites and Negroes throughout the Cotton Belt. The landowners at

Promised Land, "well, they was wheels. They *owned* their farms." And the respect and prestige they commanded within the county's landless Negro population were another kind of attraction for landless families.

The violence of Reconstruction was moderated only slightly, and a concern for personal safety was surely another reason Negroes moved to Promised Land. Few of the early settlers, those who came before the mid-1880's, could have escaped that violence, even if their contact was indirect. Wilson Nash, Willis Smith, Allen Goode, Washington Green, Wade and Eli Moragne all headed landowning households. For any who might forget, those men were constant reminders of the dangers which lay just beyond the community's perimeter.

The men at Promised Land still exercised their franchise, fully aware of both the dangers and the benefits which they knew accompanied political activity. Together they walked the three miles to Verdery and collectively cast their ballots at the post office "where Locket Frazier held the box for the niggers and Red Tolbert for the whites." Perhaps they walked together as a symbolic expression of their solidarity, but much more likely it was because of a practical concern for their own safety. They were less vulnerable to attack in a group. As it had in the past, however, this simple exercise of citizenship enraged the local whites; and, once again, in the early 1800's the men at Promised Land faced the threat of violence for their partisan political activities.

> Them old Phoenix rats, the Ku Klux, come up here to beat up the niggers 'cause they went to Verdery and voted. Them old dogs from Phoenix put on red shirts and come up here to beat the poor niggers up. Old George Foster, the white man, he told them "Don't go down in that Promiseland. Josh Wilson and Colbert Jordan and them got some boys up there, and they got shotguns and Winchesters and old guns. Any white man come in to Promiseland to beat the niggers up, some body going to die. They'll fight 'til hell freezes over. You Phoenix rats go back to Phoenix." So they went on down to Verdery, and they told them the same thing.

Their reputation, their readiness, and their willingness to defend their land were clearly well-known facts about the people at Promised Land. The "Red Shirts" heeded the warning, and white terrorists never again attempted to violate Promised Land. This, too, must have been a part of the community's attraction to landless families who moved there.

Promised Land in 1880 was a community which teemed with activity. Most of the newcomers joined in the brush arbor worship services and sent their children to the community schools. Liberty Hill School and the white schoolmaster were replaced by "schools scattered all around the woods" taught by Negro men and women who lived at Promised Land. Abbeville County maintained a public school. Crossroads School for Colored was taught by H. L. Latimer. The Mill School, maintained by the extensive Moragne family for their children, was held in James Evans' mill on Curltail Creek and was taught by J. H. Turner, Moragne brother-in-law. The Hester School, located near the southern edge of the community, was so named because it met in the Hester family's home. All three private schools supplemented the meager public support of education for Negro children; and all were filled to capacity, because "folks had big families then—ten and twelve childrens—and them schools was crowded."

The representatives to the 1868 South Carolina Constitutional Convention who formulated the state's land redistribution hoped to establish an economically independent Negro yeomanry in South Carolina. The Land Commission intended the purchase and resale of Dr. Marshall's farm to solidify the interests of radical Republicanism in Abbeville County, at least for a time. Both of these designs were realized. A third and unintended consequence also resulted. The land fostered a socially autonomous, identifiable community. Drawing on resources and social structures well established within an extant Negro culture, the men and women who settled Promised Land established churches and schools and a viable economic system based on landownership. They maintained that economic autonomy by subsistence farming and supported many of their routine needs by patronizing the locally owned and operated grist mills and general store. The men were actively involved in Reconstruction politics as well as other aspects of civil life, serving regularly on county juries and paying their taxes. Attracted by the security and prestige Promised Land afforded and the possible hope of eventual landownership, fifty additional landless households moved into the community during the 1870's, expanding the 1880 population to almost twice its original size. Together the eighty-nine households laid claim to slightly more than four square miles of land, and within that small territory they "carved out their own little piece of the world."

The artist's imagination pictures America
seeking her destiny westward

The Westward Route

ALAN TRACHTENBERG

In the middle of the nineteenth century American leaders announced that they were pursuing a course of "manifest destiny." By this they meant that the nation would move westward, under the guidance of divine providence, until the United States reached from coast to coast and, possibly, from pole to pole (the latter intention was subsequently dropped). In order to accomplish what was seen as its divine mission, the United States engaged in war with Mexico.

After annexing the territory that was formerly a part of Mexico and in order to fulfill American destiny, there remained two major tasks. First, a plan that would open up the West to exploitation and settlement needed to be devised and secondly, the people who lived in the newly acquired territory needed to be subdued. The first task was accomplished with the completion of the transcontinental railroad in 1869. This development, along with the passing of the Homestead Act, enabled the land of the West to pass from public control into the hands of private individuals and corporations.

The conquest of the people of the West, however, was another matter. There was the question of how to incorporate the former Mexican citizens of the Southwest into American society. But this was not as important at the time as was the issue regarding the Indians. The Native American population had proved to be an obstacle to American expansion ever since the initial settlement of the New World. However, this problem was near solution by the last quarter of the nineteenth century. Two vastly different solutions were considered—kill them all ("the only good Indian is a dead Indian") or assimilate them into American society. Few Americans were willing to accept the possibility of a large, foreign community with a distinctly different culture living in their midst. Fortunately, the recommended genocide policy was set aside in favor of assimilation. Although the latter policy did not succeed, its adoption enabled Indian communities to continue to exist, however marginal to changing American society.

During the conquest of the West, it was necessary to justify the actions of the American government and its citizens in terms of developing American values. In the selection from his book on the impact of corporate culture on American life in the Gilded Age, Alan Trachtenberg of Yale University discusses the ways in which the fulfillment of manifest destiny was explained and justified. Also in this narrative, professional historians and molders of public opinion describe their version of the settlement of the West. Again, results show the progressive and inevitable victory of "civilization" over "savagery."

I

"The Western wilds, from the Alleghenies to the Pacific," wrote the historian Frederick Jackson Turner in 1903, "constituted the richest gift ever spread out before civilized man." It was a gift, he had argued ten years earlier, from which America derived all that was distinctive in its brief history: democratic institutions, national unity, a rugged independence, and individualism. Turner had propounded his famous "frontier thesis" at a propitious moment and place: in 1893, at a meeting of the American Historical Association during the World's Columbian Exposition in Chicago. What more apt site for reflection on "the first period in American history"? Four hundred years earlier, Columbus had inaugurated the westward route; now the 1890 census disclosed that a distinct "frontier line" no longer existed. No more "Western wilds" lay ahead of the American nation.

Had the gift run out? A mere three generations earlier, it had seemed inexhaustible: Thomas Jefferson and others among the revolutionary generation guessed it would take a thousand years to reach the Pacific. They counted on free land as perpetual assurance of independence from Europe, of unending prosperity flowing from a vast inland empire. Agriculture then seemed to most Americans the truest foundation of national wealth, and uncharted acres beyond the Appalachians stirred visions of a Western "garden" tended by yeoman-farmers. The vision became policy, and through purchase, exploration, and conquest, expansion proceeded steadily westward. The founders timed their calculations by a pre-industrial clock. But railroads, appearing in the 1840's and 1850's, stepped up the tempo, and the discovery of gold in California in 1849 inspired a veritable "rush" toward the western edge of the continent.

Of course, in the rush it became clear that the gift would be costly. A war with Mexico in 1848, and persistent, apparently fanatical resistance from native inhabitants, the North American Indians, indicated what price in violence and its shabby rationalizations the westward route would exact. What had seemed "vacant," "unredeemed," and "virgin" land often disclosed places of habitation by societies with different but no less self-justifying practices of land ownership and sustenance. With different notions of possession, Indians saw their land as already possessed, occupied, integrated with a human culture. The gift, in short, had to be wrested by force. The period of expansion and settlement witnessed incessant warfare. Indeed, fighting intensified in the decades following the Civil War, ending only with the collapse of Indian resistance by the early 1890's. The year 1893 marked, then, not only four hundred years of "progress" but also of destruction: the end not only of "frontier" but of independent native societies.

The westward route had drawn its unshakable sanctions from both religious and economic indicators, from "mission" as well as "progress." "The *untransacted* destiny of the American people is to subdue the continent," trumpeted William Gilpin in 1846; he repeated the resounding phrase in 1873 in *The Mission of the North American People*. Journalist, adviser to pre-Civil War Presidents, publicist for railroads and for a "Northwest Passage" to Asia, Gilpin described that destiny in provincial terms: "to establish a new order in human affairs." That prospect was a key plank in the evangelical Protestant "Home Mission" movement represented by Josiah Strong, who in *Our Country* (1886) expatiated on Gilpin's theme: "Like the star in the East which guided the three kings with their treasures westward until at length it stood still over the cradle of the young Christ, so the star of empire, rising in the East, has ever beckoned the wealth and power of the nations westward, until today it stands over the cradle of the young empire of the West." The star standing still would mark the end of profane time. The mission promised nothing short of sacred redemption, the remaking of "West" into a temple of God.

It was also, as Theodore Roosevelt explained in his popular *The Winning of the West* (1889), a half-mystical imperative of "race-history," a culminating moment in the drive of "the English-speaking peoples" for dominance in the world. The work of the new racial mix called "American"—an Anglo-Saxon mix in which English strains held sway— "Western conquest" had begun simultaneously with the appearance of this new breed, "at the moment when they sprang into national life." The pioneers responded to racial urges: "In obedience to the instincts working half blindly within their breasts, spurred ever onward by the fierce desires of their eager hearts, they made in the wilderness homes for their children, and by so doing wrought out the destinies of a continental nation."

In his momentous address in Chicago, Frederick Jackson Turner drew on such popular beliefs, the scattered dreams of an agrarian empire, of a providential mission for a newly forged race of white fighters and settlers. His vision coincided with Roosevelt's in many ways, though only Turner transposed the prophesied destiny into a different discourse. Reviewing Roosevelt's book in 1889, he had argued that "American history needs a connected and unified account of the progress of civilization across the continent." The nation needed, that is, a coherent, integrated story of its beginnings and its development. Connectedness, wholeness, unity: these narrative virtues, with their implied telos of closure, of a justifying meaning at the end of the tale, Turner would now embody in the language of historical interpretation. And an interpretation not merely accurate according to the canons of historical writing but serviceable according to the needs of politics and culture: the needs of the nation at a moment of crisis. "Aside from the scientific importance of such a work," he added in his review, "it would contribute to awakening a real national self-consciousness and patriotism." Neither apocalyptic in style nor explicitly visionary in purpose, Turner would speak in the tempered voice of "science," in the perspective of a belated recognition: now that the story had run its course, the historian stood poised in the White City of the Chicago Exposition to gather its meaning, to trace the "significance of the frontier in American history."

It is difficult to ignore the irony of the occasion, of Turner in Chicago, proclaiming what would become the most vital interpretation of the United States for at least the next fifty years. The moment proved a cultural as well as a scholarly event: a drama of confrontation. A scholar born and bred in the Middle West, nurtured by the rural culture of Wisconsin, where his father owned a newspaper and ran for political office, Turner urged his fellow historians to break with "eastern" intellectual proclivities, to pay more mind to "western" experience. Only recently had the profession itself emerged, with the founding of the American Historical Association in 1884. Turner himself came to his task in 1893 shaped as much by the structures of the profession as by his youth on the frontier. As a graduate student in the East, at the new center of advanced historical studies at Johns Hopkins, and as an assistant professor at the state university in Wisconsin (he would later move to Harvard), he had cut his teeth within a newly organized world of academic scholarship.

In his argument, "West" meant the pioneer sturdiness, independence, scorn of social constraint: "that coarseness and strength combined with acuteness and inquisitiveness; that practical, inventive turn of mind, quick to find expedients; that masterful grasp of material things, lacking in the artistic but powerful to effect great ends; that restless, nervous energy; that dominant individualism, working for good and for evil, and withal that buoyancy and exuberance which comes from freedom." Turner celebrated these heroic masculine traits even as he lamented the passing of the conditions which produced them. And he did so in a manner which not only described their demise but also dramatized it. For there, in the great new metropolis of Chicago, he performed a decidedly urban feat. The style itself of his discourse—neither a narrative in the grand manner nor a monograph freighted with citations, but an essay of analysis—represented the historian as a *professional,* one who performs his work according to academic standards. Moreover, the frontier thesis presupposed both a subject—"society"—and an outlook toward it neither romantic nor sentimental but "scientific," a view based on presumably sound Darwinian assumptions of evolution and organism, a subject available for research, for collective investigation. Unlike Roosevelt, Turner does not speak of "half-blind instincts' but of environment and institutions.

"In a very real sense," Richard Hofstadter has observed, "the Turner thesis and the historical profession grew up together." In its account of "progress" from simplicity to complexity, from "frontier" to "society," the thesis thus offered an account of its own origins. Indeed, Chicago itself seemed a product of the logic Turner described: "At last the slender paths of aboriginal intercourse have been broadened and interwoven into the complex mazes of modern commercial lines; the wilderness has been interpenetrated by lines of civilization growing ever more numerous. It is like the steady growth of a complex nervous system for the originally simple, inert continent." Thus the very propounding of the thesis in the new metropolis of Chicago declared the conclusion of a process, the inevitability of its end.

Thus we can see that in the contours of its argument as well as in the sinews of its sentences, the Turner thesis belongs to the new world made palpable and vivid in Chicago in 1893; it is of a piece with White City. Like the Columbian Exposition, the Turner thesis portrayed an American at a critical juncture. Both affirmed drastic change since the days when it might have been possible to imagine the nation as a society of freeholders. Both embraced the change—the rise of cities, industrial capitalism, corporate forms of business and social activities—and yet they attempted to preserve older values and traditional outlooks. Both served cultural missions: White City overtly, indeed in the very forms of culture, of high art and architecture; the Turner thesis covertly, in the guise of professional "scientific" discourse.

But the specific crisis Turner faced in the deepest levels of his argument centered on the paradox typified by Chicago. If the frontier had provided the defining experience for Americans, how would the

values learned in that experience now fare in the new world of cities—
a new world brought into being as if blindly by the same forces which
had proffered the apparent gift of land? Would the America fashioned
on the frontier survive the caldrons of the city? Turner responded to
the challenge by an act of distillation. To be sure, he argued, the story
of the frontier had reached its end, but the product of that experience
remains. It remains in the predominant *character*, the traits of selfhood,
with which the frontier experience had endowed Americans, that
"dominant individualism" which now must learn to cope with novel
demands. The thesis projects a national character, a type of person fit
for the struggles and strategies of an urban future.

The prominence Turner gives to character, to a "composite nationality," in the resounding conclusion of the essay, clarifies his strategy.
His response to the crisis of having reached the end of the frontier
story shows in the meaning he gives to "land," treating it as he does
less as an economic resource (he hardly mentions minerals and extrac-
tive industries in his 1893 essay) than as an environmental force, virtually as a character in its own right. "The wilderness masters the
colonist," he writes. And the process he describes rings of a ritual event,
a set of actions echoed throughout American fiction and poetry in recounted excursions into an archaic wilderness, in Cooper's tales of Natty
Bumpo, in Faulkner's *The Bear*, in "The River" and "The Dance" in
Hart Crane's *The Bridge*. The colonist arrives a "European," but instantly commences a descent, stepping from the railroad car into a
birchbark canoe, shedding "civilized" clothing and habits. He descends, strips himself of "society," transforming himself into the very
image of "land" he then sets out to transform into the image of
"progress." This descent and ascent, this "continual beginning over
again" and "perennial rebirth" at the "meeting point between savagery
and civilization" becomes, for Turner, the authentic source not simply
of a process which culminates in Chicago but of the sound fiber of
American character itself. Thus, he writes, "the frontier is the line of
the most rapid and effective Americanization," giving rise to "a composite nationality for the American people." The "connected and unified account" of the American past required by the times coheres, then,
in the figure of the typical, the composite American.

Seeking a "connected and unified account" of the American past
at a time of disunity, of economic depression and labor strife, of immigrant urban workers and impoverished rural farmers challenging a
predominantly Anglo-Saxon Protestant economic and social elite, Turner
thus arrived at his conception of the American character as an emblem
of national coherence. The nation incorporated itself, he insisted, through
that figure and its traits of inventive individualism. To be sure, the
account slights crucial aspects of the Western experience stressed by
later historians. It fails to acknowledge cultural multiplicity; in the

Southwest alone, Anglo-Americans, Spanish Americans, Roman Catholics, Mormons, and Indians all contributed to a heterogeneous culture. It makes its claims on the basis of a decidedly partial experience—of chiefly Anglo-Saxon settlers and farmers flowing from New England into the Midwest. Moreover, the thesis ignores or obscures the real politics of the West, where, as Howard Lamar has shown, federal territorial policy held much of the region in a dependent, colonial status (prior to admission to statehood) through most of the post-Civil War period. "By 1889," writes Lamar, "every territory in the West was calling its federal officials colonial tyrants and comparing its plight to that of one of the thirteen colonies." Turner's frontier, then, is as much an invention of cultural belief as a genuine historical fact: an invention of an America "connected and unified" in the imagination if nowhere else. The invention proclaims that, even in Chicago, some fundamental residue of the nation persists, an idea of hardy manhood, of inventive genius and originality. Only partially hidden within its overtly "scientific" historical discourse, then, the Turner thesis held another discourse of uncertainty and concern over America in a time of cities, immigrants, and corporate power.

II

An invention of cultural myth, the word "West" embraced an astonishing variety of surfaces and practices, of physiognomic differences and sundry exploitations they invited. The Western lands provided resources essential as much to industrial development after the Civil War as to cultural needs of justification, incentive, and disguise. Land and minerals served economic and ideological purposes, the two merging into a single complex image of the West: a temporal site of the route from past to future, and the spatial site for revitalizing national energies. As myth and as economic entity, the West proved indispensable to the formation of a national society and a cultural mission: to fill the vacancy of the Western spaces with civilization, by means of incorporation (political as well as economic) and violence. Myth and exploitation, incorporation and violence: the processes went hand in hand.

The gift of geography to American society consisted of unimaginable natural wealth in the manifest form of a picturesque landscape. Of course, nature is manifestly neither romantic nor picturesque: the descriptive terms convey cultural meanings that live in perceptions. American painters had fastened onto conventions of landscape painting in the antebellum period with a unique intensity, and produced, in the Hudson River School, a body of work which lent to American terrain an almost mystical power. They depicted nature as the stage of dramas of growth and decay, of aspiration and defeat—and invested it with emotions appropriate to visions of national destiny. Landscape painting served as an approximation to the heroic historical canvases that academic European art crowned as the highest, most spiritual of paintings. The habit of confronting history in American nature found an even more grandiose scale, as painters and explorers turned their eyes toward views newly disclosed in expeditions in the Far West. In his experiences recounted in *Mountaineering in the High Sierras* (1872), geologist Clarence King found evidence of geological upheavals aeons old, cataclysms representing a history more antique and awesome than any possessed by European societies. In the path of America's future seemed to lie a *natural* history that gave to the Western settlement a biblical cast.

The term "natural wealth" implies another cultural perception, another way of interpreting the strata of rock and mineral deposits that gave to the mountain and desert regions of the West a look of prehistoric enchantment. Ways of interpreting the land tend to become equivalents to acting upon it, consuming it as an aesthetic object, as a resource. King's memoir registers an often tortured division of outlooks, in his case between aesthetic (and moral) perception and scientific knowledge. The division took another form in popular publications that flooded the country, especially as the nation approached the centennial year of 1876. In William Cullen Bryant's preface to *Picturesque America* (1874), a lavish two-volume set of texts and reproductions of paintings in steel engraving, we read:

> By means of the overland communications lately opened between the Atlantic coast and that of the Pacific, we have now easy access to scenery of a most remarkable character. For those who would see Nature in her grandest forms of snow-clad mountain, deep valley, rocky pinnacle, precipice, and chasm, there is no longer any occasion to cross the ocean. A rapid journey by railway over the plains that stretch westward from the Mississippi, brings the tourist into a region of the Rocky Mountains rivalling Switzerland in its scenery of rock piled on rock, up to the region of the clouds. But Switzerland has no such groves on its mountainsides, nor has even Libanus, with its ancient cedars, as those which raise the astonishment of the visitor to that Western region—trees of such prodigious height and enormous dimensions that, to attain their present bulk, we might imagine them to have sprouted from the seed at the time of the Trojan War.

The buried contradiction here between the appeal of wild grandeur and the comfort of mechanized access to the site where such an appeal can be satisfied is not merely comic in its blithe leap over wagon tracks and rotting carcasses that marked a mode of access only a few years past; it indicates a special kind of denial of social fact that afflicted sections of American culture in these years. Thus the railroad, the prime instrument of the large-scale industrialization which re-created American nature into "natural resources" for commodity production, appears as a chariot winging Americans on an aesthetic journey through the new empire. Tourism, already implicit in the landscape conventions, becomes yet another form of acting upon the land.

The "vast, trackless spaces," as Whitman put it, of open land, forest, and mountain—the Great Plains and the Rockies—not only fired the imagination but figured quite concretely in the industrial program. While perceptions of Western space often diminished the sense of human significance and worked their effects on the hardy folk who people the legends of Western settlement, perceptions of potential wealth inspired more calculating responses. The federal government had sponsored systematic exploration of unsettled regions as early as the Lewis and Clark expeditions in 1804–6. Mapmaking preceded settlement and had perhaps an even greater effect on conceptualization of the land than landscape paintings. About 1845, the government outfitted army explorations to find suitable routes for railroad lines to the Pacific.

The overt aim of these early probings was to chart the way to an agricultural empire—a "new garden of the world"; they explored regions for settlement and military defense. Reflecting a different emphasis and a new set of needs, explorations during the Civil War and continuing to the end of the century were concerned with natural resources; they were explicitly "scientific" expeditions, typified by the meticulously planned United States Geological Survey established in 1879. Such surveys collected detailed information about terrain, mineral and timber resources, climate, and water supply. One of the tangible products of the several postwar surveys were thousands of photographs, displayed in mammoth-sized plates and in three-dimensional stereo images, an astonishing body of work that when viewed outside the context of the reports it accompanied seems to perpetuate the landscape tradition. Many of the photographers, such as William Henry Jackson, clearly followed conventions of painting in depicting panoramic landscapes, while others, like Timothy O'Sullivan, worked more closely to the spirit of investigation of the surveys and produced more original visual reports. The photographs represent an essential aspect of the enterprise, a form of record keeping; they contributed to the federal government's policy of supplying fundamental needs of industrialization, needs for reliable data concerning raw materials, and promoted a public willingness to support government policy of conquest, settlement, and exploitation.

That policy held ambiguities and contradictions. Undertaken at first on behalf of agricultural settlement, it fostered in fact a massive industrial campaign. As Henry Nash Smith has shown, by the Civil War the West had gathered to itself connotations of a peaceful New World garden, a symbolic wish for prosperity safe from the tragedies of Europe. Fertile soil on the high plains, open spaces, seemingly "virgin" lands beckoned the independent yeoman Jefferson had celebrated as America's best hope, and seemed an assurance of permanent tranquillity. The logic of events in the 1870's and 1880's disclosed, however, not an agrarian but an industrial capitalist scenario. Penetrating the West with government encouragement, the railroad and the telegraph opened the vast spaces to production. Following the lead of the railroads, commercial and industrial businesses conceived of themselves as having the entire national space at their disposal: from raw materials for processing to goods for marketing. The process of making themselves national entailed a changed relation of corporations to agriculture, an assimilation of agricultural enterprise within productive and marketing structures. The rapid appearance of grain elevators after the 1850's indicated the change and its character; the need for storage facilities, and for standardized grading and weighing and inspecting, implied sales in high volume, direct purchases by dealers from farmers, and a distant exchange for commercial transaction. Agricultural products entered the commodities market and became part of an international system of buying, selling, and shipping. The farmer's work in every section of the nation thus gained a cosmopolitan character. Marketing and exchange left his hands, the work now of dealers and brokers. Where processing was necessary, as in meat and tobacco, mass producers soon incorporated the entire process, from farm to factory to consumer.

Especially with the opening of vast fertile tracts in the Western plains, farmers turned to "cash crops," attempting to anticipate prices in commodity markets centered in distant cities here and abroad. The effect of almost instantaneous telegraphic communication of prices on his plans and expectations was often cataclysmic. Controlled by private corporations, the new technologies came to be enemies of the farmer; steep rates for elevator storage, for railroad transport, for middleman services, claimed the better part of his harvests, even in years of bumper crops. Overmortgaged, overcapitalized, overmechanized, independent farmers even on the fertile plains increasingly felt the chill winds of financial disaster in the very place once promised as a New World garden.

The promise embodied in the idea of the West as a yeomen's garden had seemed so much the closer to fulfillment with the passage of the Homestead Act by the Civil War Congress in 1862, which offered 160 acres of the public domain to individuals for the nominal fee of $10. Republicans had joined with Free Soil Democrats in supporting the measure with two goals in mind: to provide an agricultural "safety valve" for surplus or discontented urban workers, and a Western population base for an enlarged domestic market for manufactured goods. Free or cheap land had tempted some labor spokesmen in the antebellum years to envision cooperative colonies in the West as an alternative to the wage system, and such a notion remained a plank of some labor organizations as late as the 1880's. But from the very beginning of the administration of the Homestead Act, it was clear that a society of small homesteaders in the West was not its functional goal. The act did not provide necessary credit for people without savings to take up their cherished 160 acres. And its clauses permitted land grabbing by speculative companies, and the eventual concentration of large tracts in private hands. As historian Fred Shannon has shown, perhaps only a tenth of the new farms settled between 1860 and 1900 were acquired under the Homestead Act; the rest were bought either directly from land or railroad companies (beneficiaries of huge land grants), or from the states.

Rather than fostering a region of family farmers, the Homestead Act would prove instrumental in furthering the incorporation of Western lands into the Eastern industrial system. Until the practice was discontinued in 1871, the Republican Congress had enthusiastically donated more than a million and a half acres of public domain in the form of "land grants" to railroad companies operating west of the Mississippi. In turn, the railroads became private colonizers in their own right, selling off large sections of their grants to individuals and companies. Responding to business lobbies, Congress passed additional acts between 1866 and 1873 virtually giving away lands and rights of access to mining and timber interests. Continuing government-sponsored surveys of exploration culminated in the establishment in 1879 of the United States Geological Survey, whose voluminous reports and maps facilitated the private development of lands rich in timber, oil, natural gas, coal, iron ore, and other minerals. Privatization of the public domain continued as large companies bought out or pushed aside individual entrepreneurs, replacing small-scale mining, timber cutting, and farming with capital-intensive methods. Hit-or-miss prospectors and miners found themselves slowly forced into day labor in Eastern-owned mines and factories employing improved machinery for more efficient extraction and processing—an experience Mark Twain recounts from his own days in the Nevada Comstock region in *Roughing It* (1871). New methods of mining, drilling, loading ores by automatic machinery, shipping oil through long-distance trunk lines, appeared in short order, stepping up the tempo of a massive conversion of nature into the means and ends of industrial production.

Thus, incorporation took swift possession of the garden, mocking those who lived by the hopes of cultural myth, and those who thought of machines as chariots for tourists. Abuses in the treatment of land did arouse an outcry for control and regulation, but not until the basic apparatus of exploitation already stood in place. A movement for preservation and the protection of certain regions as national parks emerged in the 1870s; with John Wesley Powell (who explored the Grand Canyon region) and John Muir as leading advocates, Congress established Yellowstone National Park (1872) and preserved Yosemite as well (1890). Powell and others, including a growing number of landscape architects, as J. B. Jackson has pointed out, proposed plans for orderly land use of remaining public resources, especially water supplies for desert regions. But public planning was anathema to Congress and private entrepreneurs, who did not flinch from public subsidy of business. So the unimaginable wealth of nature's gift was funneled by the people's representatives into private hands.

The West poured its resources into the expanding productive system, contributing decisively to the remaking of that system into a national incorporated entity. Wheat and cattle enterprises came under control of Eastern capitalists, for whom the agricultural surplus provided a major source of new capital. Newly established meat-packing companies in Chicago and other Midwestern metropolises won direct control of the large herds which were their raw material. By the 1890s, food production and processing had joined mining as a capital-intensive, highly mechanized industry. The translation of land into capital, of what once seemed "free" into private wealth, followed the script of industrial progress, however much that script seemed at odds, in the eyes of hard-pressed farmers, with the earlier dream.

Another process of transformation occurred in the same decades: a remaking of the image of the West, a funneling of its powers into popular culture. The region emerged in popular consciousness as "Wild West," a terrain of danger, adventure, and violence. Through dime novels, themselves a modern artifact of mass production, and traveling Wild West shows such as Buffalo Bill's, the image impressed itself: the West as exotic romance. Especially through the dime novels, a cast of stock characters appeared: desperadoes, savage Indians, prospectors, Indian scouts and cavalrymen, marshals or "regulators," saloon-keepers, dance-hall madames, cowpunchers, and a mob of townsfolk, easily swayed toward lynchings and posses. These popular fantasies appealed to a broad stratum of Eastern readers, for whom the West served as an image of contrast to Eastern society. A simple Populism often colors these tales, in which villains appear as wealthy Eastern bankers and capitalists allied with the most notorious outlaws, and heroes often speak in praise of "honest workingmen," of "labor" in its contests with "capital." Often fugitives from Eastern injustice, men prove themselves in the West, where only personal merit and ability count. The very wildness of the West allowed native ability and honesty their due. The heroic owes nothing to social station, and often outlaws prove themselves heroes in the Robin Hood mold.

Through such popular fictions, the West in its wildness retained older associations with freedom, escape from social restraint, and closeness to nature. The ideal of solitary endurance persisted, then, even in the face of rapidly encroaching Eastern business interests: persisted especially as a proto-populist image of opposition. Heroes such as Deadwood Dick easily assume roles of outlaw and lawman, of highway robber and town marshal, always maintaining his manly virtue. The prominence of disguises and false identities in the dime novel also suggests a distrust of appearances, an unwillingness to settle for fixed social roles and obligations. Not until the end of the century, when Eastern corporations had virtually accomplished their control of Western enterprises, did the Western hero begin to shift, to accommodate itself on changed historical realities. And when the genre of the Western solidified into the form which would remain the staple of twentieth-century popular culture, it appeared as a fable of conservative values, a cultural equivalent to incorporation. The development is already complete in Owen Wister's *The Virginian* (1902). For Wister, Harvard graduate and intimate of Theodore Roosevelt (to whom the novel is dedicated), not only washes clean the literary crudities and thematic incoherences, indeed the very elements of popularity of the dime novel; he also turns the implicit egalitarianism of the earlier mode into an explicitly ruling-class vision. Wister's great tale of the cowboy hero who vaunts at once the values of personal honor and worldly success, who is prepared to kill to defend both his own reputation and his employer's property, completes the cultural appropriation of the West.

Wister appropriated freely from the popular tradition, clarifying character types, sharpening issues. In the dime novel the cowboy had been only one of many possible heroic roles along with scout, miner, outlaw, sheriff or marshal, detective. Fusing elements of several vocational types in his cowboy figure, including that of "foreman," or superintendent, over the band of migratory laborers who performed the cowpunching and herding on the ranches and plains, Wister re-created the cowboy as a romantic knight of the plains, a descendant of Sir Lancelot, as he put it in an article in 1895 on "the evolution of the cowpuncher." The medieval image is more than an idle allusion. The cowboy figure stands in a definite relation to the settled society of the plains—a relation of knightly deference to the aristocratic owner, the "Judge," and to his interests. The cowboy-knight knows his place and accepts it, and yet also insists fiercely on his own honor: a right permitted him and respected by the Judge. The code duello has a sacred place in Wister's West, as it did in the dime novels, and the defense of manly honor justifies the Virginian's occasional, always reluctant but always cool, quick, and efficient use of his gun, just as defense of private property justifies, indeed demands. "The last romantic figure upon our soil," Wister's cowboy hero is also a deadly killer.

III

"It is but little over half a dozen years since these lands were won from the Indians," wrote Theodore Roosevelt in *Hunting Trips of a Ranchman* (1886) about the Dakota Badlands. The compression of vast social change within such a narrow compass heightens the sense for Roosevelt that he is living *within* history:

> After bloody fighting and protracted campaigns they were defeated, and the country thrown open to the whites, while the building of the Northern Pacific Railroad gave immigration an immense impetus. There were great quantities of game, especially buffalo, and the hunters who thronged in to pursue the huge herds of the latter were the rough forerunners of civilization. No longer dreading the Indians, and having the railway on which to transport the robes, they followed the buffalo in season and out, until in 1883 the herds were practically destroyed.

Early cattlemen found themselves doomed by the same historical process: "The broad and boundless prairies have already been bounded and will soon be made narrow." And so history seemed for Roosevelt, for Turner, for countless others contemplating the westward experience, a foreclosed event, an inevitable advance from low to high, from simple to complex, and in more senses than one, from "Indian" to "American." For Turner, "West" offered a transparent text in which "line by line . . . we read this continental page from West to East," deciphering a "record of social evolution."

> It begins with the Indian and the hunter; it goes on to tell of the disintegration of savagery by the entrance of the trader, the pathfinder of civilization; we read the annals of the pastoral stage in ranch life; the exploitation of the soil by the raising of unrotated crops of corn and wheat in sparsely settled farming communities; the intensive culture of the denser farm settlement; and finally the manufacturing organization with city and factory system.

Thus "West" bespeaks a proof for "America" itself: the site where the process is laid bare, recapitulated as each successive "meeting point between savagery and civilization."

The proof was repeated over and over in countless popular prints such as "American Progress," published in 1873. Based on a painting by John Gast, the print displays a frank and simple allegory. It illustrates, in the words of an explanatory text on the reverse side, "the grand drama of Progress in the civilization, settlement and history of our own happy land." The picture shows a chase. On the left, a herd of buffalo, a bear and a coyote, and a family of Indians and their horses flee before an array of Americans in various "stages" of "progress": guide, hunter, trapper, prospector, pony-express rider, covered wagon followed by stagecoach, and a farmer in a field already under plow and oxen. Three railroad lines, representing the transcontinentals, join the flow, which originates from the city and its factories, schools, and churches. On the left, the text explains, we find "darkness, waste and confusion." And in the center of the scene, its presiding image, looms a white, diaphanous figure, "a beautiful and charming Female"—we are told—"floating Westward through the air, bearing on her forehead the 'Star of Empire.' " Her knee raised through her gown as if striding purposefully, she bears in one hand a book representing "Common Schools," and with the other "she unfolds and stretches the slender wires of the Telegraph" that are to "flash intelligence throughout the land." The Indians look back at her, the "wondrous presence" from which they flee. "The 'Star' *is too much for them.*"

In this "progress," this proof of "America," the profoundest role was reserved not for the abundance of land but for the fatal presence of the Indian. The Indian projected a fact of a different order from land and resources: a human fact of racial and cultural difference, not as easily incorporated as minerals and soil and timber. Here was a significant array of people—significant in number, in capacity to inflict damage and entail large military expense—occupying a world so entirely at odds with that of white Americans that their very opposition made a frontal encounter necessary for a definition of America itself. "Civilization" required a "savagery" against which to distinguish itself. Thus, native American Indians differed from blacks and Asians in several important regards. Blacks could be understood as a special category of American: formerly enslaved but now enfranchised and (presumably) on the way to equality. Chinese, on the other hand, were clear "aliens" whose right to occupy space in the country was completely at the mercy of American sovereignty. Blacks and Asians could be understood, also, as capable of productive labor, this being the ground of both fear of competition from labor groups and hope of ultimate assimilation. Both groups were targets of intensifying racial hostility in these years, in growing Ku Klux Klan terror and Jim Crow laws in the South, and exclusion legislation against Chinese in California. But the Indian represented a special case in that the right to space lay bound up with the very right to *exist.*

The character of that existence had presented challenges to white Europeans from the beginning. Were Indians true people, or demons, or "noble savages," happy innocents in a state of nature? Were their "tribes" similar to "nations," with whom treaties and land purchases might be negotiated? Essentially, the challenge concerned land; it came to a head very rapidly because the natives would fight fiercely and effectively against intrusions on their space, or violations of agreements reached with white governing bodies. The willingness of Indian tribes to enter into compacts with white invaders indicated both a willingness and a readiness to coexist. Indeed, coexistence had altered Indian life in ways not entirely negative: the introduction of horses, for example, metal utensils and tools, woven cloth, storable and transportable food, and guns enhanced the ability to hunt, to procure food and produce clothing and shelter. But steady encroachment of white trappers, hunters, traders, and finally settlers on Indian lands increased tension and hostility and produced virtually constant warfare, with the consequence of severe changes within Indian social structure (the strengthening, for example, of chiefs and warriors, and the diminishing role of women in tribal decision making), and eventual defeat. The period after the Civil War marked the conclusion of overt hostilities (after intensified fighting in the 1870's), the forced acceptance by defeated tribes of a new reservation policy, and the onset of a long period of withdrawal and apparent passivity. The Indian, by 1893, seemed a "vanishing American."

Yet, while the figure may have receded, it hardly vanished. An Indian presence persisted as the underside, the lasting bad conscience, within the prevailing conception of "West," calling for repeated ritualistic slaying in popular "Westerns." For at all junctures the real history of expansion had translated a secret script within the idea of "progress" or "manifest destiny." Bearable only in the disguise of myth and ritual, that script revealed its potentially destructive horror in the period of intensified fighting just after the Civil War, particularly as reports of unspeakable atrocities, such as those by army troops under Colonel J. M. Chivington in a massacre at the Sand Creek reservation in Colorado in 1864, reached the East. In his first message to Congress in 1869, President Grant remarked: "A system which looks to the extinction of a race is too horrible for a nation to adopt without entailing upon itself the wrath of all Christendom and engendering in the citizen a disregard for human life and rights of others, dangerous to society." Official national policy stopped short of extermination; it settled for abolishing native ways of life and their obstructive practices of communal property holding. But even this limited form of violence could not be faced directly; it must be veiled, misunderstood as an event of another kind. The Turner thesis, which defines the land as "free" and identifies Indians with "wilderness," as a "common danger," is one such veil: it fails to see Indians as other than undifferentiated "savages" in the path of "social evolution" from "frontier" to "city and factory system." To see Indians as "savage" is already to define them out of existence, to define them only in relation to their apparent opposite: "civilized" society.

The major events of Indian-white relations in these years were military and legal: more than two hundred pitched battles, not to speak of guerrilla warfare in outlying Western regions, and a reservation policy promulgated in 1887, to remain in effect until the 1930's. In each case, military action and legal solution, economic and cultural issues figured as unspoken but vital imperatives. The drama of these years was played largely on the Great Plains, but against a scenery put in place by the forced removal or expulsion of tribes east of the Mississippi in the decades before the Civil War. Executed by President Andrew Jackson in the 1830's, removal established an Indian Territory in the Southwest (now Oklahoma). The Southern tribes protested, lost an appeal to the Supreme Court, and had no choice but to accept the long march westward enforced by government troops. Chief Justice John Marshall's ruling (in 1831) was epochal: Indians were not "foreign nations" but "domestic dependent nations": "they are in a state of pupilage. Their relation to the United States resembles that of a ward to his guardian." In spite of previous treaties, Indians "occupy a territory to which we assert a title independent of their will." Or as the governor of Georgia put the matter in less judicious terms: "Treaties were expedients by which ignorant, intractable, and savage people were induced without bloodshed to yield up what civilized people had the right to possess by virtue of that command of the Creator delivered to man upon his formation—be fruitful, multiply, and replenish the earth, and subdue it."

Thus, well before the Civil War, the courts and Congress had settled the issue of conflicting "rights" by instituting as law a relation of dependency, a relation which included guarantees of protection as well as payments (in the form of annuities) for lands relinquished. "Protection," however, stood always at the mercy of "dependency," for the notion that "we assert a title independent of their will" implied that any future desire for Indian lands might well be satisfied by unilateral modification of treaties. Thus, removal imposed on Indians not only a forced abandonment of a social order and economy—many of the Eastern tribes already practiced sedentary agriculture and had a federated structure of self-government—but also an inherent legal inferiority. They were declared both inside and outside the American polity: subject to its jurisdiction, but without rights of citizenship.

The removal policy committed the government to police and military action aimed both at keeping Indians within the prescribed limits of their new territories and ostensibly protecting those limits from white incursions. But incursions increased after the Civil War as cattlemen, miners, and farmers demanded access to lands they viewed as economically desirable. The heightened friction in the West in the 1860's and 1870's resulted from stark conflicts of interest between expanding capitalist enterprises and Indian needs for sustenance. Driven westward, formerly agricultural peoples such as the Eastern Sioux were compelled to adopt a seminomadic hunting economy, based on the great roving herds of buffalo on the Great Plains. The policy of protection dwindled after the Civil War into open support of white demands to rewrite treaty boundaries, to concentrate Indian tribes within shrinking areas and enclosures called "reservations." Consistent with its economic policies of land grants and subsidies, of Homestead Act and unrestricted immigration, the federal government sponsored military campaigns to win more land and resources for exploitation. Indian policy, then, followed the logic of incorporation: expansion into space for the sake of conversion of "nature" into "raw material."

The key features of that policy in the decades after the Civil War included stepped-up military action coupled with legislative clarification of the legal status of Indian societies—their status, that is, within the purview of American polity. What needs most to be stressed is the importance of this clarification to the process of incorporation: not only as a government-sponsored clearance of an obstruction to investment and economic growth but as a crucial *cultural* definition of America itself. The method of definition was unilateral and imperial; solutions were imposed, not developed by negotiation and compromise. The problem, of course, was understood as obstruction, both by inhabitation of desirable lands and by an aggressive defense of those lands. After the Civil War, controversy arose within the national government about the most expedient solution. Earlier, in 1849, the governance of Indian affairs had been placed in the hands of the Department of the Interior; now military leaders like General William T. Sherman insisted that the Bureau of Indian Affairs be returned to the Department of War. Especially after the Sioux uprising under Chief Red Cloud in Montana and Wyoming, and the Cheyenne and Arapaho rebellion in Colorado—both following immediately after Appomattox—Sherman urged "the utter destruction and subjugation" of all Indians found outside their assigned reservations, "until they are obliterated or beg for mercy." Not only the need for costly military campaigns—millions of dollars for each expedition—but the notorious corruption of Indian agents seemed to argue for a transfer of authority to the army.

The proposal failed, and the official policy under Grant and his successors proclaimed "peace": through education, missionary work by Christians invited to replace corrupt political appointees in Indian agencies, and through a reconception of the reservation as, in John Wesley Powell's words in 1874, "a school of industry and a home for these unfortunate people." Powell and others proposed a program of "civilizing these Indians" by introducing them "to work," and requiring that they learn English in order to bring them better within the domain, and control, of "civilization": "Into their own language there is woven so much mythology and sorcery that a new one is needed in order to aid them in advancing beyond their baneful superstitions; and the ideas and thoughts of civilized life cannot be communicated to them in their own tongues," wrote Powell. And, as a decisive measure aimed at diminishing the power of tribal chiefs and thus the coherence of

Indian resistance, Congress in 1871 abolished the practice of treaty making with separate tribes, thus finally denying distinct tribes the legally troublesome status of "nation." From these measures it was thought that "peace" would follow. In fact, military campaigns continued unabated, against the Sioux under Sitting Bull and Crazy Horse in the Great Plains, Geronimo and the Apaches in the Southwest, and, most tragically, against Chief Joseph and the Nez Percé tribe in Oregon. It continued until the final defeat of the half-starved Sioux after a Ghost Dance ceremony in 1890, a massacre of about two hundred men, women, and children, including the old leader Sitting Bull, at Wounded Knee creek in the Black Hills.

By the 1880's, an influential reform group had begun to make itself heard, a group of well-placed reformers, philanthropists, clergymen, and their wives, who shared an evangelical Protestant outlook, a passion for social order, and who called themselves "Friends of the Indian." By then, the United States Army had the upper hand, and a policy which may have resulted in genocide was narrowly avoided. Genocide was in fact the logical implication and obsessive ambition of what Melville in *The Confidence Man* had called "the metaphysics of Indian-hating," a frontier habit of unremitting racial hatred. Sherman's military policy and Theodore Roosevelt's inflamed rhetoric—"treacherous, revengeful, and fiendishly cruel savages," he wrote in 1886— were stages leading to potential holocaust. Indeed, military actions, frequent armed assaults against harmless villages and women and children, massacre and atrocity—often in response to isolated guerrilla raids by desperate and vengeful young braves—had the appearance if not the official sanction of genocide. And it was an open secret that the rapid destruction of the vast buffalo herds—as many as 13 million of those imposing, shaggy creatures roamed the plains at the time of the Civil War—satisfied not only the greed of commercial hunters, leather and fur manufacturers, and railroad carriers, but government desire for a speedy resolution to the "Indian problem." Denied opportunities and land for all but marginal farming, the Plains Indians had counted on the buffalo hunt for meat, hides for clothing and shelter, bones for utensils and ornaments. "Kill every buffalo you can," advised one army officer. "Every buffalo dead is an Indian gone." "Slaughtering buffalo is a Government measure to subjugate the Indians," noted one observer. By the early 1880's, the slaughter had effectively decimated the great Southern and Northern herds. The shaggy beast receded into legend, accompanied by tidy profits for hunters and dealers in hides— and a fatal destabilization of Indian society.

The alternative to violence proposed by the "Peace Policy" had in mind, as did Grant in his remarks about the horror of genocide in 1869, the effects of such rampant slaughtering of beasts and humans on the larger society. Like their fellows among the cultivated elite and gentry throughout America, the "peace" party feared the consequences of violence, the chaos (as they saw it) of class conflict threatening in the industrial cities. A policy of military extinction might well unleash even stormier forces of disorder, such as those which had broken out in Chicago in 1886, as the riot in Haymarket Square. Instead of exterminating Indians, they proposed membership in American society in exchange for a repudiation of Indian ways. They offered, through the Dawes Severalty Act passed by Congress in 1887, to transform Indians by education and economic support into model Americans. The Dawes Act, in short, implied a theory and pedagogical vision of America itself.

That vision manifested itself in practical terms. To every male Indian "who has voluntarily taken up . . . his residence separate and apart from any tribe . . . and has adapted the habits of civilized life," the act offered not only an allotment of land for private cultivation but the prospect of full American citizenship. It offered a choice: either abandon Indian society and culture, and thus become a "free" American, or remain an Indian, socially and legally dependent. With a perverse accuracy, the act recognized the cultural power of tribal structures, of complex kinship systems, of shamanistic religion. As an alternative, it proposed, and thus helped promulgate, what it assumed to be the typical and culturally legitimate model of the male-dominated nuclear family based on private property. Linking citizenship with both propriety and property, the Dawes Act thus implied standards for the entire society.

By setting in motion a process of detribalization, the new law disclosed perhaps the rawest nerve in white-Indian relations: the conflicting practices in regard to property, especially land. The reformers on the whole shared with Roosevelt the view that Indians lacked a civilized sense of property, of spatial boundaries. "Where the game was plenty, there they hunted," wrote Roosevelt in accents in which romance clashes with economic interest; "they followed it when it moved away . . . and to most of the land on which we found them they had no stronger claim than that of having a few years previously butchered the original occupants." Reformers spoke of the despised "communistic" system of communal property relations. The vehemence aroused by Indians, fed for generations by tales of captivities and atrocities, of barbaric practices, took aim in these years of Western expansion particularly against a way of life perceived as antithetical, alien, and threatening in its implications. Again, Roosevelt provides the most vivid and blunt instances of rage. The Dawes Act, he remarked in his first message to Congress in 1901, provided "a mighty pulverizing engine to break up the tribal mass." The inner message had a wider audience in view. As he had made plain in 1889, "Indian ownership" was sometimes practiced by shiftless criminal whites as well: "To recognize the Indian ownership of the limitless prairies and forests of this continent—that is, to consider the dozen squalid savages who hunted at long intervals over a territory of a thousand square miles as owning it outright—necessarily implies a similar recognition of the claims of every white hunter, squatter, horse-thief, or wandering cattle-man." In 1886 he had warned: "The Indian should be treated in just the same way that we treat white settlers. Give each his little claim; if, as would generally happen, he declined this, why then let him share the fate of the thousands of white hunters and trappers who have lived on the game that the settlement of the country has exterminated, and let him, like those whites, who will not work, perish from the face of the earth which he cumbers." Work or perish: thus reads the inner script of the revised policy of "peace" toward the Indian.

If the Southern system of chattel slavery had obstructed industrial progress, provoking a civil war, so the Indian system of communal ownership had inspired resistance to Western expansion; it, too, required destruction, and then a policy of "reconstruction" of the defeated natives into the image of their victors: their language and costumes, their names and religion, their laws regarding work and property. By the 1890's, then, the Indian had been incorporated into America no longer simply as "savage," a fantasy object of ambivalent romantic identification or racial hatred, but as "lowest order," outcast and pariah who represented the fate of all those who do not work, do not own, do not prefer the benefits of legal status within the hierarchies of modern institutions to the prerogatives of freedom and cultural autonomy.

At the same time, and typical of the discordances of the age, knowledge of Indian cultures accumulated rapidly in these years of brutal warfare and policy formation, in the reports and monographs of the newly formed Bureau of American Ethnology (directed in its early days by John Wesley Powell). Like other academic disciplines and social sciences in these years, anthropology underwent swift professionalization, as ethnographers joined missionaries and Indian agents in native settlements, recording and analyzing their languages, customs, religions, and social structures. And scattered in their reports lay information about a way of life which might well have contributed to evolving social and cultural critiques of industrial society. Indeed, in the studies of Lewis Henry Morgan, especially in his magisterial *Ancient Society, or Researches in the Lines of Human Progress from Savagery through Barbarism to Civilization* (1877), such a contribution begins to take shape. Morgan's formulations challenged popular stereotypes of the Indian, viewing him in a perspective of history and social change deeply at odds with popular providential thought, with notions of racial superiority, and with American self-congratulatory rhetoric. Morgan carried on his research and writing despite an unlikely conventional career as a Rochester, New York, lawyer and businessman, a railroad investor and occasional member of the New York State Legislature. Refusing all university positions, he remained more or less an amateur (although he did serve as president of the prestigious American Association for the Advancement of Science), not exactly an outsider but sufficiently free of incipient professional standards to venture upon a bold theoretical enterprise in his effort to comprehend the great wealth of ethnographic data unearthed by nineteenth-century researchers. In his practical and political life, Morgan provided legal assistance to New York tribes and wrote legislation, as chairman of the State Committee on Indian Affairs, on their behalf. He never fulfilled his hope of appointment as national Commissioner of Indian Affairs.

Morgan's researches led him to a belief in the unity of mankind, and toward an evolutionary scheme in which the forms of subsistence, the level of technology, provided the basis of social change and progress. Representing earlier stages of human society and culture, the American Indian thus provided a unique opportunity for "civilized" Americans to study their own distant origins. As he put it in the preface to his remarkable study of Indian domestic architecture, *Houses and House-Life of the American Aborigines* (1881): "In studying the condition of the Indian tribes in these periods we may recover some portion of the lost history of our own race." Possessing neither the political society nor formal state of the "civilized" stage (and Morgan stresses the role of accident or fortuitous circumstances by which Semitic and Aryan peoples have arrived soonest at this condition), Indians have instead as their basic social unit what he called the gens or extended family: "a brotherhood bound together by ties of kin." Based on the arts of subsistence—hunting, gathering, some agriculture, and toolmaking—the gens functioned as communal units: "liberty, equality, and fraternity, though never formulated, were cardinal principles." About Indian dwellings he wrote: "It is evident that they were the work of the people, constructed for their own enjoyment and protection. Enforced labor never created them. On the contrary, it is the charm of all these edifices, roomy, and tasteful and remarkable as they are, that they were raised by the Indians for their own use, with willing hands, and occupied by them on terms of entire equality."

Morgan acknowledged in a letter that his work held "a tremendous thrust at privileged classes, who always have been a greater burden than society could afford to bear." "Since the advent of civilization," he wrote in the final paragraphs of *Ancient Society*, "the outgrowth of property has been so immense, its forms so diversified, its uses so expanding and its management so intelligent in the interests of its owners, that it has become, on the part of the people, an unmanageable power." Envisioning a "next higher plane of society," Morgan sees signs of its shape in forms already well established in America: "democracy in government, brotherhood in society, equality in rights and privileges, and universal education." The next plane "will be a revival, in a higher form, of the liberty, equality and fraternity of the ancient gentes."

In the face of simplistic and simplifying prevalent notions of "progress," of "civilization" and "savagery," Morgan insisted on a historical debt, "that we owe our present condition, with its multiplied means of safety and of happiness, to the struggles, the sufferings, the heroic exertions and the patient toil of our barbarous, and more remotely, of our savage ancestors." Wishing to sweep away the "misconceptions, and erroneous interpretations," the "false terminology," which have "perverted, and even caricatured" knowledge of American aboriginal history, he strove to place the Indian "in his true position in the scale of human advancement." Original errors of interpretation, he worried, have been implanted, and now "romance has swept the field."

Indeed, a fabric of fantasy, nostalgia, and idealization appeared toward the end of the nineteenth century as a kind of shroud for the "vanishing American." It was a matter of faith for Huck Finn, in Mark Twain's masterpiece of 1886, that an escape from Aunt Sally's desire to "sivilize" him lay ahead, in the Indian Territory: a place imagined as one of endless adventure, play, and freedom. Such fantasies seriously misconstrued the character of Indian cultures, but they do hold an important covert insight about the majority culture rapidly consolidating its hold on American society in these years, that "to civilize" entailed destruction or abrogation of that debt Morgan speaks of. Certainly, Frederick Jackson Turner's own notion of "progress" and stages of civilization, as indeed of the "gift" of the wilderness to white America, implies a simple passing over the inert body of Indian culture on America's way to the future. In spite of Morgan's efforts, and perhaps inevitably, "Indian" remained the utmost antithesis to an America dedicated to productivity, profit, and private property.

Tea time on the porch
of a New England home, c. 1900

The Social Defenses of the Rich

E. DIGBY BALTZELL

The myth of equality has had a powerful influence in shaping American attitudes. Beginning in the colonial period and continuing until today, foreign visitors as well as native writers have commented on what they have perceived as the high degree of social mobility available to Americans as a result of the "basic equality of opportunity that is their birthright." Of course, many of these same writers have also pointed out that certain elements of the population were left out of the equality scheme by definition, for example, women and nonwhites. But the myth persisted, even among those denied access to its rewards.

At least one group of Americans, however, knew better—the wealthy traditional elite (which did assimilate newcomers, but slowly). From the colonial period to the Civil War, many wealthy citizens of WASP (white Anglo-Saxon Protestant) ancestry believed they had a special place in society. Their wealth and traditions insulated them from the entrepreneurial clamor of the Jacksonian period, and they maintained a castelike existence in the cities of the eastern seaboard.

After the Civil War, however, traditions and family connections were no longer sufficient to maintain the exclusivity of the caste structure. The route to riches had shifted, and holders of the new wealth aspired to the life-style previously available primarily to the WASP elite. The homogeneous quality of upper-class existence began to break down under the onslaught of rapid economic growth and the extraordinary financial success of an increasing number of non-WASP families.

Initially, the traditional elite had supported open immigration from eastern and southern European countries in order to insure an overabundance of common laborers that would tend to keep wages down, but as participants in this new immigration began to rise in economic status, and in some cases to become actually wealthy, the elite began to reconsider their position. Although they were unable to restrict immigration until well into the twentieth century, they were able to take steps soon after the Civil War to insulate themselves from the society of wealthy non-WASPs.

E. Digby Baltzell, a sociologist at the University of Pennsylvania, has taken as his field of study the traditional elite of the Eastern seaboard. After publishing a book on the upper-class families of Philadelphia, he enlarged his focus to consider the exclusionary tactics of the WASP elite through the last hundred years. In the chapter reprinted below, he focuses on the anti-Semitic practices of the traditional families and enumerates the various devices by which the traditional upper class insulated itself socially from non-WASP wealth. Several features of the social life of the upper class taken so much for granted today have their origin in this period. Exclusive prep schools, college societies, restricted suburbs, summer resorts, and city clubs were founded in order to enable the traditional elite to protect what they saw as their caste privileges. Consequently, the excluded wealthy families formed their own parallel network of social organizations that were designed to reflect the class, if not the caste, prerogatives of upper-class existence.

We are still in power, after a fashion. Our sway over what we call society is undisputed. We keep the Jew far away, and the anti-Jew feeling is quite rabid.

HENRY ADAMS

The Civil War was fought, by a nation rapidly becoming centralized economically, in order to preserve the political Union. Although the Union was preserved and slavery abolished, the postwar Republic was faced with the enormously complex and morally cancerous problem of caste, as far as the formally free Negroes were concerned. The solution to this problem has now become the central one of our own age. But the more immediate effect of the Civil War was that, in the North at least, the nation realized the fabulous potential of industrial power. The Pennsylvania Railroad, for instance, began to cut back operations at the beginning of the war, only to realize a tremendous boom during the remainder of the conflict (total revenue in 1860: $5,933 million; in 1865: $19,533 million). But the profits of the war were nothing compared to those of the fabulous postwar years. Between 1870 and 1900, the national wealth quadrupled (rising from $30,400 million

From *The Protestant Establishment*, by E. Digby Baltzell. Copyright © 1964 by E. Digby Baltzell. Originally published under the title THE SOCIAL DEFENSE OF CASTE: THE TWO NATIONS IN THE 1880's. Reprinted by permission of Random House, Inc.

to $126,700 million and doubled again by 1914—reaching $254,200 million).

During this same period, wealth became increasingly centralized in the hands of a few. In 1891, *Forum* magazine published an article, "The Coming Billionaire," which estimated that there were 120 men in the nation worth over $10 million. The next year, the *New York Times* published a list of 4,047 millionaires, and the Census Bureau estimated that 9 per cent of the nation's families owned 71 per cent of the wealth. By 1910 there were more millionaires in the United States Senate alone than there were in the whole nation before the Civil War. This new inequality was dramatized by the fact, in 1900, according to Frederick Lewis Allen, the former immigrant lad Andrew Carnegie had an *income* of between $15 and $30 million (the income tax had been declared unconstitutional in a test case in 1895), while the average unskilled worker in the North received less than $460 a year in wages—in the South the figure was less than $300. It is no wonder that the production of pig iron rather than poetry, and the quest for status rather than salvation, now took hold of the minds of even the most patrician descendants of Puritan divines.

This inequality of wealth was accompanied by an increasing centralization of business power, as the nation changed, in the half century after Appomattox, from a rural-communal to an urban-corporate society. President Eliot of Harvard, in a speech before the fraternity of Phi Beta Kappa in 1888, noted this new corporate dominance when he pointed out that, while the Pennsylvania Railroad had gross receipts of $115 million and employed over 100,000 men in that year, the Commonwealth of Massachusetts had gross receipts of only $7 million and employed no more than 6,000 persons. And this corporate economy was further centralized financially in Wall Street. The capital required to launch the United States Steel Corporation, for example, would at that time have covered the costs of all the functions of the federal government for almost two years. J. P. Morgan and his associates, who put this great corporate empire together in 1901, held some three hundred directorships in over one hundred corporations with resources estimated at over $22 billion. This industrial age, in which the railroads spanned the continent and Wall Street interests controlled mines in the Rockies, timber in the Northwest, and coal in Pennsylvania and West Virginia, brought about a national economy and the emergence of a national mind.

And the prosperity of this new urban-corporate world was largely built upon the blood and sweat of the men, and the tears of their women, who came to this country in such large numbers from the peasant villages of Southern and Eastern Europe. Whereas most of the older immigrants from Northern and Western Europe had come to a rural America where they were able to assimilate more easily, the majority of these newer arrivals huddled together in the urban slums and ghettos which were characteristic of the lower levels of the commercial economy which America had now become.

Except for the captains of industry, whose money-centered minds continued to welcome and encourage immigration because they believed it kept wages down and retarded unionization, most old-stock Americans were frankly appalled at the growing evils of industrialization, immigration and urbanization. As we have seen, the closing decades of the nineteenth century were marked by labor unrest and violence; many men, like Henry Adams, developed a violent nativism and anti-Semitism; others, following the lead of Jane Addams, discovered the slums and went to work to alleviate the evils of prostitution, disease, crime, political bossism and grinding poverty; both Midwestern Populism and the Eastern, patrician led Progressive movement were part of the general protest and were, in turn, infused with varying degrees of nativism; and even organized labor, many of whose members were of recent immigrant origin, was by no means devoid of nativist sentiment.

In so many ways, nativism was part of a more generalized anti-urban and anti-capitalist mood. Unfortunately, anti-Semitism is often allied with an antipathy toward the city and the money-power. Thus the first mass manifestations of anti-Semitism in America came out of the Midwest among the Populist leaders and their followers. In the campaign of 1896, for example, William Jennings Bryan was accused of anti-Semitism and had to explain to the Jewish Democrats of Chicago that in denouncing the policies of Wall Street and the Rothschilds, he and his silver friends were "not attacking a race but greed and avarice which know no race or religion." And the danger that the Populist, isolationist and anti-Wall Street sentiment in the Middle West might at any time revert to anti-Semitism continued. As we shall see in a later chapter, Henry Ford, a multimillionaire with the traditional Populist mistrust of the money-power, was notoriously anti-Semitic for a time in the early 1920's.

Nativism was also a part of a status revolution at the elite level of leadership on the Eastern Seaboard. "The newly rich, the grandiosely or corruptly rich, the masters of the great corporations," wrote Richard Hoffstadter, "were bypassing the men of the Mugwump type—the old gentry, the merchants of long standing, the small manufacturers, the established professional men, the civic leaders of an earlier era. In scores of cities and hundreds of towns, particularly in the East but also in the nation at large, the old-family, college-educated class that had deep ancestral roots in local communities and often owned family businesses, that had traditions of political leadership, belonged to the patriotic societies and the best clubs, staffed the government boards of philanthropic and cultural institutions, and led the movements for civic betterment, were being overshadowed and edged aside in making basic political and economic decisions. . . . They were less important and they knew it."

Many members of this class, of old-stock prestige and waning power, eventually allied themselves with the Progressive movement. Many also, like Henry Adams, withdrew almost entirely from the world of power. The "decent people," as Edith Wharton once put it, increasingly "fell back on sport and culture." And this sport and culture was now to be reinforced by a series of fashionable and patrician protective associations which, in turn, systematically and subtly institutionalized the exclusion of Jews.

The turning point came in the 1880's, when a number of symbolic events forecast the nature of the American upper class in the twentieth century. Thus, when President Eliot of Harvard built his summer cottage at Northeast Harbor, Maine, in 1881, the exclusive summer resort trend was well under way; the founding of *The* Country Club at Brookline, Massachusetts, in 1882, marked the beginning of the country-club trend; the founding of the Sons of the Revolution, in 1883, symbolized the birth of the genealogical fad and the patrician scramble for old-stock roots; Endicott Peabody's founding of Groton School, in 1884, in order to rear young gentlemen in the tradition of British public schools (and incidentally to protect them from the increasing heterogeneity of the public school system) was an important symbol of both upper-class exclusiveness and patrician Anglophilia; and finally, the Social Register, a convenient index of this new associational aristocracy, was first issued toward the end of this transitional decade in 1887 (the publisher also handled much of the literature of the American Protective Association, which was active in the nativist movement at that time).

The Right Reverend Phillips Brooks—the favorite clergyman among Philadelphia's Victorian gentry, who was called to Boston's Trinity Church in 1869, the year Grant entered the White House and Eliot accepted the presidency at Harvard—was one of the most sensitive barometers of the brahmin mind. Thus, although he himself had graduated from the Boston Latin School along with other patricians and plebeian gentlemen of his generation, he first suggested the idea of Groton to young Peabody in the eighties and joined the Sons of the Revolution in 1891, because, as he said at the time, "it is well to go in for the assertion that our dear land at least used to be American."

ANCESTRAL ASSOCIATIONS AND THE QUEST FOR OLD-STOCK ROOTS

The idea of caste dies hard, even in a democratic land such as ours. Our first and most exclusive ancestral association, the Society of the Cincinnati, was formed in 1783, just before the Continental Army disbanded. Its membership was limited to Washington's officers and, in accord with the rural traditions of primogeniture, was to be passed on to the oldest sons in succeeding generations. The society's name reflects the ancient tradition of gentlemen-farmers, from Cincinnatus to Cromwell, Washington and Franklin Roosevelt, who have served their country in times of need. Just as the founding of the Society of Cincinnati reflected the rural values of the gentleman and his mistrust of grasping city ways, it was quite natural that the new wave of ancestral associations which came into being at the end of the nineteenth century was a reaction to the rise of the city with its accompanying heterogeneity and conflict. As Wallace Evan Davies, in *Patriotism on Parade*, put it:

> "The great Upheaval," the Haymarket Riot, the campaigns of Henry George, and the writings of Edward Bellamy crowded the last half of the eighties. The nineties produced such proofs of unrest as the Populist Revolt, the Homestead Strike with the attempted assassination of Henry Clay Frick, the Panic of 1893, the Pullman Strike, Coxey's Army, and finally, the Bryan campaign of 1896. Throughout all this the conservative and propertied classes watched apprehensively the black cloud of anarchism, a menace as productive of alarm and hysteria as bolshevism and communism in later generations.

These old-stock patriots, desperately seeking hereditary and historical roots in a rapidly changing world, flocked to the standards of such newly founded societies as the Sons of the Revolution (1883), the Colonial Dames (1890), the Daughters of the American Revolution (1890), Daughters of the Cincinnati (1894), the Society of Mayflower Descendants (1894), the Aryan Order of St. George or the Holy Roman Empire in the Colonies of America (1892), and the Baronial Order of Runnymede (1897). It is no wonder that genealogist, both amateur and professional, rapidly came into vogue. Several urban newspapers established genealogical departments; the Lenox Library in New York purchased one of its largest genealogical collections, in 1896, setting aside a room "for the convenience of the large number of researchers after family history"; the *Library Journal* carried articles on how to help the public in ancestor hunting; and, as of 1900, the *Patriotic Review* listed seventy patriotic, hereditary and historical associations, exactly *half* of which had been founded during the preceding decade alone.

This whole movement was, of course, intimately bound up with anti-immigrant and anti-Semitic sentiments. Thus a leader of the D.A.R. saw a real danger in "our being absorbed by the different nationalities among us," and a president-general of the Sons of the American Revolution reported that: "Not until the state of civilization reached the point where we had a great many foreigners in our land . . . were our patriotic societies successful." The Daughters of the American Revolution was indeed extremely successful. Founded in 1890, it had 397 chapters in 38 states by 1897. That the anti-immigrant reaction was most prevalent in the urban East, however, was attested to by the fact that the Daughters made slow headway in the West and South and had a vast majority of its chapters in New York and Massachusetts.

But, as Franklin Roosevelt once said, "we are all descendants of immigrants." While old-stock Americans were forming rather exclusive associations based on their descent from Colonial immigrants, newer Americans were also attempting to establish their own historical roots. Such organizations at the Scotch-Irish Society (1889), the Pennsylvania-German Society (1891), the American Jewish Historical Society (1894), and the American Irish Historical Society (1898) were concerned to establish ethnic recognition through ancestral achievement. "The Americanism of all Irishmen and Jews," writes Edward N. Saveth, "was enhanced because of the handful of Irishmen and Jews who may have stood by Washington in a moment of crisis."

The genealogically minded patrician has remained a part of the American scene down through the years. The front page of any contemporary copy of the Social Register, for instance, lists a series of clubs, universities and ancestral associations, with proper abbreviations attached, in order that each family may be identified by its members' affiliations. A recent Philadelphia Social Register listed an even dozen such societies, and a venerable old gentleman of great prestige (if little power) was listed in a later page as follows:

> Rittenhouse, Wm.   Penn—Ul.Ph.Myf.Cc.Wt.Rv.Ll.Fw.P'83 . . .
>   Union League

It was indeed plain to see (after a bit of research on page 1) that this old gentleman was nicely placed as far as his ancestral, college and club affiliations were concerned. He belonged to the Union League (Ul) and Philadelphia clubs (Ph), had graduated in 1883 from Princeton University (P'83), and was apparently devoting himself to some sort of patriotic ancestor worship in his declining years, as suggested by his ancestral association memberships: Mayflower Descendants (Myf); Society of Cincinnati (Cc); Society of the War of 1812 (Wt); Sons of the Revolution (Rv); Military Order of the Loyal Legion (Ll); and the Military Order of Foreign Wars (Fw). And, as the final entry shows, he was living at the Union League.

THE SUMMER RESORT AND THE QUEST FOR HOMOGENEITY

Americans have always longed for grass roots. In a society of cement, the resort movement in America paralleled the genealogical escape to the past. The physiological and physical ugliness of the city streets gradually drove those who could afford it back to nature and the wide-open spaces. Men like Owen Wister, Theodore Roosevelt and Madison Grant went out to the West, and the most timid, or socially minded, souls sought refuge at some exclusive summer resort. In spite of the efforts of men like Frederick Law Olmstead and Madison Grant to bring rural beauty into the heart of the city (Olmstead built some fifteen city parks from coast to coast, Central Park in New York City being the most well known), first the artists and writers, then the gentry, and finally the millionaires were seeking the beauty of nature and the simple life among the "natives" of coastal or mountain communities along the Eastern Seaboard. President Eliot and his sons spent the summers during the seventies camping in tents before building the first summer cottage in Northeast Harbor, Maine, in 1881. Charles Francis Adams, Jr., saw his native Quincy succumb to industrialism and the Irish (the Knights of Labor gained control of the Adams "race-place" in 1887), gave up his job with the Union Pacific in 1890, and finally escaped to the simple life at Lincoln, Massachusetts, in 1893.

The summer resort increased in popularity after the Civil War and went through its period of most rapid growth between 1880 and the First War. Long Branch, New Jersey, summer capital of presidents from Grant to Arthur, was filled with proper Philadelphians and New Yorkers. Further south, Cape May—where Jay Cooke, financier of the Civil War, spent every summer—was the most fashionable Philadelphia summer resort until well into the twentieth century. Boston's best retreated to the simple life at Nahant. Others went to the Berkshires, where large "cottages," large families and large incomes supported the simple life for many years (Lenox boasted thirty-five of these cottages as of 1880, and seventy-five by 1900). Between 1890 and the First War, Bar Harbor became one of America's most stylish resorts. By 1894, the year Joseph Pulitzer built the resort's first hundred-thousand-dollar "cottage," Morgan and Standard Oil partners were the leaders of the community (when a Vanderbilt bought a cottage in 1922, it was the first to change hands in fifteen years; within the next three years, forty-seven such cottages changed hands). Less fashionable, but no less genteel, Northeast Harbor grew at the same time. Anticipating modern sociology, President Eliot made a study of the community in 1890. Among other things, he found that, as of 1881, nonresident summer people owned less than one-fifth of the local real property; only eight years later, in 1889, they owned over half (and total property values had almost doubled).

Just as the white man, symbolized by the British gentleman, was roaming round the world in search of raw materials for his factories at Manchester, Liverpool or Leeds, so America's urban gentry and capitalists, at the turn of the century, were imperialists seeking solace for their souls among the "natives" of Lenox, Bar Harbor or Kennebunkport. Here they were able to forget the ugliness of the urban melting pot as they dwelt among solid Yankees (Ethan Frome), many of whom possessed more homogeneous, Colonial-stock roots than themselves. And these rustic "types" kept up their boats, taught their children the ways of the sea, caught their lobsters, served them in the stores along the village streets, and became temporary servants and gardeners on their rustic estates. But although most old-time resorters were patron- izingly proficient with the "Down East" accent, and appreciated the fact that the "natives" were their "own kind" racially, sometimes the idyllic harmony was somewhat superficial, at least as far as the more sensitive "natives" were concerned. Hence the following anecdote cir- culating among the "natives" at Bar Harbor: "They emptied the pool the other day," reported one typical "type" to another. "Why?" asked his friend. "Oh, one of the natives fell in." *Absolute exclusion*

But the simple life was, nevertheless, often touching and always relaxing. All one's kind were there together and the older virtues of communal life were abroad; Easter-Christmas-Wedding Christians usu- ally went to church every Sunday; millionaires' wives did their own shopping in the village, and walking, boating and picnicking brought a renewed appreciation of nature. And perhaps most important of all, one knew who one's daughter was seeing, at least during the summer months when convenient alliances for life were often consummated.

When J. P. Morgan observed that "you can do business with any- one, but only sail with a gentleman," he was reflecting the fact that a secure sense of homogeneity is the essence of resort life. It is no won- der that anti-Semitism, of the gentlemanly, exclusionary sort, probably reached its most panicky heights there. Thus one of the first examples of upper-class anti-Semitism in America occurred, in the 1870's, when a prominent New York banker, Joseph Seligman, was rudely excluded from the Grand Union Hotel in Saratoga Springs. This came as a shock to the American people and was given wide publicity because it was something new at that time. Henry Ward Beecher, a personal friend of the Seligmans, reacted with a sermon from his famous pulpit at Plym- outh Church: "What have the Jews," he said, "of which they need be ashamed, in a Christian Republic where all men are declared to be free and equal? . . . Is it that they are excessively industrious? Let the Yan- kee cast the first stone. Is it that they are inordinately keen on bargain- ing? Have they ever stolen ten millions of dollars at a pinch from a city? Are our courts bailing our Jews, or compromising with Jews? Are there Jews lying in our jails, and waiting for mercy. . . . You cannot find one criminal Jew in the whole catalogue. . . ."

The Seligman incident was followed by a battle at Saratoga Springs. Immediately afterwards, several new hotels were built there by Jews, and by the end of the century half the population was Jewish; as a result, it is said that one non-Jewish establishment boldly advertised its policies with a sign: "No Jews and Dogs Admitted Here." At the same time, other prominent German Jews were running into embarrassing situations elsewhere. In the 1890's Nathan Straus, brother of a member of Theodore Roosevelt's Cabinet and a leading merchant and civic leader himself, was turned down at a leading hotel in Lakewood, New Jersey, a most fashionable winter resort at that time. He promptly built a hotel next door, twice as big and for Jews only. And the resort rapidly became Jewish, as kosher establishments multiplied on all sides.

Even the well-integrated and cultivated members of Philadelphia's German-Jewish community eventually had to bow to the trend. As late as the eighties and nineties, for instance, leading Jewish families were listed in the Philadelphia Blue Book as summering at fashionable Cape May, along with the city's best gentile families. But this did not continue, and many prominent Philadelphia Jews became founding families at Long Branch, Asbury Park, Spring Lake or Atlantic City, where the first resort synagogues were established during the nineties: Long Branch (1890), Atlantic City (1893), and Asbury Park (1896).

As the East European Jews rapidly rose to middle-class status, resort-hotel exclusiveness produced a running battle along the Jersey coast and up in the Catskills. One resort after another changed from an all-gentile to an all-Jewish community. Atlantic City, for example, first became a fashionable gentile resort in the nineties. By the end of the First War, however, it had become a predominantly Jewish resort, at least in the summer months (the first modern, fireproof hotel was built there in 1902; there were a thousand such hotels by 1930). According to Edmund Wilson, it was while visiting Atlantic City in the winter of 1919 that John Jay Chapman first became anti-Semitic. "They are uncritical," he wrote to a friend after watching the boardwalk crowd of vacationing Jews. "Life is a simple matter for them: a bank account and a larder. . . . They strike me as an inferior race. . . . These people don't know anything. They have no religion, no customs except eating and drinking."

Just before the First World War, resort establishments began to advertise their discriminatory policies in the newspapers. The situation became so embarrassing that New York State passed a law, in 1913, forbidding places of public accommodation to advertise their unwillingness to admit persons because of race, creed or color.

Although the high tide of formal resort society has declined in recent years, the rigid exclusion of Jews has largely continued. As Cleveland Amory has put it:

> Certain aspects of the narrowness of the old-line resort society have continued, not the least of which is the question of anti-Semitism. Although certain Jewish families, notably the Pulitzers, the Belmonts and the Goulds have played their part in resort Society— and Otto Kahn, Henry Seligman, Jules Bache and Frederick Lewison have cut sizeable figures—the general record of resort intoler-

ance is an extraordinary one; it reached perhaps its lowest point when Palm Beach's Bath and Tennis Club sent out a letter asking members not to bring into the club guests of Jewish extraction. Among those who received this letter was Bernard Baruch, then a member of the club and a man whose father, Dr. Simon Baruch, pioneered the Saratoga Spa. Several of Baruch's friends advised him to make an issue of the affair; instead, he quietly resigned. "No one," he says today, "has had this thing practiced against him more than I have. But I don't let it bother me. I always remember what Bob Fitzsimmons said to me—he wanted to make me a champion, you know—'You've got to learn to take it before you can give it out.' "

Anti-semitism strong – exclusion from resorts.

THE SUBURBAN TREND, THE COUNTRY CLUB AND THE COUNTRY DAY SCHOOL

The resort and the suburb are both a product of the same desire for homogeneity and a nostalgic yearning for the simplicities of small-town life. Just as, today, white families of diverse, ethnic origins and newly won middle-class status are busily escaping from the increasingly Negro composition of our cities, so the Protestant upper class first began to flee the ugliness of the urban melting pot at the turn of the century. In Philadelphia, for instance, the majority of the Victorian gentry lived in the city, around fashionable Rittenhouse Square, as of 1890; by 1914, the majority had moved out to the suburbs along the Main Line or in Chestnut Hill. And this same pattern was followed in other cities.

In many ways Pierre Lorillard was the Victorian aristocrat's William Levitt. Just as Levittown is now the most famous example of a planned community symbolizing the post World War II suburban trend among the middle classes, so Tuxedo Park, New York, established on a site of some 600,000 acres inherited by Pierre Lorillard in 1886, was once the acme of upper-class suburban exclusiveness. According to Cleveland Amory, the Lorillards possessed a foolproof formula for business success which, in turn, was exactly reversed when they came to promoting upper-class exclusiveness. He lists their contrasting formulas as follows:

For Business Success:
1) Find out what the public wants, then produce the best of its kind.
2) Advertise the product so that everybody will know it is available.
3) Distribute it everywhere so that everybody can get it.
4) Keep making the product better so that more people will like it.

For Snob Success:
1) Find out who the leaders of Society are and produce the best place for them to live in.
2) Tell nobody else about it so that nobody else will know it's available.
3) Keep it a private club so that other people, even if they do hear about it, can't get in.
4) Keep the place exactly as it was in the beginning so that other people, even if they do hear about it and somehow do manage to get in, won't ever like it anyway.

At Tuxedo Park, Lorillard produced almost a caricature of the Victorian millionaire's mania for exclusiveness. In less than a year, he surrounded seven thousand acres with an eight-foot fence, graded some thirty miles of road, built a complete sewage and water system, a gate house which looked like "a frontispiece of an English novel," a clubhouse staffed with imported English servants, and "twenty-two casement dormered English turreted cottages." On Memorial Day, 1886, special trains brought seven hundred highly selected guests from New York to witness the Park's opening.

Tuxedo was a complete triumph. The physical surroundings, the architecture and the social organization were perfectly in tune with the patrician mind of that day. In addition to the English cottages and the clubhouse, there were "two blocks of stores, a score of stables, four lawntennis courts, a bowling alley, a swimming tank, a boathouse, an icehouse, a dam, a trout pond and a hatchery. . . . The members sported the club badge which, designed to be worn as a pin, was an oakleaf of solid gold; club governors had acorns attached to their oakleafs and later all Tuxedoites were to wear ties, hatbands, socks, etc., in the club colors of green and gold. . . . No one who was not a member of the club was allowed to buy property."

Tuxedo Park was perhaps a somewhat exaggerated example of an ideal. It certainly would have suggested the conformity of a Chinese commune to many aristocrats seeking real privacy (in the eighties at Nahant, for example, Henry Cabot Lodge built a high fence between his place and his brother-in-law's next door). The upper-class suburban trend as a whole, nevertheless, was motivated by similar, if less rigid, desires for homogeneity. Unlike Tuxedo, however, the country club and the country day school, rather than the neighborhood *per se*, were the main fortresses of exclusiveness. Thus the beginning of a real suburban trend can conveniently be dated from the building of *The* Country Club, at Brookline, Massachusetts, in 1882. In the next few decades similar clubs sprang up like mushrooms and became a vital part of the American upper-class way of life. Henry James, an expert on Society both here and abroad, found them "a deeply significant American symbol'' at the turn of the century, and an English commentator on our mores wrote:

> There are also all over England clubs especially devoted to particular objects, gold clubs, yacht clubs, and so forth. In these the members are drawn together by their interest in a common pursuit, and are forced into some kind of acquaintanceship. But these are very different in spirit and intention from the American country club. It exists as a kind of center of the social life of the neighborhood. Sport is encouraged by these clubs for the sake of general sociability. In England sociability is a by-product of an interest in sport.

This English commentator was, of course, implying that the real function of the American country club was not sport but social exclusion. And throughout the twentieth century the country club has remained, by and large and with a minority of exceptions, rigidly exclusive of Jews. In response to this discrimination, wealthy Jews have formed clubs of their own. When many wealthy German Jews in Philadelphia first moved to the suburbs, as we have seen, the famous merchant Ellis Gimbel and a group of his friends founded one of the first Jewish country clubs in the nation, in 1906. After the Second War, when many Jewish families began to move out on the city's Main Line, another elite club, largely composed of East European Jews, was opened.

If the country club is the root of family exclusiveness, the suburban day school provides an isolated environment for the younger generation. Thus a necessary part of the suburban trend was the founding of such well-known schools as the Chestnut Hill Academy (1895) and Haverford School (1884) in two of Philadelphia's most exclusive suburbs; the Gilman School (1897) in a Baltimore suburb; the Browne and Nichols School (1883) in Cambridge, Massachusetts; the Morristown School (1898), the Tuxedo Park School (1900), and the Hackley School (1899) in Tarrytown, to take care of New York suburbia. While not as rigidly exclusive as the country club as far as Jews are concerned, these schools have been, of course, overwhelmingly proper and Protestant down through the years. Few Jews sought admission before the Second War, and since then some form of quota system has often been applied (this is especially true of the suburban schools run by the Quakers in Philadelphia, largely because of their extremely liberal policies of ethnic, racial and religious tolerance).

The greatest monuments are often erected after an era's period of greatest achievement. Versailles was completed after the great age of Louis XIV, the finest Gothic cathedrals after the height of the Catholic synthesis, and the neoclassic plantation mansions after the South had begun to decline. As we shall see below, upper-class suburban homogeneity and exclusiveness are rapidly vanishing characteristics of our postwar era. And when the upper class reigned supreme in its suburban glory (1890–1940), discriminatory practices were genteel and subtle when compared, for example, with the methods of modern automobile magnates in Detroit. The grosser, Grosse Pointe methods, however, will serve to illustrate (in the manner of our discussion of Tuxedo Park) the anti-Semitic and anti-ethnic values of suburban upper class, especially at the height of its attempted escape from the motley urban melting pot. As a somewhat tragic, and slightly ludicrous, monument to the mind of a fading era, the following paragraphs from *Time* magazine must be reproduced in full:

> Detroit's oldest and richest suburban area is the five-community section east of the city collectively called Grosse Pointe (pop. 50,000). Set back from the winding, tree-shaded streets are fine, solid colonial or brick mansions, occupied by some of Detroit's oldest (pre-automobile age) upper class, and by others who made the grade in business and professional life. Grosse Pointe is representative of dozens of wealthy residential areas in the U.S. where privacy, unhurried tranquility, and unsullied property values are respected. But last week, Grosse Pointe was in the throes of a rude, untranquil exposé of its methods of maintaining tranquility.
>
> The trouble burst with the public revelation, during a court squabble between one property owner and his neighbor, that the Grosse Point Property Owners Association (973 families) and local real estate brokers had set up a rigid system for screening families who want to buy or build homes in Grosse Pointe. Unlike similar communities, where neighborly solidarity is based on an unwritten gentleman's agreement, Grosse Pointe's screening system is based on a written questionnaire, filled out by a private investigator on behalf of Grosse Point's "owner vigilantes."
>
> The three-page questionnaire, scaled on the basis of "points" (highest score: 100), grades would-be home owners on such qualities as descent, way of life (American?), occupation (Typical of his own race?), swarthiness (Very? Medium? Slightly? Not at all?), accent (Pronounced? Medium? Slight? None?), name (Typically American?), repute, education, dress (Neat or Slovenly? Conservative or Flashy?), status of occupation (sufficient eminence may offset poor grades in other respects). Religion is not scored, but weighted in the balance by a three-man Grosse Pointe screening committee. All prospects are handicapped on an ethnic and racial basis: Jews, for example, must score a minimum of 85 points, Italians 75, Greeks 65, Poles 55; Negroes and Orientals do not count.

On reading this questionnaire, one could not fail to see that these Detroit tycoons were, after all, only reflecting their training in the methodology of modern social science. One might prefer the less-amoral world of William James, who once said: "In God's eyes the difference of social position, of intellect, of culture, of cleanliness, of dress, which different men exhibit . . . must be so small as to practically vanish." But in our age, when the social scientist is deified, several generations of younger Americans have now been scientifically shown that men no longer seek status "in God's eyes." Instead they are asked to read all sorts of status-ranking studies, often backed by authoritative "tests of significance," which show how one is placed in society by one's cleanliness, dress, and drinking mores. How, one may ask, can one expect these suburbanites, most of whom have been educated in this modern tradition, not to use these methods for their own convenience.

THE NEW ENGLAND BOARDING SCHOOL

The growth in importance of the New England boarding school as an upper-class institution coincided with the American plutocracy's search for ancestral, suburban and resort-rural roots. At the time of Groton's founding in 1884, for example, these schools were rapidly becoming a vital factor in the creation of a national upper class, with more or less homogeneous values and behavior patterns. In an ever more centralized, complex and mobile age, the sons of the new and old rich, from Boston and New York to Chicago and San Francisco, were educated together in the secluded halls of Groton and St. Paul's, Exeter and Andover, and some seventy other, approximately similar, schools. While Exeter and Andover were ancient institutions, having been founded in the eighteenth century, and while St. Paul's had been in existence since before the Civil War, the boarding school movement went through its period of most rapid growth in the course of the half century after 1880. Exeter's enrollment increased from some 200 boys in 1880, to over 400 by 1905. The enrollment reached 600 for the first time in 1920, rose to 700 in the 1930's, and has remained below 800 ever since. St. Paul's went through its period of most rapid growth in the two decades before 1900 (the school graduated about 45 boys per year in the 1870's and rose to 100 per year by 1900, where it has remained ever since).

It is interesting in connection with the growth of a national upper class that the founding of many prominent schools coincided with the "trust-founding" and "trust-busting" era. Thus the following schools were founded within a decade of the formation of the United States Steel Corporation, in 1901:

> The Taft School in Watertown, Connecticut, was founded by Horace Dutton Taft, a brother of President Taft, in 1890; the Hotchkiss School, Lakeville, Connecticut, was founded and endowed by Maria Hotchkiss, widow of the inventor of the famous machinegun, in 1892; St. George's School, Newport, Rhode Island, which

has a million-dollar Gothic chapel built by John Nicholas Brown, was founded in 1896; in the same year, Choate School, whose benefactors and friends include such prominent businessman as Andrew Mellon and Owen D. Young, was founded by Judge William G. Choate, at Wallingford, Connecticut; while the elder Morgan was forming his steel company in New York and Pittsburgh in 1901, seven Proper Bostonians, including Francis Lowell, W. Cameron Forbes, and Henry Lee Higginson, were founding Middlesex School, near Concord, Massachusetts; Deerfield, which had been a local academy since 1797, was reorganized as a modern boarding school by its great headmaster, Frank L. Boydon, in 1902; and finally, Father Sill of the Order of the Holy Cross, founded Kent School in 1906.

While the vast majority of the students at these schools were old-stock Protestants throughout the first part of the twentieth century at least, it would be inaccurate to suppose that the schools' admission policies rigidly excluded Catholics and even Jews. Few Catholics and fewer Jews applied (Henry Morgenthau attended Exeter. As he never referred to the fact, even in his *Who's Who* biography, he probably had a pretty lonely time there). As a matter of historical fact, these schools were largely preoccupied, during the first three decades of this century, with assimilating the sons of America's newly rich Protestant tycoons, many of whom were somewhat spoiled in the style of the late William Randolph Hearst, who had been asked to leave St. Paul's.

On the whole . . . , these schools have continued to assimilate the sons of the newly rich down through the years. John F. Kennedy, for example, was graduated from Choate School in the thirties, after spending a year at Canterbury. In this connection, it was a measure of the increasingly affluent status of American Catholics that the nation's two leading Catholic boarding schools, Portsmouth Priory and Canterbury, were founded in 1926 and 1915 respectively.

THE COLLEGE CAMPUS IN THE GILDED AGE: GOLD COAST AND SLUM

The excluding mania of the Gilded Age was of course reflected on the campuses of the nation, especially in the older colleges in the East. In his book, *Academic Procession*, Ernest Earnest begins his chapter entitled "The Golden Age and the Gilded Cage" as follows:

It is ironic that the most fruitful period in American higher education sowed the seeds of three of the greatest evils: commercialized athletics, domination by the business community, and a caste system symbolized by the Gold Coast. . . . A smaller percentage of students came to prepare for the ministry, law, and teaching; they came to prepare for entrance into the business community, especially that part of it concerned with big business and finance. And it was the sons of big business, finance, and corporation law who dominated the life of the campus in the older Eastern colleges. To an amazing degree the pattern set by Harvard, Yale and Princeton after 1880 became that of colleges all over the country. The clubs, the social organization, the athletics—even the clothes and the slang—of "the big three" were copied by college youth throughout the nation. In its totality the system which flowered between 1880 and World War I reflected the ideals of the social class which dominated the period.

It is indeed appropriate that Yale's William Graham Sumner added the term "mores" to the sociological jargon, for the snobbish mass mores of the campuses of the Gilded Age were nowhere more binding than at New Haven. In the nineties, Yale became the first football factory and led the national trend toward anti-intellectualism and social snobbishness. Between 1883 and 1901, Yale plowed through nine undefeated seasons, piled up seven hundred points to its opponents' zero in the famous season of 1888, and produced Walter Camp, who picked the first All-American eleven and who produced Amos Alonzo Stagg, who, in turn, taught Knute Rockne everything he knew about football. By the turn of the century, "We toil not, neither do we agitate, but we play football" became the campus slogan. And cheating and the use of purchased papers almost became the rule among the golden boys of Yale, most of whom lived in "The Hutch," an expensive privately owned dormitory where the swells patronized private tailors, ruined expensive suits in pranks, sprees and rioting, ordered fine cigars by the hundred-lot, and looked down on those poorer boys who had gone to public high schools. The Yale Class Book of 1900, appropriately enough, published the answer to the following question: Have you ever used a trot? Yes: 264, No: 15. At the same time, in a survey covering three floors of a dormitory, it was found that not a single student wrote his own themes. They bought them, of course. After all, this sort of menial labor was only for the "drips," "grinds," "fruits," "meatballs," and "black men" of minority ethnic origins and a public school education. But at least one gilded son was somewhat horrified at the mores of Old Eli in those good old days before mass democracy had polluted gentlemenly education. A member of the class of 1879, this young gentleman asked an instructor in history to recommend some outside reading. The reply was "Young man, if you think you came to Yale with the idea of reading you will find out your mistake very soon."

This anti-intellectual crowd of leading Yale men was composed primarily of boarding school graduates who began to dominate campus life at this time. Owen Johnson, graduate of Lawrenceville and Yale (1900), wrote about this generation in his best seller, *Stover at Yale*.

Stover soon learned that the way to success at Yale meant following the mores established by the cliques from Andover, Exeter, Hotchkiss, Groton and St. Paul's: "We've got a corking lot in the house—Best of the Andover crowd." Even in the famous senior societies, caste replaced the traditional aristocracy of merit. Thus a committee headed by Professor Irving Fisher found that, whereas twenty-six of the thirty-four class valedictorians had been tapped by the senior societies between 1861 and 1894, after 1893 not a single one had been considered.

By the turn of the century, the College of New Jersey which had only recently changed its name to Princeton was far more homogeneously upper class than Yale. "The Christian tradition, the exclusiveness of the upper-class clubs, and the prejudices of the students," wrote Edwin E. Slosson in *Great American Universities* in 1910, "kept away many Jews, although not all—there are eleven in the Freshman class. Anti-Semitic feeling seemed to me to be more dominant at Princeton than at any of the other universities I visited. 'If the Jews once get in,' I was told, 'they would ruin Princeton as they have Columbia and Pennsylvania.' "

Football mania and the snobberies fostered by the eating-club system gradually dominated campus life at Princeton. Thus in 1906, Woodrow Wilson, convinced that the side shows were swallowing up the circus, made his famous report to the trustees on the need for abolishing the clubs. Although many misunderstood his purpose at the time, Wilson actually desired to make Princeton an even more homogeneous body of gentlemen-scholars. His preceptorial and quadrangle plans envisioned a series of small and intimate groups of students and faculty members pursuing knowledge without the disruptive class divisions fostered by the existing club system. Wilson was defeated in his drive for reform (partly because of his tactlessness) and was eventually banished to the White House, where he would be less of a threat to the system so dear to the hearts of many powerful trustees.

One should not dismiss Princeton's idea of homogeneity without mentioning one of its real and extremely important advantages. Princeton is one of the few American universities where an honor system is still in force, and presumably works. In this connection, Edwin E. Slosson's observations on the system as it worked in 1910 should be quoted in full:

> At Harvard I saw a crowd of students going into a large hall, and following them in, I found I could not get out, that no one was allowed to leave the examination room for twenty minutes. The students were insulated, the carefully protected papers distributed, and guards walked up and down the aisles with their eyes rolling like the search lights of a steamer in a fog. Nothing like this at Princeton; the students are on their honor not to cheat, and they do not, or but rarely. Each entering class is instructed by the Se-

niors into the Princeton code of honor, which requires any student
seeing another receiving or giving assistance on examination to report him for a trial by his peers of the student body. . . . I do not
think the plan would be practicable in the long run with a very
large and heterogeneous collection of students. It is probable that
Princeton will lose this with some other fine features of its student
life as the university grows and becomes more cosmopolitan. The
semimonastic seculsion of the country village cannot be long maintained.

In contrast to Princeton, and even Yale, Harvard has always been
guided by the ideal of diversity. A large and heterogeneous student
body, however, is always in danger of developing class divisions. Like
his friend, Woodrow Wilson, A. Lawrence Lowell was disturbed by
this trend at Harvard at the turn of the century. In a letter to President
Eliot, written in 1902, he mentioned the "tendency of wealthy students
to live in private dormitories outside the yard" and the "great danger
of a snobbish separation of the students on lines of wealth." In a committee report of the same year, he noted how one of the finest dormitories was becoming known as "Little Jerusalem" because of the fact
that some Jews lived there.

Samuel Eliot Morison, in his history of Harvard, shows how the
college gradually became two worlds—the "Yard" and the "Gold
Coast"—as Boston society, the private schools, the club system and the
private dormitories took over social life at the turn of the century. "In
the eighties," he writes, "when the supply of eligible young men in
Boston was decreased by the westward movement, the Boston mam-
mas suddenly became aware that Harvard contained many appetizing
young gentlemen from New York, Philadelphia, and elsewhere. One
met them in the summer at Newport, Beverly, or Bar Harbor; naturally
one invited them to Mr. Papanti's or Mr. Foster's 'Friday Evenings'
when they entered College, to the 'Saturday Evening Sociables' soph-
omore year, and to coming-out balls thereafter." These favored men
were, at the same time, living along Mount Auburn Street in privately
run and often expensive halls, and eating at the few final clubs which
only took in some 10 to 15 per cent of each class. Closely integrated
with the clubs and Boston Society were the private preparatory schools.
Until about 1870, according to Morison, Boston Latin School graduates
still had a privileged position at Harvard, but "during the period 1870–
90 the proportion of freshmen entering from public high schools fell
from 38 to 23 per cent." About 1890 the Episcopal Church schools and
a few others took over. "Since 1890 it has been almost necessary for a
Harvard student with social ambition to enter from the 'right' sort of
school and be popular there, to room on the 'Gold Coast' and be accepted by Boston society his freshman year, in order to be on the right
side of the social chasm . . . conversely, a lad of Mayflower or Porcel-

lian ancestry who entered from a high school was as much 'out of it' as a ghetto Jew."

During most of Harvard's history, according to Morison, a solid core of middle-class New Englanders had been able to absorb most of the students into a cohesive college life which was dominated by a basic curriculum taken by all students. The increasing size of the classes (100 in the 1860's to over 600 by the time Franklin Roosevelt graduated in 1904), the elective system which sent men off to specialize in all directions, and the increasing ethnic heterogeneity of the student body, paved the way for exclusiveness and stratification. By 1893, for example, there were enough Irish Catholics in the Yard to support the St. Paul's Catholic Club, which acquired Newman House in 1912. The situation was similar with the Jews. "The first German Jews who came were easily absorbed into the social pattern; but at the turn of the century the bright Russian and Polish lads from the Boston public schools began to arrive. There were enough of them in 1906 to form the Menorah Society, and in another fifteen years Harvard had her 'Jewish problem.' "

The "Jewish problem" at Harvard will be discussed below. Here it is enough to emphasize the fact that it grew out of the general development of caste in America in the turn of the century. And this new type of caste system was supported by all kinds of associations, from the suburban country club to the fraternities and clubs on the campuses of the nation. Not only were two worlds now firmly established at Harvard and Yale and to a lesser extent at Princeton; at other less influential state universities and small colleges, fraternities dominated campus life.

Although fraternities grew up on the American campus before the Civil War, they expanded tremendously in the postwar period. By the late 1880s, for instance, the five hundred undergraduates at the University of Wisconsin were stratified by a fraternity system which included no less than thirteen houses. As class consciousness increased, campus mores of course became more rigidly anti-Semitic and often anti-Catholic. Bernard Baruch, who entered the College of the City of New York in 1884 (as he was only fourteen at the time, his mother would not let him go away to Yale, which was his preference), felt the full weight of anti-Semitism. Although he was extremely popular among the small group of less than four hundred undergraduates, and although he was elected president of the class in his senior year, young Baruch was never taken into a fraternity at C.C.N.Y. "The Greek-letter societies or fraternities," he wrote years later in his autobiography, "played an important part at the college. Although many Jews made their mark at the college, the line was drawn against them by these societies. Each year my name would be proposed and a row would ensue over my nomination, but I never was elected. It may be worth noting, particularly for those who regard the South as less tolerant than the North, that my brother Herman was readily admitted to a fraternity while he attended the University of Virginia." In response to the "Anglo-Saxon-Only" mores which accompanied the fraternity boom in the eighties and nineties, the first Jewish fraternity in America was founded at Columbia, in 1898.

The campus mores were, of course, modeled after the adult world which the students in the Gilded Age were preparing to face. For the large corporations, banks and powerful law firms—in the big-city centers of national power—increasingly began to select their future leaders, not on the basis of ability alone, but largely on the basis of their fashionable university and club or fraternity affiliations. "The graduate of a small college or a Western university," writes Ernest Earnest, "might aspire to a judgeship or bank presidency in the smaller cities and towns; he might get to Congress, become a physician or college professor. Particularly west of the Alleghenies he might become a governor or senator. But he was unlikely to be taken into the inner social and financial circles of Boston, New York or Philadelphia." In the first half of the twentieth century, five of our eight Presidents were graduates of Harvard, Yale, Princeton and Amherst. A sixth came from Stanford, "the Western Harvard," where the social system most resembled that in the East.

THE METROPOLITAN MEN'S CLUB:
STRONGHOLD OF PATRICIAN POWER

When the gilded youths at Harvard, Yale and Princeton finally left the protected world of the "Gold Coast" to seek their fortunes in the Wall streets and executive suites of the nation, they usually joined one or another exclusive men's club. Here they dined with others of their kind, helped each other to secure jobs and promotions, and made friends with influential older members who might some day be of help to them in their paths to the top. Proper club affiliation was, after all, the final and most important stage in an exclusive socializing process. As a character in a novel about Harvard, published in 1901, put it: "Bertie knew who his classmates in college were going to be at the age of five. They're the same chaps he's been going to school with and to kid dancing classes . . . it's part of the routine. After they get out of college they'll all go abroad for a few months in groups of three or four, and when they get back they'll be taken into the same club (their names will have been on the waiting list some twenty-odd years) . . . and see one another every day for the rest of their lives." But, by the century's turn, the metropolitan club was gradually becoming more than a congenial gathering-place for similarly bred gentlemen.

British and American gentlemen, especially after the urban bourgeoisie replaced the provincial aristocracy, soon realized that the club was an ideal instrument for the gentlemanly control of social, political and economic power. For generations in England, top decisions in the City and at Whitehall have often been made along Pall Mall, where conservatives gathered at the Carlton and liberals at the Reform. But perhaps the best illustration of the role of the club in the making of gentlemen, and its use as an instrument of power, was a "gentlemanly agreement" which was made in the late nineteenth century at the frontiers of empire. And it is indeed symbolic and prophetic that it should have been made in racialist South Africa by the great Cecil Rhodes, that most rabid of racialists who dreamed of forming a Nordic secret society, organized like Loyola's, and devoted to world domination. The club served Rhodes well on his way to wealth.

The exploitation of Africa became a full-fledged imperialist enterprise only after Cecil Rhodes dispossessed the Jews. Rhodes' most important competitor in the fight for control of the Kimberley diamond mines was Barney Barnato, son of a Whitechapel shopkeeper, who was possessed by a passionate desire to make his pile and, above all, to become a gentleman. Both Rhodes and Barnato were eighteen years of age when they arrived in Kimberley in the early seventies. By 1885 Rhodes was worth fifty thousand pounds a year, but Barnato was richer. At that time Rhodes began his "subtle" and persistent dealings with Barnato in order to gain control of de Beers. Nearly every day he had him to lunch or dinner at the "unattainable," at least for Barnato, Kimberley Club (he even persuaded the club to alter its rules which limited the entertainment of nonmembers to once-a-month). At last, Barnato agreed to sell out to Rhodes for a fabulous fortune, membership in the Kimberley Club, and a secure place among the gentlemanly imperialists. Whiles Rhodes had perhaps used his club and his race with an ungentlemanly lack of subtlety, "no American trust, no trust in the world, had such power over any commodity as Rhodes now had over diamonds." But in the end, his dream that "between two and three thousand Nordic gentlemen in the prime of life and mathematically selected" should run the world became the very respectable Rhodes Scholarship Association, which supported selected members of all "Nordic Races," such as Germans, Scandinavians and Americans, during a brief stay in the civilizing atmosphere of Oxford University (the "Nordic" criterion for selection has since been abandoned). In the meantime, his friend Barney Barnato, soon after realizing his dream of becoming both a millionaire and a gentleman, drowned himself in the depths of the sea.

Many such dreams of corporate and financial empire-building have been consummated within the halls of America's more exclusive clubs. The greatest financial imperialist of them all, J. Pierpont Morgan, belonged to no less than nineteen clubs in this country and along Pall Mall. One of his dreams was realized on the night of December 12, 1900, in the course of a private dinner at the University Club in New York. Carnegie's man, Charles M. Schwab, was the guest of honor and the steel trust was planned that night.

In the 1900's the metropolitan club became far more important than the country club, the private school and college, or the exclusive neighborhood as the crucial variable in the recruitment of America's new corporate aristocracy. Family position and prestige, built up as a result of several generations of leadership and service in some provincial city or town, were gradually replaced by an aristocracy by ballot, in the hierarchy of metropolitan clubdom. In New York, for example, this process can be illustrated by the club affiliations of successive generations of Rockefellers: John D. Rockefeller belonged to the Union League; John D., Jr., to the University Club; and John D. III to the Knickerbocker. Thus is a business aristocracy recruited.

And this associational, rather than familistic, process was certainly democratic, except for one thing. That is the fact that, almost without exception, every club in America now developed a castelike policy toward the Jews. They were excluded, as a people or race, regardless of their personal qualities such as education, taste or manners. It is important, moreover, to stress the fact that this caste line was only drawn at the end of the nineteenth century, when, as we have seen, the members of the upper class were setting themselves apart in other ways. Joseph Seligman's experience at Saratoga Springs was part of a general trend which came to a head again when Jesse Seligman, one of the founders of New York's Union League, resigned from the club in 1893, when his son was blackballed because he was a Jew. Apparently this sort of anti-Semitism was not yet a norm when the club was founded during the Civil War.

Nor was it the norm among the more exclusive clubs in other cities. The Philadelphia Club, the oldest and one of the most patrician in America, was founded in 1834, but did not adhere to any anti-Semitic policy until late in the century. During the Civil War, for instance, Joseph Gratz, of an old German-Jewish family and a leader in his synagogue, was president of the club. The membership also included representatives of several other prominent families of Jewish origin. Yet no other member of the Gratz family has been taken into the Philadelphia Club since the nineties, a period when countless embarrassing incidents all over America paralleled the Seligman incident at the Union League. The University Club of Cincinnati finally broke up, in 1896, over the admission of a prominent member of the Jewish community. Elsewhere, prominent, cultivated and powerful Jews were asked to resign, or were forced to do so by their sense of pride, because of incidents involving their families or friends who were refused membership solely because of their Jewish origins. Gentlemanly anti-Semitism even invaded the aristocratic South. As late as the 1870's one of the more fashionable men's club in Richmond, the Westmoreland, had members as well as an elected president of Jewish origins. But today all the top clubs in the city follow a policy of rigid exclusiveness as far as Jews are concerned. This is the case even though the elite Jewish community in Richmond, as in Philadelphia, has always been a stable one with a solid core of old families whose members exhibit none of the aggressive, *parvenu* traits given as a reason for the anti-Semitic policies of clubs in New York, Chicago or Los Angeles.

Yet the inclusion of cultivated Jews within the halls of the Philadelphia or Westmoreland clubs in an earlier day was characteristic of a provincial and familistic age when the men's club was really social, and membership was based on congeniality rather than, as it has increasingly become, on an organized effort to retain social power within a castelike social stratum. George Apley, whose values were the product of a rapidly departing era, threatened to resign from his beloved Boston Club when he thought it was being used, somewhat in the style of Cecil Rhodes, as an agency for the consolidation of business power. At a time when his clubmates Moore and Field were apparently violating his gentlemanly code in seeking the admission of their business association Ransome, Apley wrote the admission committee as follows:

> I wish to make it clear that it is not because of Ransome personally that I move to oppose him.
> Rather, I move to oppose the motive which actuates Messrs. Moore and Field in putting this man up for membership. They are not doing so because of family connections, nor because of disinterested friendship, but rather because of business reasons. It is, perhaps, too well known for me to mention it that Mr. Ransome has been instrumental in bringing a very large amount of New York business to the banking house of Moore and Fields. This I do not think is reason enough to admit Mr. Ransome to the Province Club, a club which exists for social and not for business purposes.

Today many other clubs like Apley's Province, but unlike Pittsburgh's Duquesne, are fighting the intrusion of business affairs into a club life supposedly devoted to the purely social life among gentlemen. "A year or two ago," wrote Osborn Elliott in 1959, "members of San Francisco's sedate Pacific Union Club (known affectionately as the P.U.) received notices advising them that briefcases should not be opened, nor business papers displayed, within the confines the old club building atop Nob Hill." At about the same time, patrician New Yorkers were shocked at a *Fortune* article which reported that "at the Metropolitan or the Union League or the University . . . you might do a $10,000 deal, but you'd use the Knickerbocker or the Union or the Racquet for $100,000, and then for $1 million you'd have to move on to the Brook or the Links."

In this chapter I have shown how a series of newly created upper-class institutions produced an associationally insulated national upper class in metropolitan America. I have stressed their rise in a particular time in our history and attempted to show how they were part of a more general status, economic and urban revolution which, in turn, was reflected in the Populist and Progressive movements. All this is important as a background for understanding the present situation, primarily because it shows that upper-class nativism in general and anti-Semitism in particular were a product of a particular cultural epoch and, more important, had not always been characteristic of polite society to anywhere near the same extent. This being the case, it may well be true, on the other hand, that new social and cultural situations may teach new duties and produce new upper-class mores and values. As a measure of the success of these caste-creating associations, the following remarks made by the late H. G. Wells after a visit to this country soon after the turn of the century are interesting.

> In the lower levels of the American community there pours perpetually a vast torrent of strangers, speaking alien tongues, inspired by alien traditions, for the most part illiterate peasants and working-people. They come in at the bottom: that must be insisted upon. . . . The older American population is being floated up on the top of this influx, a sterile aristocracy above a racially different and astonishingly fecund proletariat. . . .
>
> Yet there are moments in which I could have imagined there were no immigrants at all. All the time, except for one distinctive evening, I seem to have been talking to English-speaking men, now and then, but less frequently, to an Americanized German. In the clubs there are no immigrants. There are not even Jews, as there are in London clubs. One goes about the wide streets of Boston, one meets all sorts of Boston people, one visits the State-House; it's all the authentic English-speaking America. Fifth Avenue, too, is America without a touch of foreign-born; and Washington. You go a hundred yards south of the pretty Boston Common, and behold! you are in a polyglot slum! You go a block or so east of Fifth Avenue and you are in a vaster, more Yiddish Whitechapel.

At this point, it should be emphasized that it was (and still is) primarily the patrician without power, the clubmen and resorters and the functionless genteel who, as Edith Wharton wrote, "fall back on sport and culture." It was these gentlemen with time on their hands who took the lead in creating the "anti-everything" world which Henry Adams called "Society." So often, for example, it was the men of inherited means, many of them bachelors like Madison Grant, who served on club admission committees, led the dancing assemblies and had their summers free to run the yacht, tennis and bathing clubs at Newport or Bar Harbor. And these leisurely patricians were, in turn, supported by the new men, and especially their socially ambitious wives, who had just made their fortunes and were seeking social security for their children. In all status revolutions, indeed, resentment festers with the greatest intensity among the new rich, the new poor, and the functionless genteel. And these gentlemen of resentment responded to the status revolution at the turn of the century by successfully creating, as H. G. Wells so clearly saw, two worlds: the patrician and Protestant rich, and the rest.

Suggestions for Further Reading

Few general works try to cover this period from the perspective of everyday life. One popular and entertaining work that attempts this view is J. C. Furnas, *The Americans: A Social History of the United States, 1587–1914** (New York, 1969), available in a two-volume paperback edition. Other works that present some coverage of everyday life during the Gilded Age are Ray Ginger, *Age of Excess: The United States from 1877–1914** (New York, 1965); Henry F. May, *Protestant Churches and Industrial America** (New York, 1949); and Thomas Cochran and William Miller, *The Age of Enterprise: A Social History of Industrial America** (New York, 1961). For a view of the closing decade, see Larzer Ziff, *The American 1890's: Life and Times of a Lost Generation** (New York, 1966). Tamara Hareven has edited a useful collection of essays in *Anonymous Americans: Explorations in Nineteenth Century Social History** (Englewood Cliffs, N.J., 1971). Fictional treatments of the period that are revealing are Mark Twain and Charles Warner, *The Gilded Age** (New York, 1874), and two works by William Dean Howells, *The Rise of Silas Lapham** (Boston, 1884) and *The Hazard of New Fortunes** (New York, 1889).

Carroll Smith-Rosenberg has an essay on the role of the medical profession in the adoption of anti-abortion laws in, *Disorderly Conduct: Visions of Gender in Victorian America* (New York, 1985). For a general study of birth control in this period, see Linda Gordon, *Woman's Body, Woman's Right: A Social History of Birth Control in America** (New York, 1976). For the history of and moral issues involved in the abortion controversy, see John T. Noonan, Jr. (ed.), *The Morality of Abortion: Legal and Historical Perspectives** (Cambridge, 1970) and Edward Batchelor, Jr. (ed.), *Abortion: The Moral Issues** (New York, 1982). An important prizewinning study is Rosalind Pollack Petchesky, *Abortion and Woman's Choice: The State, Sexuality, and Reproductive Freedom* (Boston, 1984).

The standard short revisionist history of Reconstruction is Kenneth M. Stampp, *The Era of Reconstruction, 1865–1877** (New York, 1965). For South Carolina specifically, see Joel Williamson, *After Slavery: The Negro in South Carolina During Reconstruction, 1861–*

*Available in paperback edition.

*1877** (Chapel Hill, 1974) and Orville Vernon Burton, *In My Father's House Are Many Mansions: Family and Community in Edgefield, South Carolina* (Chapel Hill, 1985). Leon Litwack presents a richly detailed description of the beginning of Reconstruction in *Been in the Storm So Long: The Aftermath of Slavery** (New York, 1979). In *Exodusters: Black Migration to Kansas after Reconstruction** (New York, 1977), Nell Irwin Painter tells of one attempt of the freedpeople to escape white domination. Norman Crockett describes some of the separatist settlements in *The Black Towns** (Lawrence, Kansas, 1979). The role of the federal government in land reform is explored in Claude F. Oubre, *Forty Acres and a Mule: The Freedmen's Bureau and Black Land Ownership* (Baton Rouge, 1978).

For general treatments of the ideas involved in westward movement, see Frederick Merk, *Manifest Destiny and Mission in American History: A Reinterpretation** (New York, 1963); Henry Nash Smith, *Virgin Land: The American West as Symbol and Myth** (Cambridge, 1950); and Richard A. Bartlett, *The New Country: A Social History of the American Frontier, 1776–1890** (New York, 1974). On the Indian problem, see Frederick E. Hoxie, *A Final Promise: The Campaign to Assimilate the Indians, 1880–1920* (Lincoln, Nebraska, 1984) and Francis P. Prucha, *American Indian Policy in Crisis: Christian Reformers and the Indian, 1865–1900* (Norman, Oklahoma, 1976).

For a study of the Philadelphia elite, see E. Digby Baltzell, *Philadelphia Gentleman: The Making of a National Upper Class** (Glencoe, Illinois, 1958). Glimpses of the life-style of the wealthy are found in Stewart Holbrook, *The Age of the Moguls* (Garden City, N.Y., 1953), and Stephen Birmingham, *The Right People: A Portrait of America's Social Establishment* (Boston, 1968). A contemporary critical analysis is Thorstein Veblen, *The Theory of the Leisure Class** (New York, 1899), and a more recent critique is C. Wright Mills, *The Power Elite** (New York, 1956). William G. Domhoff has probed the upper class of today in *The Higher Circles: The Governing Class in America** (New York, 1971) and *The Bohemian Grove and Other Retreats: A Study in Ruling Class Cohesiveness** (New York, 1975). Popular treatments of non-Anglo-Saxon wealth are found in Stephen Birmingham, *Our Crowd: The Great Jewish Families of New York** (New York, 1967), *The Grandees: America's Sephardic Elite** (New York, 1971), and *Real Lace: America's Irish Rich** (New York, 1973).

The Early
Twentieth Century

1900–1930

America goes to the movies

From Rum Shop to Rialto: Workers and Movies

Roy Rosenzweig

American workers began to reevaluate their lifestyles during the turn of the nineteenth century. They became more interested in shorter hours, higher wages, and improved working conditions, along with the desire to enhance the quality of their leisure time. One slogan read: "Eight hours for work, eight hours for rest, eight hours for what we will." In recent years, historians have begun carefully examining the first part of this saying regarding life in the workplace. But in order to fully understand the lives of the working people, we must understand how they are at their leisure. Roy Rosenzweig of George Mason University has begun this task in his study of the leisure time activities of Worcester's working class between the years 1870 and 1920.

The workers of Worchester often faced the same problems in dealing with factory owners and managers, but they rarely participated in united labor action. Because these people were deeply divided along ethnic and religious lines, they often found themselves at odds with each other. They allowed the owners of capital in the community to encourage disunity among the various groups thus preventing any successful union.

While industry was able to inhibit concerted worker action towards improved wages and working conditions, the workers remained relatively free to organize their leisure activities. Reform leaders sought to organize the workers' leisure activities along lines approved by the middle and upper classes, but workers resistance made this impossible.

Perhaps the most significant conflict between employers and employees concerned the role of the saloon. Both groups saw drinking establishments as fulfilling the same basic function: they were places where workers gathered entirely free from employer supervision. Almost exclusively male gatherings, the saloons provided the workers with opportunities to release the tensions accumulated throughout the long day's labor. On the other hand, the employers mistakenly saw saloons as sources of labor unrest and sub-version.

At the peak of its popularity, however, the saloon was replaced by mo-tion pictures as the primary source of working-class leisure. The process whereby the movie theater surpassed the saloon is described in the following selection. From its beginning as an almost exclusively working-class enter-tainment, the motion picture industry began to increase in popularity with all the classes in this period. This led to the breakdown of class distinctions that were made based on one's chosen leisure activity. The development of full-length feature films drew people from all walks of life into the new movie palaces being built in American cities. Rosenzweig concludes that the movies' visions of the good life helped reduce class tensions by reinforcing traditional American ideals of social mobility. By the beginning of the 1920s, prohibition further undermined the saloon as the leisure time activity of work-ers. Films had become the primary source of recreation for Americans of all classes, a position movies will maintain until television conquers the masses in the 1950s.

G. Stanley Hall

G. Stanley Hall was not alone in pointing out the close connec-tion between the decline of the saloon and the rise of the motion pic-tures. "Often when a moving picture house is set up," Vachel Lindsay wrote in 1915 in his study of *The Art of the Moving Picture*, "the saloon on the right hand or the left declares bankruptcy." Movies, according to Lindsay, had emerged as "the first enemy of King Alcohol with real power where that King has deepest hold." Saloonkeepers ruefully con-ceded Lindsay's point. Almost from the opening of the very first movie theaters in 1905, they had "protested excitedly against the nickelodeon as a menace to their trade," according to one national magazine. What saloonkeepers bemoaned, temperance leaders celebrated. "I believe the movies now occupy the attention of a great many persons who would otherwise be in a saloon," exulted a prominent Worcester no-license crusader and building contractor. While the Worcester saloon had al-ready begun a process of internal transformation, the development of a new form of working-class leisure—the movies—proved to be a much more potent force in the displacement of the saloon from the center of ethnic working-class life.

Of course, the nickelodeon's triumph over the saloon was never as complete as temperance and movie promoters liked to believe. Analyz-ing the results of a detailed 1910 study of the leisure-time pursuits of

FROM RUM SHOP TO RIALTO: WORKERS AND MOVIES   from *Eight Hours for What We Will*, by Roy Rosenzweig. Cambridge University Press, 1983. Reprinted by permission.

1,000 New York workingmen, a temperance reformer cautioned that the five-cent show "hasn't quite put the saloon out of business." But the balance had shifted: Of the men in the study, 60 percent patronized the movies, whereas only 30 percent frequented the saloon. And certainly by the dry decade of the 1920s the movies had triumphed as the most popular form of public working-class recreation. But by that time the movies were no longer merely the private preserve of the urban, immigrant working class. They had become a truly mass entertainment, attracting a weekly attendance of well over 50 million—equivalent to half the total U.S. population. This dramatic emergence of the movie theater as a center of interclass, nationally distributed mass entertainment and its impact on the late nineteenth century working-class world of the saloon and the holiday picnic forms the subject of this chapter.

THE MOVIES COME TO WORCESTER

As in most cities, moving pictures first appeared in Worcester in the late 1890s as a sporadic novelty. By 1904, however, they had found a regular spot on the program of two of the city's vaudeville theaters. The next year movies acquired their first full-time outlet when Nathan and Isaac Gordon converted a Main Street furniture store into a "penny arcade," which they filled with Edison peep-show machines. In the fall of 1906 the Gordon brothers joined with local theater managers P. F. Shea and Alf T. Wilton in opening the city's first full-fledged movie theater. With the Gordons' machines in the lobby, Shea and Wilton transformed the Palace Museum, a 1,000-seat showcase for low-priced vaudeville and Friday-night wrestling, into the Nickel Theatre, which premiered on September 24, 1906, with a program of motion pictures and illustrated songs. Other Worcester theaters continued to exhibit films as part of vaudeville programs or as special presentations, but only the Nickel offered the continuous shows and the "democratic" seating and pricing that characterized the nickelodeons, which were rapidly proliferating throughout the nation's cities.

The prices and programs proved a local success; the Nickel claimed 10,000 customers in its first week of business. Although it faced both criticism and censorship early in 1907 for showing *The Unwritten Law*, a film about the sensational Thaw-White murder case, the Nickel soon found itself surrounded by imitators. Within a few months in the spring of 1907, three other Worcester theaters, which had previously presented melodrama or vaudeville, switched to so-called pictorial vaudeville. Of course, the separation between these two entertainments was not always absolute—some theaters mixed live vaudeville and motion pictures. But the movies were now leading the way. "The unusual demand for moving pictures shows has caught the people of Worcester as it has those in every other city and town in the country," the *Worcester Gazette* reported.

Although the "nickel madness" that gripped the country equally infected Worcester, the precise pattern of growth differed from that of the largest cities. Entrepreneurs in metropolitan centers like New York and Chicago, spurred by licensing regulations, had established small storefront theaters usually seating fewer than 300 people. Only later did they open larger and more centrally located theaters. But in Worcester the movies came first to the full-sized downtown theaters and only spread to three smaller cinemas over the next two and a half years. Even more than the city's first movie houses, these smaller theaters had an ethnic or working-class management, an immigrant, working-class clientele, and the lowest prices in the city.

In 1909 John W. Raymond, a former machinist, opened the 350-seat Majestic Theatre in what had been a downtown variety store. Later Aduino Feretti and Carmine Zamarro, who ran an employment and steamship ticket agency, took it over. Also in 1909, a Jewish shoe operator, Max Graf, launched the 300-seat, five-cent Pastime Theatre. Subsequently, "Gaspard and Charlie," two French Canadians who performed between film reels, reportedly took charge. Finally, in early 1910, the larger Bijou opened its door on the site of what ten years earlier had been Michael McGaddy's saloon. For the first time in Worcester a theater had located itself well outside the city's central business district. Significantly, the Bijou chose Millbury Street, the heart of the city's multiethnic, working-class East Side. "At Last—A High Class Amusement Temple for the East Side" its advertisement proclaimed.

Thus, by 1910 Worcester had about 4,250 seats devoted exclusively to moving pictures. Furthermore, in the first ten years of the twentieth century the total number of seats in Worcester available for all forms of commercial entertainment—theater, burlesque, vaudeville, and movies—had almost tripled from 3,438 to 9,338. In the process, the number of Worcester residents for each theater seat dropped sharply from thirty-four to fewer than sixteen. The most important explanation for the rapid expansion in theatrical seats lies with the opening of the new, cheap movie houses and the development of a working-class movie audience.

WORKERS GO TO THE MOVIES

In 1912 Clark professor and social reformer Prentice Hoyt scrutinized Worcester's three cheap movie theaters, the Bijou, the Family (formerly the Nickel), and the Majestic. "All the world of a certain class meets together for an hour or two a day" at these theaters, Hoyt concluded. The poorest immigrants dominated at the Bijou, while "the slightly better class of workmen and their wives and children" filled the Family. The Majestic, located only a few steps from the Family, drew a similar crowd. Hoyt's analysis of Worcester's movie audiences confirmed the patterns found in other cities. In 1910, for example, a Russell Sage Foundation study found that in New York City blue-collar workers made up only 2 percent of the audiences at theaters showing live dramatic productions but almost three-quarters of moving picture audiences. Around the same time, a Columbia University sociology graduate student, writing his doctoral thesis on the leisure activities of New York workingmen, discovered that only reading newspapers or socializing with family or friends occurred more frequently or occupied more spare time than moviegoing for most workers. "Motion pictures," John Collier explained to a middle class suddenly noticing this new amusement, "are the favorite entertainment today of the wage earning classes of the world." And journalists and other commentators penned such phrases as "the academy of the workingman," the "drama of the multitude," "the workingman's college," and the "true theater of the people" to dramatize the new development.

While reformers, sociologists, and journalists rushed to report on this new working-class movie audience, few paused to ask where it had come from. In part, the crowds that flocked to the early nickelodeons had simply transferred their allegiances from the existing varieties of cheap commercial entertainment. As early as the 1870s, the Worcester Theatre, while primarily offering dramatic productions aimed at the city's "well-to-do," occasionally presented minstrel shows and plays appealing to Irish and German audiences. But the high tariff charged at the Worcester Theatre kept away many blue-collar workers. By 1883 Bristol's Dime Museum gave them Bohemian glass blowers, comedy sketches, ventriloquists, acrobats, and human-faced chickens at a much more affordable price. In the following decade those with only ten cents to spend could sit in the gallery of Lothrop's Opera House and watch melodramas and minstrel shows or visit the nearby Front Street Musee for burlesque or vaudeville. And such outlets for cheap amusement multiplied further in the first decade of the twentieth century.

The lower prices, the "democratic" seating, the novelty, and the excitement of the five-cent movie houses appealed strongly to the patrons of these cheap theaters. With the coming of the movies, actors in local melodramas—what a historian of Worcester theaters referred condescendingly to as "dramatic pablum of the masses for two generations"—reported "the loss of gallery patronage." Thousands of theatergoers voted with their nickels and dimes for the new entertainment sensation. Movies benefited not only from the patronage of those who had always attended the city's lower-priced theatrical amusements but even more from the general expansion of the leisure market in early twentieth century Worcester. The amusement parks discussed in the preceding chapter are one example of that boom. And the four "dime museums" featuring a combination of melodrama, farces, vaudeville, and wrestling, which opened on Front Street between 1900 and 1905, are another. Thus, even before the nickel madness of 1907 swept through Worcester, the number of theatrical seats in the city had more than doubled. In effect, a good portion of the new movie audience had found its way to older, live entertainments in the years immediately preceding the birth of the nickelodeon.

Why was commercial entertainment enjoying such prosperity around the turn of the century in both Worcester and the rest of the country? As previously noted, the rise in real incomes and the decline in work hours crucially fueled the expansion of the leisure market. Yet, significantly, movies, with their low admission price and their short programs, were also regularly accessible to workers who still had low wages and long hours. Thus, in 1912 when a Worcester labor lawyer worked out a relatively generous budget for a working-class family, he could only find room in it for a weekly expenditure of about twenty cents for amusements. In this context, the five-cent movie house had a decisive edge over not only the twenty-five-cent gallery seats at the Worcester Theatre but also the ten-cent melodrama in competing for the working-class entertainment dollar (or quarter). Similarly, nickelodeons, because their shows were continuous and short, proved compatible with long work hours. Although the U.S. Steel Corporation, a major employer in both Worcester and Pittsburgh, maintained the twelve-hour day for some workers until 1923, investigators for the 1908 Pittsburgh Survey still encountered long lines of overworked steel-mill hands at that city's nickelodeons.

Part of the success of the movies thus rested on their ability to attract the underpaid and overworked as well as those who were gaining a bit more disposable income and a few more free hours in the early twentieth century. By accommodating both kinds of schedules and pocketbooks, the movie theater managed to become—like the saloon, the church, and the fraternal lodge—a central working-class institution that involved workers on a sustained and regular basis.

Yet there was an even more obvious source for the growth in movie audiences: more people. America's cities were booming and Worcester was no exception. Its population grew by 72 percent between 1890 and 1910. Immigrants, of course, played a disproportionately large part in that population growth. In those twenty years, the city's foreign-born increased by 82 percent, adding almost 22,000 immigrants to Worcester's already substantially foreign population. These new immigrants—almost entirely non-English speaking and often from southern and eastern Europe—proved particularly important to the growth of

Worcester's movie theaters. "It doesn't matter whether a man is from Kamchatka or Stamboul, whether he can speak English or not. He can understand pictures and he doesn't need to have anyone explain that to him," commented a Worcester movie theater manager in accounting for the burgeoning of the movies. The silence of the movies beckoned immigrants unable to comprehend so many other facets of American life. "Its very voicelessness," one student of popular amusements wrote of the new medium in 1909, "makes it eloquent for Letts, Finns, Italians, Syrians, Greeks, and pigtailed Celestials. It has pulled down the Tower of Babel, abolished the hyphenated dictionary, and fulfilled the Esperantist's dearest dream."

For many Worcester immigrants—circumscribed by their language to the social institutions of their own ethnic communities—movies offered their first nonwork contact with the larger American society. "I never saw a movie in Italy," recalls Fred Fedeli, who arrived in Worcester in 1907 at age thirteen. "I was on the farm; when I came here I got interested in going to the movies." In his limited spare time from his sixty-hour per week factory job, Fedeli would spend part of the sixty cents he had left each week after paying room and board to attend the newly opened Nickel Theatre. In 1912, realizing the appeal of the new medium for his fellow immigrants, Fedeli, along with his older brother and a cousin, leased the Bijou Theatre on Millbury Street in the heart of Worcester's immigrant, working-class district. "The [Bijou] audiences," commented Professor Hoyt, "are of every nationality under the sun, every type which has its home in the region around Vernon Square." As a moviegoer and an immigrant himself, Fedeli understood this audience well. Explaining the popularity of silent films, he recalls: "My people, the Polish people and the Lithuanian and Jewish people . . . didn't talk any more English than I did."

Of course, some observers probably exaggerated the ease with which the most recent immigrants adapted to the new entertainment medium. A Worcester woman wrote that it was only through evening English-language classes that she had learned to "red a newspaper and to red de moving pekses." Reading moving captions was much less likely to be a problem for the children of immigrants, and this second generation took to the movies with even more enthusiasm than their parents. Virtually all observers of early movie theater audiences noted the presence of large numbers of children and young people. "The nickelodeon," wrote one in 1908, "is almost the creation of the child, and it has discovered a new and healthy cheap-amusement public." "Children are the best patrons of the nickelodeon," added a trade press correspondent that same year. So great was the hold of the movies on immigrant children, according to reformer Jane Adams, that a group of young girls, "accustomed to the life of a five-cent theater, reluctantly refused an invitation to go to the country for a day's outing because the return of a late train would compel them to miss one evening's performance. They found it impossible to tear themselves away not only from the excitements of the theater but from the gaiety of the crowd of young men and girls invariably gathered outside discussing the sensational posters." Children, a range of different studies agreed, composed about one-quarter to one-half of the new movie audience.

As Edward Chandler told the First Conference on Child Welfare in Worcester in 1909, the "simplest reason" why so many children and young people found their way to the movies was "the low price. A nickel or a dime is far easier to get than a quarter." But for the children of immigrants, movie houses may have had a particular attraction: freedom from the surveillance mandated by a constricted and conservative family life. One woman, a New York Italian garment worker brought up by strict parents, recalls that "the one place I was allowed to go by myself was the movies. My parents wouldn't let me go out anywhere else, even when I was 24." Another woman of the same background recalls meeting her future husband on the sly at the local movie house.

While some immigrant teen-agers relished the freedom provided by the movie house, much moviegoing was actually done in family groups. Reformer Frederic Howe noted with satisfaction that "men now take their wives and families for an evening at the movies where formerly they went alone to the nearby saloon." Mary Heaton Vorse visited a movie house on Bleecker Street in the heart of New York's Italian section and reported: "Every woman has a baby in her arms and at least two children clinging to her skirts." Whereas Worcester's Deputy Sheriff James Early complained that a mother "should be at home, attending her household duties," not patronizing "this popular form of amusement," the *Labor News* leapt to the defense of "these overworked women" who take advantage of the few hours' time during which "the older children are at school or at the playgrounds" to attend the movie theater, "very often carrying a babe in arms."

Worcester movie theater managers assiduously courted this female patronage. Press releases from the newly opened Nickel Theatre announced the management's intention "to cater especially to the patronage of women and children," and its advertisements labeled it "The Ladies and Children's Resort." After its first week of operation, it claimed that women and children made up 60 percent of the audience. The young workingwoman joined working-class mothers in this new female audience. In the early twentieth century, increasing numbers of women took jobs outside the home. In Worcester, which mirrored national trends, women's labor force participation rates went from 19.5 to 23.7 percent between 1890 and 1910. As Elizabeth Butler documented in the Pittsburgh Survey, these women—especially those living alone in cheap rooming houses—had few outlets for their hard-earned leisure time and money. Often "the only relief for nervous weariness and the desire for stimulation" was the picture show.

The working-class movie audience thus drew on a variety of sources. The movie house attracted former patrons of other cheap amusements as well as tapped what one contemporary reporter called "an entirely new stratum of people." It appeared at a moment when workers had more time and money for leisure, but its low price and convenient time schedule made it available to workers who still remained poorly paid and overworked. Finally, it had particular appeals for the non-English-speaking immigrant who was effectively shut out of other entertainment forms; the child with only a nickel to spend; the immigrant teenager seeking freedom from restrictive family life; and the wife and mother, who had traditionally shunned, or been barred from, many other working-class social centers. "As a business, and as a social phenomenon," writes historian Robert Sklar, "the motion pictures came to life in the United States when they made contact with working-class needs and desires." "The art of the photo-play," the National concluded in a similar contemporary comment, was "created for the masses and largely by them."

MOVIEGOING AS WORKING-CLASS CULTURE

Working-class audiences were decisive in the early success of the movies. But did the new medium actually reflect the values and traditions of its new patrons? Analyzing the relationship between audience and movies before 1920 is fraught with more than the usual difficulties of popular cultural analysis. Prewar films, unlike those popular in the 1920s, seem to have "dealt mostly with the working man and his world," according to one prominent film historian. Yet even this general characterization of movie content remains open to debate, given the paucity of films surviving from this period. Additionally, even if we could see all films produced in these years, how would we know which ones particularly appealed to working-class viewers or how they responded to the picture on the screen? D. W. Griffith's *The Fatal Hour*, which was shown at Worcester's Nickel Theatre in September 1908, may have offered a moralistic attack on the white slave trade, but working-class viewers may have simply seen it as an action-packed melodrama.

With these difficulties in mind, it may be more fruitful to focus on the moviegoing experience, rather than movie content. Whatever the degree of control of the middle and upper classes over movie content, the working class was likely to determine the nature of behavior and interaction within the movie theater. Although theater managers mediated the audience's self-determination, they were, like saloonkeepers, usually cut from the same cloth as their customers. They shared similar backgrounds, values, and perspectives, and even, as with Fred Fedeli, a similar language disadvantage. Together, the immigrant working-class movie manager and the immigrant working-class audience developed a style of moviegoing that accorded with, and drew upon, earlier modes of public working-class recreation.

Working-class movie theater conduct built on a long tradition of crowd behavior that could be found at a variety of earlier popular amusements from melodramas to saloons to July Fourth picnics to working-class parks. Indeed, such patterns of public sociability and boisterousness can also be discerned in eighteenth-century French and English middle- and upper-class theater audiences. But by the mid-nineteenth century, historian Richard Sennett notes, "restraint of emotion in the theater became a way for middle-class audiences to mark the line between themselves and the working class." The "silence" that descended over bourgeois public behavior in the nineteenth century did not also blanket working-class public life. Modes of conviviality, active sociability, and liveliness remained the norms for the working class. And workers brought these behavior styles with them when they entered the world of commercial amusement.

Working-class audiences at the melodramas, minstrel shows, and burlesque acts of the late nineteenth and early twentieth centuries gave repeated evidence of interactive, lively, and often rowdy public behavior. Even when the upper-class men and women of the theater boxes maintained a restrained decorum, the lower-class inhabitants of the gallery could be counted on for vocal and high-spirited spontaneity. "In all theaters," writes a historian of early nineteenth century melodrama, "the gallery was the place most suitable for rowdyism, the best point from which to bombard disliked actors, members of the orchestra who failed to play popular tunes, or even the helpless 'middling classes' ensconced in the pit." Similarly, despite a placard proclaiming "no guying, whistling, or cat-calls," the gallery of the early twentieth century urban burlesque house would rage with "whistling, stamping, and hand-clapping."

Naturally, in theaters that drew exclusively working-class patronage such lively behavior was not confined to the gallery. In the late 1890s drama critic John Corbin described the friendly and expressive audiences that filled the Teatro Italiano on New York's East Side: "They would speak to you on the slightest pretext, or none, and would relate all that was happening on stage . . . At the tragic climaxes they shouted with delight, and at the end of each act yelled at the top of their lungs." Making the reverse comparison, a letter writer to a Yiddish newspaper pointed out that "the English Theater" is "not like our Jewish theater. . . . I found it so quiet there . . . There are no cries of 'Sha!' 'Shut up!' or 'Order!' and no babies cried—as if it were no theater at all!"

Although ethnic theater companies made only occasional stops in a medium-sized industrial city like Worcester, audiences at its other low-priced commercial entertainments revealed these same patterns of theatrical behavior. At melodrama productions in the 1880s, most of the action took place "down stage," a local historian comments laconically. The "dime museums," which sprang up on Front Street in the early twentieth century, attracted particularly lively working-class crowds. At the always popular Amateur Night, singers met shouts of "If you can't sing get off the stage" and persistent howls and hisses from an audience filled with friends of their competitors. Only the presence of "several policemen in full uniform in the building put a quietus on what may have easily terminated in a miniature riot," the *Worcester Sunday Telegram* reported after one Amateur Night. Professional companies at Worcester's ten-cent music halls faced equally demanding and vocal audiences. Charles Baker, the man charged with writing, directing, performing in, and even selling tickets for productions at the Palace Museum, noted that stale jokes would never wash since "the dime audience knows more about a good joke than half of the two dollar theatre patrons." "If it isn't a go," the opening-night audience would quickly let him know, and a new production would have "to be written before the next afternoon for two o'clock."

The Nickel movie theater inherited not only the actual building of the Palace Museum but also the lively and demanding crowds that had filled it and such other centers of working-class sociability as the saloon, the fraternal lodge, and the cheap theater. Indeed, the particular structure of the moviegoing experience—especially prices, seating arrangements, time schedules, and internal conditions—reinforced and heightened preexisting behavior patterns. The lack of seating differentiation by price at the early movie house exemplified its egalitarian social style. Whereas the Worcester Theatre carefully stratified patrons according to their ability to pay, the Nickel Theatre placed all customers on an equal plane. Even many other cheap forms of commercial entertainment such as the melodrama or vaudeville had often resisted this radical "leveling."

This "democratic" pricing fostered what one critic called an "atmosphere of independence" and "a kind of proprietorship in the playhouse" and along with that an air of informality and relaxed socializing at early movie houses. The lack of a structured time schedule further encouraged these tendencies. Workers could casually stop at the movie theater on their way home from work or shopping and catch all or part of the twenty- to sixty-minute show. Since no single item on the program lasted very long, there was little pressure to arrive at a specific time. Workers, already burdened with exacting time demands on the job, undoubtedly appreciated this lack of structure. The slogan "Stay as Long as You Like," from an early Nickel Theatre advertisement, captured the casual spirit of the enterprise.

This informality sanctioned a wide variety of behaviors that were disdained at most higher-priced theaters. Commenting on the timelessness of movie shows, a reporter for the *Moving Picture World* noted that some patrons watched the same performances all day and into the night, eating their lunch in the theater along the way. In Worcester, the use of the movie house as a lunchroom brought complaints from the middle-class press: "One can go into any theatre in town prior to the noon hour and find at least one-half of the women patrons nibbling lunch biscuits, cakes, or sweet meals of some kind," one reporter grumbled. Even less acceptable to middle-class observers was drinking alcohol or exhibiting drunken behavior. Part of the job of the ticket taker at the Nickel Theatre was keeping out intoxicated patrons. Despite his efforts, "a choice collection of drunks" could be found in the back rows, perhaps sleeping off a binge. Still others undertook more animated, if still less acceptable, pursuits. "The very darkness" of the movie house, observed Jane Addams, "is an added attraction to many young people, for whom the place is filled with the glamour of love making." Newspapers labeled the last row of Worcester movie theaters "lovers' lane" and youths filled these seats well before those that provided better views.

Such unacceptable public behavior—eating, drinking, sleeping, necking—was actually incidental to the larger function of the movie house as a vehicle for informal socializing. The Bijou, for example, apparently served as a social center for Worcester's immigrant working-class East Side—"the gathering place of the women of the neighborhood with their babies and little children, a crude sort of tea-room gossiping place," according to Professor Hoyt. Similarly, in 1915, the theater correspondent of the *Worcester Sunday Telegram* complained of some Irish women at the Family Theatre who "substitute seats in the orchestra for seats at the tea table." In New York in 1909 a movie house visitor similarly observed "regulars" who "stroll up and down the aisles between reels and visit friends." "The five-cent theatre," Jane Addams reported from Chicago that same year, "is also fast becoming the general social center and club house in many crowded neighborhoods . . . The room which contains the . . . stage is small and cozy, and less formal than the regular theater, and there is much more gossip and social life as if the foyer and pit were mingled."

Overall, then, moviegoing was far from the passive experience that some critics accused it of being. The working-class audience interacted volubly not only with each other but also with the entertainment presented. The large number of children at the movie houses reinfored this boisterous atmosphere. "When the hero triumphs during a children's performance, shouting, whistling, and stomping combine in a demonstration which at times is most remarkable," noted the *Worcester Telegram*. Various nonmovie features also encouraged audience participation. The illustrated song used as a "filler" between movie reels promoted group singing with its injunction: "All Join In The Chorus." Amateur Night, of course, stimulated audience participation, with friends

and neighbors shouting for their favorites and the crowd usually selecting the winner. Other forms of working-class recreation from bike
racing to wrestling complemented movie shows and stimulated audience cheering.

Not only did movie theater conduct grow out of traditions of working-class public recreational behavior based on sociability, conviviality,
communality, and informality, but movie theater conditions also accorded with the realities of working-class life. The movie house might
offer some relief from crowded urban tenements or three-deckers, but
it did not offer a radically different environment. Unlike the ornate
movie palaces of later years, recalls an old-time Worcester manager,
the early and cheaper movie theaters were just "four walls." Another
early manager remembers the closely packed wooden seats. But a former patron paints an even less flattering picture. He recollects the old
Gem Theatre as nothing more than a "shack" and remembers rats from
the city's sewers scurring under his seat while he was watching movies
at the Bijou.

Spartan, and even unsanitary, conditions made little impression on
working-class moviegoers; such surroundings were part of their daily
lives. But middle-class commentators reacted with horror. "A room that
is stuffy and congested is not a proper place for a growing child to be,
and it doesn't look at first glance as if it were the place for the mother
either," Worcester Deputy Sheriff James Early asserted. Only the word
"filth" could adequately describe these theaters according to Professor
Hoyt: "The floors are dirty and the air is stagnant and charged with
the vileness and disease that is poured into it."

But part of the shocked reaction of middle-class observers was not
to the actual physical conditions of theaters themselves but simply to
the presence of large numbers of working-class people, who acted,
looked, and smelled differently from themselves. The *Worcester Sunday
Telegram* drama correspondent, for example, was obsessed by the odors
of theaters: "Unclean persons should be influenced to respect the rights
of others. The best ventilating system made will not rid playhouses of
odors which have become component parts of individuals." Despite
this pessimism, he offered such remedies as distributing soap to patrons or burning incense. On one occasion he recommended that patrons who "eat garlic and spread their breath promiscuously should be
given seats on the roof or in the alley." In the early twentieth century
odors had important class and cultural implications. Indeed, Rollin Lynde
Hartt, the author of a 1909 study of *The People at Play*, whimsically
suggested that "some modern saga might devote study to the graded
aromas of our entertainments." Whereas Hartt characterized the opera
as "the breath of roses," he labeled burlesque "an unwashen odor,
mitigated with vile tabacco" and the dime museum "the same and more
of it, though unfortunately without the tobacco." "With the nose we

knows," Hartt concluded. And so observers like the *Telegram*'s drama correspondent could not only see and hear working-class movie audiences, they could also smell them.

CONFLICT OVER THE WORKING-CLASS MOVIE THEATER

As the "odor issue" indicates, the development of a new entertainment medium with distinctive working-class presence and style occasioned a variety of social and cultural conflicts. On the one hand, the forces of middle-class reform, morality, and order perceived the movie house as a barrier to their efforts not only to control and redirect working-class leisure but also to shape changing middle-class leisure patterns. On the other hand, the movie theater also challenged the prevailing working-class culture and its twin institutional pillars, the saloon and the church. Accordingly, over the next twenty years advocates of the status quo within both the middle and working classes struggled to control, restrict, regulate, and redirect the new medium. In effect, both the middle and working-classes split over their willingness to accept the emerging mass culture. Nevertheless, the efforts of both groups had only limited impact. More influential in transforming the moving house were those actually assembled there: the theater owner, the working-class audience, and the new, developing middle-class audience.

In January 1910 the *Worcester Telegram* began a series of sensationalized front-page stories about the city's juvenile gangs, which stressed that many of the gangs' allegedly immoral activities centered around the city's movie theaters. According to the *Telegram*, female gang members with their "short, close fitting dresses" and "paint on their faces" could usually be found at "the opening matinees" of the downtown theatres, and male gang members also "hung about the cheap moving picture places on Front Street." The police responded swiftly to this ostensible problem of immorality and movies. Noting that girls involved in the alleged "orgies" had "confessed that their early tendencies toward evil came from seeing moving pictures . . . and from certain houses where conditions were permitted that made temptations easy," Police Chief David Matthews appointed Police Lieutenant George Hill, who had been serving as head of the police liquor squad (a job made less necessary by the impending end of no-license), as movie censor.

Just as he had fought to control working-class drinking habits, Police Censor Hill zealously battled to bring Worcester movies in line with his own narrow conceptions of propriety. Within his first two weeks as police censor in 1910, he scissored out the duel and hell scenes from *Faust*, the murder of Julius Ceasar from the Shakespeare play, and a scene from a labor film in which strikers murder a scab. The police went beyond the picture on the screen to regulate conduct within the theater. In late January, for example, Chief Matthews banned standing in theaters. And in March, Censor Hill stopped the Nickel Theatre's popular and lively Amateur Night because it "attracted lots of young girls and boys, . . . [and] it was thought best to . . . keep the girls and boys at home."

Such censorial zeal did not meet with uniform approval. The Worcester *Labor News* commented that "Hill might make an excellent rum sleuth, but that as a censor of picture films, he is an out-and-out failure," and suggested "that someone with more brains might have been selected for the position." But oppostion was not confined to the labor press. The *Worcester Evening Gazette* ran a satirical poem, which commented that "the picture shows don't have a thrill/since censored by Lieutenant Hill./There'll be no kissing scenes, you bet/no Romeo and Juliet!/ . . . No bar-room scenes—ten nights or one—/are all cut out—are simply done." The poem concluded with the suggestion that his excesses might drive movie patrons back to the saloons, which were soon to reopen with the end of no-license.

While some voices of native-American middle-class public opinion, like the *Gazette*, opposed zealous censorship, some representatives of ethnic constituencies, like the *Catholic Messenger*, gave it wholehearted support. As early as 1907 it had denounced moving pictures as "The 'Devil's Lieutenants." When the city closed *The Unwritten Law*, the paper congratulated the police, urging them to carry on an "axe raid" on the moving picture shows, particularly the Gordon Brothers' penny arcade machines. Can the mayor and City Council, they asked, "permit on Main and Front Streets a public nuisance which is being driven from the Tenderloin and the Bowery of New York?" Again, in the 1910 controversy the *Catholic Messenger* called for even more drastic action than the city had taken: "Since these shows are the breeding places of a moral plague far worse than any physical ills, why hesitate to close them?"

The *Catholic Messenger* of these years spoke more for the emerging middle-class and second-generation Irish American than it did for the laborer or the recent immigrant. Nevertheless, even such a well-known champion of the Worcester worker as the now aging James H. Mellen apparently shared the *Messenger*'s distrust of the new medium. In 1910 he urged a state investigation into the moving picture business, maintaining that "the corruption these places breed is great." "Motion pictures rightly conducted," Mellen declared, "could be made a great educational and instructive institution but the business has degraded [fallen] into the hands of men without any moral conception and the main idea is to make money at the sacrifice of the community." Mellen's moralistic strictures about popular entertainment were not simply a product of his old age. Twenty-five years earlier, as editor of the

Worcester Daily Times, he had bitterly denounced the Worcester Theatre for posting "show bills about the city . . . bedaubed with disgusting pictures of shameless women . . . exhibiting their limbs in a series of indecent gyrations."

The Swedish evangelical churches with their large immigrant working-class congregations shared Mellen's long-standing and morally based suspicion of uncontrolled commercial amusements. But they were even more absolute in their condemnation of the latest entertainment sensation. Swedish ministers considered attendance at movies, like card playing and dancing, a serious sin. So strong were the denunciations that one Swedish woman recalls that "some youngsters developed a morbid fear just walking by a movie theater." The daughter of a Swedish foundry worker who grew up in Quinsigamond Village at the beginning of the century similarly recounts how her father gave her five cents every Saturday to prove that he was not cheap but forbade her to use the money to go to the movies.

As with temperance, the motives of working-class critics of moviegoing often differed from those of their middle-class counterparts. For workers, the threat was from within rather than from without; it was an issue of maintaining ethnic and religious traditions, not controlling a disorderly mob. One Slovak commentator explained that with "a public school education" children are "lost completely to the Slovaks. Their idea of life is a breezy and snappy novel, a blood curdling *movie* and lots of money." The movies, like the amusement park, challenged traditional cultural authorities both inside and outside the ethnic working-class community.

Despite this lingering distrust, controversy over the content of movies shown in Worcester soon faded. Compulsory local censorship boards, such as that set up in Chicago in 1907, as well as the voluntary National Board of Review established in New York in 1909, began to bring movies under outside surveillance, if not total control. At the same time, the red pencil of the accountant often had more impact on film content than the blue pencil of the censor. "It is an expensive business, the making of films only to have them thrown away," noted one 1910 commentator. Indeed, as early as the 1907 controversy over *The Unwritten Law,* the nascent trade press urged the withdrawal of the film *"for the sake of the future prosperity of the five cent theaters,* all of whom are now menaced by public opinion." For businessmen interested in building a national market, self-censorship appeared to be the most prudent—and profitable—course.

Such commercial considerations also operated powerfully on the local level. "Those interested in the moving picture business realize that it is to their advantage to have picture of the highest type," the manager of the Majestic Theatre commented in 1910. Not only did managers begin to cooperate with Police Censor Hill, but they also carefully watched other sources of public disapproval. Bijou proprietor Fred Fedeli, for example, recalls that "we were amongst six [Catholic] churches in them days, and if you played a movie, that wasn't fit to be seen, they could crucify you by saying 'don't go and see it.' " So when Fedeli feared possible clerical criticism, he immediately canceled the offending film and repeated an old one. He recounts that "you would put a slide on the screen: 'By Popular Demand This Picture Brought Back.' And we were the one that was demanding it, because we were afraid; after all, you had to be careful."

Thus, by 1912 movie content rarely caused trouble in Worcester. Professor Hoyt noted that while a 1909 report on Worcester movies had revealed "a coarseness and . . . a suggestiveness of crime and sin that was frankly appalling . . . now, thanks to the most careful censorship of films we get little note of criticism." But the elimination of what he called "the story of clever vice and of trickery triumphant" did not eliminate conflict over moviegoing. "As we turn to the consideration of the conditions existing in the theatres themselves," Hoyt warned, "there is another story to tell." The reform-oriented Worcester Public Education Association agreed: "The chief weakness of the moving picture lies in the conditions of presentation rather than in the picture itself. The halls and buildings are very dirty and poorly ventilated, and the audiences [are] under no *supervision* or *surveillance* as to age or character." Other middle-class commentators also complained about poor ventilation, odor, dirt, eyestrain, and darkness at movie houses. As the now-censored films became palatable to middle-class critics, they increasingly focused their disapproval on the conditions of the theaters and the behavior of their patrons. Just as anti-saloon agitators concentrated their attacks on the saloon, not alcohol, movie reformers increasingly concerned themselves with the cheap movie theaters, not the movies. It was autonomous working-class institutions and behavior that troubled the middle class.

THE MIDDLE CLASS GOES TO THE MOVIES

Middle-class complaints about theatrical conditions and behavior reflect, in part, fears about a hidden and unknown working-class culture and a desire to control that culture and limit its autonomy. But behind all the talk about filth and body odor lay the entrance, in large numbers and for the first time, of middle-class people into movie houses and their forced encounters with a resident working-class audience, which smelled and acted in ways that jarred middle-class standards of decorum. It was the emergence of this new middle-class audience—and the theater managers' fervent efforts to cultivate it—that led to an alteration of some of the basic characteristics of the early moviegoing experience.

As late as 1914 the Worcester working class still seems to have dominated the city's movie houses. The controversy that burst forth early in that year over Sunday moving pictures confirm this alignment. Whereas the city's Protestant establishment—virtually all the Protestant ministers, the Women's Christian Temperance Union, as well as most city officials—vehemently denounced this desecration of the sabbath, "those favoring Sunday shows," according to the *Worcester Telegram*, "were composed mostly of the working class of people and persons directly or indirectly connected with the Worcester playhouses and moving picture places." To those who fought over Sunday movies, the reason for this division was obvious: "The movies always was and always will be the poor man's amusement," declared one Worcester theater manager.

Yet this very controversy also suggested that the association of the working class with the movie house was neither timeless nor total. Some of the more moderate ministers insisted that they opposed a commercialized Sunday, not moviegoing per se. "We believe in moving pictures . . . it is not moving pictures that we oppose," the Reverend Francis Poole told his Union Church congregants. Furthermore, the city's manufacturers—aligned with the Protestant clergy on the issues like drinking—do not seem to have joined in the attack on Sunday movies. Donald Tulloch, secretary of the Worcester Metal Trades Association, endorsed the idea of "well-regulated, suitable movies Sunday afternoon, leaving the forenoon and evenings entirely to the Church services and home life."

These new, more approving attitudes toward movies by middle-class Worcesterites reflected not only the success of earlier censorship efforts but also the growing appeal of movies for middle-class audiences, a trend increasingly evident in pre–World War I Worcester. In December 1913 the *Worcester Sunday Telegram*'s drama correspondent noted that Worcester theaters had suffered a bad season, and he blamed the competition of moving pictures. He pointed out that the movie version of *Quo Vadis* had attracted more Worcesterites in three days than had its live version in an entire week. "Whether the play be popular priced or of a higher scale," he concluded, "the moving pictures are drawing bigger." Vaudeville suffered less directly from the competition of movies, since many movie houses offered vaudeville acts in addition to their film programs, and most vaudeville bills included some moving pictures. Still, the balance seemed to be shifting in favor of movies. In February 1914 Sylvester Poli, Worcester's leading vaudeville promoter, recognizing "the prominent part that moving pictures have come to play in the amusement world," added feature films to the program at his flagship theater. By the following year, the *Worcester*

Sunday Telegram, distressed by the dismal quality of vaudeville shows, wondered whether "the silent drama" had given vaudeville "the count."

By the end of World War I movies had not only captured many theater and vaudeville patrons but also expanded the market for commercial entertainment in general. Between 1910 and 1918 the number of theatrical seats in Worcester nearly doubled, going from about 9,300 to about 17,600. The rate of increase greatly exceeded even Worcester's rapidly growing population; the number of people for each theatrical seat declined sharply from sixteen to ten. Even more significantly, the percentage of seats devoted primarily to moving pictures almost doubled. In 1910 moving picture houses contained only 44 percent of Worcester's theatrical seats, whereas eight years later they included 82 percent. Since moving picture houses usually had continuous or multiple performances and legitimate theater, stock, and vaudeville offered only two shows per day, these figures actually understate the ascendance of moving pictures. By 1919, according to conservative estimates, more than 128,000 Worcesterites attended the movies each week.

The burgeoning of the Worcester movie audience indicates the expansion of moviegoing into the city's middle class and the creation of the first medium of regular interclass entertaiment, a development that local observers increasingly noticed around World War I. In 1917, for example, the *Worcester Telegram* observed that the new Strand movie theater was "catering to the best class of theatrical patronage in Worcester." Pointing to the "long line of touring cars and limousines" parked in front of the theater every night, it concluded that "society folks have acquired the movie habit."

How had middle- and upper-class Worcesterites found their way into the previously disdained movie theater? In part, the theater managers and movie producers brought them there. The search for larger markets, which had motivated the movie industry to accept censorship from without and promote self-censorship within, also encouraged the quest for a middle-class audience. In pursuit of these new customers, exhibitors modernized their theaters, and producers experimented with different kinds of films. The cries of reformers to improve movie theater conditions and conduct had gone largely unheeded, but the quest for a larger and more respectable audience accomplished the same purpose: the transformation of the shabby nickelodeon into the opulent movie palace.

After 1913 Worcester movie theaters became increasingly lavish. At first the changes were rather modest. The Pleasant Theatre, reopened in November 1913 after a fire, simply advertised itself as "safe" and "clean." But a further remodeling three years later involved more extensive alterations, such as "new carpets of the finest Wilton velvet," a "colorful electric fountain," and a large rooftop electric sign. The *Worcester Telegram* theater correspondent enthusiastically celebrated this "real high-class house of feature photoplays" with its "elegance," "refinement," and "dignity." The building of the Strand Theatre in 1917 culminated the trend toward lavish theaters—until the still more impressive structures of the 1920s. Lauded as a "modern photoplay house," it included "red plush seats," no obstructed views, frosted ceiling globes, a "rich chandelier," drinking fountains, a gold fiber screen, "luxurious carpets," loges for private parties, "rich velour curtains," marble pillars, an advanced ventilating system, a $15,000 Austin organ, and, most important, "finely appointed toilet rooms."

The more elaborate accouterments of the newer Worcester theaters were often complemented by more professional theatrical management, which brought greater internal order to the theaters. Early Worcester movie managers were often local men from immigrant backgrounds who went directly from working-class jobs or small businesses to movie management. Increasingly after 1915, however, Worcester movie theaters came under the control of the theatrical chains and the direction of professional theater managers, men with long experience in theaters in different cities, who had worked their way up to the position of manager.

These more professional managers—often college graduates—hired large and well-disciplined staffs to impose order on their theaters. By way of contrast, the East Side Bijou had a staff of only four, mostly relatives. Discipline within the theater was far from tight. Fred Fedeli, who served as usher in the theater's early days, complained that "you would call people in the aisle where there were the seats and they would go the other way." But the newer and more elegant movie houses employed large corps of ushers, who strictly enforced standards of decorum. At the Plaza Theatre ushers donned summer uniforms of "military coats, white trousers and white oxfords." The military attire was perhaps deliberate, an effort to assure middle-class patrons that this was a well-run and well-ordered establishment. Indeed, by 1928 theaters like Worcester's new Plymouth were hiring army officers to drill their ushers in "bearing and discipline as well as in courteous handling of the public." The thrust of all these efforts to improve theater conditions and control theater behavior was, as historian Lary May has observed, to remove any "unease" the middle class might have over entering the previously "disreputable movie house."

While the movie exhibitor pursued middle-class patrons with carpeting and well-disciplined ushers, the movie producer enticed them with feature films, which approximated the form and length of theatrical production. By 1914 feature films had met with such success that the Paramount Pictures Corporation, the first national distributor of feature films, could guarantee exhibitors two features each week. Worcester's Pleasant Theatre, for example, immediately signed up with Paramount, believing that the combination of longer films and well-known stars would win "a patronage that will be quality and quantity combined." The exhibition of *The Birth of a Nation* sealed the marriage of middle-class audiences and movies. "It is the greatest thing I have ever seen in the way of a moving picture," Worcester's Mayor Wright declared.

Wright's enthusiasm for *The Birth of a Nation* represented a radical departure from the disapproving stance he took in the 1910 controversies. In this shift he followed the path trod by many other middle-class Worcesterites in these years. Initially perceiving movies and movie houses as a threat to the social fabric, by 1916 he joined in the home-town frenzy over the local filming of *A Romance in Worcester*. Wright even agreed to play the role of the father of the heroine, but when the Republican National Convention took him out of town, the president of the Board of Aldermen replaced him.

Mayor Wright's newfound passion for the movies reminds us of the relatively recent recognition by the middle class of its own need for non-instrumental recreation, for "fun." In going to the movies, as in playing more active sports, the middle class at least partially adapted some of the leisure patterns that characterized working-class life. As Lary May has argued, the movie theater, with its mixing of sexes and classes, its lack of formality, and its intimacy, represented a radically new experience for the native middle class. Thus, in many ways the development of moviegoing habits was a sharper break in middle-class culture than it had been in working-class culture. Moreover, it was a shift toward working-class norms.

But the process was hardly one way. The entrance of the middle class into the movie houses had altered moviegoing conduct and conditions. The new and more lavish movie theaters represented a more distinct change from the everyday conditions of working-class life than had the old storefront, five-cent theaters. More important, the new environment prescribed a more formal and structured moviegoing experience. Ushers instructed by handbooks of theater management carefully controlled conduct within the new theaters and politely guided customers to a specific seat. The longer programs made necessary by the feature films meant specific show times and even sometimes reserved seats. In effect, the new moviegoing experience was both more public and informal than that normally expected by the native middle class but also more privatistic and formal than that traditionally followed by the immigrant working class.

Still, the experience of class mixing remained limited. Many working-class people continued to view movies within their own neighborhood theaters, which more closely reflected the behavior patterns, conditions, and ownership of the early movie days. Generally, these theaters charged lower prices, showed "second-run" films, and attracted local, ethnic, and working-class crowds. Despite their downtown locations, the Family and Majestic drew what the *Worcester Telegram* called "more of a neighborhood patronage." The Family and Columbus theaters drew heavily on the Shrewsbury Street Italian community; the Gem on Quinsigamond Village Swedes; the Court on Belmont Hill Swede-Finns; and the Bijou and Vernon on the multiethnic working-class neighborhood surrounding Vernon Square. In 1917 half the city's fourteen movie theaters could be classified as "neighborhood" rather than "first-class."

Despite the strength and persistence of these neighborhood theaters, the balance was gradually shifting. Although there were equal numbers of neighborhood and first-class theaters in 1917, the larger downtown theaters held almost three-quarters of the movie seats. Moreover, whereas the ethnic working class increasingly patronized the first-class theaters, the middle-class West Siders shunned the neighborhood houses. Fred Fedeli recalls that his customers might visit the first-class theaters but that the "people uptown [i.e., middle-class West Siders] wouldn't come to us." Similarly, when the *Labor News* wrote about his cousin and partner, Jim Greeko, they felt obliged to note that "uptown folks mayhap are not acquainted with him." At the same time, however, the neighborhood theaters were becoming less Spartan. In 1918 Greeko and the Fedeli brothers opened the much larger and better appointed Rialto Theatre across the street from the Bijou. Comparing the 600 wooden seats of the Bijou with the 1,250 red-plush, spring-cushioned seats of the air-conditioned Rialto Theatre, Fedeli notes "that was a big change." The combination of the Rialto and the more lavish downtown houses forced out many of the smaller neighborhood theaters; the Bijou, Gem, Columbus, and Vernon theaters all disappeared in the next two years. "The Rialto licked them all," Fedeli recalls.

The emergence of a middle-class movie audience and the development of more lavish and formal movie houses did not, however, drive away working-class customers. Indeed, in the years during which theater owners built a middle-class clientele, the movies increasingly penetrated those working-class groups initially resistant to the lure of the nickelodeon. For example, churchgoing Irish Catholics, whose initial suspicion of the new medium was presented so vehemently by the *Catholic Messenger*, seem to have gradually warmed to it. Annual discussions in the press of whether Lent would adversely affect the movie trade were one indication of the centrality of churchgoing Catholics to the local movie audience. The competition of movies even curtailed the activities of church-affiliated groups like the Catholic total abstinence societies. This development found symbolic expression in 1914 when the Crescent movie theater temporarily took over the auditorium of the Father Mathew society.

Movies also attracted workers attached to that other pillar of traditional working-class culture: the saloon. "It is generally conceded by all," the *Worcester Sunday Telegram* reported in 1915, "that, since the increase in the number of moving picture houses, there has been somewhat of a correspondent reduction in the amounts expended for . . . booze." "Where a man was in the habit of passing much of his time in a saloon," explained the manager of the Family Theatre, "now he passes a portion, if not all of it, in the moving picture houses. They stay as long as they want to. The price is five cents. That is the cost of one beer." Particularly with Worcester's saloons under the stricter regulations imposed after 1910, the movie theater proved an increasingly enticing alternative. "Between the movies and the rigid rules of the city government our profits are cut out considerably," complained one liquor man. The situation was hardly this dismal, but one local merchant estimated that the movies had captured as much as 25 percent of the saloon trade.

Within the working class the Worcester Swedes, particularly the members of the evangelical churches, were perhaps the group least affected by the movies. But even here some signs of change could be discerned. In 1915, movie theaters opened for the first time in Worcester's two major Swedish neighborhoods. That same year the editors of *Skandinavia* noted that many Swedes still considered movies "sinful" and corrupting. But after a Saturday-night visit to the new Royal Theatre, they advised their readers that "we believe that the movies will serve our young people well."

By the 1920s, then, the movies had penetrated virtually all segments of American society and touched the lives of people who had little else in common. In 1921, for example, Socialist leader Eugene V. Debs, who languished in jail for his opposition to World War I, received a letter from a friend in which she noted that Debs and President Warren Harding shared an affection for cowboy movie star Tom Mix: "I feel sure the President will appreciate your desire to see Tom. Someday, dear Gene, we shall see Tom do his stunts and you can laugh all you want."

If Gene Debs and Warren Harding could agree on the movies, so could most Worcesterites. Thus, in 1922 Worcester voters rejected a state referendum on censorship of motion pictures by a vote of better than 3 to 1. The movie theater had become enshrined as a major mainstream cultural institution. An advertisement for Poli's Theatre summarized the new position: "As important to a city as its churches and schools is the theatre to which is entrusted the play hour of its citizens and children." Indeed, by the late 1920s new movie houses seem to have been given greater importance than new schools or churches. "As New York notes an opera opening, so does Worcester note the opening of a new movie house," the *Worcester Sunday Telegram* reported on November 25, 1928, after the premiere of the ornate, Egyptian-style Plymouth Theatre. "Its 3000 seats," the *Telegram* continued, "were filled with a moving, pulsing, vivid, throng; bankers in evening dress and newspaper men in clean collars. The city government, including the Democrats, was there." The Worcester movie house had clearly arrived.

CONTINUITY AND CHANGE IN WORKING-CLASS CULTURE

Cultures do not change overnight or even over fifty years. But over long periods of time, we can watch them slowly, and often incompletely, transforming themselves, taking on new shape and substance. The birth and triumph of the movies heralds this slow, gradual, and incomplete process of change for ethnic working-class culture. It would be foolish to see the movies as the triggering device for this glacial process of change. Deeper social and economic forces—the coming of age of second- and third-generation immigrants, the emergence of an ethnic middle class, the development of mass-production and mass-marketing techniques—are at the root of the transformation of working-class culture. Although movies themselves did not change working-class culture, the movie theater of the 1920s can serve as an important indicator of the nature and extent of changes in that world.

Like the popularity of the White City Amusement Park or the development of more businesslike saloonkeepers, the emergence and triumph of motion pictures did not signal the total obliteration of older or "residual" forms of working-class culture. Many people, for example, disdained or simply ignored the new medium. Even into the 1950s, members of Worcester's Swedish evangelical churches—particularly the Mission Covenant Church—viewed moviegoing as sinful. Age or generation could be an even more important, if less absolute, bar to movie attendance. Phyllis Williams reported in her study of New Haven Italians in the 1930s that whereas the younger generation attended the movies frequently, the older generation did not approve of this "waste of money" and was "reluctant to have any part in it." A social survey of Worcester's small black community in the 1920s found similarly that "many are positively opposed to moving pictures, but in some families the young people go as often as once or twice a week."

Even where the practice of moviegoing was wholeheartedly embraced, it often occurred within the context of an older ethnic culture. The neighborhood theater continued to foster an active and lively style of public sociability, and it often retained clear ethnic ties. When "talkies" came in, some neighborhood theaters offered foreign-language films. The Columbus Theatre on Shrewsbury Street in the heart of Worcester's Italian neighborhood was owned by Italians, who seem to have encouraged local Italian groups to meet in their theater. The Fedelis' Rialto Theatre on Millbury Street took special pains to cater to its multiethnic clientele. In 1931, when financial straits forced the theater to discontinue advertising in the daily newspapers, it continued to run ads in the local Lithuanian weekly. It even recognized religious holidays, offering *Passion Play from the Life of Jesus* for Easter-time viewers.

The persistence of ethnic patterns points to the simple fact that moviegoing did not destroy all other forms of working-class leisure; it was simply an additional—albeit particularly important—recreational option. Working people continued to go to their saloon, church, or ethnic club. Only now such activities might be punctuated by, or mixed with, visits to the movie theater. "When a man emerges from a saloon in an intoxicated condition," the *Worcester Telegram* complained in 1917, "he usually decides on one or two objective points, the retracing of his footsteps back to the saloon or going to a theatre." Fraternal and ethnic organizations often entered into a different sort of symbiotic relationship with the movie theater. Since Sunday movie shows were only permitted if classified as "benefits," such performances often assisted groups like the Lithuanian Women's Alliance, the Jewish School, the Polish Naturalization Club, and the Italian Soldiers Suffering from Tuberculosis Caused by the War.

If moviegoing coexisted with many elements of the older ethnic working-class culture, what about the actual pictures on the screen? In *Hollywood in the Twenties*, David Robinson argues that producers abandoned the "characteristically working class" settings of prewar films and "now showed predominantly a wholly imaginary leisured class, with lovely homes and lovely clothes and lovely cars and lovely lives." But given the paucity of available films from the twenties and the unreliability of existing film plot summaries, such sweeping generalizations may be open to question. Chaplin's 1920s films, for example, revolved around working-class settings and attacked the premises of middle-class life. Moreover, judging from a sample of about thirty films shown during February and March 1928 at the Rialto Theatre, Worcester's leading working-class theater, films of that era dealt not simply with the rich but with the lower class's relationships with the rich. Most commonly, the film plots seem to have revolved around the problems and possibilities of interclass and intercultural relationships. In *Spring Fever*, for example, Jack Kelly, a "wisecracking shipping clerk, secures a card to an exclusive country club, and meets Allie Monte, who after some wooing reciprocates his love."

In the films shown at the Rialto success and wealth came through marriage or such leisure-oriented careers as prizefighting, dancing, music, and baseball. Upward mobility did not even require the adoption of a middle-class life-style. In *The Babe Comes Home* (starring Babe Ruth), for example, the Babe's working-class manners (exemplified by tobacco chewing) prove intrinsic to his success as a ballplayer. Thus, neither the picture on the screen nor the behavior in the theater caused, or even necessarily represented, a sharp or sudden abandonment of an embedded ethnic working-class culture. Yet movies did presage some important, if gradual, changes in working-class life. In the shadows of the movie theater one can catch glimpses of the waning of the older ethnic, insular working-class culture and the emergence of a new outward-looking working-class culture.

The movie palace of the 1920s broke down much of the informality and communality that characterized the ethnic working-class saloon, the July Fourth picnic, and even the dime museum and the nickelodeon. The lavish setting, the militarily attired and drilled ushers, the fixed starting times, the disinfected air, the lighted clocks, and the "finely appointed toilet rooms" had all made moviegoing a more controlled, structured, and anonymous experience. Whereas before patrons might mingle in the aisles, now the nattily attired ushers directed them to a specific seat. The advent of the "talkies" heightened this trend toward formality and privatism by making in-theater conversation unacceptable. The new movie houses also imposed a more rigid time discipline than had the nickelodeon, with its slogan Stay as Long as You Like. An item from the movie page of the *Worcester Sunday Telegram* of 1925 exemplified the new moviegoing style: "*Come Early*: Are you careful to learn the starting time of a movie feature before you leave home for the theater? . . . Every week about 20,000,000 movie cash customers see movies backward because they're too lazy to telephone for the 'starting time of the features' and to get to the theatre at the right time." No longer was the movie theater a working-class refuge from the time discipline of the factory.

Naturally, the neighborhood theaters retained much of the old informality and communality with their amateur nights and perennial giveaways of dishes, linens, and turkeys. But in the downtown movie palaces, which were more likely to be attended by second-generation teen-agers than by their parents or their younger brothers and sisters, recreation became a more formal and less collective experience.

Not only did moviegoing lack the boisterous and communal style of the saloon, it also failed to challenge the legal order or the work ethic in the same way as had the rum shop. In the nineteenth century, drunkenness and liquor law violations had been the most common Worcester crimes. But, unlike the saloongoer and the saloonkeeper or even the overly exuberant July Fourth celebrant, the moviegoer and the theater owner rarely ran afoul of the law. The early movie houses came into conflict with police authorities and reformers over film content, moviegoing conduct, and theater conditions, but by the 1920s such conflicts were rare. In 1929 the Worcester Board of Motion Picture and

Theatre Review, reporting on its first thirteen years of operation, noted "a steady improvement in the nature of released films" as well as the amicable cooperation of the city's theater managers.

Worcester's manufacturers also expressed satisfaction with the new medium. Both Mayor Wright, a leading wire manufacturer, and Donald Tulloch, spokesman for the city's leading industrialists, enthusiastically embraced the movies by World War I. The reasons for such approval are not hard to find: Moviegoing posed no threat to work discipline as had the saloon. Movies encouraged neither hangovers with their absenteeism nor on-the-job drunkenness with its accidents and decreased work efficiency. With these changes in the style of working-class recreation as well as the middle- and upper-class shifts in leisure habits and attitudes, working-class recreation declined as an arena of social conflict.

A related reason for this lessening of conflict was that the movie theater lacked the sort of ominous working-class autonomy and control that had worried reformers concerned about the saloon. Movies, because of their production by a small number of large, vertically integrated corporations and their national market, were vulnerable to national censorship, as well as market and social pressures. Even the theaters themselves were much less localized and individualized than the saloons, which were always much greater in number and more diverse in ownership. Increasingly, Worcester theaters came under the control of regional and national chains, and patrons had limited influence on their operations. E. M. Loew's take-over of the Olympia and Family theaters in 1930 illustrates this waning of control of the working class over its recreational institutions. Up to that time Worcester movie houses had generally been unionized. Within two weeks, however, Loew fired his union workers and hired scabs at lower wages. Both picketing and a labor boycott failed to reverse Loew's policy. Significantly, thirty years earlier a similar boycott of Bowler Bros. beer had won a closed union shop for its employees. The more local and more exclusively working-class saloon business had been more susceptible and responsive to the pressures of Worcester's organized workers.

The nationalization and centralization of the leisure industry affected what workers saw at the movies even more than how the theaters were run. When Charles Baker wrote farces for the Palace Museum in 1904, he closely followed "the varying tastes of customers" and made sure to add "a Worcester setting" to his songs and sketches. By the 1920s even such a sporadic novelty as the local filming of *A Romance in Worcester* was inconceivable. As the production of popular culture receded from both local control and local view, the pictures on the screen were less likely to speak to the everyday lives of Worcester workers.

The loss of local working-class control over its leisure was also manifest in economic terms—a pattern noted in relation to the amusement park. Much of the money spent at the nineteenth-century saloon remained within the ethnic, working-class community in the form of wages paid to brewery workers and bartenders, profits earned by locally resident saloonkeepers, and rents paid to small landlords. Even more important, money collected at entertainments and picnics sponsored by ethnic churches, clubs, and lodges financed local charities as well as the activities of those bodies. The profits of the movie industry, however, were increasingly expropriated by oligopolistic movie corporations and national and regional theater chains located outside Worcester and its working-class neighborhoods. In such an economic structure there was little room for the reciprocity and mutuality that had characterized the saloon and the mutual benefit society. Increasingly, a national market insulated from local pressures had intruded itself into the everyday lives of working people.

The movie theater's challenge to the intense localism of the saloon also fostered the erosion of the central feature of the older working-class culture: its focus around inward-looking, ethnic separatist communities. By the 1920s the movie theater, unlike the saloon, was not the exclusive province of a specific ethnic group nor of the working class in general. Instead, it was an arena for the mixing of ethnic groups, classes, age groups, and sexes. Even the working-class-dominated neighborhood theater sometimes operated counter to the ethnic separatist communities because they mixed several ethnic groups as with the Jews, Poles, and Lithuanians who mingled at the Rialto. Of course, ethnic tensions remained strong in Worcester; the rise of a local Ku Klux Klan in the 1920s, for example, pitted not just natives against immigrants but Swedes against Irish. Still, as the rising intermarriage rate indicates, the walls of ethnic Worcester were no longer as impermeable as they had once been.

The decline of ethnic separatism and insularity had a particular impact on women. Movie theaters, unlike the saloon, courted the patronage of women. When middle-class reformers celebrated the ways that the photoplay "reunite[d] the lower class families," they failed to perceive the strains that moviegoing could create in the strongly patriarchal immigrant working-class family. Both movie content and the experience of taking leisure outside the home or the ethnic community challenged old patterns and assumptions. For many women, as Elizabeth Ewen has pointed out, the movies could mean a shift from "the constricted family-dominated culture to the more individualized values of modern urban society." But, Ewen adds with irony, "new authorities replaced the old. In the name of freedom from tradition, they trapped women in fresh forms of sexual objectification and bound them to the consumerized and sexualized household."

In the long run, of course, the greatest changes can be detected among the young, the new generations, whether male or female. They were the most regular moviegoers and the least tied to the older ethnic culture. The "models for the consumption economy" that so many recent historians have detected in 1920s films like *Charge It* and *Ladies Must Dress*, which celebrate "the new joys and pitfalls of consumption," probably had their greatest impact within the working class on the rising second and third generations. Certainly, the personal accounts of moviegoing in the 1920s collected from students and young workers by sociologist Herbert Blumer suggest that movies may have helped reorient working-class youths outward to middle-class consumer society rather than inward to Old World ethnic ties and practices. "The day-dreams instigated by the movies consist of clothes, ideas on furnishings and manners," reflected one high school student. "After seeing a wonderful picture full of thrills and beautiful scenes, my own home life would seem dull and drab," wrote another.

The ethnic industrial working class was thus moving gradually from the margins to the mainstream of American life—following, in effect, the same path marked out by the transition from the shabby neighborhood five-cent movie house to the opulent downtown movie palace. And the children and grandchildren of Worcester's immigrant working class were leading the way. Playwright S. N. Behrman, himself a son of immigrant Worcester, captured the mood of transition in his recollections of how he gradually abandoned his neighborhood gathering spot (Elkind's drugstore) for one downtown (Easton's): "The trek from the soda fountain at Elkind's to the soda fountain at Easton's was a long leap in evolution because Easton's was the centre of the world . . . The displacement of the password for rendezvous from 'meet you at Elkind's' to 'meet you at Easton's' signalized the transition from periphery to the core, from provincialism to worldliness, from naivete to sophistication."

Of course, while the children and grandchildren of the immigrant working class could join the middle class at Easton's or at the ornate Plymouth Theatre, the trek downtown only went so far. The path to full participation in the "commodity culture" advertised on the movie screen remained blocked. In another account collected by sociologist Blumer, a high school senior noted poignantly: "Fashionable pictures make me long for fine clothes. I could not see why my parents were not able to buy me all the clothes I wanted." "The movies have often made me dissatisfied with my neighborhood," added a black high school freshman, "because when I see a movie, the beautiful castle, palace, . . . and beautiful house, I wish my home was something like these." By 1930 the movie theater had brought workers closer to the mainstream of American society, but the assembly line—particularly in nonunionized, unsafe, low-paying factories—kept them out of it.

Nine-year-old boy selling newspapers

The Newsies

DAVID NASAW

Children have always worked. In agricultural societies, youngsters scarcely beyond the toddler stage could be given necessary farm chores. Indeed, having many children has usually been seen as a positive economic factor in rural areas. Prior to the development of the factory system in urban society, young children performed small tasks that were associated with shop-keeping or home industry. The important unifying factor between the above labor systems was that they both took place within the family or household.

In the nineteenth century, the position of child labor in agriculture remained unchanged, but when the children's workplace became separated from the home, the new workplace (industrial centers) called attention in new ways to the issue of child labor. Despite the issues, many children continued to perform industrial tasks, but their increased visibility, along with the genuinely horrendous conditions of factory life, caught the attention of progressive reformers. New theories on human development and the expansion of the public schools, some of which had compulsory attendance requirements, led to the enactment of laws that limited the hours and ages for child labor. The laws, however, were rarely enforced.

Most historians who have studied the child labor issue have followed the reformers' pattern. The ill effects of the industrial environment on childrens' health along with the use of low-paid child labor to subvert militant union activity have been documented and properly deplored. In most instances, because of the emphasis on reform and the desire to protect society's defenseless from the degradation of unhealthy and unsafe industrial labor, attention had been focused almost entirely on the negative impact of work on children. But there is another side to the story. All children working did not do so in lung-destroying tobacco factories, cotton mills, or back-breaking mines and foundries. As the laws restricting child labor began to take effect, children began to look elsewhere for available jobs, particularly part-time work which they could perform after school, on weekends, or during school vacations.

In his book on urban children at work and play in the early twentieth century, David Nasaw, of the College of Staten Island of the City University of New York, describes in considerable detail one particularly successful employment area for boys—the selling of newspapers. Changes in the newspaper distribution system meshed perfectly with boys' desire for after school jobs, and the "newsie" was born. The selection from Nasaw's book reprinted here explores the ways in which boys eagerly sought and performed the job of selling the new afternoon editions of city newspapers to people commuting to their homes after work or enjoying an evening on the town. While the "newsie" work was not easy or significantly rewarding, it did offer boys an opportunity to make some money and to be out from under the watchful and (to them) oppressive eyes of both school and family.

It will be quickly observed from this selection that girls were not regularly engaged in this trade. In fact, many communities specifically passed laws forbidding the employment of females in the newspaper selling business. Girls were expected by the society to stay at home, in training to become what Nasaw calls "little mothers," while their brothers were on the street hustling for pennies and the occasional nickel. This division of labor proved to reinforce the general expectation of how adults of both sexes would spend their lives in this sex-role differentiation—males in the marketplace and females in the domestic arena.

T here were dozens and dozens of ways for enterprising eleven- to fifteen-year-olds to make money in the early twentieth-century cities. Of them all, the most accessible and most fun was selling newspapers.

Newsies were as old and established an aspect of the urban landscape as the "dailies" they hawked in the streets. There was, nonetheless, something quite different about the twentieth-century boys, something that set them off from their nineteenth-century counterparts. Though every bit as streetwise, tough, and cunning as the street urchins immortalized by Horatio Alger, the newsies who peddled their papers in the turn-of-the-century cities were neither orphans nor street waifs; nor were they the sole support of ailing mothers and infant siblings. They slept at home, not in alleyways or flophouses, and ate at the dinner table, not at free lunch counters in cheap saloons. As the superintendent of a "newsboy's lodging house" explained to Jacob Riis in 1912, "The newsboy of to-day is another kind of chap, who has a home and folks." The picturesque little ragamuffins Riis had earlier written about had been replaced by "the commercial little chap who lives at home and sells papers after school-hours."

The new generation of newsies was a product of the boom in afternoon circulation that had been building through the 1880s and 1890s but took off during the Spanish-American War. The morning papers that had been the mainstay of the industry had, by the turn of the century, been eclipsed by the late editions. "By 1890, two-thirds of American dailies were published in the afternoon." By 1900, "evening papers, bought on the way home from work, outnumbered morning papers . . . about three to one."

The new metropolis had spawned the new newspaper. With the expansion of the cities outward into the urban fringes and suburbs came a new population of workers, many of whom could be enticed to buy an afternoon paper to occupy them during the commute home by ferry, streetcar, subway, or train. Better illumination on the streets and at home meant that readers had more time to read, advertisers more time to advertise, and publishers a new market of "homebound shoppers and workers and downtown evening crowds" to sell their late editions to. Technological advances in news-gathering, printing, and transportation made it possible to put out "late" editions timed to greet these new readers with "new" news and advertisements.

The newsies were reborn with the expansion of the afternoon editions. Nineteenth-century street urchins had sold the morning editions all day long. Twentieth-century newsies could sell enough papers after school to make up for what they might have lost in the morning. Hawking papers was transformed from a full-time to a part-time job, one that began, most conveniently, at four in the afternoon and extended through the evening rush hours.

Because of the timing of the editions and the hundreds of thousands of customers anxious to get their papers on their way home from work, no newspaper ever had enough newsies. As every circulation manager, city editor, advertising director, and publisher knew, the boys were the last and most vital link in the business chain. Without large numbers out on the streets, crying their wares, advertising their papers, exciting and interesting the public in the latest news and the latest edition, the newspaper business would have been in serious trouble.

In most cities the circulation managers, their assistants, and routemen welcomed the children at the downtown offices and distribution centers. Those who wanted to work steadily, every day after school and on weekends and holidays, were most welcome. But no one was turned away. Children who only wanted to sell the Sunday papers on Saturday nights or the baseball editions with the latest scores during the warm weather were free to do so. So were those who hawked the news only when they were in dire need of extra money, when they lost other jobs, or when the "news" was so hot and the headlines so bold the papers sold themselves.

In cities with more than one afternoon paper (and before World War I that included most cities), the circulation managers fought with one another to build up their stock of boys. The more boys on the street, the more papers would be available to customers. Because the profit margin on every paper was the same, the slightest incentive (negative or positive) could shift vendors from one paper to the next or give them a reason to hawk one more enthusiastically then its competitors. An editorial in *Editor and Publisher* reminded circulation managers of the dangers of alienating the boys and the benefits of treating them well. "As the newsboys can increase street sales or can, by refusing to handle a paper, cut them down, their good will and support are considered a valuable asset. Boys are humans, like grown-ups, but are much more appreciative and respond quicker to their impulses. Treat them well, that is, entertain them, give them help when they need it, and invite them to Thanksgiving and Christmas dinners and they will show their gratitude by selling your papers in preference of all others."

Publishers competing for newsies did what they could to curry the boys' favor. In Philadelphia, the *Telegram* treated twelve hundred newsies to see " 'Lover's Lane' at the Park Theater with Miss Millie James in the role of 'Simplicity Johnson.' It was the first time a majority of the boys ever had a seat below the top gallery and they appreciated the honor." In Cincinnati, the dailies competed with one another by spending between three and four thousand dollars each for theater parties, baseball leagues, and furnished recreation rooms. In Detroit, St. Paul, Baltimore, Ogden (Utah), Spokane, Fort Worth, San Antonio, Austin, Buffalo, Schenectady, Boston, Lawrence and Lynn (Massachusetts), New Orleans, Dayton, and Butte (Montana), publishers provided newsies with furnished clubhouses, tickets to ball games, trips to summer camps and free turkeys on holidays.

The publishers did it all, not for humanitarian or public relations considerations, but—as the editor of the Grand Rapids *Press* reminded his fellow editors—for pure "selfish interest."

Turkeys and theater tickets were the preferred weapons in the newspapers' war for the newsies, but there were other strategies as well. Some publishers used intimidation and violence instead of or in combination with their "welfare work." Circulation managers could, if they chose, hire thugs, arm their delivery men, and make it clear to the boys on the street that anyone not pushing their papers was headed for serious trouble. In Cincinnati, according to Edward Clopper (a reliable if somewhat histrionic reporter), the agents for two afternoon papers that were engaged in a circulation battle hired bullies "to follow the newsboys who sell the opposition paper and threaten and harass them if they are found trying to sell more than a specified number of copies." In one instance, Clopper watched as a "small band of young men . . . instead of entering into fair competition with the boys [hawking the rival newspaper], deliberately got in front of them and harassed them wherever they went, to prevent their making sales." When questioned by Clopper, the circulation manager admitted hiring five of the "bullies," but claimed to have done it in self-defense.

In Cincinnati, at least, the circulation managers used children, not adults, as strong-arms, and the violence was sporadic and short-lived. When Maurice Hexter did his study of newsboy life in Cincinnati in 1917, almost ten years after Clopper's investigation, he found no hint of such tactics. The circulation managers were instead bidding for the boys' favor with baseball leagues and theater parties. In Chicago, on the other hand, circulation battles were real battles fought by adult hoodlums hired specifically for the occasion. When William Randolph Hearst moved into the Chicago market at the turn of the century, many newsstands and newsies, bowing to pressure from the already established papers, refused to carry his papers. Hearst and the Annenberg brothers, his circulation managers, armed their delivery men and hired adult thugs to force the dealers and newsies to carry the *American* and the *Examiner*. Full-scale war broke out when Hearst's rivals enlisted their own street armies to protect the vendors still loyal to them. The newsboys were caught in the middle—and remained there for years—while the war raged through the streets. Some took advantage of the situation to sign on as "sluggers" with one of the publishers. Others made their peace as best they could and continued to sell their papers on the street.

Chicago was the only city where it took the publishers so long to discover that street battles were bad for business. Elsewhere, when violence was used, it was used selectively—to get newspapers onto the streets or temporarily scare away the competition. Circulation managers like the Annenbergs, with their arsenal of weapons, were the exception, not the rule. Their counterparts in most cities did not own guns or employ hoodlums. They were new-style managers who saw their mission as boosting circulation through efficiency and better management principles, not violence and intimidation.

In most cities and towns, the relations between circulation managers and newsies were cool but stable. The boys did not expect theater tickets or armed thugs as inducements to help them do their job. An unwritten contract existed between the boys and the adults who sold them their papers. As long as the adults honored the contract—and did nothing to cut into the boys' profit margin or disturb their laws of the street—the newsies would cooperate with them. They would push each paper with equal fervor and keep on pushing until the edition was sold out.

The children's relationship with their adult suppliers and circulation managers was a business one. The street traders were given no special consideration because of age or size. The adults they did business with treated them only as fairly as they had to. It was the children's informal organization and the conditions of street trading that protected their interests, not adult benevolence.

The street traders who hustled newspapers were blessed by circumstances not of their own making. At this point in the history of the city and of the newspapers, the publishers depended on the children for 50 percent or more of their afternoon sales. The thousands upon thousands of city workers who bought their papers on the way home from work could only have been served by a part-time work force that began work in mid-afternoon. Within a mere twenty years, there would be adults and new distribution companies to get the afternoon dailies to their customers. For the first two decades of the century, however, the newspapers had no choice but to rely on the children.

City kids who hustled papers inhabited a work world in which the pressure of self-interest was often sufficient to protect each side of the labor contract. The newspapers needed the children as much as the children needed the newspapers. The children's situation was almost unique. Their first encounter with the workplace was as workers without bosses. As independent contractors they did not have to accept management control of the workplace or work routines. They were free to set their own schedules, establish their own pace, and work when and where they chose. They, in fact, experienced more autonomy at work than in school or at home. In school, they were watched over, tested, and disciplined by teachers. At home, they were subject to the authority of parents, adult relatives, and older siblings. On the street, there were no parents, teachers, bosses, managers, or foremen to tell them what to do or how to do it. The harder and longer they hustled, the more papers they sold. The more time they took for themselves, the less they would have to bring home and to spend. In either case, the choice was theirs. When business was slow because of bad weather or dull headlines, they had no one to blame—not themselves and certainly not the publishers or suppliers. It was bad luck and bad luck alone that came between them and their profits. And today's bad luck, they knew, could easily turn better tomorrow.

Regrettably, this situation could not—and did not—last forever. The littlest hustlers would grow up and leave the streets behind. They would, however, carry with them the memory of the work world they had encountered as children and the notion that work in America need not be exploitative or unpleasant.

The newsies came from every ethnic group, in numbers roughly proportional to the adult working-class population. In New York City, three quarters of the boys were Russian-Jewish or Italian. In Chicago, over two thirds were "American," "Negro," German, or Irish. In Baltimore, more than 40 percent were "American whites." In Cincinnati,

29 percent were "American, colored." In Dallas, 80 percent were "American" or northern European.

What defined the newsie population was not ethnicity as much as class. A July 1917 study of eight hundred and six New York City news-ies found that, with the exception of four contractors and builders, five grocers, twenty-three clerks, seven salesmen, and a handful of other white-collar workers, the vast majority of the newsboys' fathers worked as laborers, tailors, drivers, peddlers, porters, pressers, longshoremen, bootblacks, skilled craftsmen, and factory hands. A 1910 St. Louis study similarly found that only 9.6 percent of newsboys' fathers were "inde-pendent business men" and 3.1 percent "public officials"; all the rest were skilled or unskilled workers.

The newsies were no exotic breed of city child. The historical re-cord suggests that selling papers on the streets was a common chil-dren's occupation. Hundreds of thousands of boys who grew up in American cities in the first decades of this century sold papers, if not regularly, then when they or their families were most in need of cash. The number of special investigative reports on "newsboy conditions" prepared by child labor reformers testifies to the widespread nature of the practice (see Appendix), as do the many biographies and autobio-graphies of boys who came of age in the early twentieth-century city. Louis Armstrong, Irving Berlin, Joe E. Brown, George Burns, Ralph Bunche, Eddie Cantor, Frank Capra, Morris Raphael Cohen, Leonard Covello, Jack Dempsey, William O. Douglas, Harry Golden, Joseph Hirschhorn, the Jolson brothers, Mervyn LeRoy, Jerre Mangione, the Marx brothers, David Sarnoff, Spyros Skouras, the Warner brothers, Earl Warren, and Bertram Wolfe, to mention a few, sold papers as boys.

Unfortunately for the historian, no accurate quantitative data are available on the number of children who hawked papers on the streets. The census figures are virtually useless, as the Bureau itself admitted in its 1924 report on *Children in Gainful Occupations*: "The characteristics of the occupations of newsboys are such that accurate enumeration of the workers is extremely difficult."

The parents and children who were the only potentially reliable sources of information on the subject could not be counted on to tell the truth—and for good reasons. By 1915, some seventeen states, the District of Columbia, and several cities had passed laws restricting chil-dren from trading on the streets. The children, more often than not, simply ignored the laws. When asked if they worked on the streets, many simply answered in the negative rather than provide some in-vestigator with incriminating information. Their parents were as cir-cumspect in their conversation with census takers and child labor investigators.

The best information we have on the percentage of city boys who sold papers comes from the local studies which used school teachers or licensing bureaus as informants. A 1911 Chicago study reported that

65 percent of fifth-graders (eleven-to-twelve-year-olds) and 35 percent of fourth-graders in a particular school were street traders. Unfortunately for our purposes, the study is suspect. It was undertaken to dramatize the plight of the child laborer for the Chicago Child Welfare Exhibit which probably chose for its survey the one school in Chicago with the greatest number of working children.

A 1909 Cincinnati study is a bit more reliable. It found that the two thousand boys, aged ten to thirteen, licensed to sell papers in the city constituted 15 percent of their age group. Had the study included newsboys who sold without licenses, the 15 percent figure would have climbed somewhat. A second Cincinnati study (1917) attempted to correct for this factor by including the unlicensed newsies but compromised its usefulness by computing the percentage of newsboys in the ten-to-sixteen age group. Since most were over eleven and under fifteen, the conclusion that 12 percent of ten- to sixteen-year-olds sold papers is less meaningful than might appear.

Anna Reed's 1916 Seattle study did not include figures on the percentage of youth who sold papers. Extrapolating from her data, however, we find that 12 percent of sixth-graders, 11 percent of seventh-graders, and 14 percent of eighth-graders regularly sold on the streets. Here, too, the figures probably under-represent the percentage of boys selling, since they exclude those who worked occasionally or were not working the day of the survey and those who, for their own reasons, preferred not to answer in the affirmative when asked if they sold papers after school.

Of the dozens of newsboy studies, these were the only ones that attempted to figure out the percentage of city boys who sold papers. The others were more concerned with collecting data to reinforce their contention that street trading led directly to juvenile delinquency. To provide themselves with evidence establishing the connection, child labor reformers scoured the juvenile courts, jails, asylums, houses of refuge, and reformatories for ex-newsies. They found what they were looking for. A 1911 memo from the secretary of the New York Child Labor Committee summarized the findings that would be used again and again to prove the connection between street work and juvenile crime:

> New York Juvenile Asylum (1911), 31% were newsboys.
> Rochester, N.Y., Industrial School (1903), 75% were newsboys. (Buffalo boys only counted.)
> Hart's Island, N.Y.C. (1906), 63% were newsboys.
> Catholic Protectory, N.Y.C. (1911), 50% were newsboys.
> House of Refuge, at Randall's Island, N.Y.C. (1911), 32% were newsboys.
> Glen Mills, Pennsylvania (1910), 77% were newsboys. (Philadelphia boys only counted.)

The data were impressive, but they proved nothing. What the reformers either did not understand or conveniently ignored was that most city boys, delinquent or not, sold papers on the street. As Justice Harvey Baker of the Boston Juvenile Court reported to a New York Child Labor Committee investigator, it was "very difficult to determine what part, if any, the selling of papers plays in the delinquency of the boys who come before this court. Since most of the Jewish boys . . . sell papers, if we are to have any delinquent Jewish boys at all, we are bound to get a large number of newspaper sellers among them." The judge's remarks could have been generalized to other city boys. Since most had, at one time or another, sold papers, most of those in trouble would have had a history of paper-selling.

The children who hawked their papers on the street enjoyed their work. The excitement, the noise, the ever-changing aspects of street life provided a needed antidote to a day spent in a crowded, stuffy classroom. Watching children from his post as superintendent of the United Jewish Charities of Cincinnati and chief investigator of a study of newsboys in that city, Maurice Hexter found few children who preferred their hours in the classroom to those spent working on the street. "The school represents a task: street work in an enjoyment."

The street was the ideal workplace: it was outdoors, alive with activity, and away from the prying eyes of teachers and parents. When, in 1918, a University of Chicago graduate student asked 378 newsies if they enjoyed their work, 87 percent responded that they did. Other investigators, employing less scientific methodologies, came to the same conclusion.

The children who worked after school were serious about earning money, but they were not ready to leave their childhood behind. Though they now had responsibilities—to their families and to themselves—these responsibilities did not prevent them from having fun whenever and wherever they could. "Children" could play all afternoon. "Adults" had to work all day. But eleven- to fifteen-year-olds, suspended somewhere in between, needed to squeeze their work and their play into the hours they had to themselves between the end of school and the moment they had to be home for dinner.

The gap between dismissal time at school—three o'clock—and working people's quitting time—after five, generally—was to the street traders' advantage. It gave them time to play before their customers hit the streets for the trip home. Unfortunately their play time, circumscribed as it was by work schedules, was too abbreviated to allow them to travel far from the streets where they would begin work later in the afternoon. Their "playgrounds" would necessarily have to be located near their workplaces.

The children who worked together came together to play before and after the rush hours. With an intensity that startled the investigators sent to observe their habits, they converted the public space they shared with adults into their "playgrounds" and proceeded to "kick the can," match pennies, and play ball—oblivious to the adults who got in their way. In midtown Manhattan, groups of newsies played in the Times Square subway station that served as the distribution point of the afternoon papers they would soon have to sell. When they were bored with "roughhousing" underground, they "went upstairs to the Square, secured a couple of tin cans, and, in the midst of the heavy traffic of Broadway between 42nd and 43rd Street, engaged themselves in a mad and aimless competition in kicking the can." An investigator from the New York Child Labor Committee looked on in amazement as the boys dashed after the can in and out of traffic, dodging automobiles and streetcars. "More than once did it seem that one or the other of them would be run over, and many a [street]car and automobile stopped in its own tracks in the middle of the block to avoid running over them. There were frequent collisions with people on the sidewalk, men and women, who might just as well not have been there for all the attention the boys paid them."

The game continued until the boys' attention was distracted by a wind-blown hat. Almost magically, they sensed its presence, halted their game, and turned "as one to pursue" it, knowing that whoever caught it was in line for a nice tip from the owner. The hat retrieved and returned, and the tip pocketed, the boys went back to the game, which continued for a time, interrupted only momentarily by the argument that broke out when the can hit Bull Head Gus in his bull head.

In Birmingham, Alabama, according to a local observer, the news ies "congregate[d]" in front of the newspaper office downtown, where they spent the "hour or so before the papers came off the press . . . matching pennies, rolling dice, fighting, using foul and profane language and creating bedlam in general."

In Chicago, where most of the action was concentrated at the Loop, the boys who sold newspapers picked them up in the alleys behind the publishers' offices. The newspapers did their best to provide the children with all the entertainment they needed—right there in the alleys. The closer the boys were kept to the presses, the sooner they could be sprung on the city with the latest editions. The *American* offered the newsies free lunches. The *Daily News* invited vendors to set up stands inside the alley. "Almost at the entrance is a small booth where 'red-hots' and ice cream are sold for a penny a-piece, and 'pop' for two cents a bottle. Just beyond this is a restaurant where cheap lunches are on sale. On one side of the alley is a man sitting under an umbrella selling ice cream from a freezer. Upstairs . . . is a penny lunch stand. . . . Just at the west entrance of the alley is a store where dime novels, dice, cards, cigarette papers and tobacco are kept on sale and

prominently displayed in the window." If the reformers who visited
the alleys are to be believed (and in this they probably are), the boys
spent their afternoons shooting craps, pitching pennies, trading dirty
stories among themselves and with the older vagrants who took shelter
there, and stuffing themselves with "trash." The newsies had no time
to waste. They had to squeeze a full day's play into the brief interval
that separated the end of school from the start of the rush hour.

The street traders lived a dual existence on the downtown streets
of the city. The street was their background, but it was their workplace
as well. Though outsiders might have been confused by the sudden
switch from child at play to little merchant at work, the children themselves knew precisely what they were doing. They played as long as
they could and then, as the rush hour began in earnest, put away their
dice, their red-hots, their baseballs, and their gossip to go to work.
Like Superman emerging from the phone booth, industrious little hustlers appeared where carefree children had stood moments before.
Alexander Fleisher, visiting a newspaper distribution center in Milwau-
kee, was amazed at the transformation worked by the arrival of the
papers. "When the edition comes from the press, the boys line up before the grating and receive their papers and rush out. . . . The place
takes on a businesslike air and everything goes with snap and order."

The children worked such miracles without the prompting of adults.
The afternoon was too short to waste. Once their papers were ready
and their customers about to hit the streets, they set to work. Schedule
and pace were determined by the rhythm of the rush hour. As it began
to build, they eased their way into their trading. By the time it had
reached its peak, they were all business. Arms and legs in perpetual
motion, they chased customers up and down the block, shouting their
wares at the top of their lungs.

The children stationed themselves along the streets with the heaviest pedestrian traffic. Their own neighborhoods were crowded with
people but not always the right kind. The newsies needed customers
with change in their pockets. They did not have to travel far to find
them. Streetcars and trolleys cost a nickel each way, a considerable
sum for part-time child workers. Fortunately the residential areas where
most of their families lived were not far from the downtown shopping,
business, and entertainment districts. In New York City, the Lower
East Side children traveled to the City Hall area or to the East River
bridges to sell their wares; the Upper East Side and West Side children
walked into midtown to do their peddling and newspaper hawking.

The children set up shop outside department store exits, in front
of the subway stations and elevated stops, and at the entrances to the
bridges, ferry terminals, and train stations, wherever they could be sure
of meeting up with homebound workers. In Mount Vernon, the boys
crowded "about the [trolley] cars that deposit passengers at the corner

of Fourth Avenue and First street. . . . Every passenger who alights is immediately besieged, and the boys tumble over each other in order to make the first sale. . . . A similar situation may be witnessed at the New Haven Railroad Station at the time the evening trains come in." In Newark, the boys gathered at the Delaware, Lackawanna, and Western depot and the Pennsylvania Railroad station. The Hoboken and Jersey City boys sold their wares outside the entrance to the "tubes" and the ferry station.

In the smaller cities, where the business, entertainment, and shopping streets were concentrated in a circumscribed area, boys hawked their papers along the main business streets. In Yonkers, they gathered along Main Street and in Getty Square. In Rutland, Vermont, a "busy town of 15,000 persons" visited by Lewis Hine for the National Child Labor Committee, the entire population of fifteen newsies worked the "principal streets from 4:30 to 6:30 every afternoon."

Hawking papers was fun, but it was also work that required physical exertion and no small amount of careful planning. Children who expected to earn decent money on the streets had to apply themselves to mastering the economics of their trade.

Newsies needed a "stake" to get started. Some borrowed money from their mothers, many got it from friends. Their "stake" bought them their first batch of papers. From that point on, they would hold back enough from each day's sales to buy tomorrow's papers from the circulation manager.

The newsies had to decide for themselves how many papers to purchase each afternoon and on Sundays. That was no easy task. Newspapers, unlike Spearmint gum, Hershey's chocolate with almonds, pencils, and handkerchiefs, went bad if not sold immediately. Every paper purchased from the circulation manager had to be unloaded before the next edition came out.

If the children bought too many papers, they would have to swallow the loss on the unsold copies or stay out all night to sell them— and that became progressively more difficult as it got later and the street traffic thinned. If, on the other hand, they bought too few, they stood in danger of losing customers. Adults were creatures of habit and creatures in a hurry. They would buy from the same boy at the same spot as long as he guaranteed them the latest edition. If he ran short once, they would cross the street to another newsie—and probably continue to do so until he too ran short.

The children could expect no help from the circulation managers they worked with. The newspapermen were entirely untrustworthy. They cared only about boosting circulation and to do so would regularly pressure the boys to buy more papers than they could sell. The newsies had to figure out what their probable sales would be—and buy just that amount of papers. To arrive at an accurate figure, they had to sift and sort a number of diverse factors: the time of day the papers were ready for distribution, the weather, the day of the week, the season of the year, the number of papers sold the day before, the number and importance of the sports scores, and, most crucially, the size and content of the headlines.

Afternoon circulations were never as constant as morning ones, which were more likely to be sold by subscription. While many readers considered the morning paper a necessity, few thought the same of the afternoon editions. Customers might forego the late papers altogether or, on big news days, buy several editions of several different papers. It was the headlines that made the difference.

The children lived for the great headlines, the red-faced, bold-type banner catastrophes that sold out editions. Murder, mayhem, riot, war, natural disaster: this was the stuff their dreams were made of. A half century after he had left the streets of Toledo, Ohio, Joe E. Brown, the comedian, still remembered vividly that "the biggest week I had in the newspaper business was the week following President McKinley's assassination. He lived for a week after he was shot at the Exposition in Buffalo and throughout that week interest in the news was at fever pitch." Brown sold more Toledo *Bees* and *Blades* than he had ever dreamed possible.

Banner headlines, no matter how dramatic, did not sell themselves. It was the boys' job to create the excitement that brought customers running. The children had no time for digesting the significance of the headlines, feeling sorrow at the tragedies, or mourning the dead. They devoted all their energy and ingenuity to communicating to the public in a language it could understand.

Harry Golden, the writer, sold papers on the Lower East Side and was on the streets the day Leo Frank was lynched for the murder of fourteen-year-old Mary Phagan. His first thought when he saw the headline of Frank's death in red ink was that "the word 'lynched' would have little meaning for Jewish immigrants." He translated it to "murder" and ran through the streets shouting the news.

When the *Titanic* sank, when the Triangle Shirtwaist Factory burst out in flames, or during the Spanish-American War, the Mexican War scare, and World War I, the newsies did their best to excite and incite the public into buying their papers. The children of the city were adept at converting disaster into profit. They played the newspapers' game as well as the city editors and reporters did. Their news as they presented it was always current, always exciting, always provocative. They took what the headline writers gave them and added the appropriate emphasis and detail. When the news was dull, they cheated a bit. George Burns jokingly recalls making up catastrophes on slow news days.

"Sometimes I'd have eight or nine papers left over, and to get rid of them I'd run through the streets hollering things like 'Extra! Extra! Ferry Boat sinks in East River!!' or 'Big Gun Battle in Sharkey's Restaurant!!' One day when I was stuck with eleven papers I took off down the street yelling, 'Extra! Extra! Huber's Museum Goes Down in Flames!!!' Well, I was selling newspapers like hotcakes, when all of a sudden I felt a hand on my shoulder. It turned out to be a disgruntled customer. He held the paper in front of my face and said, 'What are you pulling, kid? There's nothing in this newspaper about a fire at Huber's Museum!'

"For a split second I didn't know what to say. Then I blurted out, 'I know, that's such an early edition the fire hasn't started yet!' and ran."

Burns was not the only newsie who embellished the news to sell more papers. During the Great War there was a virtual epidemic of false headlines. In Cleveland, according to a story in *Editor and Publisher*, city officials were so disturbed by the boys' blatant distortion of the news that they threatened to prosecute those who shouted "false and amazing statements. . . . In extreme cases . . . offenders may be prosecuted under the Espionage Act." In New York City, where it was claimed the boys hollered louder than anywhere else in the world, the problem was even greater. In October 1917, a New York *Times* article, headed "Police Move to Stop Noise of Newsboys: Public Annoyed by Shouting of War Calamities for Which There is No Basis," reported that the police department had received scores of complaints about newsboys making up the news. "Knowing the people to be keenly interested in European events, the newsboys, to stimulate sales, often take advantage of popular concern by converting occurrences of no significance in Paris, London or Petrograd into stupendous disasters. This practice has unnerved men and women who have relatives in the service and to whom the war is of vital and personal concern. Not only in the city but in the suburbs newsboys have aroused neighborhoods late at night with their fictitious sensations." Police Commissioner Woods promised to do his best "to stop this nuisance" but made it clear that there were no specific laws forbidding the practice. Only when the citizens took the time to swear out complaints against the newsboys would the problem be solved.

In Philadelphia, the police and courts, undeterred by lack of legislation, started their own campaign to rid the streets of the newsboy menace. For "agitating and frightening mothers and others who have relatives in the war, several Philadelphia newsboys [were] fined, or given the alternative of spending a term in jail."

In those helter-skelter days of journalism between the Spanish-American War and World War I, the newsies shouting the headlines were as much a part of the urban street scene as the lampposts on

every corner. Informing the world of the latest calamities, they broadcast the news with an immediacy and enthusiasm no other medium
could approach. Not all city residents, however, appreciated the service. The boys, to be sure, made a lot of noise. They also shouted their
headlines in immigrant and working-class accents that grated on the
ears of those in the high-priced neighborhoods and hotel districts who
preferred to spend their evenings in total isolation from the raucous
elements of urban life. As one disturbed resident of New York City
wrote to the New York *Times* in the summer of 1912, the boys had
become "an unmitigated nuisance in the neighborhoods they invade"
and a serious health hazard to those "who are sick or nervous. . . .
Doctors will testify that the chances of recovery for their patients are
sometimes seriously impaired by the raucous shouts portentous of
calamity."

Had the boys been more quiet, refined, and middle-class in their
manners and accent, they might have offended fewer people. An Atlanta judge, recognizing the class bias inherent in the city ordinance
forbidding the boys to hawk their papers after eight in the evening,
threw it out of court, claiming that the boys had every right to "cry
their papers on the streets so long as they do not block traffic or disturb
the sick. . . . The sidewalks are for the newsboys as well as the millionaires." In New York City, Mayor Gaynor firmly but politely re-
buffed a series of New York *Times* letter writers who complained about
the "young foreigners" and their "offensive" pronunciation and voices.
"They do not disturb me any," declared the Mayor. The newsies of El
Paso and Seattle were not as lucky. In these cities, ordinances were
passed forbidding the boys to shout after hours or within certain areas
of the city.

The newsies made a lot of noise because it was fun, part of their
public service as unofficial town criers, and the only way they knew to
advertise their wares. When the news was a bit stale, tame, or just
plain dull, it was the newsie who sold the paper by creating the excitement the headline lacked. Regrettably there were days, weeks, even
months when the news was so slow and the headlines so tame that
not even the most imaginative and energetic hustlers could sell out the
edition. The worst times were those following extended periods of crisis. In his poem "Post-Bellum," Dean Collins, a Portland (Oregon)
newsie, described the boys' plight in the days following the close of
World War I:

> A newsboy with his papers sat sighing on the street,
> For the cruel war was over and the foe had met defeat.
> And the scare-heads in the dailies, they had vanished like a spell,
> And the liveliest thing the newsie had was market heads to yell.
> "O, maybe Sherman had it right," said he, "but wars must cease—
> And Sherman never tried to peddle papers when 'twas peace."

"They used to saw an extra off each half hour by the clock.
And we used to wake the echoes when we whooped 'em down the block.
War may be just what Sherman said it was, but just the same,
If Sherman were a newsie, O, I wonder what he'd think
Of peddling papers after peace had put things on the blink?"

"How can I jar the people loose to buy the sheet and read,
If I start yelling 'bout the rise in price of clover seed?
When they are used to war and smoke and sulphur burning blue,
Will they warm up to read about the W.C.T.U.?
O, Maybe Sherman had it right on war—but wars must cease—
And Sherman never tried to peddle papers after peace."

What is most remarkable about the poem is its candor. The poem was printed in a newspaper put out by the boys to raise money for their club, clubhouse, and organized activities. They used the publication to emphasize their patriotism and their promise as future citizens. And yet, no one at the paper, neither the poet nor his editors or publishers, saw fit to exclude or at least tone down the sentiments expressed. While the rest of the nation celebrated the cessation of hostilities, the newsboys published a poem mourning the Great War's untimely conclusion.

The newsies had been so corrupted by their business that they no longer knew when to keep quiet. They had learned to worship the bottom line. What mattered was the number of papers sold. If war, catastrophe, and tragedy sold the most, then they would gladly parade them through the streets. Modesty, humility, honesty—it was clear—won no prizes and sold no papers. The boys who shouted the loudest and twisted the headlines most creatively earned the most. All was fair on the streets. What counted was that you got the change, not how you got it.

The children, as we shall see, could be quite scrupulous in their dealings with one another. Their customers were another story.

The newsies had two sources of income: sales and tips. To sell their papers, they advertised their headlines, stretching the truth to make the news more exciting. To secure their tips, they employed all the tricks they knew. Tips didn't just happen. They had to be coaxed out of the customers' pockets.

Since most afternoon papers cost a penny, customers with a nickel had to either wait for for their four pennies in change or leave a 400 percent tip. The more frantic the customers, the more time the newsies took fishing the change out of their pockets. Early in the afternoon, they might claim to be out of change and suggest that if the customer just waited a moment, they would scurry round the corner to get it from the candy store. In such cases, the boys stood a good chance—as they knew—of being told to keep the change. Alexander Fleisher, who kept track of such things, estimated that in up to 33 percent of street sales, newsies without change or slow to make it ended up with "a larger coin than the sale call[ed] for."

Next to dashing commuters, drunks were the softest touch for newsies on the prowl. The reformers feared that the boys hung out at saloons because they wanted free drinks. The truth was different. The boys knew that the drunker the customer, the easier it was to short-change or coax a tip out of him. Harry Bremer, in his unpublished study of New York City newsies, recorded the following conversations with a twelve-year-old who claimed to specialize in squeezing tips from drunks outside saloons.

" 'A man'll give yer a quarter, and yer'll say yer ain't got change and he'll tell yer to go get some and yer'll go and won't come back.'

" 'And leave him standing on the curb?'

" 'Sure! He'll wait for yer. Last Saturday a man gave me $5, and I didn't have change—so he told me to get some. I tried one store and they didn't have it—and I went to another and they didn't have it—and I went back and saw the man standing on the corner and I went around the other way!'

" 'What did you do with it?'

" 'Gave it to my mother.'

" 'All of it?'

" 'No, I kept half for myself and spent it.' "

Prostitutes were also big tippers. Harry Golden, who "hawked papers from the corner of Delancey and Norfolk," made regular trips to Allen Street, the Lower East Side's red-light district, where he earned his tips by running "occasional errands for the whores who lived there. They always gave me an extra nickel for delivering the paper and another nickel for running to the grocery store or the soft-drink stand." In Chicago, investigators for the Vice Commission were startled and upset by similar business arrangements between prostitutes and the children who ran their errands and delivered their newspapers.

Some children stole their tips, some chased them, others performed for them, preying on the sympathy of the "Americans" who felt sorry for the poor children peddling their papers. The evenings, especially Saturday nights during the cold weather months, were the best times to perform for tips. The children dressed for the occasion and chose their locations with care. In Syracuse, Mrs. W. J. Norton, a member of the city's Social Service Club, found a "small boy of eleven" standing outside a saloon for three quarters of an hour "weeping in a most realistic fashion as a possible customer approached. Again and again he had spasms of weeping at the opportune time. His paper bag was soon empty." Florence Kelley, at the time Secretary of the National Consumers' League, reported having seen in New York City "a little boy, very ill-fed, wretched, shabby little boy, offering papers for sale at a quarter to twelve o'clock, midnight, at the door of the women's hotel, the Martha Washington Hotel. He seemed to be speculating on the pity of women who might be coming home late from theater or opera to that hotel."

The Saturday night newsies were a mixed group. Some were regulars who sold every night of the week, others hustled the Sunday papers only. The Sunday papers, a recent publishing innovation, had become a necessary source of information and entertainment for city and suburban residents. The first editions arrived on the streets late Saturday night, in time to reach the downtown crowds on their way home from the movie palaces, music halls, and restaurants.

The boys followed the crowds through the streets from the entertainment districts to the after-hours clubs and eating places and then to their train stations and ferry terminals. Saturday night was a good time for sales and tips. The streets were crowded with people who, after an evening of fun, had more trouble than usual resisting the importunings of the young merchants. Myers Diamond, who hustled Hershey's chocolate bars with almonds in front of the Lyric Theater on Market Street in Newark, sold four times more bars on Saturday nights than on weeknights. According to Scott Nearing, the Philadelphia newsies made as much on Saturday nights and Sunday mornings as "during the remainder of the week."

The newsies who sold the Sunday papers stayed up with the downtown crowds, then got up again on Sunday mornings to sell their papers to the rest of the city. Some remained downtown all night, sleeping between editions in the newspaper offices or nearby. Their work schedules were determined by the newspapers' publishing schedule. In Baltimore, the boys began the evening hawking the Philadelphia papers, which arrived about 10:00 P.M. At 1:30 A.M. they moved on to the local Baltimore editions. In Chicago, at the Loop, the boys sold from midnight, when the first edition appeared, until the early morning hours. In New York City, they could be found in the Times Square area, papers in hand, from early in the evening to well after midnight. Jersey City newsies sold from 12:30 to 2:30 A.M., then slept a few hours "under the car shed at the ferry" or in the ferry house so they'd be up and ready for their Sunday morning customers. Business was so good in Jersey City and Elizabeth that the boys took the ferry into New York City to get the papers on Saturday night rather than wait for the regular delivery later in the morning.

The newsies on the town on a Saturday night tried their best to behave as the "Americans" believed they should: with charm and servility. The newsie who tipped his cap, opened restaurant and car doors, and exhibited his respect for his betters had a good chance at a sizable tip.

According to child labor reformers, tips were so plentiful that many boys carried papers only as a front. Their real money was made begging tips. In this age of conspicuous consumers, the most conspicuous of all were the big spenders who lavished tips on doormen, waiters, cabbies, and newsies. The children went out of their way to encourage the practice. Scott Nearing, at the time Secretary of the Pennsylvania Child Labor Committee, was particularly bothered by the boys' shameless behavior in embarrassing tips out of customers who could not afford them. "A bashful young man, taking his best girl to the theater for the first time, is particularly 'easy,' and the newsboys 'spot' him at once and are sure that if they do not sell a paper, they will at least get a nickel for their pains."

Though most newsies could not have resisted teasing a tip out of a "bashful young man," they were on the lookout for bigger game. Harry Bremer, who made several outings to Time Square in his capacity as special investigator for the National Child Labor Committee, described in his own dispassionate prose the Saturday evening he spent "following two boys, one not more than eleven years old, and the other about thirteen," as they canvassed the area in search of fine-looking ladies and gentlemen with change in their pockets. Bremer trailed after the boys "from the Criterion Theatre on 44th Street, through this street to the Hudson and Belasco theatres, then on to the Hippodrome, back across 42nd Street to Broadway and down to the Knickerbocker Theatre at 38th Street. By this time it was about 11:45 and the crowd had thinned, so the boys started west across 39th Street for home. At each theatre and in the crowd on 42nd Street they thrust lighted matches at cigar ends and waited for tips, and in some cases went right up to people and asked for money. One case of this kind is worthy of note. At the Hudson a middle aged gentleman was standing with two ladies. There was nothing about him to suggest any service to be rendered yet the little fellow stepped up to him, and in a few seconds I saw the man hand the boys some change, pennies and a white coin that might have been a nickel or a dime."

As the evening wore on, the children grew bolder. Taking advantage of the late hour and adult compassion for children who should have been home in bed, the newsies practiced what the reformers called the "last paper ploy." Feigning exhaustion, cold, hunger, or all three, the children begged passers-by to buy their last papers so they could go home. As Edward Clopper, reformer and author, observed, "A kindhearted person readily falls a victim to this ruse, and as soon as he has passed by, the newsboys draws another copy from his hidden supply and repeats his importuning."

In Chicago, Else Wertheim, special officer of the Juvenile Protective Association, found a pair of brothers working this hustle. "Johnnie [seven years old] accosted the passer-by with his 'last paper,' while Harry [thirteen] concealed himself in a doorway with all the rest of their stock, and pocketed the money as soon as the customer's back was turned." On his Saturday night tour of Times Square, Harry Bremer saw the trick worked to perfection. "In front of the Republic Theatre on West 42nd Street, I saw three boys between the ages of eleven and thirteen. One had two papers, another had one, and the third had none. I bought the paper from the boy who had only one and in answer to my question he said he would now go home. . . . A half hour later, at 11:15 P.M. I returned to this spot and mixed with the crowd leaving the theatre. As I had anticipated the three boys were on the job dodging in and out of the crowd looking for opportunities to do something that would procure tips. The boy from whom I had bought the last paper, and who said he would go home, had procured another 'last' paper."

The newsies were shameless when it came to soliciting sales and tips. Far from home and family, farther yet from school and teachers, they accepted the ethics of the street huckster as their own. If a bit of chicanery, an ounce of deception, a little playacting brought more sales, so be it. "Let the Buyer Beware." They, the sellers, were doing nothing illegal. They were merely performing for their public, extending and enlarging the truth like the headlines they shouted through the streets, cultivating an image like the ads in the papers they hawked. Why not, if it would add to their earnings, accentuate their poverty? Why not parade the fact that they were cold and poorly clad and in need of the change their customers carried in their pockets? Why not put on a show?

Such business practices, though not illegal, were roundly condemned by the reformers, who urged the public not to leave tips or buy "last papers." Adults who rewarded child duplicity, they suggested, were being taken for fools and, along the way, contributing to the delinquency of minors.

It is easy to ridicule the reformers for their fears. Twelve-year-old newsies who pulled the "last paper ploy" were not in training for careers as pickpockets and hoodlums. They were, however, as the reformers understood, being swiftly corrupted by their success. The children were learning that there was no such thing as morality in the marketplace. Whatever sold goods and elicited tips was fine with them. They had absorbed the very worst lessons the business world had to offer: how to cheat, lie, and swindle customers. Eleven- to fifteen-year-olds who should have been getting their moral instruction from school, church, and, if they were fortunate, home, were growing up on the streets with the morals and values of sideshow barkers and snake oil salesmen.

The reformers broadcast their fears—and their warnings—in public meetings, pamphlets, and scores of press releases reprinted in the daily papers. Adults who should have known better ignored their pleas. They were not fooled by the child "hams" who wept for their tips. Most of them probably had a good idea what was going on, but continued, nonetheless, to buy papers and leave tips.

The more prosperous Americans, on their way home from business or pleasure, saw what they wanted to see in the city left behind. The children of the street were not, to their eyes, the exploited, deprived children the reformers had described, but a band of little merchants selling their wares. Some were dirty, some ragged; some scowled, some whimpered; but they were all on the streets for a noble cause: to make money for their families—and themselves. Here were scores of children who had adopted the American credo, who believed in hard work, hustle, and long hours, who were on their way up the ladder to success. With the help of kindly benefactors who bought their goods and left tips, these children would raise themselves from poverty to prosperity.

The children offered their customers an image of themselves that was but partially false. Their customers grabbed at it. They saw before them not simply a small army of children working hard for their pennies, but a flesh-and-blood enactment of the quintessential American morality play, a real-life Horatio Alger story on every street corner—Ragged Dick, Mark the Match Boy, Nelson the Newsboy, and Paul the Peddler, rough and ready, frank and fearless, struggling upward, bound to rise in a new world.

The image was a reassuring one to those concerned with the picture of urban crime and destitution presented by spectacle-seeking newspapers and muckraking magazines. The turn-of-the-century city was a city divided by class and geography. Only the chroniclers of life "for the other half"and the street trading children bridged the two metropolitan worlds. The reformers and journalists painted lurid pictures of the working-class, immigrant city while the children reached out across the boundaries of class and ethnicity with their papers, shoeshine boxes, and candy bars.

While the reformers watched—with anger and alarm—the children and their customers cemented a symbiotic relationship. Each gave the other what was needed: the children got their tips, and their customers the reassurance that this remained the land of opportunity, if not for the poor and downtrodden, then at least for their hardworking children.

Ricardo Flores Magon, publisher of
a newspaper in Los Angeles which supported
the Mexican Revolution of 1910

The "Brown Scare"

RICARDO ROMO

Americans of Mexican ancestry occupy a unique place in our ethnic history. Unlike blacks and American Indians, the first Mexicans were neither brought here in chains nor conquered in battle—they became Americans by treaty. After the Mexican War (1846–48), the Treaty of Guadalupe Hidalgo transferred thousands of Mexicans and Indians from Mexican sovereignty to United States jurisdiction. The treaty provided protection of their rights and claims, but, as is often the case, they found themselves deprived of land and resources promised to them by the Anglo population.

As the southwestern territories of the United States began to prepare themselves for statehood, the citizens of Mexican ancestry stood at a distinct disadvantage. They maintained three characteristics that automatically made them subject to discriminatory action by society: many were of mixed "racial" ancestry (Spanish and Indian), they were not considered white, and they were overwhelmingly Roman Catholic. These features of the population delayed the acceptance of New Mexico as a state for fifty years.

As the settlement of the Southwest and Far West increased, so did the need for unskilled labor, both in agriculture and in construction. The northern states of Mexico supplied the primary source of labor that was not available domestically. Immigrants flowed north across the border to fill the demand for labor. They worked in the expanding agricultural economy in Texas and California, toiled in the mines of the West, labored in railroad construction, migrated into the sugar-beet fields of Colorado and Idaho, and became workers in the expanding factory cities of the upper Midwest. Their traditional life-style and apparent acceptance of oppressive working conditions revealed that Mexican immigrants were an ideal source of labor for the rapidly growing economy of the West.

After the upheavals of revolution in Mexico, (a topic to be dealt with in the following selection), migration to the United States increased significantly, and more of the immigrants sought permanent residence. Much of the work they found was temporary and low paying. Many joined the stream if migratory farm workers—a situation that left them deprived of any opportunity to become economically stable or politically influential. At the same time, many others found themselves among the ranks of the urban poor, segregated from others by living on the edges of Southwest and West Coast cities; the largest urban settlement being East Los Angeles. There they met with widespread social, economic, and political discrimination.

The selection from Romo's study reprinted here discusses the strained affairs of the East Los Angeles *barrio* (neighborhood) during the Mexican Revolution and First World War. Close ties between left-wing Mexican revolutionaries in Mexico and residents of the *barrio* led the American authorities to fear the spread of the revolution north of the border. Subsequently, the possible threat of a German-Mexican alliance brought about increased government surveillance and repression within the Mexican-American community.

East Los Angeles proved to be resilient, however, and survived the "brown scare" of the early 1900s. It continued to grow and by the 1980s contained more than a million Mexican-Americans who have worked to make their community a center of political and cultural activity.

A ccelerating urbanization and industrialization in Los Angeles after 1910 brought a change in the city's social and demographic base. The vast numbers of Mexican migrants settling in the city during the period 1910–1920 contrasted with the region's traditional patterns of immigration. Prior to 1900 most immigrants to California had originated in Northern Europe, especially England, Ireland, Scandinavia, and Germany. After 1910 the majority of the newcomers to the Golden State came from Mexico and the southern regions of Europe. The influx of people from other parts of the United States as well as the increasing foreign immigration accounted for Los Angeles' rapid population growth.

These factors, along with other social conditions during the 1910s—an economic depression, the transition from a commerce and trade economy to one of industry and manufacturing, a large influx of alien population, mainly Mexican, which crowded old communities and established prominent ethnic enclaves, Mexican-U.S. border conflict, labor turmoil, and war-related hysteria—produced a situation which promoted strong nativist sentiments. Nationally, the years 1910–1921 witnessed the rise of radical labor movements and of extremist organizations espousing racial hatred; the passage of immigration quota laws based on race and nationality; and political repression.

Some scholars consider nativism a social movement whose occurrence and timing are closely related to the level of disillusionment among the majority of the population. Under these circumstances, its principal aim has been "to purge the society of unwanted aliens, or cultural elements of foreign origins, or of both." Other scholars see nativism as simply an ideology which propagandists have manipulated in order to serve their own purposes. In either case, nativists place the blame for the major ills of society on an alien or external group. When nativist sentiment surfaces, it becomes a crusade against foreigners, and usually results in increased political repression of a minority. In periods of social crisis or increased individual stress, nativism translates into "a zeal to destroy the enemies of a distinctively American way of life."

California's unique blend of nativism, which surfaced periodically during the latter half of the nineteenth century, touched the lives of Mexican residents of southern California during the early twentieth century. Californians, mostly recent arrivals themselves, expressed a deep xenophobia, which surfaced in the racial nativism of the Gold Rush era and later in the demands for anti-Chinese laws during the 1870s and 1880s. An anti-Mexican nativist crusade, unrelated to the anti-Asian campaign and directed against Mexican aliens and radicals, began early and developed peculiar dimensions on the West Coast. Among other things, during World War I Mexicans were alleged to stand on the verge of a revolution which would reclaim the entire American Southwest for Mexico. An understanding of the causes and meaning of this phenomenon in Los Angeles must take into consideration three principal factors: the fear of radicalism—political and labor-related—associated with Mexican immigration; anxiety over the spread of the Mexican Revolution and apprehension of revolution by Mexican-Americans in the Southwest; and the suspected collaboration between Mexicans—in and out of the United States—with Germany, especially during the war years.

At the national level, attempts to restrict Japanese immigration in 1905–1907, passage of the Alien Land Law in 1913, and a call for more stringent deportation and exclusionary laws figured prominently in California nativism. Additionally, during the 1910s Californians, influenced by sentiments held more generally in the United States, began to associate aliens with radicalism. Political repression of labor leaders and radicals demonstrated in police action against the Industrial Workers of the World (IWW) and socialists in California during the years 1910–1921 involved elements of hysteria and violence unknown in the Golden State since the anti-Chinese movement of the mid-1870s. In California, and in Los Angeles in particular, what has for many historians of the Southwest been seen as a transitional period—a lull before the stormy era of the Red Scare—actually constituted a crucial era for repression of aliens and radicals. During the period 1913–1918, a Brown Scare hysteria fully as great as that aimed at Communists and other radicals elsewhere, was directed at Mexicans living in Los Angeles.

As the industrial sectors in Los Angeles underwent rapid expansion and far-reaching adjustments, frequent unemployment and violent labor disputes erupted. A notable example of unrest occurred in 1911, when a mysterious explosion rocked the *Los Angeles Times* building. The *Times* had been a stinging critic of organized labor in the city, and *Times* editorials encouraged a widely accepted assumption that labor supporters had been behind this reprehensible deed. Under strange and still unexplained circumstances, two radical labor leaders took responsibility for the bombing. This violence precipitated an enormous labor setback, for over the next three years manufacturers won a prolonged battle for an open shop city. In efforts to reduce the influence of organized labor, southern California industrialists stepped up recruitment of Mexican labor. Nativists, however, attempted to stem the flow of immigration from Mexico, claiming that Mexicans were unassimilable and likely to ignite new labor conflict. Although at times the two groups undermined one another's objectives, over the years 1914–1918, Mexicans in Los Angeles became the principal scapegoats, along with alleged labor "agitators," for economic and social dislocation.

During this industrial transition, nativists paid close attention to U.S. international affairs. When the United States entered World War I, the fear of German intrigue in Mexico and in the Mexican communities of the United States surfaced as an additional "threat" to the safety of U.S. citizens. It was an era, as one historian has noted, when individuals groped "for national unity, alarmed at unheeded or widening rifts of class, or race, or ideology." Nativist leaders, especially politicians, called for immigration restrictions and U.S. military intervention in Mexican affairs.

Increased Mexican immigration did not escape the attention of nativists. This immigration came on the heels of political confrontation over Japanese immigration. The movement of Mexicans into Los Angeles, moreover, occurred during a period of intense rural-to-urban migration. In southern California, Mexican laborers filled a labor vacuum created in numerous agricultural communities by the restriction of Asian workers.

During the depression of 1913–1914, California nativists found immigrants a prime economic scapegoat. Jobs which had been considered menial or unworthy a year earlier attracted hundreds of Anglo applicants at this time. Immigration restriction had broader implications than merely jobs, as nativists raised the spectres of disease, illiteracy, and high welfare costs as the main weapons to influence public opinion. They often referred to the "learned opinions" of academic researchers to bolster their case. Samuel Bryan of Stanford University, for example, wrote in 1912, "Socially and politically the presence of large numbers of Mexicans in this country gives rise to serious problems." Bryan visited the Mexican community of Los Angeles and concluded that the Mexican quarters had become "the breeding ground" for "disease and crime." He summarized his findings in this manner: "Their low standards of living and of morals, their illiteracy, their utter lack of proper political interest, the retarding effect of their employment upon the wage scale of the more progressive races, and finally their tendency to colonize in urban centers, with evil results, combine to stamp them as a rather undesirable class of residents."

To nativists, the influx of Mexican refugees represented a serious problem. In a story of the ordeal of several hundred refugees from the Mexican Revolution who had crossed over to the U.S. side of the border under great duress, the *Los Angeles Times* warned that providing care for the "uninvited guests" would prove very costly, as officials of the State and War departments "cast about for means to defray the expense of maintaining these thousands of strangers." Chiding those who failed to seek federal assistance, the *Times* speculated that Los Angeles officials were reluctant to go to Congress for funds for fear that such an action might "precipitate an undesirable Congressional discussion on the whole Mexican problem."

Politically active refugees caused even more alarm. White Angelenos initially gained awareness of Mexican radical activity in their city through the presence of the PLM (Partido Liberal Mexicano or Mexican Liberal Party), whose exiled members established a headquarters in Los Angeles in 1907. Originally dedicated to the overthrow of the Díaz dictatorship, PLM members during the revolutionary decade worked toward social and political reform in Mexico. Indeed, during the period 1907–1911, the PLM, headed by Ricardo Flores Magón, was the most active anti-Díaz organization operating within Mexico and the United States. Flores Magón and others proposed the creation of secret PLM cells inside Mexico in order to gain the financial backing of oppositionist newspapers and impoverished or persecuted liberals inside Mexico.

Soon after arriving in Los Angeles, the Magonistas began publication of *Revolución*, a bilingual newspaper which called for political and social reform in Mexico. In political rallies hosted by the Socialist Party of Los Angeles, Flores Magón asked his Mexican compatriots to return to Mexico to overthrow Díaz. From Los Angeles, PLM leaders laid plans for the first offensive against the Díaz dictatorship. The PLM sensed that the Díaz regime was in political trouble and in 1907 called for a revolution in September 16. As PLM members in Mexico and Los Angeles worked to finalize their plans, private detectives arrested several PLM leaders. Not bothering to secure an arrest warrant, the detectives broke into their East Los Angeles headquarters and took three members of the Junta to the city jail. The police charged the PLM members with being fugitives from justice. Flores Magón spent nearly two years in the Los Angeles County jail while his lawyer, Job Harriman, fought extradition efforts by the Mexican government.

In 1911 the Magonistas once again attempted to influence the course of Mexico's political destiny from their haven in Los Angeles. The PLM political activities at the onset of the Mexican Revolution, especially the Socialist invasion of Baja California in 1911, captured local headlines in Los Angeles for nearly half a year. Angelenos learned that the PLM had joined forces with a small army of IWW and Socialist Party members to launch an attack on the principal cities of Baja California. The Mexican Embassy warned the U.S. State Department that press reports in Los Angeles placed IWW leader Simon Berthold in Los Angeles in February 1911, "recruiting adventurers" for forays into Ensenada and Mexicali in Baja California. The Mexican consul in Los Angeles informed the Mexican Secretary of Foreign Affairs two weeks later (March 9, 1911) that Flores Magón was providing arms to the rebels in Baja California and that he possessed at the time at least three cases of arms and munitions.

Once the Socialist rebel army had crossed the border into Baja California, Mexican authorities stepped up efforts to put Flores Magón out of action. Antonio Lozano, the Mexican consul in Los Angeles, obtained the services of a private detective, Fred F.Rico, to whom he assigned the duties of "secret service spy." Following a trip to the border region by Rico, the Mexican consul submitted a report to the Mexican Foreign Affairs Office which clearly implicated Flores Magón as the leader of the Baja California invasion. Lozano advised the ambassador that the "villainous conduct of Ricardo Flores Magón, the 'pseudo-socialist,' had finally managed to awaken the just rage of Mexicans" in his consulate jurisdiction.

Flores Magón did not personally join the rebel forces in Baja California. Instead he remained in Los Angeles in an effort to collect funds and arms. He also prepared a manifesto, published in English and Spanish, which described his ideological stance. In it he acknowledged the role of the PLM in "actual insurrection" in Mexico "with the deliberate and firm purpose of expropriating the land and the means of production and handing them over to the people." Criticizing President Taft for sending twenty thousand soldiers to the Mexican border, the PLM Junta asked that workers awake from their lethargy, calling for "Individual agitation of the class-conscious workers; collective agitation of labor organization and or groups organizing for liberal propaganda: Systematic agitation of the labor press and of free thought; agitation in the street, in the theatre, in the street cars, in meetings . . . in every place where you can find ears disposed to listen, consciences capable of indignation, hearts which are not calloused by injustice."

By 1914, Flores Magón had become one of the principal political organizers in the Mexican communities of southern California. At a Fourth of July gathering he spoke about class divisions and racial injustice in the United States: "Don't you know how many times a Mexican laborer has received a bullet in the middle of his chest when he has gone to pick up his paycheck from a North American boss?" Flores Magón spoke of various incidents of racial nativism directed at the Mexican worker. As Mexicanos, he stated, "You well should know that in this country we are worth nothing!" Reminding the audience of the burning at the stake of Antonio Rodríguez in Rock Springs, Texas, he asked if they had not heard that in Texas and other states it was "prohibited for Mexicans to ride in the train sections of men of white skin. Jim Crow Laws also denied Mexicans admittance to eating places, hotels, barber shops and public beaches."

Finally Flores Magón spoke about the extraordinarily high number of Mexicans sentenced to death. He warned that if the authorities took steps to hang any more Mexicans, "we, the workers, shall put our hands at the throat of the *burgueses*! Now or never! The opportunity presents itself to stop this series of infamous acts that are committed in this country against the people of our race for the only reason that we are Mexican and poor." Flores Magón's passionate orations accurately depicted conditions for most Mexicans in the United States.

Shortly after Flores Magón had given these speeches, a federal grand jury in Los Angeles convened to hear testimony regarding his activities and those of other PLM leaders. They were especially interested in the role of the Magonistas in the capture of Tijuana the previous summer. The grand jury returned indictments against the PLM members, and they were ordered to stand trial for violations of neutrality laws. The court sought to prove that the PLM had conspired to enlist men at their Los Angeles headquarters for the purpose of overthrowing the Mexican government. After a long and boisterous trial in which Magonistas and their supporters packed the courtroom on a daily basis to hear the testimony, the all-White jury found the defendants guilty as charged. Flores Magón was delcared guilty on four counts of the charges and sentenced to twenty-three months at the McNeil Island federal prison in Washington.

Mexicans who had moved north across the border and settled in communities like Los Angeles made every effort to keep up with political affairs in their former homeland. Many aspired to assist relatives and friends left behind. They organized community fund drives and collected food and medical supplies for the victims of the Revolution across the border. Former supporters of Díaz, as well as his opponents and followers of other political persuasions, active and passive, resided alongside each other in Los Angeles; bickering among them was not uncommon.

In the years following the outbreak of the Mexican Revolution, most rebel forces maintained some contact with border communities north of the Río Grande. Americans suspected that the revolutionaries depended on the United States for arms and other war supplies. Indeed Francisco (Pancho) Villa sold confiscated herds of cattle to ranchers in South Texas and maintained banking accounts in several U.S. border towns. Provisional President Venustiano Carranza frequented U.S. border cities for the purpose of buying arms and munitions. An arms embargo imposed by President Wilson eventually contributed to the fall of Victoriano Huerta, the successor to Francisco Madero. A sharp limitation on arms sales to Villistas in 1915 caused in part one of Villa's first military setbacks. The constant presence of rebel forces along the international line and reports of battles in the northern region contributed to anxiety among border state residents that the Revolution might spill over onto the American side.

Political activities of PLM members on the Mexican border and a series of articles in Los Angeles' newspapers during the fall of 1913 stirred up unrest and fears of a border invasion. On september 15, the *Los Angeles Times* reported that U.S. cavalrymen had captured several members of a band of Mexican filibusters in Texas. Authorities secured a confession from one of the leaders, Barney Cline, which revealed "the first inkling of a widespread movement to proclaim a new revolution in favor of the Flores Magón branch of Socialists who have their headquarters in Los Angeles." The article left readers unclear as to whether the revolution would occur in the United States or Mexico. Carranzistas who opposed Flores Magón increased their vigiliance in the border region as did military authorities on the U.S. side.

Although the distance from the Mexican border to Los Angeles measured 140 miles, news of border trouble greatly affected the local residents. Following the assassination of Madero, the violence in Mexico took a more pronounced course and the Los Angeles press began to give Mexico and the border region extensive coverage. The *Times* of November 9, 1913, commented on the loss of business to Los Angeles industries resulting from the rebellious activities in northern Mexico. Local lumber companies which had supplied the mining communities of Sonora and Sinaloa experienced a severe drop in sales as a result of the Revolution. Another related article appearing the same day reported that the local Carranza Junta based in Los Angeles predicted official recognition by President Wilson of the newly formed Carranza government. Reports that Carranza agent Emiliano Ocampo had circulated "in the Mexican quarters" the previous day in search of recruits for the Carranzistas received press attention.

With few exceptions *Los Angeles Times* news coverage of the Mexican Revolution prior to 1913 had been free of yellow journalism. But beginning in the fall of 1913, the *Times* joined other West Coast newspapers in using the Revolution to promote sales through an appeal to nativistic sentiments. During September, the *Times* reported the experiences of Robert Aylward, a soldier of fortune with service in the Boer War in South Africa. Aylward described the civil war in Mexico as "not war but murder" where neither side took prisoners in this "region of terror." According to Aylward, the retreating armies left their wounded behind "heaped with the dead or cremated."

The *Times* proved no more restrained in describing the Mexican situation in an editorial written on November 16, 1913. Americans living on the border could expect a terrible fate, the paper warned, for "El Paso is practically at the mercy of Villa," who could "loot it and return and entrench his army on Mexican soil" before the United States could respond with "a force adequate to cope with him." As for his rival Carranza, he was "similarly situated" with respect to the border communities of Calexico, El Centro, and San Diego in California and Yuma, Douglas, and Tucson in Arizona. Although the *Times* felt confident that a military force could drive any border invaders back to Mexico, "in the meantime, the mischief would be done; border cities and towns would be looted." The editorial ended with the observation that the Mexican people were a "desperate and despairing" lot who could be swayed "by a prospect of the rich plunder to be obtained by a combined raid upon our border cities." No doubt this type of warning heightened apprehension and increased newspaper sales as well.

The day after the *Times* editorial appeared warning of a border invasion, Los Angeles police began arresting Mexicans, and government agents stepped up their surveillance of the Mexican community. Reports surfaced that "local Carranza sympathizers" were preparing "to take advantage of a possible break between the United States and Mexico." The *Times* referred to Mexicans involved in this scheme as "reds and cholos," commenting for example that the "number of cholos" arrested for carrying concealed weapons had increased by five times. The Mexican consul did little to placate the fears of the nervous officials. Placed there by Carranza's archenemy, President Victoriano Huerta, the consul also expressed some concern over the events of that week, reporting that his office had obtained information "that numerous reds have quit work in the surrounding town and country districts" and were flocking to Los Angeles in "the expectation that something may happen."

Local authorities took the threat seriously, calling in the Justice Department to assist them in the search for revolutionaries. Police officers searched the Santa Monica hills for reported "hidden munitions of war" while "other secret agents" watched suspected leaders of the movement in the city. The *Times*, which had warned two days earlier that rebels were anxious to "plunder" the border towns, again reported that the situation was "due to the efforts of several revolutionaries who spread the news around that there might be a chance to plunder" amid "any confusion that might come from an outbreak of hostilities along the border."

Nativists expressed interest in armed intervention in Mexico two years before Villa's famous 1916 raid on Columbus, New Mexico. Nativists lauded the superiority of U.S. institutions and culture and expected President Wilson to handle the Mexican situation much as McKinley had dealt with Cuba in 1898. West Coast nativists received much of their support from business owners who wished to see their investments safeguarded. Within the Republican Party, nationalist elements argued that only armed intervention by the United States could restore peace and order. U.S. intervention came in April 1914 with the so-called Tampico Incident and the American occupation of Veracruz, Mexico's major port. In the occupation of Veracruz, nineteen Americans lost their lives and there were seventy-one reported injuries. The Mexicans lost nearly two hundred men and at least three hundred were reported wounded, many of them civilians caught in the crossfire.

Angelenos gathered their impressions of Mexicans from the local press, which in 1914 gave extensive coverage to the Revolution. For instance, in the weeks following the Veracruz incident, journalist Arthur Dunn of *Sunset* magazine (published in Los Angeles) traveled to the west coast of Mexico to investigate the situation there. He began his story with this statement: "It was war in red Mexico." Angelenos curious about the Revolution could learn from Dunn's article that "It is easier to steal and kill if need be, than to work and develop the land." He estimated that half of Mexico was hostile to the United States, "receiving its inspiration from Mexico City and such red governors as he who sits at Colima [a principal state on the west coast]."

The *Los Angeles Times*, which eventually became the leading western advocate of U.S. intervention in Mexico, had demonstrated a measured degree of restraint in earlier years. During the Díaz era, *Times* owner Harrison Gray Otis also served as president of a Los Angeles company which controlled 850,000 acres of land in Mexico. In 1908, Mexico had given Otis an additional 200,000 acres of public land in the Mexican extension of the Imperial Valley. William Randolph Hearst, owner of the *Los Angeles Examiner*, also had land interests in Mexico. They included a cattle ranch in Chihuahua, which up to 1916 had not been broken up by the Mexican revolutionaries. While many western newspapers called for the United States to play a more active role in Mexico, *Times* editorials remained remarkably subdued. On January 11, 1914, for instance, the editors buried the remarks of Benjamin Ide Wheeler, president of the University of California, concerning the Mexican situation. Upon his return from seven months abroad, Wheeler stated that European nations favored U.S. intervention in Mexico. "The foreign powers would be only too glad to have this nation straighten out the difficulties in Mexico." Moreover, on the occupation of Veracruz, the *Times* actually proposed an honorable "withdrawal of our forces" from that region in order to insure that "just claims for injuries to American property and life may be paid." The editors recommended that "we let Mexico alone to frame her own land laws and choose her own rulers."

When the Veracruz affair did not produce the ouster of President Huerta, the call for additional U.S. intervention grew ever louder. Critical of the Mexican government's failure to protect the lives and property of foreign residents, especially U.S. citizens, the *Independent* warned that "the time may come when a strong hand from without must be laid upon the clashing factions that peace may be restored." Reports circulated in Washington that Army and Navy officers expected intervention in Mexico to be "forced on the United States any day." Even Mexican citizens, observed the *Laredo Times*, viewed hostilities between the United States and Mexico as imminent. According to the Laredo paper, "most of the educated Mexicans here and in northern Mexico believe intervention is inevitable, whether started by the hostilities in Mexico or by the humanity of Americans." The border newspaper concluded that the exodus of Americans and Mexican citizens was evidence of the worsening of conditions within Mexico.

Much of the opposition to intervention betrayed nativistic underpinnings. In an article discussing the type of war that Mexico would wage upon the United States in the event of intervention, a journalist warned that a war with Mexico would be unwise because Mexicans would do everything in their power to repel the "gringo invaders" including devastating the country, poisoning it "with plague and pestilence," and "even sacrificing their women folk." Moreover, what would the American soldiers do with the Mexican people, "the nearly 14,000,000 who can neither read nor write, who are of the same class of beings whom Uncle Sam puts on reservations and sets soldiers to guard?"

With the heightening of war sentiments, the Justice Department joined Los Angeles authorities and the Mexican government in monitoring the political activities of PLM members. In 1914, Ricardo Flores Magón spoke at a meeting at the Italian Hall on the east side which attracted between seven hundred and one thousand people, 90 percent of whom were Mexican. One observer of the affair, William W. McEuen, identified the PLM as "an organization of radical Mexicans who are striving to arouse interest in the Mexican Revolution among the Mexicans here emphasizing the social and universal character of that Revolution." Although McEuen could not arrive at an accurate estimate of the party's membership, he conceded that it had a large following, evidenced by the fact that *Regeneración*, the PLM official organ, had a distribution of 10,500 copies. McEuen also said that while partisans of each Mexican leader could be found around the Mexican Plaza of Los Angeles, he had found "little evidence of active assistance of the Revolution by the Mexicans in the city."

Residents of the border region, already rocked by violence and racial discord, learned in the early months of 1915 of a proposed border invasion and insurrection to be led by Mexican Americans and accomplished through the aid of Blacks and Indians. Authorities in Texas uncovered the "Plan de San Diego" in February 1915. By the summer of that year, the national press had given the Plan extensive coverage. The *Chicago Tribune* referred to the possibility of a race war in the Southwest. "Mexican anarchy," the *Tribune* cautioned, "now thrusts its red hand across our border and with an insane insolence attempts to visit upon American citizens in their homes the destruction it has wreaked upon American persons and property abroad."

Angelenos learned about the Mexican plot when the press confirmed that local radical agitators led by Ricardo Flores Magón did indeed have plans for an insurrection in the Southwest. Speaking before a large audience of Mexicans in East Los Angeles on September 19, 1915, Flores Magón allegedly outlined "plans for a general uprising of the Mexican population of Southern California, the seizure and holding of the land by force of arms, following a programme of terrorization by pistol and bomb assassinations, looting and anarchistic demonstrations, together with wholesale jail deliveries." The "red programme" asserted to have been proposed by the Magonistas included the Mexican annexation of Texas and California following the anticipated outbreak of hostilities between the United States and Mexico. A reporter attending Flores Magón's address noted that the meeting attracted a large contingent of women and children as well as men. He commented that frequently the audience compelled the speakers "to stop until the united squalling was appeased by food for that purpose. Annexation was the idea."

Less than two weeks later, Flores Magón published an extensive report on the volatile situation in Texas. He challenged the accuracy of a *Los Angeles Tribune* article of September 7, 1915, which claimed that a territory the size of the state of Illinois had come under siege by rebel forces and that the population had been "overtaken by fear of midnight assaults, burning of ranches and murder." Flores Magón singled out a Texas Ranger report which confirmed the killing of more than 500 Mexicanos along the Texas side of the Río Grande in the previous three weeks. "Justice not bullets is what should be given to the revolutionaries in Texas," Flores Magón proclaimed.

Recruiting and fund-raising activities of the Mexican refugees in Los Angeles increased Anglo anxieties. When burglars committed a rash of robberies in Long Beach, police blamed members of Villa's army. In a December 1915 story headlined "Villa's Men Suspected of Long Beach Crime," law enforcement officers reported that in an attempt to stop the "reign of crime" they had "rounded up" a number of Mexicans seen hanging about the city "believed to have been a part of Villa's army." Such incidents did little to quell the anxieties among Los Angeles citizens that Mexican revolutionaries were now operating north of the border. Angelenos looked upon the local Mexican population with increasing suspicion.

No doubt the political intrigue of Mexican revolutionary factions did spill over to the American side of the border. Under the Carranza government, consuls kept track of anti-Carranza factions. When followers of Villa arrived in Los Angeles in January 1916, Adolfo Carrillo, the Mexican consul, sought to undermine their fund-raising activities through petty harassment and called upon the U.S. Justice Department to investigate their activities in southern California. Carrillo warned that the Villistas gathering in Los Angeles were "not altogether here for their health, as commonly reported." Their presence might not have aroused the attention of the Justice Department had Carillo not cautioned officials that "the exiles are preparing to hatch something, using Southern California as an incubator."

Perhaps no other external event, next to the European war, received more attention in the Los Angeles press during 1916 than the March 9 attack by five hundred Mexican raiders on the border town of Columbus, New Mexico. Although the claim was never decisively proven, observers placed Villa at the head of the raiders, which cost the Mexicans one hundred men and left seventeen Americans dead. National reaction to Villa's raid was almost unanimous in favor of a firm stance.

In Los Angeles, the public expressed rage and alarm at Villa's border raid. Acting on the theory that Villistas had plotted some type of "outbreak," police ordered an extension and reinforcement of a cordon thrown around the Mexican quarters. Four days after the Villista raid, police arrested three Mexican "admitted anarchists" on the charges of carrying concealed weapons. Police officers also arrested W. V. Nicovich, identified as a suspected anarchist, for "attempting to incite Mexicans to attack Americans." Hysteria gripped the community following an announcement by the mayor that he had received an anonymous tip from someone "on the inside" of a plot by local Villistas "to dynamite the federal building, the Courthouse, the power plants and the different newspaper buildings." Chief of Police Snively announced that precautions of a "drastic nature" would be instituted to forestall any outburst on the part of the Villistas. He then placed the following restrictions on the Mexican community: "No liquor will be sold to Mexicans showing the least sign of intoxication. No guns can be sold to

Mexicans, and all dealers who have used guns for window display have been ordered to take them from the windows and to show them to no Mexicans until the embargo is lifted."

The day following the local embargo of gun and liquor sales to Mexicans, Chief of Police Snively requested the creation of a special civilian force or militia in anticipation of a possible insurrection by Villa's supporters. Claiming to have received repeated threats from local Villistas, Snively sent out two thousand recruiting forms for what he termed "special policemen." Meanwhile, in the central Mexican community, referred to as Sonoratown, the chief tripled the patrol and warned that the force in that district might have to be further strengthened.

In light of the extraordinary circumstances, the city's leadership praised the police chief for taking such drastic precautionary steps. The *Times* reported that at least 10 percent of the thirty-five thousand Mexicans in the city were known to the police as "rabid sympathizers with the outlaw, Villa," and many others had spread sufficient inflammatory material "that agitators, given a free hand could stir up to fighting frenzy." Local editorials commended Snively for organizing the special force to keep Mexicans of the city under surveillance. The *Times* warned that "the firebrands—and they are not few—must be watched and snuffed out; the preachers of insurrection must be sequestered and confined."

Prohibition of the sale of guns and liquor to Mexicans and enlistment of special militia made Anglo Angelenos ever more uneasy about the presence of Mexicans in the city and sparked a tense period of nativism and racial discord. It seemed little wonder, therefore, that when the police discovered a "large metal ball" in front of the courthouse steps on March 18, they called in bomb experts and mounted a city-wide search for "two men believed to be Mexicans" seen fleeing the scene minutes after the object was found. Deputies had been alerted to threats of dynamiting public buildings "by Mexicans who were incensed because of the punitive expedition by the United States Army" into Mexico in pursuit of Villa. The police never charged anyone with the "crime," and later issues of the *Times* failed to mention the incident.

During the weeks following Villa's raid, Los Angeles civic leaders entertained numerous suggestions related to easing the tension in the city over Mexican affairs. Some groups favored deporting Mexican radicals, while others recommended that Mexicanos be placed in detention camps. Jim Goodheart, identified as the "famous superintendent of the Sunshine Rescue Mission of Denver," proposed the establishment of a "municipal workhouse and an isolation camp" which he felt would do much "toward solving the Mexican refugee problem." A large percentage of the seventy-five thousand Mexicans in Los Angeles County,

Goodheart stated, "are a menace to the health and morals of any community. Afflicted with loathsome and practically incurable diseases, as many of them are, they should be isolated if they cannot be deported."

Less than a month after Villa's raid, Los Angeles County supervisors adopted a resolution requesting federal action in the deportation of "cholos" (lower-working-class Mexicans) likely to become "public charges" and informing the federal authorities "of the dangers existing in further immigration of refugee Mexicans." The supervisors called the attention of the federal government to "the prevalence of disease, poverty, and immorality among these people" and requested "deportation of all undesirables of this class who have come here within the past three years." Federal authorities rejected the request, and Mexicans did not face deportation until after World War I.

During the remaining months of 1916, the campaign against Mexicans in southern California subsided somewhat as Americans gave greater attention to events in Europe. A small number of police officers, however, maintained a vigil on Mexican radicals and revolutionaries. During Cinco de Mayo celebrations in Los Angeles in 1917, the police kept the Mexican Plaza under constant surveillance after rumors circulated that Mexican agitators would make an appearance there.

The celebration, commemorating Mexico's defeat of the French forces at Puebla on May 5, 1862, brought out several thousand Mexicans to the Plaza for a three-day jubilee. Police units reported after the first day that they had "patrolled the Plaza so thoroughly that the loafing Mexicans [presumably PLM members] did not attempt to start trouble." On the second day of the festival, police officers arrested three members of the PLM as they attempted to address a crowd of nearly one thousand. Unable to post bail after their arrest, the three Mexicanos were sent to jail.

Arrest of these three leaders aroused community indignation. A week after the police arrested the "Mexican agitators," a group of Mexicanos distributed a circular calling for the community to unite in securing their release. Rather than advocating rebellion, the circular reflected concern over the safety of the Mexicanos in the city. The arrest of these community members for their political views alarmed some of the activists in the *colonia*. Warning of greater dangers if the community failed to show some unity, the circular accused the police of a "series of abuses" against Mexican laborers of the city. It cautioned that if the Mexican community did not "wish to be victims of greater misbehavior and injustice" by the "dogs who call themselves guardians of public order," it would be necessary to organize an opposition front. Failure of the community to unite might encourage "those savages" to "assassinate us without cause." The *colonia* must demonstrate, the circular concluded, that "we are not disposed to overlook in silence similar abuses" by the police.

Authorities continued to be alarmed by even the slightest political activity within the Mexican community. A few days after the United States declared war on Germany in April 1917, Los Angeles Sheriff John C. Cline noted an unusual disappearance of more than five thousand Mexican workers from the city. He declared that the majority of the workers seemed to be moving toward Baja California. He assumed that they had taken this action "in the belief that with all this preparation going on here trouble between this country and Mexico will follow." The sheriff told southland citizens not to worry, adding, "I have an army here that could lick all Mexico." While his agents reported that "Mexicans are quitting [their jobs] all over the country for no apparent reason, they are not mobilizing . . . The only trouble is the lack of labor." A *Times* investigation into the matter found "no serious organized movement against this part of the country" on the part of Mexicans. "It would be popular with the Mexicans, but they have not the weapons, the commanders, the numbers nor the means of transportation to accomplish it." Somewhat less reassuringly, however, the same investigation resolved that "agitators, mostly of their own race, have been working among the Mexicans hereabouts, urging them to return to Mexico and join her armies." Two residents of Los Angeles recently returned from Mexico proposed an explanation for the exodus of Mexican laborers. They noted that wages for miners in Arizona, Sonora, Sinaloa, and Chihuahua had gone up to $1.75 per day, while the prevailing rate for Mexican labor in and around Los Angeles was $1.25 per day. Another probable reason for the massive flight derived from the announcement that all aliens would be required to register for the U.S. draft and would also be eligible for service in the Allied armed forces. Still, rumors of insurrection and invasion continued to circulate in the Los Angeles area.

Angelenos, like the rest of the American public, had read about German influences in Mexico for several years prior to U.S. entry into World War I. The confrontation at Veracruz in 1914, when American marines and sailors prevented the German ship *Ypiranga* from delivering arms and munitions to the Huertistas, lent credence to the German-Mexican connection. The following year Americans learned of the Plan de San Diego and some American and Mexican authorities blamed it on the work of German agents in Mexico. Historians note that many border residents linked Villa's raid on Columbus, New Mexico, to a larger German plot designed to bring the United States and Mexico into confrontation. A *New York Times* article of June 23, 1916, "German Influence in Mexico," exemplified that argument. The New York newspaper considered the German motive for winning over Carranza as twofold: "Germans might want us [the United States] into war with Mexico in order to leave them a free hand with their U-boats. Moreover, such a war would limit American munition supplies to the Allies and Mexican oil to England."

As the war in Europe took on global proportions, the widespread fear that Mexicans supported German efforts against the Allies and might collaborate with German subversives intensified Anglo hysteria. American suspicion of Mexican-German collusion intensified in 1916, when President Carranza received recognition from the Kaiser and rumors floated around Washington and Mexico City that the Germans intended to establish submarine bases along Mexican shores.

The British informed President Wilson on February 25, 1917, that they had intercepted a telegram from German Foreign Secretary Arthur Zimmermann instructing the German minister in Mexico that in the event of war between the United States and Germany, he was authorized to offer Mexico an alliance. Mexico's support of the Central Powers would be rewarded with the opportunity to recover "her lost territory in New Mexico, Texas and Arizona." (There was no mention of California.) Mexico was also to invite Japan to join the alliance. As Karl M. Schmitt has explained, when the Zimmermann note came to light, Carranza refused to meet Washington's request to repudiate the German offer, but neither did he give the Germans satisfaction. While Carranza did not rebuff the Germans in a blunt manner, it also appears "that he did not entertain serious thoughts of entering into a German alliance."

Meanwhile the *Outlook* of February 21, 1917, had voiced the concern of many Americans when it reported that since the United States broke off relations with Germany, German agents had "been pouring into Mexico" and "anti-German Mexicans are fearful that the Kaiser's agents and his Mexican allies will succeed in embroiling Mexico with the United States by means of German-financed border raids." In April the *Los Angeles Times* carried a speech by Congressman Clarence B. Miller of the House Foreign Relations Committee asserting that "German reservists in the United States" had been flocking to Mexico for the purpose of aiding in the manufacture of arms and serving in the armed forces. Villa, Miller stated, "is now surrounded by a large number of German officers and the Carranza government is largely today in control of Germans."

After Wilson made the Zimmermann note public on March 1, 1917, a wave of anti-German sentiment swept through the nation and was especially strong in the border region. The press and public officials accused German agents not only of stirring up trouble in Mexico, but also of doing the same among Mexican workers in Los Angeles. The day before President Wilson read his war message to a joint session of Congress, the *Los Angeles Times* warned its readers once again of "German plots" being hatched in the Mexican community:

> If the people of Los Angeles knew what was happening on our border, they would not sleep at night. Sedition, conspiracy, and plots are in the very air. Telegraph lines are tapped, spies come and go at will. German nationals hob-nob with Mexican bandits,

Japanese agents, and renegades from this country. Code messages are relayed from place to place along the border, frequently passing through six or eight people from sender to receiver. Los Angeles is the headquarters for this vicious system, and it is there that the deals between German and Mexican representatives are frequently made.

When the United States entered the war in Europe, the supposed German plot in Mexico loomed even larger in scope. In 1917 the American press circulated reports that German officers had taken on training responsibilities for the armies of Obregón and Villa. Ironically, no two armed forces were more at odds than those of these two military leaders. Obregón, a brilliant field general under Carranza, had dealt Villa's forces crippling defeats in 1916. It seemed illogical that by aiding Villa, the Germans could gain favors with Carranza, the man considered by Mexicans at this juncture to be in command of national affairs. Villa adamantly denied the accusations to *Times* reporters, assuring the United States that his army of twenty thousand would cooperate in "ridding Mexico of the German menace." Although Obregón also denied the presence of any German influence in his army, Carranza had more problems convincing the American public of his neutral or pro-Allied position. Carranza, who controlled the oil fields and major ports of Mexico, supplied the British with the majority of their petroleum supplies. However, Mexico also supplied oil to the Germans. The *Los Angeles Times* extended the Mexican-German link, asserting in April 1917 that "German gold made in the United States" had been pouring into Mexico for the purpose of financing the work of German agents among Mexican rebels. Among other things, these "German plotters" had plans to commit acts of sabotage on the rich oil fields of Tampico and Tuxpan. The destruction of these oil fields, the *Times* suggested, would contribute to the collapse of the British mobile forces.

According to the California historian Cornelius C. Smith, Jr., the Justice Department suspected German agents in Los Angeles of recruiting Mexicanos to serve as spies and saboteurs. In his biography of Emilio Kosterlitzky, whom he described as a soldier of fortune and former *rural* (Mexican federal soldier employed in rural areas) under Díaz, Smith briefly discussed Kosterlitzky's role in the Mexican community of Los Angeles during the period of 1916–1918. The Justice Department, according to Smith, considered Los Angeles a "hotbed of German intrigue" and recruited Kosterlitzky as a secret agent. They assigned him to monitor the activities of German agents in this area and "to arrest them at the proper moment—not always an easy thing to do." The Justice Department considered the border area between Los Angeles and Tijuana and extending to Mexicali and Tecate as a region vulnerable to German agents. Smith characterized Los Angeles as a "clearinghouse for German agents working to enlist Mexicans in the war against the United States." He believed that men like Kosterlitzky successfully countered such activities.

World War I brought dislocation and instability to the United States in a manner unparalleled since the Civil War. Following the declaration of hostilities between the United States and Germany, the President in rapid succession signed into law the Selective Service Act, the Espionage Act, the Lever Food and Fuel Control Act, and the War Revenue Act. The Selective Service Act required the registration of all men between the ages of eighteen and forty-five, while the Espionage Act provided severe penalties for persons found guilty of aiding the enemy, obstructing recruiting, or causing insubordination, disloyalty, or refusal of duty in the armed services. All of these acts caused considerable confusion in the barrio of Los Angeles and other Mexican communities of the Southwest, since many of the immigrants had not been naturalized. Thousands of Mexicanos joined the armed services, but probably an equal number of them returned to Mexico rather than fight overseas. The Espionage Act, which empowered the Postmaster General to exclude from the mails newspapers, periodicals, and other publications containing materials alleged to be treasonable or seditious, gave government authorities the license of arrest and harass Mexican political refugees, labor organizers, and pacifists. The President also established a Committee on Public Information, for the purpose of uniting the American people behind the war efforts.

In 1917, the California state government took numerous steps designed to calm the fears of Californians worried about a border flare-up. In a speech to a Los Angeles audience on May 1, 1918, Governor William D. Stephens revealed that, at the recommendation of the State Council of the Defense, he would propose the creation of a State Defense Guard. This unit would be "called into existence" in the event that the National Guard had to respond to some danger "beyond the borders of the state." The State Defense Guard "might be called upon at any moment to deal swiftly and decisively with enemy plots anywhere within our state or with disturbances this side of our border line." He concluded his speech by commending the authorities in California cities that had "initiated drastic measures to suppress idleness and seditious disturbances."

The anti-German and anti-radical fear directed against Mexicanos in Los Angeles served as a pretext for neglecting the legitimate complaints of Mexican workers. Industrialists and civic leaders blamed German agents for nearly every labor problem or strike which occurred during the war. In the summer of 1917, the U.S. Department of State asked the Mexican Foreign Office to look into a letter published by a Mexican consul that advised Mexicans to remain out of the United States because "individuals, companies, and even the authorities" subjected them "to outrages and bad treatment." The American Embassy dismissed the validity of the charges, noting that the letter had been published in a "pro-German paper." The war situation forced the American public to grapple with a seemingly apparent contradiction concerning Mexican immigrants. On the one hand, industrialists and agricultural interests considered Mexican labor important to the war effort. On the other hand, nativists had built a public case against the importation of Mexican labor. At the request of southwestern employers, the State Department in 1917 asked the Congress to drop the literacy requirements for Mexican immigrants. This decision temporarily placed the government in favor of Mexican immigration. The State Department obviously regarded efforts by individuals working to lessen Mexican immigration as contrary to the national interest.

During the war years, authorities in Los Angeles labored not only to eliminate the German threat but also to counter any IWW activity among Mexican workers. When two hundred Mexicanos from the Pacific Sewer Pipe Company called a strike on September 21, 1918, law enforcement agents in Los Angeles labeled the strike "German-made." Deputy Sheriff Mauricio L. Reyes, a Mexican American member of the sheriff's department, spoke to the men in Spanish, attempting to convince them that they "had no grievance." Only after Reyes explained the strike as "the work of pro-German agitators" did the men return to work. With similar intentions, in June 1918 Egbert Adams of the Los Angeles Playground Commission had announced the inauguration of weekly programs of speakers at the Mexican Plaza for the purpose of "stamping out I.W.W.ism among the ignorant classes and [putting] Americanism in its place." At one of the programs, the Mexican Vice-Consul, Ramón S. Arriola, informed his audience "of the necessity of cooperation of the Mexican people with America."

While Angelenos were considering the alleged link between pro-German associations and IWW radicalism in the local Mexican community, public leaders were also speaking out against the substitution of Mexican labor for American labor. At the Commonwealth Club in San Francisco, one nativist argued that the Mexican "is dissipated, a trouble maker and has a large camp following that consumes far too much of the products of his labor. Worse than all this, he is an enemy to our country. He is at heart, a German sympathizer and would be at war with us today if he but dared fire the first gun." At the same session, a farmer observed that while a few farmers "favored" Mexican laborers, a Commonwealth Committee had been advised "that German propaganda in the Mexican press" had warned their laborers not to seek work in the United States. The farmer concluded that the committee believed that the Mexican government "had uttered similar warnings" to its people.

Seven days after President Wilson signed the declaration of war, he established the Committee of Public Information (CPI) to educate the American people about the nation's objectives in entering the conflict. By creating a system for voluntary press censorship, the committee assured that only stories which presented the war as a larger goal to promote democracy and freedom throughout the world reached the American public. Under the direction of George Creel, a former journalist, the CPI circulated on a weekly basis some twenty thousand columns of newspaper material dealing with the war.

L. N. Brunswig, a Los Angeles CPI member, personally called on U.S. Secretary of the Interior Franklin K. Lane to ask for his assistance in combatting the "German lies . . . circulated among our Mexicans." In southern California, Brunswig warned Lane, "the government has positive information that Germans attempted to interfere with food crops," and that they "especially tampered" with Mexican labor in the bean and beet fields of the lower counties of California. He suggested that the German agents sought to convince the Mexicans not to raise any more food by arguing that they would only "prolong the war." Brunswig also commented that Spanish-language newspapers would be given "the closest supervision and censorship." Though there was little evidence to support the claims linking the IWW to German national interest, nativists and employer groups effectively utilized patriotic themes to condemn and repress the local labor movement.

The CPI translated stories of war events into several foreign languages in order to reach communities it considered susceptible to German propaganda. Throughout this period of hysteria and accusations of German conspiracies, the largest Spanish-language newspaper in the United States, *La Prensa de Los Angeles*, printed Creel's propaganda and strongly supported the American cause in Europe. In June 1918, *La Prensa* reported action on the battle front in the following partisan manner: "The most horrible killing that has ever been registered in the history of the World accompanies the new offensive of the Huns." In April 1918, in a front-page article headlined "German Spies Conspire against Mexico," *La Prensa* had accused Germany of making substantial efforts to start a war between Mexico and the United States.

The debate concerning Mexico's loyalty to the Allies and suspected cooperation with Germany did not die with the Armistice. Senator Albert Fall opened his Senate "Investigations of Mexican Affairs" in late 1919, and his committee explained the major political events in Mexico during the previous ten years. The *Los Angeles Times* reported the hearings in a manner highly critical of Mexican leaders. For instance, on November 3, 1919, the *Times* published an article alleging a clandestine relationship between President Carranza and Germany: "Carranza's protestations are shown as lies. Alliance with Teutons is shown by letter." Press reports in Los Angeles also claimed that Carranza had allowed Germans to hold official government positions and permitted them to operate wireless stations in Mexico. On November 30, 1919, the *Times* published the full text of the "Plan of San Diego," claiming that it had been definitely linked to the Carranza government.

In the months following the Armistice, nationwide, Americans redirected their anti-German hysteria to political radicalism. Stanley Coben has argued that "opposition to the war by radical groups helped smooth the transition among American nativists from hatred of everything German to fear of radical revolution." During the fall of 1919 and spring of 1920, the nation experienced a "Red Scare" of unprecedented proportions. This hysteria, directed mainly at "radicals and aliens," had characteristics of the "Brown Scare" that swept through Los Angeles over the period 1913–1918.

By the beginning of the 1920s, the Los Angeles *colonia* had felt the impact of nativism, anti-radicalism, and war hysteria. Moreover, nativists in Los Angeles held Mexicanos and other radicals responsible for the rise in irresponsible acts and labor violence. Viewed with fear and contempt by those holding social and political power, physically segregated in housing and in social life, Mexicanos attempted to accommodate to the reality of Los Angeles and face the daily challenge of providing a decent existence for themselves and their families.

The moving assembly line at the Ford Motor Company

Fordization: An Idol and Its Ironies

JAMES J. FLINK

The development of the automobile and the availability of automobile ownership throughout the United States has had a major impact on American life in the twentieth century. Although the gasoline-powered vehicle appeared at the same time in Europe, it remained a luxury item there until after the Second World War. In the United States, however, inexpensive cars were being produced in large quantities before 1910 in order to fill the market demand.

One of the prime industrial movers in the dispersal of automobile ownership was Henry Ford, whose Model T has claimed a deservedly unique space in automobile folklore. As was the case with his fabled car, Ford himself took on mythic qualities as the quintessential entrepreneur and industrial innovator. James J. Flink, of the University of California at Irvine, dissects the Ford legend in the selection printed below. He indicates how Henry Ford himself worked to enhance his reputation by claiming individual credit for innovations actually developed by others. This selection explores the genuine contributions of the Ford Motor Company to the automobile industry and the subsequent collapse of the Ford mystique.

Regardless of the ambiguous place of Henry Ford in the history of capitalism, the automobile itself became the linchpin of American industry. As early as 1905, there were 121 automobile manufacturing centers. By 1921, there were 2,471, and the automobile industry was the single largest consumer of sheet steel, zinc, lead, rubber, and leather. Apart from the consumption of basic materials, the industry's impact on the national economy can be seen in other ways. By 1960, its payroll was as large as the national income was in 1890. One-tenth of consumer spending was on automotive products. According to one scholar, at least one out of seven jobs and one out of six businesses in the United States owed their existence either directly or indirectly to the automobile.

In terms of social and cultural impact, the following illustrations suggest the dimensions of the automobile craze. The average American family prizes its car second only to its home (and with the current decline in home ownership, the car value rises). The development of the automobile drastically changed the patterns of urban development, allowing satellite suburbs to supplant central cities as areas of life and work, therefore contributing to serious urban blight. Mass transit systems were allowed to decay as people moved between jobs and homes in their cars. Social habits were transformed, sexual mores changed, vacation patterns altered—all as a result of Americans spending more and more of their time in automobiles.

Both the personal and economic importance of the automobile has been proven in recent years by the occasional gasoline shortages and the negative impact foreign compact cars have on the American automobile industry. With regard to the folk mythology of capitalism, Chrysler Corporation chairman Lee Iacocca has begun to take on some of the mythic qualities earlier bestowed on Henry Ford. In the light of this development, we should look carefully at the following analysis of the Ford mystique.

No synthesis of American automobility would be complete without an interpretation of Henry Ford and the Ford Motor Company. Yet anyone compelled to write still more about Ford must reckon with Reynold M. Wik's assessment that more has already been written about the subject than any individual could read in a single lifetime. The facts are well known. Most interpretive possibilities have been attempted by one or another Ford admirer, debunker, or apologist.

An adequate interpretation of Henry Ford is difficult not only because one finds many ironic contradictions in his statements and behavior over his lifetime but even more because Ford became a symbol for the differing aspirations of many audiences. Ford the symbol was based on heroic myths that Ford the man unfortunately encouraged and deluded himself into believing. Consequently, most of Ford's many biographers have taken the position that he defies interpretation from any single point of view or consistent set of assumptions. The recent attempt of Anne Jardim, in *The First Henry Ford: A Study in Personality and Business Leadership* (Cambridge, Mass.: M.I.T. Press, 1970), to simplify Ford through a psychoanalytic interpretation must certainly be counted a failure. Yet no one has managed to get a comprehensive handle on the man through more conventional modes of analysis.

Every generation must reinterpret the American past from the perspective of its own values and problems. And this chapter attempts to

FORDIZATION: AN IDOL AND ITS IRONIES from *The Car Culture* by James J. Flink. MIT Press, 1975. Reprinted by permission.

interpret Henry Ford from the long-range perspective of the disillusioning 1970s. The interepretation inevitably is critical; even more than the mass personal automobility that Ford symbolized, the tenets of entrepreneurial capitalism and the gospel of industrial efficiency that Ford exemplified are increasingly less credible and acceptable social philosophies. Although the interpretation takes a few new twists, the factual information on which it is based will be familiar to anyone steeped in the standard sources on Henry Ford and the Ford Motor Company. Unless otherwise noted, the narrative relies upon the exhaustive three-volume study undertaken by Allan Nevins, in collaboration with Frank E. Hill: *Ford: The Times, the Man, the Company, 1865–1915; Ford: Expansion and Challenge, 1915–1933;* and *Ford: Decline and Rebirth, 1933–1962* (New York: Charles Scribner's Sons, 1954, 1957, 1963).

By May 27, 1927, when the last of over 15 million Model Ts rolled off the assembly line, a new Model T cost as little as $290 and mass automobility had become a reality. The Fordson farm tractor, introduced during World War I, promised to remove the last drudgery from farm labor and initiate a new era of agricultural abundance. The introduction of the moving-belt assembly line and the five-dollar, eight-hour day at Ford's Highland Park plant in 1913–1914, in the words of Allan Nevins and Frank E. Hill, "inaugurated a new epoch in industrial society. . . . Mass production furnished the lever and fulcrum which now shifted the globe." Roderick Nash aptly concludes in his study of American culture from 1917 to 1930: "It is possible to think of these years as the automobile age and Henry Ford as its czar. The flivver, along with the flask and the flapper, seemed to represent the 1920s in the minds of its people as well as its historians."

More was written about Henry Ford during his lifetime, and he was more often quoted, than any figure in American history. Theodore Roosevelt complained that Ford received more publicity than even the president of the United States. The *New York Times* reported that Ford's reputation had spread to peasants in remote villages in countries where only the elites had heard of Warren G. Harding or Calvin Coolidge. Will Rogers, probably the shrewdest folk psychologist in our history, said a number of times and in many witty ways that Henry Ford had influenced more lives than any man alive.

The people of what Wik calls "grass-roots America" thought Henry Ford a greater emancipator of the common man than Abraham Lincoln. They made Ford our first, and probably our last, millionaire folk hero. He received several thousand letters a day, ranging from simple requests for help and advice to demands that he solve America's remaining social and economic ills. The newspapers of his day called Ford the "Sage of Dearborn" and made him an oracle to the common man. But beyond this, Wik's analysis of letters to Ford "from farmers and middle-class folks . . . living in the typical small towns of mid-America" reveals "a widespread and simple faith in Ford and the fixed belief that an understanding existed between the writers and this man of immense wealth."

Henry Ford probably could have been elected president of the United States had he really wanted the office. In 1916 Ford spurned efforts to get him to head the tickets of the American party and the Prohibition party on a platform of peace and prohibition. And, even though he refused to campaign, he won the 1916 Michigan presidential preference primary of the Republican party by a comfortable margin.

President Woodrow Wilson, who was concerned about electing a Senate favorable to the establishment of a League of Nations, induced Ford to run for United States senator from Michigan on the Democratic ticket in 1918. The *New York World* reported of August 22 that "[Ford] hasn't spent a cent, paid for a banner, bought the boys any drinks and cigars, hired a press agent, made any speeches, or kissed a baby since the Democrats endorsed him in June." Michigan was a heavily Republican state; and Truman Newberry, Ford's Republican opponent, spent lavishly, and stooped to a mud-slinging campaign that questioned Ford's patriotism at the outbreak of World War I. (He was convicted in May 1919 of violating the Federal Corrupt Practices Law in the campaign.) Still Ford lost the election by the slim margin of 212,751 votes to Newberry's 217,088.

Ford-for-President clubs sprang up spontaneously across the nation in 1920–1923. In the summer of 1923, both a poll conducted by *Collier's Weekly* and the Autocaster nationwide survey found Ford far ahead of President Warren G. Harding. Probably no potential candidate in American political history has ever had such universal appeal to the voters: blue-collar workers were still impressed by the five-dollar, eight-hour day; farmers suffering from the agricultural depression of the 1920s had confidence in the creator of the Model T and the Fordson tractor; Southerners saw the regeneration of the South in automobility and in Ford's plans to build a nitrate plant at Muscle Shoals, Tennessee. Ford also appealed to middle-class Babbitts who thought that successful businessmen rather than politicians should run the government; his strong advocacy of prohibition made him popular among the drys; and in the disillusion that followed the Versailles Treaty, his early outspoken stand against the war was a plus. Everyone credited Henry Ford with giving America the low-priced, reliable car and recognized that the industry he led was the key to American prosperity.

The Ford-for-President boom was a major expression of the popular discontent of the early 1920s. It ended in October 1924, however, when Henry Ford announced that he would support President Calvin Coolidge, who had assumed office after Harding's death in 1923, if Coolidge would enforce prohibition. The evidence suggests that Ford traded his support for the president's endorsement of Ford's bid to develop Muscle Shoals, which was meeting stiff opposition in Congress. Many voters felt that America had lost her potentially greatest president. Others concluded that Ford, by withdrawing, had "chickened out, leaving us who thought we had a leader for the great Armageddon, the fight between right and wrong, between man and money, between freedom and slavery, between Christ and Satan. We now wonder if we haven't been worshipping a Tin God."

Americans idolized Henry Ford as a symbol of mass personal automobility—a phenomenon uniquely congruent with American values and social conditions. By 1927 the United States had about 80 percent of the world's motor vehicles and a ratio of 5.3 people for every motor vehicle registered. On the criterion of ratio of population to motor vehicles, outside the United States the automotive idea had spread most rapidly in other developing countries with low population densities that had also been settled by European immigrants and had experienced the frontier conditions that Frederick Jackson Turner proclaimed so central in shaping American institutions and character. In 1927 the United States was followed in ratio of population to motor vehicles by New Zealand (10.5:1), Canada (10.7:1), Australia (16:1), and Argentina (43:1). France and the United Kingdom tied for sixth place with ratios of 44:1.

Paradoxically, however, the Ford mystique was most pervasive abroad in the two nations whose totalitarian ideologies were soon to be considered antithetical to the American way of life. Neither Germany, with a ratio of 196 people per motor vehicle, nor the Union of Soviet Socialist Republics, with a ratio of 7,010:1, were likely prospects in 1927 for the development of automobile cultures embodying American ideals. For the Germans and the Russians, Henry Ford symbolized the mass-production and agricultural techniques essential for building self-sufficient national economies and becoming first-rate military powers.

Wik's examination of German newspapers "reveals an obsession with Henry Ford." *My Life and Work,* the autobiography that Ford wrote in collaboration with Samuel Crowther, became a best seller in Berlin in 1925, and the Germans referred to mass production as "Fordismus." "I am a great admirer of Ford," claimed Adolf Hitler. "I shall do my best to put his theories into practice in Germany." Hitler was most interested, of course, in building an industrial system that could mass-produce war materials. Automobility to him primarily meant panzer divisions moving swiftly over the express highways (*autobahnen*) feverishly constructed in Germany after he came to power. Nevertheless, it is interesting to note that the Volkswagen, Hitler's idea of a people's car, was predicated on the philosophy of product first exemplified by the Ford Model T—a static model offering basic transportation at low initial and operating expenses.

Even more incredible than a multimillionaire becoming a folk hero of grass-roots America, the world's most prominent entrepreneurial capitalist was idolized in Communist Russia. The Russians were fascinated with "Fordizatzia" and viewed Henry Ford not as a capitalist but as a revolutionary economic innovator. A visitor to the USSR in 1927 reported that the Russian people "ascribed a magical quality to the name of Ford" and found it incredible that "more people have heard of him than Stalin. . . . Next to Lenin, Trotsky, and Kalinin, Ford is possibly the most widely known personage in Russia." The 25,000 Fordson tractors shipped to the USSR between 1920 and 1927 promised the peasant a new agricultural era free from drudgery and want. Communes and babies born in communes were named "Fordson." Ford mass-production methods, widely copied in the USSR, promised an industrial horn of plenty. Progress in adopting them was chronicled in *Pravda,* and in workers' processions Ford's name was emblazoned on banners emblematic of a new industrial era. Translation of *My Life and Work* were widely read and used as texts in the universities. Wik claims that "people in Leningrad, Moscow, and Kiev used the word 'Fordize' as a synonym for 'Americanize.' "

The idolization of Henry Ford as a symbol of differing national aspiration reflected the universal human tendency to personify the impersonal forces of history—thus simplistically reducing the complexities of historical processes down to a dramatic parade of symbolic heroes and villains. Consequently, much of what passes for history in textbooks as well as in the popular imagination is merely the perpetuation of culturally meaningful, but misleading, myths. Henry Ford himself recognized this in the often misquoted, unwittingly sophisticated statement he made to Charles N. Wheeler, a newspaper reporter, in 1916: "History is more or less bunk."

Henry Ford's views about history were dredged up for public ridicule to prove that he was "an ignorant idealist" by Elliott G. Stevenson, attorney for the defense, in May 1919 during the trial of a million dollar libel suit that Ford had filed against the *Chicago Tribune* on September 16, 1916. Ford brought the suit against the newspaper in response to its editorial of June 23, 1916, entitled "Ford Is an Anarchist." Representing the interests of imperialistic American corporations who were eager to exploit Mexico's natural resources, the *Tribune* had lashed out at Ford's opposition to President Wilson for sending troops to repress Pancho Villa. The editorial erroneously charged that eighty-nine Ford employees called to border duty had lost their jobs, and it called Ford "not merely an ignorant idealist, but . . . an anarchist enemy of a nation which protects him in his wealth." Although Ford technically won the suit, he was insulted by being awarded only six cents in damages. He was further embittered by the ridicule that followed from the merciless cross-examination aimed at proving him unpatriotic and ignorant.

It is indisputable that Ford revealed an appalling ignorance of American history in his answers to the fact-laden questions asked by Stevenson. Yet Ford intuitively grasped some of the glaring faults of the prevailing historical synthesis. His main objections were that history was a bastion of tradition rather than a force for change and that history was a collection of esoteric facts that were irrelevant to understanding and solving contemporary problems. Ford explained to Charles N. Wheeler, for example: "That's the trouble with the world. We're living in books and history and tradition. We want to get away from that and take care of today. We've done too much looking back. What we want to do, and do it quick, is to make just history right now. The men who are responsible for the present war in Europe knew all about history. Yet they brought on the worst war in the world's history."

Beyond these very sensible objections, Henry Ford rebelled against a written history dominated by politics, wars, and the careers of great men. The history that Ford remembered was found in books that "began and ended with wars." Roger Butterfield points out that "Ford's matured concept of history as the appreciation and study of 'the general resourcefulness of our people' lives on in the vast collections and more than 100 buildings of the Henry Ford Museum-Greenfield Village-Edison Institute complex at Dearborn. This has become by far the most popular historical preserve in the United States (under nongovernmental operation). Its entertainment features are conspicuous, but its basic purpose is mass education." The idea for the museum complex was hatched by Ford on the ride back to Detroit from the *Tribune* trial at Mt. Clemens, Michigan, as a way to demonstrate his ideas about history. He announced to Ernest Liebold, his secretary, "I'm going to start up a museum and give people a true picture of the development of the country. That's the only history worth preserving, that you can preserve in itself. We're going to build a museum that's going to show industrial history, and it won't be bunk." Butterfield notes that, among the exhibits at Dearborne, "only one major activity of man was slighted— there were no weapons or mementos of war."

The concept of history represented by the Dearborn complex has the obvious grave deficiency that it is predicated on a primitive, visual historicism. The artifacts are assumed to speak for themselves, in Henry Ford's words, about "what actually happened in years gone by." Ford missed the essential point that raw historical data becomes history only when meaningfully interpreted and communicated in literate prose. But Ford did see that history lacking social relevance serves little purpose, that history must emphasize the forces and objects that most influenced the daily life of common people, and that technoeconomic variables are more significant than wars and politics in explaining the historical development of the American people.

The great disservice that Henry Ford did to written history—ironic for a man who complained to reporters as late as 1940 that history "isn't even true"—was that his extreme egocentrism deluded him into becoming the chief progenitor of a cult of personality based upon heroic myths. He lost no opportunity to claim personal credit for both the low-priced reliable car and the mass-production techniques that together revolutionized American life. He also cultivated the public image that the success of the giant Ford Motor Company was entirely due to his individual genius. A Chicago newspaper editor once aptly quipped, "One need not mention Ford—he mentions himself." Ford doted on articles about himself and religiously amassed for posterity what is probably the largest collection of personal data ever accumulated by an American businessman.

The man who most strongly opposed the preposterous claim that George B. Selden invented the gasoline automobile ironically came to fall just short of making the same claim for himself. As late as 1963 the Ford Motor Company advertised: "Henry Ford had a dream that if a rugged, simple car could be made in sufficient quantity, it would be cheap enough for the average family to buy." But the truth is that Ford's idea of "a car for the great multitude" was a generally held expectation, assumed to be inevitable from the introduction of the motor vehicle in the United States. Ransom E. Olds and Thomas B. Jeffery were the most important among several other automobile manufacturers who attempted prematurely to implement the idea while Henry Ford was still absorbed with building racing cars. The basic elements of automotive technology embodied in the Model T were invented and developed by scores of other automotive pioneers. The constituents of mass production—described by Henry Ford in the *Encyclopedia Britannica* as "the focusing upon a manufacturing project of the principles of power, accuracy, economy, system, continuity, speed, and repetition"—were all well-known aspects of an evolving American manufacturing tradition by the time they were adapted to the Model T.

Recognition that the Ford Motor Company led the industry in developing the mass-produced and, as a consequence, low-priced car should not obscure the fact that Ford's effort to increase output greatly in the 1908–1913 period was far from unique. Many of Ford's competitors attempted to cut manufacturing costs and capitalize on the insatiable demand for motorcars by working out similar solutions to their common production problems. For example, innovations to reduce the time and cost of final assembly similar to those worked out at Ford were independently conceived by Walter P. Chrysler, who replaced

Charles W. Nash as the head of Buick in 1910. Buick production was upped from 45 to 200 cars a day by changing outmoded procedures for finishing the body and chassis, which had amounted to "treating metal as if it were wood," and by installing a moving assembly line that consisted of "a pair of tracks made of two by fours" along which a chassis was moved from worker to worker by hand while being assembled. Chrysler recalled that "Henry Ford, after we developed our [assembly] line, went to work and figured out a chain conveyor; his was the first. Thereafter we all used them. Instead of pushing cars along the line by hand, they rode on an endless-chair conveyor operated by a motor."

Charles E. Sorensen, who was in charge of production at Ford, was keenly aware that the contribution of the Ford Motor Company to mass production lay almost entirely in its refinement of the integration and coordination of the process of final assembly. Sorensen knew that "Eli Whitney used interchangeable parts when making rifles in the early days of the Republic; and in the early days of this century Henry Leland . . . applied the same principles in the first Cadillac cars. Overhead conveyors were used in many industries, including our own. So was substitution of machine work for hand labor. Nor was orderly progress of the work anything new; but it was new to us at Ford until Walter Flanders showed us how to arrange our machine tools at the Mack Avenue and Piquette plants." The only significant contribution that Sorensen claimed for the Ford Motor Company was "the practice of moving the work from one worker to another until it became a complete unit, then arranging the flow of these units at the right time and the right place to a moving final assembly line from which came a finished product. Regardless of earlier uses of some of these principles, the direct line of succession of mass production and its intensification to automation stems directly from what we worked out at Ford Motor Company between 1908 and 1913."

The moving assembly line at Ford was conceived one Sunday morning in July 1908 at the Piquette Avenue plant during the last months of Model N production. The parts needed for assembling a car were laid out in sequence on the floor; a frame was next put on skids and pulled along by a towrope until the axles and wheels were put on, and then rolled along in notches until assembled. However, this first experiment to assemble a car on a moving line did not materialize into a moving-belt final assembly line at Ford until 1913 because the extensive changes in plant layout and procedures "would have indefinitely delayed Model T production and the realization of Mr. Ford's long cherished ambition which he had maintained against all opposition."

There was general agreement in the automobile industry that the sixty-acre Highland Park plant that Ford opened on January 1, 1910, to meet the huge demand for the Model T possessed an unparalleled factory arrangement for the volume production of motorcars and that its well-lighted and well-ventilated buildings were a model of advanced industrial construction. By 1914 about 15,000 machines had been installed. Company policy was to scrap machines as fast as they could be replaced with improved types, and by 1912 the tool department was constantly devising specialized new machine tools that would increase output. The elementary time and motion studies begun at the Piquette Avenue plant were continued and in 1912 led to the installation of continuous conveyor belts to bring materials to the assembly lines. Magnetos, motors, and transmissions were assembled on moving lines by the summer of 1913. After the production from these subassembly lines threatened to flood the final assembly line, a moving-chassis assembly line was installed. It reduced the time of chassis assembly from twelve and a half hours in October to two hours and forty minutes by December 30, 1913. Moving lines were quickly established for assembling the dash, the front axle, and the body. The moving lines were at first pulled by rope and windlass, but on January 14, 1914, an endless chain was installed. That was in turn replaced on February 27 by a new line built on rails set at a convenient working height and timed at six feet a minute. "Every piece of work in the shop moves," boasted Henry Ford in 1922. "It may move on hooks or overhead chains going to assembly in the exact order in which the parts are required; it may travel on a moving platform, or it may go by gravity, but the point is that there is no lifting or trucking of anything other than materials."

The mass-production techniques developed at Highland Park to meet the demand for the Model T became synonymous in the mind of the public with Henry Ford's name. These techniques were widely publicized and described in detail, most definitively by Horace L. Arnold and Fay L. Faurote. Ford's competitors in the automobile industry quickly installed moving-belt assembly lines, too. But the Ford Motor Company set the pace and direction of a new social order based on mass production and mass personal automobility until the early 1920s, when Hudson probably surpassed and other automobile manufacturers began to equal Highland Park's efficiency in production.

The evidence is unequivocal that both the Model T and the Ford mass-production methods, in Wik's words, "represented the efforts of a team of engineers, rather than the inspiration of one man, Henry Ford." C. Harold Wills, the chief engineer, and Joseph Galamb head a long list of Ford employees whose collective efforts were more significant than Henry Ford's inspiration in creating the Model T. Charles E. Sorensen, his assistant Clarence W. Avery, William C. Klann, and P. E. Martin deserve the lion's share of the credit for the moving-belt assembly line worked out at Highland Park, while the specialized machinery was designed by a staff of dozens of engineers headed by Carl Emde. "Henry Ford had no ideas on mass production," claimed Sorensen, the man best qualified to know. "Far from it; he just grew into it, like the rest of us. The essential tools and the final assembly line with its integrated feeders resulted from an organization which was continually experimenting and improvising to get better production." Nevins and Hill agree: "It is clear that the impression given in Ford's *My Life and Work* that the key ideas of mass production percolated from the top of the factory downward is erroneous; rather seminal ideas moved from the bottom upward."

The business success of the Ford Motor Company depended on the talents of many other individuals. For, as John Kenneth Galbraith says, "if there is any uncertainty as to what a businessman is, he is assuredly the things Ford was not." The marketing of the Model T was handled by Norval A. Hawkins, a sales and advertising whiz. Fred Diehl was in charge of purchasing. The Ford domestic and foreign branch plants were set up by William S. Knudsen. The man who oversaw the entire operation and provided the main business brains for the company until his resignation on October 12, 1915, was James Couzens, a minor stockholder as well as vice-president and treasurer. Sorensen called the period from 1903 to 1913 at Ford the "Couzens period. . . . Everyone in the company, including Henry Ford, acknowledged [Couzens] as the driving force during this period." "After Couzens left in 1915, Ford took full command and the company was never so successful again," Galbraith concludes. "In the years that followed, Ford was a relentless and avid self-advertiser. And he mobilized the efforts of many others to promote not the car but the man. Only the multitude remained unaware of the effort which Ford, both deliberately and instinctively, devoted to building the Ford myth. . . . He was the first and by far the most successful product of public relations in the industry.

The image of Henry Ford as a progressive industrial leader and champion of the common people that Americans clung to during the 1920s was incredibly incongruent with much of the philosophy of industry expounded by Ford himself in *My Life and Work* (1922), *Today and Tomorrow* (1926), and *My Philosophy of Industry* (1929).

Far from identifying with the Jeffersonian yeoman farmer glorified in Populist rhetoric, Henry Ford looked forward to the demise of the family farm. As a youth Ford had hated the drudgery of farm labor, and he longed to rid the world of unsanitary and inefficient horses and cows. But the Model T was conceived as "a farmer's car" less because Ford empathized with the plight of the small farmer than because any car designed for a mass market in 1908 had to meet the needs of a predominantly rural population. "The old kind of farm is dead," Ford wrote in 1926. "We might as well recognize that fact and take it as a starting point for something better." He looked forward in 1929 to the day when "large corporations . . . will supersede the individual farmer, or groups of farmers will combine to perform their work in a wholesale manner. This is the proper way to do it and the only way in which economic freedom can be won."

Henry Ford viewed the common man with a cynical, elitist paternalism, fundamentally at odds with the equalitarian Populist philosophy he supposedly represented. "We have to recognize the unevenness in human mental equipment," said Ford. "The vast majority of men want to stay put. They want to be led. They want to have everything done for them and have no responsibility." Ford admitted that the thought of repetitive labor was "terrifying to me. I could not do the same thing day in and day out, but to other minds, perhaps to the majority of minds, repetitive operations hold no terrors." He believed that "the average worker . . . wants a job in which he does not have to put forth much physical exertion—above all, he wants a job in which he does not have to think . . . for most purposes and most people, it is necessary to establish something in the way of a routine and to make most motions purely repetitive—otherwise the individual will not get enough done to live off his exertions."

A journalist asked Ford in 1923, "What about industrial democracy?" "The average employee in the average industry is not ready for participation in the management," Ford answered. "An industry, at this stage of our development, must be more or less of a friendly autocracy." This cynical, elitist paternalism pervaded the Ford Motor Company even during the early years that Ford's admirers peg as its brightest and most progressive. "All economists are agreed," Arnold and Faurote wrote in 1915, for example, "that the only reason why any one man works for another man is because the hired man does not know enough to be the director of his own labor. And, incontrovertibly, the employer being wiser than the employed, the wisdom of the employer should be applied to the benefit of the employed, to some extent at least."

Nevins and Hill credit Henry Ford with running his company "as a semi-public entity" in which workers and consumers shared the benefits of increased productivity at a time when profit maximization was the rule in American industry. But beyond the obvious point that the public had no voice in this "semi-public entity," Henry Ford's business philosophy boiled down to the simple observation that mass production would yield greater profits only if consumer purchasing power was increased sufficiently to enable people to buy what the machine produced. Ford called this the "wage motive" and claimed that "we have discovered a new motive for industry and abolished the meaningless terms 'capital,' 'labor,' and 'public.' . . . It is this thought of enlarging buying power by paying high wages and selling at low prices which is behind the prosperity of this country."

The liberal economist John R. Commons foolishly ranted in 1920 that "prosperity sharing" at Ford was "devoted to faith in human nature" and "good American citizenship" and that Ford was "positively too democratic for this world." More recently, Father R. L. Bruckberger reached such absurd conclusions as that money stood last in Ford's scale of values and that Ford was "infinitely more revolutionary than Marx, who was only an intellectual." The truth is that Henry Ford's philosophy of industry was a pedestrian variation of the conventional business creed that put profits first and foremost, glorified the entrepreneurial capitalist, and accepted as axiomatic the outmoded production ethic of the classical economists' economy of scarcity.

Henry Ford emphatically denied that higher wages and lower prices should follow from the technological progress of a people as a simple matter of social justice. He held, for example, that "it is untrue to say that profits or the benefit of inventions which bring lower costs belong to the worker. . . . Profits belong primarily to the business and the workers are only part of the business." Lower prices did not come at the expense of profits but resulted from increased industrial efficiency that permitted profit margins to be enhanced. Ford's policy was "to name a price so low as to force everybody in the place to the highest point of efficiency. The low price makes everybody dig for profits." The continual reinvestment of high profits in improved machinery to increase output to make still more profits for reinvestment was indeed what made the "wage motive" a workable proposition for Ford.

So in Ford's philosophy of industry, the key figure remained the entrepreneurial capitalist, whose supposed superior intelligence enabled him to organize production more and more efficiently through the continual reinvestment of his profits in improved machinery. It followed axiomatically for Ford that this industrial superman had the unquestionable prerogative to determine what were fair profits, wages, and prices free from any interference by the government, workers, or consumers. If the superman erred he would be punished by the classical economists' bogeymen, the invisible hand of the market and the unenforceable law of supply and demand.

Ford believed that "business must grow bigger and bigger, else we shall have insufficient supplies and high prices." In a new twist on the Doctrine of Stewardship, which had been the perennial rationalization of American men of wealth since it was conceived by the Puritans, Ford merely urged the men in charge of these industrial giants to consult their enlightened self-interest and "regard themselves as trustees of power in behalf of all the people. . . . It is clearly up to them now, as trustees, to see what they can do further in the way of making our system fool-proof, malice-proof, and greed-proof. It is a mere matter of social engineering." But in asking for a capitalism stripped of its traditional assumption that self-interest and greed were natural main-springs of human economic behavior, Ford never went on to call for capitalists free from hyprocrisy. Perhaps that would have been too much to expect from a "trustee of power in behalf of all the people" who also declared, "A great business is really too big to be human."

Although the Ford five-dollar, eight-hour day entailed recognition that mass consumption was a necessary corollary of mass production, Henry Ford nevertheless was still committed to most of the beliefs and values of a production-oriented society and economy. He did come to see that mass production made the worker "more a buyer than a seller," and that "the 'thrift' and 'economy' ideas have been overworked." But Ford abhorred waste and remained committed to the central tenet of a production-oriented society and economy—the work ethic. "Thinking men know that work is the salvation of the race, morally, physically, socially," claimed Ford. "Work does more than get us our living: it gets us our life."

Seeing the cure for poverty and want in terms of more efficient production, Ford held that "hiring two men to do the job of one is a crime against society" and that mass production, despite the great increase in output per worker, would always continue to create more jobs than it destroyed. To Ford, overproduction was a theoretical possibility that would mean "a world in which everybody has all that he wants." Ford feared that "this condition will be too long postponed." Nonetheless, he believed that, in the automobile industry, "We do not have to bother about overproduction for some years to come, provided our prices are right." Meanwhile, neither charity nor drones had any place in Henry Ford's conception of the good society and economy: "Fully to carry out the wage motive, society must be relieved of non-producers. Big business, well organized, cannot serve without repetitive work, and that sort of work instead of being a menace to society, permits the coming into production of the aged, the blind, and the halt. It takes away the terrors of old age and illness. And it makes new and better places for those whose mentality lifts them above repetitive work."

Mass production meant that neither physical strength nor the long apprenticeship required to become a competent craftsman was any longer a prerequisite for industrial employment. The creativity and experience on the job that had been valued in the craftsman were considered liabilities in the assembly-line worker. "As to machinists, old-time, all-around men, perish the thought!" reported Arnold and Faurote. "The Ford Company has no use for experience, in the working ranks, anyway. It desires and prefers machine-tool operators who have nothing to unlearn, who have no theories of correct surface speeds for metal finishing, and will simply do what they are told to do, over and over again from bell-time to bell-time. The Ford help need not even be able bodied."

Mass production had two clear benefits from the point of view of the worker. One was that the resulting higher wages and lower prices raised the worker's standard of living appreciably. The other was that new opportunities for remunerative industrial employment were opened to the immigrant, the Black migrant to the northern city, the physically handicapped, and the educable mentally retarded. For the machine did not discriminate and did not demand substantial training, physical strength, education, or intelligence from its operator. Except for the outspokenly anti-Semitic articles published in his *Dearborn Independent,* for which Ford publicly apologized in 1927, no employer was more immune than Henry Ford from the prevailing ethnic, racial, and social prejudices of his day. "Our employment office does not bar a man for anything he has previously done," said Ford. "He is equally acceptable whether he has been in Sing Sing or at Harvard and we do not even inquire from which place he has graduated. All that he needs is the desire to work."

By 1919 the Ford Motor Company employed hundreds of ex-convicts and 9,563 so-called "substandard men"—a group that included amputees, the blind, the deaf and dumb, epileptics, and about 1,000 tubercular employees. By 1923 Ford employed about 5,000 Blacks, more than any other large American corporation and roughly half the number employed in the entire automobile industry. As at all automobile factories, however, the bulk of the Ford labor force, probably about two-thirds, consisted of immigrants from southern and eastern Europe. The group clearly most underrepresented on the Ford assembly lines was the able-bodied, native-born Caucasian. As Nevins and Hill point out, "At the Ford plant the foundry workers, common laborers, drill press men, grinder operators, and other unskilled and semi-skilled hands were likely to be Russians, Poles, Croats, Hungarians, or Italians; only the skilled employees were American, British, or German stock."

Conditions on the assembly line repelled the worker because they were antithetical not only to basic traits of the American character but to man's basic nature. They were grudgingly accepted only by workers accustomed to even more repressive systems of labor or whose opportunities for employment elsewhere at a living wage were almost nil— immigrants, Blacks, "substandard men," and ex-convicts. Even after the inauguration of the five-dollar, eight-hour day at Ford, Arnold and Faurote recognized that "the monotony of repetitive production can be alleviated only by a satisfactory wage-rate, and is, perhaps, much more easily endured by immigrants, whose home wage stood somewhere about 60 cents for 10 hours' work than by native-born Americans."

The demands of the assembly line also put a premium on youth.

Nevins and Hill relate that "the bosses had a natural liking for young, vigorous, quick men not past thirty-five. Experienced hands past that age, if they did not possess some indispensable skill, were thus often the first to be dismissed and the last to be re-engaged." The Lynds tied mass production to the emergence of a cult of youth in the 1920s. Noting the trend toward employing younger men in Muncie, Indiana, factories, for example, the Lynds explained that "machine production is shifting traditional skills from the spoken word and the fingers of the master craftsman of the Middletown of the nineties to the cams and levers of the increasingly versatile machine. And in modern machine production it is speed and endurance that are at a premium. A boy of nineteen may, after a few weeks of experience on a machine, turn out an amount of work greater than his father of forty-five."

"I have not been able to discover that repetitive labor injures a man in any way," wrote Henry Ford. "Industry need not exact a human toll." It is true that mass production shifted many back-breaking tasks from the worker to the machine, and Highland Park exemplified the clean, safe, well-lighted, and well-ventilated factory essential to efficient mass production. Nevertheless, a human toll was exacted if only because mass production meant "the reduction of the necessity for thought on the part of the worker and the reduction of his movements to a minimum." Machines were closely spaced for optimal efficiency, and material was delivered to the worker at a waist-high level so that "wasted motion" was not expended in walking, reaching, stooping, or bending. The worker not only had to subordinate himself to the pace of the machine but had to be able to withstand the boredom inevitable in repeating the same motions hour after hour. A fifteen-minute lunch break, which included time to use the rest room and wash one's hands, was the only break from the monotonous fatigue of repetitive labor, the semihypnotic trance that workers were lulled into by the rhythmic din of the machinery.

The precise coordination of the flow of assembly that mass production demanded meant a new ironclad discipline for industrial workers. "The organization is so highly specialized and one part is so dependent upon another that we could not for a moment consider allowing men to have their own way," Ford explained. "Without the most rigid discipline we would have the utmost confusion. I think it should not be otherwise in industry." Consequently, the easy comaraderie on the job that had been normal in American industry for both unskilled and skilled workers was forbidden at Highland Park. Straw bosses and company "spotters" enforced rules and regulations that forbade leaning against the machine, sitting, squatting, singing, talking, whistling, or smoking on the job. Even smiling was frowned upon. Workers learned to communicate clandestinely without moving their lips in the "Ford whisper" and wore frozen expressions known as "Fordization of the face."

"There is not much personal contact," understated Ford. "The men do their work and go home—a factory is not a drawing room."

Mass production influenced many changes in the American way of life that were perceptible by the mid-1920s. Respect for age and parental authority was undercut in blue-collar families as sons became more valued as workers than their fathers. Being male lost some status because, theoretically at least, women could now be employed in industry on the same footing as men. Although the employment of women did not occur on any significant scale until industry experienced grave labor shortages in World War II, the democratization of the American family was furthered by mass production. The role of the housewife changed from that of a producer of many household items to a consumer of ready-made clothes, prepared foods, and electrical appliances, necessitating that she be given more control over the family budget. In addition, the mass-produced family car widened her range of associations beyond the narrow sphere of the home.

From the perspective of traditional American values, the impact of mass production on the worker was debilitating. The individual became an anonymous, interchangeable robot who had little chance on the job to demonstrate his personal qualifications for upward mobility into the echelons of management. Thus the American myth of unlimited individual social mobility, based on ability and the ideal of the self-made man, became frustrating impossibilities for the assembly-line worker. As the job became a boring, dead-ended treadmill to escape from rather than a calling in which to find fulfillment, leisure began to assume a new importance for the assembly-line worker. The meaning of work, long sanctified in the Protestant Ethic, was reduced to monetary remuneration. The value of thrift and personal economy became questionable, too, as mass consumption became an inevitable corollary of mass production.

The first significant recognition by American industry that mass production necessitated mass consumption was the inauguration of the five-dollar, eight-hour day by the Ford Motor Company on January 5, 1914. The minimum daily five-dollar wage was boldly conceived by Henry Ford as a plan for sharing profits with employees in advance of their being earned. Eligible workers consisted of those who had been at Ford for six months or more and were either married men living with and taking good care of their families, single men over twenty-two years of age of proved thrifty habits, or men under twenty-two years of age and women who were the sole support of some next of kin. Almost 60 percent of the Ford workers qualified immediately, and within two years about 75 percent were included in the profit-sharing plan.

The immediate impact of the five-dollar day on the standard of living of Ford employees was dramatic. As Nevins and Hill point out,

"When data collected at the beginning of 1916 were compared with materials gathered in the original investigation of employees beginning two years earlier, it appeared that the property of the average Ford employee in bank accounts and real estate equities had risen during the period from $196 to about $750. This figure did not include savings embodied in durable goods, nor in such intangible investments as the better education of children. Nor did the figures fully reflect the effect of the five-dollar wage upon the property of recipients even in the two limited categories named; for the average included many workers who (because of the doubling of the labor force and the six months' service rule) had participated in the plan for less than two years."

The Sociological Department was formed to check on the qualifications of employees for the five-dollar wage and to ensure that the money was put to uses considered constructive by Henry Ford. A staff of over thirty investigators (headed first by John R. Lee, who was succeeded by the Reverend Dr. Samuel S. Marquis, Ford's Episcopalian pastor) visited workers' homes gathering information and giving advice on the intimate details of the family budget, diet, living arrangements, recreation, social outlook, and morality. Americanization of the immigrant was encouraged by the Sociological Department through mandatory classes in English. The worker who refused to learn English, rejected the advice of the investigator, gambled, drank excessively, or was found guilty of "any malicious practice derogatory to good physical manhood or moral character" was disqualified from the five-dollar wage and put on probation. If he failed to reform within six months, he was discharged and his profits accumulated under the plan were used for charity. Shockingly presumptuous, repressive, and paternalistic by today's standards, the policies of the Sociological Department reflected both the long-standing assumption of American businessmen that the employer had a right to interfere in the private lives of his employees and the most advanced theories of the social workers of the Progressive Era.

In paying roughly twice the going rate for industrial labor for a shorter work day, Henry Ford defied the conventional economic wisdom of the day, which called for wages at a subsistence level. Ford implicitly acknowledged the validity of radical criticisms of income distribution under entrepreneurial capitalism when he told Samuel S. Marquis that five dollars a day was "about the least a man with a family can live on in these days." But Marquis knew that the five-dollar, eight-hour day "actually returned more dollars to [Henry Ford] than he gave out. It was unquestionably a shrewd and profitable stroke. To the credit of Mr. Ford be it said that he personally never maintained that his profit and bonus schemes were a means for distributing charity."

Ford recognized ahead of his fellow industrialists that the worker was also a consumer and that paying higher wages was profitable for several other reasons. Not only did the increased purchasing power stimulate sales; even more important, before the inauguration of the five-dollar, eight-hour day at Ford, the labor force had turned over at an incredibly costly rate. Ford recounted in 1922 that, "when the plan went into effect, we had 14,000 employees and it had been necessary to hire at the rate of about 53,000 a year in order to keep a constant force of 14,000. In 1915 we had to hire only 6,508 men and the majority of these new men were taken on because of the growth of the business. With the old turnover of labor and our present force we should have to hire at the rate of nearly 200,000 men a year—which would be pretty nearly an impossible proposition." Consistent with the primacy of profits in his wage motive, Ford reasoned in 1922 that "the payment of high wages fortunately contributes to the low costs [of production] because the men become steadily more efficient on account of being relieved of outside worries. The payment of five dollars a day for an eight-hour day was one of the finest cost-cutting moves we ever made, and the six-dollar day wage [instituted at Ford in January 1919] is cheaper than the five. How far this will go we do not know." As Arnold and Faurote had tried to explain in 1915, "The Ford Company has no socialistic leanings, and is not making any claim to placing a shining example before the world's employers of labor. It simply has the cash on hand, and it believes it will continue to have the cash on hand, to try to help its own hour-wage earners in its own way. That is the whole story up to date."

The advertising and public relations value of the five-dollar, eight-hour day alone was worth well more than the $5.8 million that the profit-sharing plan cost the Ford Motor Company during its first year of implementation. Henry Ford was roundly denounced as "a traitor to his class" by his fellow entrepreneurial capitalists, especially by his less efficient competitors in the automobile industry. On the other hand, Nevins and Hill conclude that "the public response was overwhelmingly approbatory. Nine-tenths of the newspaper comment was favorable, much of it almost ecstatic. Industrialists, labor leaders, sociologists, ministers, politicians, all hailed the innovation in glowing terms. Not a few commentators perceived the underlying connection which linked high production, high wages, and high consumption, pointing out that a new economic era might find in the Ford announcement a convenient birth date."

Although the eight-hour day, forty-eight-hour week quickly became the norm in automobile plants, Henry Ford's doubling of the daily minimum wage stood for decades as an isolated example of one capitalist's self-interested benevolence. The philosophy underlying the five-dollar, eight-hour day did not become institutionalized in American industry until after World War II. And its institutionalization was due almost entirely to the aggressiveness of the well-organized unions that had arisen during the late 1930s in our major industries, not to enlightened managerial capitalists.

Nor did the experiment in benevolent paternalism last longer than a few years at the Ford Motor Company. By 1918 the inflation of the World War I years had reduced the $5.00 minimum daily wage to only $2.80 in 1914 purchasing power, wiping out the workers' gains. The war also meant greatly reduced profit margins for Ford, and the company only survived the severe postwar recession by adopting stringent economy measures. As the 1920s wore on, the position of the Ford Motor Company in the industry declined as the Model T became outmoded and Ford's competitors became more efficient. Working conditions deteriorated with the speedup of the Ford assembly lines to meet the new competition. After the minimum daily wage of Ford workers was raised to $6.00 in January 1919, giving the workers $3.36 in 1914 purchasing power, there were no further advances in Ford wages during the 1920s. By 1925 the weekly earnings at Ford were $4.21 below the industry average, although cutting the Ford work week to five days in 1926 reduced the gap to $1.37 by 1928.

The Sociological Department folded and its records were burned after the Reverend Dr. Samuel S. Marquis, its head, resigned on January 25, 1921. He later explained: "The old group of executives, who at times set justice and humanity above profits and production, were gone. With them so it seemed to me, had gone an era of cooperation and good will in the company. There came to the front men whose theory was that men are more profitable to an industry when driven than led, that fear is a greater incentive to work than loyalty."

After the Paris taxicab fleet proved indispensable in moving troops to the front to stop the German advance at the Marne, a familiar phrase among military experts was that "in this war the exploding of gasoline is playing a more important part than the exploding of gunpowder." The automobile industry inevitably came to play a key role in American preparedness. The first call upon the industry occurred on August 10, 1915, with the appointment of Howard E. Coffin, vice-president and chief engineer at Hudson, and five other SAE dollar-a-year volunteers to the Navy Department Advisory Committee. Coffin became chairman of the Council of National Defense, which was formed in the spring of 1916 to organize our industrial system for war. Under the council, a Motor Transport Committee, chaired by Alfred Reeves of the NACC, planned for the mobilization of motor vehicles in the event of war, and

Roy D. Chapin, the president of Hudson, chaired a Highway Transport Committee to coordinate all highway transportation.

Hundreds of executives of the automobile industry volunteered, and some 463 members of the SAE alone were in government employ by the war's end on November 11, 1918. Automobile manufacturers produced aircraft engines, submarine chasers, tanks, and a variety of other military hardware that ranged from helmets to hand grenades. The industry's principal contribution, however, was made in its normal role of mass-producing motor vehicles, especially trucks. The rapid movement of troops and supplies was essential to victory at the front; and with railroad arteries to our eastern ports clogged, long-distance trucking was being developed as an alternative. By the time the United States entered the war, over 40,000 American-made trucks had been delivered to the Allies. And over half of the 238,000 motor vehicles, mainly trucks and ambulances, that the industry had contracted to make for our own government had been completed by the Armistice. In summarizing the contribution of the automobile industry to the war effort, *Motor* reported in 1919 that Earl Curzon, a member of the British War Cabinet, "said that the war could not have been won if it had not been for the great fleets of motor trucks, and that the Allied cause had been floated to victory on a wave of oil."

Industry support for preparedness and the war effort came mainly from the small automobile manufacturers that dominated the SAE. The position of these companies was deteriorating in the industry. Therefore, they not only had less to lose from a drastic curtailment of civilian production but their much smaller fixed investments in highly specialized plants and equipment made conversion to military production easier and far less costly for them than for the industry giants, Ford and General Motors.

William C. Durant at General Motors opposed undertaking war production less publicly but even more adamantly than Henry Ford. Henry M. Leland and Wilfred C. Leland, for example, resigned from Cadillac to form the Lincoln Motor Company on June 18, 1917, over Durant's vehement refusal to endorse their enthusiastic support of the war effort. When approached by the Lelands the day after war was declared with the proposition that it was a patriotic duty for Cadillac to switch over to the production of airplane engines, Durant had responded: "No! I don't care for your platitudes. This is not our war and I will not permit any General Motors unit to do work for the government." However, no automobile manufacturer could afford the reputation of being a "slacker"; so within a few months, Durant, too, succumbed to the mounting pressures of public opinion in support of the war and undertook token production of the new Liberty aircraft engine at both Buick and Cadillac.

Until the American entry into the war, Henry Ford took an outspoken stand against conscription and preparedness. "I don't believe in preparedness," he said. "It's like a man carrying a gun. Men and nations who carry guns get into trouble. If I had my way, I'd throw every ounce of gun powder into the sea and strip the soldiers and sailors of their insignia." Ford idealistically declared that he would spend half his fortune to shorten the war by one day and joined the American Peace Society, in which he came under the influence of Rosika Schwimmer, a Hungarian pacifist.

To implement Ms. Schwimmer's goals of stopping the war before either side gained a complete victory and establishing an organization for the continual mediation of international disputes, Henry Ford sponsored a "Peace Ship." On December 5, 1915, the *Oscar II* sailed on an abortive fourteen-day voyage to Oslo, Norway, carrying an array of delegates, students, technical advisers, and reporters that Charles E. Sorensen called "the strangest assortment of living creatures since the voyage of Noah's Ark." Newspapers on both sides of the Atlantic stressed the idealistic naïveté of the Peace Ship and seized upon bizarre details in an attempt to discredit "Ford's folly" as an exercise in futility and absurdity. After Ford became ill and left the delegation at Oslo, the peace party went on to Sweden and Denmark, ending up at The Hague in Holland, where it disbanded on January 15, 1916, demoralized and dissension-ridden.

Once diplomatic ties between the United States and Germany were severed on February 3, 1917, Henry Ford abruptly reversed himself, stating that "we must stand behind the President" and that "in the event of war [I] will place our factory at the disposal of the United States government and will operate without one cent of profit." After Congress declared war on April 6, Ford rationalized that "perhaps militarism can be crushed only with militarism. In that case I am in on it to the finish."

On April 8, Ford cabled the British that he would "comply with every request immediately" to help them mass-produce the Fordson farm tractor. Tractors were desperately needed by the British to help alleviate grave food shortages caused by German U-boat attacks on ships importing foodstuffs and by the loss of 80,000 farmhands to the military services. Experiments with a number of makes of tractors conducted by the Royal Agricultural Society had left the British authorities most impressed with the Fordson.

The first commercially successful gasoline-powered tractors in the United States were built by the Hart-Parr Company of Charles City, Iowa, in 1902–1903. By 1907, when Henry Ford began the experiments that led to the Fordson, about 600 gasoline-powered tractors were in use on American farms. These early machines were too heavy, clumsy, complicated, and expensive to meet the needs of the average farmer.

Between 1910 and 1915, when the Fordson was announced, several tractor demonstrations in the Middle West drew an estimated 50,000 farmers and showed that there was a large potential market for smaller machines, such as the 4,650-pound, $650 tractor introduced in 1913 by the Bull Tractor Company of Minneapolis, Minnesota. The 2,500-pound Fordson was introduced by Henry Ford personally in August 1915 at a plowing demonstration at Fremont, Nebraska. With a wheelbase of only 63 inches, the Fordson could turn in a 21-foot circle. It was cheap to operate because its four-cylinder, 20-horsepower engine ran on kerosene. And, like the Model T, the Fordson was designed to be mass-produced at low cost. Henry Ford & Son was organized to manufacture the Fordson as a separate corporation from the Ford Motor Company on July 27, 1917.

The Fordson tractor contributed little toward alleviating food shortages during the war. By March 1, 1918, only 3,600 of the 8,000 Fordsons ordered by the British government had been delivered, and privately owned steam tractors were plowing considerably more acres of British farmland than the government-owned Fordsons. Most Fordsons were bought by American farmers, who, faced for the first time in decades with expanding markets for agricultural commodities, were anxious to comply with the patriotic slogan, "Buy Tractors and Win the War." Although it was April 23, 1918, before the first Fordson for domestic use came off the assembly line, by the time of the Armistice 26,817 had been manufactured at Ford's Dearborn tractor plant. Too late to have any significant impact on winning the war, these Fordsons were distributed to the agricultural states in quotas and sold to farmers through permits granted by the County War Boards.

Despite the impression given by Henry Ford that he sold his tractors at cost as a contribution to the war effort, the $750 price of the Fordson included a tidy profit of $182.86 for Henry Ford & Son. The greatest irony was that mass production of the Fordson reached fantastic heights just as the market for American agricultural commodities rapidly evaporated in the postwar period. Some 750 Fordsons a day were being produced by 1924. Total production rose to 486,800 units in 1925 and over 650,000 units in 1927, making Ford responsible for about half the tractors manufactured in the United States up to that time. This proliferation of the Fordson farm tractor was a major factor in creating the ruinous combination of higher fixed costs and overproduction of staple commodities that plagued American farmers during the 1920s.

Even before Henry Ford abandoned his pacifist neutrality to work for the war effort "without one cent of profit," the Ford branch plants in Paris and Great Britain had disregarded Dearborn and turned out thousands of motor vehicles for the Allies. From an initial contract for 2,000 ambulances on May 30, 1917, Ford's American factors went on to produce about 39,000 motor vehicles for the war effort. They also made aircraft motors, armor plate, caissons, shells, steel helmets, submarine detectors, and torpedo tubes. Sixty Eagle Boats (submarine chasers) were completed by Ford too late to see action, and two tank prototypes developed by the company had just reached the stage where quantity production could begin when peace came.

Although the manufacture of Model Ts for the civilian market never stopped entirely, automotive work was cut back significantly at Ford during the war. By July 31, 1918, no motorcars were being made at the Highland Park plant. However, almost 3,000 a day were still being turned out at the twenty-eight Ford branch assembly plants. These plants had been established throughout the United States at freight-rate breaking points after 1909 because cars could be shipped to their ultimate destinations much more cheaply in knocked-down form. By Armistice Day the Ford branch plants were producing only about 300 cars a day, practically all for the government. The production of Ford motor vehicles declined from a high of 734,800 units in 1916 to 438,800 units in 1918. But conversion back to full civilian production was apparently no problem, for the Ford plants turned out 820,400 units in 1919. The unexpected sharp drop in Ford production to 419,500 units in 1920 shows that the postwar recession had a much greater impact than the war effort on reducing production of the Model T.

Nevertheless, participation in the war effort was costly for the Ford Motor Company in terms of profits. Net income fell from $57.1 million for the fiscal year 1915/16 to $27.2 million for 1916/17 and $30.9 million for 1917/18, and the bulk of the company's profits during the war came from its civilian production. After corporate taxes, the Ford Motor Company made only $4.357 million on its war contracts. As the owner of 58.5 percent of the Ford stock, Henry Ford's share of the company's war profits after paying personal income taxes on them came to a mere $926,780.46—a fraction of what he could have made had civilian production continued uninterrupted. The Dent Act for terminating war contracts was passed by Congress in early 1919. It gave the government until March 1, 1924, to question all settlements, and the Treasury Department did not complete its careful scrutiny of the Ford settlements until mid-1923. By then Henry Ford was angry about governmental officials probing into his business records, and the Ford Motor Company was facing tougher competitive conditions in the automobile industry. So Henry Ford reneged on his rash promise, repeated as late as his 1918 senatorial campaign, to return all his war profits to the government.

The abrupt termination of war contracts with the unanticipated coming of peace on November 11, 1918, caused little concern in the automobile industry. Automobile plants were quickly converted back to the production of passenger cars—at Highland Park it took only about three weeks—to fill the huge back orders for new cars that had accumulated during the war. Automobile manufacturers began to embark on ambitious expansion programs, confident that the demand for motorcars was insatiable.

These short-lived illusions were shattered with the onset of the postwar recession. General commodity prices continued to rise after the war, reaching a peak in May 1920 of 121.7 percent of the November 1918 level, with automobile prices continuing to rise to a peak of 124.9 percent in August. An illustration of what this meant is that a new Model T touring car that had sold for $360 in August 1916 cost $575 in August 1920. Responding to this sharply rising spiral in the cost of living, some 4.16 million U.S. workers, about 20 percent of the labor force, engaged in 3,630 work stoppages during 1919, making that year a high point of industrial unrest. Except for a major strike at Willys-Overland, the automobile industry experienced minimal direct labor-management strife. But with a million workers out on strike in the steel and coal industries and on the railroads alone, the automobile manufacturers felt the impact of work stoppages in vital ancillary industries. Most important, new car sales slackened with the general decline in purchasing power. This decline was compounded as rural America's demand for new cars, the automobile industry's mainstay for over a decade, began to evaporate. The American farmer returned to hard times with the collapse of foreign markets after 1919. Commodity prices fell rapidly in the summer of 1920. Gross agricultural income dropped from $15 billion in 1919 to only $9.2 billion in 1921 as agricultural exports declined 50 percent. The final puncture that burst the automobile manufacturers' balloon occurred when the Federal Reserve Board, concerned about a rapid expansion in the installment sales of cars, raised the rediscount rate in November 1919. The effect was to up the down payment required on automobile time sales from a fourth or a third to about half the purchase price of the car.

The recession hit Henry Ford in the midst of carrying out plans to develop an industrial colossus on the Rouge River and deeply in debt from a successful drive to buy out his minority stockholders. In the spring of 1915 Ford began buying up huge tracts of land along the Rouge River southeast of Detroit and announced plans for developing a great industrial complex there. John and Horace Dodge, still minority Ford stockholders despite having formed a rival company to build their own car, brought a lawsuit against Ford to stop his diversion of Ford profits into expanding the Rouge plant instead of distributing them as dividends, which the Dodge brothers were counting on to finance expansion at Dodge. On January 6, 1917, the lifting of a restraining order by the court permitted Ford to go ahead with developing the Rouge facilities on the condition that he post a $10 million bond to safeguard the interests of his minority stockholders. But a decision handed down on February 7, 1919, forced the Ford Motor Company to declare a special dividend of $19.275 million plus interest. Although Henry Ford as the principal Ford stockholder received the bulk of this special dividend, the experience left him determined to rid himself of his minority stockholders. Not only had his minority stockholders become wealthy on small investments while contributing nothing to the company, Ford reasoned, but these ungrateful parasites were now proving to be stumbling blocks to the expansion he deemed essential.

Henry Ford "danced a jig all around the room" when he managed to buy up the options of his minority stockholders for the bargain price of $105.8 million on July 11, 1919. Financing the transaction required a $75 million loan from a financial syndicate composed of the Chase Securities Corporation, the Old Colony Trust Company, and Bond and Goodwin. The reorganized Ford Motor Company's shares were distributed 55.2 percent to Henry Ford, 41.7 percent to Edsel Ford as Henry's only progeny and heir apparent to the throne, and 3.1 percent to Clara Ford. Edsel became titular president of the reorganized company, a position he held until his untimely death on May 26, 1943, from cancer. But no one, including Edsel, doubted that the Ford Motor Company after its reorganization was an autocracy entirely subject to the whims of its aging, egocentric founder.

Turning the giant Ford Motor Company into a family-owned and family-managed business defied precedent, business trends, rational canons of business administration, and simple common sense. Nevins and Hill point out that "never had one man controlled completely an organization the size of the Ford Motor Company. John D. Rockefeller never held more than two-sevenths of the Standard Oil Company certificates, and J. P. Morgan, who presided over the birth of the United States Steel Corporation, owned a much smaller percentage of its shares. Ford wielded industrial power such as no man had ever possessed before." The trends in American industry were toward wider dispersal of ownership among many small stockholders, the separation of ownership from management, the rise of professional managers and salaried experts within the firm, and democratic decision making by committees of executives. At the Ford Motor Company, in sharp contrast, the champion of small business against the forces of monopoly during the Selden patent suit now fastened onto his mammoth corporation the family ownership and one-man rule fit for a mom-and-pop market. By 1920 the Ford Motor Company owned, in addition to its main Highland Park and River Rouge plants, branch plants scattered across the globe, rubber plantations in Brazil, iron mines and lumber mills in Michigan, coal mines in Kentucky and West Virginia, glass plants in Pennsylvania and Minnesota, a railroad, and a fleet of ships. Family ownership and one-man rule of an enterprise of this scope defied sanity, much less Lord Acton's dictum that absolute power tends to corrupt absolutely.

As the full impact of the recession began to be felt in the summer of 1920, Henry Ford still owed $25 million, due in April 1921, on the loan to obtain control of his company; he had pledged to distribute a $7 million bonus in January; and he had to pay between $18 million and $30 million in taxes. Over the past three years $60.45 million had been spent on developing the River Rouge plant and between $15 million and $20 million on purchasing mines and timber tracts. Ford estimated that he needed $58 million, and he had only $20 million in cash on hand. The thought of seeking another loan was abandoned once it became apparent to Ford that the bankers would demand in return a voice in the management of his company. So Henry Ford turned to alternatives that preserved his sovereignty at the expense of the long-range well-being of the Ford Motor Company.

The only progressive move that Ford made was to lead the industry in a long overdue reduction in the price of cars. On September 21, 1920, the Ford Motor Company announced price cuts on the Model T that averaged $148, depending on body style. This reduction theoretically meant a short-term loss of about $20 on every car sold, but the loss was covered by the profit on the $40 worth of parts and accessories sold with every new Model T. Other automobile manufacturers claimed that the drastic Ford price cuts were ruinous for the industry, and some banded together in an attempt to preserve for old price levels. Within a few weeks, however, twenty-three of Ford's competitors followed his lead and reduced prices on their cars.

As the fall wore on, it became evident that the price cuts were failing to check the dwindling sales. By the end of 1920, automobile production was halted at Buick, Dodge, Ford, Maxwell-Chalmers, Nash, Packard, REO, Studebaker, and Willys-Overland; and the automobile plants that remained open were staffed by skeleton work forces. The number of employed automobile workers in Detroit, the geographic center of the industry, dropped from 176,000 in September to 24,000 by the end of the year.

The Ford Motor Company closed its plants "for inventory" on Christmas Eve, December 24, 1920, and remained closed until February 1, 1921, while the company disposed of "stocks on hand." Unlike most of his competitors, Henry Ford maintained full production up to the shutdown of his plants, curtailing only the purchase of raw materials. The strategy implemented at Ford was first to turn the huge inventory of raw materials that had been bought at inflated prices into a reservoir of finished cars, then to stop production until those cars were disposed of at a profit and raw material prices had declined. Consignments of unordered cars were forced on over 6,300 Ford dealers, who had the choice of borrowing heavily from local banks to pay cash on delivery for them or forfeiting their Ford franchises. Henry Ford thus avoided going to the bankers himself and preserved his one-man rule and personal profits by arbitrarily unloading his financial problems onto the backs of thousands of hard-pressed small businessmen.

The shutdown at Ford was accompanied by stringent economy measures that went beyond what was essential for survival and jeopardized the future well-being of the firm. The Ford plants were stripped of every nonessential tool and fixture—including every pencil sharpener, most desks and typewriters, and 600 extension telephones. The sale of this equipment netted $7 million. The company also benefitted from replacing some of it with improved machinery and methods that increased output per man-hour of labor. These gains were canceled out, however, by a ruthless halving of the office force from 1,074 to 528 persons as most departments, including such critical ones as auditing, were overly simplified, merged, or eliminated. Many capable executives were lost to the company. Even more important, the development of the organized bureaucracy essential to a mature corporation in a technologically sophisticated, consumer-goods industry was stultified.

Henry Ford always considered the business end of the company to be nonessential and therefore expendable. So it was inevitable that he took the first opportunity to emasculate the administrative staff after buying out Couzens, who had built it up, with the other minority stockholders. "To my mind there is no bent of mind more dangerous than that which is sometimes described as 'genius for organization,' " Ford explained in 1922. "It is not necessary for any one department to know what any other department is doing." He foolishly boasted that "the Ford factories and enterprises have no organization, no specific duties attaching to any position, no line of succession or of authority, very few titles, and no conferences. We have only the clerical help that is absolutely required; we have no elaborate records of any kind, and consequently no red tape."

The lack of "red tape" amounted to what an increasing number of ex-Ford executives called "Prussianization" as the entrepreneurial team responsible for the success of the mass-produced Model T disintegrated in the early 1920s. A complete list of the Ford executives who were arbitrarily fired or who resigned in disgust between 1919 and Henry Ford's retirement in 1945 would add up to a small town's telephone directory. Although this critical loss of executive talent defies adequate summarizing, after James Couzens the most significant losses were probably William S. Knudsen and Norval A. Hawkins. Both went to General Motors and were instrumental in Chevrolet's sales surpassing Ford's by 1927. Of more symbolic importance were the 1919 departures to build the Wills-Sainte Claire car of C. Harold Wills, the chief designer of the Model T, and John R. Lee, the first head of the short-lived Sociological Department. Charles E. Sorensen, who became Henry Ford's chief hatchet man, seemed to take a perverse pleasure in the discharges and resignations of his fellow executives, and he managed to stay in Ford's favor by saying "yes" longer than any of them. But on March 2, 1944, Sorensen too ended up by resigning—at the request of a senile Henry Ford, who feared that Sorensen had ambitions to take over his company.

Citing the Ford Motor Company as the world's outstanding example of an industrial dictatorship, the *New York Times* on January 8, 1928, called Henry Ford "an industrial fascist—the Mussolini of Detroit." As the probusiness *Fortune* magazine commented in December 1933, it was well known in the automobile industry that "Mr. Ford's organization does show extreme evidence of being ruled primarily by fear of the job." Even Edsel was mercilessly bullied by the elder Ford, who thought his son too soft and held up as a model worthy of emulation Harry Bennett, an ex-pugilist with underworld connections. Bennett enforced discipline in the Ford plants as head of a gang of labor spies and thugs called the Ford Service Department. He came to be Henry Ford's most trusted associate and comrade after the Model A replaced the Model T in 1928 and production was shifted to the River Rouge plant.

From Edsel Ford on down, the Ford executives came to fear and despise Bennett as his influence grew, and by the mid-1930s Ford workers wondered whether Hitler had derived the idea for his Gestapo from Bennett's Ford Service. "As a rule, Ford's managers, having more to lose, came to watch their jobs more nervously than the man at the Rouge who swept the floor," relates Keith Sward. "On the lower tiers of the Ford organization, Ford Service gave rise to any number of unmistakable industrial neuroses. These 'shop complaints' went all the way from mild states of anxiety to advanced nervous symptoms that were fit material for a psychopathic ward. Thus conditioned, the personality of any Ford employee was subjected to a process of subtle and profound degradation." Writing during the depths of the Great Depression, Jonathan N. Leonard, an early Ford debunker, claimed that "Detroit is a city of hate and fear. And the major focus of that hatred and fear is the astonishing plant on the River Rouge." Leonard found almost all automobile factories in Detroit "horrifying and repellent to the last degree. But the Ford factory has the reputation of being by far the worst." The main reason was that "over the Ford plant hangs the menace of the 'Service Department,' the spies and stool pigeons who report every action, every remark, every expression. . . . No one who words for Ford is safe from the spies—from the superintendents down to the poor creature who must clean a certain number of toilets an hour."

The Service Department was one manifestation of the Ford Motor

Company's deteriorating position vis-à-vis its competitors in the automobile industry. Except for minor face-liftings and the incorporation of such basic improvements as the closed body and the self-starter, the Model T remained basically unchanged long after it was outmoded. The popularity of the Model T declined in the 1920s as rural roads were improved, consumers became more style and comfort conscious, and the market for new cars shifted from a demand for low-cost, basic transportation by first-time owners to filling replacement demand. Model T owners tended to trade up to larger, faster, smoother riding, and more stylish cars; and the demand for the low-cost, basic transportation that the Model T had met tended increasingly to be filled from the backlog of used cars piling up in dealers' lots. By the mid-1920s, secondhand cars of more expensive makes in good condition could be bought for the same price as a new Model T. In addition, the onset of the market saturation for new cars forced general price reductions in 1925 that, for example, pegged only $200 higher than an obsolete Model T an annually restyled, larger, and far better equipped new Chevrolet.

Henry Ford closed his mind to the advice of his executives, the pleas of his dealers, and mounting complaints about the Model T from his customers. He denounced the new emphasis on style and comfort as extravagant and wasteful and tried to meet the competition by drastically reducing prices—to a low of $290 for the coupe by 1927—and making "everybody dig for profits." The speedup of the assembly line enforced by the Ford Service Department drove workers "to the highest point of efficiency." Ex-Ford executives were the first to testify in their reminiscences that workers were driven harder at Ford than at other automobile plants. Ford dealers, too, were forced "to the highest point of efficiency." As Model T production was cut from 1.8 million units in 1923 to 1.3 million units in 1926, the number of Ford dealerships was increased from about 8,500 to 9,800 in the hope that heightened competition among them would stimulate more aggressive salesmanship. Seven out of ten Ford dealers were losing money by 1926; and as some went bankrupt and others switched to General Motors, about a third of the Ford dealerships turned over that year.

Even Henry Ford was finally forced to recognize that the era of the Model T had ended. Its production was halted on May 27, 1927, and the Ford plants were shut down while its successor, the Model A, was hastily designed. A mild recession in 1927 was attributed in part to hundreds of thousands of automobile owners deferring their purchase of a new car until Henry Ford came out with his new new model. Some 400,000 orders were received before the Model A had been seen by the public. At a retooling cost of $18 million, for what was probably up to that time the most extensive changeover of an industrial plant in American history, the assembly lines at River Rouge began to turn out limited numbers of the Model A in November 1927.

The initial response to the four-cylinder, 40-horsepower Model A was enthusiastic. In 1929 Ford briefly regained the industry lead in sales that had been lost to Chevrolet in both 1927 and 1928. Ford production surpassed 1.5 million units in 1929 and 1.15 million units in 1930, compared with Chevrolet's 950,000 and 683,000 units for those years.

But neither the Model A nor the Ford V-8 that replaced it in 1932 could regenerate the Ford Motor Company. Between 1931 and 1970 Chevrolet outsold Ford in every year except 1935 and 1945, and the latter year was an exception only because Ford was the first automobile manufacturer to get back into civilian production following World War II. Plymouth also cut into Ford sales in the low-priced field after it was introduced in 1929. And Ford's cars in the luxury and moderately priced brackets—the Lincoln, acquired from the Lelands in 1921, and the Mercury, introduced in 1939 to compete with Pontiac and Dodge—failed to become popular. Only in the sale of light trucks did the Ford Motor Company enjoy a slight lead over its competitors. In the oligopoly that had come to dominate the automobile industry, by 1936 Ford had dropped to third place in sales of passenger cars, with 22.44 percent of the market versus 43.12 percent for General Motors and 25.03 percent for Chrysler.

The Great Depression, of course, was an even more important impediment to the revival of the Ford Motor Company than competition from General Motors and Chrysler. Automobile registrations declined for the first time in the United States during the depression, and not until 1949 did the automobile industry equal its record 1929 output of 5.3 million units. Ford production collapsed from over 1.5 million units in 1929 to a low of 232,000 units in 1932 and bounced back to only 600,000 units in 1941, the last full year of civilian automobile production before World War II. During 1931–1933 the Ford Motor Company lost $120 million after taxes. Profits of $17.9 million in 1936 and $6.7 million in 1937, during a brief revival of the economy, went far, however, toward canceling out an estimated total loss of $26 million over the preceding decade.

Henry Ford was one of the few industrial capitalists sufficiently committed to the capitalist system to make a voluntary effort to maintain the economy as it slid into the depression following the stock market crash in October 1929. Hoping to stimulate consumption by increasing purchasing power, Ford lowered prices on the Model A in November and raised the minimum daily wage of his workers to $7 in December. Early in 1930 he announced a $25 million program of branch factory construction.

Ford quickly reneged once the severity of the depression became apparent. He also reduced the profit margins of his dealers on the sale of new cars to the lowest in the industry. And by 1932 the minimum daily wage at Ford was reduced to $6 for skilled workers, $5 for semiskilled workers, and $4 for laborers. Even these rates were illusory because they did not account for the downgrading of many jobs to lower pay scales and an increase in jobbing out components to outside companies that paid lower wages than Ford. The number of Ford employees declined sharply from 170,502 in 1929 to 46,282 by 1932. Those who still had jobs were driven increasingly harder "to the highest point of efficiency." Because Ford, with the help of his Service Department, managed to resist unionization longer than General Motors or Chrysler, the company's wages for 1937–1941 fell a few cents below the average for all industry in the United States and well below the average for the automobile industry.

Outside his company, organized labor, the automobile industry, and the Detroit area, the myths that had built up around the figure of Henry Ford incredibly refused to die. A survey conducted by *Fortune* magazine in 1937 for the National Association of Manufacturers found that 47.2 percent of the respondents still approved of the policies of the Ford Motor Company, versus an insignificant 3.1 percent approval for General Motors and 1.2 percent approval for Chrysler.

Yet the Ford myths were beginning to be shattered, and Henry Ford at least was no longer being deified. In 1932 Jonathan Leonard noted the paradox that "he is hated by nearly everyone who has ever worked for him, and at one time was worshipped by nearly everyone who had not. His story is certainly the most fascinating in all the gaudy tales of American business." Henry Ford's main fault, thought Leonard, was that "he did not consider himself a mere manufacturer, like the Dodges or Chrysler. He was a prophet with a message for the world. That fact that his message was bare, ugly, tyrannical did not keep people from accepting it as long as he was the most successful industrialist in the country. In the United States a record of commercial success makes a man an authority on every subject." Leonard was optimistic that "even if the company does manage to persuade its owner to follow the rest of the industry and keep up with engineering and fashion changes, Henry Ford will never be a prophet again. He will merely be a manufacturer, and since the crash of 1929 the American people refuse to worship without reserve the god of mass production."

Even to the grass-roots Americans who had deified him for a generation, Henry Ford's rhetoric increasingly seemed irrelevant nonsense as the Great Depression wore on. The letters to the "Sage of Dearborn" dwindled and became bitter and resentful. As Wik says, "Instead of writing to Ford, farmers in increasing numbers addressed their remarks to officials in the nation's capitol where the power to affect reform resided. The letters found in the library at Hyde Park, New York, and in the National Archives in Washington, D.C., suggest that farmers believed relief could be found in federal legislation rather than in the good intentions of business leaders."

Henry Ford's mental capacities eroded rapidly after he suffered a severe stroke in 1938. He developed the hallucination that Franklin Delano Roosevelt was a warmonger controlled by General Motors and the du Ponts and that United States involvement in World War II was part of a conspiracy to get control of his company. "His memory was failing as rapidly as his obsessions and antipathies increased," Sorensen recalled. "His pet peeve was Franklin Roosevelt, but any mention of the war in Europe and the likelihood of this country's involvement upset him almost to incoherence. Edsel, who was suffering from stomach trouble, came in for unmerciful criticism."

Ford's delusions were lent substance when Roosevelt appointed William S. Knudsen, then the president of General Motors, Commissioner for Industrial Production of the National Defense Commission on May 28, 1940. Ford was already under attack for his refusal to take British war orders when he reneged on a promise, made to Knudsen at the urging of Edsel and Sorensen, that he would manufacture Rolls-Royce airplane engines, 60 percent to go to the British. Despite Ford's proclaimed neutrality, the Nazis had taken over complete control of his German and French plants. So when Knudsen called for the full cooperation of automobile manufacturers in the defense plans in late November 1940, Edsel and Sorensen recognized that Ford's failure to comply voluntarily would invite the governmental take-over that Henry Ford's paranoia led him to fear.

They managed to obtain Ford's reluctant consent to participate in the aircraft program. On November 1, 1940, the Ford Motor Company signed a contract to make Pratt & Whitney airplane engines for the U.S. Air Force. And on February 25, 1941, the government approved Ford plans for a vast bomber plant at Willow Run, near Ypsilanti, Michigan. Snags in getting "Will-It Run" into production delayed acceptance of the first B-24 bombers completely assembled by Ford until September 1942. By then the Ford Motor Company, along with the rest of the automobile industry, had completely converted over to war production and was playing an indispensable role in the war effort. Henry Ford feared that the military personnel at Willow Run were spies sent by Roosevelt to assassinate him and took to carrying an automatic pistol under the cowl of his car.

Following Edsel's death on May 26, 1943, Henry Ford again became president of the Ford Motor Company. Roosevelt, aware of Ford's mental incompetence, toyed with the idea of removing him and having the government operate the company for the duration of the war. It took the threats of Edsel's widow and Clara Ford to sell their shares of Ford stock out of the family to induce Henry Ford finally to step down in favor of his grandson Henry Ford II on September 21, 1945.

After a generation of gross mismanagement, the Ford Motor Company was losing about $10 million a month when Henry Ford II took over. The Ford Service Department had made fear and demoralization a way of life at Ford. Few executives worth their salt were left. The company lacked both a program of research and development and college-trained engineers. Accounting was so primitive that at least one department estimated its costs by weighing the invoices. There was no coordination between purchasing, production, and marketing. For years the financial statements had been closely guarded secrets even within the firm because of fear that they might damage prestige or prompt an investigation.

This was an ironic inheritance from a founder once worshiped as a deity of progress through industrial efficiency. It was even more ironic that Henry Ford II began the revitalization of the Ford Motor Company by hiring an executive team headed by Ernest R. Breech from General Motors to institute the corporate structure and modern management techniques that the first Henry Ford had sacrificed to maintain family control at Ford. More ironic still, the Ford Motor Company had over $685 million in cash on hand when Henry Ford II began its revitalization. That was not a bad bank balance for a firm that had started in 1903 with only $28 thousand of paid-in capital, that had been mismanaged for a generation, and whose founder claimed in 1916 that "we should not make such an awful profit on our cars."

Perhaps the ultimate irony turned out to be the Ford Foundation, a legal device conceived on February 3, 1936, as a means of avoiding Roosevelt's "soak-the-rich" taxes and maintaining family control of the Ford Motor Company. The Ford Foundation had a 95 percent equity in the Ford Motor Company in nonvoting common stock. A 5 percent equity of all voting common stock was retained by the Ford family. Had it not been for the Ford Foundation, the heirs of Edsel and Henry Ford would have paid federal inheritance taxes estimated at $321 million and would have lost control of the company in selling the stock necessary to raise the money. But by the end of 1955 the Ford Foundation had disposed of some $875 million of the Ford fortune and had announced plans to diversify its investments, which involved selling nearly 7 million reclassified shares of Ford common stock. Thus three-fifths of the Ford Motor Company voting common stock ended up in the hands of key Ford executives and the general public. The family control of the firm that the Ford Foundation was formed to preserve ended less than a decade after Henry Ford's death on April 7, 1947. And in September 1974 the Ford Foundation announced that because of inflation and falling securities markets it might have to reduce its annual grants by 50 percent. It was even considering dissolution.

Suggestions for Further Reading

The classic description of American life in this period is Mark Sullivan, *Our Times, 1900–1925*, 6 vols. (New York, 1926–35). Other general treatments that consider various periods of the early twentieth century are Henry May, *The End of American Innocence: A Study of the First Years of Our Time, 1912–1917** (New York, 1959); Walter Lord, *The Good Years** (New York, 1960); and Gilman Ostrander, *American Civilization in the First Machine Age, 1890–1940** (New York, 1970). J. C. Furnas has extended his popular history of American life with *Great Times: An Informal History of the United States, 1914–1929* (New York, 1974). The standard popular treatment of the 1920s is Frederick Lewis Allen, *Only Yesterday** (New York, 1931). Two recent works that challenge Allen's interpretations are Paul Carter, *The Twenties in America** (New York, 1968), and John Braeman, Robert H. Bremner, and David Brody, eds., *Change and Continuity in Twentieth-Century America: The 1920's* (Columbus, Ohio, 1968). The novelist John Dos Passos' classic trilogy, *U.S.A.** (Boston, 1937), contains much valuable material on this period.

For urban immigration, see John Bodnar, *The Transplanted: A History of Immigrants in Urban America* (Bloomington, Indiana, 1985). On working class culture, see Herbert Gutman, *Work, Culture, and Society in Industrializing America** (New York, 1976) and Milton Cantor, ed., *Working-Class Culture* (Westport, Connecticut, 1979). The drinking habits of Americans are explored in Perry Duis, *The Saloon: Drinking in Chicago and Boston, 1880–1920* (Champaign, Illinois, 1983) and K. Austin Kerr, *Organized for Prohibition: A New History of the Anti-Saloon League* (New Haven, 1985). The early history of the movies is covered in Robert Sklar, *Movie-Made America: A Social History of American Movies** (New York, 1975) and Larry May, *Screening Out the Past: The Birth of Mass Culture and the Motion Picture Industry** (New York, 1980).

For the urban background of the newsboys, see Gunther Barth, *City People: The Rise of Modern City Culture in Nineteenth Century America** (New York, 1980). For a survey of children's lives in America, see Robert H. Bremner *et al.*, eds., *Children and Youth in*

*Available in paperback edition.

America: A Documentary History*, 3 vols. (Cambridge, 1970–74). See also N. Ray Hines and Joseph M. Hawes, eds., *Growing Up in America: Children in Historical Perspective** (Champaign, Illinois, 1985). Reformers' activities on behalf of children can be found in Jeremy P. Felt, *Hostages of Fortune: Child Labor Reform in New York State* (Syracuse, 1965) and Leroy Ashby, *Saving the Waifs: Reformers and Dependent Children, 1890–1917* (Philadelphia, 1984).

The development of the Mexican-American community in the United States from 1845–1930 is covered in Albert Camarillo, *Chicanos in a Changing Society** (Cambridge, 1979). See also Richard Griswold del Castillo, *La Familia: Chicano Families in the Urban Southwest, 1848 to the Present** (South Bend, 1984). Studies of East Los Angeles include Richard Griswold del Castillo, *The Los Angeles Barrio, 1850–1890* (Berkeley, 1979); Rodolfo F. Acuna, *A Community Under Siege: A Chronicle of Chicanos East of the Los Angeles River, 1945–1975** (Los Angeles, 1984); and Joan W. Moore, *Homeboys: Gangs, Drugs, and Prison in the Barrios of Los Angeles** (Philadelphia, 1978).

The impact of Henry Ford on the American people is explored in Reynold M. Wik, *Henry Ford and Grass-roots America** (Ann Arbor, 1972). Changing manufacturing practices are described in David A. Hounshell, *From the American System to Mass Production, 1800–1832: The Development of Manufacturing Technology in the United States** (Baltimore, 1984). The standard histories of the American automobile are detailed by John B. Rae, *The American Automobile: A Brief History** (Chicago, 1965) and *The Road and the Car in American Life* (Cambridge, 1971). The impact of the automobile on mass transportation in the United States is found in Mark S. Foster, *From Streetcar to Superhighway: American City Planners and Urban Transportation, 1900–1940* (Philadelphia, 1981) and Paul Barrett, *The Automobile and Urban Transit: The Formation of Public Policy in Chicago, 1900–1930* (Philadelphia, 1983).

Depression, War, and After

1930–1960

A ''black blizzard'' over Manter, Kansas, on
April 14, 1935

The Dust Bowl

DONALD WORSTER

Coming at the same time as the Great Depression, the Dust Bowl of the 1930s on the Great Plains seemed to be adding insult to injury. Was it not enough that the American economy was at its worst point in modern times? Was nature itself, by denying rain and by increasing wind, seeking to wreak vengeance on those who were trying to make a living on the Great American Desert?

In order to understand the causes of the Dust Bowl it is necessary to consider both the nature of American agriculture and the ideology of capitalism. Donald Worster of the University of Hawaii has done both in his outstanding study of the Dust Bowl. The selection reprinted below describes the impact of the ecological disaster on people living in the area, but he indicates elsewhere in his book where the responsibility for the situation must rest.

The basic fault lies, according to Worster, with the ecological values which are expressed in the capitalist ethos. He cites three maxims: "Nature must be seen as capital. . . . Man has a right, even an obligation, to use this capital for constant self-advancement. . . . The social order should permit and encourage this continual increase of personal wealth . . ." (p. 6). The implications of these maxims are evident throughout the history of American agriculture. Farming in the United States has always been looked upon as a profit-making enterprise. Although there have been subsistence farmers in our history, they have occupied a marginal place in the business of agriculture. From the tobacco farmers of seventeenth-century Virginia to corporate agribusiness in California today, profit and not subsistence has been the goal of the nation's farmers.

Nature is not to stand in the way of profit; it is to be the capital on which the increase is to be based. Until recently nature was seen as an enemy to be feared, placated, and accommodated. The forces of nature were beyond our control, and we had to temper our desires to their demands. The expanding spirit of capitalism, however, challenged those age-old attitudes. People are now in control of nature, bending it to our will. This attitude, along with the growing mechanization of agriculture, combined to produce the conditions which made the Dust Bowl so devastating.

Cycles of drought and fertility have probably always been a part of the ecological structure of the Great Plains. Archaeologists have identified dust storms in the area as long ago as approximately 500 A.D., but the tough sod grasses which covered the plains tended to minimize their impact. In the last hundred years, however, the grasses have been destroyed in the interest of profitable agriculture. The availability of the land to settlers through the homestead acts caused thousands of people to move into the area and start carving up the sod. The First World War and the demands for American wheat from our European allies led farmers to invest in more productive and more expensive farm machinery, and to plow under millions more acres of grassland. In the 1920s when lessening demand caused the price of wheat to fall precipitously, many farmers went bankrupt and their lands were left without crops or grass. When the drought and wind hit, these farms just literally blew away.

Even though the Dust Bowl of the 1930s went the way of previous drought with the return of normal rainfall and increased irrigation, the Great Plains is still a precarious place to farm. The irrigation is seriously lowering the water table in the area, and periodic droughts threaten a return to the conditions of the 1930s. Only with reduced expectations for productivity on the plains and a careful marshaling of the available resources will it be possible to restore a relatively stable ecology to the region.

I. THE BLACK BLIZZARDS ROLL IN

The thirties began in economic depression and in droughts. The first of those disasters usually gets all the attention, although for the many Americans living on farms drought was the more serious problem. In the spring of 1930 over 3 million men and women were out of work. They had lost their jobs or had been laid off without pay in the aftermath of the stock market crash of the preceding fall. Another 12 million would suffer the same fate in the following two years. Many of the unemployed had no place to live, nor even the means to buy food. They slept in public toilets, under bridges, in shantytowns along the railroad tracks, or on doorsteps, and in the most wretched cases they scavenged from garbage cans—a Calcutta existence in the richest nation ever. The farmer, in contrast, was slower to feel the impact of the crash. He usually had his own independent food supply and stood a bit aloof from the ups and downs of the urban-industrial system. In the twenties that aloofness had meant that most farm families had not fully shared in the giddy burst of affluence—in new washing machines, silk stockings, and shiny roadsters. They had, in fact spent much of the decade in economic doldrums. Now, as banks began to fail and soup lines formed, rural Americans went on as before, glad to be spared the latest reversal and just a little pleased to see their proud city cousins humbled. Then the droughts began, and they brought the farmers to their knees, too.

During the spring and summer of 1930, little rain fell over a large part of the eastern United States. A horizontal band on the map, from Maryland and Virginia to Missouri and Arkansas, marked the hardest hit area of wilting crops, shrinking ground-water supplies, and uncertain income. Over the summer months in this drought band the rainfall shortage was 60,000 tons for each 100–acre farm, or 700 tons a day. Seventeen million people were affected. In twelve states the drought set record lows in precipitation, and among all the Eastern states only Florida was above normal. Three years earlier the Mississippi River had overflowed in banks and levees in one of the most destructive floods in American history. Now captains there wondered how long their barges would remain afloat as the river shrank to a fraction of its average height.

During the thirties serious drought threatened a great part of the nation. The persistent center, however, shifted from the East to the Great Plains, beginning in 1931, when much of Montana and the Dakotas became almost as arid as the Sonoran Desert. Farmers there and almost everywhere else watched the scorched earth crack open, heard the gray grass crunch underfoot, and worried about how long they would be able to pay their bills. Around their dried-up ponds the willows and wild cherries were nearly leafless, and even the poison ivy drooped. Drought, of course, is a relative term: it depends upon one's concept of "normal." But following the lead of the climatologists of the time, we can use a precipitation deficiency of at least 15 per cent of the historical mean to qualify as drought. By that standard, of all the American states only Maine and Vermont escaped a drought year from 1930 to 1936. Twenty states set or equaled record lows for their entire span of official weather data. Over the nation as a whole, the 1930s drought was, in the words of a Weather Bureau scientist, "the worst in the climatological history of the country."

Intense heat accompanied the drought, along with economic losses the nation could ill afford. In the summer of 1934, Nebraska reached

118 degrees, Iowa, 115. In Illinois thermometers stuck at over 100 degrees for so long that 370 people died—and one man, who had been living in a refrigerator to keep cool, was treated for frostbite. Two years later, when the country was described by *Newsweek* as "a vast simmering caldron," more than 4500 died from excessive heat, water was shipped into the West by diverted tank-cars and oil pipelines, and clouds of grasshoppers ate what little remained of many farmers' wheat and corn—along with their fenceposts and the washing on their clotheslines. The financial cost of the 1934 drought alone amounted to one-half the money the United States had put into World War I. By 1936, farm losses had reached $25 million a day, and more than 2 million farmers were drawing relief checks. Rexford Tugwell, head of the Resettlement Administration, who toured the burning plains that year, saw "a picture of complete destruction"—"one of the most serious peacetime problems in the nation's history."

As the decade reached its midpoint, it was the southern plains that experienced the most severe conditions. During some growing seasons there was no soil moisture down to three feet over large parts of the region. By 1939, near Hays, Kansas, the accumulated rainfall deficiency was more than 34 inches—almost a two-year supply in arrears. Continued long enough in such a marginal, semiarid land, a drought of that magnitude would produce a desert. Weathermen pointed out that there had been worse single years, as in 1910 and 1917, or back in the 1890s, and they repeatedly assured the people of the region that their records did not show any modern drought lasting more than five years, nor did they suggest any long-range adverse climatic shift. But farmers and ranchers did not find much comfort in statistical charts; their cattle were bawling for feed, and their bank credit was drying up along with the soil. Not until after 1941 did the rains return in abundance and the burden of anxiety lift.

Droughts are an inevitable fact of life on the plains, an extreme one occurring roughly every twenty years, and milder ones every three or four. They have always brought with them blowing dust where the ground was bare of crops or native grass. Dust was so familiar an event that no one was surprised to see it appear when the dry weather began in 1931. But no one was prepared for what came later: dust storms of such violence that they made the drought only a secondary problem— storms of such destructive force that they left the region reeling in confusion and fear.

"Earth" is the word we use when it is there in place, growing the food we eat, giving us a place to stand and build on. "Dust" is what we say when it is loose and blowing on the wind. Nature encompasses both—the good and the bad from our perspective, and from that of all living things. We need the earth to stay alive, but dust is a nuisance, or, worse, a killer. On a planet such as ours, where there is much wind, where there are frequent dry spells, and where we encounter vast expanses of bare soil, dust is a constant presence. It rises from the hooves of animals, from a wagon's wheels, from a dry riverbed, from the deserts. If all the continents were an English greensward, there would be no dust. But nature has not made things so. Nor has man, in many times and places.

Dust in the air in one phenomenon. However, dust storms are quite another. The story of the southern plains in the 1930s is essentially about dust storms, when the earth ran amok. And not once or twice, but over and over for the better part of a decade: day after day, year after year, of sand rattling against the window, of fine powder caking one's lips, of springtime turned to despair, of poverty eating into self-confidence.

Explaining why those storms occurred requires an excursion into the history of the plains and an understanding of the agriculture that evolved there. For the "dirty thirties," as they were called, were primarily the work of man, not nature. Admittedly, nature had something to do with this disaster too. Without winds the soil would have stayed put, no matter how bare it was. Without drought, farmers would have had strong, healthy crops capable of checking the wind. But natural factors did not make the storms—they merely made them possible. The storms were mainly the result of stripping the landscape of its natural vegetation to such an extent that there was no defense against the dry winds, no sod to hold the sandy or powdery dirt. The sod had been destroyed to make farms to grow wheat to get cash. But more of that later on. It is the storms themselves we must first comprehend: their magnitude, their effect, even their taste and smell. What was it like to be caught in one of them? How much did the people suffer, and how did they cope?

Weather bureau stations on the plains reported a few small dust storms throughout 1932, as many as 179 in April 1933, and in November of that year a large one that carried all the way to Georgia and New York. But it was the May 1934 blow that swept in a new dark age. On 9 May, brown earth from Montana and Wyoming swirled up from the ground, was captured by extremely high-level winds, and was blown eastward toward the Dakotas. More dirt was sucked into the airstream, until 350 million tons were riding toward urban America. By late afternoon the storm had reached Dubuque and Madison, and by evening 12 million tons of dust were falling like snow over Chicago—4 pounds for each person in the city. Midday at Buffalo on 10 May was darkened by dust, and the advancing gloom stretched south from there over several states, moving as fast as 100 miles an hour. The dawn of 11 May found the dust settling over Boston, New York, Washington, and Atlanta, and then the storm moved out to sea. Savannah's skies were hazy all day 12 May; it was the last city to report dust conditions. But there were still ships in the Atlantic, some of them 300 miles off the coast, that found dust on their decks during the next day or two.

"Kansas dirt," the New York press called it, though it actually came from father north. More would come that year and after, and some of it was indeed from Kansas—or Nebraska or New Mexico. In a later spring, New Hampshire farmers, out to tap their maples, discovered a fresh brown snow on the ground, discoloration from transported Western soil. Along the Gulf Coast, at Houston and Corpus Christi, dirt from the Llano Estacado collected now and then on windowsills and sidewalks. But after May 1934 most of the worst dust storms were confined to southern plains region; less frequently were they carried by those high-altitude currents moving east or southeast. Two types of dusters became common then: the dramatic "black blizzards" and the more frequent "sand blows." The first came with a rolling turbulence, rising like a long wall of muddy water as high as 7000 or 8000 feet. Like the winter blizzards to which they were compared, these dusters were caused by the arrival of a polar continental air mass, and the atmospheric electricity it generated helped lift the dirt higher and higher in a cold boil, sometimes accompanied by thunder and lightning, other times by an eerie silence. Such storms were not only terrifying to observers, but immensely destructive to the region's fine, dark soils, rich in nutrients. The second kind of duster was a more constant event, created by the low sirocco-like winds that blew out of the southwest and left the sandier soils drifted into dunes along fence rows and ditches. Long after New York and Philadelphia had forgotten their taste of the plains, the people out there ate their own dirt again and again.

In the 1930s the Soil Conservation Service compiled a frequency chart of all dust storms of regional extent, when visibility was cut to less than a mile. In 1932 there were 14; in 1933, 38; 1934, 22; 1935, 40; 1936, 68; 1937, 72; 1938, 61—dropping as the drought relented a bit— 1939, 30; 1940, 17; 1941, 17. Another measure of severity was made by calculating the total number of hours the dust storms lasted during a year. By that criterion 1937 was again the worst; at Guymon, in the panhandle of Oklahoma, the total number of hours that year climbed to 550, mostly concentrated in the first six months of the year. In Amarillo the worst year was 1935, with a total of 908 hours. Seven times, from January to March, the visibility there reached zero—all complete blackouts, one of them lasting eleven hours. A single storm might rage for one hour or three and a half days. Most of the winds came from the southwest, but they also came from the west, north, and northeast, and they could slam against windows and walls with 60 miles-per-hour force. The dirt left behind on the front lawn might be brown, black, yellow, ashy gray, or, more rarely, red, depending upon its source.

And each color had its own peculiar aroma, from a sharp peppery smell that burned the nostrils to a heavy greasiness that nauseated.

In the memory of older plains residents, the blackest year was 1935, particularly the early spring weeks from 1 March to mid-April, when the Dust Bowl made its full-blown debut. Springtime in western Kansas can be a Willa Cather world of meadowlarks on the wing, clean white curtains dancing in the breeze, anemones and wild verbena in bloom, lilacs by the porch, a windmill spinning briskly, and cold fresh water in the bucket—but not in 1935. After a February heat wave (it reached 75 degrees in Topeka that month), the dust began moving across Kansas, Oklahoma, and Texas, and for the next six weeks it was unusual to see a clear sky from dawn until sundown. On 15 March, Denver reported that a serious dust storm was speeding eastward. Kansans ignored the radio warnings, went about their business as usual, and later wondered what had hit them. Small-town printer Nate White was at the picture show when the dust reached Smith Center: as he walked out the exit, it was as if someone had put a blindfold over his eyes; he bumped into telephone poles, skinned his shins on boxes and cans in an alleyway, fell to his hands and knees, and crawled along the curbing to a dim houselight. A seven-year-old boy wandered away and was lost in the gloom; the search party found him later, suffocated in a drift. A more fortunate child was found alive, tangled in a barbed wire fence. Near Colby, a train was derailed by dirt on the tracks, and the passengers spent twelve dreary hours in the coaches. The Lora-Locke Hotel in Dodge City overflowed with more than two hundred stranded travelers; many of them bedded down on cots in the lobby and ballroom. In the following days, as the dust kept falling, electric lights burned continuously, cars left tracks in the dirt-covered streets, and schools and offices stayed closed. A reporter at Great Bend remarked on the bizarre scene: "Uncorked jug placed on sidewalk two hours, found to be half filled with dust. Picture wires giving way due to excessive weight of dust on frames. Irreparable loss in portraits anticipated. Lady Godiva could ride thru streets without even the horse seeing her."

The novelty of this duster, so like a coffee-colored winter snow, made it hard for most people to take it seriously. But William Allen White, the Emporia editor, called it "the greatest show" since Pompeii was buried in ashes. And a Garden City woman described her experience for the *Kansas City Times*:

> All we could do about it was just sit in our dusty chairs, gaze at each other through the fog that filled the room and watch that fog settle slowly and silently, covering everything—including ourselves—in a thick, brownish gray blanket. When we opened the door swirling whirlwinds of soil beat against us unmercifully. . . . The door and windows were all shut tightly, yet those tiny parti-

cles seemed to seep through the very walls. It got into cupboards and clothes closets; our faces were as dirty as if we had rolled in the dirt; our hair was gray and stiff and we ground dirt between our teeth.

By the end of the month conditions had become so unrelenting that many Kansans had begun to chew their nails. "Watch for the Second Coming of Christ," warned one of Topeka's unhinged, "God is wrathful." Street-corner sects in Hill City and other towns warned pedestrians to heed the signs of the times. A slightly less frenetic Concordian jotted in her log: "This is ultimate darkness. So must come the end of the world." The mood of the people had begun to change, if not to apocalyptic dread in every case, at least to a fear that this was a nightmare that might never end.

By 24 March southeastern Colorado and western Kansas had seen twelve consecutive days of dust storms, but there was worse to come. Near the end of March a new duster swept across the southern plains, destroying one-half the wheat crop in Kansas, one-quarter of it in Oklahoma, and all of it in Nebraska—5 million acres blown out. The storm carried away from the plains twice as much earth as men and machines had scooped out to make the Panama Canal, depositing it once again over the East Coast states and the Atlantic Ocean. Then the wind slackened off a bit, gathering strength, as it were, for the spectacular finale of that unusual spring season—Black Sunday, 14 April.

Dawn came clear and rosy all across the plains that day. By noon the skies were so fresh and blue that people could not remain indoors; they remembered how many jobs they had been postponing, and with a revived spirit they rushed outside to get them done. Then went on picnics, planted gardens, repaired henhouses, attended funerals, drove to the neighbors for a visit. In midafternoon the summery air rapidly turned colder, falling as many as 50 degrees in a few hours, and the people noticed then that the yards were full of birds nervously fluttering and chattering—and more were arriving every moment, as though fleeing from some unseen enemy. Suddenly there appeared on the northern horizon a black blizzard, moving toward them; there was no sound, no wind, nothing but an immense "boogery" cloud. The storm struck Dodge City at 2:40 p.m. Not far from there John Garretson, a farmer in Haskell County, Kansas, who was on the road with his wife, Louise, saw it coming, but he was sure that he could beat it home. They had almost made it when they were engulfed; abandoning the car, they groped for the fencewire and, hand over hand, followed it to their door. Down in the panhandle Ed and Ada Phillips of Boise City, with their six-year-old daughter, were on their way home too, after an outing to Texline in their Model A Ford. It was about five o'clock when the black wall appeared, and they still had fifteen miles to go. Seeing an old adobe house ahead, Ed realized that they had to take shelter, and quickly. By the time there were out of the car the dust was upon them, making it so dark that they nearly missed the door. Inside they found ten other people, stranded, like themselves, in a two-room hut, all fearing that they might be smothered, all unable to see their companions' faces. For four hours they sat there, until the storm let up enough for them to follow the roadside ditch back to town. By then the ugly pall was moving south across the high plains of Texas and New Mexico.

Older residents still remember Black Sunday in all its details—where they were when the storm hit, what they did then. Helen Wells was the wife of the Reverend Rolley Wells, the Methodist minister in Guymon. Early that morning she had helped clean the accumulated dust from the church pews, working until she was choking and exhausted. Back in the parsonage she switched on the radio for some inspiring music and what she heard was the hymn "We'll Work Till Jesus Comes." "I just had to sit down and laugh," she recalls; she had worn out her sweeper but still had a broom if that was needed. Later that day her husband, partly to please two visiting *Saturday Evening Post* reporters, held a special "rain service," which concluded in time for the congregation to get home before the dust arrived.

A Kansas cattle dealer, Raymond Ellsaesser, almost lost his wife that day. She had gone into Sublette with her young daughter for a Rebekah lodge meeting. On the way home she stopped along the highway, unable to see even the winged hood ornament on her car. The static electricity in the storm then shorted out her ignition, and foolishly, she determined to walk the three-quarters of a mile home. Her daughter plunged ahead to get Raymond's help, and he quickly piled into a truck and drove back down the road, hallooing out the window. Back and forth he passed, but his wife had disappeared into the fog-like dust, wandering straight away from the car into the field, where she stumbled about with absolutely no sense of direction. Each time she saw the truck's headlights she moved that way, not realizing her husband was in motion too. It was only by sheer luck that she found herself at last standing in the truck's beams, gasping for air and near collapse.

The last of the major dust storms that year was on 14 April, and it was months before the damages could be fully calculated. Those who had been caught outside in one of the spring dusters were, understandably, most worried about their lungs. An epidemic of respiratory infections and something called "dust pneumonia" broke out across the plains. The four small hospitals in Meade County, Kansas, found that 52 per cent of their April admissions were acute respiratory cases—thirty-three patients died. Many dust victims would arrive at a hospital almost dead, after driving long distances in storm. They spat up clods of dirt, washed the mud out of their mouths, swabbed their nostrils with Vaseline, and rinsed their bloodshot eyes with boric acid water. Old people and babies were the most vulnerable to the dusters, as were those who had chronic asthma, bronchitis, or tuberculosis, some of whom had moved to the plains so they might breathe the high, dry air.

Doctors could not agree on whether the dust caused a new kind of pneumonia, and some even denied that there were any unusual health problems in their communities. But the Red Cross thought the situation was so serious that it set up six emergency hospitals in Kansas, Colorado, and Texas, and it staffed them with its own nurses. In Topeka and Wichita volunteers worked in high school sewing rooms to make dust masks of cheesecloth; over 17,000 of those masks were sent to the plains, especially to towns where goggles had been sold out. Chewing tobacco was a better remedy, snorted some farmers, who thought it was too much of a bother to wear such gadgets when driving their tractors. But enough wore the Red Cross masks or some other protection to make the plains look like a World War I battlefield, with dust instead of mustard gas coming out of the trenches.

On 29 April the Red Cross sponsored a conference of health officers from several states. Afterward the representatives of the Kansas Board of Health went to work on the medical problem in more detail, and eventually they produced a definitive study on the physiological impact of the dust storms. From 21 February to 30 April they counted 28 days of "dense" dust at Dodge City and only 13 days that were "dust free." Dirt deposited in bakepans during the five biggest storms gave an estimated 4.7 tons of total fallout per acre. Agar plate cultures showed "no pathogenic organisms" in the accumulation, only harmless soil bacteria, plant hair, and microfungus spores. But the inorganic content of the dust was mainly fine silicon particles, along with bits of feldspar, volcanic ash, and calcite; and "silica," they warned, "is as much a body poison as is lead"—"probably the most widespread and insidious of all hazards in the environment of mankind," producing, after sufficient contact, silicosis of the lungs. These scientists also found that a measles outbreak had come with the black blizzards, though why that happened was not clear; in only five months there were twice as many cases as in any previous twelve-month period. The death rate from acute respiratory infections in the 45 western counties of Kansas, where the dust was most intense, was 99 per 100,000, compared with the statewide average of 70; and the infant mortality was 80.5, compared with the state's 62.3.

The medical remedies for the dust were at best primitive and makeshift. In addition to wearing light gauze masks, health officials recommended attaching translucent glasscloth to the inside frames of windows, although people also used cardboard, canvas, or blankets.

Hospitals covered some of their patients with wet sheets, and house-wives flapped the air with wet dish towels to collect dust. One of the most common tactics was to stick masking tape, felt strips, or paraffin-soaked rags around the windows and door cracks. The typical plains house was loosely constructed and without insulation, but sometimes those methods proved so effective that there was not enough air cir-culation inside to replenish the oxygen supply. Warren Moore of southwestern Kansas remembers watching, during a storm, the gas flame on the range steadily turn orange and the coal-oil lamp dim until the people simply had to open the window, dust or no dust. But most often there was no way to seal out the fine, blowing dirt: it blackened the pillow around one's head, the dinner plates on the table, the bread dough on the back of the stove. It became a steady part of one's diet and breathing. "We thrived on it," claim some residents today; it was their "vitamin K." But all the same they prayed that they would not ingest so much it would maim them for life, or finish them off, as it had a neighbor or two.

Livestock and wildlife did not have even those crude defenses. "In a rising sand storm," wrote Margaret Bourke-White, "cattle quickly be-come blinded. They run around in circles until they fall and breathe so much dust that they die. Autopsies show their lungs caked with dust and mud." Newborn calves could suffocate in a matter of hours, and the older cattle ground their teeth down to the gums trying to eat the dirt-covered grass. As the dust buried the fences, horses and cattle climbed over and wandered away. Where there was still water in riv-ers, the dust coated the surface and the fish died too. The carcasses of jackrabbits, small birds, and field mice lay along roadsides by the hundreds after a severe duster; and those that survived were in such shock that they could be picked up and their nostrils and eyes wiped clean. In a lighter vein, it was said that prairie dogs were now able to tunnel upward several feet from the ground.

Cleaning up houses, farm lots, and city stores after the 1935 blow season was an expensive matter. People literally shoveled the dirt from their front yards and swept up bushel-basketfuls inside. One man's ceiling collapsed from the silt that had collected in the attic. Carpets, draperies, and tapestries were so dust-laden that their patterns were indiscernible. Painted surfaces had been sandblasted bare. Automobile and tractor engines operated in dust storms without oil-bath air cleaners were ruined by grit, and the repair shops had plenty of business. Dur-ing March alone, Tucumcari, New Mexico, reported over $288,000 in property damage, although most towns' estimates were more con-servative than that: Liberal, Kansas, $150,000; Randall County, Texas, $10,000; Lamar, Colorado, $3800. The merchants of Amarillo calculated from 3 to 15 per cent damage to their merchandise, not to mention the loss of shoppers during the storms. In Dodge City a men's clothing store advertised a "dust sale," knocking shirts down to 75 cents. But the heaviest burdens lay on city work crews, who had to sweep dirt from the gutters and municipal swimming pools, and on housewives, who struggled after each blow to get their houses clean.

The emotional expense was the hardest to accept, however. All day you could sit with your hands folded on the oilcloth-covered table, the wind moaning around the eaves, the fine, soft, talc sifting in the keyholes, the sky a coppery gloom; and when you went to bed the acrid dust crept into your dreams. Avis Carlson told what it was like at night:

> A trip for water to rinse the grit from your lips. And then back to bed with washcloths over our noses. We try to lie still, because every turn stirs the dust on the blankets. After a while, if we are good sleepers, we forget.

After 1935 the storms lost much of their drama; for most people they were simply a burden to be endured, and sometimes that burden was too heavy. Druggists sold out their supplies of sedatives quickly. An Oklahoman took down his shotgun, ready to kill his entire family and himself—"we're all better off dead," he despaired. That, to be sure, was an extreme instance, but there were indeed men and women who turned distraught, wept, and then, listless, gave up caring.

The plains people, however, then as now, were a tough-minded, leatherskinned folk, not easily discouraged. Even in 1935 they managed to laugh a bit at their misfortunes. They told about the farmer who fainted when a drop of water struck him in the face and had to be revived by having three buckets of sand thrown over him. They also passed around the one about the motorist who came upon a ten-gallon hat resting on a dust drift. Under it he found a head looking at him. "Can I help you some way?" the motorist asked, "Give you a ride into town maybe?" "Thanks, but I'll make it on my own," was the reply, "I'm on a horse." They laughed with Will Rogers when he pointed out that only highly advanced civilizations—like ancient Mesopotamia—were ever covered over by dirt, and that California would never qualify. Newspaper editors could still find something to joke about, too: "When better dust storms are made," the *Dodge City Globe* boasted, "the Southwest will make them." Children were especially hard to keep down; for them the storms always meant adventure, happy chaos, a breakdown of their teachers' authority, and perhaps a holiday. When darkness descends, as it did that April, humor, bravado, or a childlike irresponsibility may have as much value as a storm cellar.

Whether they brought laughter or tears, the dust storms that swept across the southern plains in the 1930s created the most severe environmental catastrophe in the entire history of the white man on this continent. In no other instance was there greater or more sustained damage to the American land, and there have been few times when so much tragedy was visited on its inhabitants. Not even the Depression was more devastating, economically. And in ecological terms we have nothing in the nation's past, nothing even in the polluted present, that compares. Suffice it to conclude here that in the decade of the 1930s the dust storms of the plains were an unqualified disaster.

At such dark times the mettle of a people is thoroughly and severely tested, revealing whether they have the will to go on. By this test the men and women of the plains were impressive, enduring, as most of them did, discouragements the like of which more recent generations have never had to face. But equally important, disasters of this kind challenge a society's capacity to think—require it to analyze and explain and learn from misfortune. Societies that fail this test are sitting ducks for more of the same. Those that pass, on the other hand, have attained through suffering and hardship a more mature, self-appraising character, so that they are more aware than before of their vulnerabilities and weaknesses. They are stronger because they have been made sensitive to their deficiencies. Whether the dust storms had this enlarging, critical effect on the minds of southern plainsmen remains to be seen.

II. IF IT RAINS

The American plains are a "next year" country. This season the crops may wither and die, the winds may pile up dirt against the barn, but next time we will do better—we will strike a bonanza. If we are poor today, we will be rich tomorrow. If there is drought, it will rain soon. In the dirty thirties that quality of hope was strained to the breaking point. But for every discouraged resident who wanted to leave, or did so, there were two more who were determined to stick it out, hang on, stay with it. Some remained out of sheer inertia or bewilderment over what else to do, or because they had the economic means to stay where others did not. Whatever the reasons people had for not moving away, hope was commonly a part of them. The people were optimists, unwilling to believe that the dust storms would last or that their damage would be very severe. That attitude was not so much a matter of cold reason as it was of faith that the future must be better. Optimism may be an essential response for survival in this sometimes treacherous world; it certainly brought many Western farmers through to greener days. But it also can be a form of lunacy. There is about the perennial optimist a dangerous naïveté, a refusal to face the grim truths about oneself or others or nature. Optimism can also divert our attention from critical self-appraisal and substantive reforms, which is exactly what happened on the plains.

Optimism may rest either on a confidence in one's ability to affect the course of events or, paradoxically, on a happy, fatalistic belief that the world is preordained to promote one's welfare. Plainsmen in the 1930s went both ways. They were sure that they could manage the land and bring it under control, especially if Franklin Roosevelt's New Deal would give them a bit of help. Hard work and determination would pay off in the end. They were even surer that the laws of nature were on their side. A perceptual geographer, Thomas Saarinen, has concluded that Great Plains farmers consistently and habitually underrate the possibility of drought—that they minimize the risks involved in their way of life. When drought occurs, they insist that it cannot last long. Consequently, although they may become unhappy or upset by crop failures, they feel no need to seek out logical solutions or change their practices. They are prouder of their ability to tough it out than to analyze their situation rationally, because they expect nature to be good to them and make them prosper. It is an optimism at heart fatalistic—and potentially fatal in a landscape as volatile as that of the plains.

The source of that optimism is cultural: it is the ethos of an upwardly mobile society. When a people emphasize, as much as Americans do, the need to get ahead in the world, they must have a corresponding faith in the benignity of nature and the future. If they are farmers on the Western plains, they must believe that rain is on its way, that dust storms are a temporary aberration, and that one had better plant wheat again even if there is absolutely no moisture in the soil. The black blizzards said, however, that there was something seriously amiss in the plainsmen's thinking—that nature would not yield so easily, so reliably, all the riches expected, and that the future would not necessarily bring higher and higher levels of prosperity. Blowing dirt challenged the most cherished assumptions of middle-class farmers and merchants about the inevitability of progress; therefore the dirt had to be minimized, discounted, evaded, even ignored. The bedrock plainsmen's response was to shout down nature's message with a defense of the old assumptions. Changes in attitudes did occur, to be sure, but the most incredible fact of the dirty thirties was the tenacity of bourgeois optimism and its imperviousness to all warnings.

The pattern of reaction among plainsmen went something like this: fail to anticipate drought, underestimate its duration when it comes, expect rain momentarily, deny that they are as hard hit as outsiders believe, defend the region against critics, admit that *some* help would be useful, demand that the government act and act quickly, insist that federal aid be given without strings and when and where local residents want it, vote for those politicians who confirm the people's optimism and pooh-pooh the need for major reform, resent interference by the bureaucrats, eagerly await the return of "normalcy" when the plains will once more proceed along the road of steady progress. Accepting the coming of the New Deal fit into that pattern more or less easily. The region received more federal dollars than any other, along with reassurance, solicitation, and encouragement. But whenever the New Deal really tried to become new and innovative, plainsmen turned hostile. The fate of the plains lay in the hands of Providence, and Providence, not Washington, would see them come out all right.

The day after Black Sunday the Dust Bowl got its name. Robert Geiger, an Associated Press reporter from Denver, traveled through the worst-hit part of the plains, and he sent a dispatch to the *Washington Evening Star*, which carried it on 15 April 1935: "Three little words," it began, "achingly familiar on a Western farmer's tongue, rule life in the dust bowl of the continent—if it rains." That Geiger meant nothing special by the label was apparent two days later, when in another dispatch he called the blow area the "dust belt." But, inexplicably, it was "bowl" that stuck, passing quickly into the vernacular, its author soon forgotten and never really sure himself where it all began. Some liked the name as a satire on college football—first the Rose Bowl and the Orange Bowl, now the Dust Bowl—or they thought it described nicely what happened to the sugar bowl on the table. Geiger more likely had recalled the geographical image of the plains pushed forward by another Denver man, William Gilpin. In the 1850s, the continent, Gilpin had thought, was a great fertile bowl rimmed by mountains, its concave interior destined one day to become the seat of empire. If that was the unconscious precedent, then Geiger's "dust bowl" was more ironic than anyone realized.

Within weeks the southern plains had a new identity, one that they would never be able to shake off. The label came spontaneously into the speeches of the region's governors, into the pressrooms of city newspapers, and into the private letters of local residents to their distant friends—for all of them it was a handle to put on this peculiar problem. When the Soil Conservation Service capitalized it and began using it on their maps, even setting up a special office in the area, "Dust Bowl" became official. The SCS followed Geiger's own delineation rather closely: "the western third of Kansas, Southeastern Colorado, the Oklahoma Panhandle, the northern two-thirds of the Texas Panhandle, and Northeastern New Mexico." But the SCS's Region VI also covered an extensive fringe that made a total of almost 100 million acres, stretching 500 miles from north to south, 300 from east to west—about one-third of the entire Great Plains. A serious blowing hazard existed on a shifting 50 million of those acres from 1935 to 1938. In

1935 the Dust Bowl reached well down into the cotton belt of west Texas, but three years later it had moved northeastward, making Kansas the most extensively affected state. By 1939 the serious blow area within the Bowl had shrunk to about one-fifth its original size; it increased again to 22 million acres in 1940, then in the forties it disappeared.

The difficulty in making the Dust Bowl more fixed and precise was that it roamed around a good deal—it was an event as well as a locality. A puzzled tourist stopped George Taton, a Kansas wheat farmer, in Garden City one day: "Can you tell me where this Dust Bowl is?" "Stay where you are," Taton told him, "and it'll come to you." Even locals could not always discover the exact boundaries, wondering exasperatedly, "Are we in it or ain't we?" In a sense, wherever there were recurring dust storms and soil erosion there was a dust bowl, and by that test most of the Great Plains was "in it" during a part of the 1930s, some of the most severe conditions occurring as far north as Nebraska and the Dakotas. But SCS officials, surveying the entire plains, placed their Dust Bowl perimeters around the most persistent problem area, and there was no doubt which counties were at the heart of this Bowl: Morton in Kansas, Baca in Colorado, Texas and Cimarron in Oklahoma, Dallam in Texas, and Union in New Mexico.

By 1935 the landscape in those and surrounding counties had become, in Geiger's words, "a vast desert, with miniature shifting dunes of sand." The fences, piled high with tumbleweeds and drifted over with dirt, looked like giant backbones of ancient reptiles. Elsewhere the underlying hardpan was laid bare, as sterile and unyielding as a city pavement. The winds exposed long-buried Indian campgrounds, as well as arrowheads, pioneer wagon wheels, Spanish stirrups, branding irons, tractor wrenches, the chain someone had dropped in the furrow the previous year. By 1938, the peak year for wind erosion, 10 million acres had lost at least the upper five inches of topsoil; another 13.5 million acres had lost at least two and a half inches. Over all the cultivated land in the region, there were 408 tons of dirt blown away from the average acre, in some cases only to the next farm, in others to the next state or beyond. According to Roy Kimmel, the special federal coordinator assigned to the Dust Bowl, in 1938 they were still losing 850 million tons of earth a year to erosion, far more than was washed down the Mississippi. The dirt that blew away, one Iowa-deposited sample revealed, contained ten times as much organic matter and nitrogen— the basics of fertility—as did the sand dunes left behind in Dallam County, Texas.

After Geiger, other journalists came to the Dust Bowl, and they described the scene to urban Americans. They usually carried with them a license for hyperbole and a capacity for shock. George Greenfield of the *New York Times*, passing through Kansas on the Union Pacific, was the most funereal: "Today I have seen the cold hand of death on what was one of the great breadbaskets of the nation . . . a lost people living in a lost land." But more cutting was the 1937 *Collier's* article by Walter Davenport, "Land Where Our Children Die," which found in the Dust Bowl only "famine, violent death, private and public futility, insanity, and lost generations." For Davenport the source of the devastation lay in its Dogpatch residents—its Willie Mae Somethings, Jere Hullomons, Twell Murficks, all too stupid or greedy to be trusted with the land. Then there were the newsreel photographers from the *March of Time,* who had heard about Texas crows being forced to build their nests out of barbed wire and, of course, hurriedly came to exploit the rumor rather than examine it. In theaters, newspapers, and magazines, Americans began to see more of the southern plains, a place remote from their experience and heretofore ignored, but invariably what they saw was the same extreme slice of reality, the most sensationally barren parts of that land.

These outside reports, however, were not total fabrications, as many local residents admitted in their own descriptions of what they saw. Albert Law of the *Dalhart Texan* published this frank account in 1933, well before the peak years:

> Not a blade of wheat in Cimarron County, Oklahoma; cattle dying there on the range; a few bushels of wheat in the Perryton area against an average yield of from four to six million bushels; with all the stored surplus not more than fifty per cent of the seeding needs will be met—ninety per cent of the poultry dead because of the sand storms; sixty cattle dying Friday afternoon between Guymon and Liberal from some disease induced by dust—humans suffering from dust fever—milk cows going dry, turned into pasture to starve, hogs in such pitiable shape that buyers will not have them; cattle being moved from Dallam and other counties to grass; no wheat in Hartley County; new crops a remote possibility, cattle facing starvation; Potter, Seward and other Panhandle counties with one-third of their population on charity or relief work; ninety per cent of the farmers in most counties have had to have crop loans, and continued drought forcing many of them to use the money for food, clothes, medicine, shelter.

Confirmation of those details came from all over. In Moore County, Texas, for example, the welfare director, on behalf of the Dumas Chamber of Commerce, reported to federal officials in March 1935 that it was "an impossible task to describe the utter destruction": roads obliterated, the crops all gone, "no hope or ambition left," and many farmers "near starvation." Today, more than forty years later, old-timers often point out that outsiders never knew what the dirty past of the thirties was really like, never appreciated how severe the problem was.

But at the same time there were many on the plains, especially businessmen in the towns, who bitterly resented their "Dust Bowl" reputation, so much so that they formed truth squads to get the straight facts to the rest of the nation. Usually "straight" meant "most flattering," and those who did not conform, who saw things differently, could be in for trouble. Albert Law's paper lost more than $1000 in advertising after his frank article appeared, and in later years he learned to speak more carefully, even to join the truth-squad vigilantes. In 1936 he referred to that "harebrained individual" who "in an abortive fit" misnamed the plains "Dust Bowl." Leadership for the defensive campaign came from several west Texas chambers of commerce, particularly Dalhart's, and from editor John L. McCarty of Dalhart and, later, of Amarillo, McCarty's style was at its shoot-em-up best in this refutation of the *Collier's* article by Walter Davenport: "a vicious libel," "compounded of lies and half-truths," "bunk," "more bunk" "sissy." The outrage lay not only in that outside critics were condemning "a group of courageous Americans for a six-year drought cycle and national conditions beyond their control"; they were also destroying the property values, bank credit, and business prospects of the region.

A minor but extreme episode in this effort to clear away the dust from the plains' reputation centered on painter Alexandre Hogue. The son of Missouri minister, Hogue had spent much of this youth on his brother-in-law's ranch near Hartley, Texas, not far from Dalhart, where he had learned to love the country and the cowhand's life. In his mid-thirties when the dusters appeared, he began painting the ravaged panhandle landscape. Dust drifts, starved cattle, broken-down windmills, and rattlesnakes were the principal features of his works, scenes as hopeless and grim as Hogue could manage. The paintings were obviously fictions, exaggerated for dramatic effect—"superrealism" or "psycho-reality" he called his style—but brilliantly conveying the painter's ambivalent mood about the disaster. There was the utter destruction of a rural way of life, which he deeply regretted, but there was also a fascination with the forms of disorder. "They were *not* social comment," Hogue insists; "I did them because to me, aside from the tragedy of the situation, the effects were beautiful, beautiful in a terrifying way." But the Dalhart Chamber of Commerce was not ready for Hogue's aestheticism, and when *Life* magazine published some of his works in 1937 and called him "artist of the dust bowl" (he hated that phrase), the vigilantes went into action. Hogue, they insisted, was "some upstart sent down from New York who knows nothing about the region and so painted isolated cases that are not typical if they even exist." An emissary was sent to Dallas to purchase the painting "Drought Survivors" from the Pan-American Exposition there; the truth squad planned to burn it on the streets of Dalhart. But when the emissary discovered that he had been given only $50 to buy a $2000 work, he trudged back home—and art triumphed over local pride, or at least cost more.

To admit that the plains had in fact become a disaster area was to give up faith in the future and the productive potential of the land. Many simply could not bring themselves to do it. They were quick to deny, and to repress, the Dust Bowl label. But they were even quicker to announce that the Bowl was shrinking. One month after Black Sunday rain was falling everywhere; Baca County got one inch and a half— it's a "mud bowl" now, they exulted. Floods were rampaging in Hutchingson and Augusta, Kansas, just east of the blow area. It was a short-lived phenomenon, as were other moments of respite in the later part of the decade. But it was enough to renew faith in the future and to vindicate the vigilantes. One year later, in March 1936, Robert Geiger came back to Oklahoma and wrote that, with more rains, "the 'Dust Bowl' is losing its handle." Ida Watkins, a large-scale wheat farmer in southwestern Kansas, was so encouraged that she began planting, explaining to a visitor:

> I guess the good Lord is going to lead us out into the promised Land again. . . . For five years we have been living here in the desert of the dust bowl and now the abundant rains have taken us up into a high mountain and shown us close ahead the bounteous land of Canaan, blossoming with wheat and a new prosperity.

Like President Herbert Hoover, who kept reassuring the public that the Depression was almost over, these hopeful souls were false prophets. There were at least five more difficult years ahead, five years when the dust masks came out repeatedly, trains continued to be derailed by dust, and wheat fields often stood empty and dry. Most of those later storms were only "gray zephyrs" compared with those of 1935, but some could be awesomely devastating. One of the biggest ever came three years after Watkins's glimpse of the promised land—on 11 March 1939, when a Stillwater, Oklahoma, agronomist estimated there was enough dirt in the air to cover 5 million acres one foot deep. That storm raged over a 100,000-square-mile spread. A too-ready optimism was no more an effective defense against the winds of ruin than was censorship.

Even as the John McCartys were defending the region's credit rating and the Ida Watkinses were straining their eyes toward Canaan, plains residents were collecting federal aid. The benign arm of Providence could use a little government muscle, apparently. Things were not going to change for the better with time, it was feared—or at least few people were patient enough to wait around for that to happen. The plains were in serious trouble and getting worse, and no amount of faith in the inevitability of progress would save them unless prompt action were taken. What the plains wanted was a speedy restoration of "normal" expectations and the means to satisfy them. The New Deal promised that restoration, just as it offered factory workers the chance to go back to work in the same factory under the old ownership. In the mid-1930s out on the plains, federal money began raining down with the sweet smell of a spring shower, nourishing the seeds of hope that had so persistently been planted. In the absence of the real thing, such outpourings were the best available substitute. And for a while Washington became the new Providence.

It was a long way from the federal government to the Dust Bowl. The region was then, and still is, one of the most remote and rural parts of America. The largest city in the region was Amarillo, with a population of 43,000 in 1930. Denver, with almost 300,0000 inhabitants, lay at the extreme northwest corner of the Bowl, out on the fringe, as were all the other state capitals—Topeka, Oklahoma City, Austin, and Albuquerque. Scattered over the SCS's Region VI were 2 million people, most of them living not in cities, but in very small towns or on farms. And they were spiralling downward into desperate poverty as their crops failed year after year. In Hall and Childress counties in Texas, average cotton ginnings fell from 99,000 bales in the late 1920s to 12,500 in 1934. The next year Kansans cut wheat on only half their planted acreage; Stanton County reaped nothing. Those two years were especially bad, to be sure, but with the exception of 1938, a wetter year, not one in the decade saw a significantly improved harvest. As the agricultural base of the region's economy was buried under dust, extreme hardship loomed over the southern plains, and rescue by a distant government was the only hope.

In 1936, to determine which areas were in the most desperate straits, the federal government's Works Progress Administration (WPA) sent out two investigators, Francis Cronin and Howard Beers, to survey the entire Great Plains. Cronin and Beers compiled data in five categories—precipitation, crop production, status of pasturelands, changes in number of cattle, and federal aid per capita—all the way back to 1930. Taken together, the categories gave an index of "intense drought distress." Out of 800 counties they surveyed, from Minnesota and Montana to Texas, two centers of rural poverty emerged: first, an area that covered almost all of North and South Dakota, along with contiguous counties in neighboring states; and second, the Dust Bowl on the southern plains. Altogether, 125 counties from both foci qualified as "very severe" and another 127 as "severe." South Dakota led, with 41 counties in the bottom-most category; North Dakota had 23, as did Texas; Kansas, 20; Oklahoma, 5; Colorado, 2. By 1936, in each of the counties, federal aid for agricultural failure had already totaled at least $175 per person. Other studies revealed that government payments for the fourteen southwestern counties of Kansas came to $100 a year per capita, and Morton received twice that much. One-third to one-half of the farm families in that corner of the state depended upon some kind of government relief in 1935; it was still much less than the 80 per cent found in one North Dakota county, but it was well above the national average. "The prairie," observed a reader of the *Dallas Farm News* in 1939, "once the home of the deer, buffalo and antelope, is now the home of the Dust Bowl and the WPA."

Rural Americans had been more reluctant to ask for outside help than the city poor, even after they too had begun to feel the pinch of hard times. Nowhere was this aversion to "charity" more fierce than on the southern plains. To ask for aid implied personal and providential failure—the very "insult" that the McCarthy brigade had resented. In any case, there was little charity to be had, at least locally: no effective organization to give it out, public or private, in most counties; and nothing to give. State capitals were slow to learn about conditions, and slower to act, excusing themselves by reason of tight budgets. Thus there was only Washington, far away and highly suspect, but the last resort. At the onset of the drought President Hoover turned to the Red Cross, which had performed wonderfully in the Mississippi flood of 1927, to devise another rescue. But the Red Cross leaders, many of them appointed by Hoover, seriously underestimated the Western relief needs, appropriating only a third of what they had spend on the flood. At last, when it became apparent that these private efforts were pathetically inadequate, Congress set up a $45 million seed-and-feed loan fund. Hoover denounced it as "a raid on the public treasury" and a slide toward the degenerate "dole"—but he signed it into law. That was the beginning of federal initiatives to save the Great Plains from utter ruin.

The loan fund was not by any token adequate to the relief task, nor by 1932 was Hoover's gloomy mien or budget-consciousness acceptable to most Dust Bowl voters. In the national elections that year, the plains joined with the rest of the nation to elect Franklin Roosevelt, a gentleman farmer from New York, to the presidency. Traditionally Democratic Texas, Oklahoma, and New Mexico gave Roosevelt 88, 73, and 63 per cent of their votes, respectively; while in Kansas and Colorado the victory margin, although below the national level (almost 58 per cent), was a major departure from their loyal Republican past. It was time, the plainsmen agreed, for something beyond rugged individualism, even if they were unsure what and and how much the federal government ought to do for them. Perhaps Roosevelt's style, however, was more important to them than any specific program. His easy and buoyant manner appealed to a people who felt their traditional optimism slipping and wanted it shored up.

During his first year in office Roosevelt ignored the Great Plains, as his predecessor had done. It was perhaps understandable: there was a drought going on, but the dust storms had not yet reached continental proportions and he had his hands full with greater emergencies—thousands of bank failures and industrial shutdowns, national income cut in half, one out of every four workers unemployed. He did establish important new programs that would come to play a critical role in the region's recovery, such as the Agricultural Adjustment Administration, the Federal Emergency Relief Administration, and the Farm Credit Administration, all of which were set in motion during the famous first hundred days of the Roosevelt presidency in 1933. But it took the May 1934 dust storm to make the plains visible to Washington. As dust sifted down on the Mall and the White House, Roosevelt was in a press conference promising that the Cabinet was at work on a new Great Plains relief program. Desperate appeals were being heard from farmers, ranchers, politicians, and businessmen out West, some of them demanding money, others, more humble, wanting advice and comfort. "Please do something," one lady wrote, "to help us save our country, where one time we were all so happy." Alf Landon, the governor of Kansas, got letters too, as did other area governors, but in effect they forwarded them to Washington by requesting federal relief money that they could disperse to their voters—the 1930s version of states' rights.

While Roosevelt and his Cabinet worked out a drought relief package, the American public put its own ingenuity to work and sent the results to the President and other public officials. Ideas began coming in during the spring of 1934 and kept coming over the next few years, from citizens in every part of the country and even from observers in China, England, and Czechoslovakia. They came from barnyard inventors and company engineers, from immigrants eager to do something for their adopted Uncle Sam, from former plains farmers retired in Los Angeles, and from the city unemployed who hoped their notions would produce a job or a fat check. The obvious remedy, according to many of these letter writers, was simply to cover the Dust Bowl over. The Sisalkraft Company of Chicago had a tough waterproof paper that could do the job, while the Barber Asphalt Company in New Jersey recommended an "asphalt emulsion" at $5.00 an acre, and a Pittsburgh steel corporation had wire netting for sale. One man urged that the ground be covered with concrete, leaving holes for planting seeds, and another that rocks be hauled in from the mountains. Mrs. M. L. Yearby of Durham, North Carolina, saw a chance to beautify her own state by shipping its junked automobiles out to the plains to anchor the blowing fields, and several others proposed spreading ashes and garbage from Eastern cities or leaves from forests to create a mulch over the plains and restore a binding humus to the soil. Building wind deflectors also appealed to many—cement slabs or board fences, as much as 250 feet high, or shelterbelts of pine trees, alfalfa, greasewood, and even Jerusalem artichokes. An Albuquerque writer blamed the dust storms on "German agents"; a Russian-born chemist in New York City suggested

radio waves instead; the Lions Club in Perryton, Texas, pointed to pollution from local gas and oil refineries; and there were some who worried about the carbon-black plant near Amarillo.

But for plains residents the most widely favored panacea was, understandably, water. "You gave us beer," they told Roosevelt, "now
give us water." That was all they really needed, they were sure, and
the federal government was wasting its time with anything else. "Every
draw, arryo [sic], and canyon that could be turned into a lake or la-
goon," wrote a clothing store manager, "should be made into one by
dams and directed ditches & draws until there are *millions* of them thru
these mid western states." A Texas stockman wanted to use natural
gas to pump flood waters from the Mississippi River to the plains. Deep-
water irrigation wells was another scheme; 5000 of them, it was said,
would cost only $17.5 million. And then there were the perennially
hopeful rainmakers, long familiar on the southern plains, always popping up with a "scientific" method, new or old, to extract rain out of a
cloudless sky. An old soldier from Denver penciled his ideas on ruled
tablet paper: stage sham bottles with 40,000 Civilian Conservation Corps
boys and $20 million worth of ammunition—the noise would be sure
to stir up some rain, as it always did in wartime. "Try it," he finished,
"if it works send me a check for $5000 for services rendered."

Each of those letters and dozens more like them, got a patient answer from a federal administrator, but no check. The Roosevelt advisers settled on a more prosaic, if more expensive program for the Great
Plains. On 9 June 1934 the President asked Congress for $525 million
in drought relief, and it was promptly given. The biggest chunks, to-
taling $275 million, were for cattlemen—to provide emergency feed loans,
to purchase some of their starving stock, and to slaughter the animals
and can their meat for the poor. Destitute farmers would get more
public jobs, often building ponds and reservoirs, as well as cash income supplements, costing $125 million. Other features of the program
included acquiring submarginal lands, relocating rural people in better
environments, creating work camps for young men, and making seed
loans for new crops. A few days later Roosevelt squeezed in a shelter-
belt program, too. For the remainder of the thirties most of these strategies became familiar fixtures in the federal budget, evolving, along
with other farm and relief legislation, into a more specifically directed
Dust Bowl rehabilitation effort.

As for the most immediate need to stop the blowing dust, the federal government heeded regional advice and in 1935 adopted a program of emergency "listing." The lister, a standard farm implement on
the plains, was a double mold-board that dug deep, broad furrows and
threw the dirt upto high ridges. Once used for planting corn, it now
served the function of creating a corduroy-like ground surface that would
slow erosion, or at least it would if the listing were done crosswise to

the prevailing winds. In a stiff blow the ridges would still drift back into the furrows, forcing the farmer to list his fields repeatedly to keep them stabilized. Sometimes a chisel would be employed too, breaking the hard subsurface and bringing up heavy clods to hold down the dust. But when you were broke, with no money for gasoline or tractor repairs, constant lister-plowing or chiseling was impossible. Or if you lived a hundred miles away from your farm, visiting it only twice a year, once at planting and again harvesting time, the work would not get done. The government, therefore, proposed to pay plains farmers for working their own land or having it worked by someone on the scene. And the Texas and Kansas legislatures allowed counties to list the land of irresponsible neighbors, charging the expense to the owner, where all other inducements had failed. As an effort to legalize community control over recalcitrant individuals, these state laws were too hedged about with delays, and too seldom used, to be especially effective. But self-interest, along with government money, was generally adequate to put the bare fields under some control.

Emergency listing continued to get federal funds virtually every year thereafter in the decade. In the 1936 Soil Conservation and Domestic Allotment Act, $2 million was the sum allowed for this work. Kansas and Texas received about half of the money, the other three southern plains states what was left over. In each state the money first passed through the hands of the land-grant colleges and their county extension agents, then through local committees that supervised contracts and made sure the listing was actually done, and done properly. Dust Bowl farmers listed more than 8 million acres in the 12 months prior to July 1937, for which the government paid them 20 cents an acre where they worked their own land, 40 cents where they had to hire others to do it. It was not much money; many thought they should get more. Nor did emergency listing address the deeper issues of man and the land on the southern plains or stop a full-fledged black blizzard. But it gave farmers something to do, and it kept some of the dirt from going too far.

The people of the plains made it clear in the 1936 elections how well they liked this rain of federal money. Despite the fact that the Republican party chose Alf Landon of Kansas for their presidential nominee, Roosevelt was again triumphant in the region, winning 54 per cent of the votes in Kansas, 60 in Colorado, 63 in New Mexico, 67 in Oklahoma, and 87 in Texas. Landon, who conducted a fumbling and waffling campaign, had nothing fresh or appealing to offer the Dust Bowl states and had been regionally upstaged and outmaneuvered by Roosevelt's "fact-finding" swing through the northern Great Plains in September. Two years later Roosevelt and the New Deal were still immensely popular in the Southwest. When the President went to Amarillo on 11 July 1938, in his only venture into the Dust Bowl itself, the city assembled the largest massed marching band in the history of the nation to greet him, thousands lined the streets, and, *mirabile dictu,* rain began to fall shortly before he arrived. As he stood hatless in the downpour, uttering genial platitudes in his clear ringing style, a woman in the audience exclaimed: "I am ready to make him king, anybody who can smile like that." So warm a reception was bound to cool, of course, and by 1940 portions of the dust belt began to defect, reverting to their traditional political views. But throughout the dirty thirties it was all New Deal country.

Some of the most insistent proponents of government intervention were Dust Bowl businessmen. While farmers tended to resist too much interference with their freedom to do as they liked with the land, there were business groups that demanded more authoritarian control by Washington, including a declaration of martial law. The Liberal, Kansas, Chamber of Commerce, for instance, insisted on "a force program, under government supervision," which would see that every field was listed properly. The federal soil erosion agent there noted in 1937 that businessmen, who had been arguing that "the conditions were being over emphasized and this area was getting more than its share of adverse publicity," now were agreed that "the control of wind erosion in the dust bowl is well out of hand and are willing to allow any action that the federal government may take to put into operation." Down in Dalhart the truth squad had to send out a new emissary, this one to a Washington congressional committee, to admit there was some truth in Alexandre Hogue's paintings and to plead for passage of a $10-million water-facilities bill.

But there was one government proposal that never failed to arouse hostility—resettlement or relocation. Leaving the plains meant giving up, admitting defeat, and possibly losing the future altogether; Providence never rewards the quitters. Resettlement was never really a serious idea in Washington either, not at least to the extent of removing all of the people from the Dust Bowl, but plains residents were forever on their guard after the Harold Ickes incident. Secretary of the Interior Ickes, when presented in November 1933 with a proposal to build expensive dams in the Oklahoma panhandle, turned thumbs down; he felt that it would be a waste of money. "We'll have to move them [the people] out of there," he said, "and turn the land back to the public domain." The howls of protest from 40,000 Oklahomans could be heard all the way to Capitol Hill. Ickes is "entirely ignorant of the possibilities this country affords," retorted the *Boise City News.* But the subsequent setting up of a Resettlement Administration in 1935 under Rexford Tugwell, a Columbia University professor, kept the plains wall-eyed. Following Black Sunday, as more rumors of forced evacuation came from the East Coast, John McCarty and his Dalhart boosters organized a Last Man's Club, each member pledging on his sacred honor never to abandon the plains. And farther west, in New Mexico, where the prospects of removal were just as unwelcome, a farmer spoke for many when he warned: "They'll have to take a shotgun to move us out of here. We're going to stay here just as long as we damn please."

That fierce resolve to stay, even as the tawny dust was making their land of opportunity a dreary wasteland, followed in large part from an assumption that the plains people made. It was drought, they were confident, and drought alone, that had made the Dust Bowl: "That drought put the fixins to us." But with a gambler's trust in better luck, they knew the rains would return. "This land will come back," most were sure: "it'll make good agin—it always has." Franklin Roosevelt, although he hardly knew what real drought was, or poverty, for that matter, shared the plainsmen's optimism, and, to a large extent, their analysis of the problem. "Drought relief" was what they most needed, he believed, and when the rains returned the people would be back on their feet, restoring the land to the rich agricultural empire it had been. That confidence was not absolutely misplaced, as later history showed. But it was all too simple and easy, and the farmers too quick to blame nature for the dust storms, too ready to lay all their misfortunes on the lack of rain. Although drought assistance was obviously needed, as flood or earthquake aid was needed elsewhere, a few of Roosevelt's administrators soon began to see that something more was required: a more far-reaching conservation program that would include social and economic changes.

Without the abrupt drop in precipitation the southern plains would never have become so ravaged a country, nor would they perhaps have needed, even during the Depression, much government aid: this much is true. But the drought, though a necessary factor, is not sufficient in itself to explain the black blizzards. Dry spells are an inevitable fact of life on the plains, predictable enough to allow successful settlement, but only if the settlers know how to tread lightly, look ahead, and shape their expectations to fit the qualities of the land. As the federal administrators studied the problem more fully, they came to see that the settlers of the West had never shown those qualities. They had displayed instead a naïve hopefulness that the good times would never run out, that the land would never go back on them. Some officials, therefore, began to call for major revisions in the faulty land system; others emphasized new agronomic techniques, rural rehabilitation, more diversified farming, or extensive grassland restoration. But their common theme was that staying meant changing. The Dust Bowl, in this evolving government view, must be explained as a failure in ecological adaptation—as an absence of environmental realism.

Farmers and ranchers on the plains were not so recalcitrant as to reject that analysis totally, although, understandably, it was hard for them to admit that what they had learned and had always been told was right could now be responsible for their predicament. It was natural for them to be defensive. They felt unfairly singled out for blame and criticism by many outsiders, when it was they who had to face the dust and struggle hard to save the farms that produced much of the nation's food. And they were right to this extent: it was indeed unjust and misdirected to blame everything on the Dust Bowl residents themselves, for they were largely unwitting agents—men and women caught in a larger economic culture, dependent on its demands and rewards, representing its values and patterns of thought. The ultimate meaning of the dust storms in the 1930s was that America as a whole, not just the plains, was badly out of balance with its natural environment. Unbounded optimism about the future, careless disregard of nature's limits and uncertainties, uncritical faith in Providence, devotion to self-aggrandizement—all these were national as well as regional characteristics.

The activism of the federal government was appropriate and essential; a national problem demanded national answers. But the situation also demanded a more than superficial grasp of what was responsible for the disaster and of how it could be prevented from occurring again. What the plainsmen needed was hope, of course—but the mature hope that does not smooth over failure, deny responsibility, or prevent basic change. They needed a disciplined optimism, tempered with restraint and realism toward the land. But all that required a substantial reform of commercial farming, which neither Roosevelt nor most of his New Deal advisers were prepared or able to bring about. Even as it evolved toward a more comprehensive program, the New Deal did not aim to alter fundamentally the American economic culture. Washington became and remained throughout the decade a substitute for a benign Providence, trying to give the plainsmen their "next year."

Family in Elm Grove, Oklahoma (1936)

"Fear Itself": Depression Life

ROBERT S. McCELVAINE

After a period of relative affluence and optimism in the 1920s, the American economy crashed into a shambles in late 1929. Although the Great Depression of the 1930s is usually thought to have resulted from the stock market crash of October 1929, prudent people might have foreseen the dangers as the rate of real investment began to drop and speculation increased. The Wall Street collapse and the subsequent failure of apparently stable economic institutions forced the nation and the world to see that the affluence and optimism of the 1920s had been composed of hope (that is, speculation) and promises rather than of stable economic growth.

The economic downturn led to a loss of hope and, so it seemed to some, a loss of nerve. It has been explained that lack of confidence in the business system was a major contributing factor to the spread of the Depression. Whatever the causes—and these are still being debated—the bubble burst, and the country plunged into poverty and despair.

In writing the history of the 1930s, scholars have tended to concentrate on the political developments of the time. The election of Franklin Delano Roosevelt to the presidency and the advent of what he called the New Deal have captured the imagination of historians who in turn have overemphasized the importance of the Roosevelt administration. While it is true that several important innovations in public welfare were adopted by the New Deal, these were applied only half-heartedly. And they did not end the Depression, although they did ease its effects for some of the population. The end of the Depression was brought about by the Second World War and the increased employment that resulted from the United States establishing itself as the "arsenal of democracy."

What has been slighted in historical writings, then, is the impact of the Depression on the lives of ordinary people. The best contemporary descriptions have come from the creative writers of the period; no work is likely to surpass John Steinbeck's *The Grapes of Wrath* or James Agee and Walker Evans' *Let Us Now Praise Famous Men* as portraits of despair in the 1930s. However, there is a rising concern about the effect of the depression on those who lived through it. Today many articles and books attempt to describe the suffering that afflicted so many.

One reason for the new interest in the Depression is the upshot of a new generation of historians who were very young or not yet born in the 1930s and, therefore, have no memories of the period. On the other hand, the searing experiences of the older generation, who could recall the hunger and frustration of the times, led them to try to forget, not remember.

In an attempt to realize the life situations of people during the Depression, several collections of oral history have appeared. Leading the way, and still the most comprehensive, is *Hard Times* by Studs Terkel. Another source of information are the letters written to various public authorities from people seeking help. Robert S. McElvaine of Millsaps College has published a collection of these letters in *Down and Out in the Great Depression: Letters from the "Forgotten Man."* Using this material as a basic source, McElvaine subsequently published an excellent study of the entire Depression era. The selection which follows is a chapter from that work which focuses on the life experiences of distressed Americans. While it is clear that some citizens escaped the terrors of the period, it is also clear that this was not the case for many, perhaps most, Americans. The economic hardships incurred during this period have had a profound effect on subsequent developments.

The runaway economic consumerism of the post–Second World War era may have resulted from the contrast between the affluence of the 1920s and the poverty of the 1930s. Many middle-class and would-be middle-class Americans were not able, because of the Depression, to enjoy the fruits of the consumer society that had developed in the 1920s. As the economy took off again during the Second World War, these potential consumers took off with it, and it often seems as though they attempted to ward off future terrors by surrounding themselves with as many material objects as possible.

To most Americans who escaped the ravages of the Depression, as to almost all Americans today, the unemployed of the 1930s were part of a faceless mass. Many pitied them, some despised them, most tried to ignore them. Few attempted to understand them. Such an understanding must begin with the realization that they were individuals, not statistics. They were a diverse lot, with cleavages along racial, religious, ethnic, sexual, occupational, age, regional, and other lines. Some were proud, others beaten. Some were optimistic, others had lost all hope. Some blamed themselves, others cursed businessmen, politicians, the "system," or "the Interests." They were, to be sure, victims, but they were not *only* victims. In most cases they had no part in the cause of their suffering, but the ways in which they reacted to their plight form a large—although poorly understood—portion of the history of the Depression.

Here I try to follow anthropologist Clifford Geertz's prescription for cultural analysis. "A good interpretation of anything," Geertz has said, "takes us into the heart of that of which it is the interpretation." "Mass unemployment," Cabell Phillips has noted, "is both a statistic and an empty feeling in the stomach. To fully comprehend it, you have to both see the figures and feel the emptiness." The principal goal is to go into the center of the Depression experience and attempt to feel the emptiness; in short, to blend social and intellectual history through an excursion into the minds of working-class Americans.

Undoubtedly the main reason that this topic has been so long neglected is the difficulty of approaching it. Working people are largely absent from the traditional types of historical documentation. Yet many sources do exist. The Depression and its effects upon its victims proved to be an irresistible subject for many sociologists and psychologists in the 1930s. The resulting contemporary investigations are also extremely valuable sources of information. The most important kinds of evidence are those that bring us into contact with individual working-class people of the Depression era. Several varieties of such personal sources are extant. Field investigators sent out by the Federal Emergency Relief Administration and, later, the Works Progress Administration, to report back to Federal Relief Administrator Harry Hopkins on conditions and attitudes among the poor provide us with a wealth of information. The fact that we receive our impressions of working-class thought through the eyes and words of middle-class investigators should make us cautious. Even so, the reports add much to our understanding. Interviewers hired by the WPA Federal Writers' Project collected thousands of personal histories from "ordinary" Americans in the late thirties. These, too, are a significant addition to our knowledge of working-class culture.

The most useful source of direct contact with the people of the thirties is the immense collection of letters that were addressed to public figures, especially to Franklin and Eleanor Roosevelt. These communications bring us into direct contact with more than 15 million Depression-era Americans, a majority of them laborers, clerks, and farmers. By weaving together the various types of evidence and using one kind as a check on the indications found in another, we can begin to understand the lives and values of American workers in the Great Depression. What follows is a composite of the Depression experience, using the words of Depression victims from all these sources.

For those workers who had enjoyed at least a taste of prosperity in the 1920s, the initial blow of the Depression was crushing. The twenties had seen the traditional middle-class American values, which taught that success and failure went to those who deserved them and which stressed acquisitive individualism, spread widely among workers. Such workers had been pleased to think that their modest accomplishments in the twenties were the result of their selection—whether by Calvin's God or Darwin's Nature depended upon one's viewpoint—for success. Like the Republican party, which had taken credit for good times and hence found it difficult to escape blame for bad times, Americans who had claimed responsibility for personal gains found it difficult not to feel guilty when confronted with failure.

A widespread attitude of the unemployed early in the Depression was: "There must be something wrong with a fellow who can't get a job." *Sure, I've lost my job, but I'm still a worthy provider. Work will turn up soon.* Every morning up before dawn, washed, shaved, and dressed as neatly as possible. To the factory gates, only to find a hundred others already there, staring blankly at the sign: NO HELP WANTED. The search then became more feverish. One day in 1934 a man in Baltimore walked twenty miles in search of a job. "I just stopped every place," he said, "but mostly they wouldn't even talk to me." *Perhaps an employment agency? A long wait, but it will be worth it to get a job. At last a chance.* The questions: name, age, experience. Yes, well, we'll see what we can do, but there are already more than a hundred men in our files with similar backgrounds, and most of them are younger than you. Employers can be choosy, you know. It's a buyer's market. Why hire a man who is over forty, when there are plenty of unemployed men still in their twenties? Business has to be efficient, after all. "A man over forty might as well go out and shoot himself," said a despairing Chicago resident in 1934.

Gradually those over forty, though fit physically, began to *feel* old and *look* and *act* poor. Keeping up the appearance necessary to secure employment, particularly of the white-collar variety, became increasingly difficult. As an Oklahoma woman put it in a letter to Eleanor Roosevelt in 1934, "The unemployed have been so long with out food-clothes-shoes-medical care-dental care etc-we look pretty bad-so when we ask for a job we don't get it. And we look and feel a little worse each day—when we ask for food they call us bums—it isent our fault . . . no we are not bums." Yet, "with shabby suits, frayed collars, worn shoes and perhaps a couple of front teeth gone," men *looked* like bums. "We do not dare to use even a little soap," wrote a jobless Oregonian, "when it will pay for an extra egg a few more carrots for our children."

As the days without finding a job became weeks, the weeks months, and the months years, it came to be more difficult even to look for work. ". . . You can get pretty discouraged and your soles can get pretty thin after you've been job hunting a couple of months," a Minnesota Depression victim pointed out. First you came to accept the idea of taking a job of lower quality than you thought you deserved. Then you began to wonder just what you did deserve. It came finally, for some, to be a matter of begging: "For God's sake, Mister, when are you going to give us work?" "How," asked the daughter of a long-unemployed man, "can you go up and apply for a job without crying?"

Modern industrial society does not provide a place or position for a person; rather, it requires him to make his own place—and to strive to better it. This is taken to be the measure of one's individual worth. Americans had been brought up on the belief that meaningful work is the basis of life. Without such work, people felt they had no reason for being. "Drives a man crazy," said a seventy-five-year-old former knifemaker, "or drives him to drink, hangin' around." One must, as a St. Louis man said in 1933, "get the job to keep his mind and body whole."

Community attitudes toward the unemployed sometimes added to the feelings of guilt, shame, inferiority, fear, and insecurity. Many of those who remained employed made it plain that they believed that "something is wrong with a man who can't support his family." "Taxpayers" complained of paying for the upkeep of "thieves and lazy, immoral people," "no good for nothing loafers," "human parasites," and "pampered poverty rats."

Although some of the unemployed successfully resisted the psychological effects of such verbal attacks, others were likely to hear internal as well as external voices telling them that they were to blame for their plight. "I'm just no good, I guess," a Houston woman told a caseworker in 1934. "I've given up ever amounting to anything. It's no use." "I'd kinda like to think I could get a job and hold it," an Oklahoma WPA worker said at the end of the Depression.

As scant resources ran out, self-blame often grew into the shame of having to seek assistance. In some areas, people "would almost starve rather than ask for help." Indeed, some of their fellow citizens expected no less from them. "I have had too much self respect for my self and Family to beg anything," wrote a North Carolina man in 1933. "I would be only too glad to dig ditches to keep my family from going hungry." But there were no ditches to be dug. For many, there seemed "little to look forward to save charity," with all the stigma that implied. The loss of one's "good standing" was a matter of great concern.

The thought of seeking charity was "very distasteful and humiliating."

Desperation began to take over. For many, nighttime was the worst. "What is going to become of us?" wondered an Arizona man. "I've lost twelve and a half pounds this last month, just thinking. You can't sleep, you know. You wake up about 2 A.M., and you lie and think." When you could sleep, bad dreams were likely. Worry and fear became dominant. Sometimes you would look at your children and wonder what would happen to them. Sheer terror would suddenly overcome you. Some say you appear to be shell-shocked; others tell you that you look like a frightened child. And well you should, because at times that's just the way you feel. Often you cry like a youngster; you try to do it privately, but you know the children hear you at night.

Of course you try to forget. For some, alcohol was a means of escape. It was not much help when you were hungry, though. "It's funny," a nineteen-year-old in Providence said. "A lot of times I get offered a drink. It seems like people don't want to drink alone. But no one ever offers me a meal. Most of the time when I take a drink it makes me sick. My stomach's too empty."

An alternative to drinking was withdrawal from social contacts. Convinced that you are a failure, you try to avoid your friends, fearing that they will look upon you with scorn or, what is sometimes worse, pity. Thus you are unlikely to find out that many of your friends have also fallen victim to the Depression. In this small, hothouse world, self-blame, shame, and self-pity bloom magnificently.

As desperation grows worse the choices narrow. "My children have not got no shoes and clothing to go to school with," a West Virginia man complained in 1935, "and we havent got enough bed clothes to keep us warm." You resort to using old coats in lieu of blankets. *What can be done? What of the children? They are cold and hungry, but* "to do anything desperette now they would never live down the disgrace." "What is a man to do?" You face "a complete nervous breakdown as a result of being idle. . . . What is the next move for a desperate man? To commit some crime in this time of need?" When "all else has failed," one must do something. Is it wrong to steal coal to keep your family warm? Survival becomes the goal, the justification. Much like the slaves of the Old South, some Depression victims developed a distinction between *stealing* (from a fellow sufferer) and what the slaves had called *taking* (what you need and can convince yourself is rightfully yours because its possessor has exploited you or others like you). To some, it was unacceptable to get "busy" and bring "home some extra money," as the wife of a Michigan WPA man put it. "I'd steal if I had the guts," declared a Rhode Island boy.

If not crime, what? How long can I take it? Is there no hope? Perhaps the only thing left is to "end it all." If no one will help, "than [sic] I will take my life away," said a Detroit woman in 1935. Suicide at times "seemed the only solution." "The Atlantic calls from our shores that there is plenty of room for us," a Massachusetts woman proclaimed. Suicide would be the ultimate admission of defeat, but it might appear "as the best way out," as it did to a New York woman who stated, "I am not a coward but good Lord it is awful to stand helpless when you need things." "Can you be so kind as to advise me as to which would be the most human way to dispose of my self and family, as this is about the only thing that I see left to do," a Pennsylvania man inquired in 1934. "No home, no work, no money. We cannot go along this way. They have shut the water supply from us. No means of sanitation. We can not keep the children clean and tidy as they should be."

Relatively few, of course, actually took the fatal step, but many Depression victims appear to have considered it. An FERA investigator in New York City reported late in 1934 that "almost every one of her clients" had "talked of suicide at one time or another." The programs of the New Deal may have persuaded some that life might still hold some hope. "You have saved my life," a New Jersey woman wrote, referring to assistance she had received from the Home Owners' Loan Corporation. "I would have killed myself If I would have lost my house."

Sometimes the decision of whether to seek assistance was a question of socially determined sex roles. An Italian man in Massachusetts, for instance, threatened to kill himself, his wife, and children because he was about to lose his house. It was unacceptable for *him* to ask for help. His wife saved the day by appealing to a neighbor for a loan. The bulk of the help-seeking letters of the thirties were written by women to Eleanor Roosevelt. What was inappropriate behavior for most men— "begging"—was proper for women, either because women were believed to be naturally weak or because a mother seeking help was not showing weakness, but playing her accepted role.

Thousands of the down-and-out, almost all of them women, wrote to Mrs. Roosevelt asking for old clothes. Americans facing adversity clung to their traditions and pride as long as possible, but the Depression forced many to set aside the former and swallow the latter, lest they have nothing at all to swallow. Clothing was considered an area of female responsibility. "Please do not think this does not cause a great feeling of shame to me to have to ask for old clothing," an Iowa woman wrote to the First Lady in 1936. "I am so badly in need of a summer coat and under things and dresses. oh don't think that it is not with a effort I ask you to please send me anything you may have on hand in that line which you don't care to wear yourself." "I can sew and would only be too glad to take two old things and put them together and make a new one," wrote a desperate Philadelphia woman. "I don't care what it is, any thing from an old bunch of stockings to an old Sport Suit or an old afternoon dress, in fact. Any-thing a lady 40 years of age can wear."

Although men were more plentiful among writers asking for direct financial assistance than among those seeking clothing, women appear to have outnumbered men in this category as well. Men might be as pleased as women to receive help, but their expected sex role made it more difficult for them to ask. To do so would be further admission of failure as a provider.

That so many wrote to the Roosevelts seeking help was indicative of the views most Depression-era workers had of the First Family. Such people often saw FDR in a fashion much like the European peasant who, as Oscar Handlin put it, thought "of the religious figure of the sanctified King as his distant protector who, if only he were told, would surely intercede for his devoted subjects." Letters to Roosevelt echoed this attitude. "You honor sir and your royalty. Majesty," began a 1935 letter to the President from an incapacitated black man in Georgia. When he heard Roosevelt speak over the radio in 1932, a Kansas man said, it seemed "as though some Moses had come to alleviated us of our sufferings."

The special relationship between the Roosevelts and the downtrodden made it possible to think that asking for help from that source was somehow different from seeking charity. One might even convince oneself that a modicum of independence was being preserved if help came from one's "personal friends" in the White House. Grasping at hope, a woman could ask Mrs. Roosevelt to intercede with the manager of a contest "and ask him kindly to give me a prize."

When the hope for prizes and direct assistance from the "royal family" flickered out, little was left but to apply for the dreaded dole. Any savings you once had were either lost in bank failures or long since used up. You have asked friends and relatives for a little help more times than is likely to keep them friendly. The grocer has allowed your bill to go up, but now he has said that he can do no more. Pay some of it or go hungry. By now you have been hungry—*really* hungry—for several days. A twelve-year-old boy in Chicago summed it up in a letter: "We haven't paid 4 months rent, Everyday the landlord rings the door bell, we don't open the door for him. We are afraid that will be put out, been put out before, and don't want to happen again. We haven't paid the gas bill, and the electric bill, haven't paid grocery bill for 3 months." *Something* must be done. Survival being prerequisite to independence, the latter must be sacrificed, if only temporarily. So at last it is that painful walk to the local school, which houses the relief office.

You walk by a number of times, trying to get up the nerve to go in. What if your children—or their friends—see you? Finally, it can be delayed no longer. *Why is that policeman there?* Surely *you* have recently felt like breaking something; maybe others are also on the verge of destructive acts. Still, seeing that uniform and gun does not make you any more comfortable. You tell the clerk what you are there for. You are mumbling. Speak up! he says, impatiently. (He is on relief, too, and has few qualifications and little training for the delicate position he holds.) You finally make yourself understood. *(What else would you have been there for? Why did he even have to ask?)* Take a seat. Your name will be called.

The "intake" room is crowded. You sit down, focusing your gaze on one of the holes in your shoes. After a while your eyes, thoughtlessly moving about, make contact with those of another applicant. He looks away as quickly as you do. *How can so many people be failures? . . . What's taking them so long? Do they think I have all day? . . . Come to think of it, I guess I do. What a failure I am! . . . The stink in this place is awful!*

Two hours later you realize that your name is being called—for the second time. You rise slowly and go over to the desk. The questions bother you. *Yes,* FOUR *months since we paid the rent. Yes, we have been evicted before. No, we lost the car months ago. The radio? It's paid for, and it isn't worth enough to keep us fed for a week. Can't we keep it? That's all?* You can go home and wait. An investigator will visit you in a few days. More questions, more embarrassment, further degradation. Pauperization, that's what it is. *How did this happen?* You have become "something anonymous who will presently be more or less fed." *What's that? It may be several weeks before we get any help? How do we eat in the meantime? If we had anything at all left, I wouldn't be here now.*

The shame persists, but eventually it may give way to despair and, then, apathy, particularly among those on direct relief. "Why the Hell should I get up in the morning, lady?" asked a youth of twenty. "What am I going to do with all these days? . . . I've been looking for a job for four years. I've had two. Five months in all. After a while you know it ain't getting you anywhere. There's nothing for us!" Many were bewildered. An FERA investigator described Americans in 1934 as being "terrifyingly patient." "They are sick, mentally and physically," a New York Home Relief Bureau supervisor had said of Depression victims a year earlier. "They have given up even trying to look for work. The majority have become so apathetic that they accept without questioning us whatever we give them, no matter how pitifully inadequate it is or how badly administered."

Such dole recipients were variously characterized as listless, "sinking into indifference," lethargic, and "too docile, too much licked to put up any fight." One FERA investigator described providing relief for such people as "a kind of desperate job like getting the wounded off the battlefield so that they can die quietly at the base hospital."

Apathy, too, was a stage, one beyond which many of the unemployed moved after the New Deal had taken root. Sooner or later those sets of eyes in the relief office would meet. One would see "that there were other fellows who didn't look such a bad sort or low mentality in the same fix he was." It made you feel a little better. "Bit by bit," an FERA investigator reported from Bethlehem, Pennsylvania, late in 1934, "these men discovered that it was bolstering their morale to swap experiences and reactions and to realize that their situation was the result of a social condition, not a personal failure." And if the government had accepted responsibility for providing relief, the problem must not be the fault of the individual.

For such people, resentment began to displace self-blame and apathy. If it is not your fault, why should you suffer the indignities of the relief system? Relief "clients" began to object to the young college women who often served as caseworkers. (Not always without reason. One in California visited "her clients in a very elegant riding costume—breeches, top boots, crop, and all!") "We get work from the Relief as the little young folks thinks we need it," complained a Georgia woman. "They have always been used to plenty. Don't know how hard it is for folks like us."

Among the common criticisms of relief was that recipients were treated as children: given food orders instead of cash, instructed by nutrition experts, investigated by "busybodies," and generally "regimented." "Why should it be 'dished' out to us like we were *little children*, and tell us exactly what every cent should be spent for?" asked a Californian. People who had "always managed to raise their children and feed them without advice from the outside" were unenthusiastic about such lectures. They wanted to be on their own, to have cash to buy what and where they chose, to spend it on beer every now and then, if they so desired. Although relief recipients had already become far more dependent than most of them wished to be, they wanted to retain as much independence as possible, even within the relief system.

What gave relief "clients" the chance to reassert their independence was the opportunity for work relief, first with the CWA and later with the WPA. Self-respect could finally begin to return. When a New York relief investigator told a man who had been receiving grocery orders that there was a CWA job for him, she related, "He grabbed me, swung me right up off the floor, and hugged me." When he went to work, the man left an hour earlier than necessary.

People on WPA jobs spoke with heartfelt conviction about their preference for this type of assistance. "My pride took an awful beating when I had to apply for relief," a fifty-one-year-old Minneapolis man recalled in 1940, "but I feel different about this [WPA]. Here I am working for what I'm getting." "It means," a woman said of the WPA, "that I can look people in the eye because I'm not on a dole . . . it isn't like relief. Being on relief just breaks you all up." Another man spoke of the WPA enabling him "to sleep nights instead of lying awake thinking of desperate things I might do."

By 1935 the attitude of many Depression victims toward relief had changed. Complaints increased. Shame over being on public assistance was replaced in some by anger at the smallness of payments and at relief administrators. A Muncie, Indiana, housewife expressed the latter view when she wrote, "Those in charge of relief have never lain awake at night worrying about unpaid rent, or how to make a few groceries do for the seemingly endless seven days. . . ." "It is always," she continued, "the people with full stomachs who tell us poor people to keep happy."

In the mid-thirties many of the unemployed concluded that relief simply amounted to Depression victims getting what was rightfully theirs. Social workers were reporting as early as 1934 that some people seemed to think "that the Government actually owes it [relief] to them." Lorena Hickok called such recipients "gimmies." Some, an Iowa relief administrator wrote, had "adopted a more demanding attitude" and were "willing for the government to see them through." People on public assistance in Salt Lake City developed a slang of their own. Significantly, they referred to the FERA as "Santa Claus." In many places, groups of angry unemployed people gathered at relief offices and harassed the administrators with their demands for better treatment. Within the context of a basically dependent situation, relief recipients were finding means by which to express their independence.

Whatever the changes in attitudes toward relief and dependence as the Depression continued, the psychological problems for the unemployed remained devastating. For many Americans who avoided the ravages of the Depression, it became an article of faith that relief recipients irresponsibly had children for whom they could not provide. Some conservatives charged that relief women had babies in order to qualify for higher payments. Even FERA investigators were not above accepting such notions. "On the relief rolls," wrote Martha Gellhorn in 1934, "it is an accepted fact that the more incapable and unequipped (physically, mentally, materially) the parents, the more offspring they produce." "Apparently," she concluded in another report, "the instinct of self-preservation is not very well developed in the working class American."

For the victims, however, the problem was far more complex. Some social workers excused poverty-ridden, hopeless young women who had illegitimate children, because "their lives are so empty that they fall a prey to anything which offers momentary escape from the horror of their lives." Although this view was not without some validity, the problem was more complicated. For many "forgotten women" of the thirties, the questions of intercourse, birth control, and having children were among the most gnawing of the Depression years. The wife of a Massachusetts WPA worker (and mother of his eleven children) voiced one aspect of the difficulty: "Ya know down at the Catholic Charities they tell ya your not supposed ta have children if you're on the W.P.A. An' in the church they tell ya you're not supposed ta do anything about it. An' they say you're supposed ta live with your man. Now what's a woman gonna do?"

Even for women without religious qualms about birth control sexual questions caused anguish. A woman in the San Joaquin Valley haltingly told Lorena Hickok of something "that had nearly driven her crazy" and that "she knew was one of the worst problems of women whose husbands are out of work." Almost no one in such circumstances *wanted* to have babies, but "here you are, surrounded by young ones you can't support and never knowing when there's going to be another. You don't have any money to buy anything at the drugstore. All you have is a grocery order. I've known women to try to sell some of their groceries to get a little money to buy the things needed."

This still did not describe the depth of the problem, however. "I suppose," the woman continued, "you can say the easiest way would be not to do it. But it wouldn't be. You don't know what it's like when your husband's out of work. He's gloomy and unhappy all the time. Life is terrible. You must try all the time to keep him from going crazy. And many times—that's the only way."

Pleasure in the Depression was, to be sure, often limited to such inexpensive pastimes. In many places, meat and fruit were rarities. One woman bought a dozen oranges with part of her husband's first CWA check. "I hadn't tasted any for so long," she explained, "that I had forgotten what they were like!" People were gloomy. "I know a party that has got a radio + spends some of his money for beer," a Vermont woman wrote to President Roosevelt. Her family was not so fortunate: "We don't have no pleasure of any kind."

The absence of pleasure sometimes produced family problems. "What about the children who's parents can't give their children the little things in life such as a cone of cream or a 1 *cts* piece of candy or a soft drink once a week," asked a Kentuckian. "Who will get the blame for this neglect The father of course. . . . Do you think it is right that we poor never have the pleasure of a show or a trip back home. Just stay at home and watch others have all the fun good eats fine automobiles town houses, country homes. . . ." Other family problems grew out of the quest for pleasure on empty pocketbooks. "Half the men you have Put to work taken their maney When they get Paid an spends it for whiskey," a Nashville woman complained to FDR. "If my husban new that I wrote this he would kill me," she added in a post-script.

The lack of money, work, and self-esteem caused even greater family troubles. Unemployment upset the traditional roles of father, mother, and children. Since the father's position was based upon his occupation and his role as provider, the loss of his job was likely to mean a decline in his status within the family. The man who was without a position was, well, without a position. It was he who was supposed to provide independence for the family. Having little to do, unemployed men hung around home much of the time. In doing so, they infringed upon the sphere of the wife. If the husband blamed himself for his loss of income, the wife might try to encourage him. At first most did. But as hardships grew, and as the man sitting by the kitchen stove began to irritate his wife, the latter was increasingly likely to see, and point out, faults in her mate. And as his resentment and guilt expanded, he was apt to find more in his wife's actions that displeased him. Quarrels became more numerous.

Being "on relief" stigmatized an entire family, but most especially the father. Male dominance was endangered in the Depression. It asserted itself in odd ways. In some cases, most family resources were devoted to obtaining clothes for the man. "The women," it was concluded, "can stay inside and keep warm, and the children can stay home from school." There were cases, however, where a father was obliged to share his son's clothes. "They're all we've got now," said a North Dakota farmer. "We take turns wearing 'em." The symbolism for the breadwinner must have been apparent.

The traditional role of the mother is far less dependent than that of the father on the family's status in the outside world. The Depression was, accordingly, less harmful to mothers' positions inside their families. John Steinbeck said it well in *The Grapes of Wrath*: " 'Woman can change better'n a man,' Ma said soothingly. 'Woman got all her life in her arms. Man got it all in his head.' " Some women simply took over for their unemployed husbands. In one case, a man first learned of his wife's decision to rent another house "when he came home to find the furniture had been moved." But mothers' roles were also upset by the economic breakdown. Distribution of relief commodities, Chicago social workers pointed out, "deprived the housewife of the privilege of shopping and in a sense destroyed their responsibility as housewives." Nor was it easy for "a mother to hear her hungry babe whimpering in the night and growing children tossing in their sleep because of knawing plain HUNGER," as an Oregon woman put it. "I have laid many a night & cried my self to sleep when I think of what I have to work with," wrote a Pennsylvania mother.

People did their best to maintain traditional roles. If a woman must work for her family to survive, so be it. The reemergence of a family economy of pooled resources was one means of maintaining family independence. "But soon's the men get goin' the wife's through," a Portuguese fisherman in Massachusetts said. "She stays home then. Yes ma'am, we like our wives to be home." Of course spouses who continued to cooperate during the Depression helped each other make it through with a minimum of upheaval. "We got enough ta get along on, and we got each other. That should be enough ta make any body happy," declared a shoe machinery worker. For all the problems, in fact, available evidence indicates that the families of many unemployed men continued to operate under the direction of the traditional head, with little apparent change in internal status. The principal effect of the Depression on internal family relationships, in fact, was to exaggerate the qualities and tendencies already present. The additional strain was often too much for weak families to withstand, but strong relationships usually weathered the hard times successfully.

Discrimination against women in employment became worse with the Depression. It was easy to assert that women were taking jobs that otherwise would go to male heads of households. Norman Cousins stated this argument in its most simplistic form in 1939: "There are approximately 10,000,000 people out of work in the United States today; there are also 10,000,000 or more women, married and single, who are jobholders. Simply fire the women, who shouldn't be working anyway, and hire the men. Presto! No unemployment. No relief rolls. No depression." Those who made such statements usually had little interest in facts, but most women who worked outside the home during the Depression clearly did so out of necessity. They supported themselves and their families just as did male "breadwinners." Such was the case not only with single women, but also with most working married women, whose husbands were either unemployed or paid too little to provide for their families. Nonetheless, campaigns against hiring married women were common in the 1930s. Fully 77 percent of the school districts in the United States would not hire married women to teach; 50 percent of them had a policy of firing women who married.

Despite the prejudice against women—especially married women—working, their numbers in the work force actually increased, both absolutely and as a percentage of all workers, during the Depression. In 1930, women had represented 24.3 percent of all workers; in 1940, 25.1 percent of the work force was female. Similarly, the proportion of women workers who were married increased in the face of Depression-era discrimination, from 28.8 percent at the beginning of the decade to 35 percent at its end. This seemingly remarkable development resulted from several causes.

Most women who sought employment, before as well as during the Depression, did so because the economic realities of American life obliged them to work. Most families in this country have aspired to an "American standard of living," which has always been ill defined, but is something clearly above mere subsistence. Early in the present century it was not possible for working-class families to reach that level on the wages of one adult male. The income of the father was often supplemented by the wages of children. As child labor declined, wives filled the resulting gap in family income. The living standards of most families improved in the 1920s. When the Depression hit, even those families that did not *need* the wife's extra income in an absolute sense, needed it if they were to stay close to the standard that they had enjoyed during prosperity. As husbands lost their jobs, had their wages cut, or became increasingly fearful that they *might* become unemployed, wives who had not previously worked outside the home sought jobs. Here was a distinct—and often overlooked—irony of the Depression: as jobs became much more difficult to find, far *more* people began looking for work. One estimate held that 2.5 million more people were in the work force in 1937 than there would have been had there been no depression. Most of these new workers were women, so one reason that more women found jobs in the thirties was simply that more sought them.

This might seem to support the claim that women were displacing men from jobs, but another reason for the increase in female workers refutes that argument. Women lost proportionately fewer jobs than men precisely because their types of employment were *not* considered interchangeable. There existed many positions that were identified as "women's work": domestic service, primary education, many clerical and social service jobs. Such situations remained available to women regardless of how many men were out of work. The Depression itself placed women in a relatively better position for obtaining work—poorly paid, of course—than men. "[I]deas that once had consigned women to inferior places in the labor force," historian Alice Kessler-Harris has pointed out, "now preserved for them jobs that menfolk could not get." The economic collapse hit hardest just those sectors of the economy (especially heavy industry) that had barred women workers. The fields in which women were most likely to be employed suffered a lesser decline and, in the case of clerical work (in the new government agencies), social services, and education, actually grew under the impact of the New Deal. A 1940 study found that in the five most depressed industries women represented only 2 percent of the employees. In the employment categories with the smallest drop in employment, on the other hand, women held 30 percent of the jobs. In a strange sense, women might be said to have benefited from past employment discrimination against them.

Before we become too envious of women workers during the Depression, though, it is well to remember what sort of jobs were reserved for them and what they were paid. At the end of the decade fully one-fifth of all women who worked for wages were employed as domestic servants. Live-in maids in the mid-thirties earned less than $8 per week in New York City, the highest-paying locality in the country. Other women workers were better paid, but not by much. One-fourth of the NRA codes permitted lower rates of pay for women than men. The federal government not only allowed discrimination, it practiced it. Men on WPA projects were paid $5 per day; women received only $3.

Women workers during the Depression also had to face increased psychological pressures. Antagonism from male workers and from wives who remained at home was intensified by the generally mistaken belief that women were taking jobs from men. And at a time when their traditional nurturing role seemed especially needed in the home, women who were obliged to work for wages carried a particularly heavy burden of guilt. One study placed the blame for "truancy, incorrigibility, robbery, teenage tantrums, and difficulty in managing children" on the "mother's absence at her job."

Given all the obstacles working wives faced during the Depression, it is not surprising that many people came to associate employment of women outside the home with harsh, undesirable economic conditions. In the thirties an ideal came to be formed among many Americans—women as well as men—of what American family life ought to be like. It was summed up in the answer the vice president of a United Auto Workers local made to a 1939 complaint a union member's wife had made about married women working. "Some day, Dear Sister, I hope we will reach that economic ideal where the married woman will find her place in the home caring for children, which is God's greatest gift to women and her natural birthright," Mike Mannini wrote. Here was an example of a very important part of the origins of what Betty Friedan later called "the feminine mystique." The return of the wife and mother to her "natural" sphere came during the Great Depression to be a goal, the achievement of which would be a sign of the return of "good times."

In those families where there was turmoil during the Depression, the children often suffered. Fathers (and mothers) might take out their frustrations on the children. As the effects of unemployment, shame, and worry became noticeable in parents, children grew more anxious. "The children all seem to be so excitable and high-strung these days," said a New York settlement house kindergarten teacher. "I can't help thinking it's due to the distress at home."

Why do we live like this, a child would wonder. *Things used to be better. We're not even clean anymore. Mama says the relief doesn't give enough for soap. And the bedbugs. In our old house we never had anything like that! What's wrong with Daddy? Times are hard,* they say, but "all the other little girls are getting Easter dresses." "Our friends have skates and we are not able to buy them." *Surely it's not Daddy's fault; he's the greatest. Why, he's been on relief longer than the other kids' fathers—that's* something.

How can you go to school when the other kids know your family has been evicted before and people are saying your father's not paying the rent now? *Why should I be the one who has* "to put a piece of cardboard in the sole of my shoe to go to school"? All the questions in a young mind. "My father he staying home. All the time he's crying because he can't find work. I told him why are you crying daddy, and daddy said why shouldn't I cry when there is nothing in the house. I feel sorry for him. That night I couldn't sleep."

The special times that usually bring joy to children and parents were often the hardest to bear during the Depression. Christmas could be particularly painful. "My little children talking about Santa Claus," a Texas father wrote to the President in 1934, "and I hate to see Xmas come this time because I know it will be one of the dullest Xmas they ever witnessed." A Virginia mother described a similar problem. "My little boy was speaking of Santa Claus 'He says why is it most children gets pretty toys and so many seems like they are rich and we so poor' This made tears come in my eyes," she said. "Then I told him if we are ever lucky enough to get work we will try to get him something pretty. I have to tell him of some happy day which may come."

While many adults compared Franklin Roosevelt to Lincoln, Moses, or Jesus, for some children the President was Santa Claus. Two Rhode Island boys, for instance, wrote their annual Christmas letter in 1935, but mailed it to Washington rather than the North Pole. They wanted bicycles or microscope-chemistry sets. Other children who sought gifts from the jolly man in the White House were more practical. "We have no one to give us a Christmas presents," wrote a ten-year-old Ohio girl, "and if you want to buy a Christmas present please buy us a stove to do our cooking and to make good bread." Such were the holiday thoughts of some children in 1935.

Although the children of the thirties lived through the same economic hardship as their parents did, it meant different things to the new generation. For one thing, children were largely free from the self-blame and shame that were so common among their elders. Obviously economic problems were not the fault of a child. He could rest assured that *he* had not failed. Adults might have botched things up; perhaps Dad was a failure, but few children felt any personal guilt. The Depression's most significant psychological problem was generally absent in the young.

The hardships many families faced in the thirties led children to assume greater responsibilities at an earlier age than has been customary in the years since World War II. It has been said with accuracy that there were no working-class "teenagers" in the 1930s. The generation had no time for an irresponsible, prolonged adolescence. Challenges had to be met. Often children (especially boys) were called upon to supplement meager family incomes by working after school (or in place of school). When mothers found it necessary—and possible—to get jobs, older children (especially girls) were given the responsibility of looking after their younger brothers and sisters.

Although the loss of any appreciable portion of one's childhood is tragic, there were some compensations for the youth of the thirties. The work thrust upon children in the Depression was likely to instill in them what industrial society commonly considers to be virtues: dependability, self-reliance, order, awareness of the needs of others, and practice in managing money. To the extent that the Depression furthered the development of such qualities in the young, it had a strikingly different effect on the children than on their elders. Ironically, the same family hardship that might weaken the self-reliance of a father could strengthen that quality in his child.

If being a child in the thirties was difficult, but at least on occasion rewarding, being a young adult presented problems with few compensations. Americans have always been future-oriented. If things were not quite perfect at the moment, just wait for tomorrow or next year. This attitude has been especially associated with the young.

In this as in so much else, however, the 1930s were different. Not that optimism did not survive, at least below the surface. Throughout the Depression, the slightest good news was sufficient to activate the latent hopefulness in some Americans. The creation of the CWA and the implementation of the corn loans brightened the outlook in Iowa to the point that an Irish man shouted, "In another 20 days we'll be out of the depression!" In the late spring of 1934, Lorena Hickok temporarily convinced herself that "people are in a pretty contented, optimistic frame of mind. They just aren't thinking about the Depression any more," she said, displaying at least as much optimism as she thought she detected in others. Speaking of the reaction of drought-stricken Colorado ranchers to two cloudbursts, she said, "Funny how people will cheer up if given half a chance!" "If only they will be patient, circumstances will work themselves out, and every-thing will be O.K.," a Wisconsin woman wrote in 1935. Even after a full decade of depression, WPA workers could be found in 1940 expressing faith in the future. "My idea," said an Oklahoma laborer, "is that all this is just a temporary thing, but it'll give us a chance to get another start if jobs will just pick up."

Despite the persistence of such attitudes in some quarters, though, the future looked bleak to many in the thirties. When asked "what his hope for the future was," an ex-truck driver gave a typical answer in 1934: "I just don't know." In the same year, Oklahoma relief recipients were said to "no longer have the 'chin up' attitude." Rather, they "lived in constant fear of what the next day or next week would bring." Young people simply had "nothing to look forward to." Many of the young— at just the stage in life in which the future often appears limitless— were nearly without hope during the Depression years. Older people, FERA investigator Martha Gellhorn pointed out, could "remember an easier life, a less stringent world." They refused "to believe that the end had inevitably come." "But," Gellhorn declared, "these young people have grown up against a shut door."

What hope could the future hold for the young adult of the thirties? Marriage and raising a family appeared out of the question. The CCC was all right for a while, but it was hardly a career. Work relief meant survival, but it offered no chance for advancement and no training for a "real" job. How could you get interested in it? Horatio Alger stories were fine in the old days, but what now? The traditional formula was work, save, succeed; but now you could not even reach step one. It appeared that "we shall never have good times again," we were "permanently licked." It was hard to disagree with the sobering conclusion that "it would be a cinch to run a war these days, with a good many of the world's young men having nothing better to do anyhow than get shot, and at least fed for a bit beforehand, and busy. . . ."

For most, of course, unemployment had to end sometime. The offer of a "real job" often brought tears of joy. "This will be our last week on relief," wept the wife of a skilled worker in Joplin, Missouri, after her husband obtained employment. "Next week we shall be able to take care of ourselves again." Unfortunately, such joy was often short-lived. Long unemployment had taken its physical and psychological toll. People became "nervous, muscularly soft and unconfident of their ability to do the work they formerly did." On a new job, they were so fearful of "making mistakes that they make mistakes and are promptly fired," reported a Chicago settlement official in 1934.

The Great Depression was, of course, an economic disaster for most Americans, but black people suffered a disproportionate share of the burden. The old and true saying that blacks are the last hired and the first fired cut both ways during the Depression. Unemployment in the "prosperity decade" had been much higher among blacks than whites.

"The Negro was born in depression," Clifford Burke told Studs Terkel. "It only became official when it hit the white man."

As layoffs began in late 1929 and accelerated in the following years, blacks were often the first to get pink slips. By 1932 black unemployment reached approximately 50 percent nationwide. As with women, some undesirable jobs had long been reserved for blacks. But such jobs became less undesirable when no other work was to be found. Although women's work generally remained just that in the Depression, the same was not the case with some traditionally "Negro occupations." Whites demanded that blacks be discharged as domestic servants, garbage collectors, elevator operators, waiters, bellhops, and street cleaners. A group of whites in Atlanta adopted the slogan "No Jobs for Niggers Until Every White Man Has a Job." A poorly educated Georgia woman spoke for many whites when she wrote to the President in 1935: "negroes being worked ever where instead of white men it dont look like that is rite." A year earlier a white clerk in Marianna, Florida, said in the wake of a lynch mob attack on a store that employed blacks, "A nigger hasn't got no right to have a job when there are white men who can do the work and are out of work." The number of lynchings in the United States rose from eight in 1932 to twenty-eight, fifteen, and twenty in the three succeeding years. A Depression-era study showed a positive correlation between the number of lynchings in the Deep South and economic distress. "Dust had been blown from the shotgun, the whip, and the noose," a *New Republic* article reported in 1931, "and Ku Klux practices were being resumed in the certainty that dead men not only tell no tales but create vacancies."

Those blacks who were able to keep their jobs suffered great hardship as well. A 1935 investigation in Harlem indicated that skilled workers there had experienced a drop of nearly 50 percent in their wages since the onset of the Depression. The lack of employment opportunities in northern cities cut down the extraordinary rate of black migration from the rural South, but more than 400,000 blacks did make the journey in the Depression decade. If jobs were not available in the North, at least there was not as much discrimination in the administration of relief as in the South. The continuing heavy migration of blacks into cities where they could vote, in states with large representation in the electoral college, was a political fact of growing importance.

The political influence of blacks had been minuscule since the end of Reconstruction. They voted in overwhelming majorities for the Republican party, which had come to take the "Negro vote" for granted. The Grand Old Party offered blacks little more by 1930 than the grand old platitudes of Abraham Lincoln, Thaddeus Stevens, and Charles Sumner. The Democrats, however, offered still less. The Democrats had *never* seated a single black delegate at any national convention prior to the New Deal. A few blacks were selected as alternates in 1924, but at the 1928 Democratic National Convention in Houston, the black alternates were seated in an area separated by chicken wire from the white delegates and alternates. Here was a perfect symbol of the racial attitudes of the party.

If there was little cause for blacks to hope for much from the Democratic party, there was not much more reason for optimism about the party's candidate in 1932. Like most northern Democrats, Franklin D. Roosevelt had never said anything about race that might upset southern party leaders. He went along without complaint when President Wilson ordered the institution of a complete Jim Crow system in the Navy. In 1929, FDR issued a public denial that he had eaten lunch with blacks. Both Roosevelt's administration in Albany and his 1932 campaign staff were devoid of blacks. Despite their suffering from the Depression, blacks voted for Hoover by greater majorities against Roosevelt in 1932 than they had against Smith four years before.

Yet a decade later Swedish sociologist Gunnar Myrdal wrote in his classic study of American race relations, *An American Dilemma*, that Roosevelt's presidency had "changed the whole configuration of the Negro problem." Few today would disagree with this assessment. The civil rights revolution that reached fruition in the 1960s had its origins in the Depression years. A number of factors converged to bring about this remarkable result.

In the early New Deal no direct steps were taken toward easing the plight of black Americans. To advocates of legislation to improve race relations, Roosevelt argued, with considerable justification, that pushing such bills would destroy the support of southerners in Congress needed to pass recovery legislation vital to all Americans, black as well as white. "First things come first, and I can't alienate certain votes I need for measures that are more important at the moment by pushing any measures that would entail a fight," Roosevelt said in 1933. "I've got to get legislation passed by Congress to save America," FDR explained to Walter White, the national secretary of the National Association for the Advancement of Colored People. "The Southerns by reason of the seniority rule in Congress are chairmen or occupy strategic places on most of the Senate and House committees. If I come out for the anti-lynching bill now, they will block every bill I ask Congress to pass to keep America from collapsing. I just can't take that risk."

Thus the legislation of the First Hundred Days concentrated on the immediate economic crisis, leaving the specific concerns of blacks unaddressed. The National Recovery Administration's effects on blacks were symptomatic of the impact of the early New Deal on the segment of the population. More than a hundred NRA codes established regional wage differentials under which southern workers (which in many instances meant blacks, because of the job classifications) were paid less than people doing the same work elsewhere. The Blue Eagle did not even cover the occupations in which most blacks were employed: farm labor and domestic service. Eighteen NRA codes included what one NAACP official called the "grandfather clause of the NRA." It established wage scales for types of labor based upon what wages had been at a certain date in the past. Obviously this perpetuated pay discrimination based on racial distinctions in job classifications. And in those instances where NRA codes *did* enforce equal pay for workers of either race, the result was often that blacks lost their "advantage" of working for less and were replaced by whites. Black newspapers had their own versions of what NRA stood for, including "Negro Run Around" and "Negroes Rarely Allowed."

For blacks, the Agricultural Adjustment Administration served mainly to reduce their incomes (which they could stand much less than could their large landholding white neighbors), and force black landowners into tenancy, tenants into sharecropping, and many blacks off the land entirely. These effects were extremely significant. Some 40 percent of all black workers in the United States during the Depression years were farm laborers or tenants. A 1934 investigation estimated the average annual income of black cotton farmers of all types at under $200. The AAA was not the *cause* of such deplorable conditions, but it continued them without improvement and in some cases made the problems worse.

Most early New Deal programs included the ideal of decentralized administration or "grass-roots democracy." (No one in the thirties, as far as I am aware, used the term "New Federalism.") Much could be said for the concept in the abstract. In practice, however, it meant that local elites controlled the federal programs in their areas. "[T]he releaf officials here," a black resident of Reidsville, Georgia, wrote to President Roosevelt in 1935, ". . . give us black folks, each one, nothing but a few cans of pickle meet and to the white folks they give blankets, bolts of cloth and things like that." A Georgia official confirmed a discriminatory policy: "There will be no Negroes pushing wheelbarrows and boys driving trucks getting forty cents an hour when the good white men and white women, working on the fields alongside these roads can hardly earn forty cents a day." Relief payments to blacks in Atlanta averaged $19.29 per month, while white relief clients in the same city received $32.66, nearly 70 percent more. A black person in Hattiesburg, Mississippi, summed up the effect of local control in an eloquent, if nearly illiterate, letter to FDR: "i wish you could See the poor hungry an naket half clad's at the relief office an is turned away With tears in their eyes Mississippi is made her own laws and dont treat her destituted as her Pres. had laid plans for us to live."

The need for change should have been obvious. In the 1920s, American popular culture was blatantly racist. Movies portrayed blacks as shiftless, stupid, and laughable. Radio joined in in 1928 with *Amos*

'n' Andy, a series in which white actors spoke the parts of black characters who fit all the white stereotypes of blacks. By 1929, *Amos 'n'
Andy* was radio's most popular program, heard by about 60 percent of
all radio listeners. Other broadcasts in the decade made frequent use
of "darky" jokes. Amusement parks advertised games in which whites
could "Hit the Coon and Get a Cigar." Optimists seeking signs of improvement were hard pressed for examples. Perhaps it was a significant reform when *The New York Times* began, early in 1930, to spell
"Negro" with a capital "N." Early in the New Deal, though, at least
one official of the Federal Housing Administration was still in the habit
of telling "darky" and "coon" stories in public speeches. (Administration leaders soon stopped the practice, although it did not die forever,
as Nixon-Ford Agriculture Secretary Earl Butz demonstrated in the early
1970s.)

The shift in the attitude of the federal government toward race relations was in large part the work of a few dedicated integrationist
reformers, white and black. Unquestionably, the person most responsible for beginning the change in the attitude of the federal government
toward blacks was Eleanor Roosevelt. Mrs. Roosevelt had shown no
particular concern or understanding for the problems of blacks before
her husband became president. But her empathy for the downtrodden
led her quite naturally to take up the cause of blacks. She was shocked
at the uproar that followed her having lunch with a black woman in
Florida in 1933.

In 1927, Eleanor Roosevelt met Mary McLeod Bethune, a black
woman who had risen from a sharecropper's family of seventeen children to found Bethune-Cookman College in Florida. The friendship between these two women continued over the ensuing years, and as a
result Mrs. Roosevelt's understanding of black problems expanded
greatly. She recommended Mrs. Bethune as an assistant to Aubrey Williams at the National Youth Administration, and under the leadership
of Williams, a dedicated white liberal from Alabama, and the influence
of Bethune, the NYA became a model of government assistance for
blacks.

The First Lady also became friendly with Walter White, the first
black national secretary of the NAACP. With the guidance of Bethune
and White, Eleanor Roosevelt became the leading white advocate of
racial integration in the United States. As such, she found herself the
target of virulent abuse from white racists. One of the harshest was the
ditty that put the following words in the President's mouth, speaking
to his wife:

> *You kiss the niggers,*
> *I'll kiss the Jews,*
> *We'll stay in the White House*
> *As long as we choose.*

Eleanor Roosevelt's concern for black people was a reflection of her larger attitude of compassion, which in turn meshed with the values of cooperation that were becoming popular among the American people during the Depression years. The "day of selfishness," Mrs. Roosevelt declared in a 1934 speech to a conference on black education, was over; "the day of working together has come, and we must learn to work together, all of us, regardless of race or creed or color. . . . We go ahead together or we go down together." Seen in this light, the emerging values of the American people seemed to point toward racial cooperation. But it was not so simple. A move toward racial harmony—admittedly, a very *small* move—was not the only possible effect of the Depression on racial attitudes. A glance at contemporary events in Germany is sufficient to remind us that hard times can cause an intensification of racial and religious animosity. The increase in lynching in the American South in those years indicates that such a potential existed in the United States as well. Senator Theodore Bilbo of Mississippi was one of those Americans who thought the Nazis had the right idea. "Race consciousness is developing in all parts of the world," Bilbo declared in 1938. "Consider Italy, consider Germany. It is beginning to be recognized by the thoughtful minds of our age that the conservation of racial values is the only hope for future civilization. . . . . The Germans appreciate the importance of race values."

That the United States in the Depression moved in the direction of the values of compassion and cooperation pointed to by Eleanor Roosevelt, rather than toward the "race values" outlined by Senator Bilbo (who sought a $1 billion congressional appropriation in 1939 to deport all blacks to Africa), was the result of more than Depression-bred concepts of justice, as important as they certainly were. The push given the President and his policies by Mrs. Roosevelt, Mrs. Bethune, Walter White, Harold Ickes, Will Alexander, the southern white Methodist minister who became head of the Farm Security Administration, Aubrey Williams of the NYA, and Clark Foreman, a young white Georgian who became FDR's special assistant on the economic status of Negroes, was of great importance. So was pressure from the Communist party and the CIO, both of which were in the forefront of the quest in the thirties for a larger degree of racial equality. In addition, significant pressure came from blacks themselves, both politically and in terms of organization, demonstrations, and even rioting.

The chronological proximity of President Roosevelt's shift to more forceful opposition to racial discrimination with the only major race riot of the decade, that in Harlem in 1935, may have been coincidence. Be that as it may, the growing importance of black voters in national politics surely was directly related to FDR's move to include blacks in his new Democratic coalition. Black voters began their historic desertion of the Republican party in 1934, *before* the Roosevelt administration had done much specifically for them. In the midterm elections of 1934, a majority of black voters cast their ballots for Democrats for the first time. That year Arthur Mitchell became the first black Democrat ever to win a seat in Congress, when he upset incumbent black Republican Oscar De Priest in a Chicago district. Mitchell won using the slogan "Forward with Roosevelt." The fact that Roosevelt at least attempted to prohibit discrimination in some federal programs and that his administration provided significant amounts of relief for blacks were enough to end three-quarters of a century of Republican allegiance. "Let Jesus lead you and Roosevelt feed you," a black preacher advised his congregation in 1936.

In that year, the dramatic shift in black political support was unmistakable. "Abraham Lincoln," the Baltimore *Afro-American* reminded its readers, "Is Not A Candidate in the Present Campaign." Franklin Roosevelt was, and he won an incredible 76 percent of the black vote, roughly reversing the outcome of four years earlier. The change in black voting was more decisive than that of any other group in 1936. As with working-class whites, many blacks who had never voted before were sufficiently impressed with the New Deal to cast their first ballots for Roosevelt. Even in the rural South, many blacks were by this time getting to participate in elections of a sort for the first time, as they voted in AAA referendums on such issues as crop limitations. A new political awareness and hope began to dawn among southern blacks. "They's talked more politics since Mistuh Roosevelt been in than ever befo'," one southern black said of other blacks in his area. "I been here twenty years, but since WPA, the Negro sho' has started talkin' politics."

Unsurprisingly, some Democrats did not welcome the new black members of their party. When a black minister rose to give the invocation at the 1936 Democratic National Convention in Philadelphia, Senator Ellison D. "Cotton Ed" Smith of South Carolina was horrified. "By God, he's as black as melted midnight!" Smith gasped. "Get outa my way. This mongrel meeting ain't no place for a white man!" Smith stormed out of the convention. It was the first time there had been reason for any southern delegate to walk out of a Democratic convention since 1860, but the South Carolinian's action was a foretaste of the future, not a dim reflection of the past. Some southern delegates bolted the Democratic conventions again in 1948 and 1964, as the party gave them considerably more provocation than a black minister's prayer. Senator Smith insisted that he had no objection to "any Negro praying for me, but I don't want any blue-gummed, slew-footed Senegambian praying for me *politically*." As he later embellished the story for the white folks down home, Smith said that as he left the convention, "it seemed to me that old John Calhoun leaned down from his mansion in the sky and whispered in my ear, 'You did right, Ed.' "

The attitude of such southern reactionaries as "Cotton Ed" Smith to the Democratic alliance with blacks indicates the last critical factor in the Depression-era association between liberalism and the quest for racial justice. Early in the Roosevelt administration, such vehement racists as Theodore Bilbo and John Rankin of Mississippi and Martin Dies of Texas supported the New Deal. But as southern fears grew that Roosevelt was moving toward the twin horrors of socialism and racial equality, racism and economic conservatism became intertwined. Southern conservatives combined red-baiting and race-baiting in their struggle against Roosevelt and his liberal economic policies. Charging that the President sought a second Reconstruction, southern racists created a climate in which racism was plainly identified with conservatism. For economic liberals, this provided one more incentive to come out strongly for greater equality between the races. Racism, particularly as it came increasingly to be associated with fascism and Hitler in the late thirties, was a powerful weapon to use against conservatives. In the 1930s, for the first time since the 1870s, reforms for blacks took their clear place on the liberal agenda. The groundwork was laid, but the "second Reconstruction" so dreaded by such conservative southern senators as Virginia's Carter Glass and North Carolina's Josiah Bailey would not come until a quarter century later.

Although obviously severely limited, the improvements for blacks during the Depression were discernible. In May 1935, as the "Second New Deal" was getting under way, President Roosevelt issued Executive Order 7046, banning discrimination on projects of the new Works Progress Administration. Discrimination continued, but the WPA proved to be a godsend for many blacks. In the later thirties, between 15 and 20 percent of the people working for the agency were black, although blacks constituted less than 10 percent of the national population. This, of course, was a reflection of how much worse off blacks were than whites, but the WPA did enable many blacks to survive. More than that, even minimum WPA wages of $12 a week were *twice* what many blacks had been earning previously.

Harold Ickes's Public Works Administration provided to black tenants a more than fair share of the public housing it built. The PWA went so far as to construct several integrated housing projects. PWA construction payrolls also treated blacks fairly. Some 31 percent of PWA wages in 1936 went to black workers. Ickes first made use of a quota system requiring the hiring of blacks in proportion to their numbers in the local work force. This precedent was followed again (at least in theory) by the wartime Fair Employment Practices Commission and in the civil rights legislation and court decisions of the 1960s and 1970s.

Other foundations were also laid in the New Deal for later victories in the civil rights movement. Roosevelt's Attorney General Frank Murphy created the Civil Rights Section in the Justice Department in 1939. Two years earlier, FDR appointed NAACP attorney William Hastie as the first black federal judge in American history. Robert Weaver, who had just completed a Ph.D. in economics at Harvard, was appointed in 1933 with Clark Foreman to advise the President on black economic problems. Almost a quarter century later, Lyndon Johnson named Weaver as the first black Cabinet member. Roosevelt himself was advised by a group of black leaders who came to be known in the press as his "Black Cabinet." It was, in fact, something considerably less than the name implied, but such an advisory group went far beyond anything any previous president had done in the area. By 1941 the number of blacks in regular (as opposed to WPA) government jobs exceeded their percentage in the population as a whole. But what may have been FDR's most significant legacy to the civil rights movement involved several white appointees. Seven of Roosevelt's eight choices for the United States Supreme Court were advocates of civil rights for blacks. (James F. Byrnes of South Carolina was the exception.) The Roosevelt Court set the stage for the Warren Court of the fifties and sixties.

The New Deal did more for blacks than provide for the future. There were measurable improvements at the time. Most telling was the increase in life expectancy at birth. During the 1930s this statistic rose from 63 to 67 years for white women, 60 to 62 for white men, 49 to 55 for black women, and 47 to 52 for black men. While blacks still trailed far behind their white counterparts in this key indicator of health and well-being, they narrowed the gap in the Depression years. The New Deal also helped bring about a drop in black illiteracy, from 16.4 percent at the beginning of the decade to 11.5 percent at the end.

Two well-known incidents late in the Depression symbolized both the gains blacks had made and how far they had yet to go. When, in March 1939, the Daughters of the American Revolution refused to allow black contralto Marian Anderson to give a concert in the organization's Constitution Hall in Washington, administration officials arranged for Miss Anderson to give a free concert at the Lincoln Memorial. An integrated crowd of more than 75,000 attended the event, and more than two-thirds of those asked in a nationwide Gallup poll how they felt about Eleanor Roosevelt's resignation from the DAR in protest over the organization's racist policy approved the First Lady's stand. Little more than a decade before, at the dedication of the Lincoln Memorial, blacks were segregated in a roped-off section across a road from white spectators. A notable change in white attitudes had taken place in the interim.

Less than two years after the Anderson performance, as American industry geared up for war production, A. Philip Randolph, the socialist president of the Brotherhood of Sleeping Car Porters, launched the March on Washington Movement (MOWM). The plan was to stage a massive black march on the capital to press for desegregation of the armed forces and equal opportunity in defense industries. The MOWM was, as historian Richard Dalfiume has said, "something different in black protest." The New Deal had begun a change in the American racial climate, but it had done so in such a way that blacks had been left dependent on whites in the government. Some blacks, like Randolph, were ready by 1941 to insist on doing things for themselves, on making their own gains. The New Deal approach, Ralph Bunche argued, was "in its very nature" a "defeatist attitude, since it accepts the existing patterns while asking favors and exceptions within them." The MOWM amounted to a public notice that some blacks wanted to stop asking for favors and start confronting injustice on their own. The threat of the march was sufficient to lead FDR to issue his famous Executive Order 8802, creating a Fair Employment Practices Commission to investigate charges of discrimination in defense-related industries. In exchange for this, Randolph agreed to call off the march. As it happened, the FEPC in World War II was not very effective and Randolph's militant approach declined. But another precedent had been set, and two decades later Randolph's March on Washington at last took place. Randolph was there to hear Martin Luther King, Jr., deliver his stirring "I Have a Dream" speech.

The rebirth of that dream of true racial equality, which had been crushed with the end of Reconstruction in the 1870s, was the real achievement of the New Deal years in race relations. The dream, of course, remained only that. Black expectations were raised and white liberals were enlisted in the cause. Little of substance had been accomplished by 1941 in bringing about equal rights for blacks, but the seeds of the Black Revolution of the fifties and sixties had been sown.

Women swing shifters interrupting their work at
Bethlehem Steel Shipyard for a chat (WWII)

Women, Work, and War

ALICE KESSLER-HARRIS

The long struggle for worker organization was finally attained during the mobilization for the Second World War. For thirty years thereafter, both big business and big labor seemed to agree that cooperation was a better tool than conflict in labor disputes. Since the recession of the late 1970s, however, there has been a serious decline in union membership; and industry has successfully sought to restrict the power of labor organizations. The long-established and conservative craft unions, the newly arrived industrial unions, and the increasingly active white-collar and service unions now involve less than twenty percent of the American labor force. Women make up a disproportionate number of the unorganized workers, and most of these women are in the increasingly important service sector of the economy.

Recent legislation by the federal government prohibiting discrimination by gender in the labor market and the movement to amend the Constitution to grant equal rights to women in public employment has focused national attention on working women. The history of women as a major factor in the labor force began in the nineteenth century. Women have always worked, of course, in the home, farm, and mill, but the same nineteenth-century urbanization that created the "cult of domesticity" for middle-class women forced working-class women (and their children) into the workplace to help earn a survival income.

Today, any attempt to sustain the notion that a woman's sphere is limited to the home flies in the face of reality at all class levels. Over half of all women between the ages of eighteen and sixty-four are now in the labor force. Four out of ten working women are mothers, and thirty-six percent have children under the age of six. The persistence of the traditional division of labor in the home requires many working women, particularly in families with limited income, to hold two full-time jobs—one in the workplace and one in the home.

It has long been believed that the breakthrough in female employment came with the Second World War. Fabled in song and story, "Rosie the Riveter" became a symbol for many women entering the labor force—often in occupational roles formerly restricted to males. While it is true that unprecedented numbers of women performed work in heavy industry previously barred to them, no permanent shift in the structure of the labor force seems to have followed.

Alice Kessler-Harris of Hofstra University has written a detailed history of America's working women. In the chapter on the Second World War, reprinted below, she analyzes the impact of the war on patterns of employment; concluding that most of the women who stayed in the work force after the war had been employed before the war. In the end, the rapid demobilization of both military and civilian economic sectors resulted in the restoration of formerly established labor patterns.

Kessler-Harris believes that it was the enormous growth in the consumer economy in the 1950s that led, ironically, to the permanence of females in the work force. Even though national values continued to emphasize that a woman's place was in the home, the desire, and in some cases, the need for more disposable income led women into new patterns of employment. And since it was not a time of national emergency, the jobs sought were permanent, not temporary. Gradually the female work force swelled to the point it inhabits today. This does not mean, however, that long-standing patterns of wage discrimination and restricted advancement possibilities have come to an end. Far from it. But now a more self-conscious and better organized female labor force strives to alter the misconception that woman's work is second-class in nature.

Depression and war have opposite effects on the economy. One prompts efficiency, constraint, cautious investment; the other encourages industrial expansion—even a spirit of reckless gambling. If the 1930s depression sloughed off workers, making every fourth one redundant, the war gobbled them up, then searched for more. Where workers had to plead for jobs in the thirties, in the early forties industry begged for workers. And when the army had soaked up the residue of unemployed men, employers turned to women. Unprecedented opportunity now confronted women who months earlier had pleaded for work. Was this to be a breakthrough?—a turning point that would signal the end of discrimination against women in the labor market?

It certainly looked like it. In many ways, this war duplicated the experience of World War I. Women found jobs in areas previously closed

WOMEN, WORK, AND WAR   From *Out to Work: A History of Wage-Earning Women in the United States,* by Alice Kessler-Harris. Copyright © 1982 by Alice Kessler-Harris. Reprinted by permission of Oxford University Press, Inc.

to them and, once there, proved to be effective workers. The statistical data reveal a dramatic influx of women—five million between 1940 and 1944—into the labor force and new openings in the heavy industries that had been tightly defended against them. Historians like William Chafe, Chester Gregory, and Sheila Tobias and Lisa Anderson have concluded, as a result, that World War II was, in Chafe's words, "a milestone for women in America." From that perspective, the war serves to explain and justify the new expectations of the fifties. Tobias and Anderson see demobilization as the central issue raised by the war years. The war, they argue, opened doors, changed attitudes, made women aware of possibilities they had not previously considered.

To some extent this is undoubtedly true. As in World War I, women who had always worked fought hard to retain their gains when the war ended. But viewing the war this way places too much weight on the role of a single unpredictable event in altering women's behavior. And, whereas women came to the first war out of a lengthy period of struggle for minimal wages and working conditions, they entered the second from a depression-fostered certainty of their economic importance. In fact, women had already begun to change their working patterns in the two preceding decades. They responded to war not as shiny new instruments honed to do their bit in a larger design, but out of the continuity of their own historical experience. In the twenties and thirties different women had struggled to participate in the labor market in their own ways—some seeking the challenge of a career, others organizing for higher standards of living. The war provided opportunities for both kinds of women to continue these struggles. It did not relieve the tensions surrounding their dual roles, but did cast a different light on them.

The second World War provides a place to see these tensions from a different perspective than the depression. Asked their reasons for wage-earning in both periods, women offered the same explanations. Wage work contributed to family life; financial need justified potential neglect of the home. Wartime appeals to patriotism turned the defensive posture these arguments had in the depression into an aggressive stance. Where the depression had prompted women to apologize for paid work—to present it as a last resort to preserve family life—the war focused attention on women's positive contributions to labor force needs. Satisfying family requirements, once a seemingly insurmountable barrier to wage work, became a practical problem to be solved quickly so that the nation could meet the war machine's insatiable hunger for personnel.

The changed perspective made all the difference in the reception women met in the labor force, and there is no doubt that the war raised the level of their material well-being. But whether it permanently altered their relation to wage work is another question. Women would not willingly have given up their family roles even if social sanctions were lifted and support services helped them to do so. And employers and male workers could not readily overcome a tradition of segmentation so closely related to masculinity. Economist Theresa Wolfson put it this way: "It is not easy to forget the propaganda of two decades even in the face of a national emergency such as a great war. Women themselves doubted their ability to do a man's job. Married women with families were loath to leave their homes; society had made so little provision for the thousands of jobs that a homemaker must tackle. And when they finally come into the plants, the men resent them as potential scabs." The resulting ambivalence led women to weigh the tremendous pressure to take jobs against the sacrifices required of their time and by their families. It penetrated every facet of women's work force experience.

As the European war stimulated production in 1940 and 1941, the residue of unemployment began to lessen, though men, not women, benefited from the early build-up. Women were told to "Do the home job better" or channeled into volunteer jobs. As one jocular civil defense official put it, "Give the women something to do to keep their hands busy as we did in the last war—then maybe they won't bother us." As government programs began early in 1941 to "warm up" the unemployed to heavy industry, twenty men were offered places to every woman. Some 700,000 workers received training in industrial skills in the last half of 1941. Only 1 percent of these were female. Employers believed women were not suited to most jobs and declared themselves unwilling to hire women for 81 percent of available production jobs.

Attitudes began to change after Pearl Harbor. Early in 1942, it became clear that the draft would decimate the ranks of production workers. The government issued a nondiscrimination directive. For the first time, employers sought out women, for nontraditional jobs, and occasionally offered the kinds of services that made wage work more viable for those who had households and children to care for. They sometimes provided day care centers on site. Shopping and banking facilities appeared in plants. Convenient transportation and hot lunches attracted women to factory work. As men left jobs for the armed services, women entered them. Still, from September 1942 to September 1943, the number of people in the work force remained at the 1940 level.

By mid-1942 it was clear that this was not enough. Calculating that only 29 percent of America's fifty-two million adult women had jobs, the War Manpower Commission started a campaign to recruit women in areas of labor shortage. Journalist Eleanor Herrick accused half the women in New York City of shirking their war obligations. The federal government lowered the age limit for the employment of women from eighteen to sixteen years. Patriotic appeals to women accompanied tales of their special stake in winning this war in order to stop Hitler from reducing women to "sex slaves" or driving them back to their kitchens. The Women's Bureau described desperate entrepreneurs who harangued women at street corners to come to work, or bribed high school principals to send workers to their plants. The radio did its bit, popularizing tunes like "Rosie the Riveter," which told listeners about "red, white and blue" Rosie who was "making history working for victory." Rosie kept

> . . . a sharp lookout for sabotage
> Sitting up there on the fuselage
> That little frail can do,
> More than a male can do,
> Rosie—(Brrrr) the riveter.
> Rosie's got a boyfriend, Charlie;
> Charlie, he's a marine
> Rosie is protecting Charlie
> Working overtime on the riveting machine.

By February 1943, *Fortune* magazine declared the margin for victory to be "woman power" and suggested drafting them if they did not come forward voluntarily to work in industry. And in July 1943 the War Production Board declared itself in need of a million and a half more women within a year.

Women responded to these appeals in large numbers but not with the kind of unthinking enthusiasm that the statistics seem to demonstrate. Fully three-quarters of the women who worked for pay during the war had worked before, and one and a half million more would have entered the labor force anyway in the normal course of events. Less than five million of the nineteen million women who worked for wages at some time during the war emergency had not been in the labor force before the war began.

What looks like massive mobilization of women in the war years breaks down on examination to something less startling. Nearly 11.0 million women held jobs in 1940. At the peak of wartime production in 1945, 19.5 million women were actually earning wages: an apparent increase in absolute numbers of nearly 8.7 million people or 80.5 percent. But a closer look at the figures forces us to modify our assessment of the real change this number implies. In addition to the women actually working in 1940, the Census Bureau counted some 3.0 million unemployed and looking for work. An additional number, unknown except by estimate, were discouraged but would have worked if they thought jobs were available. A million such workers seems a safe estimate. The difference between the resulting figure of 14.8 million and 19.5 million reduces the increase in women workers to 43 percent or 4.7 million new workers in the war years.

But we need to make still further modifications. What percentage of the 4.7 million would have entered the labor force anyway as a result of population growth and maturity? And what percentage would have entered as a product of the continuing twentieth-century trend of women moving into the work force? The first figure can be calculated on the basis of population growth. In 1940, 27.6 percent of the female population over fourteen was in the labor force. They constituted 25.3 percent of all workers. If the same percentage had been in the labor force in 1945, when the population of women numbered 52,860,000, an additional 750,000 workers in round numbers would have joined the labor force, war or no war. But the proportion of women wage earners had been increasing steadily since 1900 and in all likelihood would have climbed in this decade as well. From 1900 to 1940, the female labor force participation rate had increased 23.5 percent, or an average of nearly 6 percent each decade—though there were in fact wide fluctuations from decade to decade. For the half-decade from 1940 to 1945 we can safely add another 3 percent, or 400,000 women, to the 1940 figure as normal growth. In fact, the figures would in all likelihood have been higher, given the possibility that the depression, having discouraged women from wage work, had created a backlog of women eager to try their wings. Subtracting these two groups, then, one might argue that only 3.5 million workers who might not otherwise have entered the labor force did so in the war years—an addition of 25.28 percent to the female work force above the natural and expected increases. Seventy-five percent of these new female workers were married.

Wartime figures reflect the latent tendency of women to seek wage work when normative pressures to stay at home are removed. Considering the unusual (if still inadequate) child care and food services available; the absence of men to whom women ordinarily catered; attractive wages and job opportunities; and a temporary suspension of overt animosity, these data may represent a peak of the number of women willing to work for wages in that period. In the two years after the war ended, women's participation in the work force dropped by a factor of 19 percent—a figure only a trifle lower than the estimated "additional" women who entered wage work as a result of the war. In other words, after the wartime emergency receded, most of the women who remained in the labor force would have been working for wages anyway. There is no way of knowing if the three and a half million new women workers were the same women who dropped out, or were forced out, of the labor force when the war ended. But it seems clear that wartime surveys reporting that 75 to 85 percent of wage-earning women wanted to keep their jobs at the war's end probably reflected the normal proportion of wage-earning women. Of the two million additional women (above the 1940 level) still in the labor force in 1947, the Women's Bureau estimated that all but 250,000 would have been working in any event. By 1950, the rate of women's participation in the work force had increased to 32 percent—for a net gain of 16 percent over the entire decade. The Census Bureau estimated that without war, natural factors would have yielded seventeen million wage-earning women in 1950. There were in fact eighteen million in that year—only a slight increase above expected growth.

Much has been made of the number of women who entered the work force as an indication of changes in attitude and breakdown of traditional socialization patterns. But from another perspective the figures reflect continuity with previous attempts by some women to break out of traditional roles. Married women had entered the work force during the depression. In the war years, older married women contributed most of the increase that occurred among female workers. Despite publicity given to children left in locked cars while their mothers worked, a government report noted in 1943 that "practically no net expansion occurred among women between 20 and 30 years of age, and only a 6 percent increase of actual over normal employment is estimated for women in the next five year bracket." In contrast, women over forty-five appeared in the labor force in numbers about 20 percent above what would normally be expected. And of the nearly five million women at work in the spring of 1945 who had not been in the labor force five years earlier, three million were over thirty-five.

These rapid rises in participation rates exceeded those of any other age group in the labor force. They were more rapid for the married than for the unmarried, indicating both the degree to which single women had already been engaged in paid labor and the latent trend for the married with no children at home to want to work. This tendency continued after the war. By November 1946, half of all wage-earning women were over 34.8 years old. And the inclination of younger married women to leave the work force when husbands returned home meant that the proportion of older workers in the labor force would continue to rise. By 1950 there had been a net drop in the rate at which married women aged 25–34 went out to work. Correspondingly, half again as many women aged 45–54 were working for wages as had worked in 1940.

Given the high level of previous work experience among most women in the labor force during the war, it is not surprising that the emergency presented itself as an opportunity to get ahead. Memories of the depression urged women wage earners to get what they could while they could. So for those who had been accustomed to working, war-born opportunities encouraged an aggressive stance and resulted in real gains, at least for the duration of hostilities. Black women, older women, and professional women all took advantage of a reduction in discrimination to enter well-paying jobs.

For black women, the change was especially dramatic. For generations, they had been denied access to good, skilled jobs that now opened to them. The proportions who entered the labor force did not expand as rapidly as those of white women reflecting high prewar participation rates. But black women took advantage of their previous work experience and the labor shortage to move into more desirable jobs. About 20 percent of those who had been domestic servants found work in areas that had previously snubbed them. Where white women moved from laundries into factories, especially in the South, black women readily took the jobs they vacated. But it took effort to move up into factory jobs. The threat of a mass demonstration in Washington in 1941, while the United States was building up its armaments in preparation for war, drew public attention to discrimination against all blacks. To head off demonstrations, the federal government created the Fair Employment Practices Commission in July 1941.

Sustained by the FEPC as well as by rulings of the War Manpower Commission against discrimination, and actively aided by the National Council of Negro Women, black women pressed for lucrative factory jobs. In cities like Detroit, where defense work was widespread, large factories imported huge numbers of rural whites to fill jobs for which they initially refused to hire blacks. Black women there led a series of demonstrations, beginning early in 1942 and lasting for nearly two years, to force local authorities to hire them. These demonstrations—for housing as well as jobs—culminated in the storming of a Ford plant by two busloads of women protesting discriminatory hiring policies. Progress was slow. Yet for once, protesters had the active support of union locals, some civic agencies, and government policy. Members of UAW locals threatened to walk out of one plant in 1943 unless black women got jobs. At another plant, union representatives took nine months to win an agreement to hire black women, and then only after a threat of citywide action. The War Production Board and the U.S. Employment Service repeatedly urged employment of blacks in Detroit and elsewhere.

By war's end the position of black women workers had improved substantially. They never got some of the best-paying jobs—in steel mills, as welders, ship fitters, and riveters. But the numbers involved in low-paid and low-status domestic work dropped by 15 percent while the number of factory operatives more than doubled, and clerical, sales, and professional workers substantially increased. Ninety percent of the black women at work after the war had been in the labor force in 1940. Their movement into better jobs reflects not changed attitudes but their ability to take timely advantage of enlarged opportunities.

Professional women were equally aggressive. Historian Susan Hartmann has documented the extent to which they worked through their clubs and organizations to press for economic equality. Groups like the American Association of University Women and the National Federation of Business and Professional Women's Clubs met with the Women's Bureau to design "programs to promote the training, equal treatment and full utilization of women in war production," as well as "to plan for the retention of women's gains after reconversion." These organizations had little understanding of, or sympathy for, the economic problems of poor women or the racial discrimination faced by black women. Rather, they pushed to get women into policy-making positions in war agencies, even denying the need for special black representation on the Women's Advisory Committee—the only direct pipeline for women into the wartime agencies concerned with utilizing labor effectively. Despite the opposition of organizations representing poorer women, business and professional women continued to support the ERA and paid little attention to such mundane issues as day care. For them, the important thing, as always, was not resolving the home and family issues that might equalize work force opportunities for all women, but improving their own relative economic positions. They became entrenched in civil service jobs at the federal and state levels, made inroads into banking and insurance, and moved into administrative jobs in education and health. Though gains remaining after the war ended were relatively small, professional women had nevertheless succeeded in moving out of the holding pattern in which the Depression had placed them.

Two other pieces of evidence suggest that what happened in the war and immediate postwar years represented a response to emergency rather than a shift in attitude. The first emerges from a look at what women did when hostilities ceased; the second, from examining what happened to them in the demobilization period.

When war production ended, large numbers of women simply quit their jobs. The rate at which women chose to leave jobs was at least double, and sometimes triple the rate at which they were discharged. And it was consistently higher than quit rates for men. In the food, clothing, and textile industries, where they had traditionally been employed, women quit jobs at an incredible pace. Women in well-paid jobs—chemical, rubber, and petroleum—quit more slowly than from any other manufacturing jobs. Apparently, more experienced workers who had moved into better-paid jobs wanted to keep their jobs. More newer workers who had spent the war in traditionally female sectors willingly gave their places up.

Employers countered low quit rates by laying off women in the heavy industrial sectors where returning soldiers wanted jobs back. In the two months immediately following V-J Day, women were laid off at a rate of 175 per 1,000, double that of men. As the rate of layoffs slackened, women still lost their jobs at a slightly higher rate than men— especially in some durable goods industries. The biggest involuntary reduction came in the jobs where they had made the biggest gains in wartime and which presumably represented the biggest shift in social attitude—the durable heavy goods industries. Iron and steel manufactories, automobile and machinery makers fired women faster than they fired men. On the other hand, employers clearly sought to retain female employees in the nondurable goods sectors, where they were laid off more slowly than men.

Women's net gains in the war years were, therefore, negligible. They managed to retain a slightly greater share of manufacturing jobs, especially in the durable goods industries, but the general pattern of their employment remained the same as before the war. Even within manufacturing, the big gains occurred in electrical goods, where the task of assembling tiny parts was said to be suited to nimble fingers. The shift to clerical and office jobs continued. Few women retained skilled crafts jobs. The Women's Bureau concluded a study of Bridgeport, Connecticut, after the war sadly: "Only a few women have been allowed to continue in the newer fields of employment, and thus to continue to use skills learned during the war." Older women, married women, women without at least a high school education, and black women again had a hard time finding jobs.

Wartime necessity may have required women's wage work, but it did not release women who worked from the pressure to adhere to old social roles. Women's own urges for better jobs and wages met their match in the pleas for patriotism and service to the community that came from employers, the Labor Department, and the War Manpower Commission. These rationales for wage work produced policies that effectively skirted women's desires for work for its own sake. The never-ending fear that women might be unwilling to leave when the war ended led government policy makers and employers to make it clear that women ought to work only temporarily. And this too required continuing patterns of behavior that perpetuated the divided labor market with all of its psychic underpinnings.

Because of the ambivalence surrounding women's work, policies designed to make it easier for them to enter the labor force emerged erratically. Women found themselves without representation on the influential War Manpower Commission. Instead, the Commission created a Women's Advisory Committee in September 1942. That committee was authorized to recommend policy regarding women. But its recommendations were channeled through a Management-Labor Committee and thence to the WMC. The commission turned down Mary Anderson's request for one or two representatives on the Management-Labor Committee, offering instead a seat without a vote to Margaret Hickey, who chaired the Women's Advisory Committee. Three steps removed from the seat of power, the WAC operated in a vacuum. According to the Women's Bureau, it took seven months "before the WMC and its staff advisers sat down to consider the problem of how to improve communications."

While confusion persisted in administrative ranks, women in good jobs found themselves facing male pressure to be feminine, and sometimes hostility for violating traditional roles. To keep women's images of themselves as intact as possible, administrators focused attention on the ways women managed to remain feminine despite hardships. The director of War Public Services for the Federal Works Authority—in charge of expanding facilities for the war effort—told an interviewer in 1943 that women war workers deserved special commendation for the attention they paid to grooming. "They bring glamor to the job," she said. The personnel manager of a plant confirmed the importance of grooming: "We like the girls to be neat and trim and well put together. It helps their morale. It helps our prestige too." Women workers sustained and supported this stance. They struggled to be able to wear their own clothing, even where it might be dangerously floppy. One plant posted drawings of scalped women to get them to tuck hair into bonnets or nets. Overt hostility kept women in their places too. Nell Giles, a reporter for the Boston *Herald* who worked in a defense factory for a period of months, described being hooted down for carrying a black tin lunch box. Only men, it seemed, carried lunch boxes. Women used paper bags, even though they couldn't put soup or milk in them. Giles didn't have the courage, she admitted, "to buck that line." Catcalls, whistles, and hisses faced women who walked onto the production floor for the first time. Young girls who became pages on the floor of the New York Stock Exchange met wolfish whistles.

Employers adopted promotion and training policies that played into these role divisions. At the suggestion of the War Department, female training included frequent analogies to household work. Supervisors attempted to convince new recruits that any woman who could use a needle could handle a welding rod, or that cutting out sheet metal resembled cutting a pattern for a dress. Employers' willingness to use women was governed by immediate needs. They refused to integrate women into training programs that might provide access to skills beyond those essential for their initial tasks. For temporary help, management reasoned, that would have been a wasted investment. One group of women complained in late 1944 that "management is engaging in a vicious and deliberate campaign to induce women to quit by transferring them from one department to another, by assigning women the least desirable jobs, and by an unceasing psychological drive to harass women out of the plants."

The struggle for equal pay illustrates another level of ambivalence. For years, trade unions had argued for equal pay for women only when the jobs of unionists were threatened by women's lower wages. Women's quest for equal pay on the grounds of equity had met little response. Now women were literally taking men's jobs, as earlier it had been feared they would do. To pay them at a man's scale undermined the barriers that divided women's work from men's. To pay them below it undermined the value of the job and threatened men's wage scales when they returned to reclaim their jobs. Manufacturers under contract to the government, and paid on a cost-plus basis, could readily agree to raise wages. Those in the private sector preferred to retain barriers. Trade unions concerned with job protection tended to fight for equal pay (although only the left-wing unions espoused genuinely egalitarian values). Wishing to avoid chaos in the labor market as well as to promote "mobility of the labor force and maximum utilization of women workers," government agencies agreed to support labor and attempted to persuade management to go along with equal pay. A Bureau of Labor statistician acknowledged the realities involved when she wrote in 1947 that there were three reasons for granting equal pay to women: justice, sustaining men's wage rates, and increasing purchasing power. The second, she argued, was by far the most powerful.

Recognizing the pressures to sustain wages in a period when wage rises were strictly limited, the National War Labor Board issued General Order No. 16 in November 1942, permitting employers to "equalize the wage or salary rates paid to females with rates paid to males for comparable quantity of work." But the Congress failed to pass a companion bill that would have prohibited wage differentials based on sex. And only five states with about a quarter of the nation's female wage earners enacted their own laws. Furthermore, since these laws were concerned primarily with the issue of sustaining men's wages, they addressed themselves only to preventing women from wage-cutting that could depress men's earnings, not to the major source of discriminatory wages for women—the historic differentiation of male and female jobs, where jobs defined as female carried a lower wage rate. As a result, the gap between men's and women's wages increased during the war. Women were earning far more in dollar terms than before the war, and more than they would earn thereafter. Still, the average full-time woman worker earned only 55 percent of what her male co-worker earned: a drop from the 1939 figure of about 62 percent.

Women protested the vagueness of federal guidelines and agitated for additional protection. In Dayton, Ohio, angry women told Elizabeth Christman of the Women's Bureau that despite federal guidelines on equal pay embodied in General Order No. 16, the Frigidaire plant in which they worked continued to hire women at lower rates than men would be paid for the same jobs, and to violate their seniority. Book binders in the Government Printing Office complained of getting thirty to fifty-two cents an hour less than men for the same work. Christman reported that hundreds of grievances had been filed by female employees of General Motors in Ohio against rate discrimination. The same women objected to the War Labor Board's use of "comparable" to define work that should be paid equally. They wanted to substitute "same pay for same work" in order to avoid misunderstanding and confusion.

Like the struggle for equal pay, the struggle for access to trade unions suffered from the ambiguity of women's presence under sufferance owing to wartime emergency. Unions that had never had women members, like the International Boilermakers, Iron Shipbuilders, Welders and Helpers, continued to deny them membership until it was clear that the war emergency necessitated it. Unionized men complained that women would "spoil the job" or "break the morale of the plant." Women who did not understand informal work rules tended to exhaust themselves in rapid bursts of work and to work without stint. Some unionists struck to prevent women from being hired. Others, like those in steel, auto, rubber, and machine tools, accepted or actively recruited women into their ranks but denied them upgrading and frequently continued discriminatory job classifications. Most trade unions maintained separate seniority lists of men and women and tolerated job classifications and job rates on the basis of sex. They bypassed issues of particular interest to women workers. Women complained that men were not fighting hard enough for such things as equal pay. And they wanted maternity leaves without loss of seniority, good day care centers, and time off to care for sick children.

Yet the women who joined unions benefited nonetheless. In the aftermath of the great organizing drives of the 1930s, unionization had spread over the industrial Northeast. Union shops and maintenance of membership agreements—under which incoming workers automatically joined the collective bargaining unit—provided unions with a steady influx of members as war industry expanded. Recruiting three and a half million women into heavy industry where they had not previously been employed increased fourfold the number of female union members within two years. Economist Gladys Dickason estimated that at the beginning of the war only 800,000 wage-earning women were unionized. They made up 9.4 percent of unionized workers. By 1944 more than three million women constituted 22 percent of trade union membership.

Whether they fared well or ill was a matter of union politics. The strongest voice for egalitarian policies came from the left wing of the union movement. The United Electrical, Radio and Machine Workers,

whose membership was 35 percent female by 1944, had an equal proportion of women on its executive council and managed to end discriminatory pay entirely. The United Rubber Workers included an equal
pay clause in 142 of its agreements. The United Auto Workers developed perhaps the most complete policy-making apparatus. It attempted to get women involved in the union administrative structure.
It held rallies where it encouraged women to be active in their shop
committees as well as in their communities. In the spring of 1944, the
UAW War Policy Division set up its own Women's Bureau to serve the
union's 300,000 female members. R. J. Thomas, UAW president, announced that the new bureau was to "give special consideration to
seniority, safety standards, maternity leave practices, and other problems relating to the employment of women. In addition, the Bureau
will develop techniques for interesting women in general union activities and in developing their sense of union citizenship."

From the beginning, the Bureau concerned itself with the tricky
issue of how to involve women in general trade union issues while it
prepared them for inevitable postwar layoffs. Mildred Jeffrey, at its head,
began studying "the effects of cutbacks on unemployment of women
workers" as early as May 1944. She described the situation then as
"already acute in some areas" and urged a national conference to de-
fuse their objections to being fired. She wanted "our women," she wrote,
to "fully understand the problems which the International faces. . . ."

The conference that met in December covered a wide variety of
issues. Its 150 representatives passed resolutions asking for "in-plant"
cafeterias to sell hot food and requesting counseling services that would
include advice about family problems as well as work. Women complained that company counselors often attempted to "inculcate anti-
union attitudes" or acted as spies "to see if women are loitering about
in rest rooms, smoking, or wearing improper clothing." Members asked
for maternity leaves without loss of seniority, insurance plans that included maternity benefits, improved child-care facilities designed to
continue after the war emergency, a guaranteed annual wage, and unemployment benefit policies that did not discriminate against women.

For all these ambitious long-range goals, when it came to the issue
of layoffs, women workers acquiesced. They readily acknowledged that
the union faced a difficult problem in reconciling the competing interests of returning veterans with those of newly hired women. Female
representatives recognized that women would be "the first to feel the
impact of reconversion lay-offs" yet went on to endorse a seniority
system that gave job preference to a man who had worked under UAW
jurisdiction for even the briefest period before the war over a woman
who had been in the union for the duration. Better than most unions,
the UAW attempted to serve its female members. It protected and extended their rights as union members. Yet, though it supported federal

bills for full employment, it too succumbed to a pattern that saw most unions unceremoniously discard their female members at war's end.

Ambivalence toward women working during the war showed up even in the provision of support services necessary for them to work effectively. While almost everybody acknowledged the difficulties involved when a woman undertook wage labor in addition to household chores, few offered concrete suggestions for lightening the load. In fact, the opposite happened. Defense contractors asked for, and routinely got, permission to suspend maximum-hour legislation, and a woman with children to care for might be coerced into working nine or ten hours a day in a six-day week. If she took a day off for family needs, she was berated as unpatriotic. In its concern to attract "woman-power," *Fortune* sympathized with the working mother who had "marketing, cooking, laundering and cleaning to attend to" and wondered how long she could "stand up under a twelve- or fourteen-hour day." Yet when it came to setting up services, only a few plants extended more than limited help. Lest women become accustomed to amenities and too comfortable at work, little attempt was made to accommodate them even at the peak of national need. Communal kitchens and shared cleaning were rare. Most factories provided hot lunches only after a struggle. And though occasionally one reads of banking services brought to the door, only the model plants of Kaiser Industries offered anything like the British experience of factory-delivered laundry services, packaged ready-to-eat foods, and special shops. For fifty cents, Kaiser's "Home Service Food" program allowed a mother to order a family's evening meal two days ahead of time and pick up her order along with her child at the end of a day's work.

Provision of even limited services stopped short when it came to help with mothering. The WMC declared its policy to be one of actively recruiting women without children under fourteen and then added that "this principle should not be construed to mean that women who are responsible for the care of young children and who desire to work are to be deprived of an opportunity for training or employment." But such language militated against an active campaign for child-care facilities. And the Commission went on to appeal to mothers of young children to remain at home and to ask employers not to recruit them until "all other sources of local labor supply have been exhausted in order that established family life will not be unnecessarily disrupted." The Commission never spoke consistently, however. In one critical industrial area, the War Production Board noted, the WMC pleaded with women to get into the war plants, while local leaders urged them to leave the plants and stay at home with their children.

The women who worked in industry had no direct influence on developing federal child-care policy. The Children's Bureau in the Department of Labor included female early-childhood experts, and professional women and social workers sat on the Women's Advisory Committee, but much of their advice was simply ignored. The Women's Bureau later commented wryly, "It seems sound, in any case, to permit a voice in their own affairs to one-third of the working population, especially when that one-third carries a far greater proportion of responsibility for the maintenance of family and community welfare." Left almost entirely to bureaucrats, child care became a political football, tossed about in the public press as it became the focal point of hostility to women earning wages. "Experience has shown that the surest and quickest way to disrupt a family," wrote a trade union chaplain, "is to take the mother out of the home. . . . Too many mothers of families are working in war plants, not because of necessity nor for reasons of patriotism but because they are drawn by the lure of huge wages." Behind the specter of the disrupted family followed that of juvenile delinquency. In the spring of 1943, a seventeen-year-old was arrested for paying thirteen-year-old girls twenty-five cents apiece to "play" with men. Had all their mothers been at home, it was argued, this could never have happened. As if to underscore the concern, the Senate Subcommittee on Education and Labor held hearings on juvenile delinquency in the winter of 1943.

Confused by the mixed messages and divided over the child-care issue, Congress vacillated. At first it seemed satisfied to leave the problem in the hands of local communities—a solution approved by the Children's Bureau, but which completely failed to provide facilities for all those who needed them. Not content to leave child care in such disarray, and prodded by publicity about inadequately supervised children, President Roosevelt freed emergency construction funds, under the 1941 Lanham Act, to build facilities for child care. The Federal Works Administration, which supervised the funds, was to allocate them in consultation with community officials and with the Federal Security Administration, under whose charge fell most health and welfare policies.

Problems of coordinating separate federal and state agencies combined with ambivalence at all levels to produce an underfunded and entirely unsatisfactory program. The first project under the FWA's child-care program was approved in August 1942. But funds were "slow and insufficient" and even when the flow started, limited staffing reduced the numbers of children centers could care for and limited their hours. So inadequate were they that rumors circulated about executives in war industries who wanted to set up their own child-care centers. They planned to petition the Navy for permission to charge the cost to production. By August 1943, although 53,000 children were enrolled in FWA centers, reports began to spread that they were underutilized: the Chicago *Times* ran a story headlined "WAR NURSERIES LACK CHILDREN: TWO MAY CLOSE." The centers were spottily and inconveniently located.

Their hours were too short. Their fees were often too high (up to six dollars per week per child). And the FWA admitted that it had made no attempt "to sell the mother on the idea that nurseries give the child the advantage of trained care and excellent supervision." Nursery workers, often rapidly selected and poorly trained, were identified in the public mind as poor people more interested in income than in children. School boards with the facilities and expertise to implement programs had been openly hostile. By September, the FWA acknowledged that the centers were operating at only a quarter of capacity.

Interoffice squabbling finally stopped in October after the Senate had passed, and a House committee killed, a bill to provide day care funding jointly administered by the Office of Education and the Children's Bureau. The bill, sponsored by Senator Elbert Thomas, would have set aside twenty million dollars for federal grants to communities that built their own centers. It was effectively scuttled by Roosevelt, under whose leadership Congress finally gave the FWA sole prerogative over building federal centers.

But they never worked well. Those who sought to provide services for working mothers did so apologetically. "We have," said Florence Kerr, then director of the FWA child-care project, "what amounts to a national policy that the best service a mother can do is rear her children in her home. . . . But we are in a war. . . . Whether we like it or not, mothers of young children *are* at work. . . . So we do need care centers." Because they reflected the conviction that mothers of young children had no business in the labor force, the programs were geared not to the needs of mothers but to those of employers. They were, as one panel of educators and union leaders reported, "not intended as a substitute for the home, but rather as an aid to parents who face unusual problems arising from the war emergency." A proponent of the Thomas bill declared, "While none of us like the idea of mothers of infants working, many of them have essential skills and many of them, particularly soldiers' wives, need the money." The FWA came up with a most appealing slogan to handle the contradition implicit in seeking funds for children whose mothers really ought to have been at home. "Men are needed on the battle front. Women are needed at the home front. Men are needed with minds clear and steady. Women are needed with attention for their work undivided. . . ." To help their husbands, mothers needed day care.

Insistence on maintaining feminine roles had serious consequences. Since their right to be at work was never fully asserted, women were left vulnerable, after the war, to the removal of such pitiful services as existed. And this insistence accounts for the reluctance of many women to help out during the war. Faced with the failure of a massive campaign to recruit women in the Detroit area in the fall of 1942, the WMC turned to the Women's Advisory Committee to help find "the reasons for the slow response." The Committee replied swiftly. Women would not leave their homes, they argued, "in really large numbers until they had assurance that supplementary community adjustments in the form of child-care centers and other community facilities would be provided, and also, in some instances, until they had better assurance of employer acceptance."

The evidence offers little support to those who suggest that the war was either a turning point or a milestone. Neither the lives of women nor the way industry responded to them in the immediate postwar years suggests such a conclusion. Questions the war had brought to the fore—like equal pay, child care, and community services for wage-earning women—lost immediacy as women faced the reality of poorly paid jobs or none at all. The question of whether women should or should not work once again assumed ideological proportions as the labor market offered women more limited opportunities and taking advantage of them created some family stress.

Reactions to the end-of-war layoffs varied. Young women tended to accept cuts philosophically. On Wall Street, sixty-six young women who had worked as pages and clerks on the floor of the stock exchange for the first time all expected to lose their jobs as the war ended. A sympathetic reporter commented, "Most of the girls really don't care. . . . they have learned that Wall Street is not yet adjusted to the presence of women between 10 A.M. and 3 P.M." Experienced women who lost good jobs were not as quiet. They stormed employment agencies, wrote angry letters, demanded action from the Women's Bureau and queued endlessly for jobs. To no avail.

Women who had never worked before tended to move back to the home. It came as no surprise to them, according to Frieda Miller, who had succeeded Mary Anderson as director of the Women's Bureau in 1944, that they were the first to be fired, nor did they particularly want to "get ahead at the expense of veterans." Women of childbearing age gave birth to the baby boom. But the normal increase in the number of women eager to find jobs was enough to rekindle the old debate as to whether or not they ought to work. As in the thirties, even those who supported wage-earning for women made sharp distinctions between the need to work and the desire to do so. A 1946 *Fortune* survey asked if "a married women who has no children under 16 and whose husband makes enough to support her should or should not be allowed to take a job if she wants to." Only a third of the men and two-fifths of the women queried believed they should be allowed to take jobs. *Fortune* noted a sharp class division—more than half of the prosperous women answering favored women's freedom to work. But only 35 percent of the poor women agreed. They cited two main reasons in explanation: people who needed jobs would be deprived of them, and a woman's place was in the home.

But which women needed jobs? asked Lucy Greenbaum in the *New York Times Magazine*. They were, she answered, those whose husbands would not return from the war, or who would return injured; or those who would never marry because the war had decimated the ranks of men. Then she added a new category. There were those who *wanted* to work: those who found happiness in a job, who found the child-rearing role unduly restrictive or who, having experienced the relative independence and responsibility of wage earning, would simply refuse "to retreat to the home."

Against the women who wanted to work, traditionalists directed a stream of vituperation in the immediate postwar years. Family life depended on their staying at home, so it was morally wrong for such women to seek jobs. Women, argued Agnes Meyer in the *Atlantic Monthly*, were needed "to restore a security to our insecure world." She called on them to resist pressure to enter the labor market and to renounce any job except that of housewife and mother. "What ails these women," she asked, "who consciously or unconsciously reject their children? . . . The poor child whose mother has to work has some inner security because he knows in his little heart that his mother is sacrificing herself for his well-being. But the neglected child from a well-to-do home, who realizes instinctively that his mother prefers her job to him, often hates her with a passionate intensity." This was, according to Marynia Farnham and Ferdinand Lundberg, authors of the best-selling *Modern Woman: The Lost Sex*, as it should be. Women, they suggested "would do well to recapture those functions in which they have demonstrated superior capacity. Those are, in general, the nurturing functions around the home." To women who chose to enter "fields belonging to the male area of exploit or authority—law, mathematics, physics, business, industry and technology—government and socially minded organizations should . . . make it clear that such pursuits are not generally desirable for women."

If women, despite their natural bent, insisted on entering such fields, the consensus held that they deserved to be discriminated against. The psychic maladjustment that led them to leave their homes made them intrinsically poor risks in the office. They were emotionally unstable, quarreled too much, and fomented feuds in the office. They lacked the "gift for teamwork that makes for coordinated research" and did not have "the focused imagination that makes a man work steadfastly on a long project." As professionals they were indecisive, as unionists they were disloyal. Worst of all, their interest in work distracted attention from what should have been a primary concern with the home.

Few advocates of jobs for women engaged in debate at that level. Instead they responded in two ways. Women's Bureau and government policy makers proposed retraining and counseling to channel women into jobs expected to have little attraction for men. Frances Perkins, then Secretary of Labor, urged that some doors through which women had passed during the war be kept open after it ended. She advocated public health and welfare work "as professions in which 'excellent' opportunities should be available to women." Frieda Miller argued that women "would like to retain, some if not all, of the gains" made during the war. But the Women's Bureau was pragmatic about the possibilities. In 1944 it prepared a policy statement describing what would happen to women's jobs in power laundries, where they had taken over virtually all operations. "Work as washman and extractor operator may be crossed from the list for women unless the pay is so low as not to attract competent men. The Army has given many men training in these jobs, and servicemen should have first chance at the work if they want it. But since at present women are being paid less than men for washing, and the new machinery is calculated to require much less physical strength it is possible that women will be kept on in the washroom though the danger is that this will be at depressed wages."

For other women the fight to retain wartime gains revolved around their pay. By war's end, as we have seen, equal pay had been accepted in principle by some trade unions and five states. In Congress, representatives Mary Norton, Claude Pepper, and Wayne Morse introduced a bill in 1945 to insure equal pay and opportunity to women. The Women's Bureau and the WTUL waged aggressive campaigns for this bill, the Women's Equal Pay Act, and for similar legislation, from 1945 on. But opposition from chambers of commerce and management associations prevailed. By the early 1950s, equal pay was as distant as it had ever been. Maurice Tobin, then Secretary of Labor, demonstrated to an Equal Pay Conference how little progress had been made. "Dear Mr. Blank," he read, quoting a little from a company manager to an employment agency,

> We have an opening here for a combination program director and salesman. This position can be filled by either a man or a woman. We will pay a woman $20 a week for doing the office work and give her $10 a week drawing account, thus guaranteeing her $30 a week. We will pay her 20 percent commission on all sales.
> We will start a man at $30 a week for doing the office work, and $30 a week drawing account, and also pay him 20 percent on all sales. . . . the person who fills this position must have at least a year or two of business and office experience.
> . . . The gal especially should be attractive.

More radical feminists asked for full employment. The real issue, argued writer Edith Efron, was not one of turning a woman into a sort of pseudo-man who "talks, works, thinks, acts, reacts like a male." The real question, the woman worker suspected, was not " 'How come no jobs for women?' but 'How come not enough jobs?' " Women's situation, argued Lucy Greenbaum, "will depend to a large degree on the extent to which the nation's entire economy can develop a high level of employment and the extent to which the industries that require the type of work women do best can expand." *The Independent Woman,* organ of the National Federation of Business and Professional Women's Clubs, raised the issue of the right to work again. "We think that it is a right that belongs to the individual, man or woman, to decide whether or not he or she wants to work. Industry, business or government should not make that decision. If there is a job to be done, the worker should be accepted according to training and ability."

But most of the American public did not agree. Less than 22 percent of the men and 29 percent of the women interviewed by *Fortune's* pollsters thought that women "should have an equal chance with men" for any job. Only 46 percent of the men, and less than 50 percent of the women, thought even women who had to support themselves should have an "equal chance." And substantial numbers of both sexes thought men should always have the preference no matter what the woman's economic position.

As in World War I, men who worked next to women grudgingly conceded their ability to do a job. But demonstrations of effectiveness at tough jobs did not change attitudes about women's work in general or about their primary role at home. At best, militant women staged a holding action—slightly increasing the numbers out at work as they returned to stratified jobs and continuing to struggle for equal pay. The strength of the propaganda campaign to get women out of the work force reflects the extent to which perceptions of family needs still governed women's work, paid or unpaid. As family members eager to enhance economic security, women fought to retain paying jobs; but as family members anxious to preserve jobs for male breadwinners, both men and women fought to return women to the sanctity of the home.

The war turned out to be less a milestone than a natural response to the call for patriotism, to lucrative jobs, to husbands' absences, and to more readily available household and child-care services. The milestone came after. It was marked by the dawning recognition within families that women's functions of cushioning depression and fighting inflation, traditionally performed by economies within the household, might be more effectively handled by wage-earning. A woman's income, still supplementary, and her job, still less than a career, could make the difference between sheer survival and minimal comfort. If the entry of women into war work was a response to opportunity, the continuing rise in their work force participation after demobilization reflects a response to increasing economic demands on the family. Briefly, a reordered set of ideas—what Betty Friedan called the "feminine mystique"—managed in the 1950s to reconcile the competing interests of home and work. Though middle-class and working-class communities responded to postwar ideology differently, the home remained central to the aspirations of most women. It took a new set of pressures on the family and a dramatic shift in the labor market to challenge that ideology.

Jackie Robinson steals home

Jackie Robinson Breaks Baseball's Color Line

JULES TYGIEL

Looking at the world of professional athletics today, it is hard to imagine the absence of Afro-Americans in baseball's major leagues, the National Football League (NFL), or in the National Basketball Association (NBA) until the years after the Second World War. Although the kind of racial segregation that characterized the South was not as impermeable in the North and West, the major athletic organizations might as well have been located in Dixie as far as their racial policies were concerned.

The only area of professional sports where blacks had won national prominence, if not acceptance, was in boxing. The first black man to win recognition in a national boxing championship was Jack Johnson in 1909. Unfortunately, Johnson's exuberant and controversial life style alienated the American public. Joe Louis in the 1930s and 1940s became the first black champion to be taken into the hearts of the American public. Louis' extraordinarily powerful boxing style and his humble demeanor outside the ring made him an acceptable sports hero in a world divided by racial loyalties.

The Second World War proved to be as much a watershed for race relations in athletics as it was in many other areas. A key role in this development was played by the educational assistance available to veterans through the G.I. Bill. Although black colleges fielded athletic teams, white professional sports (particularly football and baseball) used white colleges as farm teams for the development of young athletes. Baseball, on the other hand, tended to use minor league systems to develop most of their players. With more black athletes attending predominantly white colleges under the G.I. Bill, their talents could hardly be ignored by the leading recruiters for professional teams. The racial barrier fell in 1945 when the Los Angeles Rams signed the first black athlete to play in the NFL. The NBA barrier fell in 1950, and today blacks make up a significant majority in professional basketball.

The most dramatic breakthrough, however, was in baseball. Major league baseball rightly considered itself "America's pastime"—by far the most popular professional sport in the post-war period. What was not widely known at the time was that there was an extensive professional league of black players. In the off-season, many teams in the Negro leagues would play teams made up of players from the white major leagues. The outstanding skills of some of the black players were well known to those in charge of major league operations, and it seemed only a matter of time until some major league team would make the recruiting leap and hire a black athlete.

As it turned out, the daring move was made by Branch Rickey, the president of the Brooklyn Dodgers; the player enlisted was Jackie Robinson, a former star athlete from U.C.L.A. who had won letters there in baseball, football, track, and basketball. And the rest, as they say, is history. But not quite. The baseball world was thrown into a turmoil by the signing of Robinson, as is seen in the following selection.

Jules Tygiel, of San Francisco State University and a long time Dodger fan, has written an exceptionally intriguing and perceptive book about what he calls "baseball's great experiment." After one year (1946) of playing with Montreal (the Dodgers' International League farm team), Robinson joined the parent club for what became one of the most outstanding careers in major league baseball. The passages from Tygiel's book that are reprinted below deal with Robinson's professional debut with Montreal and the first year of his remarkable career with the Dodgers. Robinson's exceptional skill as an athlete and his extraordinary character as a human being have made him an authentic American hero.

This is a particularly good year to campaign against the evils of bigotry, prejudice, and race hatred because we have witnessed the defeat of enemies who tried to found a mastery of the world upon such cruel and fallacious policy.

New York Times editorial,
February 17, 1946

I

Opening Day of the baseball season was always a festive occasion in Jersey City on the banks of the Passaic River. Each year Mayor Frank Hague closed the schools and required all city employees to purchase tickets, guaranteeing a sellout for the hometown Giants of the International League. The Giants sold 52,000 tickets to Roosevelt Stadium, double the ball park capacity. For those who could not be squeezed into the arena, Mayor Hague staged an annual pre-game jamboree. Jersey City students regaled the crowd outside the stadium with exhibitions of running, jumping, and acrobatics, while two bands provided musical entertainment.

On April 18, 1946, the air crackled with a special electricity. Hague's extravaganza marked the start of the first major league baseball season since the end of the war. But this did not fully account for the added tension and excitement. Nor could it explain why people from nearby New York City had burrowed through the Hudson Tubes for the event. Others had arrived from Philadelphia, Baltimore, and even greater distances to witness this contest. Most striking was the large number of blacks in the crowd, many undoubtedly attending a minor league baseball game for the first time. In the small area reserved for reporters chaotic conditions prevailed. "The press box was as crowded as the subway during rush hours," wrote one of its denizens in the Montreal *Gazette*. On the field photographers "seemed to be under everybody's feet." The focus of their attention was a handsome, broad-shouldered athlete in the uniform of the visiting Montreal Royals. When he batted in the first inning, he would be the first black man in the twentieth century to play in organized baseball. Jackie Robinson was about to shatter the color barrier.

"This in a way is another Emancipation Day for the Negro race," wrote sportswriter Baz O'Meara of Montreal's *Daily Star*, "a day that Abraham Lincoln would like." Wendell Smith, the black sportswriter of the Pittsburgh *Courier* who had recommended Robinson to Brooklyn Dodger President Branch Rickey, reported, "Everyone sensed the significance of the occasion as Robinson . . . marched with the Montreal team to deep centerfield for the raising of the Stars and Stripes and the 'Star-Spangled Banner.' We sang lustily and freely for this was a great day." And in the playing area, the black ballplayer partook in the ceremonies "with a lump in my throat and my heart beating rapidly, my stomach feeling as if it were full of feverish fireflies with claws on their feet."

Six months had passed since Rickey had surprised the nation by signing Robinson to play for the Dodgers' top farm club. It has been a period of intense speculation about the wisdom of Rickey's action. Many predicted that the effort to integrate baseball would prove abortive, undermined by opposition from players and fans, or by Robinson's own inadequacies as a ballplayer. Renowned as a collegiate football and track star, Robinson had played only one season in professional baseball with the Kansas City Monarchs of the Negro National League. Upon Robinson's husky, inexperienced shoulders rested the fate of desegregation in baseball.

Robinson's experiences in spring training had dampened optimism. Compelled to endure the indignities of the Jim Crow South, barred by racism from many ball parks, and plagued by a sore arm, Robinson had performed poorly in exhibition games. One reporter suggested that had be been white, the Royals would have dropped him immediately. Other experts also expressed grave doubts. Jim Semler, owner of the New York Black Yankees, commented before the opener, "The pace in the IL is very fast . . . I doubt that Robinson will hit the kind of pitching they'll be dishing up to him." And Negro League veteran Willie Wells predicted, "It's going to take him a couple of months to get used to International League pitching."

Robinson, the second Montreal batter, waited anxiously as "Boss" Hague threw out the first ball and lead-off hitter Marvin Rackley advanced to the plate. Rackley, a speedy center fielder from South Carolina, grounded out to the shortstop. Robinson then strode to the batter's box, his pigeon-toed gait enhancing the image of nervousness. His thick neck and tightly muscled frame seemed more appropriate to his earlier gridiron exploits than to the baseball diamond.

Many had speculated about the crowd reaction. Smith watched anxiously from the press box to see "whether the fears which had been so often expressed were real or imagined." In the stands Jackie's wife, Rachel, wandered through the aisles, too nervous to remain in her seat. "You worry more when you are not participating than when you are participating," she later explained, "so I carried the anxiety for Jack." Standing at home plate, Jackie Robinson avoided looking at the spectators, "for fear I would see only Negroes applauding—that the white fans would be sitting stony-faced or yelling epithets." The capacity crowd responded with a polite, if unenthusiastic welcome.

Robinson's knees felt rubbery; his palms, he recalled, seemed "too moist to grip the bat." Warren Sandell, a promising young left-hander opposed him on the mound. For five pitches Robinson did not swing and the count ran to three and two. On the next pitch, Robinson hit a bouncing ball to the shortstop who easily retired him at first base. Robinson returned to the dugout accompanied by another round of applause. He had broken the ice.

Neither side scored in the first inning. In the second the Royals tallied twice on a prodigious home run by right fielder Red Durrett. Robinson returned to the plate in the third inning. Sandell had walked the first batter and surrendered a single to the second. With two men on base and nobody out, the Giants expected Robinson, already acknowledged as a master bunter, to sacrifice. Sandell threw a letter-high fastball, a difficult pitch to lay down. But Robinson did not bunt. The crowd heard "an explosive crack as bat and ball met and the ball glistened brilliantly in the afternoon sun as it went hurtling high and far over the left field fence," 330 feet away. In his second at-bat in the International League, Robinson had hit a three-run home run.

Robinson trotted around the bases with a broad smile on his face. As he rounded third, Manager Clay Hopper, the Mississippian who reportedly had begged Rickey not to put Robinson on his team, gave him a pat on the back. "That's the way to hit 'em, Jackie," exclaimed Rackley in his southern drawl. All of the players in the dugout rose to greet him, and John Wright, a black pitcher recruited to room with Robinson, laughed in delight. In the crowded press box Wendell Smith turned to Joe Bostic of the *People's Voice* and the two black reporters "laughed and smiled. . . . Our hearts beat just a little faster and the thrill ran through us like champagne bubbles." Most of their white colleagues seemed equally pleased, though one swore softly, according to one account, and "there were some very long faces in the gathering" as well.

The black second baseman's day had just begun. In the fifth inning, with the score 6–0, Robinson faced Giant relief pitcher Phil Oates. The "dark dasher," as Canadian sportswriters came to call Robinson, bunted expertly and outraced the throw "with something to spare." During spring training Rickey had urged the fleet-footed Robinson "to run those bases like lightning. . . . Worry the daylights out of the pitchers." Robinson faked a start for second base on the first pitch. On the next he took off, easily stealing the base. Robinson danced off second in the unnerving style that would become his trademark. Tom Tatum, the Montreal batter, hit a ground ball to third. Robinson stepped backwards, but as the Jersey City fielder released the ball, he broke for third, narrowly beating the return throw.

Robinson had stolen second base and bluffed his way to third. He now determined to steal home to complete the cycle. He took a long lead, prompting Oates to throw to third to hold him on base. On the pitch he started toward home plate, only to stop halfway and dash back. The crowd, viewing the Robinson magic for the first time, roared. On the second pitch Robinson accelerated again, causing Oates to halt his pitching motion in mid-delivery. Oates had balked and the umpire waved Robinson in to score. Earlier Robinson had struck with power; now he had engineered a run with speed. The spectators, delighted with the daring display of baserunning, went wild, screaming, laughing, and stamping their feet. Blacks and whites, Royal fans and Giant fans, baseball buffs and those there to witness history, all joined in the ensuing pandemonium.

One flaw marred Robinson's performance. "By manner of proving that he was only human after all," according to one reporter, Robinson scarred his debut with a fielding error in the bottom of the inning. Acting as middleman in a double play, he unleashed an errant throw that allowed the Giants to score their only run. Otherwise, Robinson affirmed his reputation as an exceptional fielder.

In the seventh inning Robinson triggered yet another Royal rally. He singled sharply to right field, promptly stole another base, and scored on a triple by Johnny Jorgenson. Before the inning had ended two more runs crossed the plate to increase the Royal lead to 10–1. In the eighth frame Robinson again bunted safely, his fourth hit in the contest. Although he did not steal any bases, he scrambled from first to third on an infield hit. Once again he unveiled his act, dashing back and forth along the baseline as the pitcher wound up. Hub Andrews, the third Jersey City pitcher, coped with this tactic no better than his predecessor. Andrews balked and for the second time in the game umpires awarded Robinson home plate. According to a true baseball aficionado, this established "some kind of a record for an opening day game."

The Royals won the game 14–1. Montreal pitcher Barney DeForge threw an effortless eight-hitter and Durrett clubbed two home runs. But, as the Pittsburgh *Courier's* front page headline gleefully announced, JACKIE "STOLE THE SHOW." "He did everything but help the ushers seat the crowd," crowed Bostic. In five trips to the plate Robinson made four hits, including a three-run home run, scored four times, and drove in three runs. He also stole two bases and scored twice by provoking the pitcher to balk. "Eloquent as they were, the cold figures of the box score do not tell the whole story," indicated the New York *Times* reporter in an assessment that proved prophetic of Robinson's baseball career. "He looked as well as acted the part of a real baseball player."

"This would have been a big day for any man," reported the *Times*, "but under the special circumstances, it was a tremendous feat." Joe Bostic, who accompanied his story in the *People's Voice* with a minute-by-minute account of Robinson's feats in the game, waxed lyrical. "Baseball took up the cudgel for Democracy," wrote Bostic, "and an unassuming, but superlative Negro boy ascended the heights of excellence to prove the rightness of the experiment. And prove it in the only correct crucible for such an experiment—the crucible of white hot competition."

II

Two years before Robinson's triumphant Jersey City debut, Swedish sociologist Gunnar Myrdal had published *An American Dilemma*, a landmark study of the race problem in the United States. In it he concluded that "Not since Reconstruction has there been more reason to anticipate fundamental changes in race relations, changes which will involve a development towards the American ideal." Few people shared Myrdal's optimistic viewpoint. His work described a society characterized by northern indifference and ignorance of the plight of blacks and a firmly entrenched system of racial segregation in the South, where Jim Crow laws forbade whites and blacks from attending the same schools, riding in the same sections of trains and buses, receiving treatment in the same hospitals, or competing in the same athletic contests. In Birmingham, Alabama, it was "unlawful for a Negro and white to play together or in the company with each other" at dominoes and checkers. These legal restrictions did not adequately reflect the extent of southern discrimination and segregation. As historian C. Vann Woodward noted, "There is more Jim Crow practiced in the South than there are Jim Crow laws on the books." Common custom required separate toilets and water fountains, entrances and exits, and waiting rooms and ticket windows. "Segregation is becoming so complete," Myrdal discovered, "that the white Southerner practically never sees a Negro except as his servant and in other standardized and formalized caste situations."

Southern whites reinforced this Jim Crow regime with a combination of economic and physical coercion. Blacks who challenged racial conventions jeopardized not only their meager sources of income but their lives as well. Although violence had abated since the early decades of the century when mobs lynched scores of blacks each year, the threat of physical reprisals remained a vivid reality. In 1946 at least nine blacks were lynched; and authorities rescued twenty-one others from angry mobs. Any attempt to dismantle the southern caste system, warned Richmond *Times-Dispatch* editor Virginius Dabney, would result in an "interracial explosion" which would leave "hundreds, if not thousands, killed."

The prevalence of these conditions renders all the more remarkable Myrdal's prescient conclusion. Myrdal argued that during the 1930s, the "popular theory behind race prejudice" in the United States had gradually "decayed." The inclusion of blacks in New Deal relief programs, several Supreme Court decisions limiting discriminatory practices, and a growing exasperation with the South among northern liberals reflected this shift in attitudes. In addition, the growing militancy among blacks, whom, said Myrdal, "America can never more regard . . . as a patient, submissive minority" would contribute to the forthcoming transition. This process would be accelerated by "the world conflict and America's exposed position as the defender of the American faith." Ultimately, Myrdal argued, the opponents of segregation would discover "a powerful tool in the caste struggle" in the "American Creed"— "the glorious American ideals of democracy, liberty, and equality to which America is pledged not only by its political constitution, but also by the severe devotion of its citizens."

In the immediate aftermath of World War II the forces that Myrdal predicted would transform the nation's racial practices merged most dramatically and visibly on the playing fields of America. For a half-century, baseball had provided a mirror image of American society; blacks and whites played in two realms, separate and unequal. Within weeks of the end of the war, Brooklyn Dodger president Branch Rickey announced his intention to end Jim Crow in baseball by signing Jackie Robinson. In the eyes of some contemporary observers, Rickey had initiated a "great" or "noble experiment." Could an American institution, steeped in the traditions of racial prejudice and populated by large numbers of southerners, accept the introduction of blacks peacefully? During the following decade and a half the desegregation experiment unfolded in baseball's major and minor leagues. In a formal sense, it was completed in 1959 when the Boston Red Sox, the last all-white major league team, inserted young Elijah "Pumpsie" Green into a game as a pinch runner. In reality, the experiment continues into the present.

The integration of baseball represented both a symbol of imminent racial challenge and a direct agent of social change. Jackie Robinson's campaign against the color line in 1946–47 captured the imagination of millions of Americans who had previously ignored the nation's racial dilemma. For civil rights advocates the baseball experience offered a model of peaceful transition through militant confrontation, economic pressure, and moral suasion. In 1954 when the Supreme Court declared school segregation illegal in the famous *Brown* v. *Board of Education* decision, a majority of major league teams already fielded black athletes. Minor league integration had penetrated not only the North and West, but most of the South as well. For more than a decade before the explosion of sit-ins and freedom rides of the 1960s challenged Jim Crow accommodations in the Deep South, black athletes had desegregated playing facilities, restaurants, and hotels in many areas of the country.

Baseball was one of the first institutions in modern society to accept blacks on a relatively equal basis. The "noble experiment" thus reflects more than a saga of sport. It offers an opportunity to analyze the integration process in American life. An examination of the forces that led to Robinson's hiring, the reaction among both blacks and whites, the institutional response of the baseball establishment, and the resulting decline of the Jim Crow leagues reveals much about the United States in the 1940s and 1950s. The halting and incomplete nature of baseball's achievement notwithstanding, few other businesses have equalled its performance. The dynamics of interracial relationships among players, coaches, and managers provide rare insights into what occurs when nonwhites are introduced into a previously segregated industry.

"The American Negro problem is a problem in the heart of America," wrote Myrdal. "It is there that interracial tension has its focus. It is there that the decisive struggle goes on." From 1945 to 1959 Jackie Robinson and the blacks who followed him into baseball appealed to the "heart of America." In the process they contributed to the transformation of the national consciousness and helped to usher in a new, if still troubled, age of race relations in the United States.

*   *   *   *

> A lone Negro in the game will face caustic comments. He will be made the target of cruel, filthy epithets. Of course, I know the time will come when the ice will have to be broken. Both by the organized game and by the colored player who is willing to volunteer and thus become a sort of martyr to the cause.
>
> Washington Senators owner
> Clark Griffith, 1938

I

The Brooklyn baseball club acquired its unusual nickname in the early twentieth century. Electrified streetcars in New York's largest borough were so dangerous, joked the residents, that one had to become a skilled "trolley dodger" to survive. Brooklynites appended the name to the local baseball team and later shortened it to "Dodgers." Throughout the next several decades the team preserved the borough's identity. Brooklyn, a gathering of three million people of diverse ethnicity, populous enough to be the nation's fourth largest city, had been incorporated in 1898, against the will of most of its residents, into Greater New York. Brooklyn retained its independence from the parent metropolis only in the public mind—a community characterized by aggressive, colorful residents, distinctive Brooklyn accents, and most of all, the baseball team. In the major leagues, the Dodgers were the only franchise that hoisted the banner of a borough, rather than a city.

When Jackie Robinson arrived in Brooklyn in 1947, gasoline-powered buses were replacing the electric trolleys which had given the team its name. These two developments—the appearance of a black baseball player and the invasion of the internal combustion engine—symbolized the forces transforming Brooklyn. Wartime migrations had sprinkled the borough's predominantly white, middle-class population with blacks from the South and Latins from Puerto Rico. At the same time, the greater availability of the automobile and the rapid construction of highways faciliated the exodus of the expanding white middle class to the suburbs, and points father west. The Robinsons journeyed from California to New York; many more people traveled in the other direction. At the dawning of the age of Jackie Robinson, Brooklyn had entered its twilight era, a victim of the postwar transition affecting America's venerable industrial regions. Within a decade these changes would realign the borough's ethnic and racial composition, undermine its local economy, and, to emphasize the decline, banish its baseball club to a land of freeways. What meaning hath the term "Dodgers" in a city with no trolleys?

There is a myth which has flourished about the Brooklyn fans. It is said that they supported their team faithfully and fanatically. Through lean years and fat years, they flooded into tiny Ebbets Field, the legendary arena at the intersection of Empire Boulevard and Bedford Avenue. ("There was never another ball park like Ebbets Field," writes Red Barber. "A little small, outmoded, oldfashioned. . . . You were practically playing second base, the stands were so close to the field.") The myth nonetheless is hollow. As the Dodgers floundered in or near the second division in the 1920s and 1930s, fans stayed away in droves. By 1937 when Larry MacPhail took over the Dodgers, the team verged on bankruptcy. MacPhail rejuvenated the franchise on the field and at the box office, before turning over the reins to Rickey. The MacPhail-Rickey years marked the golden age of Brooklyn Dodger baseball. Dodger devotees flocked to Ebbets Field in record numbers and dying Hollywood soldiers asked for Brooklyn scores before passing on to their next feature film. At the war's end the Dodgers had reached the peak of their popularity.

Robinson joined a Dodger squad that had set a new Brooklyn attendance record as it tied for first place in 1946. A play-off loss to the Cardinals kept Brooklyn out of the World Series. Few people, however, predicted that the team would re-emerge as a contender. "Brooklyn is the one club which appears to lack peace of mind," wrote J. Taylor Spink in the *Sporting News*, picking the club for fifth place. "Durocher's suspension has not helped. Neither has the in-again, out-again business with Jackie Robinson." After the second game of the season, Rickey replaced Durocher with Burt Shotton, who had served as the Deacon's "Sunday Manager" in St. Louis. Shotton confronted the Dodger players, accustomed to Durocher's brassy direction, as a grandfatherly figure who wore a business suit in the dugout rather than a uniform. Unlike Durocher, writes Harold Parrott, Shotton "hardly ever raised his voice enough to be heard at the other end of the dugout, much less by an umpire; and what he did say wouldn't upset a Sunday school."

For Jackie Robinson, relative tranquility characterized the initial week of the 1947 season. In the first two contests, facing the Boston Braves, the rookie first baseman eked out one bunt single. "He seemed frantic with eagerness, restless as a can of worms," observed a Boston correspondent. On April 18 the Dodgers crossed the East River to play the New York Giants. Over 37,000 people flocked to the Polo Grounds to witness Robinson's first appearance outside of Brooklyn. Robinson responded with his first major league home run. The following day the largest Saturday afternoon crowd in National League history, more than 52,000 spectators, jammed into the Giants' ball park. Robinson stroked three hits in four at-bats in a losing cause. Rain postponed a two-game set in Boston, and on April 22 Robinson and the Dodgers returned to Brooklyn, where a swirl of events abruptly shattered the brief honeymoon. The next three weeks thrust Robinson, his family, his teammates, and baseball into a period of unrelenting crises and tension.

The Dodgers' first opponents on the homestand were the Philadelphia Phillies, managed by Alabaman Ben Chapman. While playing for the Yankees in the 1930s Chapman had gained a measure of notoriety for his anti-Semitic shouting jousts with spectators. Now he ordered his players to challenge Robinson with a stream of verbal racial taunts "to see if he can take it." From the moment the two clubs took the field for their first contest, the Phillies, led by Chapman, unleashed a torrent of insults at the black athlete. "At no time in my life have I heard racial venom and dugout abuse to match the abuse that Ben sprayed on Robinson that night," writes Harold Parrott. "Chapman mentioned everything from thick lips to the supposedly extra-thick Negro skull . . . [and] the repulsive sores and diseases he said Robinson's teammates would become infected with if they touched the towels or the combs he used." The onslaught continued throughout the series.

Bench jockeying always comprised an integral part of the national pastime. "Probably the greatest cruelty in the American sports picture is the abuse that is showered on players from the rival dugout," explained sportswriter J. Roy Stockton. These exchanges held no topic sacred. Frequent targets included personal problems, appearance, ethnicity, and race. Athletes often subjected Latin-American opponents to racial barbs. In the 1935 World Series, according to umpire George Moriarty, the Chicago Cubs "crucif[ied] Hank Greenberg for being a Jew" and taunted Jewish umpire Dolly Stark as a "Christ-killer."

The Phillies verbal assault on Robinson in 1947 exceeded even baseball's broadly defined sense of propriety. Fans seated near the Phillies dugout wrote letters of protest to Commissioner Chandler, and newsman Walter Winchell attacked Chapman on his national Sunday night radio broadcast. Chandler notified Philadelphia owner Robert Carpenter that the harassment of Robinson must cease or he would be forced to invoke punitive measures.

Chapman, while accepting Chandler's edict, defended his actions. "We will treat Robinson the same as we do Hank Greenberg of the Pirates, Clint Hartung of the Giants, Joe Garagiola of the Cardinals, Connie Ryan of the Braves, or any other man who is likely to step to the plate and beat us," said Chapman, listing some regular targets of ethnic insults. "There is not a man who has come to the big leagues since baseball has been played who has not been ridden." During his own playing career, alleged Chapman, "I received a verbal barrage from the benches that would curl your hair. . . . They wanted to see if I would lose my temper and forget to play ball." Robinson, argued Chapman, "did not want to be patronized" and had received the same test administered to all rookies.

Chapman's defense drew support from many fans and sportswriters. According to the *Sporting News,* the Phillies received "an avalanche of letters and telephone calls . . . commending Chapman for his fair stand toward Robinson." Several sportswriters also accepted Chapman's explanation. J. Roy Stockton concluded, "If the dugouts treat Jackie just as they treat any other enemy player, especially the good ones, they'll give him a riding eventually. That's baseball." Even Sam Lacy indirectly approved Chapman's stance. Lacy turned his column over to a "friend," who argued that Chapman "seems to have a pretty good explanation to me." The friend condemned Lacy and other writers who "keep on crying that you want Jackie treated like every other ballplayer. . . . The Phillies and Chapman took you at your word."

The general consensus, however, judged the Phillie behavior unacceptable. Robinson's Dodger teammates led the protest. By the second day of the series they lashed back at Chapman demanding that he cease baiting Robinson. Chapman's fellow Alabamans marched in the forefront of Robinson's defenders. Eddie Stanky called him a "coward" and challenged him to "pick on somebody who can fight back." Even Dixie Walker reprimanded Chapman, a close personal friend. Rickey later claimed that this incident, more than any other, cemented Dodger support for Robinson. "When [Chapman] poured out that string of unconscionable abuse he solidified and unified thirty men, not one of whom was willing to sit by and see someone kick around a man who had his hands tied behind his back," asserted Rickey.

Robinson publicly downplayed the incident. In his "Jackie Robinson Says" column which appeared in the Pittsburgh *Courier,* the Dodger first baseman wrote, "Some of the Phillies' bench jockeys tried to get me upset last week, but it didn't really bother me." The following week he added, "I don't think [Chapman] was really shouting at me the first time we played Philadelphia." Several writers praised Robinson for his restraint. In later years he revealed his true emotions as he withstood the barrage of insults. "I have to admit that this day of all the unpleasant days of my life brought me nearer to cracking up than I have ever been," he wrote in 1972. "For one wild and rage-crazed minute I thought, 'To hell with Mr. Rickey's "noble experiment." ' " The ordeal tempted Robinson to "stride over to that Phillies dugout, grab one of those white sons of bitches and smash his teeth with my despised black fist."

Robinson enjoyed a taste of revenge in the initial game against Philadelphia. In the eighth inning, with the teams deadlocked in a scoreless tie, he singled, stole second, and moved to third when the catcher heaved the ball into centerfield. Gene Hermanski followed with a single and Robinson answered his tormentors with the game's only run. But the final two games of the Philadelphia series marked the beginning of a prolonged batting drought. Over the next week, Robinson, plagued by a sore shoulder, failed to get a hit in twenty times at bat and rumors had him destined for the Dodger bench.

Hitting slumps are an integral part of baseball, but Robinson's early season problems came at an inopportune moment. His batting skein stemmed not only from the adjustment to major league pitching and the harassment by opponents but from the outside pressures that gathered about him. "He's not a ballplayer," complained Rickey, "He's a sideshow attraction." Even before the season had started, Rickey reported, Robinson had received 5,000 invitations to appear "at all sorts of events." "There are too many well-wishers and too many seeking to exploit him," said the Dodger president. In addition, Robinson and his wife felt obligated to answer all of the encouraging mail, making further demands on his time. "The boy is on the road to complete prostration," worried Rickey.

The daily flood of mail included not only congratulatory messages, but threats of violence. In early May, the Dodgers turned several of these notes over to the police. The letters, according to Robinson, advised "that 'somebody' was going to get hurt if I didn't get out of baseball," and "promised to kill any n——s who interfered with me." In the aftermath of the threats and in light of the burden that answering the mail placed on the Robinsons, Rickey requested that they allow the Dodgers to open and answer all correspondence. In addition, Robinson agreed to refuse all invitations to speak or be honored as well as opportunities for commercial endorsements.

The Dodgers released details of the threatening letters to the press on May 9. On that same day Robinson faced other unpublicized challenges in Philadelphia, the initial stop on the club's first extended road trip. Rickey had been forewarned that Robinson would not get a warm reception in Philadelphia. Herb Pennock, the former major league pitcher who served as the Phillies general manager, had called Rickey demanding that Robinson remain in Brooklyn. "[You] just can't bring that nigger here with the rest of your team, Branch. We're just not ready for that sort of thing yet," exhorted Pennock, according to Parrott who listened on the line. Pennock threatened that the Phillies would boycott the game. Rickey called Pennock's bluff and calmly responded that the Dodgers would accept a forfeit victory. The Phillie executive retreated.

When the Dodgers arrived in Philadelphia on May 9, the Benjamin Franklin Hotel, where the club had lodged for several years, refused to accept Robinson. Team officials had anticipated problems in St. Louis and Cincinnati, but not in the City of Brotherly Love. The preceding year, a local judge had cited the Benjamin Franklin for discrimination and the owners had signed a pledge disavowing this behavior. Before their arrival, the Dodgers had included Robinson's name on the reservation list and hotel officials raised no objections. Nonetheless, when the Brooklyn club appeared, the hotel denied Robinson entry. Rather than force a confrontation, Robinson arranged for alternative quarters. On subsequent trips, the Dodgers transferred their Philadelphia headquarters to the more expensive Warwick hotel.

At Shibe Park, Robinson endured another distasteful chore. The negative publicity inspired by the Phillies' treatment of him in Brooklyn had led both team owners to request a conciliatory photograph of Robinson and Chapman shaking hands. Chapman, pressured by the Phillies' ownership, went so far as to say that he would "be glad to have a colored player" on his team, though he continued to maintain that he had treated Robinson fairly. For Robinson the journey to the Philadelphia dugout to pose with Chapman entailed a painful necessity. "I can think of no occasion where I had more difficulty in swallowing my pride and doing what seemed best for baseball and the cause of the Negro in baseball than in agreeing to pose for a photograph with a man for whom I had only the very lowest regard," he later confessed.

Chapman's public moderation notwithstanding, the Phillies resumed their earlier harassment. Although Commissioner Chandler had limited their racial repertoire, Phillie bench jockeys replaced it with an act inspired by the recent death threats. "Some of these grown men sat in the dugout and pointed bats at me and made machine gun-like noises," Robinson later recounted.

A third, more ominous development, which also surfaced on May 9, overshadowed these incidents. New York *Herald Tribune* sports editor Stanley Woodward unveiled an alleged plot by National League players, led by the St. Louis Cardinals, to strike against Robinson. Woodward charged that the Cardinals, at the urgings of a Dodger player, had planned a strike during the first Dodger-Cardinal confrontation three days earlier. Only the stalwart actions of National League President Ford Frick and Cardinal owner Sam Breadon had averted the walkout, wrote Woodward. The two executives had confronted the players and Frick had delivered, "in effect," the following ultimatum:

> If you do this you will be suspended from the league. You will find that the friends you think you have in the press box will not support you, that you will be outcasts. I do not care if half the league strikes. Those who do it will encounter quick retribution. They will be suspended, and I don't care if it wrecks the National League for five years. This is the United States of America, and one citizen has as much right to play as another.

> The National League will go down the line with Robinson whatever the consequence. You will find that if you go through with your intention that you have been guilty of madness.

Cardinal officials immediately denied the report. Breadon called the story "ridiculous" and Manager Eddie Dyer dismissed it as "absurd." St. Louis players also refuted Woodward's charges and to this day, most team members steadfastly reject stories of a conspiracy against Robinson. "I know that there was a lot of things being written that we objected to playing against the Dodgers being Jackie Robinson was there," recalls Red Schoendienst. "But it wasn't true at all. I can't remember anybody talking about Jackie Robinson or the Dodgers for bringing up Robinson." Marty Marion, Stan Musial, and Enos Slaughter also deny contemplating a strike. "I've read stories that a strike was imminent, but I don't remember that at all," Marion told interviewer Bill Marshall.

The St. Louis Cardinal strike, although generally accepted as an integral part of the Jackie Robinson legend, remains an extremely elusive topic. Woodward's initial dispatch consisted of vague generalities. He named no names and revealed few specifics. Woodward described his story as "factually and thoroughly substantiated," but the following day he retracted major segments of his allegations. Frick, it turned out, never had met with the Cardinals and never voiced the words that Woodward attributed to him, still cited by many baseball histories as the first utterance of Frick's long career. Nonetheless, Woodward maintained his story was "essentially right and factual" and boasted, "It can now be honestly doubted that the boys from the Hookworm Belt will have the nerve to hoist their quaint sectional folklore on the rest of the country."

Reconstructed thirty-five years later, the strike saga amounts to somewhat more than the denials of the players would indicate, but quite a bit less than Woodward's allegations implied. Robinson's promotion undeniably aroused considerable discontent among the Cardinals and other teams. The idea of organizing a strike probably surfaced. Cardinal captain Terry Moore admitted as much the day the story broke. He told St. Louis sportswriter Bob Broeg that he did not doubt that there had been "high-sounding strike talk that meant nothing." How far this talk actually proceeded is difficult to discern. Dick Sisler, a rookie on the Cardinals in 1947, recalls, "Very definitely there was something going on at the time whereby they said they weren't going to play." The planning, says Sisler, was done "by a lot of the older players. I don't think the younger fellows had anything at all to say."

The Cardinal club seemed a logical fulcrum for the strike movement. Most of the Cardinal regulars came from the South, including

Moore, Marion, and Slaughter, usually identified as the ringleaders of the conspiracy. The animosity between the Dodgers and Cardinals, who had tied for first place in 1946 and expected to contend for the pennant again, was well known. Branch Rickey had assembled both teams and both bore his aggressive, hard-nosed trademark. "The Brooklyn Dodgers and Cardinals were kind of enemies," recalls Marion. "I don't think we had any personal love for anybody on the club and I don't think they had any for us." In addition, the Cardinals had started poorly, losing eleven of their first thirteen games, prompting many observers, including owner Breadon, to surmise that something other than baseball had disrupted the team.

Rumors of the impending mutiny reached Breadon in St. Louis and on May 1 he flew to New York where the Cardinals were playing the Giants. Breadon informed National League President Frick of the strike rumors. Frick, in less eloquent terms than attributed to him by Woodward, advised Breadon to warn the Cardinals that the National League would defend Robinson's right to play and that a refusal to take the field would lead to their suspensions. Breadon conferred with player representatives Moore and Marion, both of whom denied the rumors. According to Frick, Breadon reported back, "It was just a tempest in a teapot. A few of the players were upset and popping off a bit. They didn't really mean it." If an uprising indeed had been brewing, it ended with these discussions. On May 6 the Cardinals appeared as scheduled at Ebbets Field and lost to Robinson and the Dodgers.

Both Frick and Breadon assumed that this closed the matter. Meanwhile, Woodward had learned of the strike rumors and received confirmation from Frick of the warnings issued to the Cardinals. On May 9, the day after the completion of the St. Louis series, Woodward broke the story.

Woodward often receives credit for averting a player rebellion. This was not the case. As Wendell Smith wrote, the incident was "greatly exaggerated and it made a better newspaper story than anything else." If the discontent in the Cardinal locker room had reached the point of conspiratorial action, and no firm evidence exists to support this, the actions of Frick and Breadon, and not the belated revelations of the sportswriter, effectively crushed the revolt.

Nonetheless, Woodward's allegations, exaggerated or not, marked a significant turning point. The account of Frick's steadfast renunciation of all efforts to displace the black athlete, following so closely after Chapman's warning to Chapman, placed the baseball hierarchy openly in support of Robinson. In addition, the uproar created by the Woodward story dashed any lingering hopes among dissident players that public opinion, at least as reflected in the press, endorsed their opinions.

The prospect of a player strike, unlike the Chapman episode, inspired an almost totally negative response. While some writers like Stockton argued that "undue importance has been placed in some quarters on inconsequential happenings," most condemned the very idea of an effort to bar Robinson. "There is a great lynch mob among us and they go unhooded and work without the rope," wrote Jimmy Cannon denouncing this "venomous conspiracy." John Lardner labelled the accused ringleaders as "athletes of great playing ability with mental batting averages of .030." The *Sporting News* alone voiced an opposite view. It reprinted its 1942 editorial that argued that blacks and whites alike favored segregation. This view, claimed the journal, which it still adhered to, "takes on a new interest in light of the stir caused by recent events."

But even the *Sporting News* conceded that "the presence of Negroes in the major leagues is an accomplished fact." Sportswriters generally agreed that the legitimacy of baseball integration could no longer be questioned. "The universal opinion is that it is up to his admirers as well as Robinson himself whether he remains in the big leagues," wrote Edgar Brands. "What player feeling there is may be well repressed."

May 9, 1947, marked perhaps the worst day of Jackie Robinson's baseball career. Threats on his life, torment from opposing players, discrimination at the team hotel, and rumors of a player strike simultaneously engulfed the black athlete. The following day, Jimmy Cannon, describing Robinson's relations with his teammates, reported, "He is the loneliest man I have ever seen in sports." And, if as the *Sporting News* argued, "It remains only to judge Robinson on his ability as a player," he appeared to many jurors to present a weak case. Although he had curtailed his 0 for 20 slump, his batting average still languished near the .250 mark. After one month of regular season play the fate of the great experiment still seemed uncertain.

II

Amidst the swirl of controversy that followed the Dodgers on their first major road trip, the national interest in Jackie Robinson grew apparent. On Sunday, May 11, the Dodgers faced the Phillies in a doubleheader before the largest crowd in Philadelphia baseball history. Scalpers sold $2 tickets for $6, "just like the World Series." Two days later in Cincinnati 27,164 fans turned out despite an all-day rain "to size up Jackie Robinson." Bad weather diminshed the crowds for two games in Pittsburgh, but when the skies cleared, 34,814 fans appeared at Forbes Field for the May 18 series finale. The following day the Dodgers met the

Cubs in Chicago. Two hours before game time Wrigley Field had almost filled. A total of 46,572 fans crammed into the ball park, the largest attendance in stadium history. The tour concluded in St. Louis where the Dodgers and Cardinals played before the biggest weekday crowd of the National League season.

"Jackie's nimble/Jackie's quick/Jackie's making the turnstiles click," crowed Wendell Smith. Jimmy Cannon hailed him as "the most lucrative draw since Babe Ruth." By May 23 when the Dodgers returned to Brooklyn, Robinson had emerged as a national phenomenon.

Robinson had also erased all doubts about his playing abilities. At the start of the road trip many still questioned whether Robinson belonged in the big leagues. On May 13, the day of his first appearance in Cincinnati, a writer in that city commented, "But for the fact that he is the first acknowledged Negro in major league history and so much attention has been forcused on him, he would have been benched a week ago." The reaction to these remarks by Brooklyn sportswriters, however, surprised the midwesterner. The next day he reported that despite Robinson's unimpressive statistics, eastern writers agreed that Robinson was "quite a ballplayer and a cinch to stick with the Dodgers." Dodger officials felt so confident of Robinson's abilities that during the past week they had eliminated his two primary first base competitors, sending Ed Stevens to Montreal and selling Howard Schultz to the Phillies.

In city after city Robinson showed skeptical sportswriters and fans that the Dodgers had not erred. He batted safely in the first ten games of the May excursion, hitting .395 over that span. By June, Robinson had convinced even the most hardened opponents of integration of his exceptional talents. "He is a major leaguer in every respect," allowed Ben Chapman. Starting on June 14, Robinson hit safely in twenty-one consecutive games. At the end of June, he was batting .315, leading the league in stolen bases, and ranked second in runs scored. "Aside from getting up early in the morning, the thing a baseball writer dislikes most is to write about the same player day after day," complained Bill Roeder, "but there is not getting away from the fact that Jackie Robinson has been the headline man."

Robinson's impressive statistics revealed only a portion of the tale. "Never have records meant so little in discussing a player's value as they do in the case of Jackie Robinson," wrote Tom Meany. "His presence alone was enough to light a fire under his own team and unsettle his opponents." Sportswriter John Crosby asserts, "He was the greatest opportunist on any kind of playing field, seeing openings before they opened, pulling off plays lesser players can't even imagine." Robinson's intense competitiveness provided the crucial ingredient. A seasoned athlete, even in his rookie year, Robinson seemed to thrive on challenges and flourished before large audiences. At Montreal the preceding year, Dink Carroll had observed, "Robinson seems to have that same sense of the dramatic that characterized such great athletes as Babe Ruth, Red Grange, Jack Dempsey, Bobby Jones, and others of that stamp. The bigger the occasion, the more they rose to it." Robinson's drive not only inspired his own dramatic performances but intimidated and demoralized enemy players. Robinson "stirred up the Dodgers and Dodger fans in anticipation of victory and he stirred up the resentment of fans and players on other teams. To some degree because he was black, but most of all because he beat 'em." "This guy didn't just come to play," asserts Leo Durocher, "He came to beat ya. He came to stuff the goddamn bat right up your ass."

At the plate and in the field, Robinson radiated dynamic intensity, but his true genius materialized on the base paths. Sportswriters struggled to capture the striking image of Robinson in motion. They called him "the black meteor," or an "Ebony Ty Cobb," and "the Bojangles of the Basepaths." "He looks awkward, but he isn't," recorded *Time*. "He steps and starts as though turned off and on with a toggle switch. . . . Once in motion he wobbles along, elbows flying, hips swaying, shoulders rocking—creating the illusion that he will fly to pieces with every stride."

"He brought a new dimension into baseball," say Al Campanis. "He brought stealing back to the days of the twenties whereas up until that time baseball had become a long-ball hitting game." But the phenomenon went beyond base stealing. Robinson's twenty-nine steals in 1947 were actually less than the league leader of the preceding year. The style of play and the design of his baserunning antics better measure the magnitude of Robinson's achievement. He revolutionized major league baseball by injecting an element of "tricky baseball," so common in the Negro Leagues. In an age in which managers bemoaned the lost art of bunting, Robinson, in forty-six bunt attempts, registered fourteen hits and twenty-eight sacrifices, a phenomenal .913 success rate. His tactics often went against the timeworn conventional wisdom of baseball. He stole and advanced extra bases when traditional logic dictated against it. Tom Meany told the tale of a Dodger-Giant game in 1947 when Robinson doubled with one out in a tie game and then tagged up on a routine fly ball to center field. A Giant executive sitting next to Meany angrily denounced Robinson as a "showboat." "That's bush stuff," exclaimed the baseball man. "With two out he's just as valuable on second as he is on third. What's he going to do now—steal home I suppose?" On the next pitch, Robinson did just that, putting the Dodgers in the lead.

Nor did Robinson's effectiveness require the stolen base. "He dances and prances off base keeping the enemy infield upset and off balance, and worrying the pitcher," reported *Time*. In Donald Honig's *Baseball: Between the Lines*, pitchers Gene Conley and Vic Raschi, both relate incidents not of Robinson hitting or stealing, but of his talents of distraction. "Robinson had broken my concentration," recalls Raschi of a game in the 1949 World Series. "I was pitching more to Robinson [on first base] than I was to [Gil] Hodges and as a result I threw one up into Gil's power and he got the base hit that beat me." Conley tells an almost identical tale with Carl Furillo getting the game-winning blow. "Carl Furillo got all the headlines," says Conley, "but I knew it was Robinson who had distracted me just enough to hang that curve."

These attributes were much in evidence in 1947, though Branch Rickey warned, "You haven't seen Robinson yet. Maybe you won't really see him until next year. You'll see something when he gets to bunting and running as freely as he should." Rickey did not exaggerate. Robinson did not reach his peak as a ballplayer for another two seasons.

Many National League players attributed Robinson's 1947 success to an unwillingness of opponents to challenge him. "Some of the fellows may be riding Jackie, but an even greater number are going out of their way to avoid him," commented one unidentified athlete. "They just don't want to get involved in a close play where Jackie might be accidentally spiked or knocked around." Several pitchers complained privately that they feared throwing tight to Robinson to move him away from the plate, giving him an advantage in the batter's box.

There is ample evidence, however, that the majority did not adhere to this view. "Jackie Robinson can usually count on the first pitch being right under his nostrils," reported the Cincinnati *Enquirer* in July. " 'They're giving him the smell of leather,' as the boys say." By the time the season was half over, pitchers had hit Robinson seven times, more than any National Leaguer in the entire preceding season. Tom Meany later wrote, "Often his great reflexes kept him from being hit more often than he was. He boasted early in his career that though he might be hit often, he would never be beaned. He never was." Robinson himself, often joked with reporters about his league leading hit-by-pitch statistics. After being struck twice during his early season slump he cracked, "Since I can't buy a hit these days, they're doing me a favor." Later in the season he suggested, "Guess I just haven't learned to duck major league pitching." But neither Robinson nor most other observers doubted that the black athlete reigned as the most popular target among the league's pitchers.

Opponents also tested Robinson at his first base position. Playing second at Montreal, Robinson had offered an open target for runners barreling into second base trying to break up a double play. At first base fewer opportunities for physical contact existed, but the stretch required to tag the bag exposed Robinson's leg to the runner's spikes on close plays. A novice at the position, Robinson could not always protect himself. Several sympathetic players warned Robinson that he would "have to watch his tagging foot," a flaw he readily acknowledged. But some opponents deliberately attempted to spike him, making, according one account, "a pincushion out of Robinson."

Only a scattering of overt racial incidents marred Robinson's first season. On June 22 after Eddie Stanky had shattered Cincinnati pitcher Ewell Blackwell's bid for a second consecutive no-hit game, Blackwell unleashed a stream of racial epithets at Robinson, the next batter. In May, against the Cubs, who proved one of the most troublesome clubs for Robinson, shortstop Len Merullo landed on top of Robinson on a pick-off play at second base. As they untangled from the pile, Merullo deliberately kicked the black man. Robinson started to swing at the shortstop but suddenly held back. "Plenty of times I wanted to haul off when somebody insulted me for the color of my skin," Robinson told a reporter. "But I had to hold to myself. I knew I was kind of an experiment. . . . The whole thing was bigger than me."

In spring training Rickey had advised Robinson, "I want you to win the friendship of people everywhere. You must be personable, you must smile, and even if they are worrying you to death, make the public think you don't mind being bothered." Robinson created precisely this image. He publicly thanked opposing players, like Hank Greenberg and Frank Gustine, who welcomed him into the league. In his "Jackie Robinson Says" column, Robinson also diplomatically praised the St. Louis Cardinals. Robinson's obvious intelligence, self-deprecating wit, and public willingness to forgive and understand his tormentors, made him an American hero. "Throughout it all," wrote Pittsburgh sportswriter Vince Johnson, "he has remained a gentleman and a credit to the game, as well as to his race."

Robinson's exemplary demeanor won over his teammates as well. In early May when Jimmy Cannon described Robinson as the "loneliest man I have ever seen in sports," his comments were not inaccurate. But they came at a time when Robinson's isolation on the Dodger squad was receding. When Robinson had joined the Dodgers, reporters had described the locker room scene as one of "cool aloofness" amidst a tense atmosphere. In dealing with his teammates Robinson continued the policy that he had pursued at Montreal. "Jackie wouldn't sit with any white player that first year unless he was asked to," recalls Bobby Bragan. In part, this was a facet of Robinson's personality. "I sort of keep to myself by habit," he explained. "Even in the colored leagues I was that way." But, this behavior also reflected a decision to avoid forcing himself on those who objected to his presence.

Among northern teammates, playing alongside Robinson posed few problems. For southerners, on the other hand, it often required a significant adjustment. Several players feared repercussions at home for their involuntary role in baseball integration. "I didn't know if they would spit on me or not," recalled Dixie Walker of his Alabama neighbors. "It was no secret that I was worried about my business. I had a hardware and sporting goods store back home." Pee Wee Reese later said that in family discussions, "The subject always gets around to the fact that I'm a little southern boy playing shortstop next to a Negro second baseman and in danger of being contaminated." Both Walker and Kirby Higbe, before the Dodgers traded him, received insulting letters. "I got more than a thousand letters from people down South calling me 'nigger-lover,' " writes Higbe, "telling me I ought to quit playing baseball and come home rather than play with a nigger."

Robinson's relationship with some of his teammates was unpredictable. Hugh Casey, the enigmatic pitcher from Atlanta, spent hours during the early season batting balls to Robinson to help him adjust to the first base position and gently chided Robinson about his fielding after the games. Casey rushed to Robinson's defense when an opposing player spiked him. In the pitcher's Brooklyn restaurant, he displayed a picture of his black teammate and he boasted, "I'm a southerner, but I enjoyed playing with him." But Casey, a heavy drinker, could also be tactless. During a midseason card game with Robinson and others, he exclaimed, "Got to change my luck, Jackie. Tell you what I used to do down in Georgia when my poker luck got bad. I'd just go out and rub me the teat of the biggest, blackest nigger woman I could find." He then reached over and rubbed Robinson's head. Robinson required every ounce of his self-control to restrain his rage. When Roy Campanella joined the team the following season, Casey would rarely throw the type of pitch that the black catcher called for. Three years later, the alcoholic, erratic Casey committed suicide at the age of thirty-eight.

The press carefully scrutinized the interplay between Dixie Walker and Robinson. On opening day, recalls then acting manager Clyde Sukeforth, photographers urged him to arrange a picture of Robinson and Walker together. Sukeforth refused, citing Walker's business concerns. Throughout the season, if Robinson happened to be on base when Walker hit a home run, he would refrain from the customary home plate handshake, not wishing to embarrass either Walker or himself. Walker, despite his distaste for integration, never went out of his way to be unpleasant to Robinson, who later described him as a man of "innate fairness." On one occasion, the southerner approached his black teammate in the locker room and offered several batting tips. This incident prompted sportswriter Vincent X. Flaherty to report, "[Robinson's] best friend and chief advisor among the Dodgers is Dixie Walker." This represented more than a mild exaggeration. (In Robinson's personal scrapbooks this item is accompanied by the handwritten comment, "Some sportswriters fall for anything.") Nonetheless, Robinson and Walker maintained good relations throughout the season.

Rickey, recognizing the strain created by this unnatural pairing, persisted in his efforts to trade the Alabama outfielder. On June 4 he arranged a deal with the Pirates. That evening, however, Pete Reiser resumed his acquaintance with the Ebbets Field wall and Rickey, suddenly short an outfielder, cancelled the deal. After the season Walker rejected an offer from the Dodger president to manage one of Brooklyn's top farm clubs and Rickey traded him to Pittsburgh, bringing the awkward Walker-Robinson relationship to a close.

During the course of the 1947 season and subsequent campaigns, Robinson developed his closest friendship with Pee Wee Reese, the shortstop from Kentucky. The alliance emerged out of mutual respect and Reese's unaffected acceptance of Robinson as a teammate. Two incidents typified the Robinson-Reese rapport. In June the Dodgers stopped in Danville, Illinois, to play an exhibition game with one of their farm teams. Reese joined a golf foursome with pitcher Rex Barney, Harold Parrott, and reporter Roscoe McGowan. Robinson and Wendell Smith played behind them. At the fourth hole, Reese halted the game and invited the two blacks to merge with his foursome. As the three teammates joked and kidded each other, wrote one observer, "Reese and Barney showed, without knowing it, during the golf game that they like Robinson and he is one of them." Early in the following season in Boston, Brave bench jockeys rode Reese mercilessly for playing alongside a black man. Reese stode over to Robinson, placed his arm around his teammate's shoulder, and prepared to discuss the upcoming game. The gesture silenced the Boston bench.

Reese has frequently protested that people have exaggerated his role in the Robinson drama. "You know I didn't go out of my way to be nice to you," he once told Robinson. Jackie replied, "Pee Wee, maybe that's what I appreciated most."

Dan Dodson, the sociologist who assisted Rickey in his preparations for the "noble experiment," drew two prescriptions from the Dodger experience. "Don't worry about the attitudes of people who are asked to accept new members," he advised. "When relationships are predicated on the basis of goals other than integration—in the Dodger case, winning the pennant—the people involved would adjust appropriately." But equally important, according to Dodson, was an absence of coercion in interpersonal contacts. "Don't meddle with relationships between members once integration starts," he admonished. "Let members work out their relationships. Forcing relationships makes for trouble."

The Dodger clubhouse in 1947 aptly demonstrated the validity of these principles. With little outside interference from club management, the Brooklyn players gradually rallied to Robinson's side. Eddie Stanky, the second baseman from Alabama, became Robinson's leading defender against the taunts, brushbacks, and spikes of opposing players. Walker, explaining his unsolicited batting tips to Robinson, related, "I saw things in this light. When you're on a team, you got to pull together to win."

Robinson's acceptance by the Dodger players occurred with surprising rapidity, even more so than at Montreal. Within six weeks, says

Bragan, the barriers had fallen. Eating, talking, and playing cards with Robinson seemed natural. Reporters traveling with the Dodgers agreed. By the end of May, Smith could report "There is more warmth toward him these days in both the dugout and the clubhouse." Toward the end of the season, wrote white sportswriter Gordon Cobbledick, the Dodgers viewed Robinson with "something approaching genuine warmth and and affection."

III

The evolution of Dodger attitudes toward Robinson reflected a process occurring throughout the nation. Robinson's aggressive play, his innate sense of dignity, and his outward composure under extreme duress captivated the American people. Only Joe Louis, among black celebrities, had aroused the public imagination as Robinson did in the summer of 1947. Robinson's charismatic personality inspired not merely sympathy and acceptance, but sincere adulation from both whites and blacks alike.

To black America, Jackie Robinson appeared as a savior, a Moses leading his people out of the wilderness. "When times got really hard, really tough, He always send you somebody," said Ernest J. Gaines's fictional heroine Miss Jane Pittman. "In the Depression it was tough on everybody, but twice as hard on the colored, and He sent us Joe [Louis] . . . after the war, He sent us Jackie."

Thousands of blacks thronged to the ball parks wherever he appeared. At games in the National League's southernmost cities blacks swelled attendance. Many traveled hundreds of miles to see their hero in action. The Philadelphia *Afro-American* reported that orders by blacks for tickets for the first Dodger-Phillies series had "poured in" from Baltimore, Washington, and other cities along the eastern seaboard. For games in Cincinnati, a "Jackie Robinson special" train ran from Norfolk, Virginia, stopping en route to pick up black fans.

Throughout the season black newspapers continued to campaign for proper crowd behavior, and the deportment of the Afro-American spectators drew widespread praise. Blacks nonetheless found it difficult to restrain their enthusiasm. Robinson himself wrote that while the sight of so many blacks pleased him, their indiscriminate cheering sometimes proved embarrassing. "The colored fans applauded Jackie every time he wiggled his ears," complained one black sportswriter after a game in Cincinnati.

As a boy, white columnist Mike Royko attended Robinson's first game at Wrigley Field in Chicago. Twenty-five years later he described the event:

in 1947, few blacks were seen in downtown Chicago, much less up
on the white North side at a Cub game.

That day they came by the thousands, pouring off the north-
bound ELS and out of their cars.

They didn't wear baseball-game clothes. They had on church
clothes and funeral clothes—suits, white shirts, ties, gleaming shoes,
and straw hats. I've never seen so many straw hats.

. . . The whites tried to look as if nothing unusual was happening, while the blacks tried to look casual and dignified. So
everybody looked ill at ease.

For the most part it was probably the first time they had been
so close to each other in such large numbers.

When Robinson batted, recalls Royko, "They applauded, long,
rolling applause. A tall middle-aged black man stood next to me, a
smile of almost painful joy on his face, beating his palms together so
hard they must have hurt." When Robinson struck out, "the low moan
was genuine."

The scenes at the ball parks represented only the surface level of
black adulation of Robinson. "No matter what the nature of the gathering, a horse race, a church meeting, a ball game," explained Sam
Lacy, "the universal question is: 'How'd Jackie make out today?' " In
many cities pages of advertisements in the black press heralded Robinson's appearances as black businesses sought to identify themselves
with the new hero. Clothing stores advised blacks to "Dress Sporty for
the Jackie Robinson Game"; bars and nightclubs suggested they "Drop
in after the game." Robinson's visit, reported the Philadelphia *Afro-
American*, "will give the city something of a holiday setting and night
sport owners were twirling their thumbs in happy anticipation of a
boom in business."

The idolatry even reached into regions where major league baseball
remained an exercise in imagination. Bernice Franklin, a woman from
Tyronza, Arkansas, an all-black town, wrote to Robinson: "I own and
operate a rural general store and right now the farmers are gathering
for your game this afternoon. . . . There is no greater thrill than a
broadcast of a Dodgers' ball game. . . . We are so proud of you." Black
Americans affixed their loyalty not only to Robinson, but to the Brooklyn Dodgers as well. For many years, blacks throughout the nation
would be Dodger fans, in honor of the team that had broken the color
barrier.

Robinson's popularity was not confined to blacks; white fans also
stormed baseball arenas to view the new sensation. At the start of the
season the St. Louis edition of the Pittsburgh *Courier* warned its readers that tickets for the Dodger games were "going like hot cakes and it
isn't the Sepia fans that are buying the bulk of them." In Brooklyn, the

fans rallied behind Robinson "350 percent," recalls Joe Bostic. "They were with him, not just Jackie, they were with the idea. He became a state of mind in a community that was already baseball-oriented." After the games at Ebbets Field, fans waited for more than an hour for Jackie to appear. "Many wanted autographs and others simply wanted to touch him," reported Sam Lacy. "It was just as though [he] had suddenly been transformed into some kind of matinee idol."

Awards flooded in from a wide variety of sources ranging from the Freedom Awards from the United Negro and Allied Veterans of America to the "Negro Father of the Year Award" presented by the National Father's Day Committee. Local writers composed poems in his honor. *Time* magazine published a lengthy story on the Dodger rookie sensation, highlighting his ebony face in a sea of white baseballs on the cover.

As in Montreal the preceding season, Robinson found that his fame interfered with the normal processes of life. Wendell Smith reported, "He seldom gets a chance to eat a peaceful meal on the train. . . . He seldom has a moment to himself. He is the target of well-wishers, autograph hounds and indiscreet politicians who would bask in his glory to win prestige for themselves. They call him on the telephone at all hours of the morning or night."

The volume of letters that Robinson received also reflected his popularity. From the day of his promotion to the Dodgers through the end of the World Series, each day brought "piles of mail." The Dodgers hired a special secretary to handle his correspondence and Arthur Mann composed answers to all letters, both the inspirational and the insulting. Robinson reviewed, sometimes revised, and signed each response.

The Robinsons and the Dodgers disposed of most letters containing threats and insults, but a sample of the vitriolic language and personal attacks survive in letters to Branch Rickey. W. J. "Buck" Blankenship of Jackson, California, wrote criticizing the Durocher suspension, but added, "The blow that the commissioner dealt was not as severe as the one that the Brooklyn club handed itself when it signed Jackie Robinson." A Philadelphia writer told Rickey, "You should be ashamed of yourself. . . . If you want to do something for the negro, why not give some educated negro *your* job," and added, "The next time you take a shower get a negro to take one with you or does that just apply to some other man's son?" After asking Rickey if he would want his children to marry a Negro, the disgruntled critic concluded, "Well Good-Nite Dictator and Happy Dreams." Drew Linard Smith, an attorney from New Orleans, voiced similar sentiments:

> Your decision to break a big league tradition by playing a Negro on the Brooklyn team is indeed deplorable. In fact, it is inconceivable that any white man would force a Negro on other white men as

you have done. . . . I tell you Rickey anything the Negro touches he ruins and your club will be no exception. . . . The first time Robinson steps out of line you will see what I mean. He will inevitably do this too because he will be egged on by a militant and aggressive Negro press forever propagandizing for the amalgamation of the races.

This type of mail also surfaced in other places. A Columbus, Ohio, newspaper reported that it had received a "surprisingly large" number of letters from people favoring the threatened player strike. Commissioner Chandler heard from well-known vaudeville comic Bert Wheeler. Wheeler wrote that although he was a cousin of Pee Wee Reese and used to attend many games, "Then along comes a nigger, so I wrote to Pee Wee and told him I would never come to another Dodger game as long as the Nigger was on the team."

The opprobrium heaped upon the central actors in the integration drama reflects the stereotypes and the deep-seated prejudice of the era. But the torrent of sympathy and acclaim which Robinson inspired drowned out these negative sentiments. The surviving sampling of letters to Robinson reveals the thoughts of people from all sections of the country and in many walks of life: a deputy sheriff from Detroit, a black teenager from Johnson City, Tennessee, an accountant from Ontario, Canada, and a dry cleaner from Bellevue, Ohio. Robinson heard from doctors, ministers, lawyers, and college professors; from black and white students at every educational level; from a magazine editor in Rockford, Illinois and the president of a life insurance company in Durham, North Carolina. Twenty-four patients at the Oak Knoll Tuberculosis Santiarium in Mackinaw, Illinois, wrote in support. Most letters, particularly after the early weeks of the season, contained words of advice and encouragement and reflected the impact of Robinson's ordeal upon the American public.

The letters often displayed a touching warmth, as people confessed, "This is the first fan letter I've written" or identified not only their names, but small facts about their lives. "I'm no autograph hunter, only an old doctor," wrote one man. "I am white, 76, played college football, but never baseball. I am a Methodist, ex-school teacher, ex-prison warden," revealed another. At times the letters could get too personal. A twenty-year-old winner of the Miss Akron beauty contest professed her love for Robinson and invited him to visit her. "I know that you are a married man and that you have a son," she admitted, "but you don't have to be an angel." Robinson's response, signed "yours in reproof," advised the woman, "When I married Mrs. Robinson, I exchanged vows to love, honor, and cherish her for the rest of my life, 'Honor' means just that to me and any sneaking, skulking escapade would destroy the very thing that enables me to hold my head up high."

Several correspondents described their own experiences when inserted into situations as the sole representative of their race. "I know what you are going through because I went through the same thing in a much smaller way," wrote G. Gilbert Smith of Jersey City. "I was the first Negro machinist in a big shop during the war. They did all the little dirty underhanded things to me that they must be doing to you." Matt Kirwan of Bellevue, Ohio, related his experiences as the only white employee at a dry-cleaning plant in Fort Lauderdale. "At first the colored boys didn't speak to me. I didn't know what was wrong," wrote Kirwan. "When we got acquainted and they found out I was from the north, I didn't have any better friends in Florida."

Robinson's early season difficulties brought numerous letters denouncing the Philadelphia players and the accused St. Louis strikers. "I happen to be a white southerner," wrote a man from Richmond on May 19, "but I just want you to know that not all us southerners are SOB's." A letter from Corpus Christi, Texas, dated May 11 advised him to "Stay in there and fight, Jackie. For there will be others to follow you in the Big Leagues if you are successful." A midshipman at Annapolis wrote of Robinson's tormentors, "personally, I'd like to paste them on the jaw. I think it's a shame that we have such people existing in *our* country."

Correspondents repeatedly reminded the black pioneer of his responsibilities to his race and to the United States. "Whether colored men are athletes, preachers, educators, or scientists," advised a city councilman from Grove, Kansas, "if they are leaders in their line they have moral responsibilities to their race." Harold MacDowell of Newark informed Robinson that "there are thousands of American youngsters of your complexion and my different complexion who are going to learn their first lesson in sociology from your experience. . . . Remember you are on a stage all the time. Your mistakes will be attributed to all Negroes."

Robinson's correspondence reflected the changes in racial attitudes that he inspired. His dynamic presence instilled a sense of pride in black Americans and led many whites to reassess their own feelings. The affection for Robinson grew so widespread that at the year's end voters in an annual public opinion poll named him the second most popular man in America. Only Bing Crosby registered more votes.

IV

Toward the close of the 1947 season, the Philadelphia *Tribune*, a black newspaper, ran a playful story headlined, PAPERS PROVE JACKIE ROBINSON ISN'T WHITE. Sportswriters, noted the *Tribune*, repeatedly referred to Robinson as the "nimble Negro" or the "Negro flash" or myriad variations on that theme. John Drebinger of the New York *Times* referred to Robinson in this manner five times in one story. "It was so dark in the ninth inning," offered a Cleveland writer, "Jackie Robinson was only a blur."

The *Tribune* story spotlighted a significant truth about Robinson's rookie season. Despite his growing acceptance, Robinson remained an oddity in organized baseball. Throughout the season, even after he had established himself as a bona fide major league player, Robinson confronted difficulties and challenges unknown to other athletes. The burdens of racial pioneering and the restrictions imposed on his behavior still rested heavily on his shoulders.

On the road, hotel accommodations remained problematical. Throughout the Jim Crow era the issue of housing black players had loomed as a major objection to integration. Even in many northern cities, the better hotels did not allow blacks. In border cities like St. Louis and Cincinnati segregation remained the rule. Rickey and his advisers had determined that the Dodgers would not challenge local customs. "The position was taken that the Brooklyn club could not assume the responsibility for discrimination in these places," explained Dodson. Where objections to Robinson's presence were raised, other arrangements would be made. If another hotel would accept the entire team, the Dodgers would alter their future plans.

In Boston, Pittsburgh, and Chicago, Robinson had no problems. In Philadelphia and St. Louis, officials barred him and he stayed at Negro hotels. The Dodgers anticipated that Robinson would not be allowed to stay with the team in Cincinnati, but the Netherlands-Plaza Hotel accepted him under the provision that he eat his meals in his room so as not to offend other guests.

The Dodgers dared not tamper with one taboo—the prohibition on interracial roommates. One of the most common taunts that Brooklyn players heard from rival bench jockeys and fans was the charge that they were "sleeping with Robinson." In 1947 Robinson usually roomed with Wendell Smith, who traveled with the team as both a reporter and a Dodger employee.

While Jackie toured National League cities, Rachel Robinson unobtrusively learned the life of a baseball wife. She spent most of her days housecleaning, toting the considerable amount of laundry generated by Jackie, Jr., to the laundromat, and rushing off to the ball games which she never missed. "We were trying to make it as a family and that was as important and problematic as dealing with the baseball scene which was much more structured by other people," recalls Rachel. The threatening mail and crank letters unsettled them, she says, "But it wasn't in a period of kidnappings or things like that so we never worried about the baby being hurt, or our being accosted too much except by some crazy or irrational person who might shoot from the stands."

Rachel's relationship with the Dodger wives paralleled Jackie's experience. For the first month of the season, she did not know any of them, as the players' wives did not sit in a single location. "One day a young girl asked if I was Mrs. Robinson," Rachel told a reporter. "When I said I was, she introduced herself as Mrs. Clyde King. After the game she took me down under the stands, showed me where the wives usually wait for their husbands and introduced me to the other girls." By early July, Rachel recounted, "When they gossip I join right in and gossip with them." The response of the Dodger fans also encouraged Rachel. "The fans don't realize I'm his wife," she explained, "So I hear what they really think. It's wonderful the way they're pulling for Jackie to make good."

Throughout the first half of the season, the Robinsons lived on a tight budget. Despite his magnificent performance and ticket-selling feats, Robinson received only $5,000, the major league minimum. Baseball rules forbade any mid-season bonuses or salary increases. In addition, Rickey's protective prohibition on endorsements forced Robinson to turn down many lucrative offers. For the first month of the season, the family continued to live in the cramped confines of the McAlpin Hotel. In May they moved to Brooklyn where they shared a tenement apartment with a "widow courting." The tenement was filled with cockroaches and the widow and her suitor "occupied the living room all the time so Jack and I were stuck back in this little bedroom the whole season."

While their living conditions remained poor, the Robinsons' financial position improved. Rickey lifted the ban on advertisements in mid-season and Robinson's smiling face began to appear in New York and national black newspapers promoting Bond Bread, Turfee Hats, and although he did not smoke, Old Gold cigarettes. On September 23, Rickey allowed the athlete's admirers to stage a Jackie Robinson Day at Ebbets Field. The chairman of the event vowed that the gifts would add up to "as much or more than any player has received on a similar occasion." Well-wishers bestowed an estimated $10,000 worth of goods on Jackie and Rachel, including a Cadillac, a television set, and a chest of silver. Contributions came from Harlem and other black communities throughout the nation.

Robinson also received numerous money-making propositions for the winter and fall. He signed up for a theatrical tour of New York, Washington, and Chicago, traveling with three vaudeville acts. For each of his appearances Robinson would receive a minimum of $2,500. The articulate athlete became a popular radio guest and signed contracts to co-author an autobiography and to star in a Hollywood movie. Sources estimated that despite his low salary, Robinson's income for 1947 exceeded that of all major leaguers with the exception of Bob Feller and Hank Greenberg.

On the field, meanwhile, Robinson had emerged as one of the crucial figures in the Dodger pennant drive. The Dodgers moved into first place in July, but in mid-August the Cardinals, recovered from their disastrous start, challenged for the league lead. The two clubs met at Ebbets Field on August 18 and Robinson again found himself surrounded by controversy. In the opening game of the series Cardinal outfielder Joe Medwick spiked Robinson on the left foot, leaving a bloody gash. Two days later Robinson barely removed his leg in time to avoid Enos Slaughter's spikes on one occasion, but on another, Slaughter slashed Robinson on the left leg, dropping the injured athlete to the ground.

Observers disagreed as to whether the spiking was deliberate. Bill Corum of the New York *Journal-American* called it "as normal a play as anybody, whose imagination wasn't working too fast, ever saw." Robert Burnes, in the St. Louis *Gazette Democrat* argued, "If Slaughter had been trying to 'nail' Robinson, you can be sure Jackie wouldn't have been in condition to stay in the game." Slaughter, in a statement that must have surprised most National Leaguers, avowed, "I've never deliberately spiked anyone in my life. Anybody who does, don't belong in baseball." The incident, however, infuriated Robinson's teammates. Noting that the cut on his leg was located eight inches above the ankle on the outside of his leg, one player asserted, "How in the hell could Slaughter hit him way up on the side of the leg like unless he meant to do it?" Several Dodger players threatened "dire consequences" if the Cardinals continued their attacks on Robinson.

The Dodgers and Cardinals split their four-game series and Rickey, fearing his club might not withstand the St. Louis drive without pitching help, turned to the Negro Leagues for assistance. On August 23 he flew to Memphis to personally inspect right-handed pitcher Dan Bankhead of the Memphis Red Sox. After watching Bankhead strike out eleven men, Rickey purchased his contract from the Red Sox.

One of five baseball-playing brothers (Sam, the oldest was one of the finest shortstops of the age), Bankhead came to the Dodgers touted as the "next Satchel Paige" and the "colored Feller." One report labelled him "the fastest pitcher in baseball, black or white." Bankhead also batted well and boasted a league-leading .385 average in the Negro American League. Despite these superlative notices, Rickey would have preferred to give Bankhead, like Robinson, some seasoning in the minors. But, explained the Mahatma, "I can't help myself. We need pitchers and we need them badly."

Two days later Bankhead joined the Dodgers in Pittsburgh where he received "a terrific workout from photographers and newshounds." When the Pirates chased Dodger starter Hal Gregg from the mound in the second inning, manager Shotton decided to rush an admittedly nervous Bankhead into the fray. The Pirates, wrote Red Smith, "launched Bankhead by breaking a Louisville Slugger over his prow." They pounded the first black pitcher in the major leagues for eight runs and ten hits in three innings. Bankhead's only solace came at the plate. He slammed a home run in his initial at bat, the first National League pitcher to accomplish that feat. Bankhead did not prove the savior of the Dodger pitching staff. He appeared in only three more games with indifferent success and the Dodgers dispatched him to the minors for two years before recalling him in 1950.

Even without Bankhead's help the Dodgers continued to stave off the Cardinal pennant bid. When they arrived in St. Louis on September 11 for the final meetings between the two clubs, the Dodgers led the second-place Cardinals by four and a half games. The series marked the last opportunity for St. Louis to bring the Brooklyn club within striking distance.

As in the earlier series the first game was marred by a spiking incident. In the second inning Cardinal catcher Joe Garagiola caught Robinson on the heel. "I don't think Garagiola did it intentionally," Robinson said after the game, "but this makes three times in two games with the Cardinals that it's happened. He cut my shoe all to pieces." When Robinson came to the plate in the third inning he made a remark to Garagiola, who responded with a racial slur. For the first time during the long season, Robinson lost his temper. He and Garagiola "engaged in an angry teeth-to-teeth exchange" which brought coach Sukeforth out of the dugout to restrain Robinson, and required intervention by umpire Beans Reardon. *Time* magazine wrote of the episode, "That was the end of it; no fisticuffs on the field, no rioting in the stands. But it was a sign that Jackie had established himself as a big leaguer. He had earned what comes free to every other player; the right to squawk."

Time's celebration of Robinson's acceptance was premature. It would be another year before Robinson could freely retaliate against his tormentors. The outburst against Garagiola merely underscores the pent-up anger and frustration that gathered within Robinson as he submerged his naturally combative instincts and channeled them into his performances. After the spiking Robinson powered a two-run home run to lead the Dodgers to a 4–3 victory. The following night Robinson had two hits and scored two runs in a losing cause and then stroked three hits in the series finale. "In the field," wrote Dan Daniel, "Robinson's tempo was a gradual crescendo which attained the truly spectacular in the eighth inning of the last game," when the rookie first baseman hurled himself into the Brooklyn dugout to make a "brilliant catch" of a foul pop-up. The Dodgers won, 8–7, virtually assuring themselves the pennant.

"This week as the Dodgers raced toward the finish, seven games ahead," attested *Time* magazine in its cover story on Robinson, "it was at least arguable that Robinson had furnished the margin of victory." Dixie Walker agreed. "No other ballplayer on this club, with the possible exception of [catcher] Bruce Edwards, has done more to put the Dodgers up in the race than Robinson has," claimed the once recalcitrant Walker who, despite his own personal ordeal, delivered another .300 plus campaign. Another skeptic also surrendered when J. Taylor Spink and the *Sporting News* awarded Robinson the Rookie of the Year Award. The judges, wrote Spink, had "sifted only stark baseball values. . . . The sociological experiment that Robinson represented, the trail blazing that he did, the barriers he broke down, did not enter into the decisions." Spink personally flew to Brooklyn to present the award to Robinson at the pennant-clinching celebration at Borough Hall.

Throughout most of the season Robinson maintained his batting average over .300, but a late season slump after the Dodgers had clinched the pennant dropped him to .297. He finished second in the league in runs scored and first in stolen bases. Robinson also led the Dodgers in home runs with 12. Despite his reputation for being injury prone, Robinson appeared in 151 of the 154 contests, more games than anyone else on the club.

Robinson's performance also benefited other National League teams. Throughout the season fans continued to watch him in record numbers. At Pittsburgh in late July spectators overflowed the stands and lined up along the outfield wall. The grounds crew posted ropes to establish the boundaries of the playing field. By the season's end Robinson had established new attendance marks in every city except Cincinnati. Thanks to Robinson, National League attendance in 1947 increased by more than three quarters of a million people above the all-time record set in 1946. Five teams set new season records, including the Dodgers, who attracted over 1.8 millon fans for the first, and last, time in the club's Brooklyn history.

In October the Dodgers met the New York Yankees in the World Series. The 1947 series ranks as one of the most thrilling in baseball history. Fans remember it for Bill Bevens's near no-hitter in the fourth game, Al Gionfriddo's spectacular catch of Joe Dimaggio's line drive in the sixth contest, and the tightly drawn struggles in five of the seven meetings. The Dodgers challenged the Yankees into the last game before succumbing to the effective relief pitching of Joe Page. For Robinson personally, the World Series marked an anticlimax. His presence in the Fall Classic seemed natural, rather than extraordinary. On the field he performed solidly, if not spectacularly. Robinson batted well, hitting .259 despite being robbed of three hits, and he drove in three runs. His baserunning bedeviled Yankee pitchers and catchers and his fielding was flawless. But even Wendell Smith concluded of the Series,

"If we must get racial conscious about it in determining the wreath of heroism, we'll have to pass the laurels to the players of Italian extraction," noting the exploits of Dimaggio, Gionfriddo, and Cookie Lavagetto. "In short, it's been a great series," attested Smith, "No matter who your parents were."

V

The saga of Robinson's first season has become part of American mythology—sacrosanct in its memory, magnificent in its retelling. It remains a drama which thrills and fascinates, combining the central themes of the illusive Great American Novel: the undertones of Horatio Alger, the interracial comradery of nineteenth-century fiction, the sage advisor and his youthful apprentice, and the rugged and righteous individual confronting the angry mob. It is a tale of courage, heroics, and triumph. Epic in its proportions, the Robinson legend has persevered—and will continue to do so—because the myth, which rarely deviates from reality, fits our national perceptions of fair play and social progress. The emotional impact of Robinson's challenge requires no elaboration or enhancement. Few works of fiction could impart its power.

Indeed, so total was Robinson's triumph, so dominant his personality, that few people have questioned the strategies and values that underpinned Branch Rickey's "noble experiment." Rickey based his blueprint for integration both on his assessment of the racial realities of postwar America and his flair for the dramatic. He believed that the United States was ready for integrated baseball, but the balance remained so precarious that the breakthrough had to be carefully planned and cautiously advanced. Americans—both black and white, players and fans—needed time to accommodate themselves to the idea of blacks in baseball. The slightest false step, Rickey concluded, would delay the entry of nonwhites into the national pastime indefinitely. Rickey felt that the primary burden of this undertaking had to rest on the shoulders of a lone standard-bearer, upon whose success or failure the fate of the entire venture would be determined. The fact that this gradual process accrued publicity and added to the drama was never central to Rickey's thinking, but rather a natural component of his personality. Rickey conceived of schemes on the grand scale and enacted them accordingly.

Most accounts of the Robinson story unquestionably assimilate Rickey's reasoning, and several conclusions logically evolve from this: had Rickey not shattered the color line in 1945, the barrier would have remained erect for years to come; the success of integration depended upon the Mahatma's elaborate preparations and the selection of one central figure to spearhead the campaign; Robinson himself not only appears indispensable, but in most accounts emerges as the sole black athlete who could have withstood the pressures; and, had Robinson faltered, this setback would have delayed the cause of integration indefinitely. Most contemporary observers of these events shared these conceptions.

The credit for banishing Jim Crow from baseball belongs solely to Branch Rickey and the strategy that he pursued must be judged overwhelmingly effective. Yet the magnitude of his success has eradicated from memory the alternatives that existed. Rickey indeed was the only owner in 1945 with the courage and foresight to sign a black player. But with public pressure mounting, particularly in the New York area, it seems likely that political events would have forced the issue within the next few years. Rickey's action and his presentation of the Robinson case as an "experiment" actually relieved the pressure on other owners and allowed them to delay while awaiting the outcome of Rickey's gamble. It is also likely that if Rickey had not set the precedent, Bill Veeck would have. Veeck purchased the Cleveland Indians in 1946, and, given his background, he most likely would have tapped the Negro Leagues. The color line in baseball faced imminent extinction and probably would have collapsed by 1950, even if Rickey had not courageously engineered that collapse.

Rickey's preparations, in retrospect, also appear overelaborate and unnecessary. The Dodgers might have signed Robinson or another black player and immediately placed him on the Dodger roster with few adverse effects, or they might have launched wholesale signings of black players throughout the farm system and allowed the best to play their way to the major leagues. In subsequent years, the Indians pursued this strategy with great effect. Cleveland, of course, enjoyed the benefit of Robinson's prior success. Nonetheless, their less cautious tactics proved as successful as Rickey's maneuvers in the long run.

The Rickey blueprint placed tremendous pressure upon Robinson, his standard-bearer. Robinson's response to this challenge inspired a legend. His playing skills, intelligence, and competitive flair made Robinson the perfect path breaker. Still, did others exist who could have duplicated his feat? Unquestionably, many black athletes possessed major league talent, but could they have performed adequately under the intense pressure and retained their composure amidst insults? Former Negro League players differ on this matter. "I couldn't have done it," says Joe Black. "I might have taken it for a few days, or maybe a week,, but then I'd have grabbed one of them in the dugout runway or outside the ballpark and popped him . . . and right here Mr. Rickey's whole program would have gone down the drain." Other black players, however, argue that they could, and did, play in racially charged situations. Baseball was their profession, one which they plied under various conditions throughout the Americas. During the next decade, other blacks re-created Robinson's ordeal in different minor leagues; racial pressures chased few from the game.

Roy Campanella, following in Robinson's immediate wake, blazed an alternate, but nonetheless effective trail. "Roy was a calm man," says Don Newcombe. "He could withstand that kind of pressure. He was just dogged enough to really stick with it." Rickey might have introduced Robinson and Campanella together, thereby relieving the pressures endured by a lone pioneer and increasing the chances of success. It is interesting to speculate on what Rickey would have done had Robinson failed. Would he have given up and cut Campanella, already acknowledged as one of baseball's best catchers, adrift? Or, would Rickey have extended his experiment?

But Jackie Robinson did not fail and Campanella and the others who followed benefited from his example. And in Robinson, Rickey had uncovered not only an outstanding baseball player, but a figure of charisma and leadership. For blacks, Robinson became a symbol of pride and dignity; to whites, he represented a type of black man far removed from prevailing stereotypes, whom they could not help but respect. He would not fade into obscurity after retirement as most athletes do. Robinson remained an active advocate of civil rights causes and Afro-American interests. Other blacks might have sufficed in his role, concedes Dick Young, who often feuded with him, "But none, I believe, would have done it quite so well as Jackie Robinson."

The true significance of Jackie Robinson and his spectacular triumph in 1947 is reflected in the recollections of Dodger announcer Red Barber. Robinson's arrival had posed a moral dilemma for Barber, but he accepted the black man, "as a man, as a ballplayer. I didn't resent him and I didn't crusade for him. I broadcast the ball." Both Robinson and Rickey expressed their appreciation for Barber's tactful handling of the matter, but, writes Barber in his autobiography, "I know that if I have achieved any understanding and tolerance in my life . . . if I have been able to follow a little better the great second commandment, which is to love thy neighbor, it all stems from this . . . I thank Jackie Robinson. He did far more for me than I did for him."

Suggestions for Further Reading

William Manchester has provided an exhaustively detailed history of the years since 1932 in *The Glory and the Dream: A Narrative History of America, 1932–1972** (Boston, 1974). Frederick Lewis Allen followed his work on the 1920s, *Only Yesterday*, with a work on the 1930s, *Since Yesterday** (New York, 1940). Two popular histories of the Depression that consist partly of recollections are Carolyn Bird, *The Invisible Scar** (New York, 1966), and Robert Bendiner, *Just Around the Corner: A Highly Selective History of the Thirties** (New York, 1967). David A. Shannon has edited a collection of documents detailing the social impact of the Depression in *The Great Depression** (Englewood Cliffs, N.J., 1960). See also Milton Melzer, *Brother, Can You Spare a Dime? The Great Depression, 1929–1933** (New York, 1969). A view of the American workingman during this period is given in Irving Bernstein, *The Lean Years: A History of the American Worker, 1920–1933** (Boston, 1961) and *The Turbulent Years: A History of American Labor, 1933–1941** (Boston, 1970).

The impact of the Depression is measured in the essays collected by Bernard Sternsher in *Hitting Home: The Depression in Town and Country** (Chicago, 1970) and *The Negro in Depression and War: Prelude to Revolution** (Chicago, 1970). The long-term impact on children raised during the 1930s is analyzed in a unique longitudinal study by Glen H. Elder, Jr., *The Children of the Great Depression: Social Change in Life Experience** (Chicago, 1974). Robert and Helen Merrill Lynd returned to Muncie, Indiana, to measure the changes wrought by the Depression, which they describe in *Middletown in Transition** (New York, 1937). An important demographic shift is outlined by Walter J. Stein in *California and the Dust Bowl Migration** (Westport, Conn., 1973). The classic statement on this westward migration is found, of course, in John Steinbeck, *The Grapes of Wrath** (New York, 1939). For the effects of the Depression on Appalachia, see Harry M. Caudill, *Night Comes to the Cumberlands: A Biography of a Depressed Area** (Boston, 1963). Recollections of the Depression have been compiled by Studs Terkel in *Hard Times: An Oral History of the Great Depression** (New York, 1970), also available in a two-

*Available in paperback edition.

339

disc, long-playing record album. Woody Guthrie's autobiography, *Bound for Glory** (New York, 1943), contains a great deal of material on growing up in the dust bowl and bumming around the country in the 1930s.

The classic study of the Dust Bowl region is *The Great Plains** (Boston, 1931) by Walter Prescott Webb. Paul Bonnifield has studied the Depression Dust Bowl in *The Dust Bowl: Men, Dirt, and Depression* (Albuquerque, 1979). The University of Kansas has explored various aspects of Great Plains life in Brian W. Blouet and Frederick C. Leubke, eds., *The Great Plains: Environment and Culture* (Lincoln, 1979) and Merlin P. Lawson and Maurice E. Baker, eds., *The Great Plains: Perspectives and Prospects** (Lincoln, 1980).

Three additional books that use either oral history or collections of letters to describe the conditions prevailing among many Americans during the Depression are Ann Banks, ed., *First Person America** (New York, 1980); Tom E. Terrill and Jerrold Hirsch, eds., *Such As Us: Southern Voices of the Thirties** (Chapel Hill, 1978); and Robert S. McElvaine, ed., *Down and Out in the Great Depression: Letters from the "Forgotten Man"** (Chapel Hill, 1983). Susan Ware has explored the lives of women during the period in *Holding Their Own: American Women in the 1930s** (Boston, 1982). For Afro-American developments, see Harvard Sitkoff, *A New Deal for Blacks** (New York, 1978).

Recent surveys of America's working women include Barbara Mayer Wertheimer, *We Were There: The Story of Working Women in America** (New York, 1977) and Rosalyn Baxandall, Linda Gordon, and Susan Reverby, eds., *America's Working Women: A Documentary History—1600 to the Present** (New York, 1976). Studies of women during the years of the Second World War can be found in D'Ann Campbell, *Women at War with America: Private Lives in a Patriotic Era* (Cambridge, 1984); Maureen Honey, *Creating Rosie the Riveter: Class, Gender, and Propaganda during World War II* (Amherst, 1984); and Susan Hartman, *The Home Front and Beyond: American Women in the 1940s* (Boston, 1982).

A history of the early days of baseball can be found in Peter Levine, *A.G. Spaulding and the Rise of Baseball: The Promise of American Sport* (New York, 1985). A survey of the history of American sports can be found in Benjamin G. Rader, *American Sports: From the Age of Folk Games to the Age of Spectators** (Englewood Cliffs, N.J., 1983). Life in the Negro professional baseball leagues is presented in Robert Peterson, *Only the Ball Was White* (Englewood Cliffs, N.J., 1970); Donn Rogosin, *Invisible Men: Life in Baseball's Negro Leagues** (New York, 1983); and Janet Bruce, *The Kansas City Monarchs: Champions of Black Baseball* (Lawrence, Kansas, 1985). Interesting insights into the desegregation of baseball can be found in autobiographies of some of the pioneers, such as Jackie Robinson and Roy Campanella.

Contemporary America

1960–the Present

San Francisco's Haight-Ashbury hippie mecca, 1970

Rise and Fall of a Counterculture

ALLEN J. MATUSOW

If we use the term *culture* to refer to the way of life of a people, then from its very beginning American society has been made up of a variety of cultures. There has been, however, a prevailing culture that has attempted to dominate competing of conflicting cultures. Although attempts have been made to describe this dominant culture and its origins, studies show only that this "main" culture has had tremendous success in creating certain attitudes and controlling behavior.

The secret of successful studies of any culture derives from the ability of the scholar to ferret out the patterns of behavior that may, in fact, run counter to the overt attitudes of a group.

What interests us in the following selection, however, is not the conflict between attitude and behavior, but rather the conflict between a dominant culture and a deviant culture. The goal of this deviant culture is to attack the dominant culture and to bridge the gap between attitude and behavior—or what is commonly called "hypocrisy."

Since the founding of the Massachusetts Bay Colony, the body of New World society has contained deviant culture elements. This description does not refer to foreign cultures such as the American Indian or the African cultures, but to those deviations from the dominant culture that were a part of the settlers themselves. The English people who danced with Indians around a Maypole in Merry Mount in the 1630s presented a challenge within the prevailing culture. Such challenges persist to the present day. The dominant culture usually has the power of public opinion or, when necessary, the power of police authority to subdue deviants in its midst. This power, however is not always invoked. In the twentieth century there has developed a tradition often referred to as a "bohemian" culture which is restricted almost entirely to a small number of artists, writers, and composers. These creative bohemians have not sought to foster their way of life—composed as it is of a freedom from what they call "bourgeois morality"—as have the rest of America. They merely want to be left alone. And left alone they are unless they become too flagrant in their violations of community norms.

In the 1960s, an extremely powerful challenge to the dominant culture occurred. The term *counterculture*, rather than *subculture*, can correctly be applied to this movement. This counterculture saw itself as a frontal attack on what it called the "straight" world and its visionary purpose was to "turn on" the world. At the heart of the counterculture was a contempt for all traditional forms of authority and, theoretically, an intent to replace them with the authority of inner experience and interpersonal relationships. Since these new ideals were difficult to isolate and identify (much less obey), the counterculture's adherents turned many types of gurus (spiritual leaders) in an attempt to find its way.

In the following chapter, Allen J. Matusow, of Rice University, traces the rise and decline of the counterculture. Beginning with what he considers the intellectual underpinnings of the movement through the work of Norman O. Brown and the writers of the "beat generation" of the 1950s, the author traces the development of a movement based on sex, drugs, and rock and roll. Using Brown's alteration of Freud's dichotomy of Eros (sexual energy) and Thanatos (death wish), Matusow shows how the valiant but dangerous attempt to replace repression with freedom ended with the victory of the "dark side." It would be possible to trace favorable aspects of the counterculture as it made its way into the mainstream of American life, but its attempt at changing traditional culture died along with the drugged-out hippies in Haight-Ashbury.

I

America discovered hippies at the world's first Human Be-In, Golden Gate Park, San Francisco, January 14, 1967. The occasion was something special, even in a Bay Area underground long accustomed to spectacle. Political activists from Berkeley mingled with dropouts from Haight-Ashbury, ending their feud and initiating a "new epoch" in the history of man. "In unity we shall shower the country with waves of ecstasy and purification," sponsors of the Be-In prophesied. "Fear will be washed away; ignorance will be exposed to sunlight; profits and empire will lie drying on deserted beaches." Preparations for the Be-In were casual but appropriate. A hippie newspaper called the *Oracle* invited everyone "to bring costumes, blankets, bells, flags, symbols, cymbals, drums, beads, feathers, flowers." A local painter named Michael Bowen arranged with his guru in Mexico to exchange weather for the day. The Hell's Angels motorcycle gang agreed to guard the electronic equipment of the rock bands, which would play this gig for free. And poets Allen Ginsberg and Gary Snyder arrived two hours early to perform a "purificatory circumambulation" of the field, a ritual they had observed in 1963 in Sarnath, India, to drive out demons.

By early afternoon a crowd estimated at twenty thousand gathered in the park to enjoy the unseasonably warm sun and commune with the hip notables on the makeshift stage. Timothy Leary was there, dressed in white and wearing flowers in his hair. "Turn on to the scene, tune in to what is happening, and drop out—of high school, college, grad school, junior executive—and follow me, the hard way," said Leary, reciting his famous commercial for the synthetic hallucinogen LSD. Ginsberg, in a white Khader suit and blue rubber sandals, chanted a Buddhist mantra as Synder blew a conch-shell he had obtained in Kyoto while studying Zen Buddhism. "We are primitives of an unknown culture . . ." Snyder had said on the eve of the Be-In, "with new ethics and new states of mind." Music for the occasion was acid rock, performed by Quicksilver Messenger Service, Jefferson Airplane, and the Grateful Dead. Already an underground legend, the Dead had played Ken Kesey's notorious "acid tests," which had done so much to spread LSD and the psychedelic style throughout California a year or so before. Representing the new left was Jerry Rubin, released that very morning from jail, but not yet hip enough for this occasion. "Tune-In—Drop-Out—Take-Over," Rubin had said at a press conference prior to the event. But few at the Be-In were in a mood (or condition) to take over anything.

The real show was the crowd. "The costumes were a designer's dream," wrote music critic Ralph Gleason in the San Francisco Chronicle, "a wild polyglot mixture of Mod, Palladin, Ringling Brothers, Cochise, and Hells Angel's Formal." Bells tinkled, balloons floated, people on the grass played harmonicas, guitars, recorders, flutes. Beautiful girls handed out sticks of incense. A young man in a paisley parachute drifted from the sky, though no plane was in sight. An old man gave away his poems. A mysterious group called the Diggers had obtained seventy-five turkeys from a drug chemist named Owsley and supplied sandwiches, homemade bread, and oranges, free, to anyone who was hungry. When a sulfur bomb exploded under the stage, people on the grass thought it was a large cloud of yellow incense and broke into appreciative applause. Finally, after poets Michael McClure, Lenore Kandell, Snyder and Ginsberg read in the silent presence of Zen Master Suzuki Roshi who was seated on the stage, and the hours of tripping, dancing, and hugging had wound down, Ginsberg turned toward the setting sun, led a chant "om gri maitreya" (Salutations to Buddha of Futurity), and asked the people to practice "a little kitchen Yoga" by picking up their trash. Officials said that no gathering had left so little litter in the park in a generation.

Newsweek was on hand to photograph the Be-In in gorgeous color and report that "it was a love feast, a psychedelic picnic, a hippie happening." Images of hip quickly began to seep into the public consciousness, provoking intense curiosity and endless analysis in the straight world. Most of the pop sociology deserved the rebuke of Bob Dylan's "Ballad of a Thin Man": "Something is happening here but you don't know what it is. Do you, Mr. Jones?" Yet understanding was imperative, for the hippie impulse that was spreading through a generation of the young challenged the traditional values of bourgeois culture, values still underpinning the liberal movement of the 1960s—reason, progress, order, achievement, social responsibility. Hippies mocked liberal politicians, scorned efforts to repair the social order, and repudiated bourgeois society. In so doing, they became cultural radicals opposed to established authority. Among the movements arrayed against him toward the end of his tenure, none baffled Lyndon Johnson more than these hippies. Somehow, in the name of liberation, they rejected everything he stood for, including his strenuous efforts to liberate the poor and the black. Clearly, liberation meant something different to liberals like him from what it meant to radicals like them.

II

Few hippies read much, but those who did found their purpose strikingly described and anticipated in the strange books of Norman O. Brown. A classical scholar at Wesleyan University, whose underground explorations began in middle age and never strayed beyond the library, Brown published a book in 1959 called *Life Against Death*. A manifesto of cultural radicalism, this book established Brown as a prophet of the counterculture and its preeminent intellectual. Those seeking the meaning of the hippie movement could do no better than begin with him.

Brown was a Freudian who reshaped the ideas of the master to provide a happy ending; no mean feat, given Freud's pessimism. Man was unhappy, Freud argued, because his instincts were repressed. The realm of instinct was the id, wherein resided emotion, desire—above all, Eros, the sexual instinct, which sought bodily pleasure. But to accomplish the survival of the individual, Eros had to be controlled. Thus in childhood there emerged from the id the ego, which mediated between the individual and the outside world and attempted to repress the raging instincts. Eros could not be repressed entirely, however, and the ego was forced to admit it into consciousness—transformed, sublimated, desexualized. Sublimated Eros provided the energy for work, art, and culture. Hence the irony and tragedy of man: he can know happiness only in gratifying his instinctual need for bodily pleasure; but to preserve life and create civilization, that need must be denied. Freud had still other grounds for pessimism. In the id he had discovered, alongside Eros and warring against it, a second instinct, which he called the death instinct, or Thanatos. As civilization advances, Eros weakens, and the death instinct gains force. Directed outward, Thanatos becomes aggression, threatening other men with harm and civilization with extinction. "Men have gained control over the forces of nature to such an extent," Freud concluded, "that with their help they would have no difficulty in exterminating one another to the last man."

Against Freud, Brown intended to show that man could achieve his infantile dream of eternal bodily pleasure. Brown began his reconstruction of Freud by denying that there existed an instinctual dualism—life and death, Eros *vs.* Thanatos—rooted in biology. The pre-Oedipal infant at his mother's breast experiences "union of the self with a whole world of love and pleasure." In this blissful state there are no dualism, no self and other, no subject-object, no life against death, only timeless experience of being one with the world, only instinctual fusion and undifferentiated unity. Bliss ends when the infant experiences separation from the mother, producing anxiety, a sense of loss, and fear of death. According to Brown's argument, it is the infant's attempt to flee death that initiates instinctual de-fusion. Eros emerges, seeking actively to reunite with the mother, the source of bodily pleasure; Thanatos emerges, seeking the peace known at her breast. The ensuing sublimations of the instincts produce the spiritual life of man and propel history, but they cannot make man happy. The flight from death, then, is the critical event in psychic life, condemning man to sickness and removing him from nature. Brown's prescription for health was simple: If man can accept death, he can accept life, achieve instinctual re-fusion, abolish repression, and find happiness through "the resurrection of the body."

There was much in *Life Against Death* that anticipated and expressed the hippie impulse. Like the hippies, Brown was resolutely nonpolitical. Man was the animal who repressed himself; his salvation lay not in social reorganization but in self-reconstruction. Like the hippies, Brown affirmed instinctual freedom against the rational, disciplined, puritanic life that had been the life of man in Western civilization. Like the hippies, Brown was in revolt against civilized sex—exclusively genital, exclusively heterosexual, exclusively monogamous—affirming instead pan-sexualism, "polymorphous perversity," the union of many bodies: in short, erotic life based on the pre-Oedipal Eden. And finally Brown gave definition to the cultural project on which the hippies were soon to embark. Rejecting descent into the id as mere regression, Brown wished to make the unconscious conscious, incorporate the content of the id into the ego—to create, in other words, a new ego, a body ego, which Brown called the "Dionysian ego," overflowing with love, knowing no limits, affirming life. "Dionysus reunifies male and female, Self and Other, life and death," Brown wrote. The creation of the Dionysian ego, the ego in service of liberated Eros—this was a project millions of mothers would soon understand implicitly and fear with good reason.

But Dionysian ecstasy might do more than command the ego; it might overflow the ego's limits until the very self is obliterated. In *Love's Body*, published in 1966, Brown used poetic implication, nonlinear argument, and outrageous paradox to develop certain mystical implications in his earlier book. "Dionysus, the mad god, breaks down the boundaries; releases the prisoners; abolishes repression; and abolishes the *principium individuationis*, substituting for it the unity of man and the unity of man with nature," Brown wrote. The body was still there, but as a body in union with other bodies, the body lost. "The solution to the problem of identity is, get lost." The body was still there but now as universal body. "And the resurrection is the resurrection of the body"; Brown said, "but not the separate body of the individual, but the body of mankind as one body." Body existed, not as location or flesh, but as a field of energy; ego, character, personality were mere illusion. Id was now the impersonal energy embracing all mankind in "one mystical symbolical body." Indeed, knowledge of the Unity could be attained only by breaking the bonds of the ego, by having "no self." Illumination, therefore, was consciousness of void, nothingness. This was the language of the satori of the Buddha, of Oriental religion, of mysticism—and the promise of the sixties drug prophets, especially the prophets of LSD.

If Brown's books forecast the hippie projects—Dionysian ecstasies, bodily and mystic—the Human Be-In proclaimed the existence of a hippie culture, or counterculture, committed to realizing those projects through drugs, sex, and rock and roll. But just as Brown did not invent the projects, hippies did not invent their culture from scratch. Hip explorers in the realm of the Dionysian had spent a generation developing rituals and a life style from which hippies freely borrowed. Indeed, without pioneers to point the way, hippies might never have emerged to fascinate and outrage America.

III

The history of hip began with the black hipsters of the 1930s. Black folk had always constituted something of a counterculture in America, representing, at least in the white imagination, pure id. Migrating into northern ghettos after World War I, young black men used their new freedom to improvise a new variation on black deviance—the hipster—who was not only hedonistic, sensual, and sexually uninhibited, but openly contemptuous of the white world that continued to exclude him. The language that hipsters invented on Harlem street corners was jive, an action language honed in verbal duels and inaccessible to most whites. Some jive words that became part of the permanent hip lexicon were *cat, solid, chick, Big Apple, square, tea, gas, dip, flip. Ofay,* the jive word for white, meant foe in pig Latin. The hipster costume was the zoot suit, designed, as hip garb always would be, to defy and outrage conventional taste. For kicks, the hipster smoked marijuana, which heightened his sense of immediacy and helped him soar above his mean surroundings. The only bigger kick was sex.

Vital to the hipster experience was the uninhibited black music called jazz. In 1922 a writer in the *Atlantic Monthly* described jazz as the result of "an unloosing of instincts that nature wisely has taught us to hold in check, but which, every now and then, for cryptic reasons, are allowed to break the bonds of civilization." Indeed, Louis Armstrong, playing his "hot," sensual, raunchy improvisations on trumpet, was the first hipster hero. As jazz changed, the hipster persona changed with it. In the early 1940s a group of rebel black jazzmen, hostile to the commercialization of the big bands, created bebop. Bebop relied on small groups and improvisation, as before, but the sound was cool, the rhythm variable, the volume low, and the technical virtuosity of its leading performers legend. The genius of bebop was Charlie "The Bird" Parker, who lived at "the level of total spontaneity," whether he was playing alto sax or getting kicks from booze, sex, or heroin. By the mid-1940s, partly because of heroin, hot was out and cool was in. Hipster dress had become more conservative; noise and brash behavior, a breach of taste; detachment, a required pose. By then, too, the hipster had ceased to be a type restricted to blacks only. In New York and other big cities, some disaffiliates among the white young found the hipster persona so expressive of their own alienation that they adopted it as their own. Thus was born, in Norman Mailer's phrase, "the white Negro," living outside the law for sex, pot, jazz, kicks—in short, for Dionysian ecstasy.

Herbert Huncke was a white hipster who first heard the language and the music on Chicago's South Side in the thirties. Before moving to New York before World War II, he had become a junkie, a habitué of the underworld, and a petty criminal so notorious that the police would name him the Creep and bar him from Times Square. An experimenter with forbidden experience, Huncke took drugs to derange the senses and expand consciousness, and he provided rich source material for Dr. Alfred Kinsey's study of American sexual mores. When wearied of the streets, he sought refuge in a detachment so complete that he was beyond feeling. Huncke had a word to describe his weariness. He said he was "beat."

One day in 1945 Huncke encountered William Burroughs, not yet a famous writer, trying to get rid of a sawed-off shotgun and some morphine. Through Burroughs, Huncke met Allen Ginsberg, Jack Kerouac, John Clellon Holmes, and others in a circle of rebel writers and intellectuals who later became known as the beat generation. Living on the fringes of Columbia University as students or dropouts, the beats engaged in obscure resistance to the "Syndrome of Shutdown" (Ginsberg's later phrase)—the movement toward a totalitarian America based on mass consumption and mass acquiescence. They were rebels too against the official culture purveyed in academic classrooms and celebrated in the lifeless literary quarterlies. In reaction they created their literature from raw experience, which they consumed with reckless and undiscriminating abandon. When Herbert Huncke introduced the proto-beats to the hipster underground, its jive, jazz, drugs, and unconventional sex, they plunged right in. Ginsberg wrote, "As far as I know the ethos of what's charmingly Hip, and the first pronunciation of the world itself to my fellow ears first came consciously from Huncke's lips; and the first information and ritual of the emergent hip subculture passed through Huncke's person."

What the beats added to hip was the mystic quest. In the summer of 1948, living alone in East Harlem and grieving for his departed lover Neal Cassady, Allen Ginsberg had the defining experience of his life. As he lay in bed gazing at tenement roofs with a book of William Blake's *Songs of Innocence* before him, he heard the deep voice of the poet himself reciting the "Sunflower," and he knew it was the voice of God. "Looking out the window, . . ." Ginsberg remembered, "suddenly it seemed that I saw into the depths of the universe, by looking simply into the ancient sky." Ginsberg had auditory experience of other poems that evening, and there were other visions in the days that followed, until, a week later, standing in the athletic field at Columbia, Ginsberg invoked the spirit and experienced the cosmos as monster. "The sky was not a blue hand anymore but like a hand of death coming down on me." It was years before Ginsberg would seek that void again, but in the meantime he did not forget those moments when the ego had overflowed the bounds of the self and illumination had been his. A year later Huncke moved in with Ginsberg, thoughtfully stashing his stolen goods elsewhere. Arrested as an accessory, Ginsberg was committed and stayed eight months in the Columbia-affiliated New York Psychiatric Institute.

After graduating from Columbia in 1949, Ginsberg worked at straight jobs and tried to master his real vocation, which was poetry. In 1954, forsaking New York, he moved to San Francisco to visit Cassady. There a brilliant circle of poets had gathered around Lawrence Ferlinghetti's

City Lights Book Store in a neighborhood called North Beach. North Beach provided the cultural soil where the best seed, originally planted in New York, took root and flowered. With its narrow streets, high walls, and cheap houses overlooking the bay, North Beach reminded Gary Snyder of "ancient terraced fertile crescent pueblos." The beats were hipsters a decade later, explorers in the realm of the Dionysian, searching for ecstasies, bodily and mystic.

For Ginsberg San Francisco was liberation. He found a psychiatrist who told him to do what he wanted, namely write poetry and love men; and he met his "life long sex-soul union" in Peter Orlovsky. Maturing rapidly, Ginsberg also found his authentic voice as a poet. One weekend in 1955 he stayed in his apartment and wrote a poem, with little revision, which one part of him believed he could not publish out of respect for his father and another part believed would change America. In September, at an artists' co-op called the Six Gallery, with his friend Jack Kerouac there to pass around the jug and shout encouragement, Ginsberg read his astounding "Howl." Taking as its subject the life of the poet and his beat friends, "Howl" became a manifesto for the scattered disaffiliates of fifties America.

> I saw the best minds of my generation destroyed by madness,
>   starving hysterical naked,
> dragging themselves through the negro streets at dawn looking for
>   an angry fix,
> angelheaded hipsters burning for the ancient heavenly connection
>   to the starry dynamo in the machinery of night
> who poverty and tatters and hollow-eyed and high sat up smoking
>   in the supernatural darkness of cold-water flats floating across
>   the tops of cities contemplating jazz
> who bared their brains to Heaven under the El and saw Moham-
>   medan angels staggering on tenement roofs illuminated. . . .

When the authorities brought Ferlinghetti to trial for publishing "Howl," on the grounds of obscenity, the poem attained more than literary celebrity. "Howl" sold 100,000 copies in ten years, making it perhaps the most popular serious poem of the century.

Fame did not deflect Ginsberg from his Dionysian projects. Experimenting with psychedelic drugs, he deepened both his understanding of "the female principle" and his desire for women; and he tried again to transcend "this familiar rotting ginsberg" by grasping the Void. In 1961, frightened by visions of the "serpent monster," he set forth on two years of travel to the East, seeking spiritual wisdom from holy men,—from Martin Buber in Israel to Tibetan lamas in India. The holy men had a message Ginsberg had already anticipated. Get back into the body, they told him. Stop trying to "melt into the universe," stop trying to merge with the nonhuman unknown. Riding the train from

Kyoto to Tokyo in 1963, Ginsberg had an ecstatic experience as crucial to him as his Blake vision years before. The burden of his cosmic quest was instantly lifted, and he felt "suddenly free to love myself again and therefore love the people around me." Weeping with joy, still on the train, he wrote "The Change."

> Come, sweet lovely Spirit, back
> to your bodies, come great God,
> back to your only image. . . .

Ginsberg returned to America, all his demons exorcised at last, in time to become bard and shaman for the next hip generation. To the hippies, Ginsberg was a new kind of American hero-saint. He had penetrated far enough into the dark recesses of self to risk sanity, and he had returned purified, with reverence for all living things. Norman Mailer once wrote lovingly of him,

> I sometimes think
> that little Jew bastard
> that queer ugly kike
> is the bravest man
> in America.

Jack Kerouac, the beat writer who shared so many of Ginsberg's adventures, also shared his mystic quest. Kerouac had gone to Columbia to play football but rebelled against the discipline, deciding instead to write novels and probe the cultural underground. Recalling the 1940s, he wrote, "Anyway, the hipsters, whose music was bop, they looked like criminals but they kept talking about the same things I liked, long outlines of personal experience and vision, nightlong confessions full of hope that became illicit and repressed by War. . . . And so Huncke appeared to us and said, 'I'm beat' with radiant light shining out of his despairing eyes . . . a word perhaps brought from some midwest carnival or junk cafeteria. It was a new language, actually spade (Negro) jargon but you soon learned it."

Kerouac made his artistic breakthrough when he decided to write a semi-fictional account of his road experiences with Neal Cassady. Some people might have regarded Cassady as a bum. Reared on the streets of Denver by his wino father, in and out of jails mostly for stealing cars, Cassady possessed so much energy and lived so completely in the moment that the beat circle could not resist him. In April 1951 Kerouac fed a roll of teletype paper into a typewriter and let tales of Cassady flow spontaneously from his mind, in one paragraph 120 feet long. It took three weeks to write *On the Road*, six years to get it published.

On the Road portrayed Kerouac, Cassady, Ginsberg, and their hipster friends speeding across the continent in the late forties, consuming pot, jazz, and sex, envying the Negro his spontaneity, his soul, his cool. Cassady (Dean Moriarty in the book) was the natural man, the Dionysian ego, joyfully slaking his unquenchable thirst for food, sex, and life. But Kerouac saw Cassady as more than a glutton. He was "a holy con-man," "the HOLY GOOF," "Angel Dean," questing for "IT," the moment "when you know all and everything is decided forever,"—that moment in jazz, Dean explained, when the man making the music "rises to his fate and has to blow equal to it." In San Francisco, deserted by Cassady and delirious from hunger, Kerouac himself (Sal Paradise) had a mystic vision, reaching "the point of ecstasy that I always wanted to reach." Eventually, as Cassady became ensnared in complication, accusation, wounds of the body, he becomes, in Kerouac's view, "BEAT—the root, the soul of Beatific," A bestseller in 1957, *On the Road* became a literary inspiration for the restless young even then preparing to scale the walls of American suburbia in search of Dionysus.

In 1955 Kerouac, still an obscure writer, bummed his way across the country to visit Ginsberg in San Francisco. Kerouac was by then deep into Buddhism. Recognizing that the beat quest for satori had more in common with Oriental than Western religion, he vowed to end suffering and achieve nirvana by overcoming desire. In California he found that in turning East he was not alone. A pinch of Zen had by now been added to the witch's brew boiling over in North Beach. Zen's chief popularizer in the Bay Area was Alan Watts, a sometime Episcopal clergyman from England who had attained local celebrity in the early 1950s as dean of San Francisco's American Academy of Asian Studies. Watt's was an easygoing brand of Zen, based on the teachings of the Chinese founders, liberally interpreted. Zen taught, Watts explained, that it is absurd to desire the end of desire, to grasp for nirvana, which is nongrasping, to seek to liberate the nonexistent self. Let go of the passions, do not fight them; neither repress passion nor indulge it. Live naturally and spontaneously, and when satori comes, it will come without effort, as a sudden turn of consciousness. To the vast relief of the sympathetic young, Watts stressed that one of the passions that definitely did not have to be denied was sexual passion. Man was both animal and angel, Watts maintained, and can be both sexualist and mystic. Thus was born the strangest of religions—Dionysian Zen.

Kerouac met not only Watts in San Francisco but Gary Snyder. Snyder, said Watts, "*is* just exactly what I have been trying to *say*." Snyder had felt estranged from industrial civilization since, as a child growing up in backwoods Oregon, he had experienced "an undefinable awe before the natural world." He became fascinated by Indian myths at Reed College and later gave up on white civilization entirely when he discovered the East. In 1953 he began two years of study of Oriental languages at Berkeley in preparation for Zen training in Japan. Among his other accomplishments, he was a poet good enough to share the stage at the Six Gallery the night Ginsberg read "Howl."

Kerouac recounted his adventures with Snyder in *Dharma Bums*, mythologizing him as he had Cassady. When Kerouac first visited Snyder in his twenty-by-twelve shack in Berkeley, Snyder (Japhy Rider in the book) was sitting cross-legged on the floor translating the poems of the Chinese Zen lunatic Han-shan. Kerouac's admiration for the tough, wiry little Buddhist was instantaneous and complete. A pioneer dropout, Snyder was living a new kind of American life in the interstices of technological civilization. If he needed money, he shipped out on a commercial freighter; if he needed clothes, he bought them at the Goodwill store; if he was thirsty, he brewed tea of intoxicating purity, and if hungry, he could produce a delicious meal from dried vegetables, grains, and herbs. When he wanted women, which was often, he reached out and took them. "I distrust any kind of Buddhism or any kind of philosophy or social system that puts down sex," he told Kerouac. The climax of *Dharma Bums* was a climb up the Matterhorn, with Kerouac the tenderfoot learning the art from the master. Improvising haiku, leaping boulders, meditating by the campfire, the two bodhisattvas experienced ecstatic union with Nature. A thousand feet from the top of the mountain, Kerouac panicked and took refuge under a ledge. But Snyder, defying the terrifying height and wind, darted to the top, shouting "his triumphant mountain-conquering Buddha Mountain Smashing song of joy." Back on the ground Snyder delivered himself of a Zen koan. "When you get to the top of the mountain keep climbing."

And Snyder kept climbing. For most of the next ten years, while publication of his poems nourished his legend in America, Snyder studied Zen in a Japanese monastery. In 1961 he visited India to help guide Ginsberg on a mutual Buddhist pilgrimage to holy places. Five years after that he was back in America to guide a new hip generation in its own revolt against the nature-destroying civilization of the West.

By the late 1950s, a fully developed beat subculture had emerged not only in North Beach but also in Venice West (near Los Angeles), New York's Greenwich Village, and a few other hip resorts in between. The beats possessed deviant tastes in language, literature, music, drugs, and religion. Profoundly alienated from dominant American values, practicing voluntary poverty and spade cool, they rejected materialism, competition, the work ethic, hygiene, sexual repression, monogamy, and the Faustian quest to subdue nature. There were, to be sure, never more than a few thousand fulltime beats, but thanks to the scandalized media, images of beat penetrated and disconcerted the middle classes.

Beats, like hula hoops, were a fad. Indeed, by the early 1960s the San Francisco poets had scattered, and cops and tourists had driven the rest of the beats from their old haunts in North Beach. A remnant survived, however, and found convenient shelter in another congenial San Francisco neighborhood. It was Haight-Ashbury, a racially integrated community, forty square blocks, bordering magnificent Golden Gate Park. There, beat old-timers kept alive the hip style and the Dionysian projects, until hippies moved in and appropriated both.

IV

In the metamorphosis from beat to hippie, hallucinogenic drugs played an indispensable part. Indians had been using peyote and magic mushrooms for sacramental purposes since before the rise of the Aztec civilization. But in industrial civilizations, knowledge of mind-altering substances had virtually disappeared. In the 1920s chemists synthesized the active ingredient in peyote, calling it mescaline, and did the same thing in 1958 for the sacred mushrooms, producing psilocybin. Science even outdid nature in 1938 when Dr. Albert Hoffman of the Sandoz Chemical Works in Switzerland fabricated a compound many times more potent than anything imbibed by the most ecstatic Indian. Searching for a respiratory stimulant, Hoffman produced the diethylamide of lysergic acid, a colorless, odorless, apparently useless substance that he called LSD. Five years later, in the course of an experiment on animals, Hoffman accidentally ingested an "unmeasurable trace" of LSD and took the world's first acid trip. (It was, incidentally, a bummer.) Hoffman kept experimenting, and Sandoz began supplying LSD to psychiatric researchers trying to cure schizophrenia. By 1960 LSD was seeping out of the laboratory into the cultural underground.

The herald of the psychedelic revolution was the British author Aldous Huxley. Swallowing some mescaline in 1953, Huxley accidentally triggered a profound mystical experience, in which he watched "a slow dance of golden lights," discovered "Eternity in a flower" and even approached the "Pure Light of the Void," before fleeing in terror from "the burning brightness of unmitigated Reality." In *The Doors of Perception* (1954), which recounted his journey, Huxley lamented that the rich and highly educated white people of the earth were so wedded to words and reason that they had cut themselves off from mystic knowledge. Western man, he said, should accept the "gratuitous grace" of mind-expanding drugs, thus "to be shaken out of the ruts of ordinary perception, to be shown for a few timeless hours the outer and the inner world, not as they appear to an animal obsessed with survival or to a human being obsessed with words and notions, but as they are apprehended, directly and unconditionally, by Mind at Large."

The man who purveyed Huxley's holy message to the millions was Timothy Leary. Possessor of a Ph.D. in psychology, Leary quit his job as director of the Kaiser Foundation Hospital in Oakland, California, in 1958, convinced that conventional psychiatry did not work. Accepting a post at Harvard to pursue his unorthodox ideas, Leary was on his way to a productive scientific career until, one day in Mexico, he discovered the magic mushrooms.

Leary had retreated to a villa in Cuernavaca in the summer of 1960 to write a paper that he hoped would win him points in the academic game. He had never smoked marijuana and knew nothing about mind-altering drugs. But, when a friend procured the mushrooms from a local Indian, Leary thought it might be fun to try some. On a hot afternoon sitting around a pool, Leary and a few companions choked down a bowl of filthy, foul-tasting *crudos*. The game for Leary ended right there. "Five hours after eating the mushrooms it was all changed," he wrote. "The revelation had come. The veil had been pulled back. The classic vision. The full-blown conversion experience. The prophetic call. The works. God had spoken."

Back at Harvard in the fall, Leary secured Huxley's help in designing a scientific experiment to investigate the behavioral effects of psilocybin (synthesized magic mushrooms). Soon Leary was turning on graduate students, ministers, convicts, and stray seekers showing up at his rented mansion in suburban Boston. In truth, Leary was using science to cloak his real purpose, which was to give away the keys to paradise. And he did grow in spiritual knowledge. He learned that drugs alone could not produce a state of blessedness, that they "had no specific effect on consciousness, except to expand it." God and the Devil resided together in the nervous system. Which of these was summoned depended on one's state of mind. Leary, therefore, emphasized the importance of proper "set and setting" (candles, incense, music, art, quiet) to help the seeker experience God.

In December 1960 Leary made the connection with the hip underground in the person of Allen Ginsberg. Having met him in New York, Ginsberg spent a week at Leary's home to enlist the professor in his own crusade for mind expansion. The two hit it off from the start. On Sunday, with dogs, children, and hangers-on scattered about, Leary gave Ginsberg and Peter Orlovsky the sacred mushrooms. The poets repaired to their room, stripped naked, and played Wagner on the record player. Lying in bed, Ginsberg began to succumb to hellish visions, until Leary came in, looked in his eyes, and pronounced him a great man. Ginsberg arose, and with Orlovsky padding behind, descended to the kitchen to proclaim himself the Messiah. We will go into the streets and call the people to peace and love, Leary reports him as saying. And we will get on the phone and hook up Burroughs, Kerouac, Mailer, Kennedy, and Khrushchev and "settle all this warfare bit." Hello operator, Ginsberg said. This is God. Get me Kerouac. And eventually she did. Sitting in the kitchen after the drug had worn off, Ginsberg plotted the psychedelic revolution. Everybody ought to have the mushrooms, he said, beginning with the influentials. They would not listen to him, a crazy beatnik poet, but they might listen to a Harvard professor. Leary must come to New York on weekends and turn on the likes of Kerouac, Robert Lowell, LeRoi Jones, Dizzy Gillespie, Thelonious Monk, and other creative people in Ginsberg's personal telephone book. Leary was willing. "From this evening on," he wrote, "my energies were offered to the ancient underground society of alchemists, artists, mystics, alienated visionaries, dropouts and the disenchanted young, the sons arising."

Not until late 1961 did Leary try LSD—"the most shattering experience of my life." Taking him far beyond psilocybin, LSD enabled Leary to accomplish the projects of the counterculture—Dionysian ecstasies, mystic and bodily. He journeyed down the DNA ladder of evolution to the single cell at the beginning of life and then outward to the cosmic vibrations where he merged with pure energy, "the white light," nothingness. He also experienced the resurrection of the body. "Blow the mind and you are left with God and life—and life is sex," he said. Leary called LSD "a powerful aphrodisiac, probably the most powerful sexual releaser known to man. . . . The union was not just your body and her body but all of your racial and evolutionary entities with all of hers. It was mythic mating." *Playboy* asked Leary if it was true that women could have multiple orgasms under LSD. He replied with a straight face, "In a carefully prepared, loving LSD session, a woman can have several hundred orgasms."

Huxley had warned Leary that those in authority would oppose him. In April 1963, with LSD selling for a dollar a dose in Harvard Square, the university fired Leary, ostensibly because he cut classes, but really because his work had become an academic scandal. A month later, Richard Alpert, his colleague and collaborator, was fired too. After Mexico bounced the pair as well, a young millionaire came to Leary's rescue by renting him an estate in Millbrook, New York, complete with a musty sixty-four-room Victorian mansion and imitation Bavarian chalets. For the next two years Leary quit proselytizing and presided quietly over a religious commune based on drugs. The atmosphere at Millbrook was distinctly Oriental, for Leary too had discovered the East. Indeed, in 1965 Leary traveled to India where, high enough on LSD to overlook the Himalayas, he translated (from English, of course) Lao Tzu's *The Way of Life*. He called this ancient Chinese classic a "time-tested psychedelic manual."

Things began to go wrong for Leary in December 1965. On his way to Mexico with his family for a holiday, he was detained at the border and arrested with his daughter for possession of two ounces of marijuana. (Leary said he was probably the first person ever caught trying to smuggle pot *into* Mexico.) There followed more arrests, trials, convictions, appeals. The Millbrook idyll over, Leary again went public, playing to the hilt his role of unrepentant felon and high priest of the psychedelic movement. In 1966 he announced formation of a new religious organization called the League for Spiritual Discovery (LSD). That fall he conducted services in the Village Theatre in New York, where for three dollars a ticket observers could enjoy a multimedia show and a sermon by Leary. After a successful three-month run, Leary took his show on the college circuit, telling audiences to turn on, tune in, drop out. Few lines of the sixties wore so badly.

LSD was a big story in 1966. Congress outlawed it. *Newsweek, Life,* and the *Saturday Evening Post* all did cover stories on it. Sandoz stopped selling it. And the Food and Drug Administration sent a letter to two thousand colleges warning of its "widespread availability" and "profound effects on the mental processes." Years before, Leary had estimated that one million Americans would take LSD by 1967. According to *Life,* the nation had reached the million-dose mark in 1966. As for Leary himself, his reputation among heads declined rapidly after he went show biz. Many of them were already too young to know that he had once been a serious man and that at the dawn of the Aquarian Age Timothy Leary had been the Johnny Appleseed of acid.

If Leary spread the psychedelic revolution, Ken Kesey created the psychedelic style, West Coast version. In 1959, three years before publication of his modern classic *One Flew Over the Cuckoo's Nest,* Kesey took LSD as a subject in a medical experiment, and for him, then and there, the doors of perception blew wide open. In 1964, with a group of disciples called the Merry Pranksters, he established a drug commune in rural La Honda, an hour's drive from San Francisco. One of the Pranksters was Neal Cassady. On acid, Kesey and friends experienced the illusion of self, the All-in-One, the energy field of which we are all an extension. They tried to break down psychic barriers, attain intersubjectivity or group mind, and achieve synchronization with the Cosmos. And they committed themselves to a life of Dionysian ecstasy.

The Pranksters were hip, but in a new way. They were not beaten disaffiliates, warring against technology land, cursing their fate that they had not been born black. In *The Electric Kool-Aid Acid Test,* a history of Kesey in the underground, Tom Wolfe described this new hip generation, these hippies, as products of postwar affluence. Their teen years were spent driving big cars through the California suburbs, believing, like the superheroes in their Marvel comics, that anything was possible. No spade cool for them, no Zen detachment, none of Leary's "set and setting." The Pranksters used LSD to propel themselves out of their skulls toward the outer edge of Western experience. Their style was the wacko style: lurid costumes, Day-Glo paint, crazy trips in Kesey's 1939 multicolored International Harvester school bus, complete with speakers, tapes, and microphones. It was lots of kicks, of course, but it was more than kicks. For Kesey was a religious prophet whose ultimate goal was to turn America, as Michael Bowen put it, into an "electric Tibet."

Toward the end of 1965 Kesey conceived a ritual appropriate for spreading his version of cosmic consciousness. He called it the acid test. Hooking up with the rock group the Grateful Dead, he experimented with multimedia shows so noisy and frenzied that, by themselves, they menaced reason. To make sure that no one missed the point, lots of free LSD was distributed, a legal act, since California did not get around to outlawing the drug until October 1966. The purpose of the acid test was to create an experience so Dionysian that revelers would overflow the bounds of ego and plug directly into the Cosmos. After Kesey tried out the acid tests in a dozen or so road shows on the West Coast, he headed for the big time.

On January 21–23, 1966, Kesey and the Merry Pranksters produced and directed the Trips Festival at Longshoremen's Hall, San Francisco. The timing was perfect. For more than a year teenage dropouts and disillusioned campus radicals had been drifting into the beat haven of Haight-Ashbury. They were on the verge of community, but not quite there, acid freaks in search of identity. At Kesey's festival the heads of the Bay Area discovered their numbers, came out in the open, and confirmed the wacko style. The estimated twenty thousand people who attended wore every variety of wild costume, including Victorian dresses, Civil War uniforms, four-inch eyelashes, serapes, Indian headbands. Live rock propelled dancers through an electronic chaos of strobe lights, movies, tape machines, and slide projectors. High above the hall, dressed in a silver space suit, directing the whole to get the parts into sync, was Kesey himself. A few days later he took off for Mexico rather than face the consequences of a second drug bust. But Kesey's place in the history of hip was secure, no one having done more to create the hippie style that he had now to leave behind.

V

The Dionysian impulse in the hippie counterculture was made up in equal measures of drugs, sex, and music—not jazz music but rock and roll. When hippies moved in, the black jazz bars on Haight Street moved out. Spade jazz was now as irrelevant to hip as spade soul. Rock had once been black music too, but was so thoroughly appropriated by whites that many hip kids never knew its origins. Rock originated in the 1940s as "rhythm and blues," an urban-based blues music played with electric instruments, pounding beat, and raunchy lyrics—music by blacks for blacks. In 1952 the legendary Cleveland disc jockey Alan Freed hosted the first rhythm and blues record show for a white audience, calling the music "rock and roll." The music caught on among teenagers tired of sexless, sentimental ballads, and soon white performers fused pop and country styles with rhythm and blues to create white rock and roll. That's what Elvis Presley sang when he emerged in 1956 to become the biggest star in pop history. From the beginning, rock and roll was protest music, protest against Tin Pan Alley, protest against parental taste, protest against instinctual repression. Music of the id, fifties rock and roll helped create a generation of cultural subversives who would in time heed the siren song of hip.

In 1958, when Elvis went into the Army, rock entered a period of decline. Meanwhile, the black sound that had inspired it was being assimilated anew by other talented musicians, this time in England, and it would return to America, bigger than before, with the Beatles. During their long years of apprenticeship, playing lower-class clubs in Liverpool and Hamburg, John Lennon, Paul McCartney, and George Harrison explored the roots of rock and roll, even as they slowly fashioned a style of their own. By 1963 that style had fully matured. No longer just another scruffy group of Teddy Boys playing electronic guitars, they had become well-tailored professionals with a distinctive hair style (Eton long), immense stage presence, the best song-writing team in pop history (Lennon and McCartney), a fluid sound, contagious vitality, and, above all, the irrepressible beat of rock and roll. That beat helped propel the Beatles to stardom in Britain in 1963 and created Beatlemania.

Within days of its release in the United States in January 1964, "I Want to Hold Your Hand" climbed to the top of the charts, to be followed quickly by "She Loves You" and "Please, Please Me." In February the Beatles themselves arrived for a tour that began with a sensational TV performance on the *Ed Sullivan Show* and continued before hysterical teen mobs in New York, Washington, and Miami. In April all five top singles in the United States were Beatles songs and the two top albums were Beatles albums. In July the first Beatles movie, *A Hard Day's Night,* amazed critics and delighted audiences with its wit and verve. Meanwhile that year Beatles merchandise—everything from dolls to dishcloths—was grossing over $50 million. Nothing comparable to Beatlemania had ever happened in the history of pop culture.

Unlike Presley or their British rivals, the Rolling Stones, the Beatles did not menace society. They mocked it. Insouciant, irreverent, flip, they took seriously no institution or person, themselves included. "What do you think of Beethoven?" a reporter asked at the Beatles' first American press conference. "I love him," replied Ringo. "Especially his poems." Treating the adult world as absurd, they told their fans to kick off their shoes, heed their hormones, and have fun. However harmless initially, the Beatles phenomenon contained the possibility of danger. The frenzied loyalty they inspired endowed the Fab Four with immense potential power—power to alter life styles, change values, and create a new sensibility, a new way of perceiving the world. But in the early days, as they sang their songs of teen love, that power lay dormant. When Ken Kesey attended the 1965 Beatles concert in San Francisco, he was astonished by the "concentration and power" focused on the performers. He was just as astonished by their inability to exploit them. "They could have taken this roomful of kids and snapped them," said Kesey, "and they would have left that place enlightened, mature people that would never have been quite the same again. . . . They had the power to bring off this new consciousness to people, but they couldn't do it."

The artist who first seized the power of rock and used it to change consciousness was Bob Dylan. Born Robert Zimmerman, Dylan tried on every style of teen alienation available during the fifties in Hibbing, Minnesota. Though he wanted to be a rock and roll star, he discovered on enrolling at the University of Minnesota in 1959 that folk music was the rage on campus. In 1961 Dylan arrived in Greenwich Village, the folk capital of America, determined to become the biggest folkie of them all. A little over a year later, he was. Audiences responded to his vulnerability, the nasal whine with which he delivered his songs, and lyrics so riveting they transformed the folk art. Immersing himself in the left-liberal-civil-rights ethos permeating the Village in the early 1960s, Dylan wrote folk songs as protest. He did not compose from the headlines, as other protest singers did. He used figurative language and elusive imagery to distill the political mood of his time and place. Gambling that a poet could become a star, he won big. Two weeks after Peter, Paul, and Mary recorded his song "Blowin' in the Wind," it sold more than 300,000 copies. Songs like "A Hard Rain's Gonna Fall" were hailed as true art. And his "Times They Are A-Changin' " became a generational anthem. It was no less appropriate for Dylan to sing at the 1963 March on Washington than for Martin Luther King to deliver a sermon there.

Meanwhile, the Beatles arrived and Dylan was listening. "Everybody else thought they were for the teenyboppers, that they were gonna pass right away," Dylan said. "But it was obvious to me that they had staying power. I knew they were pointing the direction of where music had to go." In July 1965 Dylan outraged the folk world by appearing at the Newport Folk Festival, no longer ragged waif with acoustic guitar, but as a rock and roll singer, outfitted in black leather jacket and backed by an electric band. That summer his rock single, "Like a Rolling Stone," perhaps the greatest song he ever wrote, made it all the way to number one.

Dylan took rock and made it the medium for cultural statement—folk-rock, the critics quickly labeled it. As his music changed, so did the message. Moving with his generation, Dylan now abandoned liberal politics for cultural radicalism. The lyrics he sang in the mid-sixties were intensely personal and frequently obscure, but taken together, they formed a stunning mosaic of a corrupt and chaotic America. It is a fact of no small social consequence that in 1965 millions of radios and record players were daily pounding Dylan's message, subliminally or otherwise, into the skulls of a generation. There was, for example, "Highway 61," which depicted America as a junkyard road heading for war; "Maggie's Farm," a dropout's contemptuous farewell to the straight world; "Desolation Row," which portrayed an insane society, governed by insane men, teetering on the brink of apocalypse; "Ballad of a Thin Man," using homosexual imagery to describe an intellectual's confusion in a world bereft of reason; and "Gates of Eden," a mystical evocation of a realm beyond the senses, beyond ego, wherein resides the timeless Real. After Dylan, a host of other rock prophets arose to preach sex, love, peace, or revolution. After Dylan rock and roll became a music that both expressed the sixties counterculture and shaped it.

Among those acknowledging their debt to Dylan were the Beatles. After Dylan, they too began writing songs for the cultural opposition, to which they became increasingly committed. The Beatles induced mystic ecstasies with LSD, discovered the music and religion of the East, even took an abortive pilgrimage to India to study Transcendental Meditation with the Maharishi Mahesh Yogi. In June 1967 they released *Sergeant Pepper's Lonely Hearts Club Band,* a musically innovative album placing them at the head of the psychedelic parade. ("I'd love to turn you on," John Lennon sang on the record's best cut.) Timothy Leary, after *Sergeant Pepper,* proclaimed the Beatles "evolutionary agents sent by God, endowed with a mysterious power to create a new human species."

In the view of some, this new human species had already emerged with the San Francisco hippies, who played their own brand of rock and roll. Literally hundreds of bands had formed in the Bay Area by the mid-1960s, but because no major company recorded there, they developed in isolation from the commercial mainstream. Hippie musicians were freaks who played for freaks, having no other purpose than creation of Dionysian art. They were contemptuous of the star system, top forty stations, giant concerts for idolatrous audiences, Madison Avenue hype. They played their music live in dance halls where the musicians could jam as long as they wanted, and the dancers dressed like rock stars. The songs they wrote celebrated drugs and sex, and the music they played was music to trip on. One rock critic described the San Francisco Sound as "revelatory roaring, chills of ecstasy, hallucinated wandering, mystico-psychotic wonder."

San Francisco's dance-hall craze began in the fall of 1965 when local promoters rented seedy halls to feature hippie bands like the Jefferson Airplane, Big Brother and the Holding Company, Quicksilver Messenger Service, and the Grateful Dead. After Kesey's Trips Festival in January 1966, the acid tests merged with the dances, institutionalized at weekend freakouts at the Fillmore and the Avalon Ballroom. The quintessential San Francisco band was the Grateful Dead, who had been on Kesey's trip and never got over it. "It wasn't a *gig*, it was the Acid Tests where anything was OK," the Dead's Jerry Garcia recalled. "Thousands of people, man, all helplessly stoned, all finding themselves in a roomful of other thousands of people, none of whom any of them were afraid of. It was magic, far out, beautiful magic." In June 1966 the Dead moved into a house in Haight-Ashbury, where they lived together, jammed free for the people, got stoned, got busted, and continued to seek that magic moment in their music when performers, audience, and Cosmos were One.

By the time of the Monterey International Pop Festival, June 1967, the musical energies that had been gathering in San Francisco for two years could no longer be locally contained. Some of the hippie bands performing at the festival got their first national exposure there; others had already succumbed to the lure of fat recording contracts. By summer the San Francisco Sound was making the city the new rock mecca and its performers the newest rock superstars. The big song on the top forty stations that season was the Airplane's "White Rabbit," psychedelic variations on a theme from *Alice in Wonderland,* ending with the command to "feed a head, feed a head." That summer, too, thousands of teenagers took literally Scott McKenzie's musical invitation, with its implicit promise of Dionysian revels, to come to "San Francisco (Be Sure to Wear Flowers in Your Hair)." Ralph Gleason, San Francisco's hip music critic, understood well the cultural significance of rock. "At no time in American history has youth possessed the strength it possesses now," he wrote. "Trained by music and linked by music, it has the power for good to change the world." Significantly, he added, "That power for good carries the reverse, the power for evil."

VI

By 1967 Haight-Ashbury had attained a population large enough to merit, at last, the designation "counterculture." The question was, where was this culture tending? A few days after the famous Human Be-In, the celebrities of the movement met on Alan Watt's houseboat off Sausalito to exchange visions of utopia. Watts summed up for the others the predicament of the West: rational, technological man had lost contact with himself and nature. Fortunately, Timothy Leary said, automation could now liberate man from work and enable him to live a simpler life. Feasting off technology, dropouts from megalopolis could form tribes and move back to the land. Yes, said Gary Snyder. Turn Chicago into a center for cybernetic technology and the rest of America into buffalo pasture. After a while, as life got simpler, "Chicago would rust away." Man's destruction of his natural environment would cease. Nuclear families would give way to communes or tribes, whose members would share food, work, and sex. Like the Comanche and the Sioux, members of these tribes would go off alone to have visions, and all who knew them would know them as men. Already in Big Sur, Snyder continued, kids were using A. L. Kroeber's *Handbook of the California Indians* to learn the art of primitive survival, to learn how to be Indians. Fine, countered Allen Ginsberg, "but where are the people going to buy their Uher tape recorder machines?" which were being used to record the conversation.

Ginsberg's was the authentic voice of Haight-Ashbury. Addicted to electronic amenities, hippies merely played at being Indians, satisfied to wear Navaho jewelry and feathers. They communed with nature by picking Golden Gate Park bare of flowers; their notion of tribal harmony was to let everyone "do their own thing." As love had supposedly done for the Hopi, so it would do for them: it would conquer all. Armed with "flower power," hippies would overwhelm their enemies and live a life of ecstasy on the asphalt pavements of urban America. Real Indians were not much impressed. In the spring of 1967, when Ginsberg and Richard Alpert met Hopi leaders in Santa Fe to propose a Be-In in the Grand Canyon, the tribal spokesman brushed them off, saying according to the *Berkeley Barb*, "No, because you mean well but you are foolish. . . . You are a tribe of strangers to yourselves." If not strangers to one another, the inhabitants of Haight-Ashbury were hardly a tribe. Something of their variety, as well as the contradictory currents swirling through the community, was revealed by the local notables.

Ron Thelin was an early settler who had moved into one of Haight-Ashbury's spacious Victorian homes and founded a commune. It occurred to him that the nascent drug community needed an information center, and so in January 1966, the same month Kesey staged the Trips Festival, he opened the Psychedelic Shop on Haight Street. Beginning with a small stock of books, records, and drug paraphernalia, Ron and his brother Jay built the most famous hippie business in America. Thirty other stores catering to heads opened in the neighborhood, formed a hip proprietors association, and looked to Thelin as their spokesman. Ron, meantime, branched out into journalism, becoming one of the founders of the psychedelic San Francisco *Oracle*. Ron's problem was that he was a capitalist in Bohemia, worse yet, a capitalist who made money. It did not matter that his business returned some of its profits to the people, dispensed vital information, and maintained a free meditation room. Lots of hippies thought everything should be free. Fatally for his peace of mind, Ron Thelin thought so too. To reconcile his ideals with his money, he indulged in fantasies of a Haight Street that would be a "famous dope center." Fine teashops would display large jars of marijuana and even real tea, and fine restaurants would serve organic or macrobiotic food, "all for free or trade." In the meantime, Ron made plans to give it all up and live like an Indian in New Mexico.

Augustus Owsley Stanley III was the legendary chemist who made the acid that made San Francisco famous. Timothy Leary called him "God's Secret Agent." He called himself "Owsley." Grandson of a former U.S. senator from Virginia, Owsley was a thirty-year-old dropout when he set up a lab near the Berkeley campus in 1964 and began mass producing high-quality LSD. Though he made a fortune, he was in it for more than money. It was Owsley who soaked a Bible with acid and smuggled it into a Berkeley jail for the spiritual benefit of the Free Speech Movement. It was Owsley who supplied the LSD for Kesey's acid tests, bought the world's most expensive sound system for the Grateful Dead, and passed out free LSD at San Francisco rock concerts. It was Owsley, most of all, and the estimated ten million doses he marketed that made possible the psychedelic revolution. After Sandoz stopped selling LSD in 1966, Owsley became the world's best source. Still, few could stand his companionship very long. A compulsive talker, he lectured incessantly on meat and showers, which were good, and vegetables and baths, which were bad. Haight-Ashbury tolerated him out of necessity and hoped, for its own selfish reasons, that he could stay out of jail, which for a remarkably long time he did.

Swami A. C. Bhaktivedanta, age seventy-one, was an Indian holy man who arrived in Haight-Ashbury in January 1967 to open the Radha Krishna Temple and recruit disciples. He had been in town only a short time when the leading San Francisco bands, playing "mantra rock," gave him a benefit concert at the Avelon Ballroom. The Swami was something of an oddity in the neighborhood since he frowned on drugs and sex, but had a solution to human misery that was sufficiently simple and exotic to assure him converts. Were each man to chant the Hare Krishna mantra, the Swami taught, he would find peace in himself and bring peace to the world, for Krishna consciousness was God consciousness. Soon his ecstatic monks, dressed in cotton, shorn of hair, were chanting the Hare Krishna not only in Haight-Ashbury but on city streets across America.

Emmett Grogan was perhaps Haight-Ashbury's most influential citizen. A veteran of gang wars in New York, a student of film in Italy, a draftee who was discharged from the Army in 1966 as a schizophrenic, Grogan found a home in the San Francisco Mime Troupe, which performed radical plays free on the streets. He also plunged into the city's drug culture. Grogan, however, was no ordinary head. During his first LSD session in 1965 it had come to him in a flash of illumination that property was theft. Joined by a few others from the Mime

Troupe, Grogan began issuing anonymous mimeographed essays to provide the Haight with some politics. He called his essays "Digger Papers," after the seventeenth-century English radicals who appropriated common land and gave their surplus to the poor. The Digger Papers attacked hip capitalists like Thelin for hypocrisy, the hip *Oracle* for pansyness, and the psychedelic transcendentalism of Swami Bhaktivedanta as "absolute bullshit." But action counted with Grogan more than words, because action was theater, and theater could alter consciousness by altering frame of reference. In October 1966 the Diggers announced that every day at 4 P.M., at the panhandle on Ashbury Street, they would distribute free food to anyone who wanted it. And every day for the next year, serving food they begged and food they stole, the Diggers kept their promise. They also opened a free store, at first called the Free Frame of Reference, and after it was forced to move, the Trip without a Ticket. Anyone could take what he wanted from a free store, and floor space was always available for stray runaways. When liberals gave money, the Diggers burned it. When someone asked who was in charge, he was told he was. The media loved the Diggers and portrayed them as a hip version of the Salvation Army. In truth, there was something sinister about them, especially Grogan. Paranoid, secretive, often violent, Grogan was an anarchist moved less by visions of the beloved community than by hatred of all authority. That, too, was a tendency lurking beneath the surface of Haight-Ashbury.

Chocolate George was the hippies' favorite Hell's Angel. The Angels were the notorious motorcycle gang that had been stomping and raping its way through California for years. Ever since Kesey had invited them to a party in La Honda in 1965 and pacified them with LSD, Angels and hippies had formed an uneasy alliance—outlaw Americans sharing a taste for costumes, drugs, and defying the straights. Indeed, Angels served hippies as a private police force. At free rock concerts in the park, the Angels guarded the stage in exchange for beer. When threatened by black toughs, hippies summoned Angels to the rescue. Sometimes they summoned Chocolate George, whose signature was a large hand forever clasped around a bottle of chocolate milk. Despite his greasy jacket with its death's head insignia, Chocolate George was something of a humanitarian, having worked twelve years as a mechanic at the Recreation Center for the Handicapped. He was also a man of honor. Once when the police arrested a fellow Angel, George tried to drag him from the paddy wagon, getting himself arrested too. Irate hippies marched in protest to the precinct station and raised bail money to get him out. In August 1967 Chocolate George flipped over his Harley-Davidson and cracked open his skull. After his funeral, Angels and hippies held a wake in Golden Gate Park. The Grateful Dead and Big Brother played music, beer flowed, and mourners pelted each other with shaved ice. It was a great party, except for the visiting biker who kicked an Angel's dog and disappeared under a pile of enraged bodies, not to be seen again.

By the summer of 1967 the Haight's bizarre cast of characters was performing for a national audience. This was the summer when *Time* described the neighborhood as "the vibrant epicenter of the hippie movement," hippies estimated their full-time population nationwide at 300,000, imitation Haight-Ashburys bloomed throughout urban America, acid rock dominated the music charts, prestigious museums exhibited psychedelic posters, and doing one's own thing became the national cliché. Once school ended, San Francisco expected one to two hundred thousand kids to flood the city for the Summer of Love. But the real story that summer, unreported by the media, was that few of the thousands who did come stayed very long. Haight-Ashbury was already dying.

Its demise, so similar to the demise of hippie ghettos elsewhere, resulted from official repression, black hostility, and media hype. In San Francisco where city fathers panicked at the prospect of runaway hordes descending upon them, police began routinely roughing up hippies, health officials harassed their communes, and narcotics agents infiltrated the neighborhood. Meanwhile, black hoods from the nearby Fillmore district cruised the streets, threatening rape and violence. Blacks did not like LSD, white kids pretending to be poor, or the fact that Haight-Ashbury was, in the words of a leftover beatnik, "the first segregated Bohemia I've ever seen." Longtime residents began staying home after dark. Finally, the beguiling images of Haight-Ashbury marketed by the media attracted not only an invasion of gawking tourists, but a floating population of the unstable, the psychotic, and the criminal. By the end of the year, *reported* crime in haight-Ashbury included 17 murders, 100 rapes, and nearly 3,000 burglaries.

In October 1967 community leaders staged a pageant called "Death of Hippie." By then the Free Clinic had closed, the Diggers had stopped serving food, and Ron Thelin had put crepe on the windows of the Psychedelic Shop and headed for Katmandu. While a country fiddler made music, a parade carried an oversized coffin, filled with hippie litter, through "Hashbury." Halting at the panhandle, mourners set the coffin on fire and danced a Dionysian dance. The Diggers bravely proclaimed that the Death of Hippie signaled the "Rebirth of Free Men." In truth, the vision of an acid utopia based on love and flowers was already in ashes.

Death of community [handwritten marginal note]

VII

Though Haight-Ashbury died, the counterculture did not. If anything, in the last years of the decade the potent mix of drugs, sex, and rock and roll seduced an even larger proportion of the young. But few of these hip rebels called themselves hippies or talked of flower power any longer. Norman O. Brown had envisioned a cultural revolution in which a Dionysian ego would become the servant of Eros. But in the Freudian metaphor, Eros had to contend with Thanatos. The danger always existed that by liberating one, hip would liberate the other also. Brown himself had warned, "Not only does Dionysus without the Dionysian ego threaten us with dissolution of consciousness; he also threatens us with that 'genuine witches' brew,' 'that horrible mixture of sensuality and cruelty' (Nietzsche again), which is the result of the Dionysian against the Apollonian." After the fall from the Haight-Ashbury paradise, Thanatos, not Eros, prevailed in the counterculture. Confronted by hostile police, hysterical parents, and implacable draft boards, the freaks abandoned the rhetoric of love for the politics of rage. They became willing cannon fodder for the increasingly violent demonstrations of the new left. And they routinely threw rocks at police, rioted at rock concerts, and trashed stores. The nightmare of the Dionysian witches' brew, of Dionysus without the Dionysian ego, had become reality.

As the decade closed, it became clear that drugs, sex, and rock and roll lacked intrinsic moral content. The acid prophets had warned from the beginning that LSD did not inevitably produce the God experience. God and the Devil resided together in the nervous system, Leary had said. LSD could evoke either, depending on set and setting. The streets of Haight-Ashbury, even in the best days, had been littered with kids who deranged their senses on drugs—only to experience spiritual stupor. A fair number ended their trips in hospital emergency rooms, possessed of one or another demon. Satanic cults were not unknown in the Haight. One of them, the Process, apparently influenced Charles Manson, a hippie who lived in the neighborhood in 1967 and recruited confused young girls and a few men into his "family." Manson was an "acid fascist" who somehow found in the lyrics of the Beatles license to commit ritual murder. As violence in the counterculture mounted, LSD became chiefly a means to pierce the false rationality of the hated bourgeois world. The always tenuous link between drugs and love was broken.

Neither was sex itself necessarily the expression of Eros unalloyed with death. Sex in the counterculture did not imply love between two people, but merely gratification of the self—ecstasy through orgasm. Typical encounters in Haight-Ashbury were one-night stands. Rapists prospered, and carriers of venereal disease shared it generously. Janis Joplin, the greatest white blues singer who ever lived and the authentic voice of sexual ecstasy in Haight-Ashbury, sang Dionysian hymns to sexual climax. But for Janis the orgasm was the god that failed. How was your vacation on St. Thomas? a friend asked a year before Janis died of a heroin overdose. "It was just like anywhere else," she said. "I fucked a lot of strangers." Even orgies in the Haight were charmless. The unsuspecting clergy of the Glide Street Methodist Church once volunteered their sanctuary for an arts festival sponsored by the Diggers, among others. There were art exhibits, a symposium on obscenity, and a rock concert. But, according to Emmett Grogan, there was also a drag queen in the vestibule, Hell's Angels gangbanging a woman dressed as a Carmelite nun, couples copulating on the main altar, and hookers servicing their customers "behind a statue of Christ with blood all over the front of it from a dude who had just got his head cracked during a scuffle." No doubt real love existed somewhere in the Haight. But the case of the sixteen-year-old girl who was shot full of speed and raffled off in the streets was closer to the dominant reality.

Rock and roll was the principal art of the counterculture because of its demonstrable power to liberate the instincts. At the Woodstock Music Festival, held one weekend in August 1969 at Bethel, New York, Eros ran wild. An incredible 400,000 people gathered on a farm to hear the greatest line-up of rock talent ever assembled in one place. Overcoming conditions that could conventionally be described only as disastrous, the crowd created a loving community based on drugs, sex, and rock music. But four months later at the Altamont Raceway near San Francisco, rock revealed an equal affinity for death.

The occasion was a free concern conceived by the Rolling Stones as a fitting climax to their first American tour in three years and the documentary film that was recording it. Altamont was a calamity. Because of a last-minute cancellation elsewhere, concert promoters had only one day to ready the site for a crush of 300,000 kids. Sanitary facilities were inadequate; the sound system, terrible; the setting, cheerless. Lots of bad dope, including inferior acid spiked with speed, circulated through the crowd. Harried medics had to fly in an emergency supply of Thorazine to treat the epidemic of bad trips and were kept busy administering first aid to victims of the random violence. The violence originated with the Hell's Angels. On the advice of the Grateful Dead, the Stones had hired the Angels to guard the stage for $500 worth of beer. Armed with loaded pool cues sawed off to the length of billy clubs, high on bad dope washed down with Red Mountain vin rose, Angels indiscriminately clubbed people for offenses real or imagined. Vibrations of fear and paranoia spread from them outward through the crowd. And yet, when the Jefferson Airplane did their set, they called the Angels on stage to pay them homage. Once a hippie band singing acid rock, the Airplane had moved with the times, expressing in their music the anarchic rage surging through the counterculture. The song they sang to the Angels was "We Can Be Together."

> We should be together.
> All your private property is target for your enemy
> And your enemy is me.
> We are forces of chaos and anarchy.

> Everything they say we are we are.
> And we are proud of ourselves.
> Up against the wall
> Up against the wall motherfucker.

Minutes later, when the Airplane's Marty Balin tried to stop an Angel from beating a fan, he himself was knocked cold.

At nightfall, after keeping the crowd waiting in the cold for more than an hour, the Rolling Stones came on stage. Many critics regarded the Stones as the greatest rock and roll band in the world. Ever since their emergence, they had carefully cultivated an outlaw image—lewd, sneering, surly—to differentiate themselves from their fellow Britons, the Beatles. Their most recent music, including, notably, "Street Fighting Man" and "Sympathy for the Devil," reflected the growing violence of the culture of which they were superstars. Now at Altamont there was Mick Jagger, reveling in his image as rock's prince of evil, prancing on stage while the Angels flailed away with their pool cues below. It was too much even for him. Jagger stopped the music more than once to plead for order; but when the Angels ignored him, he had no choice except to sing on. Midway through "Sympathy for the Devil," only a few feet from the stage, an Angel knifed a black man named Meredith Hunter to death. The moment was captured by camera and made the highlight of the film *Gimme Shelter*, which as much as any counterculture document of the time revealed Thanatos unleashed.

VIII

For a variety of reasons, after 1970 the counterculture faded. Economic recession signaled that affluence could no longer be assumed and induced a certain caution among the young. The Vietnam War, which did so much to discredit authority, rapidly deescalated. And its own revels brought the hippie movement into disrepute. Carried to the edge of sanity by their Dionysian revels, many of the once hip retreated, some to rural communes in New Mexico or Vermont, most all the way back to the straight world.

Not least among the reasons for the waning of the impulse was the ease with which the dominant culture absorbed it. Indeed, despite the generational warfare that marked the late 1960s, hippies were only a spectacular exaggeration of tendencies transforming the larger society. The root of these tendencies, to borrow a phrase from Daniel Bell, was a "cultural contradiction of capitalism." By solving the problems of want, industrial capitalism undermined the very virtues that made this triumph possible, virtues like hard work, self-denial, postponement of gratification, submission to social discipline, strong ego mechanisms to control the instincts. As early as the 1920s the system of mass production depended less on saving than consumption, not on denial but indulgence. Depression and war retarded the implications of these changes until the 1950s.

Unprecedented affluence after World War II created a generation of teenagers who could forgo work to stay in school. Inhabiting a gilded limbo between childhood and adult responsibility, these kids had money, leisure, and unprecedented opportunity to test taboos. For them the Protestant ethic had no relevance, except in the lingering parental effort to enforce it. When Elvis emerged from Memphis, hammering out his beat and exuding sexuality, the teen breakout from jailhouse America began. The next step in the process of liberation was hip.

But middle-class teenagers were not alone in kicking over the traces of Puritanism. Their parents too began reckoning with the cultural implications of affluence. Critics had attacked the hippies as hedonistic and narcissistic. By the 1970s social discipline was eroding so rapidly that fashion condemned the whole of middle-class culture as the "culture of narcissism." Parental discipline declined, sexual promiscuity rose along with the divorce rate, worker productivity fell, ghetto obscenity insinuated itself into standard speech, marijuana became almost commonplace, sexual perversions were no longer deemed so, and traditional institutions like the Army, the churches, and the government lost authority. At the same time, the impulse toward ecstasy found increasing expression in Oriental religion, the New Consciousness Movement, and charismatic Christianity. Dionysus had been absorbed into the dominant culture and domesticated, and in the process routed the Protestant ethic.

Cultural change had political implications. While liberals earnestly sought to purge capitalism of traditional problems like unemployment and poverty, a vocal minority of American youth regarded unemployment as a blessing and chose poverty as a way of life. In the short run, hippie scorn was one more problem complicating the life of Lyndon Johnson, who never could understand whatever happened to earnest youth. In the long run, though it proved ephemeral, the hippie movement was profoundly significant, portending as it did the erosion of the liberal values that had sustained bourgeois society, the character type that had been its foundation, and the ethic that had undergirded efforts to accomplish its reform.

*American soldiers in Vietnam often adopted
anti-war attitudes*

The Warriors

LOREN BARITZ

Not until the end of the Second World War did military affairs occupy more than a marginal place in the American economy and culture during a time of peace. Whenever a violent war had previously broken out, the armed services moved to the forefront of public consciousness. Military commanders of these successful engagements often rode on their accomplishments into high political office.

Since the 1950s, however, establishment of what has been called the national security (or warfare) state, has dominated many aspects of American life, not the least of all, the economy. The "military-industrial complex," to use Eisenhower's often repeated designation, continues to engage the interests of politicians and public alike. Significant figures in the public eye have rarely called for a sharp reevaluation of this situation. Even though American armed forces have not had a strong record of successful completion in major military operations since the Second World War, little serious thought seems to have been undertaken in Washington as to the need to reconsider not only foreign affairs but also the basic assumptions of Pentagon policy.

While the military has overcome minimal resistance in the near comic-opera invasions of the Dominican Republic and Grenada, the major engagements of the post-war era—Korea and Vietnam—have illuminated the shortcomings of policy, strategy, and tactics which have led to a stalemate in one case and defeat in the other.

The Vietnam War has led to a flurry of agonizing reappraisals—if not recriminations—of policy. However, there seems to be no clearly articulated *official* evaluation of what went wrong (or right) in Indochina. There have been many books, articles, speeches, television programs, and even court cases that have dealt with aspects of what is often referred to as the "Vietnam syndrome." Pro- and anti-war activists, active and passive duty military officers, enlisted personnel, doctors, nurses, and journalists have recounted their experiences. No consensus appears except that somehow, something went wrong. The disagreements concern *what* went wrong, and *where*. Was the fault in Washington? In Saigon? In the streets of America? In the rice paddies and hamlets in Vietnam?

Historians and political scientists have begun a serious attempt to put the Vietnam experience in perspective. None of these efforts are completely objective accounts, nor do they try to be. Each requires the author to accept certain assumptions which then guide the organization and interpretation of the factual data. Some of these studies take a very long view, looking back into the Vietnamese and American (and sometimes Chinese and French) past, seeking the roots of the struggle in age-old imperial conflicts. Other studies concentrate on the post-Second World War era of decolonization. Still others focus their attention strictly on the period of direct American military involvement. From all of these we seek and find enlightenment of one sort or another, but still find no answers.

Loren Baritz, of the University of Massachusetts, has written a book which is critical of American policy at every turn. The most novel section of his work, reprinted below, deals with the plight of the common soldier in Vietnam and, more importantly, with the policies of the Pentagon toward military officers. Baritz' exposure of the bureaucratic nature of the military and its impact on life and death remind us again of the wisdom of our nation's founders who so structured the government as to provide for civilian control over military affairs. Indeed, war is too important a matter to be left to the generals.

T he drafted grunts who humped the boonies came from all over America. Street-smart ghetto kids, raised in the basketball wars, became battlefield buddies with dewy farm kids from Minnesota, patriotic, wide-eyed innocents who choked up a little when they sang "God Bless America." Hispanics, passionately ambivalent about Anglo culture, fought and drank alongside their closest war pals, the steelworkers, gas station attendants, and high school dropouts who never had a steady job. The entire nation went or was sent to war, except for the rich, the middle class, the vast majority of college students, and individuals who objected to war, or who objected to that war.

After LBJ decided to send combat troops, and after the draftees were moved into combat, the Vietnam War was fought by working-class teenagers. The draft was designed to produce that result. The

THE WARRIORS   From *Backfire: A History of How American Culture Led Us into Vietnam and Made Us Fight the Way We Did*, by Loren Baritz. By permission of William Morrow & Company.

average age of the American soldiers in Vietnam was just over nineteen. In World War II, the average age of the GIs who were in for the duration was about twenty-six. It was said that the military brass understood that Vietnam was a teenage war, that the kids were unruly, and that there was not much that could be done about actually imposing discipline on these postadolescents, strong boymen who were juicers and drank too much, or were smokers on skag or pot, and were too irreverent to obey by instinct or tradition. The youth of the Viet grunts, the popularity of black English, and the metastasis of military jargon help to explain why this was the slangiest war ever recorded.

As in Korea, the army, navy, and air force rotated individuals out in twelve months, and, until 1969, the marines in thirteen. They were almost always replaced one by one by new meat, or twinks, or cherries, or FNGs (fuckin' new guys) who were twelve or thirteen months younger than they were on their DEROS (date eligible for return from overseas).

When these kids enlisted or were drafted, at least after the American invasion in 1965, they knew that the so-called crazies were protesting the war, running away to Canada, hiding in colleges. Many of these soldiers had not thought much about the war, disliked the long hair of the hippies, and were offended by TV pictures of braless young women. Like most of the rest of the nation, they rejected the war protesters without thinking much about the war. Some men enlisted to get a better deal than the draft offered, or to get a new start in their young lives, or because a close friend signed up, or to escape the family, or to see the world, or to combat Communism. Some did not know why they enlisted. For some, it was an article of faith that the President knows best, and when he calls, you go.

George Ryan enlisted after he graduated from high school in Virginia. He had only read girlie magazines, sports magazines, and racing-car magazines. "If Vietnam was such a mistake," he asked, "how come the leaders of our country, the wisest men we have . . . how come they sent us in? None of the doves I ever met had any answers to *that*."

A student of the army collected more of these reactions:

> I know one thing. Before I went in, my brother could kick my ass, but now he can't. . . . He ain't nothing no more.

> The only thing I used to read was sports. . . . So I didn't have any feelings one way or the other. I figured it was more or less right, because why would I be going if it wasn't right?

> I knew almost nothing about it. The war I thought was like they taught us in high school, you know, you're fighting communism, you know, it was just the good guys against the bad guys.

A majority of the kids who were drafted thought of the draft as an event like measles, a graduation, the weather, something that happened to people. Young men got drafted as their fathers had in earlier wars. Sometimes brothers were already in. You had to do it because it had been done before, and probably would always be done, and you had to take your turn. It was usually more intimate and domestic than patriotism, although occasionally that too played a role. More often it was an unwillingness to let someone down, to hold up your end, and to do the right thing, as that was defined in the family and in the small circle of good friends. There is not much soul-searching required to honor so simple an obligation. Someday you have to earn a living, probably marry and have children, pay taxes, but first you get drafted.

There were more enlistees than conscripts, but the draftees were especially vulnerable. They were more likely than the enlistees to find themselves in the shooting war. The draftees made up 16 percent of the battle deaths in 1965; in 1969, they were 62 percent. Draftees represented 88 percent of infantry riflemen in 1970. The army apparently considered the draftees disposable—throw-away, nonreturnable men.

The Vietnam draft was an ideal model of discriminatory social policy. It kept the middle class from creating political pressure on the war administrations. So the draft was biased by level of income. The higher the income, the less chance of being drafted, importantly but not exclusively because of educational deferments. Poor young Americans, white as well as black and Hispanic, were twice as likely to be drafted and twice as likely to be assigned to combat as wealthier draft-aged youth. The draft rejected many blacks, but it was more likely to accept poor men than richer men with the same qualifications, or the same lack of qualifications. As a result, poor black Americans were swept into the fighting war in disproportionate numbers. Economic class, even more than race, except that people of color were more likely to be poor, was what determined who fought and who died. In 1980, the VA commissioned a survey of attitudes about the Viet vets and concluded that "while minority Americans may have suffered a disproportionate share of the exposure to combat and combat fatalities, their suffering was the product not of racial discrimination, but of discrimination against the poor, the uneducated, and the young. . . ." General Westmoreland reported that the state with the highest number of deaths in relation to population was West Virginia.

Alongside the deferred students was a large body of boys who could not meet the military's minimum physical or mental standards, the group Secretary McNamara called "part of America's subterranean poor" when he announced Project 100,000. This was to be a program to rehabilitate 100,000 poor men a year so they could be accepted into the military. Allegedly, they would be trained to improve their skills, earn higher incomes for the rest of their lives, and receive veterans' benefits. However, the useful training never amounted to much, although several hundred thousand of them, 40 percent black, did fight in the rice paddies. They were called the "moron corps" by other GIs. Instead of training these men to meet the military's standards, the military lowered its standards for admission, but not for the training necessary for the desirable military jobs. Senator Moynihan, then the official guru about the black family, hailed the program because he said it would teach black men some self-respect. One army officer told a plainer truth: "I'd prefer a company of riflemen with fifth-grade educations over a company of college men anytime." *educated vs. uneducated ←4x more likely to be killed*

Education in this country is a badge of class. One study of Chicago neighborhoods found that kids from areas with low educational levels were four times as likely to be killed in Vietnam than those from more schooled neighborhoods. It was as if the war had been designed to digest America's victims, the men President Eisenhower called the "sitting ducks" for the draft. Class and education also shaped the experience of the young men who enlisted. Two staff officials of President Ford's clemency board showed that a college graduate who enlisted had about a 40 percent chance of being sent to Vietnam, while a high school graduate's chance was about 65 percent, and that of a high-school dropout was 70 percent.

Something of a price was also paid by the fortunate children—the future professionals—of the families who could afford to send their sons to college. After the war, James Fallows, a writer, described his own guilt in an article called "What Did You Do in the Class War, Daddy?" The draft lottery had assigned him a low number in 1969, when he was a senior at Harvard. To avoid the draft and the risks involved in draft resistance, he chose to get a physical deferment, "the thinking man's route." His physical exam was held at the Boston Navy Yard, and he and almost all his Harvard friends managed to flunk. As the students were delightedly leaving, another contingent of potential draftees arrived, this time from Chelsea: "thick dark-haired young men, the white proles of Boston." The new arrivals were fresh out of high school "and it had clearly never occurred to them that there might be a way around the draft." About four in five of the Harvard students were deferred; about four in five of the working-class men were sent to war. Mr. Fallows concluded, "We let the boys from Chelsea be sent off to die."

One general described the troops to a journalist, as invented by James Webb in a novel that tells a truth. A general asked who are the foot soldiers, and answered: "They are the best we have. But they are not McNamara's sons, or Bundy's. I doubt they're yours. And they know they're at the end of the pipeline. That no one cares. They know."

Combat troops in Vietnam were aware that the majority of their age group was beating the draft and they hated it. It made some of them feel like fools for being there while others stayed at home, in "the World," to prepare for careers, to party, or to struggle against the war the grunts were trying to fight. For instance, Steve Harper, a poor kid from Ohio, said, "The critics are pickin' on us, just 'cause we had to fight in this war. Where were their sons? In fancy colleges?" Some campus protesters disliked this inequality, but justified their privilege on the grounds that the war was immoral. They must have assumed that less well-educated victims of the draft thought it was moral. Some of the privileged young men argued that they were so talented, and already so well educated, that they would serve the nation best if they were left alone to pursue their careers as physicians, lawyers, executives, or professors. When graduate school deferments were ended in 1967, the Harvard *Crimson* editorialized that the new policy was "careless expediency" and "unfair to students."

General Westmoreland admitted that the draft was "discriminatory, undemocratic and resulted in the war being fought by the poor man's son." He believed that the antiwar movement on the campuses was caused by a "guilt complex" suffered by the beneficiaries of injustice. He also argued that the army had to lower its standards and commission "some marginal types" because ROTC was closed down by protests on many of the best campuses. Finally, he said that when college deferments ran out, the army suffered "an education inversion," with thousands of new privates with college and graduate degrees taking orders from less well-educated officers.

Of the 27,000,000 men who constituted the male half of the post-World War II baby boom and who were eligible for the draft during the war, 2,215,000 were actually drafted, while 8,700,000 enlisted. More than 500,000 more—the group Richard Nixon called "those few hundreds"—technically became criminals to evade or resist the draft. Approximately 16,000,000 had deferments, exemptions, or disqualifications. Of these two groups, millions had their lives changed because of the threat of the draft, the moral crisis of deciding what to do about it, and the terror that some experienced, or the isolation that many more experienced, in leaving the country or going underground to resist.

The set of circumstances the grunt could expect when he arrived in Vietnam is better understood now than it was at the time. The human risks of the war are clarified by the end-of-war figures: Altogether, about 58,000 men were killed, and about 300,000 were wounded, half badly enough to be hospitalized. Only the marines had more casualties in Vietnam (105,000) than in World War II (90,000). Of the 2,700,000 men who served in Vietnam, more than 500,000 received less than honorable discharges. That made jobs harder to find after they returned.

It was worse for American blacks. In earlier wars, black Americans had to struggle for the right to fight. Now, blacks comprised 11 percent of the population. One study showed that in 1966, only about 1 percent of draft-board members were black. Seven states had no blacks on draft boards. American discrimination against blacks prevented them from getting Vietnam assignments that would improve their skills. They were assigned to combat in proportions far exceeding their numbers, and this is one of the reasons why Martin Luther King spoke against the war, against the "cruel manipulation of the poor."

None of the foot soldiers could have been prepared for Vietnam, for the climate of the land or the climate of the war. When they climbed out of the chartered plane that sped them to Vietnam—unlike earlier wars when the slower troop ships allowed time for some adjustment to the coming realities—they were physically hit by the heat, by the sensation that here is where the war is. One Braniff pilot announced as he descended into Vietnam: "The temperature outside is one hundred and three degrees; groundfire is light to moderate." They were processed, assigned a place, and went off to find the war, or to let the war find them.

Sometimes the process was not quite so routine. The novelist Tim O'Brien wrote about the reenlistment officer who would show up just before the fresh and petrified GIs were sent out to their first fight. This officer explained that some of them were about to be killed: "It's gotta happen. One or two of you men, your ass is grass." If they would reenlist for another three years, he would reassign them from combat to a safe job in the rear. "Then what?" the re-up NCO asked. "Well, I'll tell you what, it'll save your ass." On that day, none of the men accepted his offer. *So ldiers are pawns.*

One of the patterns of the grunts' life in Vietnam, as in earlier wars, was the realization, always in a fire fight, that hey, this is real, that somebody is trying to kill me, really kill me, and I might never make it out of here. A combat sergeant: "The first time you were under fire, you thought, 'How the fuck can they do this to me? If only I could talk to the cocksuckers firing at me, we'd get along.' . . . We're just pawns in this fucking thing, throwing the shit at each other." In the midst of it, in the terror of a fire fight, most of the GIs realized that one way to survive was to kill first, or kill more, not in the interest of the grand abstractions of patriotism, or freedom, or strategy, but to survive.

Survival was the strategy of the American GI, not different from soldiers in earlier wars. But, for the great majority of Vietnam grunts, there was no external purpose to the war—not defending national goals, not resisting an evil enemy, not defending motherhood and apple pie. As a result, there was no animating justification for combat or for risk. The best way to survive was to keep away from danger. This absence of external purpose made it difficult for some to develop a sense of shared enterprise with other GIs outside their own unit. Because the replacements were inserted into the war as individuals, not as members of a unit, these GIs were in fact movable parts, separate cogs in the war's machinery. Such separateness induced a sense of fragility, probably more intense and widespread than in other wars. The separate arrivals and departures, along with the absence of shared purpose, emphasized the individuality of the grunt, even while they formed the life-saving bonds of brotherhood in their small squads or platoons. It is touching and painful to hear how often the veterans felt alone.

The grunt was the instrument of General Westmoreland's "strategy" of attrition. For entirely different reasons, the grunts' war plan became identical with the general's. There was no real estate that had to be taken and held, there were no objectives to be seized. The plan was to kill the enemy, wherever and whoever he or she was. Because the body count was the scorecard, killing supposedly proved progress. This made war sense from the grunt's perspective because it was simply based on the desire to live, not necessarily callousness or moral collapse, but war through the eyes of the walking conscripts.

That is why the "other war," the ideological war, meant nothing to most of them. It did not seem, at least in the short run, the time that really mattered, to protect their lives. So they mocked the entire effort to "win the hearts and minds" of the Vietnamese by referring to it as WHAM and embroidering it even further: "Grab 'em by the balls and their hearts and minds will follow."

Luis Martinez, a Puerto Rican marine, decided he would learn something about the Vietnamese and treat them with respect because "if the Viet Cong is going to do something, he remembers you and you have a better chance of surviving." In this sense, winning hearts and minds might help him to return home in one piece. It was like money in the bank that could produce interest in the future. But in this war's twists, respect and friendship for the Vietnamese could backfire. For example, a sergeant became friends with a Vietnamese woman and her daughter. They were both killed by the NLF because they had associated with him. He decided that from then on he would leave them all alone. For most, the "other war" would take too long, was out of focus, and was therefore not a good shield for the vital or fatal 365 days they would be targets.

The grunts hated bloody fighting to take a fire base, perhaps losing buddies in the process, and then being ordered to abandon the base to fight or patrol somewhere else, and then having to endure another fire fight to recapture the first base. Some bases were retaken three or four or more times. One GI put it this way: "We don't take any land. We don't give it back. We just mutilate bodies. What the fuck are we doing here?" It seemed senseless to risk everything over and over for the same piece of turf. There was no achievement to show for the mutilations and deaths. Except the numbers. They had to train themselves to think of achievement by the numbers. Many, probably most, could not do it. They could not think of what they were doing only in terms of the body count. Even in war, death was supposed to be for something, not a thing in itself.

They recognized that the body counts were being hyped to satisfy, or shut up, corrupt officers who kept demanding higher numbers. The men could deliver any number any REMF, "rear echelon mother fucker," wanted. Of course that made the killing even more pointless. If the brass would accept fake numbers, and if the whole point of the war was numbers, why risk your life to get real kills? The war could have been fought over the radio, with a squad or company reporting whatever number was wanted. That is what sometimes happened. The grunts knew it was fraudulent and they became contemptuous of their officers. For example, after one fire fight, Herb Mock, a rifle-squad leader, said: "General Westmoreland flew in. All the news outfits and everything. It was the most hilarious thing. As these son of a bitches came out there, the GI's started lying. The newsmen would walk up to just anybody and say, 'What did you do?' 'I singlehandedly killed three hundred thousand with my bowie knife.' " Lieutenant Robert Santos spoke for many when he said, "You come home with the high body count, high kill ratios. What a fucking way to live your life."

They thought it should have been done differently, and then we would have won. Some said that American power—tanks, planes, all the sophisticated equipment, and all the American men—should have been arranged in a line across Vietnam's southernmost rice paddies. Then they should walk north. One of the grunts said that whatever the GIs left behind them in this march would be something they *wanted* behind them. They should keep walking until there was nowhere left to walk within the country. Then the war would be over, and America would win. The trouble with this, of course, was that *they* would never let it happen, and the fighting around in circles, walking point through the same treeline over and over again, ambushing and being ambushed, hunting and being hunted, instead of real soldiering, would go on forever.

Real soldiering meant that you could capture a place and hold it. It meant a sense of progress, however slow and incremental, toward a known goal. After all, if you captured enough places, you could finally win the war. Many GIs were hugely unimpressed with complicated explanations about the fact that the NLF aimed to control people, not territory. The Vietnamese guerrillas were willing for the Americans to dominate the countryside during the day, approximately from nine to five, so long as they owned the night.

Some grunts were stunned by the open hostility of some South Vietnamese, the people they had come to defend. When they had to run up chicken wire to block the objects, including grenades, that some

South Vietnamese threw at them, there was no way they could avoid wondering what they were doing there. It was maddening to discover that the food or medicine they gave to friendlies would be handed to the guerrillas after dark. It was a shock to march past an aged mama-san selling Coca-Cola on the road and notice her head nodding as each grunt passed; she was counting them. What for? What could you make of the fact that the friendlies who washed your clothes or cut your hair were found dead in your ambush of the NLF during the night? And what about the mama-san who brought you things right into your fire base and hung around a little while so she could memorize where your bunkers were so the guerrillas that night could zero in with their mortars? What about the local whores telling you where you were going next, before your own officers had announced it? This war was not like others. You could never identify the enemy. That created constant danger, not merely at the front—there was no front—but everywhere, and not merely during a battle, but anytime. Any Vietnamese could be the one. A T-shirt worn by the grunts displayed the message: KILL THEM ALL! LET GOD SORT THEM OUT!

Having no larger external purpose, there were also often no external constraints. The line beyond which an action would become a transgression was a matter of individual conscience, a Protestant formula. This was as true for the officers as for the troops. The moral formlessness of the bureaucratic war necessarily emphasized technique and means, not goals or purpose. Bureaucracies typically do not do as well at expressing where they wish to go as they do at expressing how to get there. "If you're lost, drive faster; that way you'll get it over with sooner." This left the teenage warriors to their own moral devices, such as they were. Group pressures formed one code of conduct; a watchful officer might sometimes form another. Unlike earlier wars, the Vietnam rule was the moral independence of the foot soldier and his officers.

The rapid turnover of their immediate officers—usually every six months, often less—led to the conviction that the grunts knew better than anyone else, especially better than the six-month wonders, the shake-'n'-bake lieutenants, how to stay alive. These teenage warriors were therefore thrown back into themselves in a way unusual in war. They had to take care of each other if they were to make it. After a while they could wear earrings, write almost anything they liked on their helmets and flak jackets, shoot up on drugs, get drunk, and more often than not get away with it, especially when they were in the field, which everyone called Indian country. They enjoyed getting away with it, and hated "chicken shit officers" who worried about shined shoes; but getting away with it also taught some of them that the brass did not care, and that they were on their own both as a unit and as individuals.

Because of the differences between place and time, Vietnam was not a shared experience for the men sent there. Fighting in the mountains was different from the jungles, which was different from the rice paddies, which was different from the cities. The combat grunts, however, did share the experience of danger, perhaps of killing, and of witnessing pain and death. Fighting, for the relative few who actually faced the enemy was obviously far removed from the experiences of the majority, who sat out the war in the relative safety of the rear, with easy access to palatable food, the post exchanges, television, bars, and prostitutes. Among the amenities on American installations in 1971 were 90 service clubs, 71 swimming pools, 12 beaches, 160 craft shops, 159 basketball courts, 30 tennis courts, 55 softball diamonds, 85 volleyball courts, 2 bowling alleys, and 337 libraries.

Fighting before and after 1969 was markedly different. In 1967, General Westmoreland, with his usual jut-jawed cheeriness, reported to Congress that the GIs in Vietnam were "the finest ever fielded by our nation." He reported that the troops understood and believed in the war. When General Abrams took over, he could not share such optimism, partly because he was less of an overage boy scout, and partly because by then the GIs had changed. The college students now drafted, and black militants, were both capable of finding ways to do "their own thing" regardless of military "chicken regs." More important, however, Mr. Nixon's troop withdrawals drained any vestigal meaning from the war for those who believed in any meaning in the first place. The withdrawals signaled that there would be no American victory for the Americans still fighting. By the time Mr. Nixon became President, the new recruits had experienced the antiwar movement, the tougher phase of the civil-rights movement, as well as the antiauthoritarianism of the counterculture. Blacks had been deeply angered by the murder of Martin Luther King, Jr. The civilian lives of these new grunts had prepared them to be less docile than their predecessors, and the officers permitted such independence. By 1969, too much of the army officer corps had degenerated into a self-serving, dishonest, bureaucratic organization designed to exploit the troops for the personal advancement of the leaders. The result was chaos: drugs, desertions, mutinies, riots, atrocities, and murder.

My Lai 4 was a tiny village on the northeastern coast of South Vietnam, near the South China Sea. Shortly after 8:00, on the morning of March 16, 1968, Charlie Company of Task Force Barker, 11th Brigade of the Americal Division, entered the hamlet and massacred 347 civilian women, children, and old men. Some of the younger women were raped before they were murdered. At 11:00, the Americans took a lunch break. Charlie Company burned the entire village, killed the livestock, and destroyed the food and the wells. Lieutenant Colonel Frank Barker, Colonel Oran Henderson, and Major General Samuel Koster were in their separate helicopters watching some of the action on the ground. Later, these officers could not remember seeing anything wrong. One warrant officer, Hugh Thompson, Jr., threatened over his chopper radio that he would start shooting the GIs if he saw them "kill one more woman or child." On the same day, Bravo Company of the same task force murdered civilians in another bloodbath at My Khe 4, a few miles away from My Lai. The officers and men of the Americal Division lied to each other about what had happened, expected to be rewarded for doing so, and tried to hide the truth from the world. (Seymour Hersh won the Pulitzer Prize for reporting about My Lai.)

The Americal was a hodgepodge division, with an incompetent and demoralized senior staff that was afraid of the commanding general who insisted on elegant meals, engraved china, and movies after dinner. The officers' mess, preceded by a daily cocktail hour, was almost as elegant, and drove some of the grunts to fantasize about blowing up the mess hall. A lieutenant colonel's driver had to get his boss to "the Club" in time for the daily happy hour: "It was just like they were in Washington. They would talk about promotions and all that stuff—just like a cocktail party back in the world." There was nothing in the code of the bureaucracy that required the leaders of men to be uncomfortable. Following the example of the commanding general, all the senior staff officers air-conditioned their living quarters.

The division's procedures for fact-finding was a perfect example of bureaucratic self-protection. A field report of the death of a Vietnamese would not be investigated if it was reported as "combat-related." As Mr. Hersh described it, "The men who could declare such incidents as being combat-related were the officers in charge; in effect, their choice was between a higher body count or a war crime investigation." All the bureaucratic incentives drove men to lie. Truth might make you free, but without a promotion or a pension.

In the far reaches of bureaucratic hardening of the arteries, paper becomes more important than function. Establishing the correct paper trail, ensuring that guidelines and procedures are published and filed, replaces a concern with performance. Thus, the commander of Americal, along with most of his senior aides, later testified that "directives," letters, and memos had been disseminated that specifically prohibited indiscriminate burning of people's houses, called hooches, and urged humane and friendly treatment of civilians. General Westmoreland later said that "orders were clear. Every soldier had a card on how to treat an enemy in his hands." Having issued the appropriate paper, however, there was no attempt to enforce the rules.

The existence of the paper guidelines, along with the commander's introductory remarks to FNGs, was all that was considered necessary to satisfy the bureaucratic code of the army. Lieutenant General William R. Peers, in charge of the My Lai investigating panel, understood this point. In 1970, he wrote a secret memo to General Westmoreland, then the Army Chief of Staff, to explain that paper was not the same as function: "Directives and regulations . . . are only pieces of paper unless they are enforced aggressively and firmly throughout the chain of command." This was a direct challenge to the bureaucratic instinct, and as such could not be and was not a learnable lesson. Nothing happened.

The failure to enforce rules was always someone else's fault. The general had delegated enforcement responsibility to his executive, who did not follow through; the exec delegated it to the major who passed it on to the captains and lieutenants who, in turn, charged the sergeants with this responsibility. The result of this chain of delegation, buck-passing, was always the same: Finally the grunts became responsible for self-enforcement. General Peers acknowledged this routine by condemning it: "Commanders at all echelons are responsible for the actions and the welfare of all the men under them. A commander cannot delegate such responsibility. . . ."

More concern for issuing guidelines than for ensuring compliance also typified the high military command in Saigon. General Westmoreland issued more than thirty rules of engagement that were intended to define how and when to use American firepower. But 76 percent of the 110 generals who responded to a survey conducted in 1974 said that these rules were only "fairly well adhered to" or "not particularly considered" at all.

The massacres revealed a number of important facts. Frightened and frustrated adolescents who love their weapons are capable, if pressed hard enough, of going berserk. In the context of this war, it is astonishing that it did not happen more often. The investigations of the horrors also began to reveal that a part of the officer corps of the army had become corrupt, and that the army, knowing this, refused to face the facts, and failed, as they say in the bureaucratic trade, to take corrective action. When the Department of the Army investigated what had happened, when it began to learn the facts, it expanded the Americal Division's cover-up to include the entire officer corps. The army itself covered up, and still will not explain why it failed to press charges against all the officers who had been identified, and why it still will not release all of what it knows about that grisly day.

My Lai can be explained by the bloodlust of unsupervised boymen who could not tell the difference between friend and enemy, by the official demand for killing, sometimes indiscriminate as in the free-fire zones, and by cynical officers who intended to profit from high death reports. It had partly to do with the numbers racket. Keeping the war's score by the arithmetic of kill-ratios and body counts puts an irresistible premium on good numbers.

Many of the grunts understood what was happening, but did not care about the numbers. They would report whatever they had to report to keep the CO off their backs. They were often pressed into lying by greedy officers who had only a short time to make their mark, to be "blooded" in the only available war, and to get away from the fire field as soon as they had compiled an enviable record of kills.

The malfeasance of some senior officers, the hatred of the Vietnamese, the frustration of fighting an invisible enemy, the thwarted desire for vengeance or justice, released some individual GIs from whatever restraints, if any, they had brought to Vietnam. Some of these killers were encouraged, or were not discouraged, by their officers. One grunt, for example, not connected with My Lai, described himself:

> I had a sense of power. A sense of destruction. . . . In the Nam you realized that you had the power to take a life. You had the power to rape a woman and nobody could say nothing to you. That godlike feeling you had was in the field. It was like I was a god.

The possession of exciting weaponry that converted late adolescents into potent, godlike men also changed their moral codes. It released them from whatever inhibitions they may have brought to the war. Perceiving the Vietnamese as subhuman completed the release. They sometimes would "get even" because they could. They became free, autonomous, and dangerous. Such soldiers can exist only if their officers allow them to get away with metaphorical and literal murder.

The panel the army created to inquire into the My Lai murders asked Lawrence Congleton, a radioman who was there, whether it was usual to report body counts when no one had counted the bodies. The question was asked because the military reports from the scene of the action indicated no civilian deaths, only recognizable guerrilla fighters. The soldier explained, "You can't really take too much stock in what was put on the log or something like that, because it seemed like sometimes the commanding officers were like trying to write a movie script and make it read a little more juicy for the people that were going to read it." After the massacre, the radioman said that Captain Earl R. Michles told him "to make it look good." Richard F. Silva, also present at the command post on the My Lai morning, told the investigating panel that he did not care what numbers were reported over the radio. He took them all: "They could say two thousand were dead, you know. I could care less. . . . They can say whatever they want over their radios and everything else because from past experiences I knew it was a bunch of bull anyway."

While the blood was up no officer even tried to stop the murders at My Lai or My Khe. A review of the findings of the army's investigating panel led to the conclusion that fourteen officers should be brought up on charges, including Major General Samuel W. Koster, the commander of the American Division at the time of My Lai, who was then the superintendent of West Point. He resigned to protect the academy and gave a speech to the cadets which concluded with an implicit warning about the bureaucracy: "Don't let the bastards grind you down." The cadets honored him with a standing ovation, although several said they did not mean to support the general for his alleged crimes, merely to show solidarity, to show that they understood what it meant to get squeezed by the system. Yet one cadet, perhaps speaking for most, had the typical bureaucratic defensive reaction: "Such an outstanding career, all ruined to appease the media."

The others who were charged include another general, two colonels, two lieutenant colonels, four majors, two captains, and two first lieutenants. As it finally turned out, only Lieutenant William L. Calley was convicted, to the dismay of much of the nation. President Nixon wanted to intervene on the lieutenant's behalf, an action that was probably illegal. General Westmoreland believed that the army had been forced to accept such substandard men as Lieutenant Calley because the student deferments kept better men out of reach. Most of the charges against the others were dismissed without a hearing, but Major General Koster had to endure a long secret hearing before the charges against him were dropped. Several of the high-ranking officers, including Major General Koster, were demoted and stripped of selected decorations.

My Lai was investigated only because NCOs and grunts charged that something terrible had happened. First the officers in the field were forced by the men to stage an inquiry; then the Pentagon was forced to act for the same reason. Ronald Ridenhour, an ex-GI who had not been at My Lai, was the whistle-blower who forced the Pentagon to investigate. He testified before the investigating panel that the folklore of the army had changed: "That's the first thing that you learn when you go in the Army now. We didn't learn 'Don't volunteer,' we learned 'Cover your ass.'"

The members of the prestigious panel convened to hear the cases were not corrupt. Rather, these panelists viewed their charge through the prism of their lifelong habits and allegiances. Members of the Nixon administration wanted to assist in the cover-up, but, as General Westmoreland said, "I threatened through a White House official" to go to the President "and object. . . . That," he said, "squelched any further pressure for whitewash." The assumption of the panel was simply that what went wrong at My Lai was the result of the failures of marginal individuals who probably should not have been given command responsibility in the first place. They could not see, and probably should not have been expected to see, that the army as a bureaucratic institution was implicated.

When Sam Stratton, a pro-military congressman from upstate New York, heard that the charges had been dropped against Major General

Koster, he made an angry speech to the House of Representatives: "I am afraid that this is a case where the ground rules of the mythical WPPA, the West Point Protective Association, have taken precedence over the welfare of the nation and the fundamental right of the American people to know the facts: never mind what happens to the Army or to the country, just make sure we keep our paid-up members out of embarrassment and hot water."

The congressman had perhaps unwittingly stumbled onto an important truth revealed by the Vietnam War: In modern American bureaucratic organizations, military and others, the welfare of officers as individuals takes precedence over the objectives of the institution that pays their salaries, and that is the way the organization wants it, the way rewards and punishments are distributed. As thousands of grunts came to learn, this truth was an essential aspect of their Vietnam experience.

The foot soldiers learned that parts of the army officer corps as an institution had become corrupt in specific bureaucratic ways: Personal careerism collided with the army's own code of conduct. That code had become hollow, a source of bitter humor in thousands of foxholes. The corruption made some officers dangerous to their men, which helps to explain the mutinies, fraggings, and desertions. A lieutenant was told by his colonel: "I don't care what happens to your men, but I'm not losing any more God damn tanks." Field-grade officers—majors and up—were the carriers of the pathology, generally not the company-grade officers—the captains and lieutenants—many of whom fought and lived with the men, and many of whom were good soldiers. Many GIs hated their sergeants, lieutenants, and captains, too, but this was the more normal hatred of the officers immediately in view. It was the senior brass that was tarnished. The behavior of senior officers was a significant reason why the war was so demoralizing, so crushingly absurd.

The moral decay and increasing incompetence of the army's senior officers in Vietnam was minimally caused by personal failures of individuals, despite General Westmoreland's use of Lieutenant Calley in this way. The corruption in Vietnam was systemic and was caused by procedures within the army that had been borrowed from other American bureaucratic institutions, primarily industry.

When the army adopted the "up or out" model of personnel management soon after World War II, it assumed that if an employee is not promotable, he is not employable. That meant that individuals with long and useful experience, who had found their right rung on the bureaucratic ladder, could not be retained. Up or out always devalues experience and always demands change at the price of stability. Amer-

bcur → point of position us promotion not victory

icans seem unable to imagine an individual being satisfied by doing a job for which he is suited. We insist that job advancement must be perpetual. This constant upward swimming produced the bends, maybe not for the individuals concerned, but for the army as an institution.

Although the industrial bureaucratization of the army began in the 1940s, the extent of its corrosive damage was first made undeniable in Vietnam. What had happened was that a system of rewards was imposed on the military that changed the senior officer from a military leader into a bureaucratic manager. Many senior officers in other times and places led their men into battle, shared their risks, and were respected if not loved. Vietnam proved that men cannot be "managed" into battle. *"Men cannot be Managed into battle"*

Why should a bureaucrat risk his life to manage his men? When the code of the military was replaced with that of the bureaucracy, personal risk became not only meaningless, but stupid. If the point was promotion, not victory, risk was, as they say, counterproductive. The details of the army's definition of career management assaulted military logic, morale, and honor. The My Lai slaughter was a consequence of this deformation.

The bureaucratization of the army led to a definition of officers as personnel mangers and troops as workers. It was not clear why the "workers" should have risked their lives to follow the orders of the "boss" who was not at risk himself. This sort of corruption invariably starts at the top, with the big boss. In 1966, General Westmoreland reported in unashamed industrial language and with apparent pride, "[My troops] work, and they work hard. It has been my policy that they're on the job seven days a week, working as many hours as required to get the job done." Perhaps his bureaucratic instincts, as deep as any man's could be, had been reinforced by his stint at the Harvard Business School. Vice Admiral James B. Stockdale wrote that "our business school-oriented elite tried to manipulate rather than fight the Vietnam War."

General Westmoreland was America's senior personnel manager in-country, and that is how he thought of himself. He reported to the National Press Club that by 1967 the armed forces of South Vietnam had made progress. The first reason for this good news was: "Career management for officers, particularly infantry officers, has been instituted." The second reason was: "Sound promotion procedures have been put into effect." As a consequence of these and other "improvements," he concluded, "the enemy's hopes are bankrupt."

The peculiar swagger of Americans, as John Wayne personified it, had been changed from confidence born of competence and courage to confidence wrung from ignorance. Bureaucrats are planners, and they must always believe, or pretend very hard to believe, or at least insist they believe, in the effectiveness and wisdom of their plans. The result is the sort of arrogance that drains the oxygen from a room, that makes the bureaucrat-in-chief light-headed. For example, General Westmoreland had not one doubt: "We're going to out-guerrilla the guerrilla and out-ambush the ambush . . . because we're smarter, we have greater mobility and firepower, we have endurance and more to fight for. . . . And we've got more guts."

It is written that one should know one's enemy, that pride precedes failure. The general had insulated himself from reality, was unable to hear criticism, and seemed quite pleased with himself. He was America's perfect manager of a war. As a result he was more interested in procedures and public relations than content. He wanted to engineer appearances, not substance. Every reporter who listened to his Saigon briefings understood that it was a shell game. Evidently, he himself had no idea that this was so.

Under the leadership of General Westmoreland and the rotating Chiefs of Staff, the military bureaucracy became so top-heavy that it lost its balance. There was a higher percentage of officers in the field during the Vietnam War than in other American wars, and higher than in the armies of other nations. At its peak the percentage of officers in Vietnam was almost double what it had been in World War II. In 1968, there were 110 generals in the field in Vietnam. In absolute terms there were about as many generals, admirals, colonels, and navy captains in Vietnam as there were at the height of World War II. There was a lower ratio of officer deaths than was true earlier and elsewhere. Of the seven generals who died, five lost their lives in their helicopters. There was a higher ratio of medals distributed to officers, especially as the combat began to wind down, than ever before.

Colonel John Donaldson's Vietnam career is illustrative. In 1968, he was given command of the Americal Division's 11th Brigade, which a few months earlier had sent Lieutenant Calley's platoon into My Lai. The colonel replaced Colonel Oran Henderson, who would be acquitted of the charge of a My Lai cover-up. In his first six months of command, Colonel Donaldson "earned" an "average of about one medal a week: two Distinguished Flying Crosses, two Silver Stars, a Bronze Star Medal for Valor, twenty Air Medals, a Soldier's Medal, and a Combat Infantryman Badge." He was soon promoted to brigadier general and won nine additional Air Medals and two Legions of Merit, and was transferred to the Pentagon as a strategist. During the My Lai investigation it was thought that to protect his predecessors he had destroyed key documents needed by the investigators. He denied this. In 1971, he was the first American general charged with a war crime since about 1900. He was accused of "gook hunting," shooting Vietnamese from his helicopter. He was acquitted.

In 1962, military promotion decisions had been centralized under the Chiefs of Staff. Thereafter, the military became a bureaucratic promotion machine. Meanwhile, the grunts continued to slog through the paddies and jungles. Many of them knew that something was rotten. By 1967, combat troops made up 14 percent of the troops in Vietnam; in World War II it was 39 percent; 34 percent at the end of the Korean War; and, 29 percent in 1963. Approximately 86 percent of the military in Vietnam was not assigned to combat. At the height of the buildup in 1968, when there were about 540,000 military personnel in Vietnam, 80,000 were assigned to combat. The rest, the other 460,000, constituted the grunts' enormous category of REMFs.

It is probably true that never before, in the military or anywhere, had bureaucratic officials so enthusiastically served their own interests to the detriment of the objective they were supposed to accomplish. The managerial corps finally lost to dedicated troops in black pajamas.

As the officers blamed the politicians, many grunts blamed the officers. Bruce Lawlor, a CIA case officer, knew what was happening: "The only thing the officers wanted to do was get their six months in command and then split back to the States and be promoted and go on to bigger and better things. It doesn't take long for the average guy out in the field to say, 'Fuck it!'" Or, as another example, a colonel sent troops into action without telling them (to make sure they would not evade a fight) that they would encounter an enemy base camp. Herb Mock, an infantryman who walked point on that mission, later went to find the colonel: "You made us walk right into the ambush. That's a sorry goddamn thing to do. You ain't worth shit as an officer." Herb Mock's best friend was killed in the ambush.

The army itself recognized that something was wrong. In 1970, General Westmoreland ordered the Army War College to conduct an analysis of the officer corps. The study was so damaging that he at first had it classified. What had happened, in the language of the Army War College study, was that, "careerism" in the officer corps had replaced the ethic of the officer. Careerism means that personal advancement replaces the desire to get the job done. In fact, the "job" *is* personal advancement. (This helps to explain the cheating scandals at the service academies.) Bureaucratic employees get paid to get promoted.

In April General Westmoreland ordered the commandant of the Army War College to study the moral and professional climate of the army. Although he did not believe that the army was suffering a "moral crisis," he directed the study to focus "on the state of discipline, integrity, morality, ethics, and professionalism in the Army."

In the study's preface, Major General G. S. Eckhardt, Commandant, simply stated, "This study deals with the heart and soul of the Officer Corps of the Army." The study involved interviewing about 420 above-average officers, an extensive questionnaire, and many group discussions. As a result, the study concluded that "prevailing institutional pressures" had created a divergence between the ideals and the current practices of the officers corps. "These pressures seem to stem from a combination of self-oriented, success-motivated actions, and a lack of professional skills on the part of middle and senior grade officers." The officers participating in the study described the typical Vietnam commander: "an ambitious, transitory commander—marginally skilled in the complexities of his duties—engulfed in producing statistical results, fearful of personal failure, too busy to talk with or listen to his subordinates, and determined to submit acceptably optimistic reports which reflect faultless completion of a variety of tasks at the expense of the sweat and frustration of his subordinates."

[handwritten margin note: Describes typical Viet. commander]

Many of the officers involved in the study agreed that the cause of this breakdown was that the army itself had "generated an environment" that rewarded trivial and short-run accomplishments to the neglect of significant achievement and the longer-term health of the army. The cause was not the "permissive society" at home, or the antiwar and antimilitary protests, but the army itself.

The study reported that junior officers were better officers than their own commanders, and that the younger men "were frustrated by the pressures of the system, disheartened by those seniors who sacrificed integrity on the altar of personal success, and impatient with what they perceived as preoccupation with insignificant statistics." A captain was quoted: "Many times a good soldier is treated unfairly by his superiors for maintaining high standards of professional military competence." A colonel said, "Across the border the Officer Corps is lacking in their responsibilities of looking out for the welfare of subordinates."

An important conclusion of the study was that moral failure and technical incompetence were closely connected. Incompetence seemed to come first and the need to cover it up created the thousand techniques for lying, passing the buck, and avoiding responsibility. The study acknowledged that such behavior was army-wide: "signing of false certificates; falsification of flight records; condoning of the unit thief or scrounger; acceptance by middle and upper grade officers of obviously distorted reports; falsification of . . . trips for self gain and the attendant travel pay; hiding of costs under various programs; hiding AWOLs by placing them on leave to satisfy commander's desire for 'Zero Defect' statistics."

The army's emphasis on quantification (a disease it caught when Secretary McNamara sneezed) meant that success was defined only by what could be measured. This was partly caused by the computer craze and resulted in the application to the army of "the commercial ethic." This contributed to two unfortunate consequences: ignoring characteristics that could not easily be expressed in numbers, such as leadership, and emphasizing activities that could be measured, such as

"savings bond scores and the reenlistment rate." Officers were promoted for doing well in these "programs," while they were not reprimanded for failures in areas that the computers could not be
programmed to measure, such as duty, honor, country. One captain
complained: "The fact that my leadership ability is judged by how many
people in my company sign up for bonds or give to the United Fund
or Red Cross disturbs me." (One noncom told me that his superior in
Vietnam always forced him to buy bonds, but encouraged him to cancel as soon as the good report went out.)

This definition of what mattered to the army as an institution suited
the careerist officers who were in "the business" to make a good living.
One captain described his battalion commander as a man who "had
always his mission in mind and he went about performing that mission
with the utmost proficiency. His mission was getting promoted." A
major exploded: "The only current decorations I admire are the DSC
and Medal of Honor, all others are tainted by too often being awarded
to people who do not deserve them. . . . Duty, Honor, Country is
becoming—me, my rater, my endorser, make do, to hell with it." Another major was a little more relaxed: "My superior was a competent,
professional, knowledgeable military officer that led by fear, would
doublecross anyone to obtain a star, drank too much and lived openly
by no moral code." This "superior" was soon promoted and got his
first star.

The Army War College study revealed how the officers derived
bureaucratic lessons even from My Lai. Officers got into trouble at My
Lai because they found no AK47s, Soviet-made rifles carried by both
the guerrillas and by the North's army; that made it difficult to claim
that all the villagers were combatants. "This exposure to My Lai . . .
it has driven some of the units to carry AK47s around with them so
that if they did kill someone they've got a weapon to produce with the
body."

When General Westmoreland read the study he proclaimed it a
"masterpiece," and restricted its distribution to generals only. As a group
they had quite substantial reservations about its conclusions. General
Westmoreland did, however, write a number of letters to inform the
officer corps that integrity was important. That was the most significant result of this remarkable study. Young Pentagon officers formed a
group called GROWN: Get Rid of Westmoreland Now.

Vietnam was the only available war for upwardly mobile officers,
and if they failed to get an assignment in Vietnam, called getting their
ticket punched, their careers would be thwarted. This infected the officer corps from top to bottom, beginning even before the West Point
cadets graduated. For example, James Lucian Truscott IV arrived at

West Point in 1965, where he hoped to follow his family's tradition of soldiering:

> When I was 22 years old I was pretty well convinced from having officer after officer—major, lieutenant colonel, full colonel—come and tell me, personally or in front of a class, "You've got to go to Vietnam and get your fucking ticket punched. The war sucks. It's full of it. It's a suck-ass war. We're not going to win it. We're not fighting it right, but go and do it." You know, "Duty, Honor, Country" had suddenly become "Self-Duty, Honor, Country."

A year after he graduated from West Point, Mr. Truscott resigned his commission rather than go to Vietnam.

For the office warriors, Vietnam was a marvelous opportunity to get ahead in the world. According to marine General David Shoup, some of the generals and admirals hoped to deepen America's involvement in Vietnam to speed promotions. But such motivation was not a sufficient reason to risk getting hurt or killed, or even to suffer through the war in more discomfort than was absolutely necessary.

Among the Vietnam generals he surveyed, Brigadier General Kinnard found that 87 percent believed that careerism was "somewhat of a problem" or "a serious problem." Careerist officers would not take risks in combat or in their relations with their superiors. Risk could lead to error, and a single mistake noted on an officer's efficiency report could ruin his career. This produced an equivalence of error, from incorrect table manners at "the Club" to a failure of judgment in combat. An instructor at the Command and General Staff College, said this of the rating procedure: "The system demands perfection at every level—from potatoes to strategy. It whittles away at one's ethics."

When every glitch, however petty, might end up as a black mark on the rating sheet, officers of course trained themselves to be passive, to keep quiet, and to worry more about pleasing those above them than those below. Carried to an extreme in Vietnam, the rating system produced an even conformity of thought, a religion of pleasing superiors, a very high price on dissent, and a comfortable tour for the three- and four-star generals who were not rated. Careerism inevitably forced officers to think of their subordinates as their most important resource for making them look good, to protect their "image" on paper.

Career management and sound promotion procedures, as General Westmoreland described them, motivated the bureaucratic colonels and generals who observed the war, if they observed it at all, safe in their helicopter offices fifteen hundred feet above the danger. They claimed they needed to be in the air to see the bigger picture, so as not to lose perspective by the more limited horizons of the earthbound warriors. Sometimes this was true, but the grunts hated it. Whether it was necessary or not, the chopper always gave the officers an opportunity to have the desired combat experience without the risks of combat. The availability of helicopters meshed perfectly with the imperatives of ticket-punching. Field commanders, especially lieutenants and captains, resented it also, but for obvious reasons they were less outspoken. For the grunts, the appearance of the colonel's chopper was a reminder that they and not he might get blown away. He would not be late for the happy hour at the Club, while they would remain in the field with another meal of C-rats. It reinforced a class hatred that was, in its pervasiveness, probably unique to the Vietnam War. Mike Beamon, a navy antiguerrilla scout—he called himself a terrorist—said it all: "I was more at war with the officers there than I was with the Viet Cong."

The length of time an officer in Vietnam served in a combat assignment was not a matter of established military doctrine. It was a rule of thumb of the commanders in the field. Although there were exceptions, and although some officers served more than one tour, the expectation of a twelve-month tour, even for officers, set the outer limit of a combat assignment. In 1968, the systems analysts in the Office of the Secretary of Defense studied the length of time officers served in combat. They found that the typical combat command of a maneuver battalion or a rifle company was "surprisingly short." More than half the battalion commanders, usually lieutenant colonels, were rotated out of combat command in less than six months. More than half the company commanders, usually captains, were relieved before they completed four months. One of the reasons for so short a command tour was reported in a secret document prepared in the Office of the Deputy Chief of Staff for Personnel in 1970: "Career personnel have greater opportunity for career development and progression. . . ." With short assignments more officers could get their tickets punched.

After 1970, 2,500 lieutenant colonels each hoped to command one of the 100 battalions, 6,000 colonels wanted a command of one of the 75 brigades, and 200 major generals wanted to get one of the 13 divisions. The competition for one of these assignments was fierce, and the office politicking was everywhere. As they got the right punches, the right assignments, the officers' careers flourished. Of the men who were considered for promotion to major, 93 percent succeeded, as did 77 percent to lieutenant colonel, and 50 percent to colonel. Colonel David Hackworth understood what was happening:

> We had all the assets to win this war. We had half a million troops, unlimited amounts of money and the backing of the administration. No doubt we could have won if we'd had commanders who knew how to use these assets, instead of these amateurs, these ticket punchers, who run in for six months, a year, and don't even know what the hell it's all about.

There were two important consequences of these short command assignments: Officers did get the "experience" required for their promotions; and the men under their command were killed in higher numbers
because of their commanders' inexperience. The systems analysts discovered that a maneuver battalion under a commander with more than
six months experience suffered only two thirds the battle deaths of
battalions commanded by officers with less than six months of experience. The average command lasted 5.6 months. The analysts discovered that a battalion commander with less than six months experience
lost an average of 2.5 men a month; those with more experience lost
1.6 men a month. In their technocratic, economistic, deyhdrated view
of the world, the analysts explained that "the rate of battle deaths is a
measure of the cost of success." They wanted a "cheaper price."

The analysts also found that the length of experience of a company
commander reduced the battle deaths of his troops. The average command was just under four months. These officers were themselves killed
at a higher rate than more experienced officers, a rate that rose in each
of the first four months, and that dramatically dropped by two thirds
in the fifth month, from which point it remained low and stable. In the
first four months, about 4 percent of these officers were killed; afterward, 2.5 percent were killed. "This implies," the systems analysts
concluded, "that a company commander could be left in office 6 more
months, for a total of 10, without incurring an additional risk as great
as that to which he was exposed during his first 4 months command."
Nonetheless, they were "relieved" (perhaps in several senses of that
word) in four months so that another green commander could step
onto the promotion escalator, and two thirds of them were sent out of
combat to staff positions. The typical captain in Vietnam had three different "jobs" during his twelve-month tour in Vietnam. The companies
commanded by officers with less than five-months experience had an
average of .8 killed in action each month; those with more than four
months lost .6 KIA, a drop of 25 percent.

As usual, the military was not delighted by the work of the Whiz
Kids. As usual, the military argued that the systems analysts did not
understand war. The deputy chief of staff for operations concluded,
"Our commanders in the field can best judge the length of time an
officer should remain in command of a unit in combat." The brass on
the spot had not "arbitrarily" set the average command assignments at
six months and four months. These periods of time were selected because "we know from experience that a commander begins to 'burn
out' after a period in this hazardous and exacting environment." After
the typical time in command, and after burnout, "the commander is
not fighting his unit as hard as he did during the first few months of
command when he was full of snap, zest and aggressiveness and eager
to destroy the enemy."

The analysts were unimpressed by the Pentagon's argument. They claimed there was "no data" to prove that commanders burn out. Their conclusion was ominous: "We cannot prove its existence and we suspect that the present rotation policy may be based more on considerations of providing a wide base of combat experience than on the 'burn out' factor."

The military headquarters in Saigon obviously had to join this argument, to "rebut" the analysts. MACV acknowledged that there was a "learning curve" for battle commanders, contested the statistical reliability of the figures used, and insisted that the analysts had failed to understand that battles vary in intensity. The analysts agreed about varying intensity, but added that "regrettably, data are not available," presumably unavailable in Saigon as well as Washington. They did not believe this was a serious point because their study covered so many areas of combat that differences would cancel each other out. They agreed that more information would always be helpful and might have produced different results. "But we doubt it. It was our view (and MACV confirms this) that more experienced battalion commanders are more effective: on the average fewer of their men get killed in combat."

The American military establishment took pride in its effective adoption of "sound business practices." But, on the question of the duration of command, the military borrowed from no one. There is no other institution that transfers its leaders before they can learn their jobs. There is also no other institution in which the price of ignorance is the death of other people. One scholar compared the time in office between military officers and business executives and found that military officers with less than one year's experience was 46 percent of all officers; the comparable figure for executives was 2 percent. Military officers with five or more years of experience were 6 percent of the total; 88 percent of business executives had that much experience. There were reasons why the military moved its people so quickly, but the development of competence and the safety of the troops were not among them.

General Westmoreland uncharacteristically said, "It may be that I erred in Vietnam in insisting on a one-year tour of duty. . . ." But, as he reconsidered the possibility of an error, he concluded that longer tours would have been "discrimination against officers" and would have added to his difficulties in getting enough junior officers from OCS and ROTC. Perhaps, he said, an eighteen-month tour would have been "a workable compromise." He did not mention the fate of the GIs.

Yet, every sane observer of the rotation system agreed that it interfered with conducting the war. The Army War College study of the careerism of officers cited the short tour as a major factor in the deformation of the code of officers. Careerism, it said, can be diminished "by building mutual trust and confidence, and loyalty that comes from being in one assignment long enough to be able to recover from mistakes; and to have genuine concern—as a practical matter—about the impact which expedient methods will have on the unit next year." After questioning and interviewing hundreds of officers, this study pointed out that the army had not questioned its promotion policy "for some time," and had simply continued to make the assumption that moving officers through the wide variety of jobs required for promotion was a sound policy. "The implications of this assumption," the study said, "are so far-reaching that possibly no single personnel management concept—save that of the uninhibited quest for the unblemished record—has more impact on the future competence of the Officer Corps."

Before a company commander learned his job he was sent elsewhere. Before an intelligence officer could establish all his contacts he was sent elsewhere. There was no way the military could learn from its experience. That is what John Paul Vann, a distinguished officer who had resigned in disgust from the military, meant when he said that America did not fight a ten-year war, but rather ten one-year wars. For the officers the spin was even faster. Experience obviously could not accumulate. Lessons could not be learned. It was not only a teenage war, but a war in which no one had time to become seasoned or wise. There was no institutional memory, and with every year's rotation, the war began anew, with staff trying to hold up "the old man" who always had the power of command.

It was thus a teenage war led by amateurs. The GIs did not complain, of course, about serving "only" one year, but some of them knew, as Thomas Bird, a grunt with the 1st Cavalry, admitted:

> Toward the end of my tour, when I started knowing what I was doing in the jungle and started knowing what to do under fire, it was just about time to go home. I'm going to be replaced by a guy who is as green as I was when I got here, and by the time he gets good at it he's going to be replaced by a guy who is green. It's no wonder we never got a foothold in the place.

Keeping the war's score by counting bodies, an index imposed by Washington, was made to order for careerist officers. They could and did distinguish themselves by reporting more bodies than their competitors. One general later concluded that the body count was "gruesome—a ticket punching item." Another said, "Many commanders resorted to false reports to prevent their own relief," that is, to prevent someone else from replacing them and getting ahead by filing more acceptable reports. Another general said, "I shudder to think how many of our soldiers were killed on a body-counting mission—what a waste."

When a career depends on the reported height of a pile of bodies, several sorts of decay result. Once, when the men of Charlie Company engaged the enemy, their lieutenant called for a helicopter to evacuate the wounded. "To hell with the wounded, *get those gooks,*" the lieutenant colonel radioed back from his helicopter above the action. The lieutenant turned to see his machine gunner firing at the commander's chopper.

Having instituted a process that rewarded cheating, the bureaucratic bosses simply denied that it could have happened. Most (61 percent) of the generals in Vietnam knew that the statistics were snake oil, but none complained in public. They were wedded to the system. For example, in 1973, some of the majors at the army's Command and General Staff College at Leavenworth asked the commandant to permit a discussion of the ethics of officers in Vietnam. According to a reporter:

> One general was saying that he was right on top of things in his units, that no one would dare submit a falsified report there. A young major stood up and said, General, I was in your division, and I *routinely* submitted falsified reports. The General's response was, When you speak to a general officer, stand at attention.

The most senior officers, "Old Bulls," then at Leavenworth rejected what they called this "moralistic streaking." It is an iron law of bureaucracy that the higher one is in the organization, the more optimistic one is. How could it be otherwise? If one is in charge, things must be working well. A corollary is that the more senior one is, the more one is subject to the disease of being hard-of-listening. This law and its corollary may also partly explain General Westmoreland's constant assurances that things were working out satisfactorily, and that a solution would come soon. It seems reasonably clear that he really believed his own crooning. It is extremely difficult for the chief administrative officer of an organization to think that someone else would have done a better job. The Old Bulls at Leavenworth were not different from senior supervisors in Saigon, Washington, or anywhere else where bureaucracy is a settled fact of life.   *Defending Bureaucratic Army*

Some defenders of the bureaucratic army argue that the problem in Vietnam was caused by the disorganization of American society at the time. They say that the pool of men from which the military had to draw was inadequate for military purposes. The "permissive society," the availability and use of drugs, and, most of all, the collapse of respect for authority throughout American culture apparently produced some officers who were not up to the military's legitimate expectations of correct conduct. The conclusion to this argument is that something did go wrong in Vietnam, but it was the fault of American culture, not the military.

The most careful work on this subject was done by two former officers, Richard Gabriel and Paul Savage. They argue that it was the army itself, not permissive American society, that produced the Viet-

nam officers' conduct. They show that earlier armies had always enforced conduct separate from contemporary fashions. That is what the
military must do, and formerly had done, because it is a unique institution. It cannot function if its style of command, leadership, and even
management is responsive to changing social fashions. The necessary
characteristics for an officer in combat has no useful civilian analogy.
Combat is unique. The army must train soldiers to perform specific
functions regardless of any set of social circumstances.

The Army War College study itself asserts that the failures were
inside the military and not a result of any "defects" in American society. It also concluded that the antiwar movement had no discernable
impact on the quality or motivation of "officer material." If the crisis
was, and is, internal to the army, the solution must also be. Yet, those
who rose to the most senior levels of military command were precisely
the bureaucrats who benefited by the corruption. The army's own study,
in stunning bureaucratic language, acknowledged that for this very
reason, reform was unlikely: "The fact also that the leaders of the future are those who survived and excelled within the rules of the present system militates in part against any self-starting incremental return
toward the practical application of ideal values." That is to say, reform
must and cannot be internal.

The grunts understood that they were endangered by the guerrillas, the regular army of North Vietnam, and their own temporary, rotating officers, in no particular order of threat. They knew that the
home front did not support what they were doing. If no one cared
about them, they could not care about the rules or established authority. Occasionally, around 1970, grunts would scribble UUUU on their
helmets: the unwilling, led by the unqualified, doing the unnecessary,
for the ungrateful. Other helmets proclaimed POWER TO THE PEOPLE,
KILL A NONCOM FOR CHRIST, or NO GOOK EVER CALLED ME NIGGER. It was
finally as if all they could believe and remember were pain and death.
One young man from the Bronx, for example, was cited for heroism:

> They gave me a Bronze Star and they put me up for a Silver Star.
> But I said you can shove it up your ass. I threw all of the others
> away. The only thing I kept was the Purple Heart, because I still
> think I was wounded.

A wound is the most intimate souvenir.

It cannot be surprising that the grunts found ways to resist corrupt
officers in a war that could not be understood. Desertions, excluding
AWOLs, in the army alone rose from 27,000 in 1967 to 76,634 in 1970,
a rate increase of 21 per thousand to 52 per thousand. The marines
were even worse at 60 desertions per thousand. According to the De-

partment of Defense, the rate of desertion in Vietnam was higher than in either Korea or World War II, and the rate increased as the intensity of the fighting declined and absurdity increased. As President Nixon began withdrawing troops, many of the grunts remaining on the ground lost even more conviction about why they should stay and fight. The desertion rate from 1965 to 1971 increased by 468 percent.

Fragging, defined as an attempt to murder by using a grenade, reached astonishing levels in Vietnam. It was usually a result of the fear and hatred felt by the workers toward their bosses. For example, marine Private Reginald Smith testified in a court-martial that his lieutenant was so slow in setting up a listening post that by the time he sent three marines out, the NLF was waiting and killed two of them. The troops were discussing the incompetence of this lieutenant just before he was killed by a fragmentation grenade. It was frequently said that combat squads raised a bounty to be awarded to anyone who would "waste" a particularly hated officer. The Criminal Investigating Department of the Third Marine Amphibious Force said there were more than 20 fraggings in eight months of 1969, according to the transcript of a court-martial. The Defense Department admits to 788 fraggings from 1969 to 1972. This figure does not include attempts to kill officers with weapons other than "explosive devices," such as rifles. Richard Gabriel calculated that "as many as 1,016 officers and NCOs may have been killed by their own men," but he points out that this figure includes only men who were caught and tried. There is no precedent in American military history for violence against officers on anything like this scale.

Another response of the "workers" was to "strike," that is, to disobey a combat order, that is, to commit mutiny. The Pentagon kept no records of mutinies, but Senator Stennis of the Senate Armed Forces Committee said that there were 68 mutinies in 1968 alone.

Yet another form of resistance by grunts was the pandemic use of hard drugs. In the spring of 1970, 96 percent pure white heroin appeared in Saigon; by the end of the year it was everywhere, sold in drugstores and by Vietnamese children on street corners. This junk was so pure and cheap that the troops smoked or sniffed, with only a minority reduced to injection. Its use was not remarkable in Vietnam because smoking was usually a group activity, accepted by almost everyone, and common for clean-cut midwestern boys as well as for city kids. Nothing in all of military history even nearly resembled this plague. About 28 percent of the troops used hard drugs, with more than half a million becoming addicted. This was approximately the same percentage of high school students in the States who were using drugs, but they were using softer stuff. In Vietnam, grass was smoked so much it is a wonder that a southerly wind did not levitate Hanoi's politburo.

The failure of senior officers is partly reflected in the fact that they knew what was going on and did nothing to stop it, and did not protest. Richard Gabriel and Paul Savage concluded that "the higher officer corps was so committed to expedience that the organized distribution of drugs was accepted as necessary to the support of the South Vietnamese government, which often purveyed the drugs that destroyed the Army that defended it." The CIA and the diplomatic corps in Vietnam prevented other governmental agencies from getting at the truth, while individuals with the CIA, if not the Agency itself, helped to fly drugs into Vietnam from Laos.

Despite an occasional attempt to do something—usually punishing the troops—about the blizzard of skag, neither the U.S. government nor the military ever accomplished anything worth mentioning. The much advertised urine testing (to be conducted in what the GIs called The Pee House of August Moon) was ineffective because the tests were unreliable, the troops who were not hooked could flush their bodies before the tests, and no one was prepared actually to help the soldiers who were addicts. One scholar concluded that "in not rooting out the sources of heroin in Laos and Thailand, the government had simply made a calculation that he continued political and military support of those groups profiting from the drug traffic was worth the risk of hooking U.S. soldiers." General Westmoreland, as usual, blamed everyone but his own senior officers: "The misuse of drugs . . . had spread from civilian society into the Army and became a major problem. . . . A serious dilution over the war years in the caliber of junior leaders contributed to this. . . ."

Racial conflict was suffused throughout the war, from 1968 until the end. Every service, including the previously calm air force, had race riots of varying magnitude. As some of America's cities burned, or rather as the ghettos in some cities burned, the domestic rage found its counterpart in the military. Fraggings were sometimes racially motivated. One battalion commander said, "'What defeats me is the attitude among the blacks that 'black is right' no matter who is right or wrong." One black soldier said, "I'd just as soon shoot whitey as the VC." In one incident that is what actually happened: Two white majors were shot trying to get some black GIs to turn down their tape recorder.

White officers were sometimes offended by expressions of black solidarity, including ritual handshakes, the closed fist, swearing, black jargon, and, especially, blacks arguing that they were being forced to fight "a white man's war." (The North Vietnamese and the NLF often tried to exploit that theme through various forms of psychological warfare.) The weight of the military justice system was lowered on black GIs far out of proportion to their numbers. The congressional Black Caucus did a study in 1971 that showed that half of all soldiers in jail

Blacks treated unfairly

were black. The next year, the Defense Department learned that blacks were treated more harshly than whites for identical offenses. The occasional race riots were invariably triggered by the increasing militance of American blacks in general, the peculiarly obtuse social attitudes of many older military officers, the frustrated hopes of the Great Society, the sense of an unfair draft, and an unfair shake in Vietnam.

Trying to make it to DEROS, that miraculous day one year after they had stepped foot onto Vietnam's red soil, the foot soldiers did what they could to survive the guerrillas or North Vietnam's army or their officers. For most of them, the point of the war was the clock ticking toward the shortening of their time, and, finally, the last day, the wake up call, and home. Others, in a daze of battle, tried to put home out of mind. Many others, probably most, became increasingly cautious as their "sentence" wore down, and the ingenuity expended by the short-timers in avoiding combat, occasionally simply by threatening a hard-drive officer, was inspirational, almost enough to revive the American dream of self-reliant citizens. No one wanted to die with only hours, or days, or weeks, or months, left to serve. No one wanted to die in any case, but it was even more unbearable to think about with only a short time to go. The idea of home, the idea of making it, became increasingly real as the war became increasingly surreal.

They left Vietnam as they came, suddenly, by air, usually alone, and engulfed by impressions and anxieties that were too cascading to sort out. "We went to Vietnam as frightened, lonely young men. We came back, alone again, as immigrants to a new world," William Jayne, a marine rifleman, wrote. "For the culture we had known dissolved while we were in Vietnam, and the culture of combat we lived in so intensely for a year made us aliens when we returned." They were aliens for a great variety of reasons, some because they had grown up while their former buddies who had not gone to Nam seemed as if they had been frozen in time; they were still late adolescents whose lives revolved around six-packs, cars, and chasing girls. Others because they were stunned by the nation's refusal to welcome them home as returning warriors. Others because of the continuing pain of flesh and memory. Yet others because the war had destroyed their earlier faith in "the World," in American institutions.

Important — Returning Home

The men recorded in *Charlie Company* each had his own trip home, some burdened by uncontrollable anger, flashbacks, and nightmares. Most returned relatively smoothly. Many did not. Thomas K. Bowen thought when he got home that the entire war had been a "mistake," and said, "I mean I have no—absolutely no—respect for my government." Still others could not get jobs, and some resented the women and the nonvets who were working. Joe Boxx finally decided that "bein' a Vietnam vet didn't mean shit." Skip Sommer had re-upped to survive, but finally could not endure the army and deserted; he eventually gave himself up and was later dishonorably discharged. He was a haunted, enraged man even twelve years later. But, he said, "I don't remember anything I really am ashamed of, besides the fact that I survived." Alberto Martinez was losing his mind and in despair killed himself. Edmund Lee became an expatriate in Australia. Frank Goins, back home in south Georgia, remembered the democracy of races in the foxholes, but discovered, "When we got home, they still didn't want us to go to Mr. Charlie's cafe by the front door. . . ." David Brown was not even given the usual four or five days off the line at the end of his tour; one day he was in combat and the next night the freedom bird landed him in San Francisco. He drank too much for a year or two. Charles Rupert said: "I risked my life for my country, and now nobody gives a shit. If I have a son, I won't let him go. I'll send him to Canada first." J. C. Wilson: "We were fools."

On the other side, Lieutenant Robert Kennish, a commander of Charlie Company: "I did pretty well. No problems at all, really, that are going to afflict me for the rest of my life. I think I gained more from my experience in the military and in Vietnam than I lost." What mattered to him most was that he grew in his own self-esteem as a man. An anonymous veteran grunt said that he simply grew up in the war. David Rioux, a devout Catholic who was blinded in the war, understood and approved the war as a struggle against Communism, one that he was proud to have fought. Michel, David's brother, fought in David's company and feels that David's faith prevented him from committing suicide. David said about himself and his brother: "We both knew why we were in Vietnam, and the men around us didn't, for the most part, or saw it only confusedly, but we saw why we were there and we were proud to be there, defending a people who were being oppressed by Marxist Communism. We were doing something that was commendable, in the eyes of God, our country and our family."

The stereotypes at loose in the nation when the troops began returning were largely shaped by the reports of My Lai as well as television reports of the heroin nightmare. Many Americans assumed the returning vets were junkies. Some vets were persistently asked how it felt to kill a human being. All the vets were subjected to an embarrassed national attitude about the war, and about their role in it. It got worse when the North overran Saigon, and television showed the pictures of the scramble to evacuate the remaining Americans. Then the question became even more insistent: What did we accomplish by fighting? For the veterans who had believed in the cause, Saigon's surrender was a terrible blow. Both the Rioux brothers, along with other traditionalists, believed that "giving up" was the mistake, not intervening in the first place. For the others, those who had decided the war .

was not worth fighting while they were fighting it, the fall of Saigon confirmed their opinion. In any case, the veterans faced an unprecedented social and political fact when they finally made it back: The nation did not know what to do with them, and would just as soon forget, or try to forget, the entire sorry "episode." None of the vets could forget.

They were not only not welcomed home, some of them were abused for their uniforms, their decorations, and their short hair. There was a revealing false rumor that antiwar critics were shooting vets as they climbed out of their planes. It is a mass delusion, of course, but thousands of vets claim that they were spat upon when they first arrived home. (The return of the Iranian hostages, with symbolic yellow ribbons all across the nation, with ticker-tape parades and presidential attention, brought it all back for thousands of them. It proved, once more, that only prisoners are recognized. Something was wrong.)

Most of the veterans returned home reasonably whole, as whole as returning veterans from earlier wars. The majority were not dopers, did not beat their wives or children, did not commit suicide, did not haunt the unemployment offices, and did not boozily sink into despair and futility. Yet, some prisons are still populated with black vets; the VA hospitals still do their bureaucratic thing too often and fail to help. Some vets, more than a decade later, have not yet recovered, and some never will. The government has done less for these veterans than for those of other wars. The vets had to build their own monument. Now they are struggling to force the reluctant government to face up to the hideous question of the degree to which our war technology had poisoned our own men with Agent Orange. More than a decade after most of them had come home, the government in 1984 began to make small progress in admitting its responsibility in this issue.

Nonetheless, the majority returned home and found there was life after Vietnam. Tim O'Brien, a former grunt and prize-winning novelist, thought the adjustment was too good. He feared that the vets' experience was becoming too mellow, too nostalgic. He had hoped their recoil from war would have been more of a brake on national saber-rattling. He wished they could have retained the passion and convictions that sustained them while they were boonie-rats. He wrote, "We've all adjusted. The whole country. And I fear that we are back where we started. I wish we were more troubled."

When some grunts in Vietnam heard the news that the war was over, everyone began shouting. "They were ecstatic." One of them finally asked, "Who won?" They were told the NLF won. "They didn't care."

The growing political activity of religious conservatives, such as the Moral Majority led by Rev. Jerry Falwell, has been marked by successful campaigning for favored candidates.

The Rise of the New Evangelicalism

DONALD MEYER

No phenomenon in domestic politics has aroused more interest than the recent organization of Protestant evangelicals as a conservative voting and lobbying bloc. Aided by spokesmen such as Jerry Falwell and Pat Robertson, groups such as the Moral Majority and Christian Voice, worked furiously to support the election of Ronald Reagan in 1980 and 1984. Even though the president has disappointed many in his evangelical constituency by soft-pedaling certain conservative social programs (anti-abortion laws and prayer in public schools, for example), he has retained their allegiance with his virulent anti-communism and reduction of welfare benefits.

It is a mistake, however, to assume that this new evangelical movement is in fact new. What it is is an old movement organized in a new way. Protestant evangelicalism developed out of the Great Awakening of the eighteenth and early nineteenth centuries. Reacting against the rigid and formal Puritan tradition, the evangelicals stressed a heart-warming and life-transforming conversion experience (being born again) as forming the only basis for an authentic Christian life. Although the awakening affected almost all denominations, the primary beneficiaries were the Methodist and Baptist churches which soon after became and have remained the largest Protestant groups in America.

Through an extensive network of home missionary and Bible societies, evangelicalism sought to conquer the whole of the growing United States for Christ. Accepting the constitutional mandate for the separation of church and state, these evangelicals worked towards the establishment of Protestantism as the unofficial state religion. Another important part of the evangelical program in the nineteenth century was their views against Catholicism. Genuinely fearful of a Roman Catholic takeover of American political and religious life, evangelicals sought to restrict Catholic immigration and the participation of the foreign-born in politics.

However, do to the current resurgence of evangelical participation in political organizations, many Roman Catholics have associated themselves with evangelical Protestants in order to incorporate several elements of the new conservative social agenda. Liberals (both Jewish and Protestant) and secular humanists are seen as the major impediments to the establishment of Christian civilization as the basis of American nationalism.

Twenty years ago, Donald Meyer, of Wesleyan University, published a study of the "positive religion" tradition in American life. Meyer dealt with such movements as New Thought and Religious Science and religious figures such as Joshua Liebman, Fulton Sheen, and Norman Vincent Peale. In a 1980 reissue of this work, Meyer added a chapter on the new evangelicalism which is printed below. Evan though this selection was prepared before the political resurgence of evangelicalism mentioned previously, it explores the condition of American religious culture which enabled this movement to reemerge. By charting the decline of liberal religion and focusing on such disparate evangelical figures as Jimmy Carter and Oral Roberts, Meyer sets the scene for developments which may take him and many Americans by surprise.

EVANGELICALISM AS POLITICS

If the true faith of Americans was a "civic religion," a "religion of America," Bicentennial Year 1976 challenged the ingenuity of orators, politicians, philosophers, historians, and, certainly, preachers. Watergate and the forced resignation of a President had left the "bully pulpit" empty, for despite agreement on the amiable honesty of the caretaker in the White House, he was not sensed as a voice for the nation. The national stage was unusually empty of ordained spokesmen. No prophet had succeeded Reinhold Niebuhr. Norman Vincent Peale, Fulton Sheen, and such as Joshua Roth Liebman no longer sold their millions of manuals. Billy Graham, the one major survivor from the fifties, still touring endlessly, had wounded himself, probably mortally. From the start, Graham had divided his word. "Awake, for the End is near," he had proclaimed, as had countless premillenialists before him, but at the same time he had always promised fruits in the here-and-now from being born-again. The here-and-now had nearly smothered the prophecy in his association with Richard Nixon, and Nixon's fall exposed the narrowness of Graham's social imagination. In Minneapolis and Wheaton, his mighty ecclesiastical machinery continued to turn over but increasingly with the effect of something automatic, on momentum. Of course, the one great prophet prepared by the sixties, free of all tired echoes from the fifties, Martin Luther King, who would have been only fifty-five, in his prime, at Bicentennial, had been stolen.

No confident declarations of secular identity were heard. No one could plausibly claim a happy birthday for rational Jeffersonian America. During the sixties, several liberal optimists, both in and outside the church, had discerned salvationary vitalities at work in the very "counter-cultures" then conspicuous, among environmentalists, ecologists, commune experimentalists, at Woodstock or at Haight-Ashbury, in black ghettos or in the anti-Vietnam movement. The year 1968 could seem a dawn, its confrontations holding the promise of liberating debate. Harvey Cox, the most notable religious interpreter of these secular phenomena, nicely held in suspension the "religious" question whether these vitalities testified to the "immanence" of God "in" American history or to the "grace" of a "transcendent" God still willing to re-visit American history despite its lapses. Liberal religion's determined search for reasons to hope had itself been stimulating, but by 1976 few if any of its signs any longer seemed convincing.

Perhaps this void was "sacred," however, in Paul Tillich's sense, a moment ready to be filled just because it had been so emptied, a moment for re-birth. Perhaps Bicentennial Year could be celebrated as "the Year of the Evangelical." Evangelicalism's leading magazine, *Christianity Today*, celebrating its own twentieth birthday, agreed, in a lead article by its senior editor, "The Year of the Evangelical '76." The National Association of Evangelicals, another post–World War II institution, held its annual convention in the Capitol, there addressed by the President and observed, questioned, analyzed, and reported by more journalists than had ever before attended upon evangelical affairs. Two acute observers, both Catholic, and therefore somewhat "outside," Garry Wills and Michael Novak, both opined that evangelical Christians had become the largest single element in American religious life. Media collaborated, *Time, Newsweek* and *The New York Times* each devoting major stories to something labeled the evangelical surge. Notable personalities were available for journalistic focus: Charles Colson, born-again in the ashes of Watergate; Eldridge Cleaver, saved from race hate; numerous athletes; the sister of the Democratic party's nominee for President, a proven divine healer; Marabel Morgan, converting anti-feminism into positive womanhood; and, of course, the Democratic nominee himself, soon President-elect. Statistics were available for the credulous. A bicentennial Gallup Poll indicated 50 million adult Americans—one-third the total—self-professed as born-again (one among them George Gallup, Jr., himself).

Such evidences could be—and were—taken to prove a crisis in old middle-class mainline Protestantism. All the old denominations appeared to be struggling, losing members, money, seminary candidates, in the same vortex, evidently, that was draining Roman Catholicism. No longer were Methodists, their once popular, democratic flair long cooled into respectability, the largest church. Twelve million strong, the Southern Baptists had taken a huge lead. Most sensational seemed the growth of churches long regarded as a kind of fringe on the Joseph's coat of American Protestantism, holiness, and pentecostal groups of various origins, white and black. One holiness-penticostal healing preacher, Oral Roberts, had risen, out of the obscurity that had surrounded the dozens of itinerant charismatic preachers for decades, into national visibility. The irrelevance and decadence of mainline Protestantism, so often proclaimed in the sixties by men like Cox and Episcopal Bishop James Pike, appeared confirmed, if not exactly in the way they had anticipated.

No doubt, ingredients of myth were mixed in all this. *Christianity Today's* editors, for instance, displaying professional skepticism, took pains to publish studies showing that at least 4 million of the 12 million Southern Baptists didn't seem to be living where the church rolls said they should be. And Gallup's 50 million: Why was it Americans still reported rates of religious attachment more like those of third- and fourth-world people than of other developed modern nations? Did polls somehow miss some important measure of meaningfulness in those multitudinous protestations of piety and faith and regeneration? As for being a "largest element," evangelicals still seemed adept at the infighting they had always displayed; the mighty Missouri Synod Lutherans, for instance, were slowly tearing themselves to pieces in remarkably reminiscent arguments over Bible "inerrancy." So at the very least evangelicals were not a united cohort, nor as numerous, probably, as some hoped. Yet altogether the signs did testify to a reality of some shape and of considerable dimensions that made worthwhile the efforts of observers to guess what it meant. But by far the most interesting efforts to figure out what it meant were those of the self-conscious leaders of evangelical apologetics themselves. If they could not be sure, who could?

The first "evangelical" explanation was essentially a temptation rather than a real reading of the times. Evangelism's temptation in shapeless America had always been to heighten anxiety as a cause for faith. Instead of trying to figure out the patterns of hope, evangelism won quicker results from proclaiming "the end is near." In the strictest sense, such premillenial evangelists—including Billy Graham—did not have to think badly of the world in order to insist upon the imminence of its end, but if only to preserve simplicity in the message they usually sought, as "signs" of the end, evidences of decadence, breakdown, and wickedness. Evangelicals had no particular difficulty in finding such signs in 1976. For many of them, the signs of hope made out by liberals in the sixties had already seemed signs of imminence, and the seventies brought confirmation. Some of these remained general. Technology and pollution were prompting "disillusionment about science and technology." Others were more specific: "Watergate helped us understand why humanism is on the verge of bankruptcy." Most signs contained awkward implications. Careful polls showed, for instance, that Richard Nixon owed his victories in 1968 and 1972 not to "humanists" and "secular rationalists" but to good evangelical conservative Protestants, urged on by Graham. Similarly, the leaders of movements against pollution and technological single-mindedness were more likely to be "liberals" and "experiments" than born-again evangelicals. Besides, if the end was near, it mattered little who had elected Mr. Nixon; on the other hand, should his election have induced a new conscience in the nation, perhaps the end was not near. In short, premillenialism in its old, "William Miller" purity had no meaningful hearing. Certainly Billy Graham, following his embarrassment, was in no place to revive it.

The reading of the signs, then, evinced a large pragmatism: "Human beings now experience staggering insecurity about all those structures of thought and value and community upon which we heretofore counted. . . . Despair is the pervasive reality, and any theology which does not have in it an immense amount of faith in the loving and empowering grace of God is not going to be able to cope with that reality." Here, no one was asked to become anxious because the end was nigh; rather, they were urged to consider an alternative to the anxiety and despair they already felt. For intellectual evangelicals, this was temptation indeed: it put them in the marketplace with competitive goods. The hazards, however, were great. For one thing, this competitive offer did not necessarily clarify the real roots of despair. For another, it had no leverage on those who simply denied feeling anxiety and despair in the first place. Most of all, it committed the evangelical alternative to producing results; and a few evangelicals, taking despair for granted, protected themselves by invoking the case of St. Augustine, whose offer to the faithful in the staggering insecurities of falling Rome was simply that they would be saved. It was just as impressive that there were any such "Augustinians" in 1976 as that they were few.

The part of their past the evangelicals of 1976 most usually invoked was "fundamentalism," that embattled, rigid, humiliated struggle against "modernity" within Protestantism in the 1920s. The new evangelicals, still critics of modernity and modernism, still committed to "inerrant" Scripture, still certain that only baptism by the Holy Spirit promised salvation, at the same time agreed that fundamentalism had failed for its own weaknesses. Its apology had been needlessly defensive, intellectually unsophisticated, even emotionally immature. Now and then research was directed to repristinate the image and reputation of the fundamental fathers—and grandfathers—but in essence the evangelicals of 1976 saw themselves as having shaken off the handicaps under which fundamentalists had labored. Their scholars were more resourceful, deeper, bolder. Their preachers were less crude. They had learned to use media better than the liberals did. And the modernity of the seventies enjoyed little of that glamour peculiar to the twenties, when it had seemed that all old restraints might be let go. In this, of course, the evangelicals of 1976 ascribed their new status to themselves, and not only were not proclaiming an "end" to be nigh but implicitly were interpreting American history itself as a medium for divine revelation. Just what did this heritage imply for evangelicals in 1976? So long as the model of the fundamentalists proved instructive, something very like triumphalism seemed to work, a determination that come what may evangelical forces prevail. Yet American history did not in truth yield so simple a guide. In *Discovering Our Evangelical Heritage,* the scholar Donald Dayton offered not the embattled faithful but such urgent reformers as the abolitionists Charles Grandison Finney and Sarah and Angelina Grimke as models for modern evangelicals, persons who had found American society deformed and in need of saving, rather than itself a saving history. This, of course, strongly suggested that reasons for the evangelical surge were less meaningful than what evangelicals did with their power.

The most straightforward explanation of evangelical success drew less on history than on a kind of sociology. In *Why Conservative Churches Are Growing,* Dean M. Kelley had already concluded that the old mainline denominations were in decline because they had abandoned discipline, zeal, identity, orthodoxy, had ceased being what they were supposed to be: true churches. They had pursued reform, therapy, politics, culture. By contrast, the "conservative," that is, evangelical, churches were growing precisely because they had remained true, reliable, responsible churches. Therefore, let evangelicals simply go on doing what they had been doing. This was not a wholly finished argument. For one thing, no evidence showed that the gains to evangelicalism were being won at the expense of the mainline churches. For another, the losses to mainline churches might well have been attributed to the success of those churches in fitting their members for some greater freedom beyond church boundaries. The argument, that is, betrayed a plain "church-centered" self-interest not necessarily wholly consistent with evangelism's old insistence upon the heart. Yet Kelley's approach probably best suited a consensus strategy: persist.

The end of everything; the end of liberal culture; the triumph of evangelical culture; the fulfillment of American history: these could not have been all true, but any one and some combinations might have been. Yet, the historian's eye for the sheerly accidental, "existential," and irreducible tells him the story of evangelical rising would have lacked a dramatic and organizing focus without Jimmy Carter, who could be "explained" by none of these. With Carter, evangelicals faced certain questions they might otherwise have preferred to evade. Without him, they might not have appreciated what those questions were. Surely Carter represented a great opportunity for his brethren, the Southern Baptists, and for evangelical Protestants generally. All presidential candidates testified routinely to the nation's reliance on religion, morality, values, faith, etc., etc., but Carter's testimony obviously differed. It was more personal. But what difference would that make to politics? The first puzzle was presented by his very openness. To reporters he candidly described the debt he owed his sister, Ruth Stapleton. To her he had turned in a season of doubt after defeats in Georgia, and through her he had experienced the kind of re-awakening that evangelicals took as a sign of their identity. Was this to say then that Carter could be counted on never to get discouraged whatever the frustrations of office? It might have been hard to detect the difference between this and that more familiar preservative of politicians' stamina—ambition. To interviewers from *Playboy* magazine, Carter attested his sins of the mind, specifically, lust for women other than his wife. Was this to assure citizens they need not fear arrogance in office? For non-evangelicals, the lesson might have been confusing: if being born-again did not cleanse sin from inner life, what did it do? Evangelicals were more likely to understand; it promoted humility. But was humility what Carter intended to project?

Carter's larger theme, that he would seek to make the government in Washington as "good and honest and compassionate and as filled with love" as were the American people held more complex puzzles. Did Carter really believe the American people were good and compassionate and loving? To the editors of *Christianity Today*, a black evangelical, Jesse Jackson, pointed out bluntly that white evangelicals had no Jesse Jackson because of "racism." In nothing did Carter win a more impressive success than in winning credibility with black voters and receiving 90 percent of their votes. He did not mount an open attack on racism. Rather, having already in years past, as an elder in the affairs of his church in Plains, shown that he did not share the racial views of his evangelical Southern Baptist white brothers, he relied on this record to lend credence to his addresses to blacks themselves. When confronted with difficult situations in the church, during the campaign, he avoided crusade-like rhetoric but sought, in quiet negotiations, compromises that satisfied no one eager for victory but that testified clearly both to his will to change and his skill in diplomacy. His behavior—as distinguished from his words—appeared to exemplify the theories of Reinhold Niebuhr, who had insisted that in politics love—and compassion, etc.—were unavailing in face of a general human tendency to selfishness. Justice, not love, provided the measure in politics, and politicians seeking justice did well to negotiate using the coinage of bargaining and self-interest. Report had it that Carter had in fact read, absorbed, and agreed with Niebuhr; if so, was there reason why here, as distinguished from the candor with which he exposed his personal religion, he dissimulated? And where had he got the idea the American people—or any people—were "good and honest and compassionate . . ." etc.? Surely not from evangelical orthodoxy, certainly not from Billy Graham, who knew mankind to be sinful. Fair-minded observers would agree, naturally, that no political leader in mid-twentieth-century American democracy had much to hope from discourses upon voters' sinfulness, but Carter's rhetoric seemed to go further than necessary. Had he concluded that Vietnam, Watergate, and the panoply of disorders sapping public morale justified some positive thinking? Any one of these possibilities might have been legitimate by one or another canon of political responsibility, but Carter had made a point of himself as something other than simply a superior politician. But what? His campaign left his understanding of his relationship to the American people mysterious.

Had Carter wished advice from his own people, "the Church that Produced a President," he could have read contributions sent in to *Christianity Today* in response to its editors' hypothesis, "If I Were President." Combat "secularism, egoism, luxury, and hubris," advised one contributor. Another spoke for "justice," and still another, noting "the poor, the unemployed, the aged . . . the minorities," linked their claim to the need for Americans to restrain themselves "from their increasingly affluent and often wasteful use of funds and resources, so that these can be conserved and shared with those . . . in need . . ." This echoed, no doubt deliberately, the noteworthy conclusion to the 1974 world evangelical meeting in Lausanne: "Those of us who live in affluent circumstances accept our duty to develop a simple lifestyle in order to contribute more generously to both relief and evangelism." The year before that, in Chicago, a small number of American evangelicals had organized "Evangelicals for Social Action." Their leading spokesman, Ronald J. Sider, would eventually publish *Rich Christians in an Age of Hunger,* repeating the theme struck at Lausanne. Was Jimmy Carter an Evangelical for Social Action? If so, he could only have known that ESA hardly proved to be a flourishing group, compounding the paucity of its numbers with the intensity of its own schisms. Would he attempt to promote economic justice by the same means he evidently meant to promote racial justice, quietly, by diplomacy, without rhetoric, knowing very well that not only "people" but his own people, the evangelicals, were hostile to "welfare" and "taxes" and all practical means to justice? Another of *Christianity Today*'s respondents voiced the more representative line: "cut the budget, reduce the . . . federal government." Replacing "pragmatism with idealism, cynicism with honesty" might have been taken as a reverberation from Watergate, whereas selecting the right kind of persons for office, "including, where practical, evangelical Christians," appeared one point on which Carter could not have been expected to waste any thought.

The contribution of the editors themselves best illuminated Carter's relationship of his own evangelical people. During the presidential campaign, no speculations outnumbered those devoted to how Catholics would respond to Carter, on the assumption that Catholics would remember that the tribal anti-Catholicism that had swamped Al Smith and imperiled John F. Kennedy belonged precisely to those southern evangelicals to whom Jimmy Carter belonged. Most Catholics were Democrats; how many might vote Ford out of fear of evangelical prejudice? On the other hand, most "evangelical conservative Protestants" were Republicans; could Carter win enough of them to over-balance his Catholic losses? The editors of *Christianity Today* were not in time with their suggestion, but the idea they presented on the eve of his inauguration had been in the air: "We urge that the incoming administration focus attention on the abortion issue." Here was the "issue" that offered Carter a chance to woo evangelical and Catholic votes together. His failure to seize it, in favor of carefully distinguishing between personal preferences and public policy, and thus easing the issue out of debate, suggested the familiar prudence of a middle-of-the-road politician who needed no born-again or any other kind of religious inner life to justify his prudence.

As it happened, Carter won enough ordinarily Republican "evangelical conservative Protestant" voters to compensate for his Catholic (and Jewish) losses. But the mass of his victory remained that of any Democratic winner—Catholic and Jewish Democrats, plus black Protestant Democrats—while he lost the majority of not just Protestants but of evangelical Protestants. Could evangelicals feel implicated in his victory? expect anything from him as a consequence of his religion?

By mid-1979, following Iran, the energy crisis, and the withdrawal to Camp David, Carter dropped his invocations of popular goodness in favor of the notion that a spiritual and moral crisis underlay all more specific issues. This could not have been a belated avowal of Niebuhrian principles, since, for Niebuhr, the seasons and cycles of history turned on issues of justice, with spiritual and moral conditions running along pretty much on the same level. Had Carter decided to avow the Lausanne ethic of Evangelicals for Social Action? As his energy policy and his inflation policy both seemed ineffectual, the Lausanne call for self-denial would appear to have been well-suited to the times. Let people buy less gas and spend less money, and some progress on the two most harassing problems of his administration might have been made. If Carter believed such a policy was not so much morally and spiritually justified but a necessity for long-term national survival, would he nonetheless prefer to urge its spiritual rather than its pragmatic merits? The peculiar sense gathering by late 1979 that what divided Carter from his challenger for the Democratic nomination, Edward Kennedy, was not so much matters of policy as a matter of "leadership," implied that indeed Carter had not explained himself. His Midwest campaign manager during the election, James Wall, had already anxiously tried confronting this problem. Wall, the editor of *Christian Century Magazine*, the long-time voice of ecumenical "liberal" Protestantism, had resigned his post for the campaign. Now, early in 1979, he feared something going wrong. Nominally, his target was Arthur Schlesinger, Jr.'s, much earlier attack on Carter's prescription of a government of compassion and love, but many others since had argued that Carter's personal faith and evangelical heritage provided no political guidance whatever, with the barely hidden implication they in fact made for bad politics. Wall suffered a generalized suspicion that "there are some among us who resent all things religious, especially the heart-oriented brand espoused by our current president."

But merely falling back among the evangelicals was not going to help a liberal Protestant show relevance. Wall could not demonstrate it on any terms and finally had to occupy an unusual position: "The president's homilies . . . present the simple faith of a complex public man, but they provide no magical connection between a specific political decision and the president's personal faith. . . . It is frustrating not to have more specifics on how the president relates [his] faith to his public decisions." In his frustration, Wall at times seemed to entertain the thought that the faith and the politics were not linked at all: "The nature of his task requires that he avoid the connection between his public action and his private faith." What Wall finally concluded, however, was that Carter simply couldn't talk about it: "The connection is there, but he will not make it public so long as he holds office."

EVANGELICALISM AS CULTURE

By 1976 the atmosphere of evangelical centers was that of a general flourishing, of a whole people coming into its inheritance. This inheritance was very much economic. The evangelical press published relatively few manuals of the "how to get rich" variety. Preaching the gospel of success was hardly necessary. Such aides as appeared seemed calculated more to advise people how to manage their money than how to get it. The ancient poverty of the evangelical urban fringes and rural heartlands, from the piney woods of the South to California's Central Valley and desert suburbs, but especially in the old Southwest, in Oklahoma and Texas, in Muskogee, Dallas, and Waco, at last was losing its grip. The Christian rest homes, Christian hospitals, summer institutes in California, conferences and conventions and congresses in Brazil, Africa, and Switzerland, took money, as did funding the newly flourishing seminaries and theology schools and institutes. Money was assumed in the manufacture of the cassettes and the movies of Christian meaning, and in the stream of books from evangelical publishers. This was not the kind of money that had built Catholic churches in the immigrant quarters in the nineteenth century, but rather sunbelt money, so to speak, the fruit of a spreading affluence.

The expenditure of this money might have been thought to express the Lausanne ethic, of spending not on self but on relief and evangelicalism. Statistics on giving showed that the faithful in the smaller evangelical churches gave far more than did mainline church members. Yet the single most massive fact was the expenditure of this money to upgrade and strengthen the separate world of evangelical culture itself. We have no evidence that affluent evangelicals distinguished themselves from their contemporaries as to "relief." And the evangelism this money subsidized appeared to have a narrow focus. First bemused, then proud of "growth," evangelicals soon turned to a systematic social-science study of growth, led by the influential findings of The Fuller Theological Seminary in Pasadena, one of evangelicalism's new elite intellectual centers. Church growth, studies at Fuller showed, happened where people of a kind congregated together; on the other hand, where diverse kinds of people—singles and families, say, or old and young, white and black—congregated, growth quickly proved limited. Church growth ought to exploit "homogeneous unity," then, assuming that such growth was wanted. The objectivity of the sociological finding here could be distinguished from the nature of the impulse that welcomed it. The newly prospering evangelicals were enhancing their own world, not evangelizing the world. Only the Salvation Army still remained to testify to the Lausanne ethic's roots, and still remained quite unlike any other evangelical body. At the same time, it was reasonably evident that in this evangelizing of themselves, evangelicals showed themselves aware of the need to make sure their old purity had not consisted simply of their old poverty. They used money to defend themselves against worldliness. Conspicuous in evangelical publishing lists were manuals for parents; what had once been a simple "traditional" practice of child-rearing was becoming a matter for self-consciousness, and the reason was not that of old liberal culture, to allow a new freedom to the young in the name of self-realization, but to protect the young against just those temptations money itself intensified.

The one domain in which evangelical culture appeared to have assimilated a new freedom was sex. "Intended for pleasure," as the title of one manual had it, sex by 1976 had come to be affirmed as a realm for positive experience, no longer primarily as one of danger. So much was this so that evangelicals were encouraged to learn "technique" of purely biological provenance, to supplement all spiritual, moral, psychological, and symbolic dimensions. Naturally this positive appreciation of sex applied only within marriage. Evangelicals did not succumb to those symposia among liberal churchmen common in the sixties painfully picking out new "situational" ethics for "premarital" relations. Yet, so secure was this new appropriation of sexuality as part of life's blessing that the new lines of prohibition occupied by evangelical police were not dug against premarital sexuality among the young, or even against divorce and its concomitants, "extramarital" and adulterous sexuality, but against abortion and homosexuality. Neither, on the basis of any evidence, appeared a practice troubling evangelical culture; both, however, offered opportunities for symbolic display in repudiating the old stereotype of Christian purity as mere repression. Evangelicalism was not conceding to the standards of the world but rather fulfilling biblical promises. And the Bible clearly excluded abortion and homosexuality from those promises.

But the anxiety that the new sexuality be justified by the Bible, not by the "situations" of modern experience, left the evangelicals in the position of having brought a live bomb into their own camp, since they continued to reject most of the ways of exploring sexuality generated by modern culture. Thus, the adoption of "technique" itself had aspects of unnegotiated surrender to the world.

Rather clear expression of the ambivalence with which evangelical spokesmen sought to escape fundamentalism's rigid rejections appeared in their tentative engagements with modern art. No temporizing with plain decadence would be justified by mere reputation: thus, regarding movies of Fellini and Werner Herzog, "Artistically sensitive Christians need to respond forcefully to the nihilistic anarchism filling their screens." Yet *Christianity Today* could allow a painter to observe, in "Painting as Propaganda," that as propaganda Communist and Christian art bore close resemblance: both were bad. Reviewers took note of spiritual dimensions in the work of Saul Bellow, of Andrew Wyeth, of the science fiction writer D. Keith Mano, of Bob Dylan, almost as though to find in their popularity signs that in the world too large numbers were coming to evangelical awareness, with the promise that evangelicalism's own inheritance would include expression in persuasive art. But the roots of all this in the history of American evangelical Protestantism itself were not clear; to an outside view it looked remarkably as though the new evangelicals were following behind their liberal predecessors in opening themselves to a cosmopolitan consumption of art and, like the liberals, would find no real basis for rejecting any particular art, whatever its origins.

No direct demand upon politics, and upon an evangelical politician in particular, followed from any of these commitments. No doubt a general preference for low taxes and little government fit in with the impulse to fund and improve evangelical culture itself as an autonomous world, and Carter's own campaign spoke to such feelings. On two other fronts, however, the evangelical inheritance did intersect with matters of public moment, that is, roles for women and the practice of healing. It was within the ultimate reaches of both these that the evangelicals' traditional debate with "the world," with science, "secularism" and "individualism" overflowed old prepared positions and threatened to become fusion after all. Since by 1976 the problem of healing had been given one powerful resolution, whereas the problem of women was still generating potential, I shall discuss them in that order.

The status of divine healing—at once crucial and ambiguous—was given national prominence by the President-elect's sister. Ruth Carter Stapleton's successful practice as a healer was no embarrassment to evangelicals anxious to shake the stereotypes of primitivism. Stapleton's practice derived from deep personal struggles in her own life. She had no argument with "modern" medicine. "Miracles" were not her stock-in-trade. Persons sophisticated in modern theories of psychosomatic medicine and psychological healing could interpret her two books and reports of her practice in rational ways. At the same time, Stapleton's practice fit into the tradition of healing familiar for over eighty years in American holiness and pentecostal circles. The healing power of itinerant evangelists manifested "charisma," that is, the living power in the here-and-now of the Holy Spirit. Another such power, also attested in the Bible, was speaking in tongues—"glossolalia." No doubt the patrons of healing evangelists, usually poor, often isolated on farms and in villages, had their share of medical need, perhaps a larger share of dietary origin. Yet, imputing to them a higher degree of credulity, in consequence of poor schooling, would be merely invidious, and to suggest they found spiritual healing attractive as within their economic means as orthodox doctoring would not have been requires some such imputation. Healing met the need that the group itself feel itself justified and fortified; healing itinerants provided unshakable identity to people lacking many of the other sources of identity. Almost by definition, fraud and scandal accompanied the practice of divine healing, so much so that some of the greatest itinerant preachers of the living power of the Lord, such as Billy Graham, almost conspicuously abstained from charismatic displays. But just as did "modern" medicine, politics, and other professions inherently open to fraud and scandal, divine healing survived its corruptions. In the most famous example between the world wars, that of Aimée Semple MacPherson, it remains impossible to tell whether the scandal in which she concluded her ministry implied fraud in her practice or whether the success of an honest practice led to temptation. MacPherson's case did help compromise the evangel through the Depression, but healers would not vanish and reemerged in large numbers after World War II. The instructive parallel with MacPherson was Kathryn Kuhlman, who for twenty years was the leader of an independent ministry of healing in Pittsburgh. Not only did Kuhlman's ministry benefit from the greater wisdom of modern medicine itself; but as the daughter of Methodist and Baptist parents, Kuhlman herself represented the emergence of healing within the mainline denominations. Practitioners and beneficiaries of healing were no longer drawn to leave an old church home for a new. The most famous of these "neo-pentecostals" was, of course, Ruth Carter Stapleton, loyal Southern Baptist.

Yet the significance of Stapleton for evangelicalism was ambiguous, as had been Kathryn Kuhlman's, and in fact, that of very many healers, increasingly so the more "neo-pentecostalism" spread into a variety of churches. Stapleton testified unwaveringly that the healing she facilitated in its turn testified to the power of the Holy Spirit. Her power was only a "blessing." She was an orthodox "charismatic" and eventually affirmed and practiced speaking in tongues. Nevertheless, Stapleton resisted locating these charismas exclusively within the frames of orthodox evangelical theology; nor would she "use" her powers to induce doctrinal beliefs. Her interpretation of her own experience left open the possibility that the divine power could express itself through many channels. Stapleton, in short, left doors open to pluralism, syncretism, historicism. There was no "religion of humanity" here, no "humanism," for her acknowledgment of a power that was transcendent and supernatural was unshaded. Yet it was not limited only to Southern-Baptist American evangelical supernatural transcendence. This had been a danger with Kuhlman, as it had been, too, if on less subtle, more "anarchic" grounds, with MacPherson. Stapleton herself radiated stability, responsibility, predictability; the real problem was that the "uncontrollable," anarchic potential lay in divine healing itself, whoever practiced it. Whoever practiced it, it might very well undermine the foundations of a stable evangelical culture.

An answer to this problem had already been brought nearly to completion, however, by 1976, in Tulsa, Oklahoma.

Granville Oral Roberts entered upon itinerant ministry when he was seventeen years old, in 1935, serving holiness and pentecostal churches across small-town, Depression-girt Oklahoma. Although he felt that he had been cured of tuberculosis, by a healer, he did not practice healing himself until he was nearly thirty, in 1947. Unlike many of the itinerant healers, orphaned or fatherless, both Roberts's father, a poor farmer and part-time pentecostal-holiness preacher himself, and his mother were comparatively stable folk, who allow us the inference that Roberts's ambition to rise and his ability to organize owed something to them. The beginning of Roberts's success was not 1947, when he commenced healing, but 1948, when he commenced publishing his magazine, *Healing Waters,* and forming his organization. Roberts continued to itinerate, using specially made super-size tents, but his base was now fixed. From Tulsa headquarters, books, magazines, letters, and "anointed handkerchiefs" went out by the thousands in response to growing thousands of requests. Roberts put together a radio network; soon he began televising. Theorists of the congregational community were made anxious by the new electronic evangelism; its mass audiences seemed dispersed in individual self-centeredness, without neighbors to do unto. But Roberts's ties were not only electronic. In the fifties he established ties with wealthy Midwestern businessmen, starting the Full Gospel Businessman's Fellowship. Roberts's rise won him wide notice, but well into the sixties the national press continued to present him as essentially a pentecostal primitive somehow become faddish and sleek, presumably all-too-typical of nouveau riche Oklahoma.

In 1962 Roberts began work on a university. Since it was to have his name, it was easily presumed to have purely missionary, evangelical purposes, but by 1965 Roberts was engaged in planning for a full liberal-arts program. In 1971 Oral Roberts University won accreditation from the North Central Association of Colleges, and in a few more years had won respect at first denied. Its direction appeared to be more that of James Duke University and Leland Stanford University than of, say, Bob Jones University. When Oral Roberts University came to include a medical school, it was a medical school like other medical schools, committed to modern scientific medicine. By 1977 Roberts set about to build a huge modern hospital. No more than his medical school was this to rationalize, promote, or otherwise underwrite divine healing. Interviewed on national television, Roberts had already explained that divine healing, as he knew it, utilized the understandings of modern, scientific psychosomatic medicine. Between divine healing and modern medicine there was no conflict, really. In effect, both divine healing and psychosomatic medicine testified to religious power. What more remarkable miracles could there be than modern hospitals themselves? Where but in Tulsa's whole new complex of university, medical school, and hospital might the power of Jesus Christ be seen more clearly? Embracing these, embracing Oral Roberts himself, blessed son of a stalwart poverty, Tulsa, Oklahoma, the whole Southwest, could know themselves blessed, and the condescensions of Eastern media confounded.

Roberts's most dramatic testimony had been personal, however. In 1968, son of a pentecostal minister, servant of pentecostal and holiness congregations in their dustbowl poverty, integrity, and stubbornness, Roberts joined the Methodist Church, specifically the Boston Avenue Church in Tulsa. His act caused pain; old pentecostal faithfuls, proud of him as one of theirs, grateful for his success rooted in their obscurity, felt betrayed. Yet Roberts's apostasy made sense. From 1948 he had been careful to evade any situation in which any body of church authorities might judge or control his work. The Assemblies of God, an old holiness church, were imposing discipline upon their ministers, for instance. Roberts meant to preserve his own freedom, and, ironically, protected it precisely in joining the Methodists, who, not only in their own historic intellectual permissiveness but in their new mainline liberalism nourished their ministers' individualism. Roberts himself justified his move in a brilliant simplification: without ceasing to love his father's church, he said, without ceasing to serve Jesus, he had long felt his calling was "to deal with individuals, not the denomination."

The motivation for this enterprise remained an appetite for signs, for witness, for proof of God's power, as Roberts's fight for his hospital suggests. By any prior reckoning, Tulsa had not needed a hospital. It had the largest general hospital in the state, and five private hospitals in all. It had nearly 3000 beds; almost 1000 of these ordinarily went unused. The hospital Roberts wanted left all calculations behind, entering into perhaps mystic numerology. Its 777 beds were to be paid for by contributions solicited in sums of $7, $77, $777, $7,777, $77,777, and of course, hopefully so on. Oklahoma's medical advisory board (mandated by federal legislation aimed at controlling medical costs) told Roberts "no." But Roberts had political clout. His organization, business connections, and multitude of followers were instructed to deluge Oklahoma City with letters, calls, visitations. A visitation was made to Health, Education and Welfare in Washington. Roberts's spokesman pointed out that no less than 100,000 of the 400,000 letters received at Roberts's Tulsa headquarters each month were petitions of clear medical import. What if even a modest fraction of these availed themselves of the new facilities at the City of Faith? Not only would Oral Roberts Hospital be filled, so would all the other facilities in Tulsa, and then some. Oklahoma City could not resist; neither could Washington. Roberts got only 294 beds, but that was more than a start; and he got an option for the other 483 (making the original 777), to be exercised should the need be demonstrated.

The political power evidenced here was but the means of divine power. In turn, the need being serviced was not that of old, pre-Oral Roberts Tulsa; it was that of Tulsa evangelized, Tulsa awakened to the dimensions of its real needs that provided the foundation for Oral Roberts Hospital. Awakened Tulsa and Oklahoma and the whole Southwest consisted of all those individuals who would now realize what was available to them. Their old identity, as members of divinely blessed holiness and pentecostal, and even Southern Baptist, churches and denominations, would yield to their deeper identity as individuals, with individuals' needs.

This pilgrim's progress, so remarkable in its details, at the same time conformed to a deeply conservative anxiety in evangelical culture. The rock upon which Southern, Southwestern, and Southern California popular Protestantism had always rested had been its claim to charisma, to those signs that it hosted God. The very intensity of its own folk congregational life constituted the key such sign. This intensity generated in its turn the charisma of intransigent scholars, Book-bound and embattled against "secularism" and "modernity," and of the itinerant revivalists on the other side, bringing healing, tongues, and even more emphatic evidence. So long as this folkish life knew no deep temptations from within, so long as its poverty surrounded it, it could perpetuate itself without loss. But once tempted, by an affluence that had been ever-envied but so long as it was elusive, ever-scorned, evangelical people could see their dilemma. To allow themselves to succumb to affluence, comfort, middle-class hypocrisy, to "the world," would be to lose the signs, their proof of status in the eyes of Jesus Christ, the Lord. Yet, to cling to the signs, in all their inexplicable anarchistic power, to insist upon tongues speaking no language understood by the world, to rely upon healing inexplicable in any up-to-date research laboratory, would be to remain isolated in William Jennings Bryanish dusty, out-of-date, more than slightly comical prairie backwardness. To resist this was not a matter of mere pride. Evangelicals had to remember their evangelical duty: they must convey their word, in the best, most persuasive language possible. What language could be more powerful and persuasive than that of science itself? of modern science? specifically, the language that spoke to the final unit of evangelical reckoning, the existential, real, concrete, individual himself, the evangelizable human person existent as such in his mortal, physical, biological, medically definable body? And what other language was this than that of modern medical science? Evangelical duty, it was, then, that justified Roberts's domestication of divine healing to a "materialistic" hospital. What could be more convincing—more "convicting," in an old Puritan evangelists' word—to the individual than his realization that it was only in his bodily identity that he would experience decisions for eternity? Hospitals, underwritten by evangelism, could contain much of the immense energy resident in every individual awakened to himself, made aware that no poverty, no culture, no "denomination," as Roberts said, no "world," as all evangelicals said, limited him. How to promote this awakening, on the one hand, and prevent it from creating anarchy, on the other, found an answer in universities and hospitals.

Whether or not the evangelized Tulsa of 1977 would prove a model for larger triumphs in 1980, 1984, or even 1999, its provincial limits were more obvious by the summer of that year. In July, some 40,000 charismatic Christians—*Time* magazine said 45,000—gathered from all corners of the United States for three days and four nights in Kansas City, Missouri, in the largest convention Kansas City, at least, had yet seen. Daytimes, these thousands fellowshipped all over town in workshops, conferences, and seminars. Nights, they rallied in the chief's up-to-date new Arrowhead Stadium. Preachers declaimed, priests celebrated, and the giant electronic scoreboard's computer-controllers rendered visions of love-doves, spirit-flames, exhortations—"Praise the Lord"—and Jesus' own face, twenty times life-size, in primary colors. Again, as in the bicentennial year, national media, impressed by numbers, paid attention. But again, and even more so, numbers were not what mattered.

Some of the charismatics in Kansas City belonged to the old holiness and pentecostal churches, accustomed to tongues and healing. They, like the numerous Southern Baptists present, found the appearance of "independent Bible teachers" who "travelled widely," such as "Bob" Munford of Cupertino, California, quite unsurprising. Others, though, Catholics, found the presence of Leon Joseph Cardinal Suenens, primate of Belgium, while flattering, not at all exotic. The largest single group of Protestants was Lutheran. Others from mainline denominations, each already provided with their own denominational charismatic fellowship, included Methodists, Episcopalians, and Presbyterians. A number of United Church of Christ members, attending "unaffiliated," found each other and organized a fellowship on the spot. So did some Nazarenes, accustomed to seeing Nazarene preachers professing charismatic blessing disfranchised by Nazarene headquarters. The sheer variety of churches represented at this celebration showed that charisma no longer belonged to pentecostals and holiness people or to old-line evangelicals, to domesticate as they wished. In fact, the spirit of Kansas City was much more lyric, anarchic, and ecstatic that that of a tradition coming to assured maturity in organization and affluence. The planners of the meeting were a group of Catholics; for charismatic Catholics, charisma constituted a shaking of the church, a joyful sign that despite itself the old structure could be filled with immediate divine energy. Some churchmen were emphatic about the stakes; an Episcopalian at Kansas City predicted that soon only two kinds of Episcopal churches would remain: charismatic or dead. Practically all the mainline Protestants saw themselves escaping the sterility and stagnation that had overtaken their own church traditions, and could only hope charismatics might mean their own churches' rebirth. In Ruth Carter Stapleton, the celebrants heard a charismatic whose roots were not in mainline liberalism but old evangelicalism; yet Southern Baptists were by no means with suspicion of the Word in charismatic forms, witnessing in Stapleton's evangel the powerful attraction exerted by individual needs, individual cases, individual talent, the temptation to devise individual methods. Had not Graham built the Southern Baptists into Number One by steady labor, without tongues, without healing? Was the inheritance now to be undermined by grateful patienthood and heedless rapture?

As Oral Roberts's Tulsa apotheosis suggested, classically biblical forms of divine healing were susceptible to assimilation within the forms of modern organization, modern science, modern technology, into "the magic of modern medicine." Modern medicine itself had become far more aware, on scientific grounds alone, of the unity of the person than it had been in Mary Baker Eddy's time, was far more "holistic" and "psychosomatic," proceeded in a more "person-oriented" way. The problem was to infuse the charisma of healing into the whole institution of healing, so that instead of seeming the gift of essentially unpredictable itinerants, it was obtainable as a predictable and rational expectation. Roberts's "City of Faith" in Tulsa was an inspired gesture of such institutionalization, but it was evident that the risk was too great. If "church" was allowed to become university and hospital, it would be exposed far more than the church in its usual guise to the dominance of reason, science, organization, and rationalization. The signs of divine power, diffused into the operations of the whole system, would once again seem to fade. Was there not a way that the church itself could enjoy charisma in its own operations, keep it from breaking out into schisms, yet shelter it against acculturation, institutionalization, "liberalism," and thus preserve its meaning as an evangel, as testimony that healing, revival, renewal, regeneration, rebirth, were the fundamental qualities of God?

EVANGELICALISM AS RELIGION

Along with such false philosophies of modernity as liberalism, humanism, rationalism, secularism, neo-orthodoxy, and science, evangelicals were very much inclined to include another, modern feminism. Systematic opposition to the Equal Rights Amendment flowed from evangelical sources. The counter-philosophy of positive womanhood offered sharp attacks on feminist leaders. As evangelical preoccupation with abortion and homosexuality grew, it easily linked feminism to its targets, rarely trying to distinguish one kind of feminist from another. The basic reason for the generalized caution and suspicion seemed evident. Billy Graham did not indulge in anti-feminist stereotyping; in fact, he made clear his approval of all efforts to get justice for women in equal pay, and he never questioned the equality of young women so far as higher education was concerned. Yet Graham (and his wife) opposed ERA; ERA, they feared, would overreach justice and distort those relationships in which men were expected to take the lead, bear responsibility, and provide shelter for life; relationships in which women found true leadership and felt secure fulfilling their true roles. As a culture coming into its inheritance, evangelicalism gave high priority to its own stability. Everything was connected to everything else. The parents being urged to attend to their duties were connected to the churches, both parents and churches connected to the farms and the businesses and professions underwriting them. Not at all unlike manuals of liberal and secular origin, evangelical manuals stressed the importance of fathers being fathers. The legitimate joy to be found in sex in marriage was a shared joy, in no way intended to weaken parenthood or fatherhood. Feminism threatened all this, threatened connections, threatened stability. An odd sort of double standard appeared even among those sympathetic to the "evangelical feminists" emerging in the early seventies and organizing their Evangelical Women's Caucus by 1975. Naturally, they, like the anti-feminists, made their case by citing—and interpreting—Bible texts. Was it not true, though, it was asked, that the evangelical feminists had been influenced by "feminism" first, and then went to the texts to make their case? If not disingenuous, this was unfair, for there was no evidence the anti-feminists had gone to their texts before becoming anti-feminists. In general, it was hard for evangelicals to interpret feminism sympathetically. They might often grant the "religious" origins of "humanism," of Marxism, and perhaps even plan to exploit that origin in their own effort to convert liberals, humanists, and Marxists back to faith. But feminism somehow was only secular, and no evangel adapted to feminism seemed prepared. One reason for this, evidently, was that the disturbance threatened by feminism bore, finally with most significance, not just against family order and even economic and social order but against religious order and the church. Feminism could only mean women as ministers. For most evangelicials, the ministry still carried its paternal, patriarchal, patristic charge; God was still Father and Fatherhood. Evangelical culture's attachment to the Word, Scripture, Law, still echoed of the Old Testament, of tribalism and of the tribe's patriarchs. None of this would be supportable with full enjoyment of the American inheritance, full settlement into affluence. The prospect of women ministers would then mean a culture crisis, but evangelicalism's own determination not to let culture drown religion would undermine all efforts to cope with the crisis by regression back into paternalism. Radical Protestantism would not be denied.

By 1976 some 10,000 women were ordained as ministers in American Protestantism. As only about 5 percent of the ranks of their profession, women ministers were hardly of more consequence than women lawyers, accountants, engineers, or full professors in liberal arts faculties. Still, the proportion was growing and it seemed certain to go on growing. Something like a revolution was happening in some seminaries from the early seventies: here and there entering classes enrolled more than 50 percent women. Of course, bitter struggles were still taking place, like those of the sixties, and of the more than two hundred

Protestant denominations, from the handful with millions to the scores with handfuls, hardly a third had any ordained women at all. But there seemed little doubt which way things were tending. Whether women would do as ministers, in significant numbers, would almost certainly be tested before the century was over.

By no means were these 10,000 women the fruits of feminism. Fully one-quarter were Salvation Army women. Here, women had found equality, in that supposedly most masculine of institutions, an "army," prepared, in accord with an army's reason for being, to sacrifice their own lives for others. At least another quarter were ministers in small pentecostal and holiness churches, a strong fraction of these being black. The impulse here, less that of the army's begging pennies on Main Street to succor despair on skidrow than of offering stability and reassurance midst the ghetto's terrors and the impoverished prairie's hysterias, simply reflected an equality built into the culture they helped hold together. Ironically, as pentecostal people began to thrive, the incidence of women in their ministry would begin to decline. Where women ministers were on the rise was in the mainline liberal denominations, aside from the Episcopalians, whose debate presumably reflected some higher ingredient of sacramental meanings in the ministry, which more nearly approached that of priest than the ministry of Methodists, erstwhile Congregationalists, Presbyterians, etc. Of course, one wing of Christian ministry opposition remained intransigent; obviously for Roman Catholicism to ordain women would be more revolutionary than for Unitarians or Methodists. The variety among the 10,000, then, testified clearly that there were several sources for women in the ministry; by the same token, there were several meanings, and there could be more.

The tension within evangelical culture over feminism may have been temporary. As the older leaders sensed a belated and unexpected triumph, they brought with them their memories of the old humiliation and their attachment to old styles. As Billy Graham's ministry wove toward its end, it did not suggest the need for a successor. Elsewhere, in such pulpits as W. A. Criswell's in Dallas, men of thirty, thirty-five, even forty years' service in one pulpit were recapitulating an old Puritan style of partiarchalism that had faded elsewhere a century earlier. These mighty pulpits, facing congregations of 10,000, 15,000, even 20,000, were unimaginable inhabited by a woman. Nor did they seem to fit new counsels in evangelical circles. Evangelical feminists met most welcome at the newest evangelical seminary, where the youngest new leaders were at work, at Fuller in Pasadena. There, one of the key programs was its School of Psychology, started in 1965, offering the Ph.D. in clinical psychology, fully certified by the American Psychological Association, obviously to the end of training a ministry skilled in counseling, counseling "individuals," plainly enough, in Oral Roberts's sense, not denominations. Billy Grahams and W. A. Criswells were unlikely to be generated by Fuller. But was it conceivable that Fuller was behind the times? that it was taking up "psychology" and "counseling" just as psychology and counseling may have begun to fade in the liberal denominations?

"Most clergymen who are honest with themselves would confess that pastoral counseling is too often a waste of time." There was no way the clergyman who unburdened himself this way to the readers of *Christianity Today* could prove whether he really spoke for "most" or not, but the structure of his lament had its own interest. People coming for counsel, he said, often didn't listen; or if they heard, often didn't understand; or if they understood, often didn't change their actions to suit. Their pastors then began to fret, feel guilty, suffer depression, to doubt themselves: Was it their fault? Were they inept? Had they not had a true calling? Why did counseling fail? Of course, pastoral ineptitude and even lack of true calling might provide the answers, but this disillusioned pastor thought not. He offered four thoughts. First, was it not true that the afflictions of people who came, in need, misery, despair, for counseling—a couple whose marriage had died, a community leader harassed by drink—were not the results of bad luck, bad parents, even sin, but of "will"? People willed their miseries for themselves, and "changing the will is hard work," much harder than pastoral counseling could afford. Then also: "Ministerial counseling is given free of charge." People therefore did not value it. Further: Ministers could be called any time, without appointments, again, to the devaluing of the process. Finally: "Counseling as we know it was not at the core of the New Testament Church." This last was hardly a reason for the failure of counseling; it simply provided evangelical—as distinguished from practical—grounds for dropping it. But supposing pastoral counseling was to be maintained. How would these problems be met? Should ministers charge? insist upon keeping nights and weekends, holidays and vacations, inviolate? undertake the kind of long, regular, expensive analysis adapted to affect "will"? These were not plausible. But as compared to men, women were not devalued by not being paid for their work; being always available precisely expressed a normative womanhood; and was it not possible that the "will" which resisted counseling might be at least in part provoked to resist by another will, and that a counselor who did not raise a confrontation of wills might have less of a problem?

Naturally, this prospect could be interpreted ironically from another angle: "Sexism causes work done by women to be devalued in society; when large numbers of them enter a field, the men tend to leave. . . . The entrance of large numbers of women into ordained ministry may cause it to become a 'female profession' like nursing or primary school teaching." But if sexism ruled, how could women be pouring into the ministry if it was, in fact, a "largely male caste system"? The explanation was that its gates had been opened from within: ". . . already associated with the private sphere and with feminine culture characteristics of being loving and kind . . . ," already feminized, in short, the ministry might easily become "female." The transformation would feed on itself, while, fortuitously, being fed by the outside force on economics: "budget cuts leave the largely white, male tenured faculty as the righteous remnant. . . . Seminaries may become obsolete. . . . Churches may find it cheaper to provide training schools for women like those for nurses or secretaries. . . ." The irony at work here was mostly that facing feminism, for despite the assignment of this scenario to "sexism," even its feminist author could not resist noting the fulfillment of some feminist ideals: "This development might, however, have a side benefit: an ever-increasing erosion of clergy status would diminish the line of separation between clergy and laity." Still further irony suggested that women in the ministry would most deeply suit the evangelicals themselves, more than the old mainline liberal denominations. As younger evangelical scholars got beyond the clutch of loyalty to the old fundamentalists and realized that the pursuit of "inerrant" Scripture threatened "the power of the Holy Spirit," they would be free to connect with evangelical feminism's center: "Whenever women have moved into visible church leadership, the relative importance of Scripture and tradition has been reduced and the legitimacy of personal religious experience has been enhanced. . . . Although there is not a direct correlation between the women's movement and the charismatic renewal, both developments challenge traditional sources of religious authority and open up possibilities for new forms of leadership."

Of course, the charismatics at Kansas City had not been all women, or even a majority of women. Yet, with its emphasis upon personal experience and upon healing, charismatic evangelicalism spoke directly to the evolution of the evangelical tradition as a whole toward service "to the individual, not the denomination." By comparison with Roberts's huge institutions, recapitulating and exaggerating all that was hierarchial, bureaucratic, centralized, all that tended to generate specialized medicine rather than holistic medicine, scientific care rather than person-centered care, all that had facilitated masculine competitions and masculine hegemony, a ministry of women would far more nearly fulfill evangelicalism's own deepest commitment, even as it might confront feminism with irony.

A "female ministry" would also prove compatible with deep dynamics—not structures—underlying American religious history generally. A Gallup Poll of 1978 nicely caught this long tradition in its latest stage. Sixty million adult Americans, it appeared—40 percent of the total—were "unchurched." How had a generation of widespread evangelism missed them? No people in the whole world were witness to more religious activity; was this population testimony to some basic defect in evangelism? But perhaps they had not been overlooked: these "unchurched" millions "believed" the same things that the "churched" did, it appeared, and in about the same high proportions. But the same point might be made in reverse: while 86 percent of the unchurched declared that the individual should arrive at his/her "beliefs" independently of churches and synagogues, so did not less than 76 percent of the churched. So exactly what was the challenge to evangelism? Many—a quarter—even said they had the experience of being born-again. Who were these millions? The proportion among them who were young was higher than for the population as a whole, as were the proportion who were unmarried and the proportion who were male; predictably, then, also, were the proportion who were "mobile" as to residence. Unmarried young men on the move: who would evangelize them? Surely not women ministers in the church. Once Dwight Moody may have, but in 1976 the world open to such young men had changed. Other polls indicated that 6 million adult Americans practiced TM—Transcendental Meditation, not many fewer practiced yoga, and a heavy proportion of both were under twenty-five, probably a majority of them men. The ranks of Hare Krishna were open; books of Ayn Rand and Robert Ringer were available, as was the toughening of ego, self, mind, and soul in the $250 course of training in Werner Erhard's est. There was, of course, place for young women, too, in these, as with the Reverend Sun Myung Moon and a whole display of communes, communities, communalities, farms, collectives, cooperatives, collaboratives, families, workshops, sisterhoods; and the case might have been defended that by 1976, for the first time in American history, large numbers of unmarried young women would also lead "unchurched" lives, much as had—and did—their brothers. This time, perhaps, the implacable rise of individualism, from hidden springs, like groundwater, would dissolve the old foundations. The 1978 poll indicated that despite the persistence of high rates of membership and of belief, those affirming the "importance" of religion in their daily lives were declining: 75 percent in 1952, 70 percent in 1965, 53 percent in 1978.

Was there a logic for the refreshening of religion by means of a female ministry? Certainly, focused on pastoral counseling, healing, and therapy, perfecting rites and symbols of solace, nurture, and regeneration, female-ministered churches with their "holistic" and "person-centered" approach would offer far more formidable challenges to orthodox bureaucratic medicine than mere spiritual healing did. Meanwhile, shrunken in membership, specializing in only one dimension of religious experience, they could contribute to the recognition that other kinds of religious expression were important, basic, "normal." Innovative and entrepreneurial, the healthy and vital young, no longer in need of mother-nurture, not yet in need of mother-healing, would be freed to give unambiguously religious form to their demands upon the dead, bureaucratic, command-oriented structures of that "secular" America of corporations, government, unions, schools, and media that alarmed both "humanists" and "evangelicals" alike. Their missions, communes, retreats, hermitages, pilgrimages, would no longer be condescended to as mere "cults," "fringes," or even "healthy stages" on life's way to adjustment. In other words, female-ministered "churches" might liberate the practice of utopias.

Would the evangelical churches open themselves to this logic, or at least succumb to it? Would the inert but heavy weight of patriarchalism they carried from the past-manifest in such stigmata of the traditional male ministry as the calls for submission to "inerrant" authority (rather than to "experience"), the calls for moral "leadership," and the hopes for a "spread" of the gospel—continue to seem a treasure or be recognized as a burden? So long as evangelicals suffered from the need to feel superior to the mainline churches, and thus to pursue "growth" as the plainest evidence, in a democratic society, for that superiority, they could not evolve. But Billy Graham's foundering with Nixon suggested the end of something. Oral Roberts's assimilation of spiritual healing into a civic welfare culture suggested new processes of acculturation at work within and upon the old separated folk. And Jimmy Carter's refusal to offer crusade suggested the spread not of gospel but of realism. Were his policies "Niebuhrian" or merely expedient, confused, weak? Whichever, win or lose, Carter, the only evangelical among major candidates, exposed the cries for "leadership" to his right—Reagan, Connally—and to his left—Kennedy—as functions of weakness, not of strength. Perhaps the issue for evangelicalism, whether it would persist in its triumphalistic impulses, would be settled where old-time evangelical leaders themselves had no intention of letting it be settled: among women. Would the anti-feminist evangelicals promoting "total joy" in wife- and motherhood prove up to inventing ever more refined techniques of self-persuasion? And would evangelical wives and mothers be persuaded? It seemed likely that evangelical women, just as "mainline" women, would recognize that feminism provided support for more than abortion and lesbianism, and, most of all, could be enlisted for protection of motherhood and children. Then the idea that there ought to be churches that did what good mothers did would take hold among them as well. Then evangelical manhood might realize in turn that just as it was crippling to go on tied to mother, so it was crippling to go on tied to "our kind of people." As New York's horsecars, in the heterogeneousness of their passengers, were emblematic; as Henry James, Sr., thought of the "sabbath of eternity," churches, too, even as they provided passage, might suggest the salvation to be found in leaving safe havens.

*Marriage of Cabbage Patch dolls performed by a
minister from the Universal Life Church*

Love and Marriage

ROBERT BELLAH AND ANN SWIDLER

For some years Robert Bellah, of the University of California at Berkeley, has been concerned with what he believes is an excess of individualism in American life. Recently, he assembled a talented team of scholars to explore how white middle-class Americans felt about the quality of their lives in the 1980s. The completed study was published in 1985 with the title *Habits of the Heart: Individualism and Commitment in American Life.* The title is borrowed from Alexis de Tocqueville, the French social philosopher who so brilliantly dissected the then new American nation in the 1830s. Tocqueville used the term "habits of the heart" as a synonym for mores—the norms by which people attempt to organize their lives.

Before he wrote *Democracy in America,* Tocqueville had warned about the potential dangers of runaway individualism which could separate Americans from each other and weaken what he saw as the possibility of a creative community life.

In assessing Tocqueville's projection of a possible disintegration of democratic society, Bellah's team interviewed a number of citizens about their attitudes toward and activities in a variety of institutions. These institutions included the family, religion, and politics. The interviewers sought to determine how people searched for the fabled "pursuit of happiness" which was proposed as a natural right in the Declaration of Independence. The subjects of the study—white middle-class Americans—were chosen because they were the kind of people the team saw as most likely to form the nucleus of support for the necessary free institutions of a genuinely democratic society.

The selection presented below deals with the most basic institution of any society—the family. This section was prepared primarily by Ann Swidler, of Stanford University, with some additions in the final drafting by Bellah.

Presented are two contradictory views of the way individuals approach the critical decision to marry. At one pole, represented in the study primarily by evangelical Christians, the focus is on obligation—putting the needs of the partner above one's own. The other pole is represented by what the study calls the therapeutic approach, which focuses on self-realization. As the interviews show, in actual fact few people are at the extremes. Most lie somewhere on the continuum between them, increasingly using the language of self-realization (individualism).

There is no question that the approach to marriage in modern America has changed drastically from that of the nineteenth century. The authors feel that this change is definitely an improvement over a past in which marriage partners were often trapped in situations which led to great unhappiness and misery because their initial commitments were enforced by law and divorce was difficult to procure. On the other hand, the increasing tendency to base marriage strictly on feelings of mutuality has led to a situation in which any given marriage may dissolve when the self-realization goals of either partner shift.

Unfortunately, the role of children in the family complex is not included in this selection. While the freedom to enter and leave marriage at will may be welcomed by those partners seeking fulfillment for themselves as individuals, what about the children? In order to explore fully the impact of individualism on family life, a new set of interview questions must be drawn up, questions which can show that self-realization in the parents may lead to devastation in the lives of the children.

F inding oneself" is not something one does alone. The quest for personal growth and self-fulfillment is supposed to lead one into relationships with others, and most important among them are love and marriage. But the more love and marriage are seen as sources of rich psychic satisfactions, it would seem, the less firmly they are anchored in an objective pattern of roles and social institutions. Where spontaneous interpersonal intimacy is the ideal, as is increasingly the case, formal role expectations and obligations may be viewed negatively, as likely to inhibit such intimacy. If love and marriage are seen primarily in terms of psychological gratification, they may fail to fulfill their older social function of providing people with stable, committed relationships that tie them into the larger society. As we will see in this chapter, tensions between these partially conflicting conceptions of love and marriage are endemic in our society today.

LOVE AND MARRIAGE   From *Habits of the Heart: Individualism and Commitment in American Life,* by Robert M. Bellah et al. Copyright © 1985 The Regents of the University of California, used by permission of the University of California Press.

WOMAN'S SPHERE

Tocqueville strongly argued the positive social functions of love and marriage. He saw the family, along with religion and democratic political participation, as one of the three spheres that would help to moderate our individualism. The family was central to his concern with "habits of the heart," for it is there that mores are first inculcated. At times he waxes extravagant on the importance of this sphere to the success of American democracy:

> For my part, I have no hesitation in saying that although the American woman never leaves her domestic sphere and is in some respects very dependent within it, nowhere does she enjoy a higher station. . . . if anyone asks me what I think the chief cause of the extraordinary prosperity and growing power of this nation, I should answer that it is due to the superiority of their women.

Tocqueville sees the role of religion in America as in part dependent on its influence on women. Religion, he says, "does direct mores, and by regulating domestic life it helps to regulate the state." The rigor of American mores derives from religion, but not directly through its influence on men. In America,

> religion is often powerless to restrain men in the midst of innumerable temptations which fortune offers. It cannot moderate their eagerness to enrich themselves, which everything contributes to arouse, but it reigns supreme in the souls of the women, and it is women who shape mores. Certainly of all countries in the world America is the one in which the marriage tie is most respected and where the highest and truest conception of conjugal happiness has been conceived.

Much has changed since Tocqueville's day, and we will be concerning ourselves with the changes in this chapter. Yet the conception of marriage and the family that was being worked out in the late eighteenth and early nineteenth centuries and reached a clear formulation by the 1830s, one that Tocqueville accurately grasped, is in many ways still the dominant American ideal, however subject to criticism and alternative experimentation. This modern American family pattern has been called "patriarchal," but the term is inaccurate and unhelpful here. It is better applied to an earlier phase of family life, one that lasted in America from the settlement to the late eighteenth century (and in rural contexts until much later), in which the family was an economically cooperative whole, where husband, wife, and children worked side by side on the farm or in the shop for the common good of the family. The husband-father in this earlier pattern was indeed a patriarch, responsible for the peace and order of his "family government," deciding on his children's occupations and marriage choices, and controlling the property of his wife, even her wages, if she had any. The new family that was coming into being in the early nineteenth century was not egalitarian to be sure, but it was much more voluntaristic. The power of the father over the children was greatly curtailed, and children by and large made their own choices of occupation and marriage partner. Women were no longer simply subordinate. To a certain degree, they were "separate but equal" in their own sphere—"woman's sphere." This new form of family was closely related to the new commercial and incipiently industrial economy, in which men's occupations took them outside the family into the world of business, the sphere of men. The shift involved a loss of economic functions for affluent women in that they were now confined to the home economy rather than contributing directly to the family business, but it involved a rise in status. With increasing affluence, women were now literate, educated (though mainly in "female academies"), and able to participate in the voluntary associational life of society (though largely within church-affiliated associations). Much of the literature directed to women in the 1830s, frequently written by clergymen, reflected the same attitudes expressed by Tocqueville in exalting "woman's sphere" as one of peace and concord, love and devotion, in contrast to the selfishness and immorality characteristic of "the world." This was the period in which the ideology of the family as a "haven in a heartless world" first came into prominence. It is still a common idea among those to whom we recently talked.

The two "spheres" that were clearly separating in the early nineteenth century are still very much in the minds of contemporary Americans, and the contrast between them is one of the most important ways in which we organize our world. The family, according to David Schneider and Raymond Smith, is a realm of "diffuse, enduring solidarity," as opposed to the anxiety, competitiveness, and achievement-orientation of the occupational realm. The family is a place where one is unconditionally accepted, something almost unknown in the worlds of business and politics. Americans, aware that the family these days is often not as reliable as they might hope, nonetheless define it in terms of this contrast. The family is a place of love and happiness where you can count on the other family members. The family and all familylike relationships receive a strong positive valence relative to the public world.

Given the enormous American emphasis on independence and self-reliance that we described in the previous chapter, the survival of the family, with its strong emphasis on interdependence and acceptance, is striking. In many ways, the family represents a historically older form of life. As opposed to the new time-discipline of the world of business and industry, work in the family has continued to be task-oriented, changing in character in terms of time of day and season, responsive to individual needs and their variation, and intermixing labor and social intercourse. As Nancy Cott puts it, speaking of the early nineteenth century, but in terms that still to some degree apply:

> Despite the changes in its social context adult women's work, for the most part, kept the traditional mode and location which both sexes had earlier shared. Men who had to accept time-discipline and specialized occupations may have begun to observe differences between their own work and that of their wives. Perhaps they focused on the remaining "premodern" aspects of women's household work: it was reassuringly comprehensible, because it responded to immediate needs; it represented not strictly "work" but "life," a way of being.

Morally, too, Cott points out, the family represented an older pattern: "Women's household service alone remained from the tradition of reciprocal service by family members." Thus, while men's work was turning into a career or a job, women's work had the old meaning of a calling, an occupation defined essentially in terms of its contribution to the common good. It was this aspect of unselfishness and concern for others that American clergymen and our French philosopher picked up about the role of women. Contrasting it to the self-aggrandizing individualism of the men, they linked this female familial morality to Christianity and republican virtue. They saw the future of a free society dependent on the nurturing of family mores, passed on to children by mothers and exerted by wives to restrain husbands. That the cost of the moral superiority of women in modern commercial society was their own freedom and participation in the public sphere was already evident in the early nineteenth century. Tocqueville marveled that the independent, self-reliant American girl, so much more able to hold her own in public than her European counterpart, should choose to enter the lifetime commitment of marriage, which would confine her to a limited, if noble, sphere. Probably women did not make the choice as easily as Tocqueville thought—"marriage trauma" was not infrequent and, if severe enough, could lead to women remaining unmarried for life. Yet women did accept much of the ideology of family life and "woman's sphere." Early feminists insisted that public life take on more familial qualities at the same time that they demanded greater public participation and equal rights for women.

At the crux of family life is the relationship between a man and a woman who become husband and wife, father and mother. The love that unites the marriage partners grows into the love between parents and children. It is the characteristic virtue of love that made the family appear as the locus of a morality higher than that of the world. Indeed, the "unselfish love" of a wife and mother for her husband and children was seen as the most visible example of morality itself.

The love between a man and a woman is capable of another set of extended meanings, which has given the family an additional significance in our developing culture. Love implies not only the morality of the family as against the immorality of the business world; love implies feeling as against calculation. As the primary inhabitants of the familial sphere, women were invested with all those characteristics we noted as part of the expressive, rather than the utilitarian, orientation. The nineteenth-century way of characterizing the difference was to identify women with the heart, men with the head. Women acted out of feeling, men out of reason. Nor was the contrast wholly disparaging of women, since the romantic movement exalted feeling above reason as the wellspring of genuine humanity. Women were said to have sensibility, imagination, and gaiety, whereas men were characterized by solidity, judgment, and perseverance.

However strong the contrast between these stereotypes of the sex roles, and the contrast seems to have been greater in the mid-nineteenth century than before or after, men, in one crucial respect, had to participate in what was otherwise "woman's sphere." Love was clearly a matter of the heart, not the head, and love was the essential basis of marriage for both men and women. Even in the seventeenth century, when marriages were largely arranged by parents, the couple was supposed to grow to love one another during the period of espousal and love between husband and wife was, according to Puritan theology, "a duty imposed by God on all married couples." By the nineteenth century, romantic love was the culturally recognized basis for the choice of a marriage partner and in the ideal marriage was to continue for a lifetime. Perhaps it would be too much to speak of expressive *individualism* in connection with nineteenth-century marriage, even though the full set of contrast terms by which we recognize the expressive alternative to utilitarianism was used. But in the twentieth century, marriage has to some extent become separated from the encompassing context of family in that it does not necessarily imply having children in significant sectors of the middle class. Thus marriage becomes a context for expressive individualism, or a "lifestyle enclave."

To summarize the changes in the American family since the early nineteenth century, the network of kinship has narrowed and the sphere of individual decision has grown. This is truer, even today, among the middle class than among the upper and lower reaches of our population. The nuclear family is not "isolated," as some over-zealous interpreters of that metaphor have implied, but contact with relatives outside the nuclear family depends not only on geographical proximity—not to be taken for granted in our mobile society—but also on personal preference. Even relations between parents and children are matters of individual negotiation once the children have left home.

The sphere of individual decision within the family is growing. For one thing, it is no longer considered disgraceful to remain unmarried. Social pressure to marry is not absent, but it is probably weaker than ever before in American history. Most people still want to marry, but they don't feel they have to. Further, no one has to have children. Having children is a conscious decision, as is the number of children one will have. While most couples want more than one child, large families are, with a few exceptions, a thing of the past. Finally, one can leave a marriage one doesn't like. Divorce as a solution to an unhappy marriage, even a marriage with young children, is far more acceptable today than ever before.

What does all this mean in terms of Tocqueville's claim that marriage and the family are defenses against individualism? The contrast between the family, where love is supposed to rule, and the world, where money rules, is, if anything, sharper today than in Tocqueville's time. And yet individualism is inside the family as well as outside it. Free choice in the family, which was already greater in Tocqueville's day than it had been before, is now characteristic of the decisions of all members of the family except the youngest children. The ideology of "woman's sphere" survives but has suffered severe criticism, particularly when it has been used to restrain women from participation in the occupational world or deny them equal rights in the marital relationship. Men and women both want to preserve "family values," but the justice of a fuller equality between the sexes is also widely recognized. How do all these changes affect the people we interviewed? How do they think about love and marriage in their own lives?

LOVE AND THE SELF

Americans believe in love as the basis for enduring relationships. A 1970 survey found that 96 percent of all Americans held to the ideal of two people sharing a life and a home together. When the same question was asked in 1980, the same percentage agreed. Yet when a national sample was asked in 1978 whether "most couples getting married today expect to remain married for the rest of their lives," 60 percent said no. Love and commitment, it appears, are desirable, but not easy. For, in addition to believing in love, we Americans believe in the self. Indeed, there are few criteria for action outside the self. The love that must hold us together is rooted in the vicissitudes of our subjectivity. No wonder we don't believe marriage is easy today.

Yet when things go well, love seems so natural it hardly requires explanation. A love relationship is good because it works, because it "feels right," because it is where one feels most at home. Marge and Fred Rowan have been married for twelve years and have two children. They were high school sweethearts. When asked to say how they decided to marry, Fred says "there wasn't a lot of discussion." Marge was always "the kind of girl I wanted to marry" and "somewhere along the line" he just assumed "that's wher~ our relationship was headed." There may be reasons, both practical and romantic, for marrying the person one does, but they are almost afterthoughts. What matters is the growing sense that the relationship is natural, right. One does not so much choose as simply accept what already is. Marge, Fred's wife, describes having the sense, before she married, that Fred was the "right person." "It was, like he said, very unspoken, but absolutely that's exactly how we felt. Fred was always 'my guy.' He was just 'mine.' " They were "right on ever since high school," and even when she tried to date someone else in college, "I felt stupid about it because I knew I was in love with Fred. I didn't want to be with anybody else."

Searching for a definition of "real love" becomes pointless if one "feels good" enough about one's relationship. After all, what one is looking for is the "right place" for oneself. As Fred says, "It just felt right, and it was like being caught in the flow. That's just the way it was. It wasn't a matter of deciding, so there could be no uncertainty." A relationship of the kind Fred and Marge describe seems so natural, so spontaneous that it carries a powerful sense of inevitability. For them, their relationship embodies a deep sense of their own identity, and thus a sense that the self has found its right place in the world. Love embodies one's real self. In such a spontaneous, natural relationship, the self can be both grounded and free.

Not every couple finds the easy certainty of love that Fred and Marge convey. But most couples want a similar combination of spontaneity and solidity, freedom and intimacy. Many speak of sharing—thoughts, feelings, tasks, values, or life goals—as the greatest virtue in a relationship. Nan Pfautz, a divorced secretary in her mid-forties, describes how, after being alone for many years, she fell deeply in love. "I think it was the sharing, the real sharing of feelings. I don't think I've ever done that with another man." Nan knew that she loved Bill because "I let all my barriers down. I really was able to be myself with him—very, very comfortable. I could be as gross as I wanted or I could be as funny as I wanted, as silly as I wanted. I didn't worry about, or have to worry—or didn't anyway—about what his reaction was going to be. I was just me. I was free to be me. " The natural sharing of one's real self is, then, the essence of love.

But the very sharing that promises to be the fulfillment of love can also threaten the self. The danger is that one will, in sharing too completely with another, "lose oneself." Nan struggled with this problem during her marriage, and afterward still found difficulty achieving the

right balance between sharing and being separate. "Before my relationship with Bill, seven, eight years ago now, I seemed to want to hang
on to people too much. It was almost as though I devoured them. I
wanted them totally to be mine, and I wanted to be totally theirs, with
no individuality. Melding . . . I lost all of myself that way and had
nothing of *me* left."

How is it that one can "lose" oneself in love, and what are the
consequences of that loss? Nan says she lost herself when she lost her
"own goals." At first, her marriage was "very good. It was very give
and take in those days. It really was. We went skiing the first time
together, and I didn't like skiing. From then on, he went skiing on his
own, and I did something I wanted to do." Thus not losing yourself
has something to do with having a sense of your own interests. What
can be lost are a set of independent preferences and the will to pursue
them. With the birth of her son, Nan became absorbed in the mother
role, and stopped asserting herself. She became "someone to walk on.
Very dull and uninteresting, not enthused about anything. Oh, I was
terrible. I wouldn't have wanted to be around me at all." The ironic
consequence of passively adapting to others' needs is that one becomes
less valuable, less interesting, less desirable. Nan's story is particularly
interesting because her behavior conformed fairly well to the earlier
ideology of "woman's sphere," where unselfish devotion was the ideal
of wifely behavior. But giving up one's self, a subtle shift in emphasis
from "unselfishness," may, in the contemporary middle class, as in
Nan's case, lead to losing precisely the self that was loved—and perhaps losing one's husband.

A younger woman, Melinda Da Silva, married only a few years,
has a similar way of describing her difficulties in the first years of her
marriage. She acted out the role of the good wife, trying continually to
please her husband. "The only way I knew to be was how my mother
was a wife. You love your husband and this was the belief that I had,
you do all these things for him. This is the way you show him that
you love him—to be a good wife, and the fear that if you don't do all
these things, you're not a good wife, and maybe you don't love your
husband." Trying so hard to be a good wife, Melinda failed to put her
self into the relationship. In trying so hard to "show Thomas that I
loved him," she "was putting aside anything that I thought in trying
to figure out what he thought. Everything was just all put aside." What
Melinda had "put aside" was her willingness to express her own opinions and act on her own judgment, even about how best to please her
husband.

Melinda sought help from a marriage counselor, and came to feel
that the problem with her marriage was less her husband than the loss
of her self. "That's all I thought about, was what he wanted, thinking
that he would love me more if I did what he wanted. I began to realize

when Thomas and I went for counseling I wouldn't voice my opinion, and I was doing things just for him and ignoring things for myself. The very things I was doing to get his approval were causing him to view me less favorably." Thus losing a sense of who one is and what one wants can make one less attractive and less interesting. To be a person worth loving, one must assert one's individuality. Melinda could "give a lot to our marriage" only when she "felt better" about herself. Having an independent self is a necessary precondition to joining fully in a relationship.

Love, then, creates a dilemma for Americans. In some ways, love is the quintessential expression of individuality and freedom. At the same time, it offers intimacy, mutuality, and sharing. In the ideal love relationship, these two aspects of love are perfectly joined—love is both absolutely free and completely shared. Such moments of perfect harmony among free individuals are rare, however. The sharing and commitment in a love relationship can seem, for some, to swallow up the individual, making her (more often than him) lose sight of her own interests, opinions, and desires. Paradoxically, since love is supposed to be a spontaneous choice by free individuals, someone who has "lost" herself cannot really love, or cannot contribute to a real relationship. Losing a sense of one's self may also lead to being exploited, or even abandoned, by the person one loves.

FREEDOM AND OBLIGATION

Americans are, then, torn between love as an expression of spontaneous inner freedom, a deeply personal, but necessarily somewhat arbitrary, choice, and the image of love as a firmly planted, permanent commitment, embodying obligations that transcend the immediate feelings or wishes of the partners in a love relationship. To trace out the inner logic of these conceptions, let us first contrast two modes of understanding love, each of which emphasizes one side of the dilemma. One approach is a traditional view of love and marriage as founded on obligation, a view we found most strongly held among certain evangelical Christians. The other is what we have called the therapeutic attitude, found among therapists and their clients, but also, at least in the middle-class mainstream, much more widely diffused.

Like the therapeutically inclined, the evangelical Christian worries about how to reconcile the spontaneous, emotional side of love with the obligations love entails. For the Christian, however, the tension is clearly resolved in favor of obligation. Describing how he counsels young singles who come to him with difficulties about relationships, Larry

Beckett, a youthful evangelical minister, says: "I think most people are selfish, and when they're looking at relationships romantically, they're primarily looking at it for themselves only. And the Scriptures are diametrically opposed to that. They would say, and I would teach, that there is a love that we can have for other people that is generally selfless. We have to learn it. It's actually a matter of the will. I have to decide to go out and love people by action and by will for their own good, not because I enjoy it all the time, but because God commands it. Jesus said, 'Love your enemies.' That's one of His famous sayings. When He said that, He wasn't commanding my emotions or affections, because He can't. But He can command my will and my decision process and my actions, if I allow Him to." Love thus becomes a matter of will and action rather than of feelings. While one cannot coerce one's feelings, one can learn to obey God's commands to love others in a selfless way. This obedience is not, however, necessarily in conflict with personal freedom. Through training and shaping the will, the Christian can come to want to do what he must do. People can "see their lives as a process of changing," in which they become "less selfish" as they accept "Christ as the standard" and "His ethic as their ethic. And they do that out of a desire to, not out of any compulsion. Their love for God becomes then the motivational source for loving other people," Larry continues. In Christian love, free choice and duty can be combined, but it is obligation that comes first. Then love of God can make one want to do what one is obligated to do.

Just as love is not simply a matter of feeling for Christians, it is also not expressed primarily in internal, emotional form, but in action. "The Scriptures say over and over, if you love in just lip service and not in action, then you're a hypocrite." For the Christian, love means putting another's interests ahead of one's own. The most important examples of love come when conflicts of interest are the most intense.

For the evangelical Christian, a crucial aspect of permanent commitment to marriage involves the relationship of feeling and will. Emotion alone is too unstable a base on which to build a permanent relationship, so Christians must subordinate or tame their feelings so that they follow the mind's guidance. Les Newman, a young businessman married only a few years, is an active member of an evangelical church, and already the father of two children. Describing his marriage, he says, "Before I thought it was all heart, all chemistry. Now I know that chemistry may be a good start, but the only thing that makes it real love that will endure, and the kind of love that is taken into marriages, is that mental decision that you're going to force that chemical reaction to keep going with each other. I think real love is something where there's going to be a conscious effort for two people to do what's best, instead of what's best for one individual." Emotions can be sustained, or even created, by conscious choice. Reliance on that "mental decision," in turn, guarantees a permanence or stability in relationships that would not be possible relying on feelings alone.

Howard Crossland, a scientist from a rural background and an active member of Larry Beckett's evangelical Christian church, poses the problem of reconciling feeling and obligation. Emotional and moral self-control is at the heart of Howard's theory of love. Although he feels that he and his wife, married more than a dozen years, have a good marriage, he says that without his Christian faith, he "probably would have been divorced by now." Only in the Christian faith is it "logical" to say "till death do us part." Otherwise, "if the relationship is giving you trouble, perhaps it is easier to simply dissolve the thing legally, and go your way, than it is to maybe spend five years trying to work out a problem to make a lasting relationship." The difficulty is that in any relationship there will be crises, and Christian faith allows you to "weather the storm until the calm comes back. If you can logically think through and kind of push the emotions to the back, I guess the love is always there. Sometimes it's blotted out."

Although warm, comfortable feelings of love will normally come back if one waits through difficult periods, these emotional reactions do not themselves constitute love. Love is, rather, a willingness to sacrifice oneself for others. "I have a sign hanging in my bedroom: 'Love is when another's needs are greater than your own.' I think maybe that has something to do with it. I bought it for my wife when I went on a trip one time. I felt it was appropriate." With his wife, Howard tries, where possible, to "think of ways to express my love." By this he means to do things he knows she wants, even when they are not his own preferences. These are such small matters as going out occasionally without the children, "even with a limited budget and this inflationary world." "Love" is "saying you come first, even ahead of me, where possible."

In the evangelical Christian view, then, love involves placing duty and obligation above the ebb and flow of feeling, and, in the end, finding freedom in willing sacrifice of one's own interests to others. Additional support for permanence and commitment in this view of marriage comes from an acceptance of social roles. Les Newman, the young businessman quoted earlier, stresses that marriage is a permanent bond, but one based on the fulfillment of social roles. His only expectations of marriage are that "you had that bond with another individual and you spent your lives together." But spending a lifetime together also means that one can count on one's partner. "I guess the big thing is that it's a permanent relationship between two people where they support each other all the way through life, working as a team." Les and his wife have "roles within the marriage." He is "the breadwinner and the father figure" and "the spiritual leader in the family." Susan, his wife, has "the role of the homemaker and taking care of that type of thing." Rather than being artificial, socially imposed constraints that interfere with real intimacy, roles, in this view, naturally hold people together and define their relationship. In language that would be anathema to the therapeutically inclined, the young Christian insists, "It means very much to me that a married couple is in one sense one individual, and whatever affects one, for good or bad, affects both of you. By being two of you, it just makes it that much easier to deal with the world and what's going on, and to carry out the things that you're supposed to do."

Finally, these Christians stress that, at least in modern society, there is no basis for permanent commitment in marriage apart from Christian faith itself. Larry Beckett, the evangelical minister, puts the case most strongly: the only thing that is unchangeable and can be "the foundation" of life is "the spiritual life," because "God doesn't change. Jesus Christ doesn't change." The other values on which people try to build marriage are fragile: "Whether it's career, or family, or romanticism as the center, I believe that those things are innately limited, and they are degenerative. Some time they are going to change, or get boring, or die down. If God is the center and He is unchanging, He's eternal, He is in fact our source and our maker, then by definition of who He is, He is not going to change. So what that does, it gives stability to a family. That is, the family can say, O.K., we're bored with our family life right now, but that in and of itself is not enough reason to say that I don't love you anymore. That's not enough reason to throw in the towel." Faith can tide people over when their ordinary human involvements and their changeable feelings are not enough to sustain a relationship. Les Newman, the young businessman, also insists that a marriage grounded in Christian faith is more meaningful and satisfying than one without it. "There are a lot of people who obviously have very happy marriages and get along quite well. I'd say the biggest difference would be what purpose is there, in the sense, obviously they married each other because they loved each other, but having said that, why do you get married? Why do you live the way you do? A lot of couples that I know aren't Christians are here to have a good time together and enjoy each other's company. But I guess Susan and I, our number one priority is as a pair, as a couple, to work together in the way that we think God wants us to do, and it gives direction to our lives and our relationship that I don't think other people have."

Christian love is, in the view of its practitioners, built of solider stuff than personal happiness or enjoyment. It is, first, a commitment, a form of obedience to God's word. In addition, love rests less on feeling than on decision and action. Real love may even, at times, require emotional self-denial, pushing feelings to the back in order to live up to one's commitments. Most critical in love are a firm decision about where one's obligations lie and a willingness to fulfill those obligations in action, independent of the ups and downs of one's feelings. Of course, these Christians seek some of the same qualities of sharing, communication, and intimacy in marriage that define love for most Americans. But they are determined that these are goods to be sought within a framework of binding commitments, not the reasons for adhering to a commitment. Only by having an obligation to something higher than one's own preferences or one's own fulfillment, they insist, can one achieve a permanent love relationship.

These evangelical Christians seem to be devoted to an older idea of marriage than many others to whom we talked. They are not immune to pressures for the quality of women, but they still accept a version of the traditional distinction between the sphere of men and the sphere of women. They even defend "roles" in marriage that the therapeutically inclined reject. They believe in intimacy and shared feeling in marriage, but they also believe feeling is not enough. Will and intention are also necessary. From their religious point of view, they are aware of the dangers to the family of utilitarian and expressive individualism and are concerned to resist them. But Tocqueville's linkage of religion, family, and mores seems still to some degree to apply to them.

COMMUNICATING

Most Americans long for committed, lasting love, but few are willing to accept indissoluble marriage on biblical authority alone. Rather than making a permanent choice, after which feelings of love may come and go, Americans tend to assume that feelings define love, and that permanent commitment can come only from having the proper clarity, honesty, and openness about one's feelings. At the opposite pole from evangelical Christianity, there is something we might call the therapeutic attitude, based on self-knowledge and self-realization. It emerges most fully in the ideology of many practitioners and clients of psychotherapy, but resonates much more broadly in the American middle class.

This therapeutic attitude begins with the self, rather than with a set of eternal obligations. The individual must find and assert his or her true self because this self is the only source of genuine relationships to other people. External obligations, whether they come from religion, parents, or social conventions, can only interfere with the capacity for love and relatedness. Only by knowing and ultimately accepting one's self can one enter into valid relationships with other people.

Asked why she went into therapy, a woman summed up the themes that recur again and again in accounts by therapists and their clients: "I was not able to form close relationships to people, I didn't like myself, I didn't love myself. I didn't love other people." In the therapeutic ideology, such incapacities are in turn related to a failure fully to accept, fully to love, one's self.

As the therapist Margaret Oldham puts it, many of the professionally trained, upper-middle-class young adults who come to her, depressed and lonely, are seeking "that big relationship in the sky—the perfect person." They want "that one person who is going to stop making them feel alone." But this search for a perfect relationship cannot succeed because it comes from a self that is not full and self-sustaining. The desire for relatedness is really a reflection of incompleteness, of one's own dependent needs.

Before one can love others, one must learn to love one's self. A therapist can teach self love by offering unconditional acceptance. As a Rogersian therapist observes, "There's nobody once you leave your parents who can just say you are O.K. with us no matter what you do." He continues, "I'm willing to be a motherer—to at least with certain parts of a personality, parts of them that they present to me, validate them." Another, more behavioristic therapist concurs, saying he works by "giving them just lots of positive reinforcement in their selves; continually pointing out things that are good about them, feeding them with it over and over again." Thus the initial ingredient in the development of a healthy, autonomous self may be love from the ideal, understanding surrogate parent-lover-friend—the therapist. Unlike that of lovers and friends, however, the purpose of the therapist's love is not to create a lasting relationship of mutual commitment, but to free people of their dependence so that ultimately they can love themselves.

Becoming a more autonomous person means learning self-acceptance. While another's love or approval may help, to be a firmly autonomous individual, one must ultimately become independent of others. To be able to enjoy the full benefits of a love relationship, one must stop needing another's love to feel complete. A California therapist in his forties says, "I think people have to feel somewhat whole, and that includes liking yourself—maybe hating yourself, parts of yourself—but accepting who you are, and feeling that you can make it in this world without a partner. If what a relationship means is that you can be dependent on someone, you can say I need you at times, but I think that unless you feel you also can do without that person, then you cannot say I need you. If you have been saying that I need you as a substitute because you do not think you can make it on your own, you are in trouble."

Therapy can help individuals become autonomous by affirming over and over again that they are worthy of acceptance as they are. But the ultimate purpose of the therapist's acceptance, the "unconditional positive regard" of post-Freudian therapy, is to teach the therapeutic client to be independent of anyone else's standards. Another therapist comments, "Ultimately I think people want to know that they're O.K., and they're looking for somebody to tell them that, but I think what's really needed is to be able to have themselves say that I, Richard, am O.K. personally. What people really need is a self-validation, and once people can admit that they're O.K., even though I have shortcomings, everybody has shortcomings, but once they can admit that, all right I've got these, but I'm really O.K., somehow, they get miraculously better." Thus the therapeutic ideal posits an individual who is able to be the source of his own standards, to love himself before he asks for love from others, and to rely on his own judgment without deferring to others. Needing others in order to feel "O.K." about oneself is a fundamental malady that therapy seeks to cure.

Discovering one's feelings allows one to get close to others. A behaviorist therapist describes how he teaches clients gradually to be more spontaneous by giving them positive feedback, telling them "there's a big difference in you now than last time. You seem more at ease; you tell me how you feel; you laugh; you smile." When they relax, he "provides praise for them and teaches them that it's O.K. to share your feelings." This ability to share feelings can then be carried over from therapy to other relationships. He continues: "That's how you get close to somebody, because you relax, you're spontaneous, you act like yourself and you open up to somebody and share those intimacies with somebody that in turn responds similarly." Thus sharing of feelings between similar, authentic, expressive selves—selves who to feel complete do not need others and do not rely on others to define their own standards or desires—becomes the basis for the therapeutic ideal of love.

Therapy not only teaches people to avoid problems in love relationships by overcoming excessive dependence or unrealistic demands on those they love. It also changes the ideal of love itself. When Melinda Da Silva feared she was "losing herself" in the early years of her marriage, she went to a marriage counselor, who taught her to assert what she wanted rather than always deferring to her husband's wishes. She came to feel that only by becoming more independent could she really love, or be loved by, her husband. For Melinda, the ideal of love changed from self-sacrifice to self-assertion. "The better I feel about myself, I feel I have a whole lot that I can contribute to Thomas, so I can value him more as opposed to idolize him. It's easier to love someone you're on a par with. You can be 'in love' with someone you idolize, but you can't 'love' someone you idolize." Thus she cannot really love unless she is enough of an independent person to make her own contributions to the relationship, rather than doing only what "I thought he wanted." Loving someone implies an active, free involvement that is incompatible with the helpless thralldom of being "in love."

This egalitarian love between therapeutically self-actualized persons is also incompatible with self-sacrifice. It must be based on the autonomous needs of two separate individuals—needs that may come into conflict. Melinda says, "Being in love one day can mean, like, being selfish. I mean, doing something just for yourself, which I never thought you can and still love." When asked to give an example, she replies, "I guess like just thinking about myself and sitting and telling Thomas. Not considering what his day was like when he comes home. Just when he comes in, saying I have to talk to him and sit him down and talk to him, which I never would have done before. There are times when I don't even think about his day, but I can still love him." In the therapeutic view, a kind of selfishness is essential to love.

Therapy also redefines the ideal love relationship. Indeed, therapy becomes in some ways the model for a good relationship, so that what truly loving spouses or partners do for each other is much akin to what therapists do for their clients. Melinda, now herself in training to be a counselor, expresses part of this therapeutic ideal of marriage. A "good relationship" requires, "first for both people to be able to be strong and weak together at different times. Our relationship, our marriage, changed as I became stronger. That allowed Thomas to be able to come home and say, 'My job was horrible today,' or 'I was really upset,' or 'I was in a situation where I got anxious again.' That allowed Thomas to be weaker, and for me to be stronger, so it felt a little more balanced." Both partners in a relationship become therapists in a reciprocal exchange, each willing to listen, to understand, to accept the other's weaknesses, and in turn ready to share their own anxieties and fears.

In its pure form, the therapeutic attitude denies all forms of obligation and commitment in relationships, replacing them only with the ideal of full, open, honest communication among self-actualized individuals. Like the classic obligation of client to therapist, the only requirement for the therapeutically liberated lover is to share his feelings fully with his partner. A divorced woman, now a social services administrator, feels uncomfortable with the word *love:* "I got married believing that I was in love, and that I was going to do everything for this person, and I did a lot. I gave up a lot, supported him financially through school, and I began to realize that I was not getting anything in return." The obligations and self-sacrifice promised by the word *love* turned out to be a false promise of security and a dangerous illusion, inducing her to give up protecting her own interests. Now she values relationships that are balanced, in which if she gives a lot, she gets a lot back. Asked what would be the worst thing in a relationship, she say: "If I felt communication was no longer possible, the relationship would be over. If I felt I could not really say what I felt. If I was not caring about how he felt about things, then it would be over. Lack of communication, I think it would be the end." In a world of independent individuals who have no necessary obligations to one another, and whose needs may or may not mesh, the central virtue of love—indeed the virtue that sometimes replaces the ideal of love—is communication.

For therapeutically liberated individuals, obligation of any kind becomes problematic in relationships. A counselor who runs a therapy group for divorced women tries to help them feel more independent. She wants them to enjoy doing things for themselves and one another and to develop confidence in their ability to live alone. Relationships are better when the partners "do not depend just on themselves or each other." When pressed to consider obligation in relationships, she answers, "I guess, if there is anyone who needs to owe anybody anything, it is honesty in letting each other know how they feel about each other, and that if feelings change, to be open and receptive, to accept those changes, knowing that people in relationship are not cement."

The therapeutic attitude liberates individuals by helping them get in touch with their own wants and interests, freed from the artificial constraints of social roles, the guilt-inducing demands of parents and other authorities, and the false promises of illusory ideals such as love. Equally important, the therapeutic attitude redefines the real self. Money, work, and social status are not central to the authentic self, which instead consists of the experience and expression of feelings. For such expressive selves, love means the full exchange of feelings between authentic selves, not enduring commitment resting on binding obligation.

IDEOLOGICAL CONFUSIONS

Although we have drawn a sharp contrast between the therapeutic attitude, grounded in a conception of authentic self-knowledge, and an ethic that rests on absolute and objective moral obligations, found in one form among some evangelical Christians, most Americans are, in fact, caught between ideals of obligation and freedom.

The language and some of the assumptions of the therapeutic attitude have penetrated quite deeply, at least into middle-class mainstream culture. Even Les Newman, the young Christian businessman who spoke so fervently about what makes a relationship good by saying, "I'd say a big part of it is just being able to understand, sympathize, and empathize with each other's problems. Just to be able to talk to each other and share each other's problems, sort of counsel each other a little bit. Just helping each other deal with the world." Here the ideal of mutual help and support blends with a more therapeutic image of empathy and psychological understanding as the major goods spouses can offer each other.

Even as the therapeutic attitude spreads, however, it meets, and sometimes blends with, the countervailing aspiration of many Americans to justify enduring relationships and the obligations that would sustain such relationships. For Melinda Da Silva, for example, her enthusiastic embrace of the therapeutic ideal of love is embedded in a larger sense that a marriage should last. The richer, more equal communication she and her husband worked to develop in marriage counseling was a way of sticking with her marriage rather than running away at the first sign of difficulties. "When I married him, I said that he was the person, not that I have to spend forever and ever with, but at least I'm going to make some kind of social commitment, and say I'm going to try to work things out with this person, have a family with him, and be a family with him. If we hadn't been married, I don't know that I would have gone through counseling, marriage counseling, or couple counseling." Here reasons for commitment that go beyond the terms of the therapeutic ethic are provided by the traditional social form of marriage, her sense of being a "family" with her husband, and a pride in sticking by commitments she has made. Therapy taught Melinda to "be selfish" as a way of loving, but it also gave her a way of working through the first hard times in her marriage. Yet she still has difficulty justifying her willingness to work for an enduring marriage. She gives credit to a childhood in which "family was an important value," but she hesitates to say that that value is objectively important, that it could apply to everyone. When asked whether people should stay married to the same person their whole lives she says, "Not everyone . . . I don't know how you could stop people wanting to change. I think that a lot of things that happen in divorce are that these changes occur. You're not 'in love' anymore, and being 'in love' seems so important to everyone. When they get to a point where they're not 'in love,' they don't know what else there is, so the easiest thing is to leave that and find another 'in love.' " The search for one "in love" after another strikes Melinda as unrealistic or immature, but her choice to look for more in marriage comes down fundamentally to a matter of personal preference, based on her own idiosyncratic background. The therapeutic attitude provides her with a way of deepening the bond in her own marriage, even while validating a view of the world in which people change, relationships easily end, and the self is ultimately alone.

Despite its rejection of relationships based on socially grounded obligations, the therapeutic attitude can enrich the language through which people understand their connections to others. Those influenced by the therapeutic attitude often express extreme ambivalence about ideals of obligations and self-sacrifice, particularly when they consider their own parents' marriages. They long for the unquestioning commitment their parents seemed to have, yet they are repelled by what they take to be the lack of communication, the repression of difficulties, and, indeed, the resigned fatalism such commitment seems to imply. These respondents both envy their parents and vow never to be like them.

What sometimes replaces the social obligations of marriage is a sense that relationships can be based not only on individuals maximizing their own interests and being true to their authentic feelings, but on a shared history in which two people are bound together in part by what they have been through together. Describing her sense of how her parents "love each other very much, in their sense of the word," even though they are not "in love," Melinda Da Silva says, "I never understood until the past year, after Thomas and I had gone through counseling and everything. We shared experiences together. It's different than being in love. It's real different—because we have shared things together, time and experiences, all that." For Melinda and others like her, the therapeutic attitude, with its rich description of the selves who love and the authentic feelings such selves can share, can give texture to a sense of shared history, even if it is a history of private struggles over feelings, disconnected from any larger community of memory or meaning.

The therapeutic attitude reinforces the traditional individualism of American culture, including the concept of utilitarian individuals maximizing their own interests, but stresses the concept of expressive individuals maximizing their experience of inner psychic goods. Melinda was able to blend the commitments arising from her upbringing in a large, loving traditional family with the therapeutic stress on self-assertion and communication to become a fuller participant in her own marriage. But even Ted Oster, a success-oriented young lawyer, uses aspects of the expressive individualist culture to go beyond his primarily utilitarian view of the world. It was Ted Oster who referred to life as "a big pinball game" in which in order to "enjoy it" you have to "move and adjust yourself to situations," and "to realize that most things are not absolute." He has left his family's conventional Protestantism behind, and he claims few loyalties to any ideal or standard of conduct beyond his own happiness, but this psychologically oriented pragmatist, married more than ten years, feels that he is married to the "special person" who is right for him. He acknowledges that, rationally speaking, "you see a lot of people successfully married," and "that many coincidences couldn't happen all the time." But the romantic in him insists that even if there is "more than one special person" or "quite a few people with whom you could be equally happy in a different way, you've got to find somebody from that group."

Like Melinda Da Silva, Ted Oster feels that communication and the sharing of feelings rate at the heart of a good marriage. And relationships require work. "You can't have something as good as a love relationship without putting a lot of effort into it. It's a wonderful thing, but it's not going to keep going by itself just because it's wonderful. That person is not forever just because you found that special person." Unlike Melinda, however, Ted Oster does not cite his family upbringing or the public commitment of marriage in describing why he wants a lasting relationship. In his utilitarian individualist vocabulary, the fundamental reason is that he has found the best possible partner, the one who will bring him the most happiness. He is unsure whether he has any obligations to his marriage or stays married only because he continues to prefer his wife to the available alternatives. Even when asked explicitly about obligation, he rapidly returns to what works: "I think there is an element, a small element of obligation. But I think mostly it's just, you know, this person is really good. It's worked so well up to now, and it continues to do that because you expect it to, and it does, by and large." It would be "wrong" to break up his marriage only in the sense, first, that he would feel "a sense of failure at making the relationship work, because I know you have to work at it," and, second, because it would be wrong for their children "not to be able to grow up in a family." Yet despite his utilitarian language, Ted Oster deeply values an enduring marriage. When pushed, he is finally able to say why in terms that go beyond both the romantic idea that his wife Debby is "special" and pragmatic concerns about the unpleasantness of divorce. Here he relies heavily on the idea of a shared history. When he is asked why one should not go from one relationship to another if one is tired of one's spouse or finds someone else more exciting, he begins, once again, with a statement of his preferences, but moves rapidly to a discussion of the virtues of sharing: "It [shifting relationships] is just not something that interests me. I have seen us get from a good relationship in terms of sharing with each other and so on to one that's much, much deeper. I mean, we still have our hard times and good times, but it's a deeper, deeper relationship." This "deeper" sharing in turn suggests the value of a shared life, a sense of historical continuity, a community of memory. Ted continues, "You can't develop a deeper relationship over a brief period of time, and also I think it is probably harder to develop with somebody new at this stage in your life. Your having grown through the twenties with someone is good. Having first children and doing all those things, you could never do it again with somebody else." He concludes by moving from the notion that life is more enjoyable when shared with one person to the idea that only a shared history makes life meaningful. "I get satisfaction in growth with Debby in proceeding through all these stages of life together. That's what makes it all really fun. It makes life meaning-ful and gives me the opportunity to share with somebody, have an anchor, if you will, and understand where I am. That, for me, is a real relationship."

Here the ideal of sharing, derived in part from therapy that pro-duces a "deeper relationship," goes at least part way toward filling the gap in Ted Oster's predominantly utilitarian moral language. At times, he seems to claim only that a lasting marriage is good for him because it is what he personally finds most satisfying, but he also develops a distinctive life-course argument, finally involving a larger sense of the purpose and direction of life, to explain why the value of a lifelong marriage transcends even the virtues of the "special person" he has married. Thus Ted Oster resourcefully finds ways to describe why for him a lasting relationship is, in fact, a good way to live, good not only in the pragmatic sense that it pleases him, but good in the sense that it is virtuous, given the nature of human beings and of a fulfilling life. Yet all these arguments continually threaten to collapse into the claim that for him, because of his own background or the peculiarities of his own psyche, this way of life is simply more enjoyable. His therapeutic ethic provides a partial way of describing why his bond to his wife transcends immediate self-interest. But he has difficulty, without a widely shared language of obligation and commitment, justifying his sense that a lasting relationship is more than a matter of personal preference.

We may now return briefly to Marge and Fred Rowan, the high school sweethearts, now married many years, whom we met earlier. They illustrate both the strengths and the confusions that result from the blending of a therapeutic world view with an ethic of commitment or obligation.

Marge and Fred see themselves as a traditional couple for whom marriage and family are the center of life, in Marge's words "home-body as opposed to jet-setter" types, whose love relationship is "just a way of living, just what we are." Unlike many participants in the ther-apeutic culture, they do not insist on putting self first, and indeed rel-ish a kind of old-fashioned absorption in home and family. Marge says, "I think our relationship has always been the base of just about every-thing I do. Sometimes I almost feel guilty if I'm out on my own too much." But the Rowans did go through active induction into the ther-apeutic culture through Marge's and then Fred's participation in *est* (Erhard Seminars Training). Marge, in particular, had to "find out that one little thing—that I'm O.K.," in order to assert herself more fully in her marriage and in the wider world. She echoes Melinda Da Silva's conviction that affirming herself made her a fuller participant in her own marriage. Both Marge and Fred stress the depth of communica-tion their experience of the *est* program brought to their marriage. Fred describes the new sense of security he felt after he and Marge had worked through major problems in their marriage: "It felt safer to be here. I felt more secure in the relationship. I felt like there was more support here for me as a person."

The Rowans, like the Da Silvas and the Osters, have found a way to integrate a therapeutic understanding of self and relationship (the conviction that one must know that he or she is "O.K." before one can fully enter a relationship with another) with quite traditional views of love and marriage. For the Rowans, self-discovery went hand in hand with renewed commitment to their relationship. Therapeutic language affirmed the "rightness" they had felt about each other since high school. Yet even for this stable, committed couple, therapeutic language with its stress on openness, self-development, and change, undermines a larger language of commitment. Fred stresses the excitement that their involvement in the human potential movement brought to their marriage. "I want our relationship to keep changing. I don't want it to stay exactly the way it is. Even at moments when I am just overcome with how great our relationship is, I don't even want it to stay that way. I want it to be different. I don't want it to be stagnant or boring." Marge and Fred expect their "relationship to go on forever." But they now reject any language in which permanence could be grounded in something larger than the satisfactions provided by the relationship itself. Discussing the possibility that the changes he finds so exciting might be dangerous to their relationship, Fred says, "Intellectually I think I can justify that they might be dangerous, but I feel pretty secure about our relationship, and if one of those changes happens to be something that ends our relationship, then that's probably the way the relationship was headed anyhow. If that happens it's because our relationship didn't have what it takes or took." Marge continues his thought: "Or not that it didn't have what it takes or took, but it's just what the relationship led to."

For the Rowans, as for many others, adoption of the therapeutic language leads to a paradox. They turned to the human potential movement as a way of revitalizing their marriage and working through problems. They became more committed to the marriage by doing what Americans have classically done—each, as an individual, making a fuller, freer choice of the other based on a truer, more authentic sense of self. Both Fred and Marge had to find out that they were "O.K." as individuals precisely so that they could make a genuine commitment to their relationship—because, for them, as for most Americans, the only real social bonds are those based on the free choices of authentic selves.

For the classic utilitarian individualist, the only valid contract is one based on negotiation between individuals acting in their own self-interest. For the expressive individualist, a relationship is created by full sharing of authentic feelings. But both in hard bargaining over a contract and in the spontaneous sharing of therapeutically sophisticated lovers, the principle is in basic ways the same. No binding obligations and no wider social understanding justify a relationship. It exists only as the expression of the choices of the free selves who make it up. And should it no longer meet their needs, it must end.

LOVE AND INDIVIDUALISM

How Americans think about love is central to the ways we define the meaning of our own lives in relation to the wider society. For most of us, the bond to spouse and children is our most fundamental social tie. The habits and modes of thought that govern intimate relationships are thus one of the central places where we may come to understand the cultural legacy with which we face the challenges of contemporary social life. Yet in spite of its great importance, love is also, increasingly, a source of insecurity, confusion, and uncertainty. The problems we have in thinking about love are an embodiment of the difficulty we have thinking about social attachment in general.

A deeply ingrained individualism lies behind much contemporary understanding of love. The idea that people must take responsibility for deciding what they want and finding relationships that will meet their needs is widespread. In this sometimes somber utilitarianism, individuals may want lasting relationships, but such relationships are possible only so long as they meet the needs of the two people involved. All individuals can do is be clear about their own needs and avoid neurotic demands for such unrealizable goods as a lover who will give and ask nothing in return.

Such a utilitarian attitude seems plausible for those in the throes of divorce or for single people trying to negotiate a world of short-term relationships. It is one solution to the difficulties of self-preservation in a world where broader expectations may lead to disappointment or make one vulnerable to exploitation. Then love becomes no more than an exchange, with no binding rules except the obligation of full and open communication. A relationship should give each partner what he or she needs while it lasts, and if the relationship ends, at least both partners will have received a reasonable return on their investment.

While utilitarian individualism plays a part in the therapeutic attitude, the full significance of the therapeutic view of the world lies in its expressive individualism, an expanded view of the nature and possibilities of the self. Love then becomes the mutual exploration of infinitely rich, complex, and exciting selves. Many of our respondents stress that their own relationships are much better than their parents' marriages were. They insist on greater intimacy, sharing of feelings, and willingness to "work through" problems than their parents found possible.

It is true that the evangelical Christians we interviewed and others who maintain continuity with a religious tradition—liberal Protestant, Catholic, and Jewish traditions as well—find relationships deepened by being part of a wider set of purposes and meanings the partners share. Les Newman and Howard Crossland say that their marriages are strong because they share commitment to the religious beliefs of their respective churches with their wives.

Accepting religious authority as a way of resolving the uncertainties and dilemmas of personal life was relatively unusual among those to whom we talked, as was the extreme version of the therapeutic attitude that puts self-realization ahead of attachment to others. But in the middle-class members of America's mainstream, we found therapeutic language very prevalent, even among those who also retain attachment to other modes of thinking about and experiencing the world. Therapeutic understandings fit many aspects of traditional American individualism, particularly the assumption that social bonds can be firm only if they rest on the free, self-interested choices of individuals. Thus even Americans who do not share the quest for self-actualization find the idea of loving in spite of, not because of, social constraints very appealing.

On the whole, even the most secure, happily married of our respondents had difficulty when they sought a language in which to articulate their reasons for commitments that went beyond the self. These confusions were particularly clear when they discussed problems of sacrifice and obligation. While they wanted to maintain enduring relationships, they resisted the notion that such relationships might involve obligations that went beyond the wishes of the partners. Instead, they insisted on the "obligation" to communicate one's wishes and feelings honestly and to attempt to deal with problems in the relationship. They had few ideas of the substantive obligations partners in a relationship might develop. Ted Oster began to hint at some of these when he discussed how having lived your life with someone, having a shared history, bound you to her in ways that went beyond the feelings of the moment. He seemed to reach for the idea that the interests, and indeed the selves of the partners, are no longer fully separable in a long-lasting relationship, but his utilitarian individualist language kept pulling him back. In the end, he oscillated between the idea that it might in some larger sense be wrong to leave his marriage and the simple idea that he and Debby would stay together because they were well suited to each other.

Similarly, while the evangelical Christians welcomed the idea of sacrifice as an expression of Christian love, many others were uncomfortable with the idea. It was not that they were unwilling to make compromises or sacrifices for their spouses, but they were troubled by the ideal of self-denial the term "sacrifice" implied. If you really wanted to do something for the person you loved, they said, it would not be a sacrifice. Since the only measure of the good is what is good for the self, something that is really a burden to the self cannot be part of love. Rather, if one is in touch with one's true feelings, one will do something for one's beloved only if one really wants to, and then, by definition, it cannot be a sacrifice. Without a wider set of cultural traditions, then, it was hard for people to find a way to say why genuine attachment to others might require the risk of hurt, loss, or sacrifice. They clung to an optimistic view in which love might require hard work, but could never create real costs to the self. They tended instead to believe that therapeutic work on the self could turn what some might regard as sacrifices into freely chosen benefits. What proved most elusive to our respondents, and what remains most poignantly difficult in the wider American culture, are ways of understanding the world that could overcome the sharp distinction between self and other.

MARRIAGE AND MORES

We have seen that marriage and the family continue to be important for Americans—in some ways, more important than ever. We have seen that the satisfactions of marriage and family life have been increasing, though as institutions they are more fragile and difficult to maintain than ever. We would argue that the family is not so much "fading," as some have said, as changing.

Marriage and the family, while still desirable, are now in several ways optional. The authors of *The Inner American* report as the most dramatic of their findings the change between 1957 and 1976 in "increased tolerance of people who reject marriage as a way of life." Whereas the majority of Americans believed it was "sick," "neurotic," or "immoral" to remain unmarried thirty years ago, by the late seventies only a third disapproved and 15 percent thought it was preferable, while a majority felt it was up to the individual. That getting married, having children, and staying married are now matters of choice, rather than things taken for granted, creates a new atmosphere for marriage and a new meaning for family life. In this more tolerant atmosphere, alternate forms of committed relationship long denied any legitimacy, such as those between persons of the same sex, are becoming widely accepted. To the extent that this new atmosphere creates more sensitive, more open, more intense, more loving relationships, as it seems to have done, it is an achievement of which Americans can justly be proud. To the extent that the new atmosphere renders those same relationships fragile and vulnerble, it threatens to undermine those very achievements.

All of this means that marriage and the family may be found wanting when it comes to providing "diffuse, enduring solidarity" and "unconditional acceptance." From Tocqueville's point of view, the family today is probably less able to tie individuals securely into a sustaining social order than it was in his day, though our family in many ways simply displays a further stage of the tendency he observed for "natural feeling" to increase as deference and formality declined.

It is also more difficult today for the wife and mother to be the moral exemplar that Tocqueville so admired in American women. All studies agree that women are less satisfied with family life than men. Women have entered the work force in increasing numbers, so that now the majority of married women and mothers work. This they do partly to express their feelings of self-worth and desire for public involvement, partly because today many families would not survive without two incomes, and partly because they are not at all sure their marriages will last. The day of the husband as permanent meal-ticket is over, a fact most women recognize, however they feel about "women's liberation." Yet women's work is largely low-status work and the differential between men's pay and women's pay is large, though women are increasingly breaking into formerly male occupations. On top of demeaning work and low pay, working wives and mothers come home to families where the men still expect them to do the preponderance of housework and child care. There have been considerable changes in expectation in this area but not much change in actual behavior. When women are more disgruntled with marriage than men, there is good reason. If women do more than their share of caring for others, it may not be because they enjoy it, but because custom and power within the family make them have to. We should not rule out the possibility that women have developed sex-specific moral sensitivities that have much to contribute to society. Carol Gilligan and Sara Ruddick, among others, argues as much. But women today have begun to question whether altruism should be their exclusive domain.

One resolution would be to see that the obligations traditionally associated with "woman's sphere" are human obligations that men and women should share. There is anxiety, not without foundation, among some of the opponents of feminism, that the equality of women could result in complete loss of the human qualities long associated with "woman's sphere." The present ideology of American individualism has difficulty, as we have seen, justifying why men and women should be giving to one another at all. Traditionally, women have thought more in terms of relationships than in terms of isolated individuals. Now we are all supposed to be conscious primarily to our assertive selves. To reappropriate a language in which we could all, men and women, see that dependence and independence are deeply related, and that we can be independent persons without denying that we need one another, is a task that has only begun.

What would probably perplex and disturb Tocqueville most today is the fact that the family is no longer an integral part of a larger moral ecology tying the individual to community, church, and nation. The family is the core of the private sphere, whose aim is not to link individuals to the public world but to avoid it as far as possible. In our commercial culture, consumerism, with its temptations, and television, with its examples, augment that tendency. Americans are seldom as selfish as the therapeutic culture urges them to be. But often the limit of their serious altruism is the family circle. Thus the tendency of our individualism to dispose "each citizen to isolate himself from the mass of his fellows and withdraw into the circle of family and friends," that so worried Tocqueville, indeed seems to be coming true. "Taking care of one's own" is an admirable motive. But when it combines with suspicion of, and withdrawal from, the public world, it is one of the conditions of the despotism Tocqueville feared.

Suggestions for Further Reading

A useful survey of the postwar years is found in Godfrey Hodgson, *America in Our Time: From World War II to Nixon, What Happened and Why** (Garden City, N.Y., 1976). An interesting analysis of the 1960s and 1970s can be found in Peter Clecak, *America's Quest for the Ideal Self: Dissent and Fulfillment in the 60s and 70s** (New York, 1983). A good place to begin studying the youth of the counterculture years is in two works by Kenneth Keniston that deal with nonhippie youth, *The Uncommitted: Alienated Youth in American Society** (New York, 1965) and *Young Radicals** (New York, 1968). Theodore Roszak has written a sympathetic exploration of the reasons for the growth of the counterculture in *The Making of a Counter-Culture** (New York, 1969). A recent book that describes one of the most fascinating aspects of the counterculture is Abe Peck, *Uncovering the Sixties: The Life and Times of the Underground Press* (New York, 1985).

George C. Herring has provided the most objective history of the Vietnam War in *America's Longest War: The United States and Vietnam, 1950–1975** (New York, 1979). An important new study that uses recently declassified material is Gabriel Kolko, *Anatomy of a War: Vietnam, the United States, and the Modern Historical Experience* (New York, 1985). For a study of the war by one of the generals who fought there, see Bruce Palmer, Jr., *The 25-Year War: America's Military Role in Vietnam** (Lexington, Kentucky, 1984). The issue of the draft and who ended up serving in Vietnam are covered in Lawrence M. Baskir and William A. Strauss, *Chance and Circumstance** (New York, 1978). An interesting study of the effect of the war on the servicemen is Peter Goldman and Tony Fuller, *Charlie Company: What Vietnam Did to Us** (New York, 1983). Gloria Emerson, a war correspondent, has published *Winners and Losers: Battles, Retreats, Gains, Losses, and Ruins from the Vietnam War** (New York, 1976). Novels and memoirs of the war experience continue to appear almost daily, and any student of the period will need to consult an up-to-date list of these works to get a more complete picture of conditions under which the war was fought.

George Marsden has edited a volume of historical studies of recent evangelicalism In *Evangelicalism and Modern America** (Grand

*Available in paperback edition.

Rapids, Michigan, 1984). The background of the rise of evangelicals to political power can be found in Robert Booth Fowler, *A New Engagement: Evangelical Political Thought, 1966–1976** (Grand Rapids, Michigan, 1982) and Leo Ribuffo, *The Old Christian Right: The Protestant Far Right from the Great Depression to the Cold War* (Philadelphia, 1983). Critiques of the role of evangelicals in contemporary political life can be found in Alan Crawford, *Thunder on the Right: The "New Right" and the Politics of Resentment** (New York, 1980); Daniel Maguire, *The New American Subversives: Anti-Americanism of the Religious Right* (New York, 1982); and Samuel S. Hill and Dennis E. Owen, *New Religious-Political Right in America* (Nashville, 1982).

Changing patterns in the American family can be traced in Carl N. Degler, *At Odds: Women and the Family in America from the Revolution to the Present** (New York, 1980) and Christopher Lasch, *Haven in a Heartless World: The Family Beseiged** (New York, 1977). Survey data that reflects recent changes in attitudes can be found in Joseph Veroff, Elizabeth Douvan, and Richard A. Kulka, *The Inner American: A Self-Portrait from 1957–1976* (New York, 1981) and Daniel Yankelovich, *New Rules: Searching for Self-Fulfillment in a World Turned Upside Down** (New York, 1981).